C A R S

OF THE EARLY 60'S

BRITISH AND IMPORTED MODELS 1960-1964

FORD SHOWS THE WAY!

See FORD first at the Show! Choose a model from this fine array

POPULAR	£348	plus £146.2.6 P.T.	= £494.2.6
POPULAR De Luxe	£363	plus £152.7.6 P.T.	= £515.7.6
ANGLIA	£415	plus £174.0.10 P.T.	= £589.0.10
ANGLIA De Luxe	£430	plus £180.5.10 P.T.	= £610.5.10
PREFECT	£438	plus £183.12.6 P.T.	= £621.12.6
ESCORT Estate Car	£434	plus £181.19.2 P.T.	= £615.19.2
CONSUL De Luxe	£580	plus £242.15.10 P.T.	= £822.15.10

CONSUL Saloon	£545	plus £228.4.2 P.T.	= £773.4.2
Estate Car	£710	plus £296.19.2 P.T.	= £1,006.19.2
Convertible	£660	plus £276.2.6 P.T.	= £936.2.6
ZEPHYR Saloon	£610	plus £255.5.10 P.T.	= £865.5.10
Estate Car	£775	plus £324.0.10 P.T.	= £1,099.0.10
Convertible	£725	plus £303.4.2 P.T.	= £1,028.4.2
ZODIAC Saloon	£675	plus £282.7.6 P.T.	= £957.7.6
Estate Car	£845	plus £353.4.2 P.T.	= £1,198.4.2
Convertible	£873	plus £364.17.6 P.T.	= £1,237.17.6

THERE'S A CAR FOR EVERYONE IN BRITAIN'S GREATEST RANGE FROM  FORD

* See the Ford models in full colour in FORD TIMES — essential reading for the Ford owner, present and future. Order from your newsagent. One shilling.

EXPRESS NEWSPAPERS PLC

C A R S
OF THE EARLY 60'S

BRITISH AND IMPORTED MODELS 1960-1964

PRe

This edition published 1994 by
The Promotional Reprint Company Limited,
Deacon House, 65 Old Church Street,
London SW3 5BS

Exclusively in the UK for
Bookmart Limited,
Desford Road, Enderby,
Leicester LE9 5AD

ISBN 1 85648 193 X

Printed and bound in China

CONTENTS

INTRODUCTION

Cars of the early 60's is a comprehensive guide to all the new models exhibited at the annual motor shows in England between 1960 - 1964. The book is a compilation of the Daily Express publication "Review of World Cars" and provides detailed information on all the vehicles displayed at the shows, as well as car prices and an illustrated overview of the state of the world car market as it was in the early 1960s.

The 1960 motor show was the 45th international exhibition to be held, with over 60 manufacturers from 10 countries taking part. At that time the British motor industry was suffering the effects of increased competition from foreign exports. The number of cars produced had trebled over the previous 10 years, with the result that, by 1960, there were over 8 million cars on the road, 6 million of which were privately owned.

The 1961 show was a memorable occasion due to the number of new models that were introduced. The emphasis was on combining good looks with practicality, all at rock-bottom prices. The credit squeeze was hindering the motor trade, but manufacturers were combating this by offering the customer new ideas and designs. 1961 also saw the launch of the Jaguar E Type.

The new BMC Morris 1100 with its revolutionary suspension system was launched at the 1962 show, and Ford announced the launch of the Cortina. Despite continuing to suffer from financial constraints and the high purchase tax rate, the British motor industry still managed to be the largest exporter in Britain. There were now over 9 million cars on the road, one third of which were driven by women.

The 1963 show was hailed as the best since the war. The car market was on the crest of a wave due to the car purchase tax being halved. The main theme of the show was to try to produce a car that was as maintenance free as possible. Seat belts were introduced at the 1963 show.

By the time that the 1964 show took place, the car market in Britain was booming. Exports of cars reached an all-time high. Manufacturers were determined to maintain this level by offering bright new colours, crash-free synchromesh on all forward gears, and more cars fitted with disc brakes. Disk brakes were a British invention which most of the foreign manufacturers were obliged to adopt. By the end of 1964 there were over 11 million cars on the road.

It's what YOU want

– *that is the test for the 1960 Show*

A message from the Hon.

GEOFFREY ROOTES

President of the Society of
Motor Manufacturers & Traders

To every motorist

everywhere

The Earls Court Motor Show is an event which arouses the interest of the motoring community the world over, and the desire to join the ranks of the motorist has never been greater than it is today. It is because of this that the Daily Express Review is bound to have considerable appeal.

It is indeed part of the Motor Show scene, providing its readers with news and articles on the Show and on motor cars and motoring in their everyday settings.

I recommend this Review both to visitors to the Exhibition, and to those who do not have the opportunity of going to the Motor Show this year. My congratulations go to the Daily Express on the 1960 edition.

Geoffrey Rootes.

IT is no secret that the leading British car manufacturers, displaying their latest models at the Motor Show, are expecting a sales struggle abroad more intense than any yet known in post-war days.

The struggle will be centred in America's new compact cars, of which there are as many as 10 different makes on the market. The compact car is the pared-down big U.S. model, usually two or three feet shorter and selling at a lower price.

These have met with considerable success in the United States during the last 12 months.

Now it is announced that one big U.S. manufacturer is contemplating building a baby car of the type Britain excels in producing, a further indication that tough competition lies ahead.

It is these compact cars, providing a new challenge to our own car makers, which have almost closed the American market to our saloon models. An offshoot of this has been a lessening of demand for our sports cars in America.

I believe, however, that by the spring the tension will have eased. I believe that the market will have settled down again and I believe that our car exports to the United States will be once more healthy and abundant.

Here at Earls Court you will see the big range of cars on which British manufacturers will rely in their struggle.

On the stands of more than 60 manufacturers are cars from U.S.A., Canada, France, Germany, Italy, the Netherlands, Sweden, Czechoslovakia and Russia, but the British make the largest contribution to the crowded ground-floor display.

In addition, more than 420 other stands present a vast array of carriage work, motorised caravans, accessories and components, tyres and transport service equipment.

In my view the British products reflect nothing but credit on the makers, whose wares are now the most valued of all Britain's exports.

At the Motor Show you may be surprised that there is not a large number of entirely new models exhibited. That is easily explained. Our makers no longer time the debut of their latest cars for the Earls Court exhibition.

That tradition was killed a year or two ago when it was found that by holding up presentation of cars until the Motor Show the regular flow of demand and supply was badly affected.

But, as you make your way along the plush and crowded gangways, you will see more new appointments and refinements to the cars than ever before.

You will see them, too, appearing in different shapes. What was once only a saloon model is now being offered to you as a convertible, or coupe or both. As the numerous variants come out, so you will be able to choose more exactly the precise car to suit your purpose.

You will see one or two brilliant newcomers such as the Humber Super Snipe and also the new Lea Francis, whose makers have returned to building a car after a lapse of eight years.

In the galleries you will see thousands of gadgets and aids to better motoring, and this section alone could take up a full day's inspection.

In the broad hall, under bright arc lights, you will no doubt look for the trends for 1961.

There is little mystery here. The big manufacturers have rationalised their models in order to sell them more cheaply.

by
BASIL CARDEW

Motoring Reporter of the Daily Express and Editor of the Daily Express Motor Show Review.

They have put on their cars many additions that were previously extras, such as sun visors, windscreen washers and occasionally overdrive gears.

They have placed an accent on safety, too, with disc brakes, now standard equipment on many bread-and-butter models.

They have also made their cars more gay with bright colours, many in two-tone.

So the trend is to supply the customer with more efficient motoring at the old price, which really means that he is getting his motoring more cheaply.

This is a trend to which I pay tribute, for the consumer—the private motorist—is always the most important person to be considered in any drive to sell more cars.

I believe that as there are now 8,000,000 motor vehicles on the road including 6,000,000 private cars, so motoring has become more and more important in the public eye.

In 10 years the number of cars on the road has more than trebled, and for this reason I predict that this year's Motor Show will break all records for attendance.

I confidently expect that nearly three-quarters of a million people will pass through the turnstiles—a good proportion of them people who are able to own a car for the first time as a result of the country's bouncing economy.

In the 10 days of the 45th International Motor Show there will be buyers and business leaders from more than 70 countries, anxious to get an appraisal of the British motor industry's glittering exhibits.

If you are among the less lucky ones who cannot visit the Show, I hope that this Review will bring to your home as many facts and figures about the Earls Court exhibition as you might have gathered in person had you been there.

That, in addition to its value as a guide to those attending the Show, is the object of the Review.

C A R S
OF THE EARLY 60'S
BRITISH AND IMPORTED MODELS 1960-1964

MOTOR SHOW REVIEW GUIDE
1960

A - Z
SECTION

Everyone's Doing It...!

by GORDON WILKINS

THE London Show brings together a selection of the cars built in ten countries but there are many more nations whose cars are never seen at Earls Court and the number grows almost every year.

For new nations a car factory is like a youngster's first long pants—a symbol of maturity.

It usually begins with an assembly plant putting together models imported as kits of parts from one of the established car manufacturers in Europe or the U.S.A.

As local engineering industries develop, the proportion of locally made parts is increased, until the car is a 100 per cent. local product.

Then comes the big step—the design and production of a complete local car. So another country joins the ranks of the car producers and soon it, too, will be competing for a share of the export trade in the dwindling undeveloped areas of the world.

Among the nations of Europe, Switzerland has a number of big factories assembling European and American cars, but the Swiss were building cars of their own, like the Dufaux and Pic-Pic, at the beginning of the century, and the Enzmann family are now building some highly original sports cars with VW engines and plastic bodywork.

The first Swiss Formula Junior racing car also appeared this year, driven by a modified DKW engine.

With a German accent

Many rally successes have been scored by Austria's rear-engined sports car, the Denzel, which uses VW engine and chassis parts. There are also some rather unusual versions of Fiat cars, built by Steyr-Puch in Austria, including the 500 coupe, with a flat-twin engine instead of the vertical twin used in the Italian Fiats.

The East German republic nationalised several of the factories of the German motor industry, including those formerly owned by Auto Union. They have produced a variety of cars with two-stroke engines, and front-wheel drive, including the IFA, and Wartburg with three cylinders and the Trabant with two, all drawing on the experience gained with the DKWs, which were built in this part of Germany before the last war.

Besides a saloon, convertible and sports coupe, Wartburg makes a curious station wagon with a folding roof.

In Poland, the old Russian Pobieda, first post-war car to appear in the USSR, is now made with detail improvements under the name of Warszawa.

Not many people can afford it at current prices, but there is a smaller car, the Syrena, which is very popular. It is rather heavy for its two-cylinder, two-stroke engine of 744 c.c., but it has neat modern lines, and a sports coupe has just been announced.

Many inventors are experimenting with still smaller cars, such as the odd-ball Smyk pictured on p. 3, with drop-down front entrance. One which has recently gone into production is the tiny Mikrus saloon, driven by a rear-mounted two-cylinder, two-stroke engine of only 300 c.c.

Not much has been heard of the Spanish motor industry since the magnificent Pegaso sports cars ceased appearing at the big international motor shows, but a number of assembly factories are still functioning, and SEAT build a car which is basically the new Fiat 1800 driven by the engine of the old 1400.

Depressed living standards maintain the interest in such miniature cars as the little two-cylinder T.Z. and the Autonacional Biscuter.

This began as a simple platform with two seats and four wheels, but is now made with roadster and station wagon bodies, and has a tiny engine of only 200 c.c.

Israeli and Indian

Israel has several assembly plants and has just begun exporting a new make of its own, the Sabra station wagon, which uses a British engine, gearbox and suspension parts.

Output of Indian assembly factories is curtailed by shortages of foreign exchange, but the Morris Minor and Oxford are produced locally under the name of Hindustan, and the Standard Pennant is now being built there.

Hindustan Aircraft has built the prototype of an all-Indian car, the H.A.L., which has a glass-fibre body and an Indian-built, two-stroke engine of 730 c.c.

Egypt has made many attempts to put a locally-built car on the market, and has at last succeeded with the aid of imported German engines.

An important factor in the international car trade of the future will be the fast-expanding Japanese industry. Just after the war the Japanese supplemented their tiny production of locally designed baby cars by building the Hillman Minx, Austin A50 and Renault 4CV under licence. The quality they achieved soon astonished European factory engineers, who remembered the shoddy finish of many pre-war Japanese consumer goods.

The Rising Sun

They now have seventeen modern models of their own in production and they are launching their first big export drive in Asia and South America. Japanese factories built only about 80,000 cars in 1959, but output is soaring. This year it has been hitting double last year's rate, and Japanese manufacturers are talking of achieving a million cars a year by 1970.

Japanese cars, built for island roads even narrower than our own, used to be small, low-powered models, often with two-cylinder engines, but since their makers began designing with export markets in mind, size has increased and their styling now has an international appeal.

The four-cylinder 1½-litre Prince Skyline de luxe and Toyopet Crown de luxe are fully comparable with Western models of this size. Their latest, the 1½-litre Cedric de luxe, built by Nissan in Yokohama, is a really professional styling job with a clear-cut individual line. Its over-square engine gives more than 70 horse-power, and it has four headlamps.

Communist China, working against time to turn itself into a great industrial power, is improvising madly. The picture of housewives running furnaces to produce pig iron in their backyards is now familiar to those who watch TV films, and the Chinese are beginning to build motor cars. Beginning at the top of the scale, they are producing limousines for

For instance, these are the latest from AUSTRALIA

On the left is the Holden, the first all-Australian car. It is now the best-seller down under and has been in production 11 years. The latest model is longer, roomier and more powerful, with bigger engine and restyled body.
One of the Australian models produced in the big B.M.C. plant at Sydney is the Austin Lancer—seen on the right. A similar car with oval grille and extended luggage trunk is now marketed as the Morris Major.

party bosses rather than family models for workers, but smaller cars are bound to follow.

Export plans of the Japanese and ultimately of the Chinese motor industries are of particular concern to the Australians, whose own motor industry grew out of necessity when supplies from Britain were curtailed during two world wars.

Britain and America have heavy investments in the Australian industry and Continental manufacturers are building out there too. The biggest British contribution is the £10 million B.M.C. plant on a 57-acre site outside Sydney, which is supplemented by assembly plants elsewhere in Australia.

Going up Down Under

Among the big range of vehicles it produces are two special Australian models, the Austin Lancer and Morris Major, using a body shell similar to that of the British-built Wolseley 1500.

The first completely Australian car was the General Motors Holden, and it still holds its place as top seller. It is also being exported to South-East Asia and to South Africa. The latest model has a six-cylinder engine enlarged to 2.2 litres, but retains a three-speed gearbox.

Australian-built Hillman Minx, Standard Vanguard and Triumph Herald cars hold a share of the market in competition with the locally assembled VW, and Standard has an agreement to assemble Mercedes-Benz models. Ford already assembles the Anglia and Zephyr and is planning to produce an Australian version of the American Falcon in an all-out challenge to the Holden.

There are several Australian sports cars built in small numbers, including the plastic-bodied Ascort coupe, which has a Porsche engine and VW chassis parts.

In the Far South

South Africa has a number of thriving assembly plants, but has succeeded in reversing the traditional process by producing the Dart sports car. This car, after appearing in South Africa with a variety of engines including Ford Anglia, Coventry Climax and Alfa Giulietta, is now being made in England.

Across the South Atlantic, the prosperous countries of South America are absorbing increasing numbers of cars. The big VW plant in Brazil is producing cars at such a rate that there was talk of exporting them to the U.S.A., when German-built cars were hard to get at the height of the imported car boom in North America.

The Argentine, plagued for years by financial crises, has not shared in the prosperity. Taxes are astronomical, cars are desperately scarce and improvisation is the order.

A typical example is the Bergantin, made with body pressings from the now obsolete Alfa Romeo 1900 saloon and powered by a Jeep engine. The De Tella has a Riley 1.5 body and B.M.C. engine, and the Graciela has a locally built saloon body, combined with an East German Wartburg three-cylinder engine.

It is a country where cars find a second lease of life. The Carabela, for example, is the Kaiser, which was sold in the U.S.A. in the early post-war years.

So car production goes on the world over, with one country after another striving to build its own car industry. It all adds up to ever-keener competition for our own manufacturers.

TWO BEHIND
THAT CURTAIN

East Germany's state-controlled motor industry produces the Wartburg in former Auto Union factories. Its three-cylinder two-stroke engine and front wheel drive closely resemble D.K.W. designs.

You get in at the front—eventually. The drop-down front door brings the steering wheel with it on the experimental rear-engined Smyk 2-seater—on the right—built in POLAND.

FROM THE
FAR EAST . . .

Red China enters the luxury car market with ornate Peace six-seaters (pictured above left) built at a new factory in Tientsin. Behind is a line-up of another luxury model for party bosses, the V8 Red Flag.

Japan's new 1½ litre Cedric (above right) is an up-to-the-minute styling job with clean cut lines and four headlamps.

AND FROM INDIA

H.A.L.—below—the prototype of an all-Indian car, has an Indian-built two-stroke engine of 744 c.c. and a plastic four-seater body.

← AND THIS IS FROM
SWITZERLAND

Unique lift-up top on Swiss Enzmann sports coupe.

Grace..Space..Pace – and a special kind of motoring

which no other car in the world can offer

JAGUAR

Stand 127 Earls Court

THE ENTIRE JAGUAR RANGE OF MARK IX,
MARK 2 & XK150 MODELS CONTINUES FOR 1961
London Showrooms 88 Piccadilly. W1

One of the Trophies won by Jaguar in their Le Mans victories of 1951, 1953, 1955, 1956, 1957

13

Calling ALL Cars!

—and now: OVER to YOU

ABARTH 2200

STARTING with Fiat 2100 parts, Abarth has evolved a distinguished new Gran Turismo model with coupe and convertible bodywork by Allemano. Bigger bores raise engine capacity to 2,160 c.c. to give 133 horsepower as installed in the car. Wheelbase is shortened by about 8 inches. Suspension is based on the Fiat design but a transverse stabiliser is added at the rear. Brakes are discs.

CLOSE-UP
Six-cyl.; o.h.v.; 79 × 73.5 mm.; 2,160 c.c.; 133 b.h.p.; 9 to 1 comp.; coil ign.; three Weber carbs.; 4-speed, 11.7, 6.91, 5.1, 3.64 to 1; cen. lvr.; susp. f. ind. torsion bar, r. coil and leaf; 2-door; 4-seat; hyd. disc brks.; max. 120 m.p.h.; cruise 95; m.p.g. 24; whl. base, 8ft. 0⅜in.; track f. 4ft. 4⅜in.; r. 4ft. 3⅛in.; lgth. 15ft. 0⅜in.; wdth. 5ft. 4in.; ht. 4ft. 4⅜in.; g.c. 6in.; turng. cir. 34ft. 4in.; kerb wt. 21¾ cwt.; tank 15 gals.; 12-volt.

A.C. ACE

SPORTS roadster with an international appeal, the ACE offers the choice of two six-cylinder engines—AC's own light alloy unit, or the more powerful three-carburetter Bristol. Road holding is assured by all-independent suspension with transverse leaf springs on a tubular chassis. Disc brakes are optional. There is the Aceca coupe, too, offering snug speed for two with all-weather protection.

CLOSE-UP
Six-cyl.; o.h.v.; 66 × 96 mm.; 1,971 c.c.; 125 b.h.p.; 9 to 1 comp.; coil ign.; three Solex carbs.; 4-speed, 11.42, 7.13, 5.05, 3.91 to 1; cen. lvr.; susp. f. and r. ind. trans. leaf; 2-door; 2-seat; hyd. brks.; max. 120 m.p.h.; cruise 100; m.p.g. 24; whl. base 7ft. 6in. track f. 4ft. 2in., r. 4ft. 2in.; lgth. 12ft. 8in.; wdth. 4ft. 11in.; ht. 4ft. 1in.; g.c. 6½in.; turng. cir. 34ft.; kerb wt. 16 cwt.; tank 13 gals.; 12-volt.
£1,550 + £646.19.2 p.t. = £2,196.19.2

A.C. GREYHOUND

ONCE again AC make a full four-seater with sporting performance. A three-carburetter Bristol six-cylinder engine powers a new tubular chassis with independent suspension by coil springs at front and rear. Transmission is by four-speed box with free-wheel on first and option of overdrive. Disc brakes at front complete a specialist model for the discerning driver.

CLOSE-UP
Six-cyl.; o.h.v.; 66×96 mm.; 1,971 c.c.; 125 b.h.p.; 9 to 1 comp.; coil ign.; three Solex carbs.; 4-speed, 11.97, 7.48, 5.29, 4.1 to 1; cen. lvr.; susp. f. and r. ind. coil; 2-door; 4-seat; hyd. brks. disc front; max. 120 m.p.h.; cruise 90; m.p.g. 24; whl. base 8ft. 4in.; track f. and r. 4ft. 6in.; lgth. 15 ft.; wdth. 5ft. 5½in.; ht. 4ft. 4½in.; g.c. 7in.; turng. cir. 37ft.; kerb wt. 20 cwt.; tank 12 gals.; 12-volt.
£2,116 + £882.15.10 p.t. = £2,998.15.10

ALFA GIULIETTA

CLOSED car with sports performance from factory with a world-famous name. There is something for all ages here. 52 b.h.p. in touring tune; 64 b.h.p. from the high-compression sports engine in the Giulietta T.1. Improved bodywork and new gear ratios are highlights on latest models. Twin-cam engine, all-synchromesh gearbox, rigid rear axle with coil springs and radius arms.

CLOSE-UP
Four-cyl.; o.h.v.; 74∕75 mm.; 1,290 c.c.; 64 b.h.p.; 8 to 1 comp.; coil ign.; Solex carb.; 4-speed, 16.38, 9.56, 6.17, 4.55 to 1; cen. lvr.; susp. f. ind. coil, r. coil; 4-door; 4/5-seat; hyd. brks.; max. 100 m.p.h.; cruise 80; m.p.g. 34; whl. base 7ft. 10in.; track f. 4ft. 2¾in.; r. 4ft. 2in.; lgth. 13ft. 6in.; wdth. 5ft.; ht. 4ft. 7½in.; g.c. 6in.; turng. cir. 36ft.; kerb wt. 18 cwt.; tank 10½ gals.; 12-volt.
£1,360 + £567.15.10 p.t. = £1,927.15.10

ALFA GIULIETTA SPRINT

FAST adding lustre to its success story, Italy's fabulous sports model is offered with more-tempting-than-ever choice of top-grade bodies on two lengths of wheelbase: Gran Turismo or sports racing coupes by Bertone, convertible or spider by Pinin Farina and a new super-short racing coupe by Zagato. Horsepower from 80 to 100, according to tune and temperament.

CLOSE-UP
Four-cyl.; o.h.c.; 74×75 mm.; 1,290 c.c.; 90 b.h.p.; 9.5 to 1 comp.; coil ign.; twin Weber carb.; 4-speed, 13.58, 8.03, 5.55, 4.1 to 1; cen. lvr.; susp., f., ind. coil, r., coil; 2-door; 2/4-seat; hyd. brks.; max. 112 m.p.h.; cruise, 80; m.p.g., 24-26; whl. base, 7ft. 10in.; track, f., 4ft. 2½in.; r., 4ft. 2in.; lgth., 12ft. 10½in.; wdth., 5ft.; ht., 4ft. 4in.; g.c., 5½in.; turng. cir., 36ft. 1in.; kerb wt., 17½ cwt.; tank, 18 gals.; 12-volt.
£1,825 + £761.10.10 p.t. = £2,586.10.10

ALFA ROMEO 2000

THE Italian line at its best graces the five-seater saloon body by Alfa Romeo and the short-chassis coupe with light alloy panels by Carrozzeria Touring. Two-litre engine with twin overhead camshafts zips out 100 h.p. plus in touring models, and about 112 in sports form. Gearbox has five speeds with geared-up top. Reclining seats are standard.

CLOSE-UP
Four-cyl.; o.h.c.; 84.5×88 mm.; 1,975 c.c.; 112 b.h.p.; 8.25 to 1 comp.; coil ign.; twin Solex carb.; 5-speed, 15.56 9.48, 6.48, 4.778, 4.08 to 1; cen. lvr.; susp., f., ind. coil, r. coil; 2-door; 2/4-seat; hyd. brks.; max. 112 m.p.h.; cruise 85; m.p.g. 20; whl. base 8ft. 2½in.; track f. 4ft. 7½in.; r. 4ft. 6in.; lgth. 14ft. 9in.; wdth. 5ft. 5in.; ht. 4ft. 4½in.; g.c. 6¾in.; turng. cir. 31ft.; kerb wt. 23¼ cwt.; tank 13¼ gals.; 12-volt.
£2,195 + £915.14.2 p.t. = £3,110.14.2

Abbreviations—g.c.—ground clearance; susp.—suspension; f.—front; r.—rear; comp.—compression; s.v.—side-valves; o.h.v.—overhead valves; o.h.c.—overhead camshaft; hyd.—hydraulic.

ALVIS 3-LITRE

ELEGANT car-about-town, built by a famous firm which makes fast cars, aero engines, armoured cars and fire tenders. Bodywork by Park Ward, to designs by Graber of Switzerland, gives you the choice of saloon or convertible. 100 m.p.h. performance with disc brakes to help you use it safely. Transmission is 4-speed synchromesh or Borg Warner automatic.

CLOSE-UP
Six-cyl.; o.h.v.; 84×90 mm.; 2,993 c.c.; 115 b.h.p.; 8.5 to 1 comp.; coil ign.; twin S.U. carbs.; 4-speed, 11.046, 7.740, 4.935, 3.77 to 1; cen. lvr., BW auto. opt.; susp., f., ind. coil, r., half-elliptic; 2-door; 4-seat.; hyd. brks., disc front; max. 100 m.p.h.; cruise 80; m.p.g. 18-22; whl. base 9ft. 3½in.; track f. 4ft. 7⅞in., r. 4ft. 6⅛in.; lgth. 15ft. 8½in.; wdth. 5ft. 6in.; ht. 5ft.; g.c. 7in.; turng. cir. 39ft. 6in.; kerb wt. 29½ cwt.; tank 14.3 gals.; 12-volt.

£1,995 + £832.7.6 p.t. = £2,827.7.6

ASTON MARTIN DB4

DEMAND exceeds supply as high-powered executives queue up for David Brown's sleek four-seater speed model. Tickford works at Newport Pagnell build the bodies with leisurely care, to designs by Carrozzeria Touring. The 3.7-litre engine whisks it up to around 140 m.p.h., and Dunlop disc brakes stop it in a few seconds.

CLOSE-UP
Six-cyl.; o.h.c.; 92×92 mm.; 3,670 c.c.; 240 b.h.p.; 8.25 to 1 comp.; coil ign.; twin S.U. carbs.; 4-speed, 8.82, 6.16, 4.42, 3.54 to 1; cen. lvr.; susp., f., ind. coil, r., coil; 2-door; 4-seat.; hyd. servo disc brks.; max. 140 m.p.h.; cruise 115; m.p.g. 18-20; whl. base 8ft. 2in.; track f. 4ft. 6in., r. 4ft. 5½in.; lgth. 14ft. 8¾in.; wdth. 5ft. 6in.; ht. 4ft. 4in.; g.c. 7in.; turng. cir. 34ft.; kerb wt. 26¾ cwt.; tank 19 gals.; 12-volt.

£2,800 + £1,167.15.10 p.t. = £3,967.15.10

ASTON MARTIN DB4 G.T.

SUCCESSES in this year's track races proclaim the quality of this short-chassis, two-seater coupe for the competition driver. 300 h.p. engine with three double-barrel Weber carburetters, a self-locking differential to defeat wheelspin and disc brakes on all four wheels are technical points which explain the car's ability to go from a standstill to 100 m.p.h. and stop in 20 seconds.

CLOSE-UP
Six-cyl.; o.h.c.; 92×92 mm.; 3,670 c.c.; 302 b.h.p.; 9 to 1 comp.; coil ign.; three Weber carbs.; 4-speed, 8.82, 6.16, 4.42, 3.54 to 1; cen. lvr.; susp., f., ind. coil, r., coil trailing link; 2-door; 2-seat; hyd disc brks.; max. 170 m.p.h.; cruise, 120; m.p.g. 17-20; whl. base, 7ft. 9in.; track, f., 4ft. 6in.; r., 4ft. 5½in.; lgth., 14ft. 3¾in.; wdth. 5ft. 6in.; ht. 4ft. 4in.; g.c., 7in.; turng. cir., 32ft.; kerb wt., 24 cwt.; tank 30 gals.; 12-volt.

£3,200 + £1,334.9.2 p.t. = £4,534.9.2

AUSTIN A40 COUNTRYMAN

CHEEKY car with the chunky style that set a new fashion. Family-cum-business drivers like them for the drop-down back rest and fold-away parcel shelf. Racing drivers perform incredible feats on hotted-up ones. Pat Moss and Anne Wisdom clean up in rallies. Recent addition is a station wagon version with lift-up rear window for easier loading.

CLOSE-UP
Four-cyl.; o.h.v.; 62.9×76.2 mm.; 948 c.c.; 34 b.h.p.; 8.3 to 1 comp.; coil ign.; Zenith carb.; 4-speed, 16.52, 10.8, 6.43, 4.55 to 1; cen. lvr.; susp., f., ind. coil, r., half-elliptic; 2-door; 4-seat; hyd. brks.; max. 70 m.p.h.; cruise, 60; m.p.g. 40; whl. base, 6ft. 11¼in.; track, f., 3ft. 11¼in., r. 3ft. 11in.; lgth. 12ft. 0¼in.; wdth. 4ft. 11⅜in.; ht. 4ft. 9½in.; g.c. 6in.; turng. cir. 35ft.; kerb wt. 15½ cwt.; tank 5¾ gals.; 12-volt.

£465 + £194.17.6 p.t. = £659.17.6

Abbreviations—g.c.—ground clearance; susp.—suspension; f.—front; r.—rear; comp.—compression; s.v.—side-valves; o.h.v.—overhead valves; o.h.c.—overhead camshaft; hyd.—hydraulic.

AUSTIN A55 COUNTRYMAN

NEW with an all-steel body, the actual wheel-base of the car remains the same, but the roof panel is extended to the full length of the vehicle and has the characteristic fold-under that distinguishes the Italian Farina styling. Two full-sized side windows and two rear swivel-louvre ventilating windows are added as well as a full-width window fitted in the upward opening rear half-door.

CLOSE-UP
Four-cyl.; o.h.v.; 73×89 mm.; 1,489 c.c.; 55 b.h.p.; 8.3 to 1 comp.; coil ign.; S.U. carb.; 4-speed, 17.73, 10.08, 6.69, 4.87 to 1; cen. lvr.; susp. f. ind. coil, r. half-elliptic; 4-door; 4/5-seat; hyd. brks.; max. 83 m.p.h.; cruise 60; m.p.g. 37-41; whl. base 8ft. 3½in.; track f. 4ft. ⅞in., r. 4ft. 1⅞in.; lgth. 14ft. 10in.; wdth. 5ft. 3½in.; ht. 5ft.; g.c. 6½in.; turng. cir. 37ft.; kerb wt. 22½ cwt.; tank 10 gals.; 12-volt.

£645 + £269 p.t. = £914

AUSTIN A99

THREE-LITRE engine pouring out more than 110 h.p. takes this six-seater up to 100 m.p.h. and servo-assisted disc brakes tame those wild horses at a touch on the pedal. Three-speed gearbox with overdrive on the top two creates a five-speed transmission. Crisp Farina lines enclose generous space for passengers and luggage in a car that is tops for value.

CLOSE-UP
Six-cyl.; o.h.v.; 83×89 mm.; 2,912 c.c.; 108 b.h.p.; 8.2 to 1 comp.; coil ign.; twin S.U. carb.; 3-speed, 12.1, 6.45, 3.91 to 1; col. lvr. BW overdrive; susp., f., ind. coil, r., half-elliptic; anti roll bars front and rear; 4-door; 5/6-seat; hyd. servo brks. disc front; max. 100 m.p.h.; cruise, 80; m.p.g. 22-26; whl. base, 9ft.; track f. 4ft. 6in., r. 4ft. 5½in.; lgth. 15ft. 8in.; wdth. 5ft. 8½in.; ht. 5ft. 0½in.; g.c. 6½in.; turng. cir. 38ft. 9in.; kerb wt. 30½ cwt.; tank 16 gals.; 12-volt.

£810 + £338.12.6 p.t. = £1,148.12.6

AUSTIN SEVEN

A YEAR'S trial of this little car has proved it to be brilliant in conception and splendid in performance. Its secrets include engine mounted crosswise with gears in the sump, front wheel drive and revolutionary rubber suspension. Result: top speed more than 70 m.p.h., fuel consumption more than 40 m.p.g. and seating comfort for four people with lots of parcels. An economy car for every pocket.

CLOSE-UP
Four-cyl.; o.h.v.; 63×68.26 mm.; 848 c.c.; 34 b.h.p.; 8.3 to 1 comp.; coil ign.; S.U. carb.; 4-speed, 13.657, 8.176, 5.317, 3.765 to 1; cen. lvr.; susp., f., ind. rubber r., ind. rubber; 2-door; 4-seat.; hyd. brks.; max. 73 m.p.h.; cruise, 60; m.p.g. 45; whl. base, 6ft. 8in.; track f. 3ft. 11½in.; r. 3ft. 9⅞in.; lgth. 10ft.; wdth. 4ft. 7½in.; ht. 4ft. 5in.; g.c. 6⅜in.; turng. cir. 29ft 6in.; kerb wt. 11½ cwt.; tank 5½ gals.; 12-volt.

£350 + £146.19.2 p.t. = £496.19.2

AUSTIN SEVEN COUNTRYMAN

HALF-TIMBERED brother to the sensational Seven saloon, the Countryman has extended wheelbase and a longer tail enclosing 18¾ cubic feet of cargo space, or 35½ cu. ft. if the rear seat is folded flat. Side-saddle engine and all-independent rubber suspension as on the saloon. De Luxe specification includes two wing mirrors, heater, screen washer, ashtrays and wheel discs.

CLOSE-UP
Four-cyl.; o.h.v.; 62.9×68.2 mm.; 848 c.c.; 37 b.h.p.; 8.3 to 1 comp.; coil ign.; S.U. carb.; 4-speed, 13.66, 8.178, 5.316, 3.765 to 1; cen. lvr.; susp. f. and r. ind. rubber; 4-door; 4-seat; hyd. brks.; max. 70 m.p.h.; cruise 65; m.p.g. 40-45; whl. base 7ft. 0 ⅜in.; track f. 3ft. 11 ⅞in., r. 3ft. 9¾in.; lgth. 10ft. 9¾in.; wdth. 4ft. 7½in.; ht. 4ft. 5½in.; g.c. 7in.; turng. cir. 32ft. 9in.; kerb wt. 12¾ cwt.; tank 5¾ gals.; 12-volt.

£439 + £184.0.10 p.t. = £623.0.10

Abbreviations—g.c.—ground clearance; susp.—suspension; f.—front; r.—rear; comp.—compression; s.v.—side-valves; o.h.v.—overhead valves; o.h.c.—overhead camshaft; hyd.—hydraulic.

17

AUSTIN-HEALEY SPRITE

DONALD HEALEY never designs a bad car, and the Sprite is one of his biggest successes. Its gimmick is its compactness and high cruising speed, and women go for this one as much as men. A baby sports car low priced, cheap to run, cosy and self-contained. A favourite, too, in Europe and America, this snappy model is likely to be with us for a long time.

CLOSE-UP

Four-cyl.; o.h.v.; 62.9 × 76.2 mm.; 948 c.c.; 42.5 b.h.p.; 8.3 to 1 comp.; coil ign.; twin S.U. carbs.; 4-speed, 15.31, 10.02, 5.96, 4.22 to 1; cen. lvr.; susp., f., ind. coil, r., quarter-elliptic; 2-door; 2-seat.; hyd. brks.; max. 80 m.p.h.; cruise, 70; m.p.g., 34; whl. base, 6ft. 8in.; track f., 3ft. 9¾in.; r., 3ft. 8¾in.; lgth., 11ft. 0⅝in.; wdth., 4ft. 5in.; ht. 4ft. 1¾in.; g.c. 5in.; turng. cir. 32ft. 1½in.; kerb wt., 13 cwt.; tank, 6 gals.; 12-volt.

£445 + £186.10.10 p.t. = £631.10.10

AUSTIN HEALEY 3000

PROOF of this car's brilliant characteristics is the number of expert crews who now take it on Europe's most difficult international rallies. The powerful 2.9 engine gives a top speed in excess of 110 m.p.h., with first class stopping by Girling disc brakes in front. You can have it as a two-seater or occasional four-seater for the children at the back. Extras include overdrive, wire wheels and detachable hard top.

CLOSE-UP

Six-cyl.; o.h.v.; 83.36 × 89 mm.; 2,912 c.c.; 124 b.h.p.; 9.03 to 1 comp.; coil ign.; twin S.U. carbs.; 4-speed, 10.38, 7.87, 4.64, 3.545 to 1; col. lvr. Laycock overdrive opt.; susp., f., ind. coil, r., half elliptic; 2-door; 2/4-seat opt.; hyd. servo brks., disc front; max. 115 m.p.h.; cruise 90; m.p.g. 20-24; whl. base 7ft. 8in.; track f., 4ft. 0¾in.; r. 4ft. 2in.; lgth. 13ft. 1½in.; wdth. 5ft.; ht. 4ft. 1in.; g.c. 4½in.; turng. cir. 35ft. 7in.; kerb wt. 22 cwt.; tank, 12 gals.; 12-volt.

£824 + £344.9.2 p.t. = £1,168.9.2

AUTO UNION 1000S

WITH three-cylinder two-stroke engine, four-speed all-synchromesh gearbox and front-wheel drive, the Auto Union has an individual character and excellent road holding. Two-door coupe, four-door saloon, station wagon and sports coupe complete the range. The Saxomat automatic clutch, reclining seats and sliding roof are among the optional extras. Auto Union is now associated financially with Mercedes-Benz.

CLOSE-UP

Three-cyl; two-stroke; 76 × 74 mm.; 980 c.c.; 57 b.h.p. 7.25 to 1 comp.; coil ign.; Solex carb.; 4-speed, 18, 10.47, 6.18, 4.32 to 1; col. lvr.; susp. f. ind. transv.; r. transv. leaf; 2-door; 4-seat; hyd. brks.; max. 90 m.p.h.; cruise 75; m.p.g. 32-34; whl. base 7ft. 8½in.; track f. 4ft. 2in., r. 4ft. 5in.; lgth. 13ft. 8½in.; wdth. 5ft. 6in.; ht. 4ft. 4½in.; g.c. 8in.; turng. cir. 36ft.; kerb wt. 17¾ cwt.; tank 10 gals.; 6-volt.

£886 + £370.5.10 p.t. = £1,256.5.10

BENTLEY CONTINENTAL

THE ultimate in elegance in a sporting car, this is the aristocrat of them all. A powerful light alloy V-8 engine sends it gliding along the road at speeds of two miles a minute, with consummate silence and comfort. A car for the wealthy, it has wealth stamped on every feature. Its efficiency in stopping with four-shoe front brakes matches its speed. A dream car for the sporting-minded.

CLOSE-UP

Eight-cyl.; o.h.v.; 104.14 × 91.44 mm.; 6,230 c.c.; 8 to 1 comp.; coil ign.; twin S.U. carbs.; 4-speed automatic, 11.19, 7.68, 4.23, 2.92 to 1; col. lvr.; susp. f. ind. coil, r. half-elliptic; 2/4-door; 4-seat; hyd. servo brks.; max. 120 m.p.h.; cruise, 90-100; m.p.g. 14-16; whl. base, 10ft. 3in.; track, f., 4ft. 10½in.; r., 5ft.; lgth., 17ft. 8in.; wdth., 6ft.; ht., 5ft. 2in.; g.c., 7in.; turng. cir., 41ft. 8in.; kerb wt., 39¾ cwt.; tank, 18 gals.; 12-volt.

£6,015 + £2,507.7.6 p.t. = £8,522.7.6

Abbreviations—g.c.—ground clearance; susp.—suspension; f.—front; r.—rear; comp.—compression; s.v.—side-valves; o.h.v.—overhead valves; o.h.c.—overhead camshaft; hyd.—hydraulic.

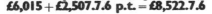

BENTLEY S2

DEFINITELY a luxury car with all the caviare-class trimmings that go with it. Its eight-cylinder engine attains a top speed well in excess of 100 m.p.h. with effortless ease. On air-conditioned cars the refrigerator is artfully concealed inside the right front wing. Automatic transmission, servo-assisted brakes and long-life chassis lubrication, and there is a ride-control switch on the steering column to deal with heavy loads or rough roads.

CLOSE-UP
Eight-cyl.; o.h.v.; 104.14×91.44 mm.; 6,230 c.c.; 8 to 1 comp.; coil ign.; twin S.U. carbs.; 4-speed automatic, 11.75, 8.10, 4.46, 3.08 to 1; col. lvr.; susp., f., ind. coil, r. half elliptic; 4-door; 5/6-seat; hyd. servo brks.; max. 110 m.p.h.; cruise, 90; m.p.g. 12-15; whl. base, 10ft. 3in.; track f., 4ft. 10in.; r. 5ft.; lgth., 17ft. 7¾in.; wdth., 6ft. 2¾in.; ht. 5ft. 4in.; g.c., 7in.; turng. cir., 41ft. 8in.; kerb wt., 41½ cwt.; tank, 18 gals.; 12-volt.

£4,195 + £1,749.0.10 p.t. = £5,944.0.10

BERKELEY QB95

A STOUT-HEARTED little sports car that is new for the Show. It is eight inches longer and four inches wider than the old B95 and there is a good sized boot for this two-seater. Engine is 692 o.h.v. Royal Enfield, giving a top speed of 85 m.p.h. and a cruising speed of 55 m.p.h. If you keep your foot well back on the accelerator pedal, this saucy little sports model will give you 50 m.p.g. at 50 m.p.h.

CLOSE-UP
Two-cyl.; o.h.v. air cooled; 70×90 mm.; 692 c.c.; 40 b.h.p.; 7½ to 1 comp.; coil ign.; Amal carb.; 4-speed, 13.7, 8.62, 5.95, 4.31 to 1; cen. lvr.; susp. f. and r. ind. coil; 2-door; 2-seat; hyd. brks.; max. 85 m.p.h.; cruise 55; m.p.g. 45-60; whl. base 5ft. 10in.; track f. 3ft. 6½in.; r. 3ft. 6in.; lgth. 10ft. 5½in.; wdth. 4ft. 2in.; ht. 3ft. 10in.; g.c. 3½in.; turng. cir. 28ft.; kerb wt. 7 cwt.; tank 5½ gals.; 12-volt.

£442.8.8 + £185.9.5 p.t. = £627.18.1

B.M.W. 507

LONG, lean and speedy lines that stand out in any company distinguish the fastest of the B.M.Ws. The V-8 engine is offered in two versions—the most powerful now said to give 173 b.h.p., enough for 135 m.p.h. Bodies are coupe or roadster, panelled in light alloy. Extras on request: disc front brakes, detachable hard top for the roadster.

CLOSE-UP
Eight-cyl.; o.h.v.; 82×75 mm.; 3,168 c.c.; 173 b.h.p.; 7.8 to 1 comp.; coil ign.; 2 Solex carbs.; 4-speed, 12.54, 7.66, 5.03, 3.7 to 1; cen. lvr.; susp., f., ind. torsion bar, r., torsion bar; 2-door; 2-seat; hyd. servo brks.; max. 135 m.p.h.; cruise, 95; m.p.g., 15-17; whl. base, 8ft. 1½in.; track f., 4ft. 8¾in., r., 4ft. 8in.; lgth., 14ft. 5in.; wdth., 5ft. 5in.; ht., 4ft. 1½in.; g.c. 6in.; turng. cir., 36ft.; kerb wt., 23½ cwt.; tank, 21 gals.; 12-volt.

£3,100 + £1,292.15.10 p.t. = £4,392.15.10

B.M.W. 502 SUPER

SOBER styling and craftsman-finished interior combined with a 100-plus maximum make this the car for the busy director with conservative tastes. Light alloys are used in V-8 engine and four-speed all-synchromesh gearbox. Suspension is by extra-long torsion bars, and German-built Dunlop discs are now optional braking equipment at the front. Other extras: rev counter and reclining seats.

CLOSE-UP
Eight-cyl.; o.h.v.; 82×75 mm.; 3,168 c.c.; 140 b.h.p.; 7.3 to 1 comp.; coil ign.; two Solex carbs.; 4-speed, 15.9, 9.2, 5.8, 4.22 to 1; col. lvr.; susp. f. ind. torsion bar, r. torsion bar; 4-door; 5/6-seat; hyd. brks. disc front opt.; max. 110 m.p.h.; cruise 90; m.p.g. 22-24; whl. base 9ft. 3½in.; track f. 4ft. 4½in.; r. 4ft. 7½in.; lgth. 15ft. 6in.; wdth. 5ft. 10in.; ht. 5ft.; g.c. 7in.; turng. cir. 39ft.; kerb wt. 27 cwt.; tank 15½ gals.; 12-volt.

£2,165 + £903.4.2 p.t. = £3,068.4.2

Abbreviations—g.c.—ground clearance; susp.—suspension; f.—front; r.—rear; comp.—compression; s.v.—side-valves; o.h.v.—overhead valves; o.h.c.—overhead camshaft; hyd.—hydraulic.

B.M.W. 700

SELLING as fast as B.M.W. can make them, these neat, nimble economy cars have style and zip for people with young ideas. Flat-twin, air-cooled engine is at the rear, and suspension is all-independent. Two models: four-seater saloon and two-seater coupe. Synchromesh on all gears including first; rack and pinion steering. Sliding roof or folding top are optional extras.

CLOSE-UP

Two-cyl.; o.h.v. air cooled; 78×73 mm.; 696 c.c.; 35 b.h.p.; 7.5 to 1 comp.; coil ign.; downdraught carb.; 4-speed, 19.22, 10.53, 6.89, 4.59 to 1; cen. lvr.; susp. f. and r., ind. coil; 2-door; 2/4-seat; hyd. brks.; max. 78 m.p.h.; cruise, 60; m.p.g. 45-50; whl. base, 6ft. 11½in.; track f., 4ft. 2in., r., 3ft. 11½in.; lgth., 11ft. 7½in.; wdth., 4ft. 10½in.; ht. 4ft. 1⅝in.; g.c. 6in.; turng. cir., 29ft.; kerb wt., 12½ cwt.; tank, 6½ gals.; 12-volt.

£513.1.9 + £214.18.3 p.t. = £728

B.M.W. ISETTA

THIS is a well-proven runabout seen everywhere. You get into it by opening the front lid and find ample space for two grown-ups. It can be parked in spaces where others cannot get, and gives moderate comfort at medium speeds. The home version is built near Brighton. A useful little car, with only minor moderations this year, its popularity is assured.

CLOSE-UP

Single-cyl.; o.h.v.; air cooled; 72×73 mm.; 295 c.c.; 13 b.h.p.; 7 to 1 comp.; coil ign.; single carb.; 4-speed, 23.21, 12.14, 8.17, 6.1 to 1; side lvr.; susp. f., ind. coil; r., quarter-elliptic; 1-door; 2/3-seat; hyd. brks.; max. 55 m.p.h.; cruise 45-50; m.p.g. 65-75; whl. base, 4ft. 10in.; track f., 4ft., r., 1ft. 9in.; lgth., 7ft. 6in.; wdth., 4ft. 7in.; ht., 4ft. 5in.; g.c., 6½in.; turng. cir., 30ft.; kerb wt., 6⅖ cwt.; tank, 2¾ gals.; 12-volt.

£257.10.10 + £108.8.8 p.t. = £365.19.6

BORGWARD ISABELLA

SPRIGHTLY Isabella finds ways to please everyone. Saloon, sports saloon, coupe, convertible or station wagon form a range that meets most needs in the 1½-litre market. Standard engine gives 60 b.h.p.; Touring Sports unit turns out 75 b.h.p. Suspension is all-independent, and gearbox has synchromesh on all four speeds. Optional extras include folding or sliding roof, reclining seats.

CLOSE-UP

Four-cyl.; o.h.v.; 75×84 mm.; 1,493 c.c.; 60 b.h.p.; 7 to 1 comp.; coil ign.; Solex carb.; 4-speed, 15.05, 8.38, 5.3, 3.9 to 1; col. lvr.; susp. f. and r. ind. coil; 2-door; 4-seat; hyd. brks.; max. 80 m.p.h.; cruise 70; m.p.g. 32; whl. base 8ft. 6½in.; track f. and r. 4ft. 5⅜in.; lgth. 14ft. 4in.; wdth. 5ft. 7in.; ht. 4ft. 9in.; g.c. 6⅜in.; turng. cir. 36ft.; kerb wt. 20½ cwt.; tank, 8¾ gals.; 6-volt.

£845 + £353.4.2 p.t. = £1,198.4.2

BORGWARD 2.3 LITRE

FIRST German car to be offered with option of self-levelling air springs, this is Borgward's prestige model for the busy executive. 2¼-litre six-cylinder engine gives it 100 h.p. for fast motorway cruising and the gearbox is fully synchronised. Safety features include padded steering wheel and flexible instrument cowl. Two-speed wipers, headlamp flasher, fuel reserve warning lamp and fog lamps are standard.

CLOSE-UP

Six-cyl.; o.h.v.; 75×84.5 mm.; 2,240 c.c.; 98 b.h.p.; 8.2 to 1 comp.; coil ign.; Solex carb.; 4-speed, 15.05, 8.38, 5.3, 3.9 to 1; col. lvr.; susp. f. and r., ind. coil; 4-door; 5-seat; hyd. brks.; max. 100 m.p.h.; cruise, 80; m.p.g. 23-25; whl. base, 8ft. 8½in.; lgth., 15ft. 5⅝in.; wdth., 5ft. 8½ir.; ht. 4ft. 9¾in.; turng. cir., 36ft.; tank, 10 gals.; 12-voit.

BRISTOL 406

FOLLOWING the upheavals which concentrated the famous names of the aircraft industry into new corporations for greater efficiency, Bristol's car division has become an independent company producing individualistic quality cars. Three-carb 2.2-litre hemispherical-head engine, Laycock overdrive and servo-operated disc brakes are features. Spare wheel is stored in a front wing to leave maximum free trunk space in the tail.

CLOSE-UP

Six-cyl.; o.h.v.; 68.69 × 99.64mm.; 2,216 c.c.; 105 b.h.p.; 8.5 to 1 comp.; coil ign.; 3 Solex carbs.; 4-speed, 15.42, 7.79, 5.52, 4.27 to 1; cen. lvr. Laycock overdrive; susp., f., ind. transv. leaf, r., torsion bar; 2-door; 4-seat; disc Servo brks.; max. 100 m.p.h.; cruise, 85; m.p.g., 20-23; whl. base, 9ft. 6in.; track, f., 4ft. 5in.; r., 4ft. 8in.; lgth., 16ft. 6in.; wdth., 5ft. 8in.; ht., 5ft.; g.c. 6½in.; turng. cir., 37ft. 6in.; kerb wt., 26¾ cwt.; tank, 18 gals.; 12-volt.

£2,995 + £1,249.0.10 p.t. = £4,244.0.10

BUICK SPECIAL

CASHING in on the swing to smaller cars, Buick sheds its excess avoirdupois to tempt the economy-minded buyer with this space-saving family model powered by a light alloy V8 engine of 3½ litres. Another technical feature is a new lightweight automatic transmission offered as an alternative to the normal synchromesh gearbox. Specification below refers to the larger Le Sabre.

CLOSE-UP

Eight-cyl.; o.h.v.; 104.775 × 86.36 mm.; 5,957 c.c.; 233 b.h.p.; 9 to 1 comp.; coil ign.; Carter carb.; 2-speed automatic, 6.11, 3.36 to 1; col. lvr.; susp. f. ind. coil, r. coil; 4-door; 6-seat; hyd. servo brks.; max. 106 m.p.h.; cruise 80; m.p.g. 16-19; whl. base 10ft. 3in.; track f. 5ft. 2⅜in.; r. 5ft.; lgth. 18ft. 1⅛in.; wdth. 6ft. 8⅜in.; ht. 4ft. 9in.; g.c. 6½in.; turng. cir. 44ft.; kerb wt. 39 cwt.; tank 16¾ gals.; 12-volt.

BUICK ELECTRA

BIGGEST of the big Buicks, this is the luxury model on the long wheelbase, powered by a great V8 engine of 6½ litres, fitted with four-barrel carburetter and twin exhausts. Transmission is automatic, through a fluid torque converter and two-speed planetary gears. The body range includes saloons, hard-top coupes and convertibles, all bold, broad and low-built.

CLOSE-UP

Eight-cyl.; o.h.v.; 101.36 × 92.45 mm.; 6,571 c.c.; 312 b.h.p.; 10.25 to 1 comp.; coil ign.; Stromberg carb.; 2-speed auto, 5.88, 3.23 to 1; col. lvr.; susp. f. ind. coil, r. coil; 2-door; 6-seat; hyd. servo brks.; max. 112 m.p.h.; cruise 80; m.p.g. 14-18; whl. base 10ft. 3in.; track f. 5ft. 2⅜in., r. 5ft.; lgth. 18ft. 1⅛in.; wdth. 6ft. 8⅜in.; ht. 4ft. 9in.; g.c. 6½in.; turng. cir. 44ft.; kerb wt. 41 cwt.; tank 16¾ gals.; 12-volt.

£2,335 + £974.0.10 p.t. = £3,309.0.10

CADILLAC 62

WORLD'S top-selling prestige car, Cadillac has a new body for 1961, but retains its opulent extrovert character. Engines are V8s of 6.4 litres, giving more than 300 h.p.; and there is a more compact automatic transmission to reduce the hump in the floor. Equipment on dream-car scale includes electric controls for windows, sliding seats, and automatic operation for tops on convertibles.

CLOSE-UP

Eight-cyl.; o.h.v.; 101.6 × 98.42 mm.; 6,384 c.c.; 345 b.h.p.; 10.5 to 1 comp.; coil ign.; Carter carb.; 4-speed auto, 11.66, 7.49, 4.55, 2.94 to 1; col. lvr.; susp. f. ind. coil, r. coil; 4-door; 6-seat; hyd. servo brks.; max. 110 m.p.h.; cruise 80; m.p.g. 13-15; whl. base 10ft. 9½in.; track f. and r. 5ft. 1in.; lgth. 18ft. 6in.; wdth. 6ft. 7in.; ht. 4ft. 8½in.; g.c. 5in.; turng. cir. 45ft.; kerb wt. 42⅗ cwt.; tank 20 gals.; 12-volt.

£3,200 + £1,334.9.2 p.t. = £4,534.9.2

Abbreviations—g.c.—ground clearance; susp.—suspension; f.—front; r.—rear; comp.—compression; s.v.—side-valves; o.h.v.—overhead valves; o.h.c.—overhead camshaft; hyd.—hydraulic.

CADILLAC 75

MORE than 20 feet long, the limousine is a favourite with crowned heads, oil sheikhs and city tycoons who leave their chauffeurs to cope with the parking problems. Brakes and steering have servo assistance. Automatic transmission, four headlamps, fog lamps, reversing lamps, heater, screen washer, radio, clock and electric press-button window controls are included in the lavish equipment.

CLOSE-UP
Eight-cyl.; o.h.v.; 101.6×98.42 mm.; 6,384 c.c.; 325 b.h.p.; 10.5 to 1 comp.; coil ign.; Rochester carb.; 4-speed auto., 13.32, 8.56, 5.20, 3.36 to 1; col. lvr.; susp. f. ind. coil, r. coil; 4-door; 6-seat; hyd. servo brks.; max. 110 m.p.h.; cruise 80; m.p.g. 12-14; whl. base 12ft. 6in.; track f. and r. 5ft. 1in.; lgth. 20ft. 4½in.; wdth. 6ft. 7½in.; ht. 4ft. 11½in.; g.c. 5⅞in.; turng. cir. 50ft. 9in.; kerb wt. 51 cwt.; tank 16¾ gals.; 12-volt.

CHEVROLET BEL AIR

STILL the best-selling big car with American buyers, the Chevrolet has undergone major styling changes for 1961. Fins are still a feature and the trunk is unusually large, with special storage space for packages and a bigger-than-usual opening. Choice of six- or eight-cylinder engines and an immense range of bodies: saloons, coupes, convertibles and station wagons.

CLOSE-UP
Eight-cyl.; o.h.v.; 98.48×76.2 mm.; 4,637 c.c.; 170 b.h.p.; 8.5 to 1 comp.; coil ign.; Rochester carb.; 3-speed, 8.76, 5.43, 3.55 to 1; col. lvr., auto trans. opt.; susp. f. ind. coil, r. coil; 4-door; 6-seat; hyd. servo brks.; max. 103 m.p.h.; cruise 80; m.p.g. 15-17; whl. base 9ft. 11in.; track f. 5ft. 0⅞in., r. 4ft. 11⅜in.; lgth. 17ft. 5in.; wdth. 6ft. 6⅜in.; ht. 4ft. 8½in.; g.c. 6in.; turng. cir. 40ft. 8in.; kerb wt. 32 cwt.; tank 16½ gals.; 12-volt.

£1,479 + £619 p.t. = £2,096

CHEVROLET CORVAIR

BLAZING a new trail with air-cooled flat six engine in the tail, all-independent suspension and option of synchromesh or automatic transmission, this is the most radical of the "compacts" which have transformed the American motorist's attitude to automobiles. Body is improved for 1961. Mechanical changes ensure longer life for fan belts, freedom from carburetter icing. Fuel tank is in front under the trunk.

CLOSE-UP
Six-cyl.; o.h.v.; air-cooled; 2,376 c.c.; 80 b.h.p.; 8 to 1 comp.; coil ign.; two Rochester carbs.; 3-speed, cen. lvr.; susp. f. and r. ind. coil; 4-door; 5/6-seat; hyd. brks.; max. 86 m.p.h.; cruise 75; m.p.g. 22; whl. base 9ft.; track f. and r. 4ft. 6in.; lgth. 15ft.; wdth. 5ft. 6⅞in.; ht. 4ft. 3⅜in.; g.c. 6in.; kerb wt. 21½ cwt.; tank 9¼ gals.; 12-volt.

£1,235 + £515.14.2 p.t. = £1,750.14.2

CHEVROLET CORVETTE

AN all-American sports car, distinguished by its lack of chrome and trimmings. Built to travel at nearly two miles a minute, this gracefully curved model has been a big winner in sports car races in the United States. Petrol consumption is 17 miles to the gallon, which means that you pay for the speed. But in a snazzy car like this it is worth it.

CLOSE-UP
Eight-cyl.; o.h.v.; 98.42×76.19 mm.; 4,637 c.c.; 230 b.h.p.; 9.5 to 1 comp.; coil ign.; 2-choke carb.; 3-speed, 8.17, 4.88, 3.7 to 1; cen. lvr.; 4-speed, 8.14, 6.14, 4.84, 3.7 auto. opt.; cen. lvr.; susp. f. ind. coil, r. coil; 2-door; 2-seat; hyd. brks.; max. 110 m.p.h.; cruise 80; m.p.g. 15; whl. base 8ft. 6in.; track f. 4ft. 9in., r. 4ft. 11in.; lgth. 14ft. 9in.; wdth. 6ft. 1in.; ht. 4ft. 3in.; g.c. 8in.; turng. cir. 37ft.; kerb wt. 25¾ cwt.; tank 16 gals.; 12-volt.

£2,050 + £855.5.10 p.t. = £2,905.5.10

Abbreviations—g.c.—ground clearance; susp.—suspension; f.—front; r.—rear; comp.—compression; s.v.—side-valves; o.h.v.—overhead valves; o.h.c.—overhead camshaft; hyd.—hydraulic.

CHRYSLER NEW YORKER

THE grille made famous on the 150 m.p.h. Chrysler 300 F now extends to all the range. Under the bonnet is a V8 engine giving about 350 h.p. on the test bed. Chrysler puts power to work inside with electricity to slide seats and move windows, hydraulic assistance to take the effort out of steering, and vacuum servo to help the braking.

CLOSE-UP
Eight-cyl.; o.h.v.; 106.2×95.30 mm.; 6,768 c.c.; 350 b.h.p.; 10 to 1 comp.; coil ign.; Carter carb.; 3-speed auto., 8.11, 4.79, 3.31 to 1; push buttons; susp. f. ind. torsion bar, r. half-elliptic; 4-door; 6-seat; hyd. servo brks.; max. 115 m.p.h.; cruise 80; m.p.g. 13-15; whl. base 10ft. 6in.; track f. 5ft. 1½in., r. 5ft.; lgth. 18ft. 4in.; wdth. 6ft. 7½in.; ht. 4ft. 7in.; g.c. 6in.; turng. cir. 47ft.; kerb wt. 37½ cwt.; tank 19½ gals.; 12-volt.

CITROEN BIJOU

AT high tax-paid prices, the rustic charms of the little 2 CV's corrugated coachwork had little appeal for English buyers, so the Bijou brings modern lines in glass-reinforced plastic to augment the appeal of Citroen's almost unbreakable economy chassis: flat-twin, air-cooled engine, front-wheel drive, all-independent suspension, interconnected between front and rear and oversize inboard front brakes.

CLOSE-UP
Two-cyl.; o.h.v.; air cooled; 66×62 mm.; 425 c.c.; 12 b.h.p.; 7 to 1 comp.; coil ign.; Solex carb.; 4-speed, 25.9, 12.56, 7.5, 5.7 to 1; dash lvr.; susp. f. and r. ind. coil; 2-door; 4-seat; hyd. brks.; max. 55-60 m.p.h.; cruise 45; m.p.g. 54-58; whl. base 7ft. 9½in.; track f. and r. 4ft. 1⅜in.; lgth. 12ft. 11in.; wdth. 5ft. 2in.; ht. 4ft. 7in.; g.c. 7in.; turng. cir. 34ft. 6in.; kerb wt. 11 cwt.; tank 4¾ gals.; 6-volt.
£490 + £205.5.10 p.t. = £695.5.10

CITROEN DS

UNIQUE in style and sales points, the years-ahead car with the revolutionary hydraulic-pneumatic self-adjusting suspension. Disc front brakes with a clever device to distribute braking according to load. Screen washer worked by compressed air in spare wheel. One-spoke safety steering wheel. Quick release wings removed by undoing one nut. Translucent plastic roof. Front wheel drive.

CLOSE-UP
Four-cyl.; o.h.v.; 78×100 mm.; 1,911 c.c.; 75 b.h.p.; 7.5 to 1 comp.; coil ign.; Weber or Zenith carb.; 4-speed, 13.79, 6.96, 4.77, 3.31 to 1; dash lvr.; susp. f. and r. ind. hyd. pneu.; 4-door; 5/6-seat; hyd. power brks., disc front; max. 85-90 m.p.h.; cruise 70; m.p.g. 28; whl. base 10ft. 3in.; track f. 4ft. 11⁷₁₆in., r. 4ft. 3⅛in.; lgth. 15ft. 9in.; wdth. 5ft. 10½in.; ht. 4ft. 10in.; g.c. 6⅛in.; turng. cir. 36ft.; kerb wt. 24 cwt.; tank 14 gals.; 12-volt.
£1,196 + £499.9.2 p.t. = £1,695.9.2

CITROEN ID

SAME self-levelling air-oil suspension that turns driving into gliding, but without the DS's servo aid for steering, clutch and gearshift. Engine is less powerful, with a different cylinder head. The station wagon seats eight and has constant ground clearance regardless of load—in fact you can vary ground clearance to suit road conditions by a lever inside the car.

CLOSE-UP
Four-cyl.; o.h.v.; 78×100 mm.; 1,911 c.c.; 66 b.h.p.; 7.5 to 1 comp.; coil ign.; Solex carb.; 4-speed, 13.79, 7.35, 4.77, 3.31 to 1; col. lvr.; susp. f. and r. hyd. pneu.; 4-door; 8-seat; hyd. brks., disc front; max. 85 m.p.h.; cruise 70; m.p.g. 25-30; whl. base 10ft. 3in.; track f. 4ft. 11⁷₁₆in., r. 4ft. 3⅛in.; lgth. 16ft. 4in.; wdth. 5ft. 10½in.; ht. 4ft. 11⅜in.; g.c. 6⅛in.; turng. cir. 36ft. 1in.; kerb wt. 25¾ cwt.; tank, 14 gals.; 12-volt.
£1,308 + £546.2.6 p.t. = £1,854.2.6

COMET

A STAGE larger than the Falcon, this is Ford's entry in the area between the compact and the colossal. As introduced in mid-1960 it had the Falcon engine but a larger power unit is on the way. Unit body-chassis, coil spring front suspension and option of synchromesh or automatic transmission are technical points. Bodies are saloons with two or four doors.

CLOSE-UP
Six-cyl.; o.h.v.; 88.9 × 63.5 mm.; 2,364 c.c.; 90 b.h.p.; 8.7 to 1 comp.; coil ign.; downdraught carb.; 3-speed, 11.71, 6.23, 3.56 to 1; col. lvr., auto. trans. opt.; susp. f. ind. coil, r. half-elliptic; 4-door; 5/6-seat; hyd. brks.; max. 84 m.p.h.; cruise 75; m.p.g. 20-22; whl. base 9ft. 6in.; track f. 4ft. 7in., r. 4ft. 6½in.; lgth. 16ft. 3in.; wdth. 5ft. 10½in.; ht. 4ft. 6½in.; g.c. i2$\frac{9}{10}$in.; turng. cir. 39ft.; tank 11 gals.; 12-volt.

DAF

SMALLEST car in the world with fully automatic transmission, a chassis that needs no greasing, an air-cooled flat-twin engine that cannot boil or freeze, and all-independent suspension for jolt-free road holding. This is the unique sales story for the DAF, the only Dutch family car. Silent automatic drive is by long-lasting, non-slip rubber and nylon belts.

CLOSE-UP
Two-cyl.; o.h.v. air cooled; 76 × 65 mm.; 590 c.c.; 22 b.h.p.; 7.1 to 1 comp.; coil ign.; downdraught carb.; variomatic between 20 and 4.4 to 1; cen. lvr.; susp. f. trans. leaf spring, r. swing axles, coil springs; 2-door; 4/5-seat; hyd. brks.; max. 57 m.p.h.; cruise 57; m.p.g. 48; whl. base 6ft. 9in.; track f. and r. 3ft. 10½in.; lgth. 11ft. 10in.; wdth. 4ft. 9in.; ht. 4ft. 6½in.; g.c. 7in.; turng. cir. 31ft.; kerb wt. 12$\frac{2}{5}$ cwt.; tank 6¼ gals.; 6-volt.

£480 + £201.2.3 p.t. = £681.2.3

DAIMLER SP250

A LIGHT alloy overhead-valve V8 engine of advanced design gives this Daimler sports model its high performance while disc brakes on all wheels ensure swift fade-free stopping power. The convertible body, with winding side windows, is made from easily repairable plastic mouldings and a detachable hard top turns it into a snug coupe for winter driving.

CLOSE-UP
Eight-cyl.; o.h.v.; 76.2 × 69.5 mm.; 2,530 c.c.; 140 b.h.p.; 8.2 to 1 comp.; coil ign.; twin S.U. carb.; 4-speed, 10.5, 6.236, 4.41, 3.58 to 1; cen. lvr.; susp. f., ind. coil, r., half-elliptic; 2-door; 2/3-seat; hyd. disc brks.; max. 120 m.p.h.; cruise, 90; m.p.g. 28; whl. base, 7ft. 8in.; track f., 4ft. 2in., r., 4ft.; lgth. 13ft. 4½in.; wdth., 5ft. 0½in.; ht., 4ft. 2½in.; g.c., 6in.; turng. cir., 33ft.; kerb wt., 19½ cwt.; tank, 12 gals.; 12-volt.

£983.18.3 + £411.1.9 p.t. = £1,395

DAIMLER MAJESTIC

AFTER Jaguar's recent take-over the question arose: will they continue with Daimlers? Answer is yes and the Majestic is one of the favoured models. It is really a car for the business executive who likes to drive himself—and to drive fast. With this beauty it is possible to register 100 m.p.h. on the clock, along with power-assisted disc brakes, and a great deal of interior room to carry brother executives.

CLOSE-UP
Six-cyl.; o.h.v.; 86.36 × 107.95 mm.; 3,794 c.c.; 147 b.h.p.; 7.5 to 1 comp.; coil ign.; twin S.U. carbs.; 3-speed BW auto., 9.04, 5.62, 3.92 to 1; col. lvr.; susp., f., ind. coil, r., half-elliptic; 4-door; 6-seat; disc servo brks.; max. 100 m.p.h.; cruise, 80; m.p.g., 17-22; whl. base, 9ft. 6in.; track, f., 4ft. 8in.; r., 4ft. 9in.; lgth., 16ft. 4in.; wdth., 6ft. 1½in.; ht., 5ft. 2½in.; g.c., 7in.; turng. cir., 42ft.; kerb wt., 36 cwt.; tank, 18 gals.; 12-volt.

£1,760.7.8 + £734.12.4 p.t. = £2,495

Abbreviations—g.c.—ground clearance; susp.—suspension; f.—front; r.—rear; comp.—compression; s.v.—side-valves; o.h.v.—overhead valves; o.h.c.—overhead camshaft; hyd.—hydraulic.

DAIMLER MAJESTIC MAJOR

HERE is the big boy in the Daimler range. It is a large and graceful car, with tremendous power in the engine, and lots of space for the chauffeur and his passengers. Jaguar, who bought up Daimlers this year, have plenty of faith in the model which is really for the well-to-do. This big Daimler is the latest addition to a long line of prestige cars.

CLOSE-UP

Eight-cyl.; o.h.v.; 95.25 × 80.01 mm.; 4,500 c.c.; 220 b.h.p.; 8 to 1 comp.; coil ign.; two S.U. carbs.; auto. 3-speed, 8.7, 5.41, 3.77 to 1; col. lvr.; susp. f. ind. coil, r. half-elliptic; 4-door; 5/6-seat; hyd. disc brks.; max. 120 m.p.h.; cruise 95; m.p.g. 20-22; whl. base 9ft. 6in.; track f. and r. 4ft. 9in.; lgth. 16ft. 10in.; wdth. 6ft. 1⅛in.; ht. 5ft. 2¼in.; g.c. 7in.; turng. cir. 42ft.; kerb wt. 37¾ cwt.; tank 16 gals.; 12-volt.

£2,113.6.6 + £881.13.6 p.t. = £2,995

DE SOTO FIREFLITE

MEDIUM model from the Chrysler group, the Fireflite has distinctive new front-end styling for 1961. There are more tolerant engines, that will take ordinary grades of fuel without pinking. Unit body chassis, with torsion bar front suspension. Around six litres of V8 engine, and choice of three-speed synchromesh transmission, or two different automatics with two and three speeds.

CLOSE-UP

Eight-cyl.; o.h.v.; 108 × 85.9 mm.; 6,260 c.c.; 325 b.h.p.; 10 to 1 comp.; coil ign.; Carter carb.; 3-speed auto. 8.1, 4.79, 3.31 to 1; push buttons; susp. f. ind. torsion bar, r. half-elliptic; 2-door; 6-seat; hyd. servo brks.; max. 112 m.p.h.; cruise 80; m.p.g. 14-15; whl. base 10ft. 6in.; track f. 5ft. 1in., r. 5ft.; lgth. 18ft. 5in.; wdth. 6ft. 6½in.; ht. 4ft. 9in.; g.c. 5½in.; turng. cir. 47ft.; kerb wt. 36 cwt.; tank 19 gals.; 12-volt.

DKW JUNIOR

CATCHING on fast with Continental buyers, the lively Junior is a new model made by Auto Union in a new factory. Its three-cylinder two-stroke engine is lubricated by oil in the fuel. The gearbox has four speeds, steering is by rack and pinion, suspension is by torsion bars, and front brakes are mounted inboard to reduce unsprung weight.

CLOSE-UP

Three-cyl.; two-stroke; 68 × 68 mm.; 741 c.c.; 39 b.h.p.; 8.1 to 1 comp.; coil ign.; downdraught carb.; 4-speed, 14.45, 8.6, 5.45, 3.62 to 1; col. lvr.; susp. f. ind. tors. bar, r. tors. bar; 2-door; 4-seat; hyd. brks.; max. 75 m.p.h.; cruise 70; m.p.g. 37; whl. base 7ft. 3in.; track f. 3ft. 10½in., r. 3ft. 11½in.; lgth. 13ft.; wdth. 5ft. 2⅛in.; ht. 4ft. 7½in.; g.c. 7in.; turng. cir. 31ft.; kerb wt. 14 cwt.; tank 8 gals.; 6-volt.

£563.15 + £236.2.6 p.t. = £799.17.6

DODGE DART

DIMENSIONED in between the American "compact" cars and the mammoth petrol guzzlers, the Dart scored a bull's-eye in this year's sales contest and continues with improvements for 1961. Choice of 3.7-litre six-cylinder engine or a 5.2-litre V8 and vast range of transmissions, colour schemes and body styles. All have unit body-chassis with torsion bar front suspension.

CLOSE-UP

Six-cyl.; o.h.v.; 86.36 × 104.77 mm.; 3,682 c.c.; 145 b.h.p.; 8.5 to 1 comp.; coil ign.; Ball & Ball carb.; 3-speed, 8.85, 5.94, 3.54 to 1; col. lvr., auto trans. opt.; susp. f. ind. torsion bar, r. half-elliptic; 4-door; 5-seat; hyd. brks.; max. 88 m.p.h.; cruise 75; m.p.g. 14-18; whl. base 9ft. 10in.; track f. 5ft. 1⅛in., r. 5ft.; lgth. 17ft. 4in.; wdth. 6ft. 6in.; ht. 4ft. 6⅛in.; g.c. 5⅛in.; turng. cir. 43ft. 3in.; kerb wt. 35¼ cwt.; tank 16½ gals.; 12-volt.

£1,965 + £820 p.t. = £2,785

Abbreviations—g.c.—ground clearance; susp.—suspension; f.—front; r.—rear; comp.—compression; s.v.—side-valves; o.h.v.—overhead valves; o.h.c.—overhead camshaft; hyd.—hydraulic.

DODGE LANCER

SPURRED by the success of the Valiant, Chrysler have used the same body shell with various small styling changes and a different grille for this new six-seater in the Dodge range. Its slanting six-cylinder engine has long inlet pipes for high efficiency, and transmission is synchromesh or automatic. Front suspension by torsion bars. Electricity by alternator with high output at low revolutions.

CLOSE-UP

Six-cyl.; o.h.v.; 86.36 · 79.4 mm.; 2,789 c.c.; 101 b.h.p.; 8.2 to 1 comp.; coil ign.; Carter carb.; 3-speed, 9.62, 6.49, 3.55 to 1; col. lvr., auto. trans. opt.; susp. f. ind. torsion bar, r. half-elliptic; 4-door; 5/6-seat; hyd. servo brks.; max. 96 m.p.h.; cruise 80; m.p.g. 20; whl. base 8ft. 10½in.; track f. 4ft. 8in., r. 4ft. 7½in.; lgth. 15ft. 9in.; wdth. 6ft. 0¾in.; ht. 4ft. 6in.; g.c. 5½in.; turng. cir. 37ft. 9in.; kerb wt. 24 cwt.; tank 10½ gals.; 12-volt.

FACEL VEGA EXCELLENCE

RUE DE RIVOLI—Rue de la Paix—The Opera—Longchamps or the Bois de Boulogne —France's most luxurious car is ideal for the social round in Paris; perfect setting for the gowns of the haute couture. Its vast trunk holds the luggage for holidays on the Cote d'Azur. Chrysler-built V8 engine gives sports-car acceleration and a 125 m.p.h. maximum.

CLOSE-UP

Eight-cyl.; o.h.v.; 108 × 85.8 mm.; 6,286 c.c.; 330 b.h.p.; 10 to 1 comp.; coil ign.; Carter carb.; 3-speed auto.; col. lvr.; susp. f. ind. coil, r. half-elliptic; 4-door; 4/5-seat; hyd. servo disc brks.; max. 125 m.p.h.; cruise 110; m.p.g. 14-17; whl. base 10ft. 5in.; track f. 4ft. 8in., r. 4ft. 9in.; lgth. 17ft. 3in.; wdth. 6ft.; ht. 4ft. 6½in.; g.c. 7in.; turng. cir. 38ft.; kerb wt. 37¾ cwt.; tank 27 gals.; 12-volt.

£4,500 + £1,876.2.6 p.t. = £6,376.2.6

FACEL VEGA HK 500

ONE of the world's fastest and most opulent sports touring cars. Beautiful French-built coachwork, American-style wrap-round windscreen and four-lamp front, Chrysler-built American V8 engine, British Dunlop disc brakes and Italian light alloy wheels, with triple-eared hub nuts. The price is not peanuts, but electrically winding windows, radio with retractable aerial and lavish equipment are included.

CLOSE-UP

Eight-cyl.; o.h.v.; 108 · 85.8 mm.; 6,286 c.c.; 360 b.h.p.; 10 to 1 comp.; coil ign.; twin Carter carbs.; 4-speed, 11.4, 6.5, 4.5, 3.36 to 1; cen. lvr.; susp., f. ind. coil, r. half-elliptic; 2-door; 4-seat; hyd. servo disc brks.; max. 140 m.p.h.; cruise 120; m.p.g. 12-18; whl. base 8ft. 8½in.; track f. 4ft. 8in., r. 4ft. 9in.; lgth. 15ft. 1in.; wdth. 5ft. 11in.; ht. 4ft. 5in.; g.c. 7in.; turng. cir. 38ft.; kerb wt. 34½ cwt.; tank 22 gals.; 12-volt.

£3,345 + £1,394.17.6 p.t. = £4,739.17.6

FACEL VEGA FACELLIA

FAMILY resemblance is strong in this sleek sprout from Facel-Vega. Its clear-cut lines and luxurious finish closely follow those of the larger models, and its high-efficiency 1,647 c.c. twin camshaft twin-carburetter engine has already sped it over the measured kilometre at a mean of 114.9 m.p.h. The gearbox has synchromesh on all ratios and disc brakes are available.

CLOSE-UP

Four-cyl.; twin o.h.c.; 82 × 78 m.m.; 1,600 c.c.; 115 b.h.p.; 9.4 to 1 comp.; coil ign.; two Solex carbs.; 4-speed, 14.1, 8.0, 5.2, 4.1 to 1; cen. lvr.; susp. f. ind. coil, r. half-elliptic; 2-door; 2-seat; disc brks.; max. 115 m.p.h.; cruise 100; m.p.g. 25; whl. base 8ft. 0½in.; track f. and r. 4ft. 3½in.; lgth. 13ft. 7½in.; wdth. 5ft. 4in.; ht. 4ft. 1½in.; g.c. 7in.; turng. cir. 32ft.; kerb wt. 19¾ cwt.; tank 12½ gals.; 12-volt.

£1,900 + £792.15.10 p.t. = £2,692.15.10

Abbreviations—g.c.—ground clearance; susp.—suspension; f.—front; r.—rear; comp.—compression; s.v.—side-valves; o.h.v.—overhead valves; o.h.c.—overhead camshaft; hyd.—hydraulic.

FAIRTHORPE ELECTRON MINOR

TOP speed about 90 miles an hour; fuel consumption 45 to 55 miles a gallon when normally cruising. These are two of many first-class characteristics of this car, built by ex-Pathfinder ace Don Bennett. Other good points include a really sturdy engine, plastic body and tubular chassis. All this adds up to a minimum of weight providing speed and economy. Fairthorpe also produces a number of other models, like the six-cylinder Zeta shown here.

CLOSE-UP
Four-cyl.; o.h.v.; 63×76 mm.; 948 c.c.; 42 b.h.p.; 8.5 to 1 comp.; coil ign.; twin S.U. carbs.; 4-speed, 19.4, 11.19, 6.6, 4.55 to 1; cen. lvr.; susp. f. ind. coil, r. coil; 2-door; 2-seat; hyd. brks.; max. 90 m.p.h.; cruise 60; m.p.g. 48; whl. base 6ft. 9in.; track f. 4ft. 1in.; r. 4ft. 0½in.; lgth. 11ft.; wdth. 4ft. 10in.; ht. 3ft. 10in.; g.c. 7½in.; turng. cir. 23ft.; kerb wt. 8 cwt.; tank 10 gals.; 12-volt.

£563.10 + £235.18.4 p.t. = £799.8.4

FERRARI 250 G.T.

FIRST four-seater version of Ferrari's fabulous 250 GT is this hairy but airy saloon by Pinin Farina. Engine and gearbox have been moved forward to give the extra space without increasing length or wheelbase. Radiator grille is slightly smaller than on two-seaters. Technical items include thermostatically controlled fan clutch, Dunlop disc brakes on all wheels and (for the first time) a Laycock overdrive.

CLOSE-UP
Twelve-cyl.; o.h.c.; 73×58.8mm.; 2,953 c.c.; 240 b.h.p.; 8.8 to 1 comp.; coil ign.; 3 Weber carbs.; 4-speed, 10.59, 7.76, 5.73, 4.57 to 1; cen. lvr.; susp., f., ind. coil, r., half-elliptic and torque arms; 2-door; 4-seat; hyd. brks.; max. 140-150 m.p.h.; cruise, 120; m.p.g. 15-17; whl. base, 8ft. 6⅜in.; track, f., 4ft. 5 5/16 in.; r., 4ft. 5½in.; lgth., 15ft. 3in.; wdth., 5ft. 2½in.; ht., 4ft. 7½in.; g.c., 6in.; turng. cir., 32ft. 9in.; kerb wt., 25½ cwt.; tank, 22 gals.; 12-volt.

£4,400 + £1,834.9.2 p.t. = £6,234.9.2

FIAT 500 GIARDINIERA

LONGER than the saloon, Fiat's 60 m.p.h. station wagon is a thrifty baby with seats for four adults. Air-cooled two-cylinder engine is larger (499 instead of 479 c.c.) and lies on its side under the rear floor, fed with air through grilles behind the windows. Folding roof is standard. Rear seat folds away, and the single back door forms the tradesman's entrance for goods or luggage.

CLOSE-UP
Two-cyl.; air-cooled; o.h.v.; 67.4×70 mm.; 499.5 c.c.; 21.5 b.h.p.; 7.1 to 1 comp.; coil ign.; Weber carb.; 4-speed, 18.96, 10.59, 6.66, 4.48 to 1; cen. lvr.; susp. f. ind. transv. leaf, r. ind. coil; 3-door; 4-seat; hyd. brks.; max. 60 m.p.h.; cruise 50; m.p.g. 55; whl. base 6ft. 4¼in.; track f. 3ft. 8¼in.; r. 3ft. 8¼in.; lgth. 10ft. 5¼in.; wdth. 4ft. 4¼in.; ht. 4ft. 5¼in.; g.c. 5in.; turng. cir. 28ft. 2½in.; kerb wt. 11 cwt.; tank 4½ gals.; 12-volt.

£412.10 + £173 p.t. = £585.10

FIAT 600

ITALY'S thrifty best-seller in the small car market, perfected by years of development. Take your choice from four-seater saloons with fixed or folding tops. They have water-cooled rear engines and all-independent suspension. See the Multipla, too, with the same versatile rear engine in a forward-control body that seats six. And there's a new version of the 600 Saloon with engine enlarged to 750 c.c.

CLOSE-UP
Four-cyl.; o.h.v.; 60×56 mm.; 633 c.c.; 24.5 b.h.p.; 7.5 to 1 comp.; coil ign.; Weber carb.; 4-speed, 18.19, 11.04, 7.16, 4.82 to 1; cen. lvr.; susp., f., ind. coil; r., ind. coil; 2-door; 4-seat; hyd. brks.; max. 63 m.p.h.; cruise, 50; m.p.g. 50; whl. base, 6ft. 6⅜in.; track, f., 3ft. 9¼in.; r., 3ft. 9 7/16 in.; lgth. 10ft. 9⅜in.; wdth. 4ft. 6⅜in.; ht. 4ft. 7⅜in.; g.c. 6¼in.; turng. cir. 28ft. 6in.; kerb wt. 11¾ cwts.; tank, 6 gals.; 12-volt.

£415.10 + £174.5 p.t. = £589.15

Abbreviations—g.c.—ground clearance; susp.—suspension; f.—front; r.—rear; comp.—compression; s.v.—side-valves; o.h.v.—overhead valves; o.h.c.—overhead camshaft; hyd.—hydraulic.

27

FIAT 1100

ITALY'S idea of a sprightly, medium-sized family car. A good example it is, too. It is a strictly functional car, uncluttered with embellishments, made for hard work. Its 1,089 four-cylinder engine goes well over the 70 m.p.h. mark, and it purrs along cruising at 65 m.p.h. A best-seller in Italy in the four-seater-with-luggage class, it sells well abroad, too.

CLOSE-UP

Four-cyl.; o.h.v.; 68×75 mm.; 1,089 c.c.; 48 b.h.p.; 7 to 1 comp.; coil ign.; Solex carb.; 4-speed, 16.59, 10.23, 6.75, 4.3 to 1; col. lvr.; susp. f. ind. coil, r. half-elliptic; 4-door; 4-seat; hyd. brks.; max. 75 m.p.h.; cruise 65; m.p.g. 36; whl. base 7ft. 8in. track f. 4ft. 0½in., r. 3ft. 11½in.; lgth. 12ft. 10½in.; wdth. 4ft. 9½in.; ht. 4ft. 10½in.; g.c. 5in.; turng. cir. 34ft. 6in.; kerb wt. 17½ cwt.; tank 8½ gals.; 12-volt.

£578.10 + £242.3.4 p.t. = £820.13.4

FIAT 1500

NOW available with right-hand drive, Fiat's fast sports model has folding-head coachwork by Pinin Farina. The Maserati brothers, famous for their racing cars, produced the prototype of the twin carburetter twin overhead camshaft engine, which turns out 90 horse-power from 1½ litres. High speed, high style and luxurious finish in a sporting, all-weather car. There is a detachable hard top, too.

CLOSE-UP

Four-cyl.; o.h.c.; 78×78 mm.; 1,491 c.c.; 90 b.h.p.; 8.6 to 1 comp.; coil ign.; twin-choke Weber carb.; 4-speed, 13.27, 8.50, 5.93, 4.30 to 1; cen. lvr.; susp. f., ind. coil, r., half-elliptic; 2-door; 2/4-seat.; hyd. brks.; max. 105 m.p.h.; cruise, 85; m.p.g. 28; whl. base, 7ft. 8½in.; track, f., 4ft. 0½in.; r., 3ft. 11½in.; lgth., 13ft.; wdth., 4ft. 11½in.; ht. 4ft. 3⅜in.; g.c., 5in.; turng. cir., 34ft. 5½in.; kerb wt., 18½ cwts.; tank, 8½ gals.; 12-volt.

£1,300 + £544 p.t. = £1,844

FIAT 1800/2100

QUALITY cars from across the Alps with choice of engine sizes, both silent six cylinders. Full of ingenious ideas for pleasurable motoring: reminder lights for handbrake and parking lamps, extra direction indicators on the sides, grab handles and interior lights above the doors, map-reading lamp in back of anti-dazzle mirror. Reclining seats, too, for a refreshing nap on a long trip.

CLOSE-UP

Six-cyl.; o.h.v.; 72×73.5 mm.; 1,795 c.c.; 75 b.h.p.; 8.8 to 1 comp.; or 77×73.5 mm.; 2,054 c.c.; 82 b.h.p.; coil ign.; twin Weber carb.; 4-speed, 13.80, 8.12, 6.02, 4.3 to 1; col. lvr.; susp. f., ind. tors. bar.; 4-door; 4/5-seat.; hyd. servo brks.; max. 90 m.p.h.; cruise, 75; m.p.g. 27-29; whl. base, 8ft. 8½in.; track, f., 4ft. 4½in.; r., 4ft. 3½in.; lgth., 14ft. 7½in.; wdth., 5ft. 3½in.; ht., 4ft. 9½in.; g.c., 5½in.; turng. cir., 37ft. 9in.; kerb wt., 24½ cwt.; tank, 13.2 gals.; 12-volt.

1800 **£950 + £396.19.2 p.t. = £1,346.19.2**
2100 **£987 + £412.7.6 p.t. = £1,399.7.6**

FORD ANGLIA

POWERED by the super-smooth, over-square, overhead valve engine which has helped to make British cars invincible in this year's Formula Junior racing, the New Anglia enters its second year on a wave of success. The back-slope rear window was a bold idea which succeeded. Road holding is excellent and fuel consumption makes this one of the thriftier family cars.

CLOSE-UP

Four-cyl.; o.h.v.; 80.96×48.41 mm.; 997 c.c.; 39 b.h.p.; 8.9 to 1 comp.; coil ign.; Solex carb.; 4-speed, 16.987, 9.884, 5.826, 4.125 to 1; cen. lvr.; susp. f. ind. coil, r. half-elliptic; 2-door; 4-seat; hyd. brks.; max. 75 m.p.h.; cruise 65; m.p.g. 40-43; whl. base 7ft. 6½in.; track f. 3ft. 10in., r. 3ft. 9½in.; lgth. 12ft. 9½in.; wdth. 4ft. 9½in.; ht. 4ft. 8½in.; g.c. 6⅜in.; turng. cir. 32ft.; kerb wt. 14½ cwt.; tank 7 gals.; 12-volt.

£415 + £174.0.10 p.t. = £589.0.10

Abbreviations—g.c.—ground clearance; susp.—suspension; f.—front; r.—rear; comp.—compression; s.v.—side-valves; o.h.v.—overhead valves; o.h.c.—overhead camshaft; hyd.—hydraulic.

FORD CONSUL DE LUXE

THIS is one of the most popular cars on the market, noted for its durability, good line and lion-hearted engine. It is an ideal car if you want a twixt-and-between model, neither too small nor too big. It has been glamorised with extra chrome, extended rear wings and a lower roof. Power-assisted disc brakes in front are optional.

CLOSE-UP

Four-cyl.; o.h.v.; 82.55 × 79.5 mm.; 1,703 c.c.; 59 b.h.p.; 7.8 to 1 comp.; coil ign.; Zenith carb.; 3-speed, 11.67, 6.75, 4.11 to 1; col. lvr.; susp., f., coil, r., half-elliptic; 4-door; 6-seat; hyd. brks., disc opt.; max. 80 m.p.h.; cruise 65; m.p.g. 28; whl. base 8ft. 8½in.; track f. 4ft. 5in., r. 4ft. 4in.; lgth. 14ft. 5¾in.; wdth. 5ft. 8½in.; ht. 5ft.; g.c. 6½in.; turng. cir. 35ft.; kerb wt. 22¼ cwt.; tank 10½ gals.; 12-volt.

£580 ÷ £242.15.10 p.t. = £822.15.10

FORD POPULAR

ONE of the best buys of any on the market and still priced under £500 with purchase tax, it is really the old Anglia in a simplified and cheapened guise. The familiar and well-tried 1,172 c.c. side-valve engine is retained in unchanged form, so you have reliability plus cheapness. It is a jolly good little car for the motorist with the restricted pocket.

CLOSE-UP

Four-cyl.; s.v.; 63.25 × 92.5 mm.; 1,172 c.c.; 36 b.h.p.; 7 to 1 comp.; coil ign.; Solex carb.; 3-speed, 17.246, 8.889, 4.429 to 1; cen. lvr.; susp., f., ind. coil, r., half-elliptic; 2-door; 4-seat; hyd. brks.; max. 70 m.p.h.; cruise, 60; m.p.g., 28-32; whl. base, 7ft. 3in.; track f., 4ft., r., 3ft. 11½in.; lgth., 12ft. 5¾in.; wdth., 5ft. 0½in.; ht., 4ft. 10¾in.; g.c., 7in.; turng. cir., 34ft. 6in.; kerb wt., 15 cwt.; tank, 7 gals.; 12-volt.

£348 + £146.2.6 p.t. = £494.2.6

FORD PREFECT

A NEW overhead valve engine of 996 c.c. and a new four-speed gearbox rejuvenated the Prefect a year ago, enhancing its appeal for the family man who must have a four-door saloon. Performance was increased, fuel consumption reduced, and interior trim and colour schemes were brightened to complete the transformation. No basic changes are being made for 1961.

CLOSE-UP

Four-cyl.; o.h.v.; 80.96 × 48.11 mm.; 997 c.c.; 39 b.h.p.; 8.9 to 1 comp.; coil ign.; Solex carb.; 4-speed, 18.239, 10.612, 6.254, 4.429 to 1; cen. lvr.; susp., f. ind. coil, r. half-elliptic; 4-door; 4-seat; hyd. brks.; max. 75 m.p.h.; cruise 65; m.p.g. 38; whl. base 7ft. 3in.; track f. 4ft., r. 3ft. 11½in.; lgth. 12ft. 5¾in.; wdth. 5ft. 0¾in.; ht. 4ft. 11½in.; g.c. 6½in.; turng. cir. 34ft. 6in.; kerb wt. 16 cwt.; tank 7 gals.; 12-volt.

£438 + £183.12.6 p.t. = £621.12.6

FORD ZEPHYR

OPTIONAL disc brakes are the arresting new feature of Dagenham's swift six. The numbers you see on the road endorse the appeal of the Zephyr's style, space and speed at a strictly moderate price. Saloon, convertible and station wagon are on offer with extra-cost options of overdrive or fully automatic transmission. A firm favourite matured by years of careful development.

CLOSE-UP

Six-cyl.; o.h.v.; 82.55 × 79.5 mm.; 2,553 c.c.; 85 b.h.p.; 7.8 to 1 comp.; coil ign.; Zenith carb.; 3-speed, 11.08, 6.40, 3.90 to 1; BW overdrive or auto. trans. opt.; col. lvr.; susp., f., ind. coil, r., half-elliptic; 4-door; 6-seat; hyd. brks., disc opt.; max. 90 m.p.h.; cruise 75; m.p.g. 23-26; whl. base 8ft. 11in.; track f. 4ft. 5in., r. 4ft. 4in.; lgth. 14ft. 11in.; wdth. 5ft. 8½in.; ht. 5ft.; g.c. 6½in.; turng. cir. 36ft.; kerb wt. 23¾ cwt.; tank, 10½ gals.; 12-volt.

£610 + £255.5.10 p.t. = £865.5.10

Abbreviations—g.c.—ground clearance; susp.—suspension; f.—front; r.—rear; comp.—compression; s.v.—side-valves; o.h.v.—overhead valves; o.h.c.—overhead camshaft; hyd.—hydraulic.

29

FORD ZODIAC

THIS is the caviare-and-champagne car of the brilliant Ford range—big, bold and beautiful. It has all the extra trimmings and accoutrements of the show-piece model from Dagenham, including plenty of chrome, special safety locking devices, electric clock, passenger vanity mirror and new-type sun visors. Power-assisted disc brakes in front are optional.

CLOSE-UP

Six-cyl.; o.h.v.; 82.55 × 79.5 mm.; 2,553 c.c.; 85 b.h.p.; 7.8 to 1 comp.; coil ign.; Zenith carb.; 3-speed, 11.08, 6.40, 3.90 to 1; BW overdrive or auto. trans. opt.; col. lvr.; susp., f., ind. coil, r., half-elliptic; 4-door; 6-seat; hyd. brks., disc opt.; max. 90 m.p.h.; cruise 75; m.p.g. 23-26; whl. base 8ft. 11in.; track f. 4ft. 5in.; r., 4ft. 4in.; lgth., 15ft. 0½in.; wdth., 5ft. 8½in.; ht. 5ft. 0½in.; g.c. 6¾in.; turng. cir., 36ft.; kerb wt., 23½ cwt.; tank, 10½ gals.; 12-volt.

£675 + £282.7.6 p.t. = £957.7.6

FORD TAUNUS 17M COMBI

BIGGEST of the German Fords which are built at Cologne, the Taunus 17M is available as a two- or four-door saloon and as a station wagon. It has a big over-square four-cylinder engine, and for transmission there is a choice of three- or four-speed gearboxes, with option of automatic clutch. Other options include a sliding roof.

CLOSE-UP

Four-cyl.; o.h.v.; 84 × 76.6 mm.; 1,698 c.c.; 60 b.h.p.; 7.1 to 1 comp.; coil ign.; Solex carb.; 3-speed, 12.75, 6.59, 3.9 to 1; col. lvr. 4-speed opt.; susp., f., ind. coil, r., half-elliptic; 2-door; 4/5-seat; hyd. brks.; max. 78 m.p.h.; cruise 60; m.p.g. 28; whl. base, 8ft. 6½in.; track f. and r., 4ft. 2in.; lgth., 14ft. 4½in.; wdth., 5ft. 5¾in.; ht. 4ft. 11½in.; g.c., 7in.; turng. cir., 37ft. 9in.; kerb wt., 22 cwt.; tank, 10 gals.; 6-volt.

£830 + £346.18.4 p.t. = £1,176.18.4

FORD FALCON

FLYING high with a successful year behind it, the American Falcon is not changed radically for 1961. Its neat uncluttered styling is retained but the radiator grille is new. Body-chassis form a unit, front suspension is by coil springs and power plant is a 2.4 litre six giving 90 horsepower. Choice of two- or four-door saloons and a station wagon.

CLOSE-UP

Six-cyl.; o.h.v.; 88.9 × 63.5 mm.; 2,365 c.c.; 85 b.h.p.; 8.7 to 1 comp.; coil ign.; Holley carb.; 3-speed, 10.2, 5.43, 3.10 to 1; col. lvr. auto. trans. opt.; susp. f. ind. coil, r. half-elliptic; 2 or 4-door; 6-seat; hyd. brks.; max. 90 m.p.h.; cruise 70; m.p.g. 26; whl. base 9ft. 1½in.; track f. 4ft. 7in., r. 4ft. 6½in.; lgth. 15ft. 1in.; wdth. 5ft. 10½in.; ht. 4ft. 7in.; kerb wt. 21 cwt. 35 lb.; 12-volt.

FORD GALAXIE

THE basic models of the big American Ford range go back to a more aggressive front. The big round tail lamps which have become a Ford identification feature return for 1961. Sailing against the compact car and moderate power current by offering long lines and more power than ever, these handsome cars go swishing at more than 100 m.p.h. with insolent ease.

CLOSE-UP

Eight-cyl.; o.h.v.; 101.6 · 83.8 mm.; 5,441 c.c.; 225 b.h.p.; 8.9 to 1 comp.; coil ign.; twin Venturi carbs., automatic choke; 3-speed, std. trans. 8.86, 5.37, 3.56 to 1; col. lvr.; susp. f. ind. coil, r. half-elliptic; 4-door; 6-seat; hyd. brks.; max. 100 m.p.h.; cruise 75; whl. base 9ft. 11in.; track f. 5ft. 1in.; r. 5ft.; lgth. 17ft. 6in.; wdth. 6ft. 8in.; ht. 4ft. 7in.; g.c. 7¹⁄₁₆in.; turng. cir. 40ft.; kerb wt. 34½ cwt.; tank 16½ gals.; 12-volt.

£1,899.0.3 + £792.7.7 p.t. = £2,691.7.10

Abbreviations—g.c.—ground clearance; susp.—suspension; f.—front; r.—rear; comp.—compression; s.v.—side-valves; o.h.v.—overhead valves; o.h.c.—overhead camshaft; hyd.—hydraulic.

FORD THUNDERBIRD

FORD'S popular family sports saloon bounds into the spotlight with radically new styling featuring long, angular lines and a low-swept front end. Two-door hardtops and convertibles are available, powered by hefty V8 engines of 5.8 or 7 litres. For transmission the choice is three-speed synchromesh gearbox with optional overdrive or an automatic box with torque converter and three speeds.

CLOSE-UP

Eight-cyl.; o.h.v.; 101.6×88.9 mm.; 6,391 c.c.; 375 b.h.p.; 10.6 to 1 comp.; coil ign.; 4 Venturi carbs. with automatic choke; 3-speed, 7.34, 5.70, 3.10 to 1; col. lvr.; susp. f. ind. coil, r. half-elliptic; 2-door; 4-seat; hyd. brks.; max. 120 m.p.h.; cruise 80; whl. base 9ft. 5in.; track f. and r. 5ft.; lgth. 17ft. 1in.; wdth. 6ft. 4in.; ht. 4ft. 4in.; g.c. 7⅕in.; turng. cir. 40ft.; kerb wt. 35 cwt. 37 lb.; tank 16 gals.; 12-volt.

FRAZER-NASH

ONE of the last survivors of the true bespoke hand-built performance cars, built to order only with all the customer's personal preferences incorporated. Made in London, with V8 B.M.W. engine in a tubular chassis clothed with light alloy body to give 90 m.p.h. cruising and a 130-plus maximum. Gearbox has synchromesh on all four speeds; rear axle is de Dion.

CLOSE-UP

Eight-cyl.; o.h.v.; 82 × 75 mm.; 3,168 c.c.; 8.2 to 1 comp; 173 b.h.p.; coil ign.; twin down-draught carbs.; 4-speed 11.6, 7.1, 4.6, 3.4 to 1; cen. lvr.; susp., f., ind. trans., r., de Dion; 2-door; 2-seat; hyd. brks. disc front; max. 135 m.p.h.; cruise 90-100; m.p.g., 18-28; whl. base, 8ft. 3in.; track, f., 4ft. 2in.; r., 4ft. 5⅛in.; lgth., 13ft. 5in.; wdth., 5ft.; ht., 4ft. 3in.; g.c. 6⅛in.; turng. cir., 32ft.; kerb wt., 16½ cwt.; tank, 17 gals.; 12-volt.

£2,300 + £959.9.2 p.t. = £3,259.9.2

GOGGOMOBIL T.300

THIS is a neat little German runabout, distinctive in many respects. The twin-cylinder, air-cooled engine at the back is cheap to run, robust and snappy. Women like the car for its gay colours and ease of parking. Relaxed drivers like it because the gears are changed by a flick of a switch on the optional electrically controlled gearbox. A car that is as good tempered on the open road as in congested city streets.

CLOSE-UP

Two-cyl.; two-stroke; air-cooled; 58 × 56 mm.; 293 c.c.; 17 b.h.p.; 6 to 1 comp.; coil ign.; Bing carb.; 4-speed, 20.624, 10.966, 7.177, 5.073 to 1; cen. lvr.; susp. f. and r. ind. coil; 2-door; 4-seat; hyd. brks.; max. 60 m.p.h.; cruise 50; m.p.g. 58-60; whl. base 5ft. 10⅜in.; track f. and r. 3ft. 7in.; lgth. 9ft. 6in.; wdth. 4ft. 2½in.; ht. 4ft. 3in.; g.c. 7in.; turng. cir. 24½ft.; kerb wt. 8 cwt.; tank 5½ gals.; 12-volt.

£329 + £138.4.2 p.t. = £467.4.2

GOGGOMOBIL T700

THE spare wheel on this gay German baby for the small and thrifty family lies in the front, just above the flat-twin, air-cooled engine. Transmission goes to the rear wheels by way of a gearbox with Porsche synchro-shift for all four speeds. Body styles include saloon and station wagon. A folding sun roof is an optional extra.

CLOSE-UP

Two-cyl.; o.h.v. air-cooled; 78 × 72 mm.; 688 c.c.; 30 b.h.p.; 7.2 to 1 comp.; coil ign.; Solex carb.; 4-speed, 22.4, 11.35, 6.65, 5.0 to 1; cen. lvr.; susp., f., ind. coil, r., half-elliptic; 2-door; 4-seat; hyd. brks.; max. 69 m.p.h.; cruise, 55-60; m.p.g. 50; whl. base, 6ft. 7in.; track f., 3ft. 11½in.; r., 3ft. 10in.; lgth., 11ft. 3in.; wdth., 4ft. 10in.; ht. 4ft. 6⅜in.; g.c. 7½in.; turng. cir., 29ft. 6in.; kerb wt., 14½ cwt.; tank, 8¾ gals.; 12-volt.

£473 + £198.4.2 p.t. = £671.4.2

Abbreviations—g.c.—ground clearance; susp.—suspension; f.—front; r.—rear; comp.—compression; s.v.—side-valves; o.h.v.—overhead valves; o.h.c.—overhead camshaft; hyd.—hydraulic.

HILLMAN HUSKY

SMALL-SIZE station wagon with a sprightly performance, the Husky puts on style with a new grille, cowled headlamps, thinner screen pillars and a new ribbed roof with projecting edges at front and rear. Rear window is larger, seats are lower and wider, back-rests are more comfortable. The new gearbox has a remote control sports-type lever, and the engine has detail improvements.

CLOSE-UP
Four-cyl.; o.h.v.; 76.2 × 76.2 mm.; 1,390 c.c.; 51 b.h.p.; 8 to 1 comp.; coil ign.; Zenith carb.; 4-speed, 15.24, 9.75, 6.34, 4.55 to 1; cen. lvr.; susp. f. ind. coil, r. half-elliptic; 3-door; 4-seat.; hyd. brks.; max. 75 m.p.h.; cruise 65; m.p.g. 28; whl. base 7ft. 2in.; track f. 4ft. 1in., r. 4ft. 0½in.; lgth. 12ft. 5½in.; wdth. 5ft. 0½in.; ht. 4ft. 11¼in.; g.c. 6¼in.; turng. cir. 33ft. 6in.; kerb wt. 18¾ cwt.; tank 6½ gals.; 12-volt.

£475 + £199.0.10 p.t. = £674.0.10

HILLMAN MINX

A LOW-PRICED Minx saloon, replacing the Special, has the de luxe type instrument panel, with new bumpers and side mouldings. All models can be supplied with Easidrive, the remarkable high-efficiency automatic transmission which uses electro-magnetic powder clutches for a smooth, foolproof flow of power. 1961 Minxes have new hypoid final drive to replace the spiral bevels.

CLOSE-UP
Four-cyl.; o.h.v.; 79 × 76.2 mm.; 1,494 c.c.; 56.5 b.h.p.; 8.5 to 1 comp.; coil ign.; Zenith carb.; 4-speed, 14.872, 9.513, 6.187, 4.44 to 1, Smith's auto. opt.; col. or cen. lvr.; susp., f., ind. coil, r., half-elliptic; 4-door; 4-seat; hyd. brks.; max. 80 m.p.h.; cruise, 65; m.p.g., 30-34; whl. base, 8ft.; track, f., 4ft. 1in., r., 4ft. 0½in.; lgth., 13ft. 6in.; wdth., 5ft. 0½in.; ht. 4ft. 11½in.; g.c., 7in.; turng. cir., 36ft.; kerb wt., 20 cwt.; tank, 7¼ gals.; 12-volt.

£539 + £225.14.2 p.t. = £764.14.2

HILLMAN ESTATE CAR

MOTHERS use this car often to take their children to school. Men use it to carry loads they cannot stow aboard the normal saloon. In fact this estate wagon is more than a two-purpose car, it serves almost every field. It has been given fresh elegance with minor body changes, and the bigger front brakes make it safe and sure and wonderfully easy to handle.

CLOSE-UP
Four-cyl.; o.h.v.; 79 × 76.2 mm.; 1,494 c.c.; 56.5 b.h.p.; 8.5 to 1 comp.; coil ign.; Zenith carb.; 4-speed, 14.872, 9.513, 6.187, 4.44 to 1, Smith's auto opt.; col. or cen. lvr.; susp., f., ind. coil, r., half-elliptic; 5-door; 4/5-seat; hyd. brks.; max. 80 m.p.h.; cruise, 65; m.p.g., 25-33; whl. base, 8ft.; track, f., 4ft. 1in., r., 4ft. 0½in.; lgth., 13ft 6in.; wdth., 5ft. 0½in.; ht., 5ft. 1in.; g.c., 7in.; turng. cir., 36ft.; kerb wt., 21 cwt.; tank, 7¼ gals.; 12-volt.

£605 + £253.4.2 p.t. = £858.4.2

HUMBER HAWK

SISTER car to the Super Snipe, this 2.2 litre Humber Hawk now has disc brakes fitted as standard for 1961. It also has more interior space and a heater fitted as standard. The car for the family man in the upper salary brackets or the business executive who wants a hard-working model at medium price. Fully automatic transmission or overdrive are extras.

CLOSE-UP
Four-cyl.; o.h.v.; 81 × 110 mm.; 2,267 c.c.; 78 b.h.p.; 7.5 to 1 comp.; coil ign.; Zenith carb.; 4-speed; 14.128, 9.038, 5.877, 4.22 to 1; Laycock overdrive opt.; col. lvr.; susp. f., ind. coil, r., half-elliptic; 4-door; 6-seat; hyd. servo brks., disc front; max. 85 m.p.h.; cruise 70-75; m.p.g. 20-25; whl. base 9ft. 2in.; track, f. 4ft. 9in., r., 4ft. 7½in.; lgth. 15ft. 4¼in.; wdth. 5ft. 9¼in.; ht., 5ft. 1in.; g.c., 7in.; turng. cir. 38ft.; kerb wt. 28 cwt.; tank 12¼ gals.; 12-volt.

£840 + £351.2.6 p.t. = £1,191.2.6

HUMBER SUPER SNIPE

FOUR headlamps in a bolder front light the way to 1961 for the most luxurious car of the Rootes range. Three litres of engine to give effortless acceleration with option of three-speed, all-synchromesh gears and overdrive or Borg-Warner's two-pedal automatic box. A car for chauffeur drive or for private owners. Power assistance for steering and disc front brakes.

CLOSE-UP
Six-cyl.; o.h.v.; 87.3×82.55 mm.; 2,965 c.c.; 129 b.h.p.; 8 to 1 comp.; coil ign.; Zenith carb.; 3-speed, 12.77, 7.34, 4.55 to 1; col. lvr., Laycock overdrive or B.W. auto trans. opt.; susp., f., ind. coil, r., half-elliptic; 4-door; 6-seat; hyd. servo brks. disc front; max. 98 m.p.h.; cruise, 80; m.p.g., 20-25; whl. base, 9ft. 2in.; track, f., 4ft. 9in.; r., 4ft. 7½in.; lgth., 15ft. 8in.; wdth., 5ft. 9½in.; ht., 5ft. 1in.; g.c., 7in.; turng cir., 38ft.; kerb wt., 30 cwt.; tank, 12½ gals.; 12-volt.

£875 + £365.14.2 p.t. = £1,240.14.2

IMPERIAL

EYE-CATCHING feature of Chrysler's elite model for 1961 is a reversion to separate head-lamps four in a row mounted on stalks in deep recesses flanking the broad, squat grille. Its great V8 engine delivers about 350 horsepower, enough to deal with lavishly equipped limousine coachwork. Automatic transmission and servo assistance for brakes and steering are standard. Self-locking differential is optional.

CLOSE-UP
Eight-cyl.; o.h.v.; 106.20 × 95.30 mm.; 6,768 c.c.; 350 b.h.p.; 10 to 1 comp.; coil ign.; Carter carb.; auto. 3-speed, 7.17, 4.24, 2.93 to 1; push-button control; susp. f. ind. tors. bar, r. half-elliptic; 4-door; 6-seat; hyd. servo brks.; max. 112 m.p.h.; cruise 85; m.p.g. 12-15; whl. base 10ft. 9in.; track f. 5ft. 2in.; r. 5ft. 2⅛in.; lgth. 18ft. 9in.; wdth. 6ft. 9in.; ht. 4ft. 9in.; g.c. 5¾in.; turng. cir. 48ft. 2in.; kerb wt. 42 cwt.; tank 19 gals.; 12-volt.

JAGUAR 2.4 LITRE MARK 2

WITH a lighter engine than 3.8 or 3.4, some judges rate this the best balanced of the Jaguar saloons. Wider rear track gives surer road holding and all-round vision is greatly improved on Mark 2. Front suspension has been strengthened this year as on the 3.8. Note the safety eye which flashes a warning if brake fluid runs low.

CLOSE-UP
Six-cyl.; o.h.c.; 83 × 76.5 mm.; 2,483 c.c.; 120 b.h.p.; 8 to 1 comp.; coil ign.; 2 Solex carb.; 4-speed, 14.42, 7.94, 5.48, 4.27 to 1; cen. lvr. Laycock overdrive or BW auto. trans. opt.; susp., f., ind. coil, r., cantilever leaf; 4-door; 5-seat; hyd. servo disc brks.; max., 105 m.p.h.; cruise, 75-80; m.p.g., 23; whl. base, 8ft. 11¾in.; track, f., 4ft. 6⅝in.; r., 4ft. 2⅛in.; lgth., 15ft. 0¾in.; wdth., 5ft. 6⅝in.; ht., 4ft. 9½in.; g.c., 7in.; turng. cir., 33ft. 6in.; kerb wt., 27 cwt.; tank, 12 gals.; 12-volt.

£1,082 + £451.19.2 p.t. = £1,533.19.2

JAGUAR 3.4/3.8 LITRE MARK 2

SLIMMER pillars and larger glass areas, new front suspension and wider rear track, new instrument panel with dials in line for at-a-glance viewing, heater ducts to rear compartment and picnic tables on backs of front seats are points which have spelled success for the Mark 2 series. Choice of two engine sizes, and manual or automatic transmissions.

CLOSE-UP
Six-cyl.; o.h.c.; 83 × 106 mm.; 3,442 c.c.; 210 b.h.p.; 8 to 1 comp. or 87 × 106 mm.; 3,781 c.c.; 220 b.h.p.; coil ign.; 2 S.U. carbs.; 4-speed, 11.95, 6.58, 4.54, 3.54 to 1; BW auto. trans. or Laycock overdrive opt.; cen. lvr.; susp., f., ind. coil; r., cantilever leaf; 4-door; 5-seat; hyd. servo disc brks.; max. 120 m.p.h.; cruise 90-100; m.p.g., 16-23; whl. base, 8ft. 11¾in.; track, f., 4ft. 6⅝in.; r., 4ft. 2⅛in.; lgth., 15ft. 0¾in.; wdth., 5ft. 6⅝in.; ht., 4ft. 9½in.; g.c., 7in.; turng. cir., 33ft. 6in.; kerb wt., 27½ cwt.; tank, 12 gals.; 12-volt.

3.4 £1,177 × £491.10.10 p.t. = £1,618.10.10
3.8 £1,255 × £524.0.10 p.t. = £1,779.0.10

Abbreviations—g.c.—ground clearance; susp.—suspension; f.—front; r.—rear; comp.—compression; s.v.—side-valves; o.h.v.—overhead valves; o.h.c.—overhead camshaft; hyd.—hydraulic.

JAGUAR MARK IX

ONE of the fastest saloon cars built anywhere in the world, the Mark IX stems from a family of brilliant models, astounding in performance, graceful in looks. It is the car for the family man who likes to hurry, or the business boss with a minimum of time for a maximum of duties. Every year it gets slight new touches—mechanical and bodywise—to keep it predominately successful.

CLOSE-UP

Six-cyl.; o.h.c.; 87×106 mm.; 3,781 c.c.; 220 b.h.p.; 8 to 1 comp.; coil ign.; 2 S.U. carbs.; 4-speed, 14.42, 7.94, 5.48, 4.27 to 1; Laycock overdrive or BW auto. trans. opt.; cen. lvr.; susp., f., ind. torsion bar; r., half-elliptic; 4-door; 5-seat; hyd. servo disc brks.; max. 115 m.p.h.; cruise, 80-85; m.p.g., 16-19; whl. base, 10ft.; track, f., 4ft. 8½in., r., 4ft. 10in.; lgth., 16ft. 4½in.; wdth., 6ft. 1in.; ht., 5ft. 3in.; g.c., 7½in.; turng. cir., 36ft.; kerb wt., 34¾ cwt.; tanks, 17 gals.; 12-volt.

£1,329 + £554.17.6 p.t. = £1,883.17.6

JAGUAR XK150

FAST motoring with tremendous power, splendid road holding and consummate good looks—these are main points of this well-tried sports car, which piles miles into minutes with effortless ease. Its maximum speed, well over 120 m.p.h., is so high that some may question its practical value, at least on British roads. But couple that speed with Dunlop disc brakes on all four wheels. Result: motoring at its most exciting.

CLOSE-UP

Six-cyl.; o.h.c.; 83×106 mm.; 3,442 c.c.; 210 b.h.p.; 8 to 1 comp.; coil ign.; twin S.U. carbs.; 4-speed, 11.95, 6.58, 4.54, 3.54 to 1; Laycock overdrive opt.; cen. lvr.; susp., f., ind. torsion bar, r., half-elliptic; 2-door; 2/3-seat; disc servo brks.; max. 125 m.p.h.; cruise 90; m.p.g., 18-22; whl. base, 8ft. 6in.; track, f. and r., 4ft. 3½in.; lgth., 14ft. 9in.; wdth., 5ft. 4½in.; ht. 4ft. 7in.; g.c., 7½in.; turng. cir., 33ft.; kerb wt., 28¼ cwt.; tank, 14 gals.; 12-volt.

£1,175 + £490.14.2 p.t. = £1,665.14.2

JENSEN 541 S

THIS is the car for fast and elegant motoring. Its fibre glass body retains the lithe, graceful lines typical of this make, mounted on a robust tubular body. Rolls Royce automatic transmission is fitted as standard, and there are now Dunlop self-adjusting disc brakes on all four wheels. So you have power, speed and ease of handling with this new model that is hard to match anywhere.

CLOSE-UP

Six-cyl.; o.h.v.; 87×111 mm.; 3,993 c.c.; 133 b.h.p.; 7.6 to 1 comp.; coil ign.; 3 S.U. carbs.; 4-speed auto. trans. opt., 10.79, 7.70, 4.24, 2.93 to 1; cen. lvr.; susp., f., ind. coil, r., half-elliptic; 2-door; 4-seat; disc servo brks.; max. 125 m.p.h.; cruise, 93; m.p.g., 20-22; whl. base, 8ft. 9in.; track f. and r., 4ft. 4in.; lgth., 14ft. 10in.; wdth., 5ft. 7in.; ht., 4ft. 6½in.; g.c., 7in.; turng. cir., 34ft.; kerb wt., 28¾ cwt.; tank, 15 gals.; 12-volt.

£1,910 + £796.19.2 p.t. = £2,706.19.2

LANCIA FLAMINIA

ADVANCED engineering, tailored in high style. V-6 o.h.v. engines in chassis with three lengths of wheelbase from a famous Italian factory. Clutch and gearbox are grouped aft with the de Dion axle. Pinin Farina styled the saloon and coupe (see photograph). Touring do the four-headlamp Superleggera coupe, and Zagato build the feather-weight competition job with 117 b.h.p. engine and disc brakes.

CLOSE-UP

Six-cyl.; o.h.v.; 80×81.5 mm.; 2,458 c.c.; 112 b.h.p.; 8 to 1 comp.; coil ign.; Solex carb.; 4-speed, 12.3, 7.6, 5.6, 3.75 to 1; col. lvr.; susp., f., ind. coil, r., de Dion half-elliptic; 4-door; 5/6-seat; disc brks.; max. 100 m.p.h.; cruise, 80; m.p.g., 22; whl. base, 9ft. 5in.; track, f. and r., 4ft. 6in.; lgth., 15ft. 11in.; wdth., 5ft. 9in.; ht., 4ft. 8in.; turng. cir., 39ft. 6in.; kerb wt., 30 cwt.; tank, 12½ gals.; 12-volt.

Saloon £2,620 + £1,092.15.10 p.t. = £3,712.15.10

Abbreviations—g.c.—ground clearance; susp.—suspension; f.—front; r.—rear; comp.—compression; s.v.—side-valves; o.h.v.—overhead valves; o.h.c.—overhead camshaft; hyd.—hydraulic.

LEA FRANCIS LYNX

LONG famous for high performance sports cars with an individual style, Lea Francis stage a come-back after eight years of absence with a new 2½-litre model, featuring hand-built saloon and roadster bodywork of their own design on a chassis of classic layout. Front suspension by torsion bars and rigid rear axle with semi-elliptics. Overdrive transmission and disc brakes all round.

CLOSE-UP

Six-cyl.; o.h.v.; 82.55×79.5 mm.; 2,553 c.c.; 7.8 to 1 comp.; coil ign.; 3 S.U. carbs.; 4-speed, cen. lvr. overdrive std.; susp. f. ind. torsion bar, r. half-elliptic; 2-door; 2/4-seat; disc brks.; max. 100 m.p.h.; cruise 85; m.p.g. 20-22; whl. base 8ft. 3in.; track f. and r. 4ft. 4in.; lgth. 15ft.; wdth. 5ft. 10in.; ht. 4ft. 6in.; turng. cir. 30ft.; tank 14 gals.; 12-volt.

LINCOLN

OUTWARDLY this is all new, with lines more graceful than the heavily sculptured colossi of recent years. Interior finish strikes the same note, with appointments of luxury and refinement calculated to re-establish Lincoln as a car for discerning members of the international set. A V8 engine of more than 7-litres and the twin range Turbo Drive send it loafing along at a hundred.

CLOSE-UP

Eight-cyl.; o.h.v.; 109.2×94 mm.; 7,045 c.c.; 315 b.h.p.; 10 to 1 comp.; coil ign.; 4-choke carb.; 3-speed auto., 6.8, 4.27, 2.89 to 1; col. lvr.; susp. f. ind. coil, r. coil; 4-door; 6-seat; hyd. servo brks.; max. 108 m.p.h.; cruise 80; m.p.g. 10-15; whl. base 10ft. 11in.; track f. and r. 5ft. 1in.; lgth. 17ft. 8½in.; wdth. 6ft. 8in.; ht. 4ft. 5½in.; g.c. 6in.; turng. cir. 44ft.; kerb wt. 42 cwt. 67 lb.; tank 17½ gals.; 12-volt.

£3,937 + £1,641.10.10 p.t. = £5,578.10.10

LOTUS ELITE

TWIN carburetters for extra power, improved rear suspension, more comfortable interior and better sound proofing are key quotes on the latest issue of this coupe with the brilliant sporting record. Its unique body chassis in resin-bonded glass fibre slashes weight to the minimum. All-independent suspension holds it rock steady at racing speeds and discs guarantee fade-free stopping power.

CLOSE-UP

Four-cyl.; o.h.c.; 76.2×66.6 mm.; 1,216 c.c.; 75 b.h.p.; 10 to 1 comp.; coil ign.; S.U. carb.; 4-speed, 16.5, 9.9, 5.94, 4.5 to 1; cen. lvr.; susp., f., ind. coil, r., ind. coil; 2-door; 2-seat; disc brks.; max. 120 m.p.h.; cruise, 90; m.p.g., 28-33; whl. base, 7ft. 4in.; track, f. and r., 3ft. 11in.; lgth., 12ft. 6in.; wdth., 4ft. 10in.; ht., 3ft. 10in.; g.c., 6½in.; turng. cir., 31ft.; kerb wt., 11 cwt.; tank, 6½ gals.; 12-volt.

£1,375 + £574.0.10 p.t. = £1,949.0.10

LOTUS SEVEN

FAMOUS build-it-yourself sports car (or ready to roll if you prefer it and can afford the purchase tax). Improved chassis, smaller wheels and revised rear suspension give still better road holding. Nose cowl and wings are now glass fibre. Instrument panel is more functional. Hood, spare wheel and windscreen wipers are now included in the price. Choice of Ford Anglia, B.M.C. or Coventry Climax engines.

CLOSE-UP

Four-cyl.; s.v.; 63×92.5 mm.; 1,172 c.c.; 36 b.h.p.; 8.5 to 1 comp.; coil ign.; S.U. carb.; 3-speed, 17.3, 9.78, 4.875 to 1; cen. lvr.; susp. f. ind. coil, r. coil; 2-seat; hyd. brks.; max. 95 m.p.h.; cruise 80; m.p.g. 35-40; whl. base 7ft. 4in.; track f. and r. 3ft. 11in.; lgth. 10ft. 3in.; wdth. 4ft. 5in.; ht. 2ft. 11in.; g.c. 5in.; turng. cir. 00ft. 0in.; kerb wt. 7½ cwt.; tank 7¼ gals.; 12-volt.

£587 Components only

Abbreviations—g.c.—ground clearance; susp.—suspension; f.—front; r.—rear; comp.—compression; s.v.—side-valves; o.h.v.—overhead valves; o.h.c.—overhead camshaft; hyd.—hydraulic.

35

MASERATI 3500 G.T.

MODENA, cradle of countless fast cars, is where Maserati build this luxurious Gran Turismo model for road and track. High efficiency six-cylinder engine with twin-overhead camshafts and three twin-choke Webers. Four-speed, all-synchro ZF box with option of overdrive. British Girling discs on front wheels. Choice of Superleggera coupe body by Touring, or convertible by Vignale.

CLOSE-UP

Six-cyl.; o.h.c.; 86 × 100 mm.; 3,458 c.c.; 226 b.h.p.; 8.5 to 1 comp.; dual ign.; three Weber carbs.; 4-speed, 10.62, 6.53, 4.61, 3.55 to 1; cen. lvr.; susp. f. ind. coil, r. half-elliptic; 2-door; 4-seat; hyd. brks., disc front, drum rear; max. 150 m.p.h.; cruise 120; m.p.g. 19-21; whl. base 8ft. 6in.; track f. 4ft. 6½in., r. 4ft. 5½in.; lgth. 15ft. 9in.; wdth. 5ft. 8in.; ht. 4ft. 3in.; g.c. 7in.; turng. cir. 40ft.; kerb wt. 26 cwt.; tank 18 gals.; 12-volt.

£4,130 + £1,722.2 p.t. = £5,852.2

MERCEDES-BENZ 180

CHOICE of four-cylinder petrol or diesel engines attracts big-milage drivers to this practical model designed for hard work. Appearance now harmonises with the 220 series thanks to a lower, broader grille and stronger bumpers. Front brake drums have turbo cooling fins. Equipment, up to usual Mercedes standards, includes safety padded steering wheel, screen washer and headlamp flasher.

CLOSE-UP

Four-cyl.; o.h.c.; 85 × 83.6 mm.; 1,897 c.c.; 78 b.h.p.; 7 to 1 comp.; Bosch ign.; Solex carb.; 4-speed, 15.79, 9.28, 5.96, 3.96 to 1; col. lvr.; susp. f. and r. ind. coil; 4-door; 4/5-seat; hyd. brks.; max. 84 m.p.h.; cruise 70; m.p.g. 26; whl. base 8ft. 8½in.; track f. 4ft. 8½in., r. 4ft. 10in.; lgth. 14ft. 9in.; wdth. 5ft. 8½in.; ht. 5ft. 1½in.; g.c. 7½in.; turng. cir. 35ft.; kerb wt. 23 cwt.; tank 12 gals.; 12-volt.

£1,195 + £499.0.10 p.t. = £1,694.0.10

MERCEDES-BENZ 190 SL

A BEST-SELLER in the proud Mercedes-Benz range, this fast two-seater has a touch of the aristocrat about it. Beautifully finished, it has a four-cylinder, overhead camshaft engine of 1,897 c.c. and synchromesh on all four forward speeds. Built for sunny climates, it can be converted into a hard top in a trice when the weather turns foul. A brilliant car worthy of its name.

CLOSE-UP

Four-cyl.; o.h.c.; 85 × 83.6 mm.; 1,897 c.c.; 120 b.h.p.; 8.5 to 1 comp.; coil ign.; twin Solex carbs.; 4-speed, 13.7, 9.10, 5.92, 3.89 to 1; cen. lvr.; susp., f. and r., ind. coil; 2-door; 2-seat; hyd. servo brks.; max. 112 m.p.h.; cruise, 96; m.p.g., 22-26; whl. base, 7ft. 10½in.; track, f., 4ft. 8½in., r., 4ft. 9½in.; lgth., 13ft. 10in.; wdth., 5ft. 8½in.; ht., 4ft. 4in.; g.c., 6½in.; turng. cir., 36ft.; kerb wt., 22½ cwt.; tank, 14½ gals.; 12-volt.

£1,950 + £813.12.6 p.t. = £2,763.12.6

MERCEDES-BENZ 220 S

THERE are three models in this series, all with steering, braking, road holding and finish to delight the most critical driver. 220 is the lowest-priced model. 220S has different carburetters, servo brakes and even more elaborate equipment. 220SE is the star performer, with fuel injection engine. Safety-padded steering wheels, hand-holds in doors and roof and adjustable back rests.

CLOSE-UP

Six-cyl.; o.h.c.; 80 × 72.8 mm.; 2,195 c.c.; 134 b.h.p.; 8.7 to 1 comp.; coil ign.; 2 Solex carb.; 4-speed, 14.92, 9.68, 6.27, 4.1 to 1; col. lvr.; susp., f., ind. coil, r., ind. coil; 4-door; 5/6-seat; hyd. servo brks.; max., 102 m.p.h.; cruise, 90; m.p.g. 26; whl. base, 9ft. 0½in.; track f., 4ft. 9½in.; r., 4ft. 10½in.; lgth., 16ft. 0½in.; wdth., 5ft. 10½in.; ht., 4ft. 11½in.; g.c., 7½in.; turng. cir., 37ft. 5in.; kerb wt., 26½ cwt.; tank, 14½ gals.; 12-volt.

£1,757 + £733.4.2 p.t. = £2,490.4.2

Abbreviations—g.c.—ground clearance; susp.—suspension; f.—front; r.—rear; comp.—compression; s.v.—side-valves; o.h.v.—overhead valves; o.h.c.—overhead camshaft; hyd.—hydraulic

MERCEDES-BENZ 300 SL

WORLD famous as the quintessence of speed and style, the 300SL translates long racing experience into a practical road car of terrific performance. Three-litre engine with fuel injection, servo brakes and independent rear suspension with transverse compensator spring are among the mechanical features. Bodywork is a superbly finished two-seater convertible, with hard top listed as an optional extra.

CLOSE-UP

Six-cyl.; o.h.c.; 85 × 88 mm.; 2,996 c.c.; 250 b.h.p.; 8.55 to 1 comp.; coil ign.; Bosch injection; 4-speed, 12.16, 7.17, 5.06, 3.64 to 1; cen. lvr.; susp. f. and r., ind. coil; 2-door; 2-seat; hyd. servo brks.; max. 129-155 m.p.h.; cruise, 100-110; m.p.g., 15-24; whl. base, 7ft. 10½in.; track f., 4ft 7$\frac{7}{16}$in., r., 4ft. 9in.; lgth., 15ft.; wdth, 5ft. 10½in.; ht., 4ft. 3½in.; g.c., 5¼in.; turng. cir., 37ft. 6in.; kerb wt., 26¾ cwt.; tank, 22 gals.; 12-volt.

£3,750 + £1,563.12.6 p.t. = £5,313.12.6

MERCURY MONTEREY

A STEP up from the big Fords in price and finish, the Mercury offers an immense range of body styles in innumerable colour schemes: saloons, hard-tops, coupe convertibles and station wagons, all with powerful V8 engines from five to seven litres. Extras include automatic transmission, press-button operation for windows and seat adjustment, servo brakes and power-assisted steering.

CLOSE-UP

Eight-cyl.; o.h.v.; 3.75 × 3.30 mm.; 4,786 c.c.; 185 b.h.p.; 8.8 to 1 comp.; coil ign.; Holley carb.; 3-speed auto., 6.89, 4.3, 2.91 to 1; col. lvr.; susp. f. ind. coil, r. half-elliptic; 2/4-door; 6-seat; hyd. servo brks.; max. 105 m.p.h.; cruise 80; m.p.g. 12-15; whl. base 10ft.; track f. 5ft. 1in., r. 5ft.; lgth. 17ft. 10in.; wdth. 6ft. 5in.; ht. 4ft. 7in.; g.c. 7in.; turng. cir. 43ft. 8in.; kerb wt. 34 cwt.; tank 16½ gals.; 12-volt.

METROPOLITAN 1500

HOME on the range for British buyers after a year with an export-only tag, the Metropolitan now has an exterior opening to the luggage trunk for easier access. Built by B.M.C. for American Motors, these colourful little coupes and convertibles are generously powered with a 1½-litre engine, which supplies the torque needed for flexible top-gear performance.

CLOSE-UP

Four-cyl.; o.h.v.; 73.02 × 89 mm.; 1,489 c.c.; 51 b.h.p.; 8.3 to 1 comp.; coil ign.; Zenith carb.; 3-speed, 11.98, 6.28, 4.22 to 1; col. lvr.; susp., f., ind. coil, r., half-elliptic; 2-door; 2/3-seat; hyd. brks.; max. 74 m.p.h.; cruise, 60; m.p.g., 26-30; whl. base, 7ft. 1in.; track, f., 3ft. 9$\frac{5}{16}$in., r., 3ft. 8½in.; lgth., 12ft. 5½in.; wdth., 5ft. 1½in.; ht., 4ft. 8in.; g.c., 6⅜in.; turng. cir., 37ft.; kerb wt., 16¾ cwt.; tank, 8¾ gals.; 12-volt.

£498.10 + £208.16.8 p.t. = £707.6.8

M.G. MGA 1600

THIS is still a big favourite in the United States, where their compact cars have temporarily set back the sale of British saloons. One of the smallest 100 miles-an-hour cars built, the M.G.A. 1600 gathers further support with its bigger engine and Lockheed disc brakes on the front. A splendid little sports car at a remarkably reasonable price. It stems from a well-established line.

CLOSE-UP

Four-cyl.; o.h.v.; 75.39 × 88.9 mm.; 1,588 c.c.; 79.5 b.h.p.; 8.3 to 1 comp.; coil ign.; S.U. carb.; 4-speed, 15.652, 9.52, 5.908, 4.3 to 1; cen. lvr.; susp. f., ind. coil, r., half-elliptic; 2-door; 2-seat; hyd. brks. disc front; max. 100 m.p.h.; cruise, 80; m.p.g. 28; whl. base, 7ft. 10in.; track, f., 3ft 11½ in. r., 4ft 0¾ in.; lgth., 13ft.; wdth., 4ft. 10in.; ht., 4ft. 2in.; g.c., 6in.; turng. cir., 30ft. 6in.; kerb wt., 18 cwt.; tank, 10 gals.; 12-volt.

£663 + £277.7.6 p.t. = £940.7.6

Abbreviations—g.c.—ground clearance; susp.—suspension; f.—front; r.—rear; comp.—compression; s.v.—side-valves; o.h.v.—overhead valves; o.h.c.—overhead camshaft; hyd.—hydraulic

37

M.G. MAGNETTE MARK III

THIS is a honey of a car for those who like a fast saloon beautifully turned out. B.M.C.'s new Farina-body look particularly suits the Magnette which has gay two-colour finishes and leather upholstery. There are loads of other good points, including particularly fine driver's vision, child-proof door locks, safety padded instrument panel and a large and practical luggage trunk.

CLOSE-UP

Four-cyl.; o.h.v.; 73 × 88.9 mm.; 1,489 c.c.; 63.5 b.h.p.; 8.3 to 1 comp.; coil ign.; S.U. carb.; 4-speed, 15.64, 9.52, 5.91, 4.3 to 1; cen. lvr.; susp. f., ind. coil, r., half-elliptic; 4-door; 4/5-seat; hyd. brks.; max. 85 m.p.h.; cruise, 70; m.p.g. 23-30; whl. base, 8ft. 3⅞in.; track, f., 4ft. 0⅞in.; r., 4ft. 1⅞in.; lgth., 14ft. 10in.; wdth., 5ft. 3½in.; ht., 4ft. 11½in.; g.c., 6½in.; turng. cir., 37ft. 6in.; kerb wt., 22½ cwt.; tank, 10 gals.; 12-volt.

£714 + £298.12.6 p.t. = £1,012.12.6

MORGAN PLUS FOUR

DISC brakes and lowered steering ratios to make its handling lighter are the main changes in next year's model. These will appeal particularly to the enthusiast who wants his motoring low priced, sporting and distinctive, for the Plus Four stems from a privately owned firm which operates from the West Country and always produce a car that is interesting and a little different.

CLOSE-UP

Four-cyl.; o.h.v.; 83 × 92 mm.; 1,991 c.c.; 100 b.h.p.; 8.5 to 1 comp.: coil ign.; twin S.U. carbs.; 4-speed, 12.85, 7.38, 5.24, 3.73 to 1; cen. lvr.; susp., f., ind. coil, r. half-elliptic; 2-door; 2/4-seat; hyd. brks., disc front; max. 105 m.p.h.; cruise 85; m.p.g. 32; whl. base 8ft.; track f. and r. 3ft. 11in.; lgth. 12ft.; wdth. 4ft. 8in.; ht. 4ft. 3in.; g.c. 7in.; turng. cir. 33ft.; kerb wt. 16½ cwt.; tank 11 gals.; 12-volt.

£655 + £274.0.10 p.t. = £929.0.10

MORRIS MINI TRAVELLER

A NEW baby estate car with an entirely new body fitted to the now-famous transverse-mounted engine. Front ends are identical with the saloons, but the body is nine inches longer, with an extra four inches on the wheelbase, although it still has a turning circle of 32 feet 9 inches. Height of the back compartment is 2 feet 10½ inches—adequate for the medium-sized baby carriages now so popular.

CLOSE-UP

Four-cyl.; o.h.v.; 63 × 68.26 mm.; 848 c.c.; 37 b.h.p.; 8.3 to 1 comp.; coil ign.; S.U. carb.; 4-speed, 13.657, 8.176, 5.317, 3.765 to 1; cen. lvr.; susp. f. ind. rubber, r. ind. rubber; 2-door; 4-seat; hyd. brks.; max. 73 m.p.h.; cruise 60; m.p.g. 45; whl. base 7ft.; track f. 3ft. 11¾in., r. 3ft. 9¾in.; lgth. 10ft. 9¾in.; wdth. 4ft. 7½in.; ht. 4ft. 5in.; g.c. 6¼in.; turng. cir. 32ft. 9in.; kerb wt. 13 cwt.; tank 6½ gals.; 12-volt.

£439 + £184.0.10 p.t. = £623.0.10

MORRIS MINOR 1000

EXPECT to hear that the millionth Morris Minor has been built and sold. Announcement will be made a few days after the Motor Show has folded. For 12 years this grand little car has been a best-seller and has thoroughly merited it. Ideal as a family runabout or as the wife's second car, this splendid road holder shows no sign of waning popularity. Its 950 c.c. engine does all that is asked of it.

CLOSE-UP

Four-cyl.; o.h.v.; 62.9 × 76 mm.; 948 c.c.; 37 b.h.p.; 8.3 to 1 comp.; coil ign.; S.U. carb.; 4-speed, 16.507, 10.802, 6.425, 4.555 to 1; cen. lvr.; susp., f., ind. torsion bar, r., half-elliptic; 2-door; 4-seat; hyd. brks.; max. 75 m.p.h.; cruise, 55; m.p.g. 36-48; whl. base, 7ft. 2in.; track, f. 4ft. 2⅝in., r., 4ft. 2⅛in.; wdth., 5ft. 1in.; lgth., 12ft. 4in.; ht., 5ft.; g.c., 6½in.; turng. cir., 33ft.; kerb wt., 14¾ cwt.; tank, 6½ gals.; 12-volt.

£416 + £174.9.2 p.t. = £590.9.2

Abbreviations—g.c.—ground clearance; susp.—suspension; f.—front; r.—rear; comp.—compression; s.v.—side-valves; o.h.v.—overhead valves; o.h.c.—overhead camshaft; hyd.—hydraulic.

MORRIS OXFORD SERIES V

VITAL inches of extra space make it possible for even families of six to travel in comfort. Note the extra wide opening doors suggesting no more laddered nylons. The car has a superb panoramic windshield to reduce driver fatigue by giving an uninterrupted view of both front wings. The spare wheel, in a separate compartment, leaves the Oxford's luggage trunk with a tremendous appetite for cases.

CLOSE-UP

Four-cyl.; o.h.v.; 73×88.9 mm.; 1,489 c.c.; 53 b.h.p.; 8.3 to 1 comp.; coil ign.; S.U. carb.; 4-speed, 16.55, 10.08, 6.25, 4.55 to 1; cen. lvr. or st. col.; susp., f., ind. coil, r., half-elliptic; 4-door; 4/5-seat; hyd. brks.; max. 79 m.p.h.; cruise, 60; m.p.g. 25-35; whl. base, 8ft. 3¾in.; track, f., 4ft. 0⅝in.; r., 4ft. 1⅞in.; lgth. 14ft. 10in.; wdth., 5ft. 3½in.; ht., 4ft. 11¾in.; g.c., 6½in.; turng. cir., 37ft. 6in.; kerb wt., 21½ cwt.; tank, 10 gals.; 12-volt.

£575 + £240.14.2 p.t. = £815.14.2

MORRIS OXFORD TRAVELLER

A NEW Farina-styled station wagon with attractive lines and practical design features. Rear seats fold away as usual, but the backrest can be split horizontally to form a pillow for a 6 ft. sleeping compartment. Wheel-changing can be done without moving all the luggage, thanks to a tool box at the extreme rear and a drop-down spare wheel cradle.

CLOSE-UP

Four-cyl.; o.h.v.; 73.025×89 mm.; 1,489 c.c.; 53 b.h.p.; 8.3 to 1 comp.; coil ign.; S.U. carb.; 4-speed, 17.74, 10.79, 6.69, 4.875 to 1; cen. lvr.; susp. f. ind. coil, r. half-elliptic; 5-door; 4/5-seat; hyd. brks.; max. 78 m.p.h.; cruise 65; m.p.g. 28; whl. base 8ft. 3¾in.; track f. 4ft. 0⅝in., r. 4ft. 1⅞in.; lgth. 14ft. 10½in.; wdth. 5ft. 3½in.; ht. 5ft.; g.c. 6½in.; turng. cir. 37ft. 5in.; kerb wt. 23½ cwt.; tank 10 gals.; 12-volt.

£655 + £274.0.10 p.t. = £929.0.10

MOSKVITCH

RUGGED small car built in Moscow for the Russian family man and now available on the British market. Its low-compression 1.3-litre engine uses cheap grades of fuel. Equipment includes radiator blind, reclining seats and a full tool kit. Other models in the range include a station wagon and a four-wheel drive cross-country saloon with high ground clearance.

CLOSE-UP

Four-cyl.; o.h.v.; 76×75 mm.; 1,358 c.c.; 45 b.h.p.; 7 to 1 comp.; coil ign.; downdraught carb.; 4-speed, 17.89, 11.39, 7.83, 4.71 to 1; col. lvr.; susp. f. ind. coil, r. half-elliptic; 4-door; 4-seat; hyd. brks.; max. 72 m.p.h.; cruise 50; m.p.g. 35; whl. base 7ft. 9in.; track f. and r. 4ft.; lgth. 13ft. 4in.; wdth. 5ft. 1in.; ht. 5ft. 1½in.; g.c. 8in.; turng. cir. 39½ft.; kerb wt. 19½ cwt.; tank 7¾ gals.; 12-volt.

£535 + £224.0.10 p.t. = £759.0.10

NSU PRINZ

SPOTLIGHTED on this stand is the Sport Prince coupe with pretty Bertone-designed body in production at last. Its air-cooled vertical twin engine of only 583 c.c. mounted at the rear is said to give it a top speed of about 80 m.p.h. Also on view is the nippy little four-seater saloon. Suspension is all-independent by coil springs.

CLOSE-UP

Two-cyl.; o.h.c., air-cooled; 75×66 mm.; 583 c.c.; 36 b.h.p.; 7.6 to 1 comp.; coil ign.; Bing carb.; 4-speed, 18.74, 10, 6.39, 4.52 to 1; cen. lvr.; susp., f., ind. coil, r., ind. coil.; 2-door; 4-seat; hyd. brks.; max. 75 m.p.h.; cruise, 55; m.p.g. 45-50; whl. base, 6ft. 6½in.; track, f., and r., 3ft. 11in.; wdth., 4ft. 7½in.; ht., 4ft. 5¼in.; g.c., 7in.; turng. cir., 27ft.; kerb wt., 9¼ cwt.; tank, 5¼ gals.; 12-volt.

£392 + £155.8.6 p.t. = £547.8.6

Abbreviations—g.c.—ground clearance; susp.—suspension; f.—front; r.—rear; comp.—compression; s.v.—side-valves; o.h.v.—overhead valves; o.h.c.—overhead camshaft; hyd.—hydraulic.

OLDSMOBILE SUPER 88

ALWAYS among the fastest American cars, the big Oldsmobiles have high-powered V8 engines and new styling in the spirit of the space-travel age. A practical advantage of the new bodywork is increased leg room especially at the rear. A smaller automatic transmission reduces the size of the centre hump, too. Power aids your efforts in steering, braking or erecting convertible tops.

CLOSE-UP

Eight-cyl.; o.h.v.; 104.7 × 93.7 mm.; 6,456 c.c.; 325 b.h.p.; 10 to 1 comp.; coil ign.; Rochester carb.; 3-speed, 7.82, 4.47, 3.64 to 1; col. lvr. auto trans. opt.; susp. f. ind. coil, r. coil; 2-door; 6-seat; hyd. brks.; max. 115 m.p.h.; cruise 90; m.p.g. 14; whl. base 10ft. 3in.; track f. and r. 5ft. 1in.; lgth. 17ft. 8in.; wdth. 6ft. 5½in.; ht. 4ft. 7⅞in.; g.c. 5½in.; turng. cir. 46ft. 3in.; kerb wt. 38½ cwt.; tank 17 gals.; 12-volt.

£2,400 + £1,086.2.6 p.t. = £3,486.2.6

OLDSMOBILE F.85

DESCRIBED as a de luxe front-engined small car the Olds is no miniature by European standards. Almost 16 ft. long, with a V8 engine developing nearly 150 horsepower it sells quality in a parkable package. The body shell is the same as that of the rear-engined Chevrolet Corvair but the engine is at the front. There is a new lightweight automatic transmission.

CLOSE-UP

Eight-cyl.; o.h.v.; 5,118 c.c.; 155 b.h.p.; 8.75 to 1 comp.; coil ign.; Rochester carb.; 3-speed, col. lvr., 4-speed auto. opt.; susp. f. ind. coil, r. coil; 4-door; 6-seat; hyd. brks.; max. 100 m.p.h.; cruise 90; m.p.g. 20; whl. base 9ft. 4in.; lgth. 15ft. 8in.; wdth. 5ft. 11⅝in.; ht. 4ft. 4⅝in.; kerb wt. 24 cwt.; 12-volt.

£2,320 + £968 p.t. = £3,288

PANHARD PL 17

ROOMY four-door body for comfort, flat twin air-cooled engine for economy, front wheel drive for sure road grip—this is the formula that has kept Panhard buyers coming for many years. Front doors are now hinged on the forward edge to meet new French regulations and interior trim is redesigned. Normal engine gives 42 h.p. Tiger sports produces 50.

CLOSE-UP

Two-cyl.; o.h.v.; air-cooled; 85 × 75 mm.; 850 c.c.; 42 b.h.p.; 7.2 to 1 comp.; coil ign.; Zenith carb.; 4-speed, 16.495, 9.277, 6.148, 4.525 to 1; col. lvr.; susp. f., transv. ind., r., tors. bar; 4-door; 5/6-seat; hyd. brks.; max. 80 m.p.h.; cruise, 70; m.p.g., 47; whl. base, 8ft. 5 7/16in.; track, f. and r., 4ft. 3 7/16in.; lgth., 15ft. 0⅜in.; wdth., 5ft. 5 5/16in.; ht., 4ft. 9¼in.; g.c., 6¼in.; turng. cir., 31ft.; kerb wt., 16 cwt.; tank, 9½ gals.; 12-volt.

£633 + £264.17.6 p.t. = £897.17.6

PEUGEOT 403

FRENCH family five-seater with a proud reputation for rugged reliability. You see them cruising at 80 on France's long highways but they are economical, too, thanks to the unusual gearbox with a geared-up cruising ratio. Reclining seats and a big trunk are bull points for the long-distance driver. Latest addition is a 1,300 c.c. economy version to replace the recently withdrawn 203.

CLOSE-UP

Four-cyl.; o.h.v.; 80 × 73 mm.; 1,468 c.c.; 65 b.h.p.; 7 to 1 comp.; coil ign., d/d carb.; 4-speed, full syncromesh, 17.5, 9.44, 5.75, 4.33 to 1; col. lvr.; susp. f. ind. transv. leaf, r. coil; 4-door; 5/6-seat; hyd. brks.; max. 85 m.p.h.; cruise 70-75; m.p.g. 30-32; whl. base 8ft. 9in.; track 4ft. 4¾in. f., r. 4ft. 4in.; lgth. 14ft. 8in.; wdth. 5ft. 6in.; ht. 4ft. 11¼in.; g.c. 6in.; turng. cir. 28ft. 9in.; kerb wt. 21 cwt.; tank 11 gals.; 12-volt.

£796.2.11 + £332.17.1 p.t. = £1,129

Abbreviations—g.c.—ground clearance; susp.—suspension; f.—front; r.—rear; comp.—compression; s.v.—side-valves; o.h.v.—overhead valves; o.h.c.—overhead camshaft; hyd.—hydraulic.

PEUGEOT 404

COMPACT, fast and practical new car for keen drivers from one of France's oldest manufacturers. 1.6 litre 4-cylinder engine is laid on its side to lower centre of gravity and simplify maintenance. Four-speeds, all synchronised. Top is direct, not geared up as on 403. New strut-type front suspension. Controllable fresh-air louvres on instrument panel. Adjustable back-rests and sockets in the roof for a roof rack.

CLOSE-UP
Four-cyl.; o.h.v.; 84×73 mm.; 1,618 c.c.; 72 b.h.p.; 7.2 to 1 comp.; coil ign.; Solex carb.; 4-speed, 17.4, 9.29, 5.97, 4.2 to 1; col. lvr.; susp. f. ind. coil, r. coil; 4-door; 5/6-seat; hyd. brks.; max. 90 m.p.h.; cruise 75-80; m.p.g. 30-32; whl. base 8ft. 8¼in.; track f. 4ft. 5in., r., 4ft. 2¾in.; lgth. 14ft. 7in.; wdth. 5ft. 5¾in.; ht. 4ft. 9in.; g.c. 6in.; turng. cir. 31ft. 7in.; kerb wt. 20½ cwt.; tank 11 gals.; 12-volt.

£915 + £382.7.6 p.t. = £1,297.7.6

PLYMOUTH FURY

PIONEER of the high-tailed, sharp-finned American style, Plymouth retracts for 1961 with a smoother line which many will find more attractive. Buyers have a bewildering choice of six or eight cylinder engines with manual or automatic transmissions in saloons, hard tops, convertibles and station wagons. Option lists are equally extensive, including radio, electric seat adjustment, servo steering and servo brakes.

CLOSE-UP
Eight-cyl.; o.h.v.; 99.3×84 mm.; 5,208 c.c.; 230 b.h.p.; 9 to 1 comp.; coil ign.; Stromberg carb.; 3-speed auto, 8.11, 4.79, 3.31 to 1; push buttons; susp. f. ind. torsion bar, r. half-elliptic; 4-door; 6-seat; hyd. servo brks.; max. 108 m.p.h.; cruise 80; m.p.g. 16-18; whl. base 9ft. 10in.; track f. 5ft. 1in., r. 4ft. 11½in.; lgth. 17ft. 5¾in.; wdth. 6ft. 6in.; ht. 4ft. 8½in.; g.c. 5¼in.; turng. cir. 42ft.; kerb wt. 31½ cwt.; tank 17 gals.; 12-volt.

£1,970 + £822 p.t. = £2,792

PONTIAC TEMPEST

TOPICS for technical discussion abound here. A new front-mounted four-cylinder engine (first four-cylinder in an American saloon for over 25 years) driving to a combined gearbox and differential mounted at the rear. Canted-over engine lowers the bonnet line and the fixed drive shaft keeps down the size of the centre tunnel. Choice of saloon or station wagon. Specification is for larger Bonneville.

CLOSE-UP
Eight-cyl.; o.h.v.; 103.1×95.25 mm.; 6,364 c.c.; 260 b.h.p.; 8.6 to 1 comp.; coil ign.; Rochester carb.; 4-speed auto., 12.8, 8.23, 5.0, 3.23 to 1; col. lvr.; susp. f. ind. coil, r. coil; 4-door; 6-seat; hyd.-servo brks.; max. 105 m.p.h.; cruise 80; m.p.g. 14-17; whl. base 10ft. 2in.; track f. 5ft. 3¼in., r. 5ft. 4in.; lgth. 17ft. 9¾in.; wdth. 6ft. 8¼in.; ht. 4ft. 10⅜in.; g.c. 6¼in.; turng. cir. 42ft. 9in.; kerb wt. 42½ cwt.; tank 17½ gals.; 12-volt.

£1,665 + £693.15 p.t. = £2,358.15

PONTIAC PARISIENNE

BUILT in a General Motors Canadian factory, the Pontiac Strato Chief, Laurentian and Parisienne differ in numerous details from the models made in U.S.A. Six-cylinder o.h.v. engines of 4.3 litres are normally used, but Laurentian four-door saloon and Parisienne hard top can also be had with V8 engines of 4.7 litres. Transmission is Powerglide two-speed automatic.

CLOSE-UP
Six-cyl.; o.h.v.; 95.25×100 mm.; 4,278 c.c.; 150 b.h.p.; 8.5 to 1 comp.; coil ign.; Rochester carb.; 2-speed auto., 7.11, 3.36 to 1; col. lvr.; susp. f. ind. coil, r. coil; 2-door; 5-seat; hyd. servo brks.; max. 90 m.p.h.; cruise 80; m.p.g. 15-18; whl. base 9ft. 11in.; track f. 5ft. 0½in., r. 4ft. 11½in.; lgth. 17ft. 7in.; wdth. 6ft. 8½in.; ht. 4ft. 8½in.; g.c. 6in.; turng. cir. 40ft. 6in.; kerb wt. 38 cwt.; tank 16½ gals.; 12-volt.

£1,626 + £679 p.t. = £2,305

Abbreviations—g.c.—ground clearance; susp.—suspension; f.—front; r.—rear; comp.—compression; s.v.—side-valves; o.h.v.—overhead valves; o.h.c.—overhead camshaft; hyd.—hydraulic.

PORSCHE STANDARD

LIGHT alloy engine, worn in the tail, and squat low drag coachwork give Porsche its unrivalled name for speed with economy. Latest headlamps in higher front wings give clearer night vision and massive front bumpers fend off careless parkers. The range includes streamlined coupe, convertible and spyder with detachable hard top. Small rear seats convert to a flat luggage platform.

CLOSE-UP

Four-cyl.; o.h.v. air-cooled; 82.5 × 74 mm.; 1,582 c.c.; 75 b.h.p.; 7.5 to 1 comp.; coil ign.; twin Zenith carbs.; 4-speed, 13.9, 7.7, 4.9, 3.5 to 1; cen. lvr.; susp., f. and r., ind. torsion bar; 2-door; 2/4-seat; hyd. brks.; max. 100 m.p.h.; cruise, 80-85; m.p.g., 33-35; whl. base, 6ft. 11in.; track f., 4ft. 3⅓in.; r., 4ft. 1⅓in.; lgth. 12ft. 11½in.; wdth., 5ft. 5¼in.; ht., 4ft. 3⅓in.; g.c., 6in.; turng. cir., 36ft.; kerb wt., 16¼ cwt.; tank, 11½ gals.; 6-volt.

£1,410 + £588.12.6 p.t. = £1,998.12.6

PORSCHE SUPER 90

LAZING along at 90 with that durable flat-four engine purring away at the rear, you wonder how any car can go so fast on so little fuel with so little fuss. What other gearbox matches this job with its servo-ring synchromesh on all four speeds? And for utmost grip on corners, there is the latest rear suspension with transverse compensator spring.

CLOSE-UP

Four-cyl.; o.h.v.; air-cooled; 82.5 × 74 mm.; 1,582 c.c.; 90 b.h.p.; 9. to 1 comp.; coil ign.; twin Zenith carbs.; 4-speed, 15.5, 8.57, 5.49, 3.96 to 1; cen. lvr.; susp., f., and r., ind. torsion bar; 2-door; 2/4-seat; hyd. brks.; max. 105 m.p.h.; cruise, 90; m.p.g., 30-35; whl. base, 6ft. 11in.; track, f., 4ft. 3⅓in., r., 4ft. 1⅓in.; lgth., 12ft. 11½in.; wdth., 5ft. 5¾in.; ht., 4ft. 3⅓in.; g.c., 6in.; turng. cir., 36ft.; kerb wt., 16¼ cwt.; tank, 11½ gals.; 6-volt.

£1,700 + £709.9.2 p.t. = £2,409.9.2

RAMBLER AMERICAN

PIONEER of the American compact cars, the little Rambler has pulled American Motors finances out of the red and forced the big corporations to come into line. Now re-styled for 1961, it is more competitive than ever and just what many family men are looking for, with six-cylinder 3.2 litre engine for lively performance and a choice of manual or automatic transmission.

CLOSE-UP

Six-cyl.; s.v.; 79.37 × 107.95 mm.; 3,205 c.c.; 90 b.h.p.; 8 to 1 comp.; coil ign.; Carter carb.; 3-speed, 9.4, 6.15, 3.78 to 1; col. lvr.; susp. f. ind. coil, r. semi-elliptic; 4-door; 5-seat; hyd. brks.; max. 85 m.p.h.; cruise 70; m.p.g. 28; whl. base 8ft. 4in.; track f. 4ft. 6in., r. 4ft. 7in.; lgth. 14ft. 5in.; wdth. 5ft. 10in.; ht. 4ft. 8in.; g.c. 7in.; turng. cir. 36ft.; kerb wt. 22½ cwt.; tank 16½ gals.; 12-volt.

RENAULT DAUPHINE

FRANCE'S best-selling motor car, the Dauphine is light, fast and sprightly. Its rear engine provides ample space for luggage under the bonnet, and from only an 845 c.c. power plant comes a top speed of 70 m.p.h. and 40 m.p.g. An outstanding little car sold in vast numbers all over the world. The manufacturers assemble it in England, too, which suggests first-class servicing arrangements.

CLOSE-UP

Four-cyl.; o.h.v.; 58 × 80 mm.; 845 c.c.; 31 b.h.p.; 7.75 to 1 comp.; coil ign.; Solex carb.; 3-speed, 16.1, 7.88, 4.52 to 1; cen. lvr.; susp., f., ind. coil, r., ind. coil and pneu.; 4-door; 4-seat; hyd. brks.; max. 75 m.p.h.; cruise, 60; m.p.g., 43-48; whl. base, 7ft. 5⅓in.; track, f., 4ft. 1⅓in., r., 4ft. 1in.; lgth., 12ft. 11in.; wdth., 5ft.; ht., 4ft. 9in.; g.c., 6in.; turng. cir., 29ft.; kerb wt., 12⅝ cwt.; tank, 7 gals.; 6-volt.

£486 + £203.12.6 p.t. = £689.12.6

Abbreviations—g.c.—ground clearance; susp.—suspension; f.—front; r.—rear; comp.—compression; s.v.—side-valves; o.h.v.—overhead valves; o.h.c.—overhead camshaft; hyd.—hydraulic.

RENAULT FLORIDE

A FAVOURITE with the ladies, who like its graceful lines, chic finish and gay colour schemes, the Floride uses mechanical parts of the Dauphine. There are seats for four, and the bonnet contains space for lots of luggage. The engine, the same as that used in the Dauphine Gordini four-speed saloon, gives 40 b.h.p. Choose from convertible or fixed head coupe bodywork.

CLOSE-UP
Four-cyl.; o.h.v.; 58×80 mm.; 845 c.c.; 40 b.h.p.; 8 to 1 comp.; coil ign.; Solex carb.; 4-speed, 16.1, 9.1, 6.3, 4.52 to 1; cen. lvr.; susp., f., ind. coil, r., ind. coil and pneu.; 2-door; 2/4-seat; hyd. brks.; max. 80 m.p.h.; cruise, 60; m.p.g. 39-43; whl. base, 7ft. 5½in.; track, f., 4ft. 1½in.; r., 4ft.; lgth., 14ft.; wdth., 5ft. 1⅜in.; ht., 4ft. 3⅜in.; g.c., 7in.; turng. cir., 29ft. 10in.; kerb wt., 15 cwt.; tank, 7 gals.; 6-volt.

£858 + £358.12.6 p.t. = £1,216.12.6

RILEY 4/68

MOST expensive of the Farina-styled 1½-litre saloons from the B.M.C., the Riley 4/68 has a twin-carburetter engine for lively performance. Luxurious interior finish is in leather and walnut veneers and the instruments include a tachometer. As a four/five seater with a big luggage trunk, it has space for a family and pace to suit the enthusiastic driver.

CLOSE-UP
Four-cyl.; o.h.v.; 73.025×88.9 mm.; 1,489 c.c.; 63.5 b.h.p.; 8.3 to 1 comp.; coil ign.; twin S.U. carb.; 4-speed 15.64, 9.52, 5.91, 4.3 to 1; cen. lvr.; susp., f., ind. coil, r., half-elliptic; 4-door; 4/5-seat; hyd. brks.; max. 85 m.p.h.; cruise 70; m.p.g. 23-30; whl. base, 8ft. 3¾in.; track f., 4ft. 0⅞in., r., 4ft. 1⅞in.; lgth., 14ft. 10in.; wdth., 5ft. 3½in.; ht., 4ft. 11½in.; g.c., 6½in.; turng. cir., 37ft.; 6in.; kerb wt., 22½ cwt.; tank, 10 gals; 12-volt.

£725 + £303.4.2 p.t. = £1,028.4.2

RILEY ONE-POINT-FIVE

DASH with elegance is the keynote of this year's model. With surging power from the 1½-litre engine which has twin carburetters, you get also a beautifully finished walnut veneer dashboard and leather seats. Inside hinges are now fitted to the bonnet and boot lid, the shape of the combustion chamber has been modified, and tappet noise has been reduced through a new camshaft with modified cam forms, and a longer oil level dipstick is now supplied.

CLOSE-UP
Four-cyl.; o.h.v.; 73.025×88.9 mm.; 1,489 c.c.; 63.5 b.h.p.; 8.3 to 1 comp.; coil ign.; twin S.U. carbs.; 4-speed, 13.56, 8.25, 5.12, 3.73 to 1; cen. lvr.; susp., f., ind. torsion bars, r., half-elliptic; 4-door; 4-seat; hyd. brks.; max. 85 m.p.h.; cruise 70; m.p.g. 25-35; whl. base, 7ft. 2in.; track, f., 4ft. 2½in., r., 4ft. 2⅝in.; lgth., 12ft. 9in.; wdth., 5ft. 1in.; ht., 4ft. 11½in.; g.c., 6½in.; turng. cir., 34ft. 3in.; kerb wt., 18½ cwt.; tank, 7 gals.; 12-volt.

£575 + £240.14.2 p.t. = £815.14.2

ROLLS ROYCE PHANTOM V

WHEN you buy this car there is little change out of £10,000. But oh! it is worth it, for this is the largest Rolls Royce ever built. An eight-seater limousine (including the chauffeur) it is the caviare and pink champagne car of the world. Mostly patronised by crowned heads and business tycoons, the chassis has the light alloy V-8 engine, power assistance for steering and brakes, automatic transmission and two refrigeration systems. Bodies are built by Park Ward, H. J. Mulliner and James Young.

CLOSE-UP
Eight-cyl.; o.h.v.; 104.14×91.44 mm.; 6,230 c.c.; 8 to 1 comp.; coil ign.; 2 S.U. carb.; 4-speed automatic, 14.86, 10.23, 5.64, 3.89 to 1; col. lvr.; susp., f., ind. coil, r., half-elliptic; 4-door; 7-seat; hyd. servo brks.; max. 100 m.p.h.; cruise 85; m.p.g. 12; whl. base, 12ft. 0in.; track f., 5ft. 0¾in.; r., 5ft. 4in.; lgth., 19ft. 10in.; wdth., 6ft. 7in.; ht., 5ft. 9in.; g.c., 7⅛in.; turng. cir., 48ft. 9in.; tank, 23 gals.; 12-volt.

£6,960 + £2,901.2.6 p.t. = £9,861.2.6

Abbreviations—g.c.—ground clearance; susp.—suspension; f.—front; r.—rear; comp.—compression; s.v.—side-valves; o.h.v.—overhead valves; o.h.c.—overhead camshaft; hyd.—hydraulic.

ROLLS ROYCE SILVER CLOUD II

WHISPERING along in the eighties with power to spare for a silent surge up to the hundred you find why this is acclaimed as the world's best. Closed bodywork gives the choice of four side windows for the private owner, or six on a longer wheelbase, with glass partition for chauffeur drive. Optional air conditioning completes the enjoyment, even in temperate climes.

CLOSE-UP

Eight-cyl.; o.h.v.; 104.14 × 91.44 mm.; 6,230 c.c.; 8 to 1 comp.; coil ign.; 2 S.U. carb.; 4-speed automatic, 11.75, 8.10, 4.46, 3.08 to 1; col. lvr.; susp., f., ind. coil, r., half-elliptic; 4-door; 5/6-seat; hyd. servo brks.; max., 110 m.p.h.; cruise 90; m.p.g. 12-15; whl. base, 10ft. 3in.; track f., 4ft. 10in.; r., 5ft.; lgth., 17ft. $7\frac{3}{4}$in.; wdth., 6ft. $2\frac{3}{4}$in.; ht., 5ft. 4in.; g.c., 7in.; turng. cir., 4ft. 8in.; kerb wt., $41\frac{1}{2}$ cwt.; tank, 18 gals.; 12-volt.

£4,300 + £1,792.15.10 p.t. = £6,092.15.10

ROVER 80

IMPECCABLE finish and an economical four-cylinder engine make this the car for the mature citizen, more interested in comfort than speed. But it is no sluggard. 82 m.p.h. maximum and 65 m.p.h. cruising are possibilities. Front brakes are discs, overdrive is standard and the chassis has only four greasing points. Valves are overhead (other Rovers have overhead inlet, side exhaust).

CLOSE-UP

Four-cyl.; o.h.v.; 90.47 × 88.8 mm.; 2,286 c.c.; 77 b.h.p.; 7 to 1 comp.; coil ign.; Solex carb.; 4-speed, 14.51, 8.78, 5.92, 4.3 to 1; cen. lvr. Laycock overdrive; susp., f., ind. coil, r., half-elliptic; 4-door; 4/5-seat; hyd. servo brks. disc front; max. 82 m.p.h.; cruise 65; m.p.g. 18-25; whl. base, 9ft. 3in.; track f., 4ft. $4\frac{1}{2}$in., r., 4ft. $3\frac{1}{2}$in.; lgth., 14ft. $10\frac{1}{4}$in.; wdth., 5ft. $5\frac{5}{8}$in.; ht., 5ft. $3\frac{3}{4}$in.; g.c., $7\frac{1}{8}$in.; turng. cir., 37ft.; kerb wt., 29 cwt.; tank, $11\frac{1}{2}$ gals.; 12-volt.

£963 + £402.7.6 p.t. = £1,365.7.6

ROVER 100

ACCLAIMED by critics as one of the best cars Rover ever built, the 100 shows how quality grows with steady development. No gaudy gimmicks to mark the passing years, but a wealth of thoughtful detail, sound engineering and conscientious craftsmanship make the difference between a hack and an heirloom. Engine is a short-stroke version of the 3-litre. Overdrive is standard.

CLOSE-UP

Six-cyl.; o.h. inlet, s. exhaust.; 77.3 × 92.075 mm.; 2,625 c.c.; 104 b.h.p.; 7.8 to 1 comp.; coil ign.; S.U. carb.; 4-speed, 14.51, 8.78, 5.92, 4.3 to 1; cen. lvr. Laycock overdrive; susp. f., ind. coil, r., half-elliptic; 4-door; 4/5-seat; hyd. servo brks. disc front; max., 94 m.p.h.; cruise 75; m.p.g. 18-25; whl. base, 9ft. 3in.; track f., 4ft. $4\frac{1}{2}$in.; r., 4ft. $3\frac{1}{2}$in.; lgth., 14ft. $10\frac{1}{4}$in.; wdth., 5ft. $5\frac{5}{8}$in.; ht., 5ft. $3\frac{3}{4}$in.; g.c., $7\frac{1}{8}$in.; turng. cir., 37ft.; kerb wt., $29\frac{1}{2}$ cwt.; tank, $11\frac{1}{2}$ gals.; 12-volt.

£1,085 + £453.4.2 p.t. = £1,538.4.2

ROVER 3-LITRE

POWER-ASSISTED steering now eases away the effort when you drive the most powerful of the Rovers. Interior furnishings, discreet and comfortable as those of an English club lounge, have received finishing touches and detail mechanical changes have been made in pursuit of silence. Rubber-insulated front end, choice of manual or automatic transmission, disc front brakes and adjustable facia air ducts are points to note.

CLOSE-UP

Six-cyl.; o.h. inlet, s. exhaust 77.8 × 105 mm.; 2,995 c.c.; 115 b.h.p.; 8.75 to 1 comp.; coil ign.; S.U. carb.; 4-speed, 14.5, 8.78, 5.92, 4.3 to 1; cen. lvr. Laycock overdrive; BW. auto trans. opt.; susp. f. ind. torsion bar, r., half-elliptic; 4-door; 5/6-seat; hyd. servo brks. disc front; max. 98 m.p.h.; cruise 75; m.p.g. 18-25; whl. base 9ft. $2\frac{1}{2}$in.; track f. 4ft. $7\frac{1}{4}$in., r. 4ft. 8in.; lgth. 15ft. $6\frac{1}{2}$in.; wdth. 5ft. 10in.; ht. 5ft.; g.c. $7\frac{1}{2}$in.; turng. cir. 38ft. 6in.; kerb wt. $32\frac{1}{2}$ cwt.; tank, 14 gals.; 12-volt.

£1,258 + £525.5.10 p.t. = £1,783.5.10

Abbreviations—g.c.—ground clearance; susp.—suspension; f.—front; r.—rear; comp.—compression; s.v.—side-valves; o.h.v.—overhead valves; o.h.c.—overhead camshaft; hyd.—hydraulic.

SAAB 96

IT IS first time in London for Sweden's nimble front-drive economy model. Built by a famous aircraft manufacturer it ran without major change from early post-war days to this summer when the body was redesigned and the engine enlarged. Better vision, wider rear seat, more luggage space and higher performance resulted. Three-cylinder two-stroke engine is now 841 c.c. giving 42 b.h.p.

CLOSE-UP
Three-cyl.; two-stroke; 70×72.9 mm.; 841 c.c.; 42 b.h.p.; 7.3 to 1 comp.; coil ign.; Solex carb.; 3-speed, 17.19, 8.53, 5.23 to 1; col. lvr.; susp. f. ind. coil, r. coil; 2-door; 4/5-seat; hyd. brks.; max. 75 m.p.h.; cruise 70; m.p.g. 34; whl. base 8ft. 2in.; track f. and r. 4ft.; lgth. 13ft. 2in.; wdth. 5ft. 2in.; ht. 4ft. 10in.; g.c. 7½in.; turng. cir. 36ft.; kerb wt. 16½ cwt.; tank 8½ gals.; 12-volt.

£623.17.6 + £261.2.6 p.t. = £885

SIMCA ARONDE

FIVE times round the world in 80 days is the distance covered with Simca's new five-bearing engine in a recent endurance demonstration. Power is increased to 51 b.h.p. for Monaco saloon; 61 for Monaco hardtop, Castel station wagon, Plein Ciel sports convertible and Oceane sports coupe. New exterior bright work in stainless steel, new instrument panels and reclining seats with new cushion contours.

CLOSE-UP
Four-cyl.; o.h.v.; 74×75 mm.; 1,290 c.c.; 51 b.h.p.; 7.5 to 1 comp.; coil ign'; Solex carb.; 4-speed, 16.4, 10.57, 6.52, 4.44 to 1; col. lvr.; susp., f., ind. coil, r., half-elliptic; 4-door; 4-seat; hyd. brks.; max. 80-85 m.p.h.; cruise, 70; m.p.g., 32-35; whl. base, 8ft. 10½in.; track, f., 4ft. 0¼in., r., 4ft. 1¼in.; lgth. 13ft. 6in.; wdth., 5ft. 1¾in.; ht., 4ft. 11¾in.; g.c., 5½in.; turng. cir., 31ft.; kerb wt., 18¾ cwt.; tank, 9½ gals.; 12-volt.

£563 + £235.14.2 p.t. = £798.14.2

SIMCA VEDETTE

A FRENCH car built by a company in which Chrysler has a large interest, the Vedette gets its speed from a 2.4-litre V8 engine which was originally a Ford design. Standard transmission is three-speed synchromesh but as an extra-cost option there is the Rushmatic, a semi-automatic push-button affair built round the British Laycock de Normanville overdrive.

CLOSE-UP
Eight-cyl.; s.v.; 60.06×85.72 mm.; 2,351 c.c.; 84 b.h.p.; 7.5 to 1 comp.; coil ign.; Zenith carb.; 3-speed, 14.18, 8.06, 4.55 to 1; col. lvr.; susp., f., ind. coil, r., half-elliptic; 4-door; 6-seat; hyd. brks.; max., 90 m.p.h.; cruise, 75; m.p.g., 25; whl. base, 8ft. 10in.; track, f., 4ft. 6in.; r., 4ft. 4¾in.; lgth., 15ft. 7in.; wdth., 5ft. 8¾in.; ht., 4ft. 10½in.; g.c., 6in.; turng. cir., 37ft. 6in.; kerb wt., 24 cwt.; tank, 13 gals.; 12-volt.

£965.10 + £403.18.6 p.t. = £1,369.8.6

SINGER GAZELLE

CLAIMED to be the lowest-priced luxury car, its attractions include fitted carpets, polished walnut panelling, lockable glove box, courtesy lights, twin-windtone horns, windscreen washers, twin sun visors, a full range of instruments and wheel-finishers. Automatic transmission optional. The non-automatic model can be fitted with a floor-mounted, or steering-column, gear shift. Compact, economical and a good-looker.

CLOSE-UP
Four-cyl.; o.h.v.; 79×76.2 mm.; 1,494 c.c.; 60 b.h.p.; 8.5 to 1 comp.; coil ign.; Solex carb.; 4-speed, 14.872, 9.513, 6.187, 4.44 to 1; col. or cen. lvr.; Laycock overdrive or Smith's auto. opt.; susp. f. ind. coil, r. half-elliptic; 4-door; 5-seat; hyd. brks.; max. 87 m.p.h.; cruise, 70; m.p.g., 28-32; whl. base, 8ft. 1in.; r., 4ft. 0¼in.; lgth., 13ft. 7½in.; wdth., 5ft. 0¾in.; ht., 4ft. 11¾in.; g.c., 7in.; turng. cir., 36ft.; kerb wt., 20¾ cwt.; tank, 10 gals.; 12-volt.

£598 + £250.5.10 p.t. = £848.5.10

Abbreviations—g.c.—ground clearance; susp.—suspension; f.—front; r.—rear; comp.—compression; s.v.—side-valves; o.h.v.—overhead valves; o.h.c.—overhead camshaft; hyd.—hydraulic.

STUDEBAKER HAWK V8

BUCKET-TYPE front seats and the option of a four-speed gearbox with central lever are new features of this American five-seater coupe. Less enterprising pilots can still have three speeds or automatic self-mixing gears. With the extra-cost four-barrel carburetter, engine power rises to 225 b.h.p. Servo brakes, power steering and air conditioning are also available.

CLOSE-UP

Eight-cyl.; o.h.v.; 76.2 / 101.6 mm.; 4,247 c.c.; 180 b.h.p.; 8.8 to 1 comp.; coil ign.; Stromberg carb.; 3-speed auto., 8.49, 5.2, 3.54 to 1; col. lvr.; susp. f. ind. coil, r. half-elliptic; 2-door; 4-seat; hyd. brks.; max. 102 m.p.h.; cruise 80; m.p.g. 20; whl. base 10ft. 0½in.; track f. 4ft. 9½in., r. 4ft 8½in.; lgth. 17ft.; wdth. 5ft. 11½in.; ht. 4ft. 7½in.; g.c. 6¾in.; turng. cir. 42ft. 4in.; kerb wt. 28¾ cwt.; tank 15 gals.; 12-volt.

£1,374 + £573.12.6 p.t. = £1,947.12.6

SUNBEAM ALPINE

A BIGGER engine serves up man-sized performances for 1961, but this tender trap also has the comforts for girl appeal. Wrap-round windscreen, wind-up windows and a fully fashioned soft top temper the wind to the shingled lamb, and for winter evenings there is a clip-on hard top. A sophisticated sports car that was an instant success. Front brakes are discs.

CLOSE-UP

Four-cyl.; o.h.v.; 81.5 / 76.2 mm.; 1,592 c.c.; 85.5 b.h.p.; 9.1 to 1 comp.; coil ign.; two Zenith carbs.; 4-speed, 13.013, 8.324, 5.413, 3.89 to 1; cen. lvr.; Laycock overdrive opt.; susp. f. ind. coil, r. half-elliptic; 2-door; 2-seat; hyd. brks. disc front; max. 100 m.p.h.; cruise 80; m.p.g. 25; whl. base 7ft. 2in.; track f. 4ft. 3in., r. 4ft. 0½in.; lgth. 12ft. 11½in.; wdth. 5ft. 0½in.; ht. 4ft. 3½in.; g.c. 5in.; turng. cir. 34ft.; kerb wt. 19½ cwt.; tank, 9 gals.; 12-volt.

£685 + £286.10.10 p.t. = £971.10.10

SUNBEAM RAPIER

THE Rapier matches sparkling performance with low fuel consumption. Its 1½ litre engine, which has an aluminium cylinder head, inclined overhead valves, twin carburetters and a high compression ratio of 9.2 to 1, develops 78 b.h.p. All this accounts for the Rapier having dominated the 1½ litre class in Europe's major rallies this year, including the Monte Carlo Rally, the International Alpine Rally and the International Greek Acropolis Rally.

CLOSE-UP

Four-cyl.; o.h.v.; 79 × 76.2 mm.; 1,494 c.c.; 78 b.h.p.; 9.2 to 1 comp.; coil ign.; twin Zenith carbs.; 4-speed, 14.128, 9.038, 5.877, 4.22 to 1, Laycock overdrive opt.; cen. lvr.; susp., f., ind. coil, r., half-elliptic; 2-door; 4-seat; hyd. brks., disc front; max., 90 m.p.h.; cruise, 70; m.p.g., 27-30; whl. base, 8ft.; track f., 4ft. 1½in.; r., 4ft. 0½in.; lgth. 13ft. 6½in.; wdth., 5ft. 1in.; ht., 4ft. 10½in.; g.c., 5¾in.; turng. cir., 36ft.; kerb wt., 21 cwt.; tank, 10 gals.; 12-volt.

£695 + £290.14.2 p.t. = £985.14.2

TRIUMPH HERALD COUPE

THIS one combines the roadworthiness of the sports car and the amenities of a completely furnished saloon. It carries two children in the back with reasonable comfort, or provides loads of space for luggage. Compared with the four-seater Herald saloon the coupe has extra power from a higher compression, twin-carburetter engine, and is slightly lighter in weight. A tremendous favourite both here and in many foreign countries.

CLOSE-UP

Four-cyl.; o.h.v.; 63 × 76 mm.; 948 c.c.; 50½ b.h.p.; 8.5 to 1 comp.; coil ign.; 2 S.U. carbs.; 4-speed, 19.45, 11.2, 6.62, 4.55 to 1; cen. lvr.; susp., f., ind. coil, r., ind. trans. leaf; 2-door; 2-seat; hyd. brks.; max. 78-80 m.p.h.; cruise, 70; m.p.g., 35; whl. base, 7ft. 7in.; track f. and r., 4ft.; lgth., 12ft. 9in.; wdth., 4ft. 3½in.; g.c., 6½in.; turng. cir., 25ft.; kerb wt., 15½ cwt.; tank, 7 gals.; 12-volt.

£515 + £215.14.2 p.t. = £730.14.2

Abbreviations—g.c.—ground clearance; susp.—suspension; f.—front; r.—rear; comp.—compression; s.v.—side-valves; o.h.v.—overhead valves; o.h.c.—overhead camshaft; hyd.—hydraulic.

SKODA OCTAVIA

CZECHOSLOVAKIA'S small family saloon is brought up to date with coil spring front suspension, safety steering wheel and new grille. The chassis has all-independent springing attached to a tubular backbone. Windscreen and rear window are interchangeable. Reclining seats are available at extra cost. Octavia has 1,089 c.c. engine; Octavia Super has 1,221 c.c. The range also includes the Felicia sports convertible.

CLOSE-UP

Four-cyl.; o.h.v.; 68∕75 mm.; 1,089 c.c.; 43 b.h.p.; 8.2 to 1 comp.; coil ign.; Jikov carb.; 4-speed, 20.4, 11.8, 7.6, 4.78 to 1; col. lvr.; susp. f. ind. coil, r. ind. transv.; 2-door; 4-seat; hyd. brks.; max. 77 m.p.h.; cruise 60; m.p.g. 40; whl. base 7ft. 10½in.; track f. 3ft. 11⅜in., r. 4ft. 1in.; lgth. 13ft. 4in.; wdth. 5ft. 3in.; ht. 4ft. 8½in.; g.c. 8½in.; turng. cir. 32ft. 9in.; kerb wt. 17¾ cwt.; tank 6 gals.; 12-volt.

£525 + £220 p.t. = £745

STANDARD ENSIGN

IF YOUR pocket does not quite run to a Vanguard this is a very good second best. It is cheaper and the 1,670 c.c. engine is slightly smaller. Its wet liner engine construction results in a longer run before a major overhaul is needed. A notable feature is the detachable front wings which help to cut down repairs considerably. A well established car, well proven.

CLOSE-UP

Four-cyl.; o.h.v.; 76×92 mm.; 1,670 c.c.; 60 b.h.p.; 8 to 1 comp.; coil ign.; Solex carb.; 4-speed, 14.5, 8.61, 5.66, 4.1 to 1; cen. lvr. overdrive opt.; susp., f., ind. coil, r., half-elliptic; 4-door; 5/6-seat; hyd. brks.; max., 80 m.p.h.; cruise, 60; m.p.g. 32-38; whl. base, 8ft. 6in.; track f. and r., 4ft. 3½in.; lgth., 14ft. 3½in.; wdth., 5ft. 7½in.; ht., 5ft.; g.c., 7½in.; turng. cir., 37ft.; kerb wt., 23½ cwt.; tank, 12 gals.; 12-volt.

£599 + £250.14.2 p.t. = £849.14.2

STANDARD VANGUARD LUXURY SIX

ONE of the first true post-war cars to emerge in Britain, the Vanguard has seen a number of styling changes, culminating in the successful Vignale transformation, but the engine has always been a four-cylinder. Now a six-cylinder unit adds a new injection of smooth power to rejuvenate a sound, solid, proved design. Saloon and estate car are available.

CLOSE-UP

Six-cyl.; o.h.v.; 74.7∕76 mm.; 1,998 c.c.; 85 b.h.p.; 8 to 1 comp.; col. ign.; 2 Solex carbs.; 4-speed, 14.5, 8.61, 5.66, 4.1 to 1 (3-speed box with col. change opt.); cen. lvr.; susp. f. ind. coil, r. half-elliptic; 4-door; 5/6-seat; hyd. brks.; max. 90 m.p.h.; cruise 70; m.p.g. 25-35; whl. base 8ft. 6in.; track f. and r. 4ft. 3in.; lgth. 14ft. 3½in.; wdth. 5ft. 7½in.; ht. 5ft.; g.c. 7½in.; turng. cir. 39ft.; kerb wt. 23½ cwt.; tank 12 gals.; 12-volt.

£720 + £301.2.6 p.t. = £1,021.2.6

STUDEBAKER LARK

THE Skybolt Six, an overhead valve engine replacing the previous side-valve unit, gives a spirited performance to this pioneer of the American "compact" car movement. With it come a larger clutch and the option of a new torque converter transmission. Manual gearbox and overdrive are also offered. There is a choice of axle ratios and power steering is now listed.

CLOSE-UP

Six-cyl.; o.h.v.; 76.1×101.5 mm.; 2,779 c.c.; 110 b.h.p.; 8.3 to 1 comp.; coil ign.; Carter carb.; 3-speed, 8.62, 5.39, 3.31 to 1; col. lvr.; susp. f. ind. coil, r. half-elliptic; 2/4-door; 5-seat; hyd. brks.; max. 80 m.p.h.; cruise 70; m.p.g. 22-25; whl. base 9ft. 0½in.; track f. 4ft. 9¾in., r. 4ft. 8½in.; lgth. 14ft. 7in.; wdth. 5ft. 11½in.; ht. 4ft. 11¼in.; g.c. 6in.; turng. cir. 40ft.; kerb wt. 23½ cwt.; tank 15 gals.; 12-volt.

£1,160 + £484.9.2 p.t. = £1,644.9.2

Abbreviations—g.c.—ground clearance; susp.—suspension; f.—front; r.—rear; comp.—compression; s.v.—side-valves; o.h.v.—overhead valves; o.h.c.—overhead camshaft; hyd.—hydraulic.

47

TRIUMPH HERALD CONVERTIBLE

LATEST addition to the Herald range, this fresh-air four-seater has sporting lines and a folding top which can be raised or lowered without leaving the car. All-independent suspension, a taxi-like steering lock, unmatched engine accessibility, easy-change body panels for quick repair and a chassis which has almost banished lubrication problems, are the main sales points.

CLOSE-UP
Four-cyl.; o.h.v.; 63 × 76 mm.; 948 c.c.; 50½ b.h.p. (gross); 8.5 to 1 comp.; coil ign.; 2 S.U. carbs.; 4-speed, 19.45, 11.2, 6.62, 4.55 to 1; cen. lvr.; susp. f. ind. coil, r. swing axle trans. leaf; 2-door; 2-seat; hyd. brks.; max. 78 m.p.h.; cruise 70; m.p.g. 35; whl. base 7ft. 7½in.; track f. and r. 4ft.; lgth. 12ft. 9in.; wdth. 5ft.; ht. 4ft. 0½in. (hood down); g.c. 6½in.; turng. cir. 25ft.; kerb wt. 15¾ cwt.; tank 7 gals.; 12-volt.

£540 + £226 p.t. = £766

TRIUMPH TR3

ANOTHER best-seller in the United States in spite of the set-back in the sale of our saloons. It is a relatively low-priced sports car with a top speed well above 100 m.p.h. Yet it handles as docilely as a lamb in congested streets. Power comes from a well developed 2-litre engine with plenty of stopping power through disc brakes. Extras include overdrive, wire wheels and detachable top.

CLOSE-UP
Four-cyl.; o.h.v.; 83 × 92 mm.; 1.991 c.c.; 100 b.h.p.; 8.5 to 1 comp.; coil ign.; twin S.U. carbs.; 4-speed, 12.5, 7.4, 4.9, 3.7 to 1; cen. lvr.; Laycock overdrive opt.; susp., f., ind. coil., r., half-elliptic; 2-door, 2-seat; hyd. brks. disc front; max. 110 m.p.h.; cruise, 85-90; m.p.g., 26-32; whl. base, 7ft. 4in.; track, f. and r., 3ft. 9in.; lgth., 12ft. 7in.; wdth., 4ft. 7½in.; ht., 4ft. 2in.; g.c., 6in.; turng. cir., 35ft.; kerb wt., 19¾ cwt.; tank, 12 gals.; 12-volt.

£699 + £292.7.6 p.t. = £991.7.6

VALIANT

CHRYSLER'S first competitor in the "compact car" stakes—a handsome six-seater with six-cylinder engine canted on its side to lower the centre of gravity and leave space for long, free-flow inlet pipes. Pioneer feature is an alternator instead of a dynamo. Its hefty charge, even at tick-over, should banish troubles with flat batteries. Bodies are saloons and station wagons.

CLOSE-UP
Six-cyl.; o.h.v.; 86.36 × 79.37 mm.; 2,789 c.c.; 100 b.h.p.; 8.5 to 1 comp.; coil ign.; Carter carb.; 3-speed, 9.62, 6.49, 3.55 to 1; col. lvr., auto. trans. opt.; susp. f. ind. torsion bar, r. half-elliptic; 4-door; 6-seat; hyd. brks.; max. 95 m.p.h.; cruise 80; m.p.g. 18-22; whl. base 8ft. 10½in.; track f. 4ft. 8in.; r. 4ft. 7½in.; lgth. 15ft. 4in.; wdth. 5ft. 8½in.; ht. 4ft. 6in.; g.c. 6½in.; turng. cir. 36ft. 6in.; kerb wt. 25¼ cwt.; tank 10¾ gals.; 12-volt.

£1,575 + £657.7.6 p.t. = £2,232.7.6

VANDEN PLAS PRINCESS

A PRESTIGE car of surprisingly modest price, the Vanden Plas 3-litre saloon and touring limousine sells for less than £1,400 with overdrive, and only £1,467 with automatic transmission. Following the impact made by the car at last year's Motor Show it was decided to establish the famous coach building firm as a car manufacturing company. It is the sort of large and comfortable car you can drive yourself or you can leave it to the chauffeur.

CLOSE-UP
Six-cyl.; o.h.v.; 83 × 89 mm.; 2,912 c.c.; 112 b.h.p.; 8.3 to 1 comp.; coil ign.; two S.U. carbs.; 3-speed, 12.1, 6.45, 3.91, to 1; B.W. overdrive, auto. trans. opt.; susp. f. ind. coil, r. half-elliptic; 4-door; 5/6-seat; hyd. servo brks., disc front; max. 100 m.p.h.; cruise 80; m.p.g. 20-22; whl. base 9ft.; track f. 4ft. 6in.; r. 4ft. 5¼in.; lgth. 15ft. 8½in.; wdth. 5ft. 8½in.; ht. 4ft. 11in.; g.c. 6¾in.; turng. cir. 40ft.; kerb wt. 31. cwt.; tank 16 gals.; 12-volt.

£985 + £412 p.t. = £1,397

Abbreviations—g.c.—ground clearance; susp.—suspension; f.—front; r.—rear; comp.—compression; s.v.—side-valves; o.h.v.—overhead valves; o.h.c.—overhead camshaft; hyd.—hydraulic.

VAUXHALL CRESTA

RIBBON-TYPE speedometer recording in green, then yellow, then red, tells the tale of flashing performance, and improved braking on the Luton-built luxury model from General Motors. Bigger engine, wheels and brakes, higher axle ratio, stronger frame and springs. New sealed beam headlamps for greater power and longer filament life. New anodised wheel discs. Overdrive or automatic transmission optional.

CLOSE-UP

Six-cyl.; o.h.v.; 82.55 × 82.55 mm.; 2,651 c.c.; 113 b.h.p.; 8.1 to 1 comp.; coil ign.; Zenith carb.; 3-speed, 11.18, 6.38, 3.90 to 1; col. lvr.; susp. f. ind. coil, r. half-elliptic; 4-door; 6-seat; hyd. brks.; max. 95 m.p.h.; cruise 75-80; m.p.g. 20-25; whl. base 8ft. 9in.; track f. and r. 4ft. 6in.; lgth. 14ft. 10in.; wdth. 5ft. 8½in.; ht. 4ft. 9in.; g.c. 7in.; turng. cir. 36ft.; kerb wt. 23½ cwt.; tank 10¾ gals.; 12-volt.

£715 + £299.0.10 p.t. = £1,014.0.10

VAUXHALL FRIARY

IF YOU have a lot of family or a lot of luggage or both this is the model for you. Powered by the big Velox engine you can now have it with overdrive—a station wagon that is a glutton for work. I have driven it thousands of miles on Continental roads with six up and lots of cases behind. Its body is specially built for Vauxhalls, and a first-class job they have made of it.

CLOSE-UP

Six-cyl.; o.h.v.; 82.55 × 82.55 mm.; 2,651 c.c.; 113 b.h.p.; 8 to 1 comp.; coil ign.; Zenith carb.; 3-speed, 11.18, 6.38, 3.90 to 1; col. lvr.; susp. f. ind. coil, r. half-elliptic; 4-door; 6-seat; hyd. brks.; max. 94 m.p.h.; cruise 75; m.p.g. 20-23; whl. base 8ft. 9in.; track f. and r. 4ft. 6in.; lgth. 14ft. 10in.; wdth. 5ft. 8½in.; ht. 4ft. 9in.; g.c. 6⅝in.; turng. cir. 36ft.; kerb wt. 24¾ cwt.; tank 14 gals.; 12-volt.

£862 + £360.5.10 p.t. = £1,222.5.10

VAUXHALL VELOX

BIGGER engine of 2.6 litres, higher axle ratio and bigger wheels guarantee surging acceleration and effortless hill climbing on Vauxhall's popular six. To cope with the extra urge the clutch is stronger, and front brakes are bigger. Front springs and frame are strengthened. Changes to parking lamps, rear lamps and indicators improve the exterior. An entirely new automatic transmission is the latest option.

CLOSE-UP

Six-cyl.; o.h.v.; 82.55 × 82.55 mm.; 2,651 c.c.; 113 b.h.p.; 8.1 to 1 comp.; coil ign.; Zenith carb.; 3-speed, 11.18, 6.38, 3.90 to 1; col. lvr.; susp. f. ind. coil, r. half-elliptic; 4-door; 6-seat; hyd. brks.; max. 95 m.p.h.; cruise 75-80; m.p.g. 20-25; whl. base 8ft. 9in.; track f. and r. 4ft. 6in.; lgth. 14ft. 10in.; wdth. 5ft. 8½in.; ht. 4ft. 9in.; g.c. 7in.; turng. cir. 36ft.; kerb wt. 23 cwt.; tank 10¾ gals.; 12-volt.

£655 + £274.0.10 p.t. = £929.0.10

VAUXHALL VICTOR

VICTOR'S international appeal is boosted by new grille, new colours, larger rear window and different instrument cluster for 1961. De luxe headlamp cowls are chromium-capped, and side mouldings are heavier. The trunk lid is re-styled, and can be shut without using the key. Re-sited driving mirror gives better driving vision. Engine bearings are redesigned to stand up to motorway driving.

CLOSE-UP

Four-cyl.; o.h.v.; 79.4 × 76.2 mm.; 1,508 c.c.; 55 b.h.p.; 7.8 to 1 comp.; coil ign.; Zenith carb.; 3-speed, 13.14, 6.74, 4.125 to 1; col. lvr.; susp. f., ind. coil, r., half-elliptic; 4-door; 4/5-seat; hyd. brks.; max. 78 m.p.h.; cruise, 65; m.p.g. 30-35; whl. base, 8ft. 2in.; track, f., and r., 4ft. 2in.; lgth., 14ft.; wdth., 5ft. 3½in.; ht., 4ft. 10in.; g.c., 6½in.; turng. cir., 34ft.; kerb wt., 19½ cwt.; tank, 8 gals.; 12-volt.

£510 + £213.12.16 p.t. = £723.12.6

Abbreviations—g.c.—ground clearance; susp.—suspension; f.—front; r.—rear; comp.—compression; s.v.—side-valves; o.h.v.—overhead valves; o.h.c.—overhead camshaft; hyd.—hydraulic.

49

VOLGA

STRESSED for a hard ride over the Russian steppes, the Volga is heavily constructed, but weight is saved by its aluminium engine and gearbox. For transmission, the choice is three-speed synchromesh or fully automatic. The front backrest drops to form a bed. Radiator shutters, heater and a comprehensive do-it-yourself tool kit are in the standard equipment.

CLOSE-UP

Four-cyl.; o.h.v.; 92×92 mm.; 2,445 c.c.; 75 b.h.p.; 7.5 to 1 comp.; coil ign.; downdraught carb.; 3-speed, 14.191, 8.072, 4.556 to 1; col. lvr. auto. trans. opt.; susp., f., ind. coil, r., half-elliptic; 4-door; 5-seat; hyd. brks.; max. 84 m.p.h.; cruise 60; m.p.g. 31; whl. base, 8ft. 10½in.; track, f., 4ft. 7½in., r., 4ft. 8in.; lgth., 15ft. 10in.; wdth., 5ft. 11in.; ht., 5ft. 4in.; g.c., 7½in.; turng. cir., 42ft.; kerb wt., 26 cwt.; tank, 13 gals.; 12-volt.

£785 + £328.4.2 p.t. = £1,113.4.2

VOLKSWAGEN DE LUXE

DURABLE veteran that remains Europe's best seller. Now rejuvenated with new engine, giving more power, better acceleration, faster hill climbing and maximum speed of 72 m.p.h. Countless other improvements, too—all-synchromesh gearbox, front luggage space nearly doubled, twin-jet screen washer, transparent brake fluid reservoir, flashing direction indicators, asymmetrical headlamp beams for long anti-dazzle range, visor for passenger—all at no extra cost.   CLOSE-UP

Four-cyl.; o.h.v.; air-cooled; 77×64 mm.; 1,192 c.c.; 40 b.h.p.; 7 to 1 comp.; coil ign.; Solex carb.; 4-speed 16.63, 9.01, 5.77, 3.89 to 1; cen. lvr.; susp. f. and r., ind. torsion bars; 2-door; 4-seat; hyd. brks.; max. 72 m.p.h.; cruise, 72; m.p.g., 38; whl. base, 7ft. 10½in.; track, f., 4ft. 3in., r., 4ft. 2¾in.; lgth., 13ft. 4in.; wdth., 5ft. 0½in.; ht., 4ft. 11in.; g.c., 6in.; turng. cir., 36ft.; kerb wt., 14½ cwt.; tank, 8¾ gals.; 6-volt.

£505 + £211.10.10 p.t. = £716.10.10

VOLKSWAGEN KARMANN-GHIA

NEW engine, as in saloon models, gives an extra four horsepower. Automatic choke, stronger crankshaft, vacuum spark advance, new camshaft and bigger valves, boost performance, but fuel consumption is said to be reduced at cruising speeds. Engine revs faster and gear ratios are slightly lower. Compression is higher, but normal fuel is still good enough. Warm air feed to the carburetter prevents winter icing. Synthetic coat hooks and padded visors for greater safety.

CLOSE-UP

Four-cyl.; o.h.v. air-cooled; 77×64 mm.; 1,192 c.c.; 40 b.h.p.; 7 to 1 comp.; coil ign.; Solex carb.; 4-speed, 16.63, 9.01, 5.77, 3.89 to 1; cen. lvr.; susp. f. and r. ind. torsion bars; 2-door; 2/4-seat; hyd. brks.; max. 75 m.p.h.; cruise, 75; m.p.g., 38; whl. base, 7ft. 10½in.; track, f., 4ft. 3in., r., 4ft. 2¾in.; lgth., 13ft. 7in.; wdth., 5ft. 4¾in.; ht., 4ft. 4½in.; g.c., 6in.; turng. cir., 37ft.; kerb wt., 16 cwt.; tank, 8¾ gals.; 6-volt.

£843.10 + £352.11.8 p.t. = £1,196.1.8

VOLVO 122 S

THIS well-built high-performance family car from Sweden is familiar to British race-goers from its successes in production car events. Twin carburetters help in producing 85 b.h.p. from the 1,600 c.c. four-cylinder engine and the gearbox has synchromesh on all four speeds. Heater and screen washer are standard. Reclining front seats are available at extra cost.

CLOSE-UP

Four-cyl.; o.h.v.; 79.4×80 mm.; 1,583 c.c.; 85 b.h.p.; 8.2 to 1 comp.; coil ign.; twin S.U. carbs.; 4-speed, 15.7, 9.9, 6.0, 4.6 to 1; cen. lvr.; susp., f., ind. coil, r., coil; 4-door; 5-seat; hyd. brks.; max. 95 m.p.h.; cruise 85; m.p.g. 28-36; whl. base, 8ft. 6½in.; track, f. and r., 4ft. 3½in.; lgth., 14ft. 5in.; wdth., 5ft. 4in.; ht., 4ft. 11½in.; g.c., 7½in.; turng. cir., 32ft.; kerb wt., 21 cwt.; tank, 10 gals.; 6-volt.

£916 + £382.15.10 p.t. = £1,298.15.10

Abbreviations—g.c.—ground clearance; susp.—suspension; f.—front; r.—rear; comp.—compression; s.v.—side-valves; o.h.v.—overhead valves; o.h.c.—overhead camshaft; hyd.—hydraulic.

VOLVO P.1800

HERE comes Scandinavia's slick sports coupe for export markets, with body-chassis built and trimmed in England, and British disc brakes, completed by a Swedish engine, gearbox and other parts. Five-bearing four-cylinder 1.6 litre engine gives a maximum of 100 horse-power and the gearbox has all four speeds synchronised. Thief-proof armoured cables connect ignition switch to coil.

CLOSE-UP

Four-cyl.; o.h.v.; 84.14×80 mm.; 1,780 c.c.; 100 b.h.p.; 9.5 to 1 comp.; coil ign.; Two S.U. carbs.; 4-speed, 12.83, 8.15, 5.57, 4.1 to 1; cen. lvr., Laycock overdrive opt.; susp. f. ind. coil, r. coil; 2-door; 2-seat; hyd. servo brks., disc front; max. 110 m.p.h.; cruise 95; m.p.g. 28-30; whl. base 8ft. 0½in.; track f. and r. 4ft. 4in.; lgth. 14ft. 5in.; wdth. 5ft. 7in; ht. 4ft. 3in.; g.c. 6in.; turng. cir. 31ft.; tank 10 gals.; 12-volt.

WOLSELEY FIFTEEN HUNDRED

A SMALL saloon from the B.M.C. with an ample-sized engine which gives it a lively performance. The standard model has the traditional Wolseley finish inside, with walnut veneered instrument panel and leather upholstery, but there is a Fleet model at a much lower price, which has simpler trim and, being lighter, is bought by enthusiasts in search of maximum performance.

CLOSE-UP

Four-cyl.; o.h.v.; 73.025×88.9 mm.; 1,489 c.c.; 48 b.h.p.; 7.2 to 1 comp.; coil ign.; S.U. carb.; 4-speed, 13.56, 8.25, 5.12, 3.73 to 1; cen. lvr.; susp., f., ind. torsion bars, r., half-elliptic; 4-door; 4-seat; hyd. brks.; max. 79 m.p.h.; cruise 75; m.p.g. 32-38; whl. base, 7ft. 2in.; track, f., 4ft. 2⅞in.; r., 4ft. 2⅝in.; lgth., 12ft. 7¾in.; wdth., 5ft. 1in.; ht., 4ft. 11¾in.; g.c., 6½in.; turng. cir., 34ft. 3in.; kerb wt., 18½ cwt.; tank, 7 gals.; 12-volt.
£530 + £221.19.2 p.t. = £751.19.2

WOLSELEY 15/60

SILKY, smooth motoring is provided by this medium-sized car for the family or the business man. This model has a modified combustion chamber to minimise pre-ignition, a new camshaft to reduce tappet noise and a longer oil level dipstick, plus new ashtrays with stubbing plates, all designed for better motoring. This is one of the best Farina-styled 1½-litre models produced by the British Motor Corporation, and a well established winner.

CLOSE-UP

Four-cyl.; o.h.v.; 73 / 88.9 mm.; 1,489 c.c.; 53 b.h.p.; 8.3 to 1 comp.; coil ign.; S.U. carb.; 4-speed, 16.55, 10.08, 6.25, 4.55 to 1; cen. lvr.; susp., f., ind. coil, r., half-elliptic; 4-door; 4/5-seat; hyd. brks.; max. 79 m.p.h.; cruise, 60; m.p.g. 25-35; whl. base, 8ft. 3³⁄₁₆in.; track f., 4ft. 0⅞in., r., 4ft. 1⅞in.; lgth., 14ft. 10in.; wdth., 5ft. 3½in.; ht., 4ft. 11¾in.; g.c., 6½in.; turng. cir., 37ft. 6in.; kerb wt., 22¼ cwt.; tank, 10 gals.; 12-volt.
£660 + £276.2.6 p.t. = £936.2.6

WOLSELEY 6/99

BIG express carriage combines the best of both worlds: Wolseley grille with illuminated name plate, leather upholstery, walnut veneers and pile carpets for traditionalists, Farina's long Italian line for admirers of contemporary style; three-litre 112 b.h.p. engine for swift speed; three-speed gearbox with Porsche crash-proof synchromesh on all ratios and overdrive on the top two; disc front brakes with vacuum servo.

CLOSE-UP

Six-cyl.; o.h.v.; 83×88.9 mm.; 2,912 c.c.; 108 b.h.p.; 8.23 to 1 comp.; coil ign.; 2 S.U. carb.; 3-speed, 12.1, 6.45, 3.91 to 1; col. lvr. BW. overdrive; susp., f., ind. coil, r., half-elliptic; 4-door; 5/6-seat; hyd. servo brks. disc. front; max. 99 m.p.h.; cruise, 80; m.p.g., 22-26; whl. base, 9ft.; track f., 4ft. 6in., r., 4ft. 5¼in.; lgth., 15ft. 8in.; wdth., 5ft. 8½in.; ht., 5ft.; g.c., 6¾in.; turng. cir., 38ft. 9in.; kerb wt., 30½ cwt.; tank, 16 gals.; 12-volt.

£885 + £369.17.6 p.t. = £1,254.17.6

Abbreviations—g.c.—ground clearance; susp.—suspension; f.—front; r.—rear; comp.—compression; s.v.—side-valves; o.h.v.—overhead valves; o.h.c.—overhead camshaft; hyd.—hydraulic.

51

AUSTIN A55.
Also available with countryman body.

GET INTO AN AUSTIN
AND SEE WHAT YOU GET OUT OF IT!

This year, at the Motor Show, you will see nine highly individual Austin cars. You can look over them. You can look into them too. And the moment you do you'll find your first impressions eloquently confirmed—by the comfort, the sweeping visibility, the sheer convenience of the Austin range.

If you can't visit the Motor Show, your Austin dealer has a show of his own going on right now. So after the Motor Show (or instead of it) ask your nearest Austin dealer for a trial run demonstration in the Austin car of your choice. What wonderful cars these Austins are! THE AUSTIN MOTOR COMPANY LTD · LONGBRIDGE · BIRMINGHAM

AUSTIN A40   AUSTIN A55   METROPOLITAN 1500   AUSTIN SEVEN

AUSTIN A99   AUSTIN HEALEY SPRITE   AUSTIN HEALEY 3000

By Appointment to Her Majesty The Queen Motor Car Manufacturers The Austin Motor Company Limited

Backed by BMC 12-month warranty and BMC service

AUSTIN LOOKS YEARS AHEAD

52

Pioneers O Pioneers!

You can bet someone thought of the
"latest" invention back in the old
red-flag days

"NOW why didn't somebody think of *that* before?", marvelled the B.M.C. Mini-twins' countless admirers at the '59 Motor Show. *That* was designer Alec Issigonis's stunningly simple space-saving recipe—across-the-frame engine mounting combined with front wheel drive.

Well, somebody *did* think of it before. In 1911, when Mr. Issigonis was in his minipram, a British car called the FD had its engine and transmission arranged exactly the same way.

Look around Earls Court and you'll find engineering and styling ideas galore that had their origin in the distant past, then petered out, finally petered back in again, to be hailed as master strokes.

Disc brakes are a case in point. Lanchester had them first about 53 years ago. Unitary construction, with the chassis and body in divorce-proof wedlock, dates back further still—Queen Victoria was on the throne when Lanchester sprang that one. Two French makes, Bollée and Decauville, featured independent front suspension before the turn of the century.

Independent rear suspension, which constantly threatens to sweep old-fashioned "cart springing" off the face of Earls Court, and never quite succeeds, was pioneered by two long-forgotten firms in 1913—Parnacott and Imp, British and American respectively.

But invention hasn't always been the road to extinction. Indeed, many of the modern motorist's greatest boons were originated by 1960 Show exhibitors, with the honours fairly well shared between American, Continental and British brains.

Cadillac, for instance, was first with electric self-starters (1912), dipping headlamps (1915), automatic windscreen wipers (early 20's), and synchromesh gearboxes (1928). Pierce Arrow, also American, fitted its 1919 models with screen wipers by Trico, but these were worked manually.

Rubber engine mountings were another Detroit brainwave—the Chrysler group simulated six-cylinder smoothness in a four-cylinder power unit by this cushioning technique on its 1932 Plymouths. First European emulator—under licence from Chrysler—was Citroen in France.

But the deeper you dig into history, the more instances you find of features that are popularly supposed to have originated in America but didn't. Examples? Tail fins, for one. Full-width bodies, with running boards banished and wings merged in, for another. Steering-column gear changes for a third.

Tail fins, so fixedly associated with Cadillac that they became known as "Cad. fins", were a Cisitalia idea . . . one up to Italy (1946).

Prototype of the currently universal envelope car body scored a first for Bugatti in 1923; admittedly, though, M'sieu Bug only used this anti-cranny architecture for racing, and quickly abandoned it anyway . . . for twelve years.

Which actual make was first off the mark with steering-column shifts it would be hard to say. Practically all the cars of the horseless-carriage era, European and American alike,

had them, then they virtually vanished until Vauxhall exhumed them in 1927. Subsequently, American fashion copied Vauxhall and, in the roundabout way that these things happen, most of the popular British makes copied the Americans.

A second look at suspension systems reveals that a Briton, more exactly a Welshman, J. G. Parry Thomas, famous racing driver and three-time breaker of the Land Speed Record, thought up the torsion bar spring (1923 or thereabouts). Its first application in volume production, however, was by Mathis in France, whose designer was an Austrian, the late Dr. Ferdinand Porsche, father of the VW.

Genesis of the road spring damper takes us back to 1899, when Mors—French again—added "shock-absorber" to the motoring glossaries. Nine years later, Mercedes in Germany hit on a half-way answer to a

by
DENNIS MAY

problem whose final solution is still baffling the boffins, evolving a damper that automatically damped harder as you piled on the load.

And these were the milestones—some of them, anyway—on the road to mid-century braking efficiency:—

1909: Four-wheel brakes launched almost neck and neck by Spyker in Holland, Crossley, Sheffield Simplex, Arrol Johnston and Newton Bennet in Britain.

1914: Rather confusingly, an American by the name of Lougheed invented the Lockheed system of hydraulic brake operation; this was standardised on some U.S. makes around 1921/22 but wasn't taken up in Britain until about 1930 (by Triumph on its Super Seven).

1919: Power braking originated by Hispano-Suiza in Spain.

Until early Edwardian times, metal had graunched complainingly on metal when you hit your brakes. It was Ferodo who beat this bogy with fabric-based friction materials distantly foreshadowing today's phenomenally durable liners.

Did the Americans, who now produce more automatic transmissions in a week than the rest of the world in a year, get in first with these devices? Well, yes and no.

Behind the NO vote is the fact that in 1913 a French cycle-car, the Bedelia, was rigged to "shift for itself", with an exposed and flapping drive belt running over split pulleys that adjusted their own effective diameter by centrifugal means.

Next significant step towards two-pedal motoring came a decade later, with the birth of the Constantinesco torque converter system (its inventor, George Constantinesco, was a British citizen but Hungarian born). Almost

simultaneously, in France, de Lavaud unveiled an automatic transmission harnessing a swash-plate to triple connecting rods whose length varied under changing conditions of engine speed and load. But neither of these devices was ever standardised by an established make.

Austin's 1933 catalogue listed Hayes automatic transmission as an option on some of its larger models; but the Hayes box being American (by Buick), who gets the pioneer stripe—U.S. or U.K.? It's a hair-split, really, because probably not more than a dozen Hayes-equipped Austins were ever delivered.

Taking the wider view, however, the Americans win this verdict, for if they weren't first on the drawing-board with automatics, they certainly were first in production on a scale that mattered. The earliest practical overdrive was transatlantic too—Borg-Warner's kickdown job, a deb of the early 'thirties.

The V8 engine talks with an American accent but don't be fooled; its earliest ancestor was French and bore the de Dion nameplate (1909). More than sixty years ago, de Dion also originated a back axle layout which until this season was consistently on the front of the grid in racing. It had lain mouldering in the grave between about 1902 and '37, when it was resuscitated by Auto Union in Germany.

Who fathered the six-cylinder engine? That depends on your definition of paternity, but neither of the rival claimants is at Earls Court this week, or ever was. Spyker (Dutch, you remember) showed a six that worked in 1904, and Napier was in production with one the following year.

Superchargers? Another mark to America. A Yankee make called Chadwick blazed the blower trail in 1907, driving a three-stage centrifugal compressor off the engine flywheel. Earliest European copyist was Hispano-Suiza (1912).

Aluminium pistons? This was W. O. Bentley's brain-child. He fitted them first on a car called the D.F.P. in 1912.

Sparking plugs? Karl Benz, Germany 1885.

High-tension ignition? Another German breakthrough. Bosch was the pioneer, 1903 the date.

Automatic chokes? Cadillac, U.S.A., 1922. (By nineteen-*sixty*-two there probably won't be a car at Earls Court without one).

Desmodromic valve gear? (*You* know—holiday-for-springs idea that helped Mercedes to win its racing World Championship in 1954). A French make—I forget its name—used it at Le Mans around 1924 or '25.

Hemispherical cylinder heads, as now worn by Jaguar, Aston Martin and other technical pace setters? Chalk one up to Belgium. The make: Pipe. The date: 1904.

Safety glass for screens and windows? The French invented it (1912), the British Triplex company led with it commercially, shortly before the first world war.

Curved screens? Studebaker in America, 1948 . . .

All right, just tell us something that *is* new under the sun. We'll buy it.

What is a girl to do with a fortune on wheels in her lily-white hands?

by

JILL BUTTERFIELD

WOMAN at the wheel

by ARTIE

PUT me anywhere in this rough, tough, man's world and I am at home—anywhere, that is, but sitting in comparative comfort behind the wheel of a modern motor-car.

The very minute I curl into the driver's seat I develop every music-hall feminine failing in the book.

I have to practise imaginary writing to tell my right hand from my left. I develop momentary colour blindness at every set of traffic lights.

In a voice five notes higher and fifteen tones squeakier than normal I tell the world that my brakes need oiling, and ask where I can buy a dip-stick, as mine does not seem to reach the oil.

Needless to say, my husband drives our car, which is probably why we are still married.

But with new cars pouring on to the roads at a rate of a thousand a day, with every manufacturer attempting to woo the little woman with pictures of great, uncluttered motorways bathed in a perpetual sunlight glow, and with promises of everlasting "togetherness" if she chooses his car, isn't it time they *really* got down to considering what we *really* want?

To begin with, we want a car that caters for the passengers. It is no good trying to win us with fantastic statistics of revs per minute (most of us think they are a television rating anyway) and completely ignoring the fact that the back seats of most modern cars were designed solely for children under six.

Yet children under six demand to sit in the front with Daddy, and you know who is left with her knees tucked neatly underneath her chin behind.

Talking of children, whether we choose a two-door or a four-door car, cannot something be done about safety locks? Any right-minded inquisitive infant can hurl himself to certain death with the present door fastenings. I am only surprised that more of them do not.

It is no use offering us a lovely cinemascopic window to see out of, when we have to wind the whole thing down to get a breath of clean air.

What every woman wants is a car with gently circulating fresh air, which does not make a complete bird's nest of her hair-do. I mean really fresh air, not the backwash from someone else's exhaust, which blows in from the air inlets, however cunningly placed.

It is just plain frustrating when those mouth-watering filmstar colour schemes we settle for in the shiny catalogues turn out to be either unavailable or have a six months' delay.

No woman will ever feel the same about a nice, sound, sober grey car when she has set her heart on and builds her wardrobe around, something rather flashy in cream and pale blue.

We want room to put our parcels, room to spread our legs, a place to put the pram, and a make-up mirror that is big enough to see our whole face in—not one which means we have to do our powdering in three horizontal sections.

When I have all these things, with a little more gentle persuasion I might even venture behind the steering wheel again. But the persuasion would have to be a bit more practical than it is at the moment.

First, I would need a car that would park itself. Preferably sideways.

Men, I am told, are so selfish that they do not mind holding up the traffic while they manoeuvre themselves in. To a woman the jeers and catcalls from the waiting cars, which come when, in her panic, she muffs it, are the biggest agony of motoring.

Second, I would need a wheel that changes itself at the press of a button, for the main joy of owning a car is that it gets you from A to B immaculately. A virtue which is lost if you have to stop on the way and struggle with a wheel in your pencil-slim skirt and fresh white gloves.

Third, I want windscreen wipers and washers on my back window as well as just the front one. What is the good of the man in your life screaming at you to keep your eye on the driving mirror when your back window is so caked with mud and mess that you cannot see a single thing out of it?

If, after all this, the manufacturers still see women as potential purchasers, the quickest way to our hearts would be to reduce the price of the cars on sale.

I mean, what girl feels safe with half the price of a country cottage, two years' school fees, a nice mink coat or a world-wide cruise held, somewhat insecurely, in her little, lily-white hands?

C A R S
OF THE EARLY 60'S
BRITISH AND IMPORTED MODELS 1960-1964

MOTOR SHOW REVIEW GUIDE
1961

A - Z
SECTION

GLAMOUR for all

A Message from D. G. STOKES, President of the Society of Motor Manufacturers and Traders, Sales Director of the Leyland Group of Companies and Standard-Triumph International.

¶ Of all the annual events in Britain perhaps the Earls Court Motor Show captures the public imagination more than any other. Year after year the glamour and excitement of shining new cars and all the equipment that goes with motoring bring people in their hundreds of thousands from far and wide. Whether they are young or old, rich or poor, motorist or pedestrian, the Motor Show has a special fascination for them all.

¶ To the fortunate ones who are able to visit the Motor Show this year I send my good wishes, and hope that they enjoy themselves as much as, if not more than they have done in previous years.

¶ Whether you come to Earls Court or stay at home, the Daily Express Motor Show Review is bound to have a tremendous appeal. With a full coverage of the scene, providing illustrations, articles and news of the Show, this Review is both a guide and a souvenir. Congratulations to the Daily Express on such an excellent contribution to the Earls Court Motor Show of 1961.

Donald Stokes

Never so much that's NEW

ONE undeniable point stands out at the Motor Show this year. There are more new models on the stands than at any car exhibition I remember.

Apart from the spate of newcomers from the United States and Europe, the British manufacturers have made a tremendous effort to give the motoring public new shapes, new engineering feats, and new refinements.

These improvements are to be seen in every car—in the baby cars, the medium-sized family saloons, the sports cars and the limousines. The keynote of construction throughout has been to provide something new with good looks, something functional, and at a minimum cost.

I view this fascinating and exciting development as a resurgence on the part of our manufacturers, a brilliant effort to overcome the lean months caused by the sales recession which in turn was caused by the credit squeeze.

The credit squeeze is still with us, and the motoring producers are seeking to offset it by courting the customer with an abundance of new ideas and new designs.

Their efforts have been directed as much towards women motorists—now estimated to constitute a third of our drivers—as to the men who in the end usually foot the bill.

One example of their wooing of the women motorists is the distinct improvement in the positioning of the control pedals to suit women's shorter legs, and the greater use of treadle-type accelerators.

Here are others: the new cars are roomier inside to take the family shopping and the dog . . . . The colours have been artfully blended with modern fashion hues . . . . Models have an uncluttered surface and wide-opening doors to allow for the sweep of long evening dresses. There are fewer protuberances (including

by
BASIL CARDEW
Daily Express Motoring Reporter

smooth handles), thus reducing the danger of ladders in stockings.

From the man's viewpoint, perhaps, interest will be focused more on the new trend towards less owner maintenance. The latest ideas include sealed lubrication, which means that a car needs greasing only once or twice a year.

Sealed engine-cooling systems and self-adjusting brakes are other maintenance-free solutions which give more leisure to the motorist who usually does his own servicing at the weekend.

As you tour the plush corridors at Earls Court you may note that there are important developments in transmissions. Some car-makers are offering a choice of gear controls, either on the floor or on the steering column.

There are improved automatic transmissions, and more cars are being fitted with synchromesh on first gear and with overdrives. Here the trend is to simplify the driving, and make it easier for the man—or woman—at the controls to handle the car.

Another tendency seen at Earls Court is to incorporate previous additions to a car as standard equipment. This applies to such functional aids as heaters, windscreen-washers and mirrors.

It is a move which I heartily endorse, for the customer—the private motorist—will be saving money, and the private motorist is always the most important person to be considered, when it comes to selling cars in the world's markets.

This year there are 62 car stands and the latest models from no fewer than 10 countries—Britain, Canada, France, Germany, Italy, Holland, Czecho-Slovakia, Sweden, Russia and the United States.

More than 410 stands present a vast array of bodywork, motorised caravans and the hundred-and-one ancillaries to motoring. These include accessories and components, tyres and transport service equipment, and even the hire-purchase finance houses.

With 9,000,000 vehicles on the road and many more thousands being taxed for the first time every week, I forecast that the attendance of 428,538 at Earls Court in 1960 will be easily exceeded this year.

Motoring, our most vital and biggest currency-earning export, is now on the crest of popularity. It is not only our main means of transport, but it is an escape for people from their humdrum workaday life.

In the 10 days of the 46th International Motor Show more than 70 countries are sending their buyers and business executives to inspect and appraise the British motor industry's shining new products.

For those who are coming to the Show this Daily Express Motor Show Review will be a guide and an aid in the exciting hours ahead.

For the less fortunate, who will not be able to visit Earls Court, but can only read about it, this Review will bring the Exhibition to them.

That is its double object.

*PATRICIA LEWIS, strictly with it as cars go,
is frank and feminine about this question—*

What happens when there's a girl at the wheel?

I LIVE in my car. Wherever I go, whatever I do we practically always go through it together—particularly the occasional brush with the law.

So as a day-in day-out all-weather driver I remain poker-faced at those hackneyed cracks about women at the wheel.

The latest in this exclusively masculine brand of mirth comes from America and tells of a new car especially designed for women: they deliver it al-*ready* smashed up.

Hmmmmmmmmmmm!

Bad joke though this may be it does provoke an entertaining train of thought.

Supposing, supposing someone finally did design a completely feminine car. . . . ? Well, it would not be a car at all really—more of a hybrid between Cleopatra's barge and something out of Jules Verne, with a touch of Emmett's genius to bind the two.

But I digress. Motoring is something sacred to the rev-happy Englishman, and I would hate to be thought sacrilegious. So, turn off the fantasy and turn on the facts.

This is what I, as a bachelor-girl about most towns and countries, want of my dream car—dammit!

I WANT . . .

I want: long, lean, speedy lines (for impressing doormen who look the other way when one drives up in a tiny-tip run-about) . . . a body with a Pinin Farina flavour (for keeping up with the international jet-set) . . . a stout-hearted engine (for chasing eloping heiresses across the Highlands) . . . caviar-class trimmings (because they are so ME) . . . a vast boot (to hold *all* my fur coats) . . . a maximum speed of well over 120 m.p.h. (for over-taking motor coaches) . . . all-independent suspension (because I don't want my right wheel to know what my left wheel is doing) . . . disc brakes (because I like music when motoring) . . . split-second convertibility from open to hard-top (because that bit about rain being good for the complexion is just so much jazz) . . . head-room (for Ascot hats) . . . leg-room

(for lovers) . . . 360-degree vision (because my blind spot is *everywhere*) . . . atomic-radiation proof glass (because I shall be taking to the hills with John Osborne any day now) . . . padded instrument panel (for Joey, my boxer dog, who is already punch-drunk on his first birthday) . . . gauges that tell me exactly what is going on inside (for is there another way to find out?) . . . a speedo that flashes red when I am creeping at more than 30 m.p.h. in a built-up area (for *your* sake, officer darling!) . . . a bell that rings when I am passing the last garage for 20 miles (because otherwise it's a long walk) . . . swivel seats for elegant arrivals (because whoops! I've torn it again) . . . and completely puncture-proof tyres (for not only do I not know *where* my jack is, but that legend about handsome, helpful truck drivers went out with Jean Harlow).

All right, the whole project is either impossible or fantastically expensive so let me indulge my dizzy desires a little further.

How about windscreen washers that spout Chateau de Selle, so that even when the courtesy driver in front is spattering the car with mud the outlook is Rosé?

Or a horn that plays the most recognisable piece from Colonel Bogey when you finally pass that man who won't get over?

I WANT . . .

And, while we are at it, we might as well have push-button wings to lift us over traffic jams . . . a swimming-pool under the off-side front wing and a telescopic hair-dryer beneath the back seat . . . a switch-sword-blade that flicks out à la Ben Hur's chariot race to tear road-hog's tyres to shreds . . . and why not a 60-second spray-gun to change the colour of the coach-work to match one's dress (or hair)? . . . or, best of all, chinchilla bumpers to caress jay-walkers into admitting that "it-didn't-really-hurt-anyway?"

Oh, well . . . I go too far!

Or do I?

With women at the wheel you never know.

new grace .. new space .. new pace

a completely new JAGUAR .. *a successor*
to the Mark IX, now joins the famous Mark 2 and 'E' Type models

The Jaguar Mark X, although an entirely new car in construction, design and appearance, stems from a long and illustrious line of outstanding models which have been identified during the past decade by the symbols Mark VII, Mark VIII and Mark IX. All have been highly successful in their own right and have formed important links in a chain of development culminating in the creation of the finest car yet to be produced in the Jaguar big saloon tradition—the Jaguar Mark X.

This elegant model is of monocoque construction and is powered by the world-famous Jaguar XK 'S' Type 3.8 litre twin overhead camshaft engine with three carburettors. This highly versatile engine by reason of its flexibility, smoothness and silence is ideally suited for use in such a car as the Mark X where every emphasis has been placed upon refinement of performance. Producing 265 horsepower, the engine, save for minor details, is identical with that fitted to the recently introduced 'E' Type Grand Touring Models, and it endows the Mark X with a degree of performance superior even to the Mark IX which it now supplants. Independent suspension front and rear and disc brakes on all four wheels enable full advantage to be taken of this performance with safety and comfort, whilst the luxurious furnishings and appointments include such refinements as reclining seats, folding tables and high efficiency dual-control heating installation.

With new grace in its smooth flowing lines, with new space in its roomier interior and with new pace in its magnificent road performance, the Jaguar Mark X provides a special kind of motoring which no other car in the world can offer.

The Mark Ten

ON STAND 121 EARLS COURT

London Showrooms: 88 Piccadilly, W.1

1962

— it's the year
for bold design
& new ideas

*charted here
for you from*
A *(for Abarth)* **to**
Z *(for Zaporogiets)*
and **EVERY CAR in between**

ABARTH 1000 BIALBERO
CARLO ABARTH has moved fast and far since he started tuning baby Fiats. Now his Fiat-based sports cars range from 700 to 2,300 c.c., with bodies by leading coachbuilders. One of the world's fastest 1,000 c.c. cars is his miniature 1,000 Bialbero with his own twin overhead camshaft rear engine, all-independent suspension, Girling disc brakes and streamlined body by Zagato.

CLOSE-UP
Four-cyl.; o.h.c.; 65 × 74 mm.; 982 c.c.; 105 b.h.p.; 10.4 to 1 comp.; coil ign.; 2 Weber carbs.; 4-speed, 16.44, 9.95, 6.45, 4.33 to 1; cen. lvr.; susp., f. ind. trans. leaf, r. ind. coil; 2-door; 2-seat; disc brks.; max 130 m.p.h.; cruise, 115; m.p.g. 30-32; whl. base, 6ft. 6¾in.; track f. 3ft. 9½in., r. 3ft. 9¾in.; lgth., 11ft. 3¾in.; wdth., 4ft. 7in.; ht. 3ft. 11in.; g.c. 6⅛in.; turng. cir. 28ft. 8in.; kerb wt., 11¼ cwt.; tank, 6½ gals.; 12-volt.

A.C. ACE
ALWAYS trumps with those who want a hand-built, made-to-order sports car, the Ace enters a new phase of its career with option of the Ford Zephyr engine as alternative to the A.C. or Bristol units. Suspension is independent and disc brakes are optional. Fuel tank holds 12 gallons, which will take you quite a long way cruising at 110 m.p.h. at 24 m.p.g. Demand for this quality sports car is rising.

CLOSE-UP
Six-cyl.; o.h.v.; 66 × 96 mm.; 1,971 c.c.; 125 b.h.p.; 9 to 1 comp.; coil ign.; 3 Solex carbs.; 4-speed, 11.42, 7.13, 5.05, 3.91 to 1; cen. lvr.; susp. f. and r. ind. trans. leaf; 2-door; 2-seat; hyd. brks, disc. opt.; max. 120 m.p.h.; cruise 100; m.p.g. 24; whl. base 7ft. 6in; track f. and r. 4ft. 2in., lgth. 12ft. 8in.; wdth. 4ft. 11in.; ht. 4ft. 1in.; g.c. 6½in.; turng. cir. 34ft.; kerb wt. 16 cwt.; tank 13 gals.; 12-volt.
£1,295 + £594.11.1 p.t. = £1,889.11.1

Abbreviations—g.c.—ground clearance; susp.—suspension; f.—front; r.—rear; comp.—compression; s.v.—side-valves; o.h.v.—overhead valves; o.h.c.—overhead camshaft; hyd.—hydraulic.

A.C. GREYHOUND

A HIGH performance, grand touring car with accommodation for rear-seat passengers. Its unusual four-wheel independent suspension and rigid steel chassis went through the mill for long periods over all types of conditions on Belgian pavé, tram lines, third-class tracks, high-speed motorways—in good and bad weather. Extensive use of fibre glass gives good heat insulation, and helps silent running.

CLOSE-UP

Six-cyl.; o.h.v.; 66×96 mm.; 1,971 c.c.; 125 b.h.p.; 9 to 1 comp.; coil ign.; 3 Solex carbs.; 4-speed, 11.97, 7.48, 5.29, 4.1 to 1; cen. lvr.; susp. f. and r. ind. coil; 2-door; 4-seat; hyd. brks. disc front; max. 120 m.p.h.; cruise 90; m.p.g. 24; whl. base 8ft. 4in.; track f. and r. 4ft. 6in.; lgth. 15ft.; wdth. 5ft. 5½in.; ht. 4ft. 4½in.; g.c. 7in.; turng. cir. 37ft.; kerb wt. 20 cwt.; tank 12 gals.; 12-volt.

£2,116 + £970.16.11 p.t. = £3,086.16.11

ALFA GIULIETTA SALOON

BY slashing prices and producing a right-hand drive model, Alfa Romeo have brought the Giulietta saloon within reach of many British motorists who could not consider it before. There are two versions, normal with 60 horse-power and TI sports saloon with higher compression, and twin-choke carburettor giving 75 horsepower. Gearbox has synchromesh on all four speeds, brakes are turbo-cooled.

CLOSE-UP

Four-cyl.; o.h.c.; 74×75 mm.; 1,290 c.c.; 64 b.h.p.; 8 to 1 comp.; coil ign.; Solex carb.; 4-speed, 16.38, 9.56, 6.17, 4.55 to 1; cen. lvr.; susp. f. ind. coil, r. coil; 4-door; 4/5-seat; hyd. brks.; max. 100 m.p.h.; cruise 80; m.p.g. 34; whl. base 7ft. 10in.; track f. 4ft. 2¾in., r. 4ft. 2in.; lgth. 13ft. 6in.; wdth. 5ft.; ht. 4ft. 7½in.; g.c. 6in.; turng. cir. 36ft.; kerb wt. 18 cwt.; tank 10½ gals.; 12-volt.

£1,125 + £516.17.3 p.t. = £1,641.17.3

ALFA ROMEO 2000 SPRINT

THIS elegant coupe by Bertone made its debut at the Turin Motor Show last year and was an instant success. Clean-cut, uncluttered lines for top performance with no fuss, four head-lamps for easy night-driving and a fine all-synchromesh five-speed gearbox make this 2/3 seater the kind of car you might use for a quick week-end run to Nice and back. There is also a convertible.

CLOSE-UP

Four-cyl.; o.h.c.; 84.5×88 mm.; 1,975 c.c.; 112 b.h.p.; 8.25 to 1 comp.; coil ign.; 2 Solex carbs.; 5-speed, 15.56, 9.48, 6.48, 4.778, 4.08 to 1; cen. lvr.; susp., f., ind. coil, r. coil; 2-door; 2/4-seat; hyd. brks.; max. 112 m.p.h.; cruise 85; m.p.g. 20; whl. base 8ft. 2½in.; track f. 4ft. 7½in., r. 4ft. 6in.; lgth. 14ft. 9in.; wdth. 5ft. 5in.; ht. 4ft. 4½in.; g.c. 6½in.; turng. cir. 31ft.; kerb wt. 23½ cwt.; tank 13½ gals.; 12-volt.

£2,045 + £938.10.7 p.t. = £2,983.10.7

ALVIS 3-LITRE

IDEAL combination of elegant bodywork designed by the Swiss, with chassis built by a famous and long established British firm. Result: a fast, graceful car that will top 100 m.p.h., will brake well with discs on the front and will look good as a saloon or a convertible. And there is a choice of a 4-speed synchromesh or Borg Warner automatic. No changes for 1962.

CLOSE-UP

Six-cyl.; o.h.v.; 84×90 mm.; 2,993 c.c.; 115 b.h.p.; 8.5 to 1 comp.; coil ign.; 2 S.U. carbs.; 4-speed, 11.046, 7.740, 4.935, 3.77 to 1; cen. lvr.; BW auto. or overdrive opt.; susp., f., ind. coil, r., half-elliptic; 2-door; 4-seat; hyd. brks., disc front; max. 100 m.p.h.; cruise 80; m.p.g. 18-22; whl. base 9ft. 3½in.; track f. 4ft. 7⅞in., r. 4ft. 6½in.; lgth. 15ft. 8½in.; wdth. 5ft. 6in.; ht. 5ft.; g.c. 7in.; turng. cir. 39ft. 6in.; kerb wt. 30 cwt.; tank 14.3 gals.; 12-volt.

£2,195 + £1,007.5.7 p.t. = £3,202.5.7

ASTON MARTIN DB4

THIS 140 m.p.h. beauty with the 3.7-litre engine is one of the fastest cars on the road today. 1962 changes include a slightly redesigned bonnet and grille, and hooded tail lamps. Transmission now has twin-plate clutch and new gear ratios. It is the car for high-powered executives who want to go places quickly and (with Dunlop disc brakes) safely. A David Brown masterpiece.

CLOSE-UP
Six-cyl.; o.h.c.; 92×92 mm.; 3,670 c.c.; 240 b.h.p.; 8.25 to 1 comp.; coil ign.; 2 S.U. carbs.; 4-speed, 8.82, 6.16, 4.42, 3.54 to 1; cen. lvr.; susp., f., ind. coil, r., coil; 2-door; 4-seat; servo disc brks.; max. 140 m.p.h.; cruise 115; m.p.g. 16-20; whl. base 8ft. 2in.; track f. 4ft. 6in., r. 4ft. 5½in.; lgth. 14ft. 8¾in.; wdth. 5ft. 6in.; ht. 4ft. 4in.; g.c. 6¼in.; turng. cir. 34ft.; kerb wt. 26¾ cwt.; tank 19 gals.; 12-volt.
£2,800+£1,284.11.5 p.t.=£4,084.11.5

ASTON MARTIN DB4 G.T.

ZAGATO'S lightweight coupe coachwork steps up the speed of this short-chassis competition model. Light alloy panels, with slim frames for screen and windows pare off pounds, smooth lines with faired-in headlamps help the airflow. A 300 h.p. engine provides the urge and a self-locking differential defeats wheelspin to permit 0-100 and back to a stop in 20 seconds.

CLOSE-UP
Six-cyl.; o.h.c.; 92×92 mm.; 3,670 c.c.; 302 b.h.p.; 9 to 1 comp.; coil ign.; 3 Weber carbs.; 4-speed, 9.67, 6.14, 4.14, 3.31 to 1; cen. lvr.; susp. f., ind. coil r., coil; 2-door; 2-seat; disc brks.; max. 160 m.p.h.; cruise 120; m.p.g. 14-18; whl. base, 7ft. 9in.; track, f., 4ft. 6in., r., 4ft. 5½in.; lgth., 14ft. 3¾in.; wdth. 5ft. 6in.; ht. 4ft. 4in.; g.c. 6¼in.; turng. cir. 32ft.; kerb wt., 25 cwt.; tank 30 gals.; 12-volt.
£3,200+£1,467.18.1 p.t.=£4,667.18.1

AUSTIN A40 MARK II

EXTRA length in the wheelbase and extra power from the engine add to the attractions of this popular small car, first of the B.M.C. range to adopt Pininfarina styling. Rear passengers now have more leg-room. Italian sales have soared since Innocenti began building them under licence. There are two versions, saloon with fixed rear window, and station wagon with lift-up rear door.

CLOSE-UP
Four-cyl.; o.h.v.; 62.9×76.2 mm.; 948 c.c.; 37 b.h.p.; 8.3 to 1 comp.; coil ign.; S.U. carb.; 4-speed, 16.52, 10.8, 6.43, 4.55 to 1; cen. lvr.; susp., f., ind. coil, r., half-elliptic; 2-door; 4-seat; hyd. brks.; max. 73 m.p.h.; cruise, 60; m.p.g. 40; whl. base, 7ft. 3 1/16in.; track, f., 3ft. 11½ in., r., 3ft. 11 in.; lgth.12ft. 0¼in.; wdth. 4ft. 11⅜in.; ht. 4ft. 9¾in.; g.c. 6in.; turng. cir. 36ft.; kerb wt. 15 cwt.; tank 5¼ gals.; 12-volt.
£450+£207.9.9 p.t.=£657.9.9

AUSTIN A60 CAMBRIDGE

BRITISH Motor Corporation's well-established medium-sized family car now comes out with body refinements, a more powerful engine, and new Borg-Warner automatic gearbox as alternative to the normal four-speed type. Power plant is now 1,622 c.c. developing 61 b.h.p., and there are new gear ratios. This is a car which is equally useful for taking the family about or for making business trips.

CLOSE-UP
Four-cyl.; o.h.v.; 76.2×88.9 mm.; 1,622 c.c.; 61 b.h.p; 8.3 to 1 comp.; coil ign.; S.U. carb.; 4-speed, 15.63, 9.52, 5.91, 4.3 to 1; cen. or col. lvr.; susp, f. ind. coil r. half-elliptic; 4-door; 4/5-seat; hyd. brks.; max. 80 m.p.h.; cruise 70; m.p.g. 30-32; whl. base, 8ft. 4½in.; track f. 4ft. 2⅝in., r. 4ft. 3⅞in.; lgth 14ft. 6 in.; wdth., 5ft. 3in.; ht. 4ft. 10in.; g.c. 5⅜in.; turng. cir. 37ft.; kerb wt. 21 cwt.; tank 10 gals.; 12-volt.
£585+£269.7.3 p.t.=£854.7.3

AUSTIN A/110

A HEFTY boost in engine power brings still more sparkling performance to the lowest-priced six-cylinder model in the BMC range, and a two-inch increase in wheelbase adds to the leg-room inside. Normal transmission is three-speed all-synchromesh box, and it now has a central instead of steering column lever. Overdrive and disc front brakes are standard. Automatic transmission is optional.

CLOSE-UP
Six-cyl.; o.h.v.; 83×89 mm.; 2,912 c.c.; 120 b.h.p.; 8.2 to 1 comp.; coil ign.; 2 S.U. carbs.; 3-speed, 12.1, 6.45, 3.91 to 1; cen. lvr. BW overdrive; susp., f., ind. coil, r., half-elliptic; 4-door; 5/6 seat; servo brakes. disc front; max. 104 m.p.h.; cruise, 80; m.p.g. 22-26; whl. base, 9ft. 2in.; track f. 4ft. 6in.; r. 4ft. 5¼in.; lgth. 15ft. 8in.; wdth. 5ft. 8½in.; ht. 5ft. 0½in.; g.c. 6½in.; turng. cir. 38ft. 9in.; kerb wt. 30½ cwt.; tank 16 gals.; 12-volt.
£870+£400 p.t.=£1,270

AUSTIN SEVEN COUNTRYMAN

NEW export version of this brilliant runabout drops the half-timber and leaves the body bare. It is optional, of course, and the stark model is mostly for the hot countries where wood wilts. Longer in wheelbase and tail than its sensational brother, the Seven saloon, this is one of the nippiest all-purpose cars in the world. Monthly its popularity increases.

CLOSE-UP
Four-cyl.; o.h.v.; 62.9×68.2 mm.; 848 c.c.; 37 b.h.p.; 8.3 to 1 comp.; coil ign.; S.U. carb.; 4-speed, 13.66, 8.178, 5.316, 3.765 to 1; cen. lvr.; susp. f. and r. ind. rubber; 4-door; 4-seat; hyd. brks.; max. 70 m.p.h.; cruise 65; m.p.g. 40-45; whl. base 7ft.; track f. 3ft. 11in., r. 3ft. 9⅞in.; lgth. 10ft. 9¾in.; wdth. 4ft. 7½in.; ht. 4ft. 5½in.; g.c. 7in.; turng. cir. 32ft. 9in.; kerb wt. 12¾ cwt.; tank 5¾ gals.; 12-volt.
£439+£202 p.t.=£641

AUSTIN SUPER SEVEN

HIGH grade finish to match the brilliant road behaviour of B.M.C.'s famous baby. Better seats and door trim, new instrument panel with oil gauge and thermometer, bright frames for doors, better sound proofing, fully lined luggage trunk. Common to all models are longer gear lever, improved roof gutters, quieter 16-blade fan. See the high-speed Cooper Seven with disc brakes, too.

CLOSE-UP
Four-cyl.; o.h.v.; 63×68.26 mm.; 848 c.c.; 34 b.h.p.; 8.3 to 1 comp.; coil ign.; S.U. carb.; 4-speed, 13.657, 8.176, 5.317, 3.765 to 1; cen. lvr.; susp., f. and r. ind. rubber; 2-door; 4-seat; hyd. brks.; max. 73 m.p.h.; cruise, 60; m.p.g. 45; whl. base, 6ft. 8in.; track f. 3ft. 11½in.; r. 3ft. 9⅞in.; lgth. 10ft.; wdth. 4ft. 7½in.; ht. 4ft. 5in.; g.c. 6⅜in.; turng. cir. 29ft. 6in.; kerb wt. 11¾ cwt.; tank 5½ gals.; 12-volt.
£405+£186.17.3 p.t.=£591.17.3

AUSTIN SEVEN

AS the Mini family grows the choice becomes bewildering but many thrifty buyers stick to the original versions: Standard with small wheel hub plates, fixed rear-quarter windows and durable rubber floor covering, or de luxe with wheel discs (now an improved spring-on type), pivoted quarter windows, screen washer and better trim. Every car now is given a thorough leak test at the factory.

CLOSE-UP
Four-cyl.; o.h.v.; 63×68.26 mm.; 848 c.c.; 34 b.h.p.; 8.3 to 1 comp.; coil ign.; S.U. carb.; 4-speed, 13.657, 8.176, 5.317, 3.765 to 1; cen. lvr.; susp., f. and r. ind. rubber; 2-door; 4-seat; hyd brks.; max. 73 m.p.h.; cruise, 60; m.p.g. 45; whl. base, 6ft. 8 in.; track f. 3ft. 11½in., r. 3ft. 9⅞in.; lgth., 10ft.; wdth., 4ft. 7½in.; ht. 4ft. 5in.; g.c. 6⅜in.; turng. cir., 29ft. 6in.; kerb wt., 11¾ cwt.; tank, 5½ gals.; 12-volt.
£350+£161 p.t.=£511

Abbreviations—g.c.—ground clearance; susp.—suspension; f.—front; r.—rear; comp.—compression; s.v.—side-valves; o.h.v.—overhead valves; o.h.c.—overhead camshaft; hyd.—hydraulic.

AUSTIN HEALEY SPRITE MARK II

WORLD'S top-selling sports car is now better looking, quieter and more comfortable. Headlamps move to the wings. Lighter-to-lift bonnet makes the engine more accessible. Luggage trunk with external lid is easier to load. High compression, bigger inlet valves, modified camshaft raise power output. De luxe model has adjustable passenger seat, screen washers, rev. counter.

CLOSE-UP
Four-cyl.; o.h.v.; 62.94×76.2 mm.; 948 c.c.; 50 b.h.p.; 9 to 1 comp.; coil ign.; 2 S.U. carbs.; 4-speed, 13.50, 8.08, 5.73, 4.22 to 1; cen. lvr.; susp., f. ind. coil, r. quarter-elliptic; 2-door; 2-seat; hyd. brks.; max. 86 m.p.h.; cruise, 70; m.p.g. 33-38; whl. base, 6ft. 8in.; track, f. 3ft. 9¾in., r. 3ft. 8¾in.; lgth., 11ft. 4in.; wdth. 4ft. 5in.; ht. 4ft. 1½in.; g.c. 7in.; turng. cir., 29ft. 3in.; kerb wt., 13½ cwt.; tank, 6 gals.; 12-volt.

£452+£208 p.t.=£660

AUSTIN HEALEY 3000 MARK II

LATEST version is faster through the gears while using less fuel. Its 2,912 c.c. six-cylinder engine now has three S.U. carburettors boosting its output from 124 b.h.p. to 132 b.h.p. With a body basically similar to its predecessor, the new car is recognisable by a radiator grille with vertical slats and a new badge. Seat belt points and disc brakes on the front wheels are standard.

CLOSE-UP
Six-cyl.; o.h.v.; 83.34×88.9 mm.; 2,912 c.c.; 132 b.h.p.; 9.03 to 1 comp.; coil ign.; 3 S.U. carbs.; 4-speed, 10.209, 7.302, 4.743, 3.545 to 1; de Normanville overdrive opt.; cen. lvr.; susp., f. ind. coil, r. half-elliptic; 2-door; 2-seat; hyd. brks., disc front; max. 112 m.p.h.; cruise 95; m.p.g. 20; whl. base, 7ft. 8in.; track, f. 4ft. 0¾in., r. 4ft. 2in.; lgth., 13ft. 1½in.; wdth., 5ft.; ht. 4ft. 1in.; g.c. 4½in.; turng. cir., 32ft. 7in.; kerb wt. 21¾ cwt.; tank, 12 gals.; 12-volt.

£824+£378 p.t.=£1,202

AUTO UNION 1000S

VERTICAL stowage of spare wheel increases luggage space, and fittings for safety belts increase passenger security in the 1962 version of this three-cylinder front-drive car. Safety catches prevent front seats folding during heavy braking. The trunk lid is easier to lift, there is a new oil metering device (two strokes use oil in their petrol) and disc brakes are optional.

CLOSE-UP
Three-cyl; two-stroke; 76×74 mm.; 980 c.c.; 57 b.h.p. 7.25 to 1 comp.; coil ign.; Solex carb.; 4-speed, 18, 10.47, 6.18, 4.32 to 1; col. lvr.; susp. f. ind. transv., r. transv. leaf; 2-door; 4-seat; hyd. brks.; max. 90 m.p.h.; cruise 75; m.p.g. 32-34; whl. base 7ft. 8½in.; track f. 4ft. 2in., r. 4ft. 5in.; lgth. 13ft. 10½in.; wdth. 5ft. 6in.; ht. 4ft. 9¾in.; g.c. 8in.; turng. cir. 36ft.; kerb wt. 17¾ cwt.; tank 10 gals.; 6-volt.

£807+£372 p.t.=£1,179

BENTLEY CONTINENTAL

A CAR with the wealthy look for the well-heeled sporting driver who deals naturally in superlatives. Light alloy V8 engine provides speeds up to 120 m.p.h. Patrician styling, fine design and superb appointments—all combine for the ultimate in silence, comfort and handling. Automatic transmission, power-assisted steering and servo brakes with choice of saloon, coupe or convertible bodies.

CLOSE-UP
Eight-cyl.; o.h.v.; 104.14×91.44 mm.; 6,230 c.c.; 8 to 1 comp.; coil ign.; 2 S.U. carbs.; 4-speed automatic, 11.75, 8.10, 4.46, 3.08 to 1; col. lvr.; susp. f. ind. coil, r. half-elliptic; 2/4-door; 4-seat; hyd. servo brks.; max. 120 m.p.h.; cruise, 90-100; m.p.g. 14-16; whl. base, 10ft. 3in.; track, f., 4ft. 10½in., r., 5ft.; lgth., 17ft. 8in.; wdth., 6ft.; ht. 5ft. 2in.; g.c. 7in.; turng. cir. 41ft. 8in.; kerb wt., 39¾ cwt.; tank, 18 gals.; 12-volt.

£6,250+£2,865.16.5 p.t.=£9,115.16.5

BENTLEY S2

DEFYING the Chancellor's efforts to prevent people from acquiring them, buyers in a steady stream make the financial sacrifice to enjoy the best that money can buy. A body-line that is never dated by passing fashions, a silent V8 engine made of light alloys, automatic transmission and power assistance for brakes and steering are the main features, plus matchless finish in every detail.

CLOSE-UP

Eight-cyl.; o.h.v.; 104.14×91.44 mm.; 6,230 c.c.; 8 to 1 comp.; coil ign.; 2 S.U. carbs.; 4-speed auto.; 11.75, 8.10, 4.46, 3.08 to 1; col. lvr.; susp., f., ind. coil, r. half-elliptic; 4-door; 5/6-seat; hyd. servo brks.; max. 110 m.p.h.; cruise, 90; m.p.g. 12-15; whl. base, 10ft. 3in.; track, f., 4ft. 10in.; r., 5ft.; lgth., 17ft. 7¾in.; wdth., 6ft. 2¾in.; ht. 5ft. 4in.; g.c. 7in.; turng. cir. 41ft. 8in.; kerb wt. 41½ cwt.; tank, 18 gals.; 12-volt.

£4,195+£1,923.18.11 p.t.=£6,118.18.11

B.M.W. 3.2 SUPER

CONCENTRATION on the successful rear-engined small cars has eliminated the big V8 sports cars, but the luxurious V8 saloon continues as BMW's representative in the executive transport category. Light alloy 140 h.p. engine ensures swift acceleration, and disc front brakes take care of the deceleration. Engine oil heat exchanger, adjustable back-rests are among the quality features. And watch for the new Bertone Coupe.

CLOSE-UP

Eight-cyl.; o.h.v.; 82×75 mm.; 3,168 c.c.; 140 b.h.p.; 7.3 to 1 comp.; coil ign.; 2 Solex carbs.; 4-speed, 14.43, 9.60, 5.79, 3.89 to 1; col. lvr.; susp. f. ind. torsion bar, r. torsion bar; 4-door; 5/6-seat; hyd. brks. disc front; max. 112 m.p.h.; cruise 90; m.p.g. 22-24; whl. base 9ft. 3½in.; track f. 4ft. 4½in. r. 4ft. 7¾in.; lgth. 15ft. 6in.; wdth. 5ft. 10in.; ht. 5ft.; g.c. 7in.; turng. cir. 39ft.; kerb wt. 29 cwt.; tank 15½ gals.; 12-volt.

B.M.W. 700

SOON to be available with right-hand drive, this rear-engined, small car from Germany has provided tough competition for our own babies in international races. Basic model is the two-door saloon. There are also a sports coupe and a convertible, with flat-twin air-cooled engine fitted with twin carburettors, giving 40 horse-power. Each of these should be good for about 84 m.p.h.

CLOSE-UP

Two-cyl.; o.h.v. air cooled; 78×73 mm.; 696 c.c.; 35 b.h.p.; 7.5 to 1 comp.; coil ign.; downdraught carb.; 4-speed, 19.22, 10.53, 6.89, 4.59 to 1; cen. lvr.; susp. f. and r., ind. coil; 2-door; 2/4-seat; hyd. brks.; max. 78 m.p.h.; cruise, 60; m.p.g. 45-50; whl. base, 6ft. 11½in.; track, f., 4ft. 2in., r., 3ft. 11½in.; lgth., 11ft. 7½in.; wdth., 4ft. 10¼in.; ht. 4ft. 1½in.; g.c. 6in.; turng. cir., 29ft.; kerb wt., 12½ cwt.; tank, 6½ gals.; 12-volt.

£612.2.5+£281.16 p.t.=£893.18.5

B.M.W. ISETTA

MORE than 100,000 of these eager ovoids have been built, some with four wheels and some with three, but all with the single front door, which makes entry so easy. The engine is an economical single-cylinder four-stroke, fan-cooled. An excellent runabout in city streets, it does 65-75 m.p.g. and makes the most of every parking spot. But it is also fast enough for week-end outings.

CLOSE-UP

Single-cyl.; o.h.v.; air cooled; 72×73 mm.; 295 c.c.; 13 b.h.p.; 7 to 1 comp.; coil ign.; single carb.; 4-speed, 23.21, 12.14, 8.17, 6.1 to 1; side lvr.; susp. f., ind. coil; r., quarter-elliptic; 1-door; 2/3-seat; hyd. brks.; max. 55 m.p.h.; cruise 45-50; m.p.g. 65-75; whl. base, 4ft. 10in.; track, f., 4ft.; r., 1ft. 9in.; lgth., 7ft. 6in.; wdth., 4ft. 7in.; ht., 4ft. 5in.; g.c. 6½in.; turng. cir., 30ft.; kerb wt., 7¼ cwt.; tank, 2⅓ gals.; 12-volt.

£257.10+£119.10.11 p.t.=£377.0.11

Abbreviations—g.c.—ground clearance; susp.—suspension; f.—front; r.—rear; comp.—compression; s.v.—side-valves; o.h.v.—overhead valves; o.h.c.—overhead camshaft; hyd.—hydraulic.

65

BRISTOL 407

SWIFT sign of enterprise by the new company which has taken over the former Bristol Aeroplane Company's Car Division is the new 5.2-litre V8 model. Low-drag shape enhances the performance obtained from its 250 horse-power. Front suspension is new, with coil springs and wishbones, and torsion bars are used at the rear. Brakes are Dunlop discs with servo assistance.

CLOSE-UP
Eight-cyl.; o.h.v.; 98.55×84.07 mm.; 5,130 c.c.; 250 b.h.p.; 9 to 1 comp.; coil ign.; Carter carb.; 3-speed auto., 8.10, 4.80, 3.31 to 1; push button control; susp., f. ind. coil, r. torsion bar; 2-door; 4-seat; disc servo brks.; max 122 m.p.h.; cruise, 100; m.p.g. 18-20; whl. base, 9ft. 6in.; track f. 4ft. 5in.; r. 4ft. 6½in.; lgth., 16ft. 7in.; wdth., 5ft. 8in.; ht. 5ft.; g.c. 6½in.; turng. cir., 39ft. 6in.; kerb wt., 32 cwt.; tank, 18 gals.; 12-volt.

£3,525+£1,617 p.t.=£5,142

BUICK ELECTRA

ELECTRA and Invicta are the big Buicks for the buyer who still wants acres of space and power to spare. Massive chassis, coil spring front suspension and coil springs at the rear, with radius arms to locate the axle. The automatic fluid transmission has variable-angle guide vanes for increased efficiency. You are given a big choice of saloon, coupe and convertible bodies.

CLOSE-UP
Eight-cyl.; o.h.v.; 101.36×92.45 mm.; 6,571 c.c.; 312 b.h.p.; 10.25 to 1 comp.; coil ign.; Stromberg carb.; 2-speed auto., 5.88, 3.23 to 1; col. lvr.; susp., f. ind. coil, r. coil; 4-door; 6-seat; hyd. Servo brks.; max. 112 m.p.h.; cruise, 80; m.p.g. 14-17; whl. base, 10ft. 3in.; track f. 5ft. 2⅜in.; r. 5ft.; lgth., 18ft. 1½in.; wdth., 6ft. 8¾in.; ht. 4ft. 9in.; g.c. 6⅝in.; turng. cir., 44ft.; kerb wt., 41 cwt.; tank, 16¾ gals.; 12-volt.

£2,465+£1,130 p.t.=£3,595

BUICK SPECIAL

ONE of the more luxurious of the smaller-sized American cars. Its original much praised 3½-litre V8 engine, made of light alloy is now offered as an extra-cost option. The new standard power unit is a cast-iron V6, the first time such an engine has gone into mass production for U.S. cars, although one is used on G.M. trucks. Manual or automatic transmission is available to order.

CLOSE-UP
Eight-cyl.; o.h.v.; 88.9×70.9 mm.; 3,523 c.c.; 150 b.h.p.; 8.8 to 1 comp.; coil ign.; Rochester carb.; 3-speed, 8.6, 5.2, 3.4 to 1; col. lvr.; susp., f. ind. coil, r. coil; 4-door; 6-seat; hyd. brks.; max. 92 m.p.h.; cruise, 80; m.p.g. 18-22; whl. base, 9ft. 4in.; track f. and r. 4ft. 8in.; lgth., 15ft. 8½in.; wdth., 5ft. 11½in.; ht. 4ft. 4½in.; g.c. 6½in.; turng. cir., 36ft.; kerb wt., 23¾ cwt.; tank, 16½ gals.; 12-volt.

£1,830+£840 p.t.=£2,670

CADILLAC 62

SAFETY is the keynote in the world's top-selling luxury car for 1962, with twin fluid circuits for the brakes and new cornering lights, which are switched on by the direction indicator switch. Other features are automatic vacuum release for parking brake, and trunk-lid lock. Many detail improvements to body and chassis make the silence more silent and the smoothness still smoother.

CLOSE-UP
Eight-cyl.; o.h.v.; 101.6×98.42 mm.; 6,384 c.c.; 345 b.h.p.; 10.5 to 1 comp.; coil ign.; Carter carb.; 4-speed auto., 11.66, 7.49, 4.55, 2.94 to 1; col. lvr.; susp., f. ind. coil, r. coil; 4-door; 6-seat; hyd. servo brks.; max.110 m.p.h.; cruise, 80; m.p.g. 13-15; whl. base, 10ft. 9½in.; track f. and r. 5ft. 1in.; lgth., 18ft. 6in.; wdth., 6ft. 7in.; ht. 4ft. 8½in.; g.c. 5in.; turng. cir., 45ft.; kerb wt., 42¾ cwt.; tank, 20 gals.; 12-volt.

£3,660+£1,678 p.t.=£5,338

CADILLAC 75

THE utmost in luxury, American style, this 20-foot 9-seater cruises in silence at 100 m.p.h. Power assisted brakes and steering plus the fine 4-speed Hydra-matic gearbox simplify the chauffeur's task. The automatic transmission even releases the parking brake as you move away. Among the optional extras are air conditioning, a photo-electric headlamp dipper and cruise control which maintains a steady speed on motorways.

CLOSE-UP

Eight-cyl.; o.h.v.; 101.6 × 98.43 mm.; 6,384 c.c.; 330 b.h.p.; 10.5 to 1 comp; coil ign.; Carter carb.; 4-speed auto., 13.31, 8.57, 5.21, 3.36 to 1; col. lvr.; susp. f. ind. coil, r. coil; 4-door; 9-seat; hyd. servo brks.; max. 118 m.p.h.; cruise 100; m.p.g. 9-13; whl. base 12ft. 5⅝in.; track f. and r. 5ft. 1in.; lgth. 20ft. 4¾in.; wdth. 6ft. 8in.; ht. 4ft. 11in.; g.c. 6⅜in.; turng. cir. 52ft.; kerb wt. 50½ cwt.; tank, 17½ gals.; 12-volt.

CHEVROLET CORVAIR

MOST radical of America's compact cars, the Corvair has a flat-six air-cooled engine at the rear with choice of three or four speeds or automatic transmission. Spare wheel is now over engine to leave more luggage space in front. Corvair 700 two-door coupe has 99 h.p. There is a station wagon too, with the engine under the rear floor.

CLOSE-UP

Six-cyl.; o.h.v.; air-cooled 87.3 × 66 mm.; 2,372 c.c.; 80 b.h.p.; 8 to 1 comp.; coil ign.; 2 Rochester carbs.; 3-speed, 11.44, 6.50, 3.27 to 1, 4-speed or auto. opt.; cen. lvr.; susp. f. and r. ind. coil; 4-door; 5/6-seat; hyd. brks.; max. 84 m.p.h.; cruise 75; m.p.g.18-24; whl. base 9ft.; track f. and r. 4ft. 6in.; lgth. 15ft.; wdth. 5ft. 6⅞in.; ht. 4ft. 3in.; g.c. 6in.; turng. cir. 39ft. 11in.; kerb wt. 22 cwt.; tank, 9¼ gals.; 12-volt.

CHEVROLET CORVETTE

A BRAND new V8 engine of 5.3 litres is the latest news in Chevrolet's plastic-bodied sports car. In standard form, with four-barrel carburettor, it gives 250 horse power; fuel injection and other changes push it up to 360. A lighter automatic transmission with aluminium casing is an alternative to the excellent synchromesh gearbox. The grille is changed, and there are four colours for the upholstery.

CLOSE-UP

Eight-cyl.; o.h.v.; 5,358 c.c.; 250 b.h.p.; coil ign.; 4-speed, 8.14, 6.14, 4.84, 3.7 to 1, auto opt.; cen. lvr.; susp. f. ind. coil, r. coil; 2-door; 2-seat; hyd. brks.; max. 114 m.p.h.; cruise, 90; m.p.g. 15; whl. base, 8ft. 6in.; track f. 4ft. 9in., r. 4ft. 11in.; lgth. 14ft. 9in.; wdth., 6ft.; ht. 4ft. 3in.; g.c. 8in.; turng. cir., 37ft.; kerb wt., 26 cwt.; tank, 16 gals.; 12-volt.

£2,750 + £1,261 p.t. = £4,011

CHEVROLET CHEVY II

ALONGSIDE the rear-engined, air-cooled, independently sprung Corvair, this new popular-sized car from General Motors looks highly conventional, and is designed to compete against Ford's orthodox, but successful, Falcon. It is larger than the Corvair, smaller than normal Chevrolet. There is a choice of four or six-cylinder engines, and single-leaf rear springs are a new design feature.

CLOSE-UP

Four-cyl.; o.h.v.; 2,507 c.c.; 90 b.h.p.; coil ign.; 3-speed. col lvr.; susp., f. ind. coil, r. single-leaf half-elliptic; 2 or 4-door; 6-seat; hyd. brks.; whl. base, 9ft. 2in ; lgth., 15ft. 3in.; wdth., 5ft.10⅞in.; ht. 4ft. 7in.; 12-volt.

Abbreviations—g.c.—ground clearance; susp.—suspension; f.—front; r.—rear; comp.—compression; s.v.—side-valves; o.h.v.—overhead valves; o.h.c.—overhead camshaft; hyd.—hydraulic.

CHRYSLER NEW YORKER

BESIDES external re-styling, there is a new automatic transmission with aluminium casing that saves 59 lb., and a high-speed starter with reduction gear that saves 5 lb. Brakes have a suspended-vacuum servo, which cuts out the reservoir. Anti-glare headlamps stop the stray beams that go downwards to reflect off the bumper and electrical circuits are guarded by easy-change, household-type fuses.

CLOSE-UP
Eight-cyl.; o.h.v.; 106.3 × 95.3 mm.; 6,767 c.c.; 350 b.h.p.; 10 to 1 comp.; coil ign.; downdraught carb.; 3-speed auto., 8.11, 4.79, 3.31 to 1; push button control; susp., f. ind. torsion bar, r. half-elliptic; 4-door; 6-seat; hyd. servo brks.; max. 115 m.p.h.; cruise, 80; m.p.g. 13-16; whl. base, 10ft. 6in.; track f. 5ft. 1⅛in.; r. 5ft.; lgth., 18ft. 3in.; wdth., 6ft. 7⅜in.; ht. 4ft. 7⅜in.; g.c. 6in.; turng. cir., 47ft.; kerb wt., 37½ cwt.; tank, 19½ gals.; 12-volt.

CITROEN AMI 6

THIRD completely new Citroen produced since 1934, the Ami is well in the revolutionary tradition both in looks and performance. 3 CV flat-twin engine gives more than 60 m.p.h. at very high fuel economy. Independent swinging arm suspension with interconnection between front and rear. A raked rear window, rectangular headlamps, and windows covering more than a quarter of body surface, produce an arresting appearance.

CLOSE-UP
Two-cyl.; o.h.v.; 74 × 70 mm.; 602 c.c.; 22 b.h.p.; 7.25 to 1 comp.; coil ign.; Solex carb.; 4-speed, 20.365, 10.505, 6.97, 4.77 to 1; dash lvr.; susp. f. and r. ind. coil; 4-door; 4-seat; hyd. brks.; max. 60 m.p.h.; cruise 50; m.p.g. 38-45; whl. base 7ft. 10½in.; track f. 4ft. 1⅜in.; r. 4ft.; lgth. 12ft. 8⅝in.; wdth. 4ft. 11¾in.; ht. 4ft. 10½in.; g.c. 7¼in.; turng. cir. 36ft.; kerb wt. 12 cwt.; tank, 5¼ gals.; 6-volt.

CITROEN DS 19

THE car of the future, with revolutionary hydraulic-pneumatic self-adjusting suspension, load-adjustable front disc brakes, quick-release body sections, one-spoke safety steering wheel and insulating plastic roof. It is in a class of its own. The unique Belbrace safety harness is an interesting available extra. Newly improved engine gives extra power. Automatic clutch and fully reclining front seats are standard.

CLOSE-UP
Four-cyl.; o.h.v.; 78 × 100 mm.; 1,911 c.c.; 83 b.h.p.; 8.5 to 1 comp.; coil ign.; Weber carb.; 4-speed, 13.79, 6.96, 4.77, 3.31 to 1; dash lvr.; susp. f. and r. ind. hyd. pneu.; 4-door; 5/6-seat; hyd. servo brks., disc front; max. 95 m.p.h.; cruise 75; m.p.g. 29; whl. base 10ft. 3in.; track f. 4ft.11in., r. 4ft. 3½in.; lgth. 15ft. 9in.; wdth. 5ft. 10½in.; ht. 4ft. 11½in., g.c. 6½in.; turng. cir. 36ft.; kerb wt. 23 cwt.; tank 14 gals.; 12-volt.
£1,196 + £549.8.1 p.t. = £1,745.8.1

CITROEN ID SAFARI

CHOICE of many rally drivers and the winner of many events, the ID has normal controls with front-wheel drive and self-levelling air-oil suspension. It has a lively engine, a smooth gearbox and it handles well, with a good turning circle. Engine is less powerful with a different cylinder head from its bigger brother, but it is cheaper to buy and cheaper to run. The station wagon seats eight.

CLOSE-UP
Four-cyl.; o.h.v.; 78 × 100 mm.; 1,911 c.c.; 66 b.h.p.; 7.5 to 1 comp.; coil ign.; Solex carb.; 4-speed, 13.79, 7.35, 4.77, 3.31 to 1; col. lvr.; susp. f. and r. hyd. pneu.; 4-door; 8-seat; hyd. servo brks., disc front; max. 85 m.p.h.; cruise 70; m.p.g. 25-30; whl. base 10ft. 3in.; track f. 4ft. 11in., r. 4ft. 3½in.; lgth. 16ft. 4in.; wdth. 5ft. 10½in.; ht. 4ft. 11½in.; g.c. 6½in.; turng. cir. 36ft 1in.; kerb wt. 25¼ cwt.; tank, 14 gals.; 12-volt.
£1,298 + £596.3.1 p.t. = £1,894.3.1

COMET

ONE of the models with which Ford have carved themselves a large share of the American compact-car market, the Comet now forms part of the Mercury range. It appeals to those who want quality without excessive size. Of last year's buyers, 53 per cent ordered the bigger 101 h.p. engine, 62 per cent chose automatic transmission, and 58 per cent took white side-wall tyres.

CLOSE-UP
Six-cyl.; o.h.v.; 88.9×74.64 mm.; 2,786 c.c.; 101 b.h.p. 8.7 to 1 comp.; coil ign.; Ford carb.; 2-speed auto., 6.6, 3.2 to 1; col. lvr.; susp., f. ind. coil, r. half-elliptic; 4-door; 6-seat; hyd. brks.; max. 85 m.p.h.; cruise, 70 m.p.g. 22; whl. base, 9ft. 1½in.; track f. 4ft. 7in., r. 4ft. 6½in.; lgth., 16ft. 3in.; wdth., 5ft. 10in.; ht., 4ft. 6½in.; g.c. 6¾in.; turng. cir., 39ft. 10in.; kerb wt., 21½ cwt.; tank, 11 gals.; 12-volt.

DAF

THE unique Dutch family car with enlarged engine for 1962—a two-cylinder, air-cooled engine which, incidentally, cannot freeze or boil. It boasts fully automatic transmission, a chassis that needs no greasing, and fully independent suspension for extra-smooth road holding. Here is the economy car for the family driver who likes care-free motoring, with no clutch pedal and no gears to shift.

CLOSE-UP
Two-cyl.; o.h.v. air cooled; 85.5×65 mm.; 746 c.c.; 30 b.h.p.; 7.1 to 1 comp.; coil ign.; downdraught carb.; Variomatic between 16.4 and 3.9 to 1; cen. lvr.; susp. f. ind. trans. leaf; r. ind. coil; 2-door; 4-seat; hyd. brks.; max. 65 m.p.h.; cruise, 65; m.p.g. 38-48; whl. base 6ft. 9in.; track f. and r. 3ft. 10½in.; lgth. 12ft. 1in.; wdth. 4ft. 9in.; ht., 4ft. 6½in.; g.c. 6¾in.; turng. cir. 31ft.; kerb wt. 13 cwt.; tank, 6¼ gals.; 6-volt.

DAIMLER SP250

SCOTLAND YARD is now using these fast sports cars in its battle to beat the road-hog. Soon all London's divisions will have one or more of them. For the chase the machines have fade-free disc brakes on all four wheels, and in a crash the convertible body will be easily repairable with plastic mouldings. For winter driving there is a detachable hard top.

CLOSE-UP
Eight-cyl.; o.h.v.; 76.2×69.5 mm.; 2,530 c.c.; 140 b.h.p.; 8.2 to 1 comp.; coil ign.; 2 S.U. carbs.; 4-speed, 10.5, 6.236, 4.41, 3.58 to 1; cen. lvr.; susp. f., ind. coil, r., half-elliptic; 2-door; 2/3-seat; disc brks.; max. 120 m.p.h.; cruise, 90; m.p.g. 28; whl. base, 7ft. 8in.; track f., 4ft. 2in., r. 4ft.; lgth., 13ft. 4½in.; wdth., 5ft. 0½in.; ht., 4ft. 2½in.; g.c., 6in.; turng. cir., 33ft.; kerb wt. 19½ cwt.; tank, 12 gals.; 12-volt.
£1,054+£485 p.t.=£1,539

DAIMLER LIMOUSINE

THE new, sleeker limousine, following the style of the Majestic Major and powered by its hefty 4½-litre V8 engine. Automatic transmission, plus power assistance for steering and disc brakes lighten the task of the driver in this luxurious two-tonner. On each side of the rear seat are cigarette-lighter, heater controls, reading and roof lamps. Separate heaters front and rear.

CLOSE-UP
Eight-cyl.; o.h.v.; 95.25×80.01 mm.; 4,561 c.c.; 220 b.h.p.; 8 to 1 comp.; coil ign.; 2 S.U. carbs.; auto. 8.701, 5.418, 3.77 to 1; col. lvr.; susp., f. ind. coil, r. half-elliptic; 4-door; 8-seat; disc servo brks.; max. 110 m.p.h.; cruise, 90; m.p.g. 17-20; whl. base, 11ft. 6in.; track f. and r. 4ft. 9in.; lgth., 18ft. 10in.; wdth., 6ft. 1½in.; ht., 5ft. 5½in.; g.c. 7 in.; turng. cir., 44ft.; kerb wt., 40 cwt.; tank, 16 gals.; 12-volt.
£2,738.11.7+£1,256.8.5 p.t.=£3,995

Abbreviations—g.c.—ground clearance; susp.—suspension; f.—front; r.—rear; comp.—compression; s.v.—side-valves; o.h.v.—overhead valves; o.h.c.—overhead camshaft; hyd.—hydraulic.

69

DAIMLER MAJESTIC

SPACE, comfort, speed and prestige are provided in this fine car which is ideal for the business man who likes to drive himself and his business contacts at up to 100 m.p.h. Power-assisted disc brakes make stopping from these speeds safe and the interior might well be just what is needed to clinch a business deal. Daimler is now a member of the dynamic Jaguar group.

CLOSE-UP

Six-cyl.; o.h.v.; 86.36 × 107.95 mm.; 3,794 c.c.; 147 b.h.p.; 7.5 to 1 comp.; coil ign.; 2 S.U. carbs.; 3-speed BW auto., 9.04, 5.62, 3.92 to 1; col. lvr.; susp., f., ind. coil, r., half-elliptic; 4-door; 6-seat; disc servo brks.; max. 100 m.p.h.; cruise, 80; m.p.g., 17-22; whl. base 9ft. 6in.; track, f., 4ft. 8in.; r., 4ft. 9in.; lgth., 16ft. 4in.; wdth., 6ft. 1¼in.; ht., 5ft. 2¾in.; g.c., 7in.; turng. cir., 42ft.; kerb wt., 36 cwt.; tank, 18 gals.; 12-volt.

£1,760 + £808.9.3 p.t. = £2,568.9.3

DAIMLER MAJESTIC MAJOR

HERE is time-saving transport for the busy executive, with the prestige of the oldest name in the industry now backed by Jaguar's flair for efficient production of quality cars. Its 4½ litre V8 engine with pushrod-operated valves produces a very adequate 220 horsepower; transmission is Borg Warner automatic, and brakes are discs all round. No significant changes are made for 1962.

CLOSE-UP

Eight-cyl.; o.h.v.; 95.25 × 80.01 mm.; 4,500 c.c.; 220 b.h.p.; 8 to 1 comp.; coil ign.; 2 S.U. carbs.; auto. 3-speed, 8.7, 5.41, 3.77 to 1; col. lvr.; susp. f. ind. coil, r. half-elliptic; 4-door; 5/6-seat; servo disc brks.; max. 120 m.p.h.; cruise 95; m.p.g. 20-22; whl. base 9ft. 6in.; track f. and r. 4ft. 9in.; lgth. 16ft. 10in.; wdth. 6ft. 1¼in.; ht., 5ft. 2¾in.; g.c. 7in.; turng. cir. 42ft.; kerb wt., 37¾ cwt.; tank 16 gals.; 12-volt.

£2,113 + £970.3.4 p.t. = £3,083.3.4

DKW JUNIOR

THE special equipment model introduced this year is now joined by a Junior de luxe, with engine increased to 796 c.c. and automatic engine lubrication. On this model you do not mix oil with the fuel; you put it in a separate tank holding enough for 1,500 to 2,000 miles. It is fed to the carburetter automatically. Advantages: reduced oil consumption, no blue smoke or oiled plugs.

CLOSE-UP

Three-cyl.; two-stroke; 68 × 68 mm.; 741 c.c.; 39 b.h.p.; 8.1 to 1 comp.; coil ign.; downdraught carb.; 4-speed, 14.45, 8.6, 5.45, 3.62 to 1; col. lvr.; susp. f. ind. torsion bar, r. torsion bar; 2-door; 4-seat; hyd. brks.; max. 75 m.p.h.; cruise 70; m.p.g. 37; whl. base 5ft. 1⅜in.; track f. 3ft. 10½in., r. 3ft. 11¼in.; lgth. 13ft.; wdth. 5ft. 2¼in.; ht. 4ft. 7⅛in.; g.c. 7in.; turng. cir. 31ft; kerb wt. 14 cwt.; tank, 8 gals.; 6-volt.

£614.4.9 + £282.15.3 p.t. = £897

DODGE DART 440

ENGINE improvements cut fuel consumption and there is a new lighter automatic transmission. The brakes are self-adjusting for 1962. Printed circuit instrument wiring links to a single connector on the bulkhead with single plug on the engine side. The Polara is a new sporting model with coupe or convertible body. Dart has choice of six or eight-cylinder engines in saloons, coupes and station wagons.

CLOSE-UP

Eight-cyl.; o.h.v.; 98.55 × 84.07; 5,130 c.c.; 230 b.h.p.; 9 to 1 comp.; coil ign.; Carter carb.; 3-speed auto., 6.76, 3.0, 2.76 to 1; push button auto; susp., f. ind. torsion bar, r. half-elliptic; 4-door; 6-seat; hyd. servo brks.; max. 108 m.p.h.; cruise, 90; m.p.g. 16-21; whl. base 9ft. 8in.; track f. 4ft. 11½in., r. 4ft. 9in.; lgth. 16ft. 10in.; wdth., 6ft. 4½in.; ht. 4ft. 6in.; g.c. 5in.; turng. cir., 42ft. 9in.; kerb wt. 30 cwt.; tank 17 gals.; 12-volt.

Abbreviations—g.c.—ground clearance; susp.—suspension; f.—front; r.—rear; comp.—compression; s.v.—side-valves; o.h.v.—overhead valves; o.h.c.—overhead camshaft; hyd.—hydraulic.

FACEL VEGA EXCELLENCE

A BIGGER Chrysler-built V8 engine boosts power and speed in this prestige car which the French produce. It is the model you see at the world's most fashionable haunts—elegant, and made for the pockets of the rich. Not the least of its attractions is a boot so vast that it takes six good-sized cases. Truly a car *par excellence*. Automatic transmission and disc brakes are features of a well designed chassis.

CLOSE-UP

Eight-cyl.; o.h.v.; 107.9×85.8 mm.; 6,286 c.c.; 330 b.h.p.; 10 to 1 comp.; coil ign.; Carter carb.; 3-speed auto. 8.10, 4.79, 3.31 to 1; col. lvr.; susp. f. ind. coil, r. half-elliptic; 4-door; 4/5-seat; servo disc brks.; max. 125 m.p.h.; cruise, 110; m.p.g. 14–17; whl. base 10ft. 5in.; track f. 4ft. 8in., r. 4ft. 9in.; lgth. 17ft. 3in.; wdth. 6ft.; ht. 4ft. 6½in.; g.c. 7in.; turng. cir. 38ft.; kerb wt. 37½ cwt.; tank 27 gals.; 12-volt.
£4,500+£2,063.10.3 p.t.=£6,563.10.3

FACEL VEGA FACELLIA

GOOD things in a small package. On France's luxurious Facellia you choose from two-seater coupe, convertible or close-coupled four-seater coupe, all with Facel's clean-cut lines and chic interiors. Twin overhead camshaft engine gives 114 h.p. in standard form, 120 on the high performance F.2. Gearbox with synchromesh for all four speeds increases the pleasure of driving. Disc brakes are optional.

CLOSE-UP

Four-cyl.; o.h.c.; 82×78 mm.; 1,600 c.c.; 115 b.h.p.; 9.4 to 1 comp.; coil ign.; Solex carb.; 4-speed, 14.1, 8.0, 5.2, 4.1 to 1; cen. lvr.; susp. f. ind. coil, r. half-elliptic; 2-door; 2-seat; disc brks.; max. 115 m.p.h.; cruise 100; m.p.g. 25; whl base. 8ft. 0½in.; track f. and r. 4ft. 3½in.; lgth. 13ft. 7½in.; wdth. 5ft. 4in.; ht. 4ft. 1½in.; g.c. 7in.; turng. cir. 32 ft.; kerb wt. 19¼ cwt.; tank 12½ gals.; 12-volt.
£1,770+£812.5.3 p.t.=£2,582.5.3

FAIRTHORPE ELECTRON

A NEW, lighter version of the Electron sports model is now available with Coventry Climax engines of 1,089 or 1,220 c.c. Nearly 200lb has been saved by changes to wheels and suspension, and use of smaller disc brakes. The small Electron Minor is now offered with a choice of four engines: Triumph Herald twin carburetter 948 c.c., Triumph Herald 1200 c.c., Ford Anglia 998 c.c., or Ford Classic 1,340 c.c.

CLOSE-UP

Four-cyl.; o.h.c.; 72.4×66.6 mm.; 1,098 c.c.; 93 b.h.p.; 10.5 to 1 comp.; coil ign.; 2 S.U. carbs.; 4-speed, 14.5, 8.6, 5.6, 4.1 to 1; cen. lvr.; susp., f. and r. coil; 2-door; 2-3 seat; hyd. brks., disc front; max. 110 m.p.h.; cruise, 85; m.p.g. 35–45; whl. base, 6ft. 10in.; track f. 4ft., r. 3ft. 9½in.; lgth., 11ft. 5in.; wdth., 4ft. 10in.; ht. 3ft. 10in.; g.c. 7½in.; turng. cir., 23ft.; kerb wt., 9½ cwt.; tank, 10 gals.; 12-volt.
£563.10+£259.5.8 p.t.=£822.15.8

FERRARI 250 G.T.

THIS fabulous car is now available as either a two- or four-seater. In the four-seater saloon version by Pininfarina, both engine and gearbox are moved forward to provide extra room without modification in either length or wheelbase. De Normanville overdrive, thermostatically controlled fan clutch, and Dunlop disc brakes on all wheels are standard fittings. The Berlinetta is the lightweight T.T. winner.

CLOSE-UP

Twelve-cyl.; o.h.c.; 73×58.8 mm.; 2,953 c.c.; 240 b.h.p.; 8.8 to 1 comp.; coil ign.; 3 Weber carbs.; 4-speed 10.59, 7.76, 5.73, 4.57 to 1; cen. lvr.; susp., f., ind. coil, r., half-elliptic; 2-door; 4-seat; servo disc brks.; max. 140–150 m.p.h.; cruise 120; m.p.g. 15–17; whl. base, 8ft. 6⅜in.; track, f. 4ft. 5in., r. 4ft. 5⅛in.; lgth. 15ft. 3in.; wdth. 5ft. 2½in.; ht. 4ft. 7½in.; g.c. 6in.; turng. cir. 32ft. 9in.; kerb wt. 25½ cwt.; tank 22 gals.; 12-volt.
£4,500+£2,166.17.2 p.t.=£6,666.17.2

FIAT GIARDINIERA 500

MINIMUM motoring, Italian style, with smooth running, economical two-cylinder engine, air-cooled mounted at rear. In the coupe it is vertical; in the Giardiniera station wagon it lies flat under the floor. Both models are now available with the enlarged engine of 499.5 c.c although 479 c.c. coupes are still sold where utmost economy is the objective. A folding roof is standard on the station wagon.

CLOSE-UP

Two-cyl.; o.h.v.; air-cooled; 67.4×70 mm.; 499.5 c.c.; 21.5 b.h.p.; 7.1 to 1 comp.; coil ign.; Weber carb.; 4-speed, 18.96, 10.59, 6.66, 4.48 to 1; cen. lvr.; susp. f. ind. transv. leaf, r. ind. coil; 3-door; 4-seat; hyd. brks.; max. 60 m.p.h.; cruise 55; m.p.g. 55; whl. base 6ft. 4⅜in.; track f. 3ft. 8⅛in., r. 3ft. 8½in.; lgth. 10ft. 5¼in.; wdth. 4ft. 8½in.; ht. 4ft. 5¼in.; g.c. 5¼in.; turng. cir. 28ft. 2½in.; kerb wt. 11-cwt.; tank, 4½ gals.; 12-volt.

£410.10+£189.7.8 p.t.=£599.17.8

FIAT 600 D

ITALY's best-selling cheap little car now has a larger engine (767 c.c.) and new gear ratios providing livelier pick-up, a higher top speed of 70 m.p.h., and less fuel thirst. Other modifications include improved ventilation and silencing, and a new air filter. It is also built as a convertible or 6-person Multipla. All versions have water-cooled rear engines and all-independent suspension.

CLOSE-UP

Four-cyl.; o.h.v.; 62×63.5 mm.; 767 c.c.; 32 b.h.p.; 7.5 to 1 comp.; coil ign.; Weber carb.; 4-speed, 14.47, 8.78, 5.69, 3.83 to 1; cen. lvr.; susp. f. ind. trans leaf r. ind. coil; 2-door; 4-seat; hyd. brks.; max. 69 m.p.h.; cruise, 60; m.p.g. 45; whl. base, 6ft. 6¾in.; track, f., 3ft. 9¼in., r., 3ft. 9⅝in.; lgth. 10ft. 9⅜in.; wdth. 4ft. 6⅜in.; g.c. 6¼in.; turng. cir. 28ft. 6½in.; kerb wt. 11¾ cwt.; tank, 6 gals.; 12-volt.

£438+£201.19.9 p.t.=£639.19.9

FIAT SPECIAL 1100

UNEMBELLISHED and clean cut, this is a strictly functional family car made for hard work. Easy cruising at 65 m.p.h. is possible, and speeds of more than 70 can be reached. With a hint of that Latin look, this is a best seller in Italy in the medium family range, and with ample luggage space and comfort for four it is exporting well, too. The range also includes a well-finished station wagon.

CLOSE-UP

Four-cyl.; o.h.v.; 68×75 mm.; 1,089 c.c.; 55 b.h.p.; 7.8 to 1 comp.; coil ign.; twin-choke Weber carb.; 4-speed, 16.59, 10.23, 6.75, 4.3 to 1; col. lvr.; susp. f. ind. coil, r. half-elliptic; 4-door; 4-seat; hyd. brks.; max. 80 m.p.h.; cruise 70; m.p.g. 36; whl. base 7ft. 8⅛in.; track f. 4ft. 0½in., r. 3ft. 11⅞in.; lgth. 13ft.; wdth. 4ft. 9½in.; ht. 4 ft. 10⅝in.; g.c. 5⅛in.; turng. cir. 34ft. 5⅛in.; kerb wt. 17½ cwt.; tank 8⅜ gals.; 12-volt.

£563+£259.5.8 p.t.=£822.5.8

FIAT 1300/1500

ITALY'S new family car with choice of engine sizes, both fast performers. Four headlamps, disc front brakes, forward-opening bonnet, four-speed all-synchromesh gearbox and flush-fitting door handles are modern features. Twin-choke carburetter with differential throttle control ensures high power with flexibility. Instrumentation includes warning lights for handbrake, reverse gear, fuel reserve.

CLOSE-UP

Four-cyl.; o.h.v.; 72×79.5 mm.; 1,295 c.c.; 72 b.h.p.; 8.8 to 1 comp.; or 77×79.5 mm.; 1,481 c.c.; 80 b.h.p.; coil ign.; Weber carb. or Solex; 4-speed, 15.37, 9.43, 6.12, 4.1 to 1; col. lvr.; susp., f. ind. coil, r. half-elliptic; 4-door; 4-seat; hyd. brks., disc front; max. 86-93 m.p.h.; cruise, 80-85; m.p.g. 30-35; whl. base, 7ft. 11¼in.; track f. 4ft. 3in., r. 4ft. 2in.; lgth., 13ft. 2⅝in.; wdth., 5ft. 0⅞in.; ht. 4ft. 5¾in.; g.c. 8¼in.; turng. cir. 33ft. 5in.; kerb wt., 18⅛ cwt.; tank, 10 gals.; 12-volt.

1300—£753+£346.7.4 p.t.=£1,099.7.4
1500—£785+£351.0.8 p.t.=£1,136.0.8

Abbreviations—g.c.—ground clearance; susp.—suspension; f.—front; r.—rear; comp.—compression; s.v.—side-valves; o.h.v.—overhead valves; o.h.c.—overhead camshaft; hyd.—hydraulic.

FIAT 2300

LARGEST car in the Fiat range, based on the 2100 but recently redesigned with a larger engine, disc brakes, semi-elliptic suspension (instead of coil springs and flexible radius arms) and a new front with four headlamps. Other features are reminder lights for handbrake and parking lamps, and extra direction indicators on the sides. The 1800, the economy six-cylinder, is also improved.

CLOSE-UP

Six-cyl.; o.h.v.; 78 × 79.5 mm.; 2,279 c.c.; 117 b.h.p.; 8.8 to 1 comp.; coil ign.; twin choke Weber carb.; 4-speed, 13.82, 8.15, 6.03, 4.30 to 1; col. lvr.; susp., f. ind. coil, r. half-elliptic; 4-door; 4/5-seat; disc brks.; max. 100 m.p.h.; cruise, 90; m.p.g. 22; whl. base, 8ft. 8½in.; track f. 4ft. 4⅜in., r. 4ft. 3½in.; lgth., 14ft. 7⅞in.; wdth., 5ft. 5⅜in.; ht. 4ft. 9⅞in.; g.c. 5⅜in.; turng. cir., 37ft. 8½in.; kerb wt., 24 cwt.; tank, 13½ gals.; 12-volt.

£1045 + £480.3.11 p.t. = £1525.3.11

FORD ANGLIA ESTATE CAR

THIS eye-catching Ford is now available as saloon or estate car, both using the same basic structure. Low fuel consumption, excellent road holding, and a maximum speed well over 70 m.p.h., obtained from a silent, over-square, overhead valve engine, all combine to make this car a winner in its class. There are 18 colour schemes for the estate car which has a surprising amount of room in the rear seats.

CLOSE-UP

Four-cyl.; o.h.v.; 80.96 × 48.41 mm.; 997 c.c.; 39 b.h.p.; 8.9 to 1 comp.; coil ign.; Solex carb.; 4-speed, 16.987, 9.884, 5.826, 4.125 to 1; cen. lvr.; susp., f. ind. coil, r. half-elliptic; 3-door; 4-seat; hyd. brks.; max. 75 m.p.h.; cruise, 65; m.p.g. 40-43; whl. base, 7ft. 6½in.; track f. 3ft. 10in.; r. 3ft. 9¾in.; lgth., 12ft. 10½in.; wdth., 4ft. 9⅜in.; ht. 4ft. 7½in.; g.c. 6⅜in.; turng. cir., 32ft.; kerb wt., 15¾ cwt.; tank, 7 gals.; 12-volt.

£465 + £214.7.3 p.t. = £679.7.3

FORD CONSUL CAPRI

LOW, sleek lines of specialist coachwork, but at a practical price are here in Ford's new venture for the owner who wants individual coupe styling and plenty of luggage space allied to the Consul Classic features. 1,340 c.c. engine, four-speed gearbox with steering-column control or central lever as you wish, four headlamps and disc front brakes. Side windows and rear quarter lights retract.

CLOSE-UP

Four-cyl.; o.h.v.; 80.96 × 65.07 mm.; 1,340 c.c.; 56.5 b.h.p.; 8.5 to 1 comp.; coil ign.; Zenith carb.; 4-speed, 16.99, 9.88, 5.83, 4.13 to 1; col or cen. lvr.; susp., f. ind. coil, r. half-elliptic; 2-door; 2-seat; hyd. brks., disc front; max. 80 m.p.h.; cruise, 70; m.p.g. 30-33; whl. base, 8ft. 3in.; track f. and r. 4ft. 1½in.; lgth., 14ft. 2½in.; wdth., 5ft. 5½in.; ht. 4ft. 4in.; g.c. 6½ in.; turng. cir., 34ft.; kerb wt., 18 cwt.; tank, 9 gals.; 12-volt.

£627 + £288.12.0 p.t. = £915.12.0

FORD CONSUL CLASSIC

THIS is Ford's big winner which came out new this summer. It has loads of new points—the first medium-priced car to incorporate twin headlamps and the first British car of its class with disc brakes in front as standard equipment. It cruises comfortably at 70 m.p.h. with little sense of speed, and no drumming or wind noise. The Classic's new 1,340 c.c., 56 b.h.p. engine is the smoothest and quietest in its class.

CLOSE-UP

Four-cyl.; o.h.v.; 80.96 × 65.07 mm.; 1,340 c.c.; 56 b.h.p.; 8.5 to 1 comp.; coil ign.; Zenith carb.; 4-speed, 16.99, 9.88, 5.83, 4.13 to 1; col. or cen. lvr.; susp., f. ind. coil, r. half-elliptic; 2 or 4-door; 4/5-seat; hyd. brks., disc front; max. 80 m.p.h.; cruise, 70; m.p.g. 30-33; whl. base, 8ft. 3in.; track f. and r. 4ft. 1½in.; lgth., 14ft. 2½in.; wdth., 5ft. 5½in.; ht. 4ft. 6½in.; g.c. 6½in.; turng. cir. 34ft.; kerb wt., 18 cwt.; tank, 9 gals.; 12-volt.

£525 + £241.17.3 p.t. = £766.17.3

Abbreviations—g.c.—ground clearance; susp.—suspension; f.—front; r.—rear; comp.—compression; s.v.—side-valves; o.h.v.—overhead valves; o.h.c.—overhead camshaft; hyd.—hydraulic.

73

FORD CONSUL DE LUXE

POWER-ASSISTED disc brakes as standard equipment now make this six-seater saloon super safe. The de luxe customer will also have the cosseting of two-tone colours, deep carpets, twin horns, a front-seat centre arm-rest, windscreen washers, bright metal wheel discs, a cigar lighter and coat hooks. A car that is tops in popularity and well deserves it. Its performance is matched by its road holding.

CLOSE-UP

Four-cyl.; o.h.v.; 82.55 × 79.5 mm.; 1,703 c.c.; 59 b.h.p.; 7.8 to 1 comp.; coil ign.; Zenith carb.; 3-speed, 11.67, 6.75, 4.11 to 1; col. lvr.; susp., f., coil, r., half-elliptic; 4-door; 6-seat; hyd. brks., disc front.; max. 80 m.p.h.; cruise 65; m.p.g. 28; whl. base 8ft. 8⅛in.; track f. 4ft. 5in., r. 4ft. 4in.; lgth. 14ft. 5⅞in.; wdth. 5ft. 8⅛in.; ht. 5ft.; g.c. 6⅜in.; turng. cir. 35ft.; kerb wt. 22¼ cwt.; tank 10½ gals.; 12-volt.

£598 + £275.6.5 p.t. = £873.6.5

FORD POPULAR

JUST topping the £500 tag the Popular is still one of the cheapest and best buys on the market. The 1,172 c.c. side-valve engine continues to give first-class service. People who have to look after the pence as well as the pounds cannot do better than consider this well-tried car which is really the old Anglia in a simplified and cheapened guise.

CLOSE-UP

Four-cyl.; s.v.; 63.25 × 92.5 mm.; 1,172 c.c.; 36 b.h.p.; 7 to 1 comp.; coil ign.; Solex carb.; 3-speed, 17.246, 8.889, 4.429 to 1; cen. lvr.; susp., f., ind. coil, r., half-elliptic; 2-door; 4-seat; hyd. brks.; max. 70 m.p.h.; cruise, 60; m.p.g. 28-32; whl. base, 7ft. 3in.; track, f., 4ft., r., 3ft. 11⅛in.; lgth. 12ft. 5¾in.; wdth., 5ft. 0⅛in.; ht., 4ft. 10¾in.; g.c., 7in.; turng. cir., 34ft. 6in.; kerb wt. 15 cwt.; tank, 7 gals.; 12-volt.

£348 + £160.14.9 p.t. = £508.14.9

FORD ZODIAC

WHILE Fords this year have been producing exciting new models, this one, their biggest and most powerful, continues to command maximum popularity. Showpiece from Dagenham, it has much more chrome and more luxury inside and out. A bold and beautiful car, it is a best-seller in many parts of the world. Power-assisted disc brakes in front are now standard.

CLOSE-UP

Six-cyl.; o.h.v.; 82.55 × 79.5 mm.; 2,553 c.c.; 85 b.h.p.; 7.8 to 1 comp.; coil ign.; Zenith carb.; 3-speed, 11.08, 6.40, 3.90 to 1; BW overdrive or auto. opt.; col. lvr.; susp., f., ind. coil, r., half-elliptic; 4-door; 6-seat; hyd. brks., disc front; max. 90 m.p.h.; cruise 75; m.p.g. 23-26; whl. base 8ft. 11in.; track f. 4ft. 5in., r., 4ft. 4in.; lgth. 15ft. 0½in.; wdth., 5ft. 8⅞in.; ht. 5ft. 0½in.; g.c. 6½in.; turng. cir. 36ft.; kerb wt., 23½ cwt.; tank, 10½ gals.; 12-volt.

£693 + £318.17.3 p.t. = £1,011.17.3

FORD TAUNUS 17M ESTATE CAR

ONE of the most-discussed styling jobs of recent years, Ford's German Taunus strikes a new note with its clean, curved lines and oval headlamps. Bodies include station wagon and two or four-door saloons. There is a choice of three- or four-speed gearboxes, each fully synchronised, and for countries where taxes are based on engine size, there is a 1.5-litre engine. Latest addition is a hotted-up sports saloon.

CLOSE-UP

Four-cyl.; o.h.v.; 84 × 76.7 mm.; 1,698 c.c.; 67 b.h.p.; 7 to 1 comp.; coil ign.; Solex carb.; 4-speed, 12.2, 7.01, 4.88, 3.56 to 1; col. lvr.; susp. f. ind. coil, r. half-elliptic; 3-door; 5-seat; hyd. brks.; max. 86 m.p.h.; cruise 75; m.p.g. 28-35; whl. base 8ft. 7⅛in.; track f. 4ft. 3in., r. 4ft. 2⅜in.; lgth. 14ft. 7⅛in.; wdth. 5ft. 5¾in.; ht. 4ft. 9in.; g.c. 7in.; turng. cir. 35ft.; kerb wt. 20 cwt.; tank, 10 gals.; 6-volt.

£860 + £395.8.1 p.t. = £1,255.8.1

Abbreviations—g.c.—ground clearance; susp.—suspension; f.—front; r.—rear; comp.—compression; s.v.—side-valves; o.h.v.—overhead valves; o.h.c.—overhead camshaft; hyd.—hydraulic.

FORD FALCON

MOST conventional of the American Compact cars, but also the most popular to date, the Falcon is now available in a big range of body styles and colour options, and its original 2.4-litre, six-cylinder engine has been supplemented by a 2.8-litre giving 100 horse-power for those who want more performance. Automatic transmission with fluid torque converter and two-speed epicyclic gearbox is an extra.

CLOSE-UP
Six-cyl.; o.h.v.; 88.9 × 74.64 mm.; 2,786 c.c.; 85 b.h.p.; 8.7 to 1 comp.; coil ign.; Ford carb.; 2-speed auto., 6.6, 3.2 to 1; col. lvr.; susp., f. ind. coil, r. half-elliptic; 2 or 4-door; 6-seat; hyd. brks.; max. 75 m.p.h.; cruise, 65; m.p.g. 22-24; whl. base, 9ft. 1½in.; track f. 4ft. 7in., r. 4ft. 6½in.; lgth., 15ft. 1in.; wdth., 5ft. 10½in.; ht. 4ft. 7in.; g.c. 6½in.; turng. cir., 38ft.; kerb wt., 21 cwt.; tank, 11½ gals.; 12-volt.

FORD THUNDERBIRD

LOW, clean-cut lines, armchair seats for four and the thrust of 300 horsepower make this America's most popular performance car; a success symbol for the younger executive or telepersonality. With passengers, it weighs two tons, but automatic transmission and power-assisted steering make it light to handle. Servo brakes are optional. Bodies are convertible and hard top coupe.

CLOSE-UP
Eight-cyl.; o.h.v.; 102.8 × 96 mm.; 6,384 c.c.; 300 b.h.p.; 9.6 to 1 comp.; coil ign.; Ford carb.; 3-speed auto., 7.2, 4.41, 3.0 to 1; col. lvr.; susp. f. ind. coil, r. half-elliptic; 2-door; 4-seat; hyd. servo brks.; max. 120 m.p.h.; cruise 90; m.p.g. 12-16; whl. base 9ft. 5in.; track f. 5ft. 1in., r. 5ft.; lgth. 17ft. 1in.; wdth. 6ft. 4in.; ht. 4ft. 4½in.; g.c. 5½in.; turng. cir. 41ft. 6in.; kerb wt. 37½ cwt.; tank, 16 gals.; 12-volt.
£2,800.5.9 + £1,284.14.6 p.t. = £4,085.0.3

FORD GALAXIE

BUILT in Detroit but also assembled in Canada for Commonwealth markets, the big Fords include this fine-looking 100 m.p.h. model offered in an immense range of body-styles and colour schemes. The choice of engines for the big Fords ranges from a 3.6-litre six giving a mere 135 h.p. to a great V8 of 6.3 litres producing 370 horse-power. Transmissions are manual, plus optional overdrive, or automatic.

CLOSE-UP
Eight-cyl.; o.h.v.; 101.6 × 88.9 mm.; 5,769 c.c.; 220 b.h.p.; 8.9 to 1 comp.; coil ign.; 2-choke carb.; 3-speed, 7.46, 4.45, 3.10 to 1; col. lvr., auto. opt.; susp., f. ind. coil, r. half-elliptic; 4-door; 6-seat; hyd. brks.; max. 95 m.p.h.; cruise, 70; m.p.g. 17-18; whl. base, 9ft. 11in.; track f. 5ft. 7in., r. 5ft. 7in.; lgth., 17ft. 5in.; wdth., 6ft. 8in.; ht. 4ft. 7in.; g.c. 7 in.; turng. cir., 41ft.; kerb wt., 33½ cwt.; tank, 16 gals.; 12-volt.

FRAZER-NASH

THIS is a London-built car for the individualist who likes his motoring tailored to suit himself. A first-class example of a well-proven model with a powerful engine, high cruising speed and more than a two-mile-a-minute maximum. Much of this comes from a splendid power-weight ratio, which stems from a tubular chassis and a light alloy body. It deserves its continued success.

CLOSE-UP
Eight-cyl.; o.h.v.; 82 × 75 mm.; 3,168 c.c.; 173 b.h.p.; 8.2 to 1 comp.; coil ign.; 2 downdraught carbs.; 4-speed 11.6, 7.1, 4.6, 3.4 to 1; cen. lvr.; susp., f., ind. trans. leaf, r., de Dion; 2-door; 2-seat; disc brks.; max. 135 m.p.h.; cruise 100; m.p.g. 28; whl. base, 8ft. 3in.; track, f., 4ft. 2in., r., 4ft. 5½in.; lgth. 13ft. 5in.; wdth., 5ft.; ht., 4ft. 3in.; g.c., 6½in.; turng. cir., 32ft.; kerb wt., 16½ cwt.; tank, 17 gals.; 12-volt.
£2,500 + £1,147.1.5 p.t. = £3,647.1.5

Abbreviations—g.c.—ground clearance; susp.—suspension; f.—front; r.—rear; comp.—compression; s.v.—side-valves; o.h.v.—overhead valves; o.h.c.—overhead camshaft; hyd.—hydraulic.

GLAS FLEETWING S1004

A BELT-DRIVEN overhead camshaft is a revolutionary feature of the four-cylinder engine on the Glas 1004 coupe, latest model from a German factory that specialises in economy cars. Original Goggomobils had two-stroke engines, air-cooled, mounted at the rear. This one has a front engine, water-cooled, driving the rear wheels. There are a number of other lively Goggomobil babies.

CLOSE-UP
Four-cyl.; o.h.c.; 72×61 mm.; 992 c.c.; 42 b.h.p.; 8.5 to 1 comp.; coil ign.; Solex carb.; 4-speed, 16.68, 8.466, 5.64, 4.25 to 1; cen. lvr.; susp., f. ind. coil, r. half-elliptic; 2-door; 2-seat; hyd. brks.; max. 84 m.p.h.; cruise, 75; m.p.g. 40; whl. base, 6ft. 10½in.; track f. 4ft. r. 3ft. 11½in.; lgth., 12ft. 6½in.; wdth., 4ft. 11in.; ht. 4ft. 5½in.; g.c. 7in.; turng. cir., 31ft. 3in.; kerb wt., 14¼ cwt.; tank, 8¾ gals.; 6-volt.

GOGGOMOBIL ROYAL

SALOON and estate car are the models in this range of sprightly economy cars from Germany. Motive power comes from a fan-cooled flat twin engine at the front, driving the rear wheels. The spare wheel lies flat above the engine, leaving extra space in the trunk accessible from inside or outside. A folding sun roof is among the optional extras. Also continued are the smaller Goggomobils with two-stroke engines at the rear.

CLOSE-UP
Two-cyl.; o.h.v. air-cooled; 78×72 mm.; 688 c.c.; 30 b.h.p.; 7.2 to 1 comp.; coil ign.; Solex carb.; 4-speed, 22.4, 11.35, 6.65, 5.0 to 1; cen. lvr.; susp., f., ind. coil, r., half-elliptic; 2-door; 4-seat; hyd. brks.; max. 69 m.p.h.; cruise, 55-60; m.p.g. 50; whl. base, 6ft. 7in.; track f., 3ft. 11½in., r., 3ft. 10in.; lgth., 11ft. 4in.; wdth., 4ft. 10in.; ht. 4ft. 6in.; g.c. 7½in.; turng. cir., 29ft. 6in.; kerb wt., 14½ cwt.; tank, 8¾ gals.; 12-volt.

£473+£217.16.1 p.t.=£690.16.1

HILLMAN HUSKY

THIS sprightly, small-sized station wagon continues as the smallest car from the Rootes Group, pending arrival of the much-publicised baby car for which a new factory is being built in Scotland. The Husky is a handy small-family car, with saloon and station wagon features. Rear seats fold flat and there is a big rear door. The car's snappy appearance remains unchanged.

CLOSE-UP
Four-cyl.; o.h.v.; 76.2×76.2 mm.; 1,390 c.c.; 51 b.h.p. 8 to 1 comp.; coil ign.; Zenith carb.; 4-speed, 14.87, 9.51, 6.8, 4.44 to 1; cen. lvr.; susp. f. ind. coil, r. half-elliptic; 3-door; 4-seat; hyd. brks.; max. 75 m.p.h.; cruise 60; m.p.g. 30; whl. base 7ft. 2in.; track f. 4ft. 1in., r. 4ft. 0½in.; lgth. 12ft. 5½in.; wdth. 5ft. 0½in.; ht. 4ft. 11½in.; g.c. 6½in.; turng. cir. 33ft. 6in.; kerb wt. 18¼ cwt.; tank, 6½ gals.; 12-volt.

£475+£218.18.11 p.t.=£693.18.11

HILLMAN MINX DE LUXE

THE new de luxe saloon now has the well-proved 1,592 c.c. engine raising its power output to 56½ b.h.p. With a higher rear axle ratio, top speed is now in excess of 80 m.p.h. The car has greater acceleration through the gears for safe overtaking and the brakes a total lining area of 121 square inches for better fade resistance and high efficiency.

CLOSE UP
Four-cyl.; o.h.v.; 81.5×76.2 mm.; 1,592 c.c.; 56.5 b.h.p.; 8.3 to 1 comp.; coil ign.; Zenith carb.; 4-speed, 15.816, 9.038, 5.877, 4.22 to 1; cen. lvr.; Easidrive auto. opt.; susp., f. ind. coil., r. half-elliptic; 4-door; 5-seat; hyd. brks.; max. 82 m.p.h.; cruise 70; m.p.g. 30-35; whl. base 8ft.; track f. 4ft. 1in., r. 4ft. 0½in.; lgth., 13ft. 6in.; wdth., 5ft. ½in.; ht. 4ft. 11½in.; g.c. 7in.; turng. cir., 36ft.; kerb wt., 20 cwt.; tank, 7¼ gals.; 12-volt.

£498+£229 p.t.=£727

Abbreviations—g.c.—ground clearance; susp.—suspension; f.—front; r.—rear; comp.—compression; s.v.—side-valves; o.h.v.—overhead valves; o.h.c.—overhead camshaft; hyd.—hydraulic.

HILLMAN SUPER MINX

THIS new roomier addition to the Minx line is planned for the family man. A longer wheelbase and smaller wheels give extra leg-room and the interior is wider. Safety-harness anchorages are built in, greasing points are reduced to three, and Easidrive automatic transmission is an optional extra. Power unit is the latest 1.6-litre engine with stronger crankshaft and larger big-end bearings.

CLOSE-UP

Four-cyl.; o.h.v.; 81.5×76.2 mm.; 1,592 c.c.; 66.25 b.h.p.; 8.3 to 1 comp.; coil ign.; Zenith carb.; 4-speed, 14.128, 9.038, 5.877, 4.22 to 1; cen. lvr.; susp., f. ind. coil, r. half-elliptic; 4-door; 4/5-seat; hyd. brks.; max. 84 m.p.h.; cruise 70; m.p.g. 28-32; whl. base, 8ft. 5in.; track f. 4ft. 3½in., r. 4ft. 0½in.; lgth., 13ft. 9in.; wdth, 5ft. 2½in.; ht. 4ft. 10½in.; g.c. 6.5in.; turng. cir., 36ft.; kerb wt. 21 cwt.; tank 11 gals.; 12-volt.

£585 + £269.7.3 p.t.= £854.7.3

HUMBER HAWK

DISC brakes and heater are now standard on this roomy upper-bracket family car. Bodywork is both elegant and imposing and the 2.2-litre Humber engine makes this model just the thing for hard but smart motoring in real comfort for up to six people. Fully automatic transmission or de Normanville overdrive in conjunction with a manual gearbox are available as extra-price options.

CLOSE-UP

Four-cyl.; o.h.v.; 81×110 mm.; 2,267 c.c.; 78 b.h.p.; 7.5 to 1 comp.; coil ign.; Zenith carb.; 4-speed, 14.128, 9.038, 5.877, 4.22 to 1; de Normanville overdrive opt.; col. lvr.; susp. f., ind. coil, r., half-elliptic; 4-door; 6-seat; servo brks., disc front; max. 85 m.p.h.; cruise 70-75; m.p.g. 20-25; whl. base 9ft. 2in.; track, f. 4ft. 9in., r., 4ft. 7½in.; lgth., 15ft. 4½in.; wdth. 5ft. 9½in.; ht., 5ft. 1in.; g.c., 7in.; turng. cir. 38 ft.; kerb wt. 28 cwt.; tank 12½ gals.; 12-volt.

£875 + £402.5.7 p.t.= £1,277.5.7

HUMBER SUPER SNIPE

FIRST example of four headlamps on a British car, this is the most luxurious and best-equipped model in the Rootes range. Built for the tycoon, it is silent and elegant, with a three-litre engine for effortless pick-up. Power-assisted steering and disc front brakes are matched by the luxury interior, which includes deeply upholstered seats, folding tables, ashtrays and cigar-lighter.

CLOSE-UP

Six-cyl.; o.h.v.; 87.3×82.55 mm.; 2,965 c.c.; 129 b.h.p; 8 to 1 comp.; coil ign.; Zenith carb.; 3-speed, 12.77, 7.34, 4.55 to 1; col. lvr., de Normanville overdrive or BW auto. opt.; susp., f., ind. coil, r., half-elliptic; 4-door; 6-seat; servo brks. disc front; max. 98 m.p.h.; cruise, 80; m.p.g., 20-25; whl. base, 9ft. 2in.; track, f., 4ft. 9in., r., 4ft. 7½in.; lgth., 15ft. 8in.; wdth., 5ft. 9½in.; ht., 5ft. 1in.; turng. cir., 38 ft.; kerb wt., 30 cwt.; tank, 12½ gals.; 12-volt.

£1,050 + £482.9.9 p.t.= £1,532.9.9

IMPERIAL

POWERFUL prestige model from the Chrysler group is identified by its four "free standing" headlamps. Improvements for 1962 include new lighter starter and automatic transmission, new suspended vacuum brake servo. No greasing is needed for the first 32,000 miles. New shrouds on headlamp filaments reduce glare, wiring connectors are simplified. Air conditioning with refrigeration is optional. Safety-harness anchorages are built-in.

CLOSE-UP

Eight-cyl.; o.h.v.; 106.2×95.25 mm.; 6,768 c.c.; 350 b.h.p.; 10 to 1 comp.; coil ign.; downdraught carb.; 3-speed auto., 7.18, 4.25, 2.93 to 1; press button control; susp., f. ind. torsion bar. r. half-elliptic; 2 or 4-door; 6-seat; hyd. brks.; max. 120 m.p.h.; cruise, 100; m.p.g. 18-22; whl. base, 10ft. 9in.; track f. 5ft. 5in., r. 5ft. 2½in.; lgth., 18ft. 11in.; wdth., 6ft. 9½in.; ht. 4ft. 9in.; g.c. 5½in.; turng. cir., 48ft. 9in.; kerb wt., 43½ cwt.; tank, 17 gals.; 12-volt.

Abbreviations—g.c.—ground clearance; susp.—suspension; f.—front; r.—rear; comp.—compression; s.v.—side-valves; o.h.v.—overhead valves; o.h.c.—overhead camshaft; hyd.—hydraulic.

JAGUAR E-TYPE

A REAL breakthrough in high-performance car design, this Jaguar gives racing speeds and handling with docility, gentle suspension and town appointments. Available in open two-seater and coupe models its streamlined unit-construction body shell hints at the power produced by its twin-cam six-cylinder engine. All-independent suspension, disc brakes and thermostatically controlled fan are featured.

CLOSE-UP

Six-cyl.; o.h.c.; 87×106 mm.; 3,781 c.c.; 265 b.h.p.; 9 to 1 comp.; coil ign.; 3 S.U. carbs.; 4-speed, 11.18, 6.16, 4.25, 3.31 to 1; cen. lvr.; susp., f. ind. torsion bar, r. ind. coil; 2-door; 2-seat; servo disc brks.; max. 150 m.p.h.; cruise, 130; m.p.g. 18-22; whl. base, 8ft.; track f. and r. 4ft. 2in.; lgth., 14ft. 7⅜in.; wdth., 5ft. 5¼in.; ht. 4ft. 0⅛in.; g.c. 5½in.; turng. cir., 39ft.; kerb wt. 24 cwt.; tank, 14 gals.; 12-volt.

£1,480+£679.6.11 p.t.=£2,159.6.11

JAGUAR 2.4 LITRE MARK 2

SMALLER-ENGINED than its lustier brothers, the Jaguar 2.4 continues to be a best-seller in its class in a score of markets. Many believe that it strikes just the right note, being a 100-miles-an-hour-plus car with a moderate fuel thirst. It is noted for its first-class road holding, splendid all-round vision and wonderful durability. A typical Jaguar, with luxurious finish at a moderate price.

CLOSE-UP

Six-cyl.; o.h.c.; 83×76.5 mm.; 2,483 c.c.; 120 b.h.p.; 8 to 1 comp.; coil ign.; 2 Solex carbs.; 4-speed, 14.42, 7.94, 5.48, 4.27 to 1; cen. lvr. de Normanville overdrive or BW auto. opt.; susp., f., ind. coil, r., cantilever leaf; 4-door; 5-seat; servo disc brks.; max. 105 m.p.h.; cruise, 75-70; m.p.g. 23; whl. base 8ft. 11¾in.; track, f., 4ft. 7in., r., 4ft. 5⅜in.; lgth. 15ft. 0¾in.; wdth., 5ft. 6⅝in.; ht., 4ft. 9in.; g.c. 7in.; turng. cir. 33ft. 6in.; kerb wt. 28¼ cwt.; tank, 12 gals.; 12-volt.

£1,082+£496.14.2 p.t.=£1,578.14.2

JAGUAR 3.4/3.8 LITRE MARK 2

BRILLIANT in conception as in performance, these cars continue in the Jaguar range, with many minor refinements—such things as new door sealing and higher efficiency heater, and a dozen other well-thought-out improvements. Put together they make the blueprint for another bumper year for sales not only here but throughout the world. Choice of two engine sizes, with manual or automatic gearboxes.

CLOSE-UP

Six-cyl.; o.h.c.; 83×106 mm.; 3,442 c.c.; 210 b.h.p.; 8 to 1 comp. or 87×106 mm.; 3,781 c.c.; 220 b.h.p.; coil ign.; 2 S.U. carbs.; 4-speed, 11.95, 6.58, 4.54, 3.54 to 1; BW auto. or de Normanville overdrive opt.; cen. lvr.; susp., f., ind. coil; r., cantilever leaf; 4-door; 5-seat; servo disc brks.; max. 120 m.p.h. (3.4), 125 m.p.h. (3.8); cruise 90-100; m.p.g. 16-23; whl. base 8ft. 11⅜in.; track, f., 4ft. 7in., r., 4ft. 5⅜in.; lgth. 15ft. 0¾in.; wdth. 5ft. 6¾in.; ht. 4ft. 9in.; g.c. 7in.; turng. cir. 33ft. 6in.; kerb wt. 29¼ cwt.; tank, 12 gals.; 12-volt.

3.4 — £1,177+£540.9.5 p.t.=£1,717.9.5
3.8 — £1,255+£576.4.5 p.t.=£1,831.4.5

JAGUAR MARK X

THIS is possibly the best-looking car ever built by Jaguars, who specialise in good-looking cars. Stemming from the Mark X and "E" type models, it is an entirely new 4/5-seater of unit construction. Engine is the XKS type developing 265 b.h.p, and it has independent suspension and disc brakes fitted on all four wheels. A real thoroughbred beauty with a racing pedigree.

CLOSE UP

Six-cyl.; o.h.c.; 87×106 mm.; 3,781 c.c.; 265 b.h.p.; 9 to 1 comp.; coil ign.; 3 S.U. carbs.; 4-speed, 11.95, 6.58, 4.54, 3.54 to 1; (overdrive or auto. opt.); cen. lvr.; susp., f. and r. ind. coil; 4-door; 5-seat; servo disc brks.; max. 115 m.p.h.; cruise, 90; m.p.g. 15-20; whl. base, 10ft.; track f. and r. 4ft. 10in.; lgth., 16ft. 10in.; wdth., 7ft. 4⅜in.; ht., 4ft. 6¾in.; g.c. 6¾in.; turng. cir., 36ft.; tank, 20 gals.; 12-volt.

£1,640+£752.18.1 p.t.=£2,392.18.1

Abbreviations—g.c.—ground clearance; susp.—suspension; f.—front; r.—rear; comp.—compression; s.v.—side-valves; o.h.v.—overhead valves; o.h.c.—overhead camshaft; hyd.—hydraulic.

JENSEN 541

BIGGER body and lower rated engine modify Jensen's character; more comfort, lower maximum, but still an easy 100 m.p.h. cruising speed. Four-speed gearbox is an alternative to the automatic. Body panels are plastic on a tubular chassis. Front wings and bonnet lift for access to engine. Four luxurious armchair seats, with safety harness for those in front.

CLOSE-UP
Six-cyl.; o.h.v.; 87×111 mm.; 3,993 c.c.; 7.4 to 1 comp.; coil ign.; 3 S.U. carbs.; 4-speed auto., 11.19, 7.70, 4.24, 2.93 to 1; col. lvr.; susp. f. ind. coil, r. half-elliptic; 2-door; 4-seat; disc servo brks.; max. 110 m.p.h.; cruise, 100; m.p.g. 16-20; whl. base, 8ft. 9in.; track f. 4ft. 6 5/16 in., r. 4ft. 7½in.; lgth. 14ft. 10in.; wdth. 5ft. 7in.; ht. 4ft. 6⅜in.; g.c. 7in.; turng. cir. 37ft. 7in.; kerb wt. 30 cwt.; tank, 15 gals.; 12-volt.
£2,255+£1,034.15.7 p.t.=£3,289.15.7

LAGONDA RAPIDE

NEW touring flier from the David Brown Group has a 4-litre light alloy engine, automatic transmission and disc brakes. Superleggera 5-seater body styled by Touring of Milan has light alloy panels on steel tube frame welded to a platform chassis. Fuel tanks in the wings free extra luggage space. Rear window de-mister, radio with electrically controlled aerial and electric window lifts are included.

CLOSE-UP
Six-cyl.; o.h.c.; 96×92 mm.; 3,995 c.c.; 236 b.h.p.; 8.25 to 1 comp.; coil ign.; 2 Solex carbs.; 3-speed auto., 8.7, 5.41, 3.77 to 1; col. lvr.; susp., f. ind. coil, r. de Dion, torsion bar; 4-door; 5-seat; disc servo brks.; max. 125 m.p.h.; cruise, 100; m.p.g. 16-18; whl. base, 9ft. 6in.; track f. 4ft. 6in., r. 4ft. 7½in.; lgth. 16ft. 3½in.; wdth., 5ft. 9½in.; ht. 4ft. 8in.; g.c. 6in.; turng. cir., 40ft. 6in.; kerb wt., 33¾ cwt.; tank, 16½ gals.; 12-volt.
£3,600+£1,651.4.9 p.t.=£5,251.4.9

LANCIA FLAMINIA

THIS light-weight Zagato coupe with 117 b.h.p. engine and disc brakes is the fastest of the Flaminia models. Other models include the four-headlamp Superleggera coupe and convertible, the Pininfarina coupe and the standard four-door saloon, also Farina-styled. The V6 o.h.v. engine driving to a rear-mounted gearbox in unit with the differential anticipated recent American developments.

CLOSE-UP
Six-cyl.; o.h.v.; 80×81.5 mm.; 2,458 c.c.; 102 b.h.p.; 8 to 1 comp.; coil ign.; Solex or Weber carb.; 4-speed, 12.3, 7.6, 5.6, 3.75 to 1; col. lvr.; susp., f., ind. coil, r., de Dion half-elliptic.; 4-door; 6-seat; disc brks.; max. 105 m.p.h.; cruise 90; m.p.g. 24-28; whl. base 9ft. 5in.; track, f. and r. 4ft. 6in.; lgth. 15ft. 11in.; wdth. 5ft. 9in.; ht. 4ft. 9½in.; g.c. 5½in.; turng. cir. 40ft.; kerb wt. 29½ cwt.; tank, 12¾ gals.; 12-volt.
£2,469+£1,132.17.3 p.t.=£3,601.17.3

LANCIA FLAVIA

HUNDREDS of Lancia's chunky new front-drive cars are coming into England, for this car succeeds the Aprilia, an old favourite with British drivers. Flat-four light alloy engine and four-speed all-synchromesh gearbox, in a rubber-insulated sub frame to damp out noise. Disc brakes by Dunlop. Interior in Lancia's discreet quality style, with an unusual grouping of instruments and controls.

CLOSE-UP
Four-cyl.; o.h.v.; 82×71 mm.; 1,500 c.c.; 78 b.h.p.; 8.3 to 1 comp.; coil ign.; Solex or Weber carb.; 4-speed, 16.16, 9.53, 6.71, 4.09 to 1; col. lvr.; susp. f. ind. trans. leaf, r. half-elliptic; 4-door; 5-6 seat; disc brks.; max. 95 m.p.h.; cruise 85; m.p.g. 26-32; whl. base 8ft. 8¼in., track f. 4ft.3in., r. 4ft. 2in.; lgth. 15ft. 0½in.; wdth. 5ft. 3in.; ht. 4ft. 11in.; g.c. 5in.; turng. cir. 36ft.; kerb wt. 24 cwt.; tank, 10½ gals.; 12-volt.
£1,499+£688.12.0 p.t.=£2,187.12.0

LINCOLN CONTINENTAL

TOP-PRICE luxury car of the Ford line with a range that includes America's only four-door convertible. Guaranteed for two years, including parts and labour. The price includes power operation for steering, brakes and windows, radio, heater and automatic transmission. A warning light flashes if a rear door is not properly closed. Bumpers and grille are modified for 1962.

CLOSE-UP

Eight-cyl.; o.h.v.; 109.2×93.9 mm.; 7,045 c.c.; 300 b.h.p.; 10 to 1 comp.; coil ign.; Carter carb.; 3-speed auto, 6.85, 4.04, 2.89 to 1; col. lvr.; susp., f. ind. coil, r. half-elliptic; 4-door; 5-seat; hyd. servo brks.; max. 110 m.p.h.; cruise, 90; m.p.g. 11-15; whl. base, 10ft. 3in.; track f. and r. 5ft. 2in.; lgth., 17ft. 9in.; wdth., 6ft. 6in.; ht. 4ft. 5¾in.; g.c. 5⅛in.; turng. circ., 48ft.; kerb wt., 44¼ cwt.; tank, 17½ gals.; 12-volt.

£3,515+£1,612 p.t.=£5,127

LOTUS ELITE

THE unique race-winning coupe, almost unbeatable in its class. Body-chassis in plastic, all-independent suspension developed from Grand Prix experience, Coventry Climax engine and disc brakes. Gran Turismo model has more than 100 horsepower and does more than 120 m.p.h., but it is practical, too, with a surprising amount of luggage space. ZF gearbox is optional, with synchromesh on all speeds.

CLOSE-UP

Four-cyl.; o.h.c.; 76.2×66.6 mm.; 1,216 c.c.; 75 b.h.p.; 10 to 1 comp.; coil ign.; S.U. carb.; 4-speed, 16.5, 9.9, 5.94, 4.5 to 1; cen. lvr.; susp. f. ind. coil, r. ind. coil; 2-door; 2-seat; disc brks.; max. 116 m.p.h.; cruise 90; m.p.g. 28-33; whl. base 7ft. 4in.; track, f. and r., 3ft. 11in.; lgth. 12ft. 6in.; wdth. 4ft. 10in.; ht. 3ft. 10in.; g.c. 6½in.; turng. cir. 31ft.; kerb wt. 11 cwt.; tank, 6½ gals.; 12-volt.

£1,375+£631 p.t.=£2,006

LOTUS SEVEN

LATEST development of the simple lightweight sports car that helped to found the Lotus fame. Available fully assembled or sold separately as parts for the do-it-yourself enthusiast, this lean light-weight is available with Ford, B.M.C. or Coventry Climax engines. Latest option is the Ford Classic engine of 1,340 c.c. Tubular space frame, with panels of light alloy and cowlings in glass fibre.

CLOSE-UP

Four-cyl.; s.v.; 63×92.5 mm.; 1,172 c.c.; 36 b.h.p.; 8.5 to 1 comp.; coil ign.; S.U. carb.; 3-speed, 17.3, 9.78, 4.875 to 1; cen. lvr.; susp. f. ind. coil, r. coil; 2-seat; hyd. brks.; max. 95 m.p.h.; cruise 80; m.p.g. 35-40; whl. base 7ft. 4in.; track f. and r. 3ft. 11in.; lgth. 10ft. 3in.; wdth. 4ft. 5in.; ht. 2ft. 11in.; g.c. 5in.; turng. cir. 30ft. 3in.; kerb wt. 7¼ cwt.; tank 7¼ gals.; 12-volt.

Kit form: £499 basic

MERCEDES BENZ 180

LOWEST-PRICED model in the Mercedes range, the 180 is well equipped with padded steering-wheel, windscreen washer, padded visors and instrument panel, heater with air ducts to demist side windows, anti-dazzle mirror and safety locks. The 180D is the diesel-engined version with a new, larger overhead camshaft power unit of 1,988 c.c., giving 52.4 h.p. It does 68 m.p.h. and 37-45 m.p.g.

CLOSE-UP

Four-cyl.; o.h.c.; 85×83.6 mm.; 1,897 c.c.; 78 b.h.p.; 7 to 1 comp.; coil ign.; Solex carb.; 4-speed, 15.79, 9.28, 5.96, 3.9 to 1; col. lvr.; susp., f. and r. ind. coil; 4-door; 5-seat; hyd. brks.; max. 84 m.p.h.; cruise, 75; m.p.g. 25-27; whl. base, 8ft. 8in.; track f. 4ft. 8¾in., r. 4ft. 10½in.; lgth., 14ft. 9½in.; wdth., 5ft. 8½in.; ht. 5ft. 10in.; g.c. 7½in.; turng. cir., 35ft. 1in.; kerb wt., 23 cwt.; tank, 12¼ gals.; 12-volt.

£1,275+£585.12.3 p.t.=£1,860.12.3

Abbreviations—g.c.—ground clearance; susp.—suspension; f.—front; r.—rear; comp.—compression; s.v.—side-valves; o.h.v.—overhead valves; o.h.c.—overhead camshaft; hyd.—hydraulic.

MERCEDES BENZ 190

A NEW Mercedes with wide appeal, the 190 now has the same body as the sixes but with slightly shorter wheelbase. Swing axle rear suspension with compensating spring, all-synchromesh gearbox, safety pad on steering wheel. 190D is the same car with newly enlarged diesel engine of 1988 cc. giving 60 b.h.p. It is said to do 78 m.p.h. and 33–43 m.p.g.

CLOSE-UP

Four-cyl.; o.h.c.; 85×83.6 mm.; 1,897 c.c.; 90 b.h.p.; 8.7 to 1 comp.; coil ign.; Solex carb.; 4-speed, 16.6, 9.75, 5.53, 4.1 to 1; col. lvr.; susp. f. and r. ind. coil; 4-door; 5/6-seat; hyd. brks. servo opt.; max. 90 m.p.h.; cruise 75; m.p.g. 25-34; whl. base 8ft. 10⅜in.; track f. 4ft. 9¾in., r. 4ft. 10¼in.; lgth. 15ft. 6½in.; wdth. 5ft. 10¼in.; ht. 4ft. 10¾in.; g.c. 7¼in.; turng. cir. 37ft. 5in.; kerb wt. 24½ cwt.; tank, 11¼ gals.; 12-volt.

£1,362+£625.9.9 p.t.=£1,987.9.9

MERCEDES BENZ 220S

MEDIUM-PRICED model in the 220 six-cylinder range, the 220S has twin carburetters, servo brakes. The 220SE has fuel injection engine. Recent additions are 220SE coupe and convertible with less marked tail fins, disc front brakes by Girling and central gear levers. Equipment includes safety padded steering-wheel, hand grips in the roof, recessed interior door handles and padded instrument panel.

CLOSE-UP

Six-cyl.; o.h.c.; 80×72.8 mm.; 2,195 c.c.; 124 b.h.p.; 8.7 to 1 comp.; coil ign.; 2 Solex carbs.; 4-speed, 14.92, 9.68, 6.27, 4.1 to 1; col. lvr.; susp. f. and r. ind. coil; 4-door; 5/6-seat; hyd. servo brks.; max., 102 m.p.h.; cruise, 90; m.p.g. 26; whl. base 9ft. 0½in.; track f. 4ft. 9¾in., r. 4ft. 10½in.; lgth. 16ft. 0½in.; wdth. 5ft. 10¼in.; ht. 4ft. 11½in.; g.c. 7½in.; turng. cir. 37ft. 5in.; kerb wt. 26½ cwt.; tank 14½ gals.; 12-volt.

£1,847+£847.15.7 p.t.=£2,694.15.7

MERCEDES BENZ 300SE

HIGH-SPEED luxury from Stuttgart. An advanced design with light alloy fuel injection engine, four-speed automatic transmission with manual override, all-independent air suspension, power-assisted steering and disc brakes with anti-dive device to prevent skids if you brake in a corner. The cooling fan is thermostatically controlled to reduce noise and fuel consumption. Air conditioning with refrigerator is optional.

CLOSE-UP

Six-cyl.; o.h.c.; 85×88 mm.; 2,996 c.c.; 250 b.h.p.; 8.55 to 1 comp.; coil ign.; Bosch injection; 4-speed, 12.16, 7.17, 5.06, 3.64 to 1; cen. lvr.; susp. f. and r. ind. coil; 2-door; 2-seat; servo disc brks.; max. 120 m.p.h.; cruise 100-110; m.p.g. 15-24; wh. base 7ft. 10½in.; track f. 4ft. 10⅜in., r. 4ft. 10⅜in.; lgth. 15ft.; wdth. 5ft. 10½in.; ht. 4ft. 3½in.; g.c. 5¼in.; turng. cir. 37ft. 6in. kerb wt. 26¾ cwt.; tank, 22 gals.; 12-volt.

MERCURY MONTEREY

COST of maintenance is slashed on this luxurious medium-priced model from the Ford group. The chassis needs no greasing for 30,000 miles, engine oil is changed every 6,000 miles and brakes are self-adjusting. Choose from a six-cylinder engine giving 138 b.h.p. or three V.8s giving from 170 to 300 h.p. Transmission is three-speed manual or two-speed automatic with torque converter.

CLOSE-UP

Eight-cyl.; o.h.v.; 95.25×83.82 mm.; 4,785 c.c.; 170 b.h.p.; 8.8 to 1 comp.; coil ign.; Ford carb.; 2-speed auto., 5.25, 3.00 to 1; col. lvr.; susp., f. ind. coil, r. half-elliptic; 4-door; 6-seat; hyd. brks. servo opt.; max. 105 m.p.h.; cruise, 85; m.p.g. 14-17; whl. base, 10ft.; track f. 5ft. 1in., r. 5ft.; lgth. 17ft. 11½in.; wdth., 6ft. 7½in.; ht. 4ft. 7in.; g.c. 7in.; turng. cir., 41ft. 6in.; kerb wt., 35 cwt.; tank, 16½ gals.; 12-volt.

£1,916+£879 p.t.=£2,795

M.G. MIDGET

SPORTS-CAR enthusiasts champion the re-appearance of the famous little Midget which comes from a line of M.G.s dating back to 1929. Re-introduced version has a modern, full-width body, which gives exceptional elbow room for the passengers, and an engine, a little under a litre in capacity, which produces a top speed of 86 m.p.h. It follows the M.G. tradition of speed with safety.

CLOSE-UP

Four-cyl.; o.h.v.; 62.9×76.2 mm.; 948 c.c.; 50 b.h.p.; 9 to 1 comp.; coil ign.; 2 S.U. carbs.; 4-speed, 13.50, 8.08, 5.73, 4.22 to 1; cen. lvr.; susp., f. ind. coil, r. quarter-elliptic; 2-door; 2/3-seat; hyd. brks.; max. 86 m.p.h.; cruise 70; m.p.g. 33-38; whl. base 6ft. 8in.; track f. 3ft. 9¾in., r. 3ft. 8¾in.; lgth. 11ft. 4¼in.; wdth. 4ft. 5in.; ht. 4ft. 1¾in.; g.c. 5in.; turng. cir. 31ft. 2½ in.; kerb wt. 13¾ cwt.; tank, 6 gals.; 12-volt.

£472 + £217.11.5 p.t. = £689.11.5

MGA 1600 MARK II

ENGINE capacity increase of 34 c.c. plus minor styling changes identify this year's model. Maximum speed is now comfortably clear of 100 m.p.h. Scuttle top and facia are covered in matt plastic, the radiator grille and rear lamp clusters have been redesigned, and safety-belt attachments are standard. For competition work the MGA now enters the international category for cars up to 2 litres.

CLOSE-UP

Four-cyl.; o.h.v.; 76.2×88.9 mm.; 1,622 c.c.; 90 b.h.p.; 8.9 to 1 comp.; coil ign.; 2 S.U. carbs.; 4-speed, 14.909, 9.079, 5.632, 4.1 to 1; cen. lvr.; susp. f. ind. coil, r. half-elliptic; 2-door; 2-seat; hyd. brks. disc front; max. 101 m.p.h.; cruise 85; m.p.g. 22-26; whl. base 7ft. 10in.; track, f. 3ft. 11½in., r. 4ft. 0¾in.; lgth. 13ft.; wdth. 4ft. 10in.; ht. 4ft. 2in.; g.c. 6in.; turng. cir. 30ft. 6in.; kerb wt. 18 cwt.; tank 10 gals.; 12-volt.

£663 + £305.2.3 p.t. = £968.2.3

M.G. MAGNETTE Mk.IV

EXTRA punch from the bigger 1,622 c.c. engine means still more sparkling performance from the Farina-bodied Magnette which has already outsold all its predecessors. Wider track at front and rear improves high-speed stability, and the expert eye will spot many other improvements to this popular family sports saloon. The luggage trunk is enormous, and the colour schemes are new.

CLOSE-UP

Four-cyl.; o.h.v.; 76.2×88.9 mm.; 1,622 c.c.; 65 b.h.p.; 8.3 to 1 comp.; coil ign.; 2 S.U. carbs.; 4-speed, 15.64, 9.52, 5.91, 4.3 to 1; cen. lvr., auto. opt.; susp., f. ind. coil, r. half-elliptic; 4-door; 4-seat; hyd. brks.; max. 88 m.p.h.; cruise, 75; m.p.g. 23-29; whl. base, 8ft. 4½in.; track f. 4ft. 2⅝in.; r. 4ft. 3⅞in.; lgth. 14ft. 6½in.; wdth. 5ft. 3½in.; ht. 4ft. 10⅞in.; g.c. 5⅞in.; turng. cir., 37ft.; kerb wt., 22¾ cwt.; tank, 10 gals.; 12-volt.

£725 + £333.10.7 p.t. = £1,058.10.7

MORGAN PLUS FOUR

THIS is a 100-mile-an-hour plus car that comes at a relatively low price. It is built by a privately owned company which operates in the west country. They have been making distinctive 2/4-seat tourers for a long time. The 1962 models continue with disc brakes and lowered steering ratios for driving ease. There is plenty of power from the sturdy 2-litre engine. The 4/4 now has the Ford Classic 1,340 c.c unit.

CLOSE-UP

Four-cyl.; o.h.v.; 83×92 mm.; 1,991 c.c.; 100 b.h.p.; 8.5 to 1 comp.; coil ign.; 2 S.U. carbs.; 4-speed, 12.85, 7.38, 5.24, 3.73 to 1; cen. lvr.; susp., f. ind. coil, r. half-elliptic; 2-door; 2/4-seat; hyd. brks.; disc front; max. 105 m.p.h.; cruise 85; m.p.g. 32; whl. base 8ft.; track f. and r. 3ft. 11in.; lgth. 12ft.; wdth. 4ft. 8in.; ht. 4ft. 3in.; g.c. 7in.; turng. cir. 33ft.; kerb wt. 16½ cwt.; tank, 11 gals.; 12-volt.

£655 + £301.8.11 p.t. = £956.8.11

Abbreviations—g.c.—ground clearance; susp.—suspension; f.—front; r.—rear; comp.—compression; s.v.—side-valves; o.h.v.—overhead valves; o.h.c.—overhead camshaft; hyd.—hydraulic.

MORRIS MINI-COOPER

BIGGER engine and disc front brakes in a Gran Turismo version which takes full advantage of the Mini's amazing road holding. Designed in collaboration with Coopers, builders of World Champion Grand Prix cars, the twin carburetter 997 c.c. engine produces an extra 21 horsepower to give a near-90 maximum speed. Remote control gear lever, proper inside door-handles, de luxe finish throughout.

CLOSE-UP

Four-cyl.; o.h.v.; 62.43×81.28 mm.; 997 c.c.; 55 b.h.p.; 9 to 1 comp.; coil ign.; 2 S.U. carbs.; 4-speed, 12.05, 7.213, 5.11, 3.765 to 1; cen. lvr.; susp., f. and r. ind. rubber; 2-door; 4-seat; hyd. brks., disc front; max. 88 m.p.h.; cruise, 75; m.p.g. 36-40; whl. base, 6ft. 8$\frac{5}{32}$in.; track f. 3ft. 11$\frac{7}{16}$in.; r. 3ft. 9$\frac{7}{8}$in.; lgth., 10ft. 0$\frac{1}{4}$in.; wdth., 4ft. 7$\frac{1}{2}$in.; ht. 4ft. 5in.; g.c. 6$\frac{3}{8}$in.; turng. cir., 31ft.; kerb wt., 11$\frac{1}{2}$ cwt.; tank, 5$\frac{1}{2}$ gals.; 12-volt.

£465+214.7.3 p.t.=£679.7.3.

MORRIS MINOR 1000

MORE than a million sold—first time for any British car. A family favourite for the past 13 years the Minor is the perfect runabout, easy to park and with a cruising speed on the flat of anything up to 70 m.p.h. With exceptional luggage capacity, elegance and economical running, this model should continue to attract the discriminating small car driver for some time to come.

CLOSE-UP

Four-cyl.; o.h.v.; 62.9×76 mm.; 948 c.c.; 37 b.h.p.; 8.3 to 1 comp.; coil ign.; S.U. carb.; 4-speed, 16.507, 10.802, 6.425, 4.555 to 1; cen. lvr.; susp., f. ind. torsion bar, r. half-elliptic; 2-door; 4-seat; hyd. brks.; max. 75 m.p.h.; cruise 55; m.p.g. 36-48; whl. base 7ft. 2in.; track f. 4ft. 2$\frac{5}{8}$in., r. 4ft. 2$\frac{1}{4}$in.; lgth. 12ft. 4in.; wdth. 5ft. 1in.; ht. 5ft.; g.c. 6$\frac{3}{4}$in.; turng. cir. 33ft.; kerb wt. 14$\frac{3}{4}$ cwt.; tank, 6$\frac{1}{2}$ gals.; 12-volt.

£416+£191.17.3 p.t.=£607.17.3

MORRIS OXFORD VI

THIS new Morris Oxford has been given a clever face-lift and a bigger heart. This is to say it now comes out with improvements to the bodywork and with a larger engine. Under the bonnet is a 1,622 c.c. power plant developing six b.h.p. more than its predecessor. A first-class car that serves as brilliantly for private use as for business purposes, it is roomier and more comfortable than ever.

CLOSE-UP

Four-cyl.; o.h.v.; 76.2×88.9 mm.; 1,622 c.c.; 55 b.h.p.; 8.3 to 1 comp.; coil ign.; S.U. carb.; 4-speed, 15.64, 9.52, 5.91, 4.3 to 1; col. or cen. lvr.; susp., f. ind. coil, r. half-elliptic; 4-door; 4-seat; hyd. brks.; max. 80 m.p.h.; cruise, 65; m.p.g. 25-33; whl. base, 8ft. 4$\frac{1}{4}$in.; track f. 4ft. 2$\frac{5}{8}$in., r. 4ft. 3$\frac{3}{8}$in.; lgth., 14ft. 6$\frac{1}{2}$in.; wdth. 5ft. 3$\frac{1}{2}$in.; ht. 4ft. 10$\frac{7}{8}$in.; g.c. 5$\frac{7}{8}$in.; turng. cir., 37ft.; kerb wt., 21$\frac{3}{4}$ cwt.; tank, 10 gals.; 12-volt.

£595+£273.18.11 p.t.=£868.18.11

MOSKVITCH

DISTINCT improvement in finish is apparent as Russia's car manufacturers set out to sell in western markets. The Moskvitch, like all Soviet cars, is solidly built with a high ground clearance to cope with rutted dirt roads, and its engine is designed for low-grade fuels. A radiator blind and powerful heater deal with severe winters. A full tool-kit helps maintenance where there are no garages.

CLOSE-UP

Four-cyl.; o.h.v.; 76×75 mm.; 1,360 c.c.; 45 b.h.p.; 7 to 1 comp.; coil ign.; downdraught carb.; 4-speed, 17.89, 11.39, 7.83, 4.71 to 1; col. lvr.; susp. f. ind. coil, r. half-elliptic; 4-door; 4-seat; hyd. brks.; max. 72 m.p.h.; cruise 50; m.p.g. 35; whl. base 7ft. 9in.; track f. and r. 4ft.; lgth. 13ft. 4in.; wdth. 5ft. 1in.; ht. 5ft. 1$\frac{1}{4}$in.; g.c. 7$\frac{3}{4}$in.; turng. cir. 39$\frac{1}{2}$ft.; kerb wt. 18$\frac{3}{4}$ cwt.; tank 7$\frac{3}{4}$ gals.; 12-volt.

£535+£246 p.t.=£781

Abbreviations—g.c.—ground clearance; susp.—suspension; f.—front; r.—rear; comp.—compression; s.v.—side-valves; o.h.v.—overhead valves; o.h.c.—overhead camshaft; hyd.—hydraulic.

NSU PRINZ 4

NEW roomier body with seats for four, and a big front trunk, propelled by the Sport Prinz 36 horsepower engine, rear mounted, make this version of the Prinz a practical small family car. Air cushions supplement coil springs in its independent rear suspension, and the gearbox has synchromesh on all four speeds. There are only two greasing points on the chassis, which keeps down maintenance costs.

CLOSE-UP

Two-cyl.; o.h.c. air-cooled; 76×66 mm.; 598 c.c.; 36 b.h.p.; 7.5 to 1 comp.; coil ign.; Solex carb.; 4-speed, 19.89, 10.61, 6.77, 4.80 to 1; cen. lvr.; susp., f. and r. ind. coil; 2-door; 4-seat; hyd. brks.; max. 74 m.p.h.; cruise, 65; m.p.g. 50; whl. base, 6ft. 8in.; track f. 4ft. 0½in., r. 3ft. 11½in.; lgth., 11ft. 6in.; wdth., 4ft. 10½in.; ht. 4ft. 5½in.; g.c. 7in.; turng. cir., 28ft.; kerb wt., 11 cwt.; tank, 8 gals.; 12-volt.

OLDSMOBILE SUPER 88

THE Holiday Sedan, one of the re-styled Super 88 models, features longer, lower, sportier lines. There are 17 body styles. For engines there is a choice of 8.75 to 1 compression, giving 260 b.h.p., or the 10.25 to 1 unit running on top-grade fuel to produce 330 h.p. A high capacity heater is standard, and chassis greasing has been almost eliminated. Power-assisted brakes (optional) are self-adjusting.

CLOSE-UP

Eight-cyl.; o.h.v.; 104.7×93.7 mm.; 6,456 c.c.; 330 b.h.p.; 10.25 to 1 comp.; coil ign.; Rochester carb.; 3-speed, 6.94, 3.97, 3.23 to 1; col. lvr., auto. opt.; susp., f. ind. coil, r. coil; 4-door; 6-seat; hyd. brks.; max. 115 m.p.h.; cruise, 90; m.p.g. 14; whl. base, 10ft. 3in.; track f. 5ft. 1in., r. 5ft. 1in.; lgth., 17ft. 9¾in.; wdth., 6ft. 5⅞in.; ht. 4ft. 7¾in., g.c. 5½in.; turng. cir., 46ft. 3in.; kerb wt., 37½ cwt.; tank, 17 gals.; 12-volt.

£2,540+£1,165 p.t.=£3,705

OLDSMOBILE F-85

THE new Cutlass convertible, an addition to the range of compact Oldsmobiles with light alloy V8 engines, has bucket front seats, four-barrel carburetter and extra-high compression. There is also a Cutlass coupe. Saloons have extra rear leg-room and the output of the optional air conditioning system is increased. Styling changes include new bonnet, grille and body side mouldings and re-designed interiors.

CLOSE-UP

Eight-cyl.; o.h.v.; 88.9×71.12 mm.; 3,531 c.c.; 155 b.h.p.; 8.75 to 1 comp.; coil ign.; twin-choke carb.; 3-speed, 7.91, 4.77, 3.08 to 1, auto opt.; col. lvr.; susp. f. ind. coil, r. coil; 4-door; 5-seat; hyd. brks.; max. 93 m.p.h.; cruise 80; m.p.g. 17-23; whl. base 9ft. 4in.; track f. and r. 4ft. 8in.; lgth. 15ft. 8½in.; wdth. 5ft. 11½in.; ht. 4ft. 2½in.; g.c. 5in.; turng. cir. 37ft.; kerb wt. 22¾ cwt.; tank, 13 gals.; 12-volt.

£1,830+£840 p.t.=£2,670

PANHARD PL17

A FRENCH car of unique character. See its roomy interior and cavernous trunk. See it cruising in the seventies on main roads and motorways, then marvel at the tiny flat-twin engine that drives the front wheels. Torsion bars are used for valve springs as well as for rear suspension. Tiger is the Monte Carlo Rally winner with hotter engine developing 50 h.p. and special interior finish.

CLOSE-UP

Two-cyl.; o.h.v.; air-cooled; 85×75 mm.; 850 c.c.; 42 b.h.p.; 7.2 to 1 comp.; coil ign.; Zenith carb.; 4-speed, 16.495, 9.277, 6.148, 4.525 to 1; col. lvr.; susp. f. transv. ind., r. torsion bar. 4-door; 5-seat; hyd. brks.; max. 80 m.p.h.; cruise 70; m.p.g. 47; whl. base 8ft. 10 1/16 in.; track f. and r. 4ft. 3½in.; lgth. 15ft. 0¾in.; wdth. 5ft. 5 5/16 in.; ht. 4ft. 9½in.; g.c. 6¼in.; turng. cir. 31ft.; kerb wt. 15¾ cwt.; tank, 9½ gals.; 12-volt.

£633+£291 p.t.=£924

Abbreviations—g.c.—ground clearance; susp.—suspension; f.—front; r.—rear; comp.—compression; s.v.—side-valves; o.h.v.—overhead valves; o.h.c.—overhead camshaft; hyd.—hydraulic.

PEUGEOT 403

TOURISTS in France see this rugged five-seater everywhere. At a glance it is a large 1½-litre car with a good deal that is unorthodox. Example: of the four forward speeds in an all-synchromesh gearbox, third is a direct drive and fourth is a geared-up indirect ratio for 80 m.p.h. cruising. A big boot and reclining seats also make an appeal.

CLOSE-UP
Four-cyl.; o.h.v.; 80×73 mm.; 1,468 c.c.; 65 b.h.p.; 7 to 1 comp.; coil ign.; Solex carb.; 4-speed, 17.5, 9.44, 5.75, 4.33 to 1; col. lvr.; susp. f. ind. transv. leaf, r. coil.; 4-door; 5/6-seat; hyd. brks.; max. 85 m.p.h.; cruise 70-75; m.p.g. 30; whl. base 8ft. 9in.; track f. 4ft. 4⅜in., r. 4ft. 4in.; lgth. 14ft. 8in.; wdth. 5ft. 6in.; ht. 4ft. 11½in.; g.c. 6in.; turng. cir. 28ft. 9in.; kerb wt. 21 cwt.; tank, 11 gals.; 12-volt.

£775+£356.8.11 p.t.=£1,131.8.11

PEUGEOT 404

PROVING reliable and selling well, the 404 looks like making itself a reputation as respected as that of the 403, which is already a byword for reliable motoring in France. The 404 has a four-cylinder engine canted on its side, four synchronised gears and strut-type front suspension. Styled by Pininfarina, it looks both solid and swift—and it is. A convertible has just been added to the range.

CLOSE-UP
Four-cyl.; o.h.v.; 84×73 mm.; 1,618 c.c.; 72 b.h.p.; 7.2 to 1 comp.; coil ign.; Solex carb.; 4-speed, 17.4, 9.29, 5.97, 4.2 to 1; col. lvr.; susp. f. ind. coil, r. coil; 4-door; 5-seat; hyd. brks.; max. 90 m.p.h.; cruise 75-80; m.p.g. 30-32; whl. base 8ft. 8½in.; track f. 4ft. 5in., r. 4ft. 2⅜in.; lgth. 14ft. 7in.; wdth 5ft. 5⅜in.; ht. 4ft. 9in.; g.c. 6in.; turng. cir. 31ft. 7in.; kerb wt. 20½ cwt.; tank 11 gals.; 12-volt.

£915+£420.12.3 p.t.=£1,335.12.3

PLYMOUTH FURY

ONCE among America's top-selling popular makes, Plymouth is promoted into the medium-price class by arrival of the cheaper "compacts". The high-powered Fury V8, with engine of over 5-litres giving 225 h.p. has terrific performance. Other models have six-cylinder engines of 3.7 litres, or V8s. of 5.9, with a vast choice of bodies: saloons, hardtop coupes, convertibles and station wagons.

CLOSE-UP
Eight-cyl.; o.h.v. 98.55×84.07 mm.; 5,130 c.c.; 225 b.h.p.; 9 to 1 comp.; col. ign.; Carter carb.; 3-speed auto., 6.76, 3.0, 2.76 to 1; press button control; susp., f. ind. torsion bar, r. half-elliptic; 4-door; 6-seat; hyd. servo brks.; max. 102 m.p.h.; cruise, 85; m.p.g. 13-18; whl. base, 9ft. 8in.; track f. 4ft. 11½in., r. 4ft. 9in.; lgth., 16ft. 10in.; wdth., 6ft. 3in.; ht. 4ft. 6in.; g.c. 7¾in.; turng. cir., 40ft. 3in.; kerb wt. 30 cwt.; tank 16½ gals.; 12-volt.

PONTIAC CATALINA

ONE of the lower-priced models among the big Pontiacs, with seven different body styles. Wheelbase and over-all length are increased, against the compact trend, the V8 engines are improved and the chassis requires no greasing for 35,000 miles. Pontiac's range extends from the compact four-cylinder Tempest, with front engine and rear gearbox, to the Bonneville with V8 engine delivering up to 348 horse-power.

CLOSE-UP
Eight-cyl.; o.h.v.; 106×95.25 mm.; 6,374 c.c.; 267 b.h.p.; 8.6 to 1 comp.; coil ign.; Rochester carb.; 4-speed auto., 12.8, 8.23, 5.0, 3.23 to 1; col. lvr.; susp., f. ind. coil, r. coil; 4-door; 6-seat; hyd. servo brks.; max. 105 m.p.h.; cruise, 80; m.p.g. 14-17; whl. base, 10ft.; track f. 5ft. 3½in.; r. 5ft. 4in.; lgth., 17ft. 7⅜in.; wdth., 6ft. 6½in.; ht. 4ft. 10⅞in.; g.c. 6½in.; turng. cir., 42ft. 9in.; kerb wt., 42½ cwt.; tank, 17½ gals.; 12-volt.

Abbreviations—g.c.—ground clearance; susp.—suspension; f.—front; r.—rear; comp.—compression; s.v.—side-valves; o.h.v.—overhead valves; o.h.c.—overhead camshaft; hyd.—hydraulic.

PORSCHE STANDARD

THOUGH retaining the low-drag contours which have given it an unbeatable combination of high speed and fuel economy, the Porsche is now available in a variety of styles—streamlined coupe, convertible, roadster, hard-top. A new shape for the fuel tank frees extra luggage space in front, glass areas are larger. Variable-speed wipers, electric clock and gear-lever lock are now standard.

CLOSE-UP

Four-cyl.; o.h.v. air-cooled; 82.5 × 74 mm.; 1,582 c.c.; 75 b.h.p.; 7.5 to 1 comp.; coil ign.; 2 Zenith carbs.; 4-speed, 13.9, 7.7, 4.9, 3.5 to 1; cen. lvr.; susp. f. and r. ind. torsion bar; 2-door; 2/4-seat; hyd. brks.; max. 100 m.p.h.; cruise 80-85; m.p.g. 33-35; whl. base 6ft. 11in.; track f. 4ft. 3½in., r. 4ft. 1½in.; lgth. 12ft. 11½in.; wdth. 5ft. 5½in.; ht. 4ft. 3½in.; g.c. 6in.; turng. cir. 36ft.; kerb wt. 16½ cwt.; tank, 11½ gals.; 6-volt.

£1,530 + £702.5.3 p.t. = £2,232.3.2

PORSCHE SUPER 90

CONTINUING the conservative policy of steady development and improvement which has earned them a world-wide reputation, Porsche have made few but useful changes. Windscreen and rear window are bigger, giving better all-round vision, a re-designed fuel tank gives more space for luggage and the filler is now accessible externally. Latest addition is the 2-litre o.h.c. Carrera.

CLOSE-UP

Four-cyl.; o.h.v. air-cooled; 82.5 × 74 mm.; 1,582 c.c.; 90 b.h.p.; 9 to 1 comp.; coil ign.; 2 Solex carbs.; 4-speed, 15.5, 8.57, 5.49, 3.96 to 1; cen. lvr.; susp. f. and r. ind. torsion bar; 2-door; 2/4-seat; hyd. brks.; max. 105 m.p.h.; cruise 90; m.p.g. 30-35; whl. base 6ft. 11in.; track f. 4ft. 3½in., r. 4ft. 1½in.; lgth. 12ft. 11½in.; wdth. 5ft. 5½in.; ht. 4ft. 3½in.; g.c. 6in.; turng. cir. 36ft.; kerb wt. 16½ cwt.; tank, 11½ gals; 6-volt.

£1,824 + £837.0.3 p.t. = £2,661.0.3

RAMBLER AMERICAN

CONTINUING its highly successful David-and-Goliath act, the Rambler American challenges the best the big American corporations can do, for it was the pioneer Compact car, and still has a strong attraction with its clean-cut confident styling. There is a choice of two six-cylinder engines with side or overhead valves, manual or automatic transmission, and a full range of body styles.

CLOSE-UP

Six-cyl.; o.h.v.; 79.37 × 107.95 mm.; 3,205 c.c.; 90 b.h.p.; 8 to 1 comp.; coil ign.; Carter carb.; 3-speed, 9.4, 6.15, 3.78 to 1; col. lvr.; susp., f. ind. coil, r. half-elliptic; 2 or 4-door; 5-seat; hyd. brks.; max. 85 m.p.h.; cruise, 70; m.p.g. 28; whl. base, 8ft. 4in.; track f. 4ft. 6in., r. 4ft. 7in.; lgth., 14ft. 5in.; wdth., 5ft. 10in.; ht. 4ft. 8in.; g.c. 7in.; turng. cir., 36ft.; kerb wt., 22½ cwt.; tank, 16½ gals.; 12-volt.

RELIANT SABRE

RACY new sports model from a company which has previously specialised in three-wheeler utility vehicles. A Ford Consul engine in a light chassis is the recipe for performance with low upkeep costs. The gearbox has synchromesh on all speeds; front brakes are discs. Front suspension is by coil struts; rear axle is located by Watt linkage. Equipment includes cigarette-lighter, windscreen washers.

CLOSE-UP

Four-cyl.; o.h.v.; 82.6 × 79.5 mm.; 1,703 c.c.; 61 b.h.p.; 7.8 to 1 comp.; coil ign.; Zenith carb.; 4-speed, 9.0, 6.0, 4.37, 3.55 to 1; cen. lvr.; susp.; f. ind. coil strut, r. coil; 2-door; 2-seat; hyd. brks. disc front; max. 90 m.p.h.; cruise, 75; m.p.g. 25-28; whl. base, 7ft. 6in.; track f. and r. 4ft.; lgth., 13ft. 9in.; wdth., 5ft. 1in.; ht. 4ft. 2in.; g.c. 6in.; turng. cir., 30ft.; tank, 8½ gals.; 12-volt.

£773 + £355.10.7 p.t. = £1,128.10.7

RENAULT R4

THE new go-anywhere, do-anything car with countless uses—family saloon, light van, station wagon, camping car all in one. Lightweight seats, quickly removable. Four side doors and a big one at the back. Folding top optional. High ground clearance and all independent suspension. Successor to the famous 4 CV with the same engine, but front-mounted and driving the front wheels.

CLOSE-UP

Four-cyl.; o.h.v.; 54.5×80 mm.; 747 c.c.; 26.5 b.h.p.; 8.5 to 1 comp.; coil ign.; Solex carb.; 3-speed, 15.675, 7.598, 4.282 to 1; dash lvr.; susp., f. and r. torsion bar; 5-door; 4-seat; hyd. brks.; max. 61 m.p.h.; cruise, 50; m.p.g. 45-50; whl. base, 8ft.; track f. 4ft. 1in.; r. 3ft. 11½in.; lgth., 11ft. 11½in.; wdth., 4ft. 10½in.; ht. 5ft. 4in.; g.c. 7½in.; turng. cir., 31ft.; kerb wt., 11¼ cwt.; tank, 5¾ gals.; 6-volt.

£399 + £184.2.3. p.t. = £583.2.3

RENAULT DAUPHINE

FOUR speed gears are now offered on this French best seller. Speeds up to 70 m.p.h., 40 m.p.g. and high manoeuvrability made this car a natural for London's new minicab service. Its rear engine leaves plenty of room for luggage beneath the bonnet. Heater, town and country horns and parking lights are standard. This is a really good looking practical "baby" with a French air and a lively performance.

CLOSE-UP

Four-cyl.; o.h.v.; 58×80 mm.; 845 c.c.; 30 b.h.p.; 7.75 to 1 comp.; coil ign.; Solex carb.; 3-speed, 16.1, 7.88, 4.52 to 1; 4-speed opt.; susp., f. ind. coil, r. ind. coil and pneu.; 4-door; 4-seat; hyd. brks.; max. 75 m.p.h.; cruise, 60; m.p.g. 42-48; whl. base, 7ft. 5½in.; track f. 4ft. 1½in.; r. 4ft.; lgth., 12ft. 11½in.; wdth., 5ft.; ht. 4ft. 9in.; g.c. 6in.; turng. cir., 29ft.; kerb wt., 12⅜ cwt.; tank, 7 gals.; 12-volt.

£479 + £220.15.7 p.t. = £699.15.7

RENAULT DAUPHINE GORDINI

HERE is the high performance version of the Dauphine, with Floride-type engine, four-speed gearbox, special colour schemes and much more luxurious finish. Extra features include adjustable backrests and foam overlays for front seats, plastic foam under-carpets, different wheels, screen-washer and lock on engine compartment. Add the normal Dauphine features: steering lock, town and country horns, parking lamps.

CLOSE-UP

Four-cyl.; o.h.v.; 58×80 mm.; 845 c.c.; 40 b.h.p.; 8 to 1 comp.; coil ign.; Solex carb.; 4-speed, 16.1, 9.1, 6.3, 4.52 to 1; cen. lvr.; susp., f. ind. coil, r. ind. coil and pneu.; 4-door; 4-seat; hyd. brks.; max. 80 m.p.h.; cruise, 70; m.p.g. 40-45; whl. base, 7ft. 5½in.; track f. 4ft. 1½in.; r. 4ft.; lgth., 13ft.; wdth., 5ft.; ht. 4ft. 9in.; g.c. 6in.; turng. cir., 29ft.; kerb wt., 12½ cwt.; tank, 7 gals.; 12-volt.

£546 + £251.9.9 p.t. = £797.9.9

RENAULT FLORIDE

IN spite of its name, the Floride looks really French and feminine and the ladies quickly fall for its chic. Mechanically based on the Dauphine, and available as fixed-head coupe or convertible, this spirited little filly from the Renault stables gives up to 80 m.p.h. and cruises comfortably at 60 m.p.h. Special cylinder head gives an extra eight horsepower. Gearbox has four speeds.

CLOSE-UP

Four-cyl.; o.h.v.; 58×80 mm.; 845 c.c.; 40 b.h.p.; 8 to 1 comp.; coil ign.; Solex carb.; 4-speed, 16.1, 9.1, 6.3, 4.52 to 1; cen. lvr.; susp. f. ind. coil, r. ind. coil and pneu.; 2-door; 2/4-seat; hyd. brks.; max. 83 m.p.h.; cruise 60; m.p.g. 39-43; whl. base 7ft. 5½in.; track f. 4ft. 1½in.; r. 4ft.; lgth. 14ft.; wdth. 5ft. 1½in.; ht. 4ft. 3½in.; g.c. 7in.; turng. cir. 29ft. 10in.; kerb wt. 15 cwt.; tank, 7 gals.; 12-volt.

£818 + £376.3.1 p.t. = £1,194.3.1

Abbreviations—g.c.—ground clearance; susp.—suspension; f.—front; r.—rear; comp.—compression; s.v.—side-valves; o.h.v.—overhead valves; o.h.c.—overhead camshaft; hyd.—hydraulic.

RILEY ELF

APPOSITE name for a clever version of the B.M.C.'s twin babies. With the new Riley radiator treatment the car takes on fresh good looks, and there is a slight addition to the engine output, power going up from 34 to 38 b.hp. Interior refinements also raise the class of the car to suit the faithful enthusiasts of the Riley badge. An addition well worth while, to bring you mini motoring in style.

CLOSE-UP
Four-cyl.; o.h.v.; 62.94×68.26 mm.; 848 c.c.; 37 b.h.p.; 8.3 to I comp.; coil ign.; S.U. carb.; 4-speed, 13.657, 8.176, 5.31, 3.765 to I; cen. lvr.; susp., f. and r. ind. rubber; 2-door; 4-seat; hyd. brks.; max. 73 m.p.h.; cruise, 65; m.p.g. 42-45; whl. base, 6ft. 8 5/32 in.; track f. 3ft. 11¾in.; r. 3ft. 9⅞in.; lgth., 10ft. 8⅜in.; wdth., 4ft. 7½ in.; ht. 4ft. 5in.; g.c. 6⅜in.; turng. cir., 31ft.; kerb wt., 11¾ cwt.; tank, 5½ gals.; 12-volt.

£475+£218.18.11 p.t.=£693.18.11

RILEY 4/72

SUCCESSOR to the 4/68, this most opulent of the medium-sized B.M.C. cars boasts a larger engine for 1962, and the new Borg Warner automatic transmission is an optional extra. Front suspension has an anti-roll bar, and a stabiliser bar is added at the rear. A wider track makes more room in the rear seat, and a change in steering ratio produces lighter steering.

CLOSE-UP
Four-cyl.; o.h.v.; 76.2×88.9 mm.; 1,622 c.c.; 65 b.h.p.; 8.3 to I comp.; coil ign.; 2 S.U. carbs.; 4-speed, 15,64, 9.52, 5.91, 4.3 to I; cen. lvr.; susp., f. ind. coil, r. half-elliptic; 4-door; 4-seat; hyd. brks.; max. 88 m.p.h.; cruise, 75; m.p.g. 23-29; whl. base, 8ft. 4¼in.; track f. 4ft. 2⅝in.; r. 4ft. 3⅜in.; lgth., 14ft. 6½in.; wdth., 5ft. 3in.; ht. 4ft. 10⅞in.; g.c. 5⅞in.; turng. cir., 37ft.; kerb wt., 22¾ cwt.; tank, 10 gals.; 12-volt.

£745+£342.13.11 p.t.=£1,087.13.11

RILEY ONE-POINT-FIVE

THIS well-known, lively small family car, which has had its share of sporting successes, is identified for 1962 by revised front grille. Inside, modifications to seats increase the comfort. Figured walnut instrument panel and leather upholstery supply the touches of quality in the Riley tradition. The engine has twin carburetters and a neat remote control gear-lever complements the sporting character.

CLOSE-UP
Four-cyl.; o.h.v.; 73.025×88.9 mm.; 1,489 c.c.; 60 b.h.p.; 8.3 to I comp.; coil ign.; 2 S.U. carbs.; 4-speed, 13.56, 8.25, 5.12, 3.73 to I; cen. lvr.; susp. f. ind. torsion bar, r. half-elliptic; 4-door; 4-seat; hyd. brks.; max. 85 m.p.h.; cruise 70; m.p.g. 25-35; whl. base 7ft. 2in.; track f. 4ft. 2⅝in., r. 4ft. 2 5/16 in.; lgth. 12ft. 9in.; wdth. 5ft. 1in.; ht. 4ft. 11¾in.; g.c. 6½in.; turng. cir. 34ft. 3in.; kerb wt. 18½ cwt.; tank, 7 gals.; 12-volt.

£580+£267.1.5 p.t.=£847.1.5

ROLLS-ROYCE SILVER CLOUD II

YOU glide up to 90 m.p.h. for cruising and top 110 m.p.h. in this magnificent, silent showpiece. So popular has it proved that no changes have been thought to be necessary. For the wealthy private owner there is a shorter wheelbase with closed bodywork and a choice of four windows. For the chauffeur there is a longer wheelbase, a glass partition and six windows.

CLOSE-UP
Eight-cyl.; o.h.v.; 104.14×91.44 mm.; 6,230 c.c.; 8 to I comp.; coil ign.; 2 S.U. carbs.; 4-speed auto. 11.75, 8.10, 4.46, 3.08 to I; col. lvr.; susp. f. ind. coil, r. half-elliptic; 4-door; 5/6-seat; hyd. servo brks.; max. 110 m.p.h.; cruise 90; m.p.g. 12-15; whl. base 10ft. 3in.; track f. 4ft. 10in., r. 5ft.; lgth. 17ft. 7¾in.; wdth. 6ft. 2¾in.; ht. 5ft. 4in.; g.c. 7in.; turng. cir. 41ft. 8in.; kerb wt. 41½ cwt.; tank, 18 gals.; 12-volt.

£4,300+£1.972.1.5 p.t.=£6,272.1.5

ROLLS ROYCE PHANTOM V

A CAR fit for a queen. Regal presence, spacious nine-seater interior and silence even at 100 m.p.h. V8 engine, automatic transmission, power-assisted brakes and steering in a long chassis with coachwork by Britain's top craftsmen at Park Ward and James Young. Cocktail cabinet, pigskin fittings, electric division, dual heater are standard. Extras include electric window lifts and air conditioning with refrigerator.

CLOSE-UP

Eight-cyl.; o.h.v.; 104.14×91.44 mm.; 6,230 c.c.; 8 to 1 comp.; coil ign.; 2 S.U. carbs.; 4-speed auto. 14.86, 10.23, 5.64, 3.89 to 1; col. lvr.; susp. f. ind. coil, r. half-elliptic; 4-door; 7-seat; hyd. servo brks.; max. 100 m.p.h.; cruise 85; m.p.g. 12; whl. base 12ft.; track f. 5ft. 0⅜in., r. 5ft. 4in.; lgth. 19ft. 10in.; wdth. 6ft. 7in.; ht. 5ft. 9in.; g.c. 7¼in.; turng. cir. 48ft. 9in.; tank, 23 gals.; 12-volt.

£7.050+£3,232.9.9 p.t.=£10,282.9.9

ROVER 80

HIGH-speed long-distance driving, sight-seeing or just shopping—are all tasks well within the capabilities of this smart, versatile saloon. De Normanville overdrive and front disc brakes are provided. Standard fittings include fitted tool kit, tinted transparent sun visors and hide upholstery throughout. An exceptionally quiet four-cylinder engine maintains cruising speeds of 70 m.p.h. and an 80 m.p.h. maximum.

CLOSE-UP

Four-cyl.; o.h.v.; 90.47×88.8 mm.; 2,286 c.c.; 77 b.h.p.; 7 to 1 comp.; coil ign.; Solex carb.; 4-speed, 14.51, 8.78, 5.92, 4.3 to 1; cen. lvr.; de Normanville overdrive; susp. f. ind. coil, r. half-elliptic.; 4-door; 4/5-seat; servo brks. disc front; max. 82 m.p.h.; cruise 65; m.p.g. 18-25; whl. base 9ft..3in.; track f. 4ft. 4½in., r. 4ft. 3½in.; lgth. 14ft. 10½in.; wdth. 5ft. 5⅝in.; ht. 5ft. 3½in.; g.c. 7¼in.; turng. cir. 37ft.; kerb wt. 29 cwt.; tank, 11½ gals.; 12-volt.

£985+£452.13.11 p.t.=£1,437.13.11

ROVER 100

TOP craftsmanship with years of Rover know-how combine to make the 100 one of Britain's best-built cars. Its keynote is quality throughout, coupled with good looks and a well-designed engine. It is the car favoured by the class who spurn gimmicks. Twin S.U. petrol pumps have been fitted to give more reliability. The additional pump is operated by a switch mounted on the instrument panel.

CLOSE-UP

Six-cyl.; o.h. inlet, s. exhaust; 77.3×92.075 mm.; 2,625 c.c.; 104 b.h.p.; 7.8 to 1 comp.; coil ign.; S.U. carb.; 4-speed, 14.51, 8.78, 5.92, 4.3 to 1; cen. lvr.; de Normanville overdrive; susp. f. ind. coil, r. half-elliptic; 4-door; 4/5-seat; servo brks. disc front; max. 94 m.p.h.; cruise 75; m.p.g. 18-25; whl. base 9ft. 3in.; track f. 4ft. 4½in., r. 4ft. 3½in.; lgth. 14ft. 10in.; wdth. 5ft. 5⅝in.; ht. 5ft. 3¾in.; g.c. 7¼in.; turng. cir. 37ft.; kerb wt. 29½ cwt.; tank, 11½ gals.; 12-volt.

£1,085+£498.10.7 p.t.=£1,583.10.7

ROVER 3-LITRE

POWER is the keynote of this, the most powerful of the Rovers. Power-assisted steering takes the effort out of parking. Cruising at 80 m.p.h. is easy with this lusty six-cylinder engine, while discreet design ensures lasting comfort. Disc front brakes, adjustable facia air ducts, and rubber insulated front sub frame are standard. Choose between automatic or manual transmission with the addition of de Normanville overdrive.

CLOSE-UP

Six-cyl.; o.h. inlet, s. exhaust; 77.8×105 mm.; 2,995 c.c.; 115 b.h.p.; 8.75 to 1 comp.; coil ign.; S.U. carb.; 4-speed, 14.5, 8.78, 5.92, 4.3 to 1; cen. lvr. de Normanville overdrive; BW auto. opt.; susp. f. ind. torsion bar, r. half-elliptic; 4-door; 5/6-seat; servo brks. disc front; max. 98 m.p.h.; cruise 75; m.p.g. 18-25; whl. base 9ft. 2½in.; track f. 4ft. 7½in., r. 4ft. 8in.; lgth. 15ft. 6½in.; wdth. 5ft. 10in.; g.c. 7¼in.; turng. cir. 38ft. 6in.; kerb wt. 32½ cwt.; tank, 14 gals.; 12-volt.

£1,258+£577.16.5 p.t.=£1,835.16.5

Abbreviations—g.c.—ground clearance; susp.—suspension; f.—front; r.—rear; comp.—compression; s.v.—side-valves; o.h.v.—overhead valves; o.h.c.—overhead camshaft; hyd.—hydraulic.

SAAB 96

DESIGNED for Sweden's dusty summers and hard winters, the Saab has scored many international successes, including an outright win in the R.A.C. rally. Three-cylinder, two-stroke engine, and front-wheel drive within a streamlined shape. This gives surprising passenger space. Radiator blind for engine temperature control, air extractors on the body to demist the rear window. There is a station wagon, too.

CLOSE-UP
Three-cyl.; two-stroke; 70×72.9 mm.; 841 c.c.; 42 b.h.p.; 7.3 to 1 comp.; coil ign.; Zenith carb.; 3-speed, 17.19, 8.53, 5.23 to 1; col. lvr.; susp. f. ind. coil, r. coil; 2-door; 4/5-seat; hyd. brks.; max. 75 m.p.h.; cruise 70; m.p.g. 34; whl. base 8ft. 2in.; track f. and r. 4ft.; lgth. 13ft. 2in.; wdth. 5ft. 2in.; ht. 4ft. 10in.; g.c. 7½in.; turng. cir. 36ft.; kerb wt. 16¼ cwt.; tank, 8½ gals.; 12-volt.

£624 + £287.4.9 p.t. = £911.4.9

SIMCA ARONDE

A BRIGHT medium family car, the Aronde is available as Etoile Saloon, Monaco hardtop, Oceane coupe, Plein Ciel convertible or Castel station wagon. Its five-bearing engine has proven reliability and endurance with cruising speeds over the 70 m.p.h. mark, and 35 m.p.g., economy. Reclining seats and special cushion contours give comfort for the family. Montlhery Special engine now develops 70 b.h.p.

CLOSE-UP
Four-cyl.; o.h.v.; 74×75 mm.; 1,290 c.c.; 62 b.h.p.; 8.5 to 1 comp.; coil ign.; Solex carb.; 4-speed, 16.4, 10.43, 6.53, 4.44 to 1; col. lvr.; susp., f. ind. coil, r. coil and half-elliptic; 4-door; 4-seat; hyd. brks.; max. 82 m.p.h.; cruise, 70; m.p.g. 32-35; whl. base, 8ft. 0½in.; track f. 4ft. 1½in.; r. 4ft. 1½in.; lgth., 13ft. 9½in.; wdth., 5ft. 1½in.; ht. 4ft. 8½in.; g.c. 5½in.; turng. cir., 35ft. 4in.; kerb wt., 18½ cwt.; tank, 9⅝ gals.; 12-volt.

SIMCA ARONDE MONTLHERY

IN the Simca constellation the Montlhery is the sports saloon with the latest 70 h.p. version of the four-cylinder, five-bearing engine. Monaco is the four-seater, two-door coupe with the same engine. Seats have 10-position adjustable back-rests; heater, windscreen-washer, horn ring are standard equipment; a sliding roof is optional. Latest addition to the Simca range is the rear-engined small car.

CLOSE-UP
Four-cyl.; o.h.v.; 74×75 mm.; 1,290 c.c.; 70 b.h.p.; 8.5 to 1 comp.; coil ign.; Solex carb.; 4-speed, 18.25, 11.20, 7.0, 4.77 to 1; col. lvr.; susp., f. ind. coil, r. half-elliptic; 4-door; 4/5-seat; hyd. brks.; max. 87 m.p.h.; cruise, 75; m.p.g. 27-34; whl. base, 8ft. 0½in.; track f. 4ft. 1½in.; r. 4ft. 1½in.; lgth., 13ft. 9in.; wdth., 5ft. 1½in.; ht. 4ft. 8½in.; g.c. 5½in.; turng. cir., 35ft. 4in.; kerb wt., 18½ cwt.; tank, 9⅝ gals.; 12-volt.

SIMCA ARIANE

SIMCA'S Rush Super engine with five-bearing crankshaft boosts the performance of the roomy Ariane economy model. Body and chassis are developed from those originally used for the French Ford V8, acquired when Simca took over the works at Poissy outside Paris. A fold-down rear seat creates extra luggage space, and an adjustable back-rest for the front bench seat is an optional extra.

CLOSE-UP
Four-cyl.; o.h.v.; 74×75 mm.; 1,290 c.c.; 62 b.h.p.; 8.5 to 1 comp.; coil ign.; Solex carb.; 4-speed, 17.8, 11.2, 4.77 to 1; col. lvr.; susp., f. ind. coil, r. half-elliptic; 4-door; 5/6-seat; hyd. brks.; max. 78 m.p.h.; cruise, 65; m.p.g. 25-30; whl. base, 8ft. 10in.; track f. 4ft. 6in.; r. 4ft. 5in.; lgth., 14ft. 10in.; wdth., 5ft. 9in.; ht. 4ft. 10½in.; g.c. 6in.; turng. cir., 37ft. 6in.; kerb wt., 21¾ cwt.; tank, 13 gals.; 12-volt.

SINGER GAZELLE

BIGGER 1.6 litre engine and higher rear-axle ratio in the 1962 car gives higher cruising speed and a better petrol consumption. The heater is now standard equipment, and there are many other refinements in this well-established luxury family car. It has a four-speed gearbox operated by a short remote control floor lever, and both automatic or manual transmission are available. The frame is strengthened for greater stiffness.

CLOSE-UP
Four-cyl.; o.h.v.; 81.5×76.2 mm.; 1,592 c.c.; 56.5 b.h.p.; 8.3 to 1 comp.; coil ign.; Zenith carb.; 4-speed, 15.816, 9.038, 5.877, 4.22 to 1; cen. lvr. de Normanville overdrive or Easidrive auto. opt.; susp. f. ind. coil, r. half-elliptic; 4-door; 4/5-seat; hyd. brks.; max. 82 m.p.h.; cruise 70; m.p.g. 30-35; whl. base 8ft.; track f. 4ft. 1in., r. 4ft. 0½in.; lgth. 13ft. 7½in.; wdth. 5ft. 0¾in.; ht. 4ft. 11½in.; g.c. 7in.; turng. cir. 36ft.; kerb wt. 20¾ cwt.; tank, 10 gals.; 12-volt.

£575+£264.15.7 p.t.=£839.15.7

SINGER VOGUE

HERE is a new quality model in the Rootes range, for buyers interested in the popular 1.6-litre class. Longer wheel-base than Gazelle and smaller wheels ensure extra interior space, and the trunk is big enough for holiday touring, but over-all size remains compact. Mechanical features: heftier crankshaft than in previous Singers; paper element air-cleaner, rubber anti-vibration sleeve on propeller shaft, longer and wider rear springs.

CLOSE-UP
Four-cyl.; o.h.v.; 81.5×76.2 mm.; 1,592 c.c.; 66 b.h.p.; 8.3 to 1 comp.; coil ign.; Solex carb.; 4-speed, 14.128, 9.038, 5.877, 4.22 to 1; de Normanville overdrive or Easidrive auto. opt.; cen. lvr.; susp. f. ind. coil, r. half-elliptic; 4-door; 4/5-seat; hyd. brks.; max. 84 m.p.h.; cruise 70; m.p.g. 28-32; whl. base 8ft. 5in.; track f. 4ft. 3½in., r. 4ft. 0½in.; lgth. 13 ft. 9½in.; wdth. 5ft. 2½in.; ht. 4ft. 10½in.; g.c. 6½in.; turng. cir. 36ft.; kerb wt. 22 cwt.; tank, 11 gals.; 12-volt.

£655+£301.8.11 p.t.=£956.8.11

SKODA OCTAVIA

BUILT round a tubular backbone, this small family car from Czecho-Slovakia has a highly individual character. Take your choice from 1,089 or 1,221 c.c. engines both water-cooled and front mounted, with saloon, station wagon or convertible bodywork. Windscreen and rear window are interchangeable, and reclining seats with fully adjustable back-rests are among the optional equipment. Octavia Touring Sport saloon has a twin-carburetter 53 h.p. engine.

CLOSE-UP
Four-cyl.; o.h.v.; 68×75 mm.; 1,089 c.c.; 43 b.h.p.; 7.5 to 1 comp.; coil ign.; Jikov carb.; 4-speed, 20.4, 11.8, 7.6, 4.78 to 1; col. lvr.; susp. f. ind. coil, r. ind. transv. leaf; 2-door; 4-seat; hyd. brks.; max. 77 m.p.h. cruise 60; m.p.g. 40; whl. base 7ft. 10½in.; track f. 3ft. 11⅝in., r. 4ft. 1in.; lgth. 13ft. 4in.; wdth. 5ft. 3in.; ht. 4ft. 8½in.; g.c. 8½in.; turng. cir. 32ft. 9in.; kerb wt. 17¾ cwt.; tank, 6 gals.; 12-volt.

£415+£191.18.11 p.t.=£606.18.11

STANDARD ENSIGN

A CHEAPER edition of the Vanguard with a smaller 1,670 c.c. engine, this is the car that appeals to the Standard-Triumph enthusiast with a limited pocket. It is a family five-seater, which retains its four-speed gearbox and four-cylinder power plant, and incorporates mechanical modifications made to the Vanguard models. A trusty, well-established saloon that does not strive for the highlights.

CLOSE-UP
Four-cyl.; o.h.v.; 76×92 mm.; 1,670 c.c.; 60 b.h.p.; 8 to 1 comp.; coil ign.; Solex carb.; 4-speed, 14.5, 8.61, 5.66, 4.1 to 1; cen. lvr. overdrive opt.; susp. f. ind. coil, r. half-elliptic; 4-door; 5/6-seat; hyd. brks.; max. 80 m.p.h.; cruise, 60; m.p.g. 32-38; whl. base, 8ft. 6in.; track f. and r. 4ft. 3½in.; lgth., 14ft. 3½in.; wdth., 5ft. 7½in.; ht. 5ft.; g.c. 7½in.; turng. cir., 37ft.; kerb wt., 23½ cwt.; tank, 12 gals.; 12-volt.

£554+£225.3.1 p.t.=£779.3.1

Abbreviations—g.c.—ground clearance; susp.—suspension; f.—front; r.—rear; comp.—compression; s.v.—side-valves; o.h.v.—overhead valves; o.h.c.—overhead camshaft; hyd.—hydraulic.

STANDARD VANGUARD SIX

OPTIONAL disc brakes at only £15 extra, including tax, are an addition to this well-tried, good-looking Vanguard. It is a sturdy, well-built family and business car, powered by a six-cylinder engine, and you can have it in saloon and estate car versions. Easy to handle on long-distance runs or for nipping into town, the Six is a favourite with a wide class of motorists.

CLOSE-UP

Six-cyl.; o.h.v.; 74.7×76 mm.; 1,998 c.c.; 85 b.h.p.; 8 to 1 comp.; col. ign.; 2 Solex carbs.; 4-speed, 14.5, 8.61, 5.66, 4.1 to 1, 3-speed opt.; cen. lvr.; susp., f. ind. coil, r. half-elliptic; 4-door; 5/6-seat; hyd. brks.; max. 90 m.p.h.; cruise, 70; m.p.g. 25-35; whl. base, 8ft. 6in.; track f. and r. 4ft. 3in.; lgth. 14ft. 3½in.; wdth. 5ft. 7½in.; ht. 5ft.; g.c. 7½in.; turng. cir., 39ft.; kerb wt. 23½ cwt.; tank, 12 gals.; 12-volt.

£720+£331.4.9 p.t.=£1,051.4.9

STUDEBAKER HAWK

A GRILLE mighty close to that of a Mercedes is a new feature on this low-built coupe—America's nearest approach to a Gran Tourismo machine. Studebaker are associated with Mercedes distribution in U.S.A, which may explain the resemblance. With the big V8 engine there is power to spare, and for transmission there is the option of three or four speeds, or an automatic box.

CLOSE-UP

Eight-cyl.; o.h.v.; 90.5×92 mm.; 4,735 c.c.; 210 b.h.p.; 8.25 to 1 comp.; coil ign.; down draught carb.; 3-speed, 8.49, 5.2, 3.54 to 1; col. lvr., overdrive or auto. opt.; susp., f. ind. coil, r. half-elliptic; 2-door; 4-seat; hyd. brks.; max. 104 m.p.h.; cruise, 85; m.p.g. 20; whl. base, 10ft. 0½in.; track f. 4ft. 9 in., r. 4ft. 8½in.; lgth., 17ft.; wdth., 5ft. 11¾in.; ht. 4ft. 7½in.; g.c. 6¾in.; turng. cir., 42ft. 4in.; kerb wt., 28¾ cwt.; tank, 14¾ gals.; 12-volt.

STUDEBAKER LARK

THE choice of six- or eight-cylinder engines and a big range of body styles on two lengths of wheelbase broaden the appeal of this successful American "compact" car. The Regal is the long wheelbase six-cylinder four-door saloon with luxurious finish. The Cruiser is the same-sized car with V.8 engine and automatic transmission. Manual gearboxes are available with optional overdrive.

CLOSE-UP

Six-cyl.; o.h.v.; 76.2×101.6 mm.; 2,785 c.c.; 112 b.h.p.; 8.25 to 1 comp.; coil ign.; Stromberg carb.; 3-speed, 9.58, 5.78, 3.73 to 1 auto. opt.; col. lvr.; susp., f. ind. coil, r. half-elliptic; 4-door; 5-seat; hyd. brks. servo opt.; max. 88 m.p.h.; cruise, 75; m.p.g. 20-24; whl. base, 9ft. 5in.; track f. 4ft. 9in., r. 4ft. 8½in.; lgth., 15ft. 8in.; wdth., 5ft. 11in.; ht. 4ft. 8½in.; g.c. 6in.; turng. cir., 41ft.; kerb wt., 28 cwt.; tank, 14¾ gals.; 12-volt.

SUNBEAM ALPINE

HERE is a snappy, elegant sports two-seater that is good for town or country. You see these cars driven Citywards by bowler-hatted men, you see them driven by pretty girls in the country—a car easily managed by either sex. Its backbone, of course, is the traditional Rootes bringing-up the hard way through rallies and races. Disc brakes curb its speed, and there are a number of refinements.

CLOSE-UP

Four-cyl.; o.h.v.; 81.5×76.2 mm.; 1,592 c.c.; 85.5 b.h.p.; 9.1 to 1 comp.; coil ign.; 2 Zenith carbs.; 4-speed, 13.013, 8.324, 5.413, 3.89 to 1; cen. lvr.; de Normanville overdrive opt.; susp. f. ind. coil, r. half-elliptic; 2-door; 2-seat; hyd. brks. disc front; max. 100 m.p.h.; cruise 80; m.p.g. 25; whl. base 7ft. 2in.; track f. 4ft. 3in. r. 4ft. 0½in.; lgth. 12ft. 11½in.; wdth. 5ft. 0½in.; ht. 4ft. 3½in.; g.c. 5in.; turng. cir. 34ft.; kerb wt. 19½ cwt.; tank, 9 gals.; 12-volt.

£695+£319.15.7 p.t.=£1,014.15.7

SUNBEAM RAPIER

HEATER-DEMISTER with booster fan, and a windscreen washer are now included in the price of this well-equipped and glamorously finished sports saloon which has won an impressive list of successes in tough international sporting events. Its engine went up to 1.6 litres earlier this year in line with the Alpine and other Rootes cars, and front brakes are discs. De Normanville overdrive is optional.

CLOSE-UP

Four-cyl.; o.h.v.; 81.5 × 76.2 mm.; 1,592 c.c.; 80.25 b.h.p.; 9.1 to 1 comp.; coil ign.; 2 Zenith carbs.; 4-speed, 14.128, 9.038, 5.877, 4.22 to 1; cen. lvr.; susp., f. ind. coil, r. half-elliptic; 2-door; 4-seat; hyd. brks., disc front.; max. 93 m.p.h.; cruise 80; m.p.g. 25-30; whl. base, 8ft.; track f. 4ft. 1¾in., r. 4ft. 0½in.; lgth., 13ft. 6½in.; wdth., 5ft. 1in.; ht. 4ft. 10½in.; g.c. 6½in.; turng cir., 36ft.; kerb wt., 21 cwt.; tank 10 gals.; 12-volt.

£705 + £324.7.3 p.t. = £1,029.7.3

TRIUMPH HERALD 'S' SALOON

A SMALL car that cuts out the frills for economy, the S model retains all the advanced technical features of the present Triumph Herald. These include the 948 c.c. engine, independent four-wheel suspension, and the 25-foot turning circle which is like a taxi. A down-to-the-bones car that is good value for money. Heralds can now be had with disc front brakes at £15 extra, including tax.

CLOSE UP

Four-cyl.; o.h.v.; 63 × 76 mm.; 948 c.c.; 34½ b.h.p.; 8.5 to 1 comp.; coil ign.; Solex carb.; 4-speed, 20.8, 11.9, 7.0, 4.8 to 1; cen. lvr.; susp., f. ind. coil, r. ind. trans. leaf; 2-door; 4-seat; hyd. brks.; max. 72 m.p.h.; cruise 65; m.p.g. 35; whl. base, 7ft. 7½in.; track f. and r. 4ft.; lgth., 12ft. 9in.; wdth., 5ft.; ht., 4ft. 4in.; g.c. 6¼in.; turng. cir., 25ft.; kerb wt., 15½ cwt.; tank 6½ gals.; 12-volt.

£457 + £210.13.11 p.t. = £667.13.11

TRIUMPH HERALD 1200

A BIGGER engine gives extra power, torque and speed, which the Herald's all-independent suspension handles nicely without loss of road holding. Higher axle ratio reduces engine revs for restful, fast cruising. Besides the saloon, coupe and convertible, there is a handsome new station wagon. All have telescopic safety steering column, detachable body panels for easy repair, and no chassis points to grease.

CLOSE-UP

Four-cyl.; o.h.v.; 69.3 × 76 mm.; 1,147 c.c.; 43 b.h.p.; 8 to 1 comp.; coil ign.; Solex carb.; 4-speed, 15.42, 8.88, 5.74, 4.11 to 1; cen. lvr.; susp., f. ind. coil, r. ind. transv. leaf; 2-door; 4-seat; hyd. brks.; max. 75 m.p.h.; cruise, 70; m.p.g. 33-37; whl. base, 7ft. 7½ in.; track f. and r. 4ft.; lgth., 12ft. 9in.; wdth., 5ft.; ht. 4ft. 6in.; g.c. 6¼in.; turng. cir., 25ft. kerb wt., 15¾ cwt.; tank, 7 gals.; 12-volt.

£479 + £220.15.7 p.t. = £699.15.7

TRIUMPH TR4

DURING 1961 Triumph reached top place in British sales to U.S.A. Now comes the TR4 with TR3 ruggedness plus modern styling, roomier body, wider track, bigger, more powerful engine and synchromesh on all four speeds. Bodies are convertible, with optional hard top. There is a new hot weather idea, too. Replace the hardtop's roof panel with a flexible "surrey" top—but with no fringe.

CLOSE-UP

Four-cyl.; o.h.v.; 86 × 92 mm.; 2,138 c.c.; 105 b.h.p.; 9 to 1 comp.; coil ign.; 2 S.U. carbs.; 4-speed, 11.61, 7.44, 4.9, 3.7 to 1; cen. lvr.; susp. f. ind. coil, r. half-elliptic; 2-door; 2-seat; hyd. brks. disc front; max. 110 m.p.h.; cruise 95; m.p.g. 25; whl. base 7ft. 4in.; track f. 4ft. 1in., r. 4ft.; lgth. 13ft.; wdth. 4ft. 9½in.; ht. 4ft. 2in.; g.c. 6in.; turng. cir. 33ft.; kerb wt. 20 cwt.; tank, 11¾ gals.; 12-volt.

£750 + £344.19.9 p.t. = £1,094.19.9

Abbreviations—g.c.—ground clearance; susp.—suspension; f.—front; r.—rear; comp.—compression; s.v.—side-valves; o.h.v.—overhead valves; o.h.c.—overhead camshaft; hyd.—hydraulic.

VALIANT

ONE of the smaller cars from the Chrysler Group. Chassis greasing is practically eliminated, brakes are self-adjusting, and the parking brake now acts on rear wheels instead of transmission. Printed circuits simplify instrument wiring. There is the option of a bigger engine with die-cast cylinder block, and the Signet sports saloon with bucket front seats is a new addition.

CLOSE-UP
Six-cyl.; o.h.v.; 86×79 mm.; 2,786 c.c.; 101 b.h.p.; 8.2 to 1 comp.; coil ign.; down draught carb.; 3-speed auto., 9.53, 5.85, 3.23 to 1; press button control; susp., f. ind. torsion bar, r. half-elliptic; 4-door; 6-seat; hyd. brks.; max. 101 m.p.h.; cruise, 85; m.p.g. 18-22; whl. base, 8ft. 10½in.; track f. 4ft. 8in.; r. 4ft. 7½in.; lgth., 15ft. 4½in.; wdth., 5ft. 10½in.; ht. 4ft. 6½in.; g.c. 6½in. turng. cir., 36ft. 4in.; kerb wt., 24 cwt.; tank, 11 gals.; 12-volt.

VANDEN PLAS PRINCESS 4-LITRE

THE B.M.C.'s magnificent prestige car with coach-built body mounted on an extra long wheelbase chassis can seat nine. It has a host of fittings to suit individual tastes, right down to a reading lamp for the chauffeur and separate heating control for the rear passengers. If you can think of it, this formal limousine probably has it and you see it at all the formal functions where limousines are in demand.

CLOSE-UP
Six-cyl.; o.h.v.; 87.3×111 mm.; 3,993 c.c.; 6.8 to 1 comp.; coil ign.; Stromberg carb.; 4-speed, 15.1, 10.3, 6.4, 4.4 to 1; col. lvr., auto. opt.; susp., f. ind. coil, r. half-elliptic; 4-door; 8-seat; hyd. brks.; max. 100 m.p.h.; cruise, 80; m.p.g. 16-19; whl. base, 11ft. 0⅜in.; track f. 4ft. 10½in.; r. 5ft. 2½in.; lgth., 17ft. 11in.; wdth., 6ft. 2½in.; ht. 5ft. 10in.; g.c. 6½ in.; turng. cir., 45ft. 6in.; kerb wt., 41¾ cwt.; tank, 16 gals.; 12-volt.
£2,150+£987 p.t.=£3,137

VAUXHALL CRESTA

BUYERS have more options for 1962: disc or drum front brakes, individual or bench front seats, centre arm-rests at front and rear, automatic transmission or 3-speed manual with or without overdrive, leather or nylon upholstery, more colours in a new enamel with long-lasting lustre. Padded sun visors, longer wiper blades and "safety-zone" windscreen are common to Cresta and less expensive Velox.

CLOSE-UP
Six-cyl.; o.h.v.; 82.55×82.55 mm.; 2,651 c.c.; 113 b.h.p.; 8.1 to 1 comp.; coil ign.; Zenith carb.; 3-speed, 11.18, 6.38, 3.90 to 1; col. lvr., De Normanville overdrive or auto opt.; susp. f. ind. coil, r. half-elliptic; 4 door; 6-seat; hyd brks., disc front opt.; max 95 m.p.h.; cruise 75-80; m.p.g. 20-25; whl. base 8ft. 9in.; track f. and r. 4ft. 6in.; lgth. 14ft. 10in.; wdth. 5ft. 8½in.; ht. 4ft. 9in.; g.c. 7in.; turng. cir. 39 ft.; kerb wt. 23¾ cwt.; tank, 10¾ gals.; 12-volt.
£715+£328.18.11 p.t.=£1,043.18.11

VAUXHALL VELOX

1962 policy for the Velox is to give the customer a wider choice, so he may now decide between disc or drum brakes on front wheels; individual front seats or bench-type seat; centre arm-rests fore and aft, or at the back only. These go with many other improvements inside. The Velox is now finished in a hard cellulose-synthetic enamel that retains its lustre longer than the previous paint finish.

CLOSE-UP
Six-cyl.; o.h.v.; 82.55×82.55 mm.; 2,651 c.c.; 113 b.h.p.; 8.1 to 1 comp.; coil ign.; Zenith carb.; 3-speed, 11.18, 6.38, 3.90 to 1; col. lvr., De Normanville overdrive or auto opt.; susp. f. ind. coil, r. half-elliptic; 4-door; 6-seat; hyd. brks., disc front opt.; max. 95 m.p.h cruise 75-80; m.p.g. 20-25; whl. base 8ft. 9in.; track f. and r. 4ft. 6in.; lgth. 14ft. 10in.; wdth. 5ft. 8½in.; ht. 4ft. 9in.; g.c. 7in.; turng. cir. 39ft.; kerb wt. 23 cwt.; tank, 10¾ gals.; 12-volt.
£655+£301.8.11 p.t.=£956.8.11

VAUXHALL VICTOR

A GOOD-LOOKING, thrifty new model with practical features to cut motoring costs. No chassis greasing, no draining of gearbox or axle oil. Roomy, well-styled interior, and an enormous luggage trunk with spare wheel inside the right rear wing. Choice of three-speed gearbox with steering column lever, or four-speed with central lever. And don't miss the high-performance VX4/90 with disc brakes.

CLOSE-UP
Four-cyl.; o.h.v.; 79.4×76.2 mm.; 1,508 c.c.; 56.3 b.h.p.; 8.1 to 1 comp.; coil ign.; Zenith carb.; 3-speed, 12.42, 6.37, 3.9 to 1; col. lvr., 4-speed opt.; susp. f. ind. coil, r. half-elliptic; 4-door; 5-seat; hyd. brks.; max. 80 m.p.h.; cruise 68; m.p.g. 28-35; whl. base 8ft. 4in.; track f. 4ft. 2¾in., r. 4ft. 3in.; lgth. 14ft. 5½in.; wdth. 5ft. 4in.; ht. 4ft. 7½in.; g.c. 6½in.; turng. cir. 34ft.; kerb wt. 18½ cwt.; tank, 10 gals.; 12-volt.
£510+£234.19.9 p.t.=£744.19.9

VAUXHALL VICTOR ESTATE CAR

JUST as crisp in style as the new saloon, the Victor Estate car has a full-width counter-balanced lift-up rear door giving access to goods carrying space, which reaches 45 cubic feet when the rear seat is folded away. There is an option of separate front seats, four-speed all-synchro gearbox with central lever, dual or single colour schemes in high lustre enamel over phosphate anti-rust coating.

CLOSE-UP
Four-cyl.; o.h.v.; 79.4×76.2 mm.; 1,508 c.c.; 56.3 b.h.p.; 8 to 1 comp.; coil ign.; Zenith carb.; 3-speed, 13.5, 6.74, 4.125 to 1, 4-speed opt.; col. lvr.; susp., f. ind. coil, r. half-elliptic; 5-door; 5-seat; hyd. brks.; max. 80 m.p.h.; cruise, 70; m.p.g. 28-34; whl. base, 8ft. 4in.; track f. 4ft. 2¾in., r. 4ft. 3½in.; lgth., 14ft. 5½in.; wdth., 5ft. 4in.; ht. 4ft. 8½in.; g.c. 7in.; turng. cir., 36ft.; kerb wt., 19¾ cwt., tank; 10 gals.; 12-volt.
£590+£271.13.1 p.t.=£861.13.1

VOLGA

SOLIDLY built for bouncing over dirt roads, Russia's Volga is designed for owner maintenance without benefit of service stations, if necessary. Very full tool-kit and a tin of paint are supplied. Radiator blind and powerful heater cope with winter cold. Reclining seats help with summer camping. Three-speed gearbox with steering column lever. A transmission handbrake is an unusual item.

CLOSE-UP
Four-cyl.; o.h.v.; 92×92 mm.; 2,445 c.c.; 80 b.h.p.; 7.5 to 1 comp.; coil ign.; downdraught carb.; 3-speed, 14.911, 8.072, 4.556 to 1; col. lvr.; susp. f. ind. coil, r. half-elliptic; 4-door; 6-seat; hyd. brks.; max. 84 m.p.h.; cruise 60; m.p.g. 31; whl. base 8ft. 10in.; track f. 4ft. 7½in., r. 4ft. 8in.; lgth. 15ft. 10in.; wdth. 5ft. 11in.; ht. 5ft. 4in.; g.c. 7½in.; turng. cir. 42ft.; kerb wt. 27¾ cwt.; tank, 13 gals.; 12-volt.

VOLKSWAGEN DE LUXE

EUROPE's best-selling small car is always having bits and pieces added to keep it in the forefront. On the 1962 models additions will include brake lights and rear flashing indicators, differently coloured, in twin-compartment housings. There will be a pneumatic windscreen washer, two warm-air outlets below the rear seat, and standard safety-belt mounting points. The bonnet will be spring loaded.

CLOSE-UP
Four-cyl.; o.h.v.; air-cooled; 77×64 mm.; 1,192 c.c.; 40 b.h.p.; 7 to 1 comp.; coil ign.; Solex carb.; 4-speed, 16.63, 9.01, 5.77, 3.89 to 1; cen. lvr.; susp. f. and r. ind. torsion bars; 2-door; 4-seat; hyd. brks.; max. 72 m.p.h.; cruise 72; m.p.g. 38; whl. base 7ft. 10½in.; track f. 4ft. 3in., r. 4ft. 2¾in.; lgth. 13ft. 4½in.; wdth. 5ft. 0½in.; ht. 4ft. 11in.; g.c. 6in.; turng. cir. 36ft.; kerb wt. 14½ cwt.; tank, 8¾ gals.; 6-volt.
£521+£240.0.7 p.t.=£761.0.7

Abbreviations—g.c.—ground clearance; susp.—suspension; f.—front; r.—rear; comp.—compression; s.v.—side-valves; o.h.v.—overhead valves; o.h.c.—overhead camshaft; hyd.—hydraulic.

VOLKSWAGEN KARMANN-GHIA

ECONOMY at cruising speeds of 70 m.p.h. or more has been obtained by clever styling and light stressing. This VW gives 40 m.p.g. motoring. Features include automatic choke, all-synchromesh gearbox, slender pillars for maximum visibility and three-position adjustable back-rests. Air-cooled, flat-four engine, and all-independent torsion-bar suspension. Room for children or extra luggage in the rear.

CLOSE-UP
Four-cyl.; o.h.v. air-cooled; 77×64 mm.; 1,192 c.c.; 40 b.h.p.; 7 to 1 comp.; coil ign.; Solex carb.; 4-speed, 16.63, 9.01, 5.77, 3.89 to 1; cen. lvr.; susp. f. and r. ind. torsion bars; 2-door; 2/4-seat; hyd. brks.; max. 75 m.p.h.; cruise 75; m.p.g. 38; whl. base 7ft. 10½in.; track f. 4ft. 3in., r. 4ft. 2¾in.; lgth. 13ft. 7in.; wdth. 5ft. 4¼in.; ht. 4ft. 4½in.; g.c. 6in.; turng. cir. 37ft.; kerb wt. 16 cwt.; tank, 8¾ gals.; 6-volt.
£820+£377.1.5 p.t.=£1,197.1.5

VOLKSWAGEN 1500

MIXTURE as before, but in an up-to-date package. VW's big brother has torsion-bar springing and rear-mounted flat-four air-cooled engine like the original best-seller, but the engine is bigger and the cooling fan, at the end instead of above, leaves space for a second luggage trunk. Roomier body, too, in modern but durable style.

CLOSE-UP
Four-cyl.; o.h.v. air cooled; 83×69 mm.; 1,493 c.c.; 53 b.h.p.; 7.2 to 1 comp.; coil ign.; Solex carb.; 4-speed, 15.67, 8.50, 5.44, 3.67 to 1; cen. lvr.; susp. f. and r. ind. torsion bar; 2-door; 4-seat; hyd. brks.; max. 81 m.p.h.; cruise, 81; m.p.g. 30; whl. base, 7ft. 10½in.; track f. 4ft. 3½in.; r. 4ft. 5in.; lgth. 13ft. 10½in.; wdth., 5ft. 3½in.; ht. 4ft. 10in.; g.c. 6in.; turng. cir., 36ft.; kerb wt., 17½ cwt.; tank, 8¾ gals.; 6-volt.

VOLVO 122 S/B.18

THIS well-built Swedish family car, already a familiar sight in production car races, will soon add to its reputation for high performance. A new version is offered with the option of the sports coupe 1,780 c.c. engine, overdrive and disc front brakes. All four forward speeds in the gearbox have synchromesh. Heater and screen washer are standard. Reclining front seats are an optional extra.

CLOSE-UP
Four-cyl.; o.h.v.; 84.14×80 mm.; 1,780 c.c.; 90 b.h.p.; 8.5 to 1 comp.; coil ign.; 2 S.U. carbs.; 4-speed 12.8, 8.16, 5.58, 4.1 to 1; opt. overdrive, cen. lvr.; susp. f. ind. coil, r. coil; 4-door; 5-seat; hyd. brks., disc front; max. 100 m.p.h.; cruise 85; m.p.g. 28-36; whl. base 8ft. 6½in.; track f. and r. 4ft. 3½in., lgth. 14ft. 7½in.; wdth. 5ft. 3½in.; ht. 4ft. 11½in.; g.c. 7½in.; turng. cir. 32ft.; kerb wt. 22 cwt.; tank, 10 gals.; 12-volt.
£940+£432.1.5 p.t.=£1,372.1.5

VOLVO P.1800

"INTERNATIONAL" describes this lively sports car with saloon comfort. The body is British built, engine and gearbox are from Sweden, and the car is assembled in England by Jensen Motors. Components also come from other European countries—all chosen by Volvo with an eye to quality. A car for 100 m.p.h. motoring, at a price which should prove competitive even after import duties.

CLOSE-UP
Four-cyl.; o.h.v.; 84.14×80 mm.; 1,780 c.c.; 100 b.h.p.; 9.5 to 1 comp.; coil ign.; 2 S.U. carbs. 4-speed, 14.27, 9.07, 6.2, 4.5 to 1; overdrive; cen. lvr.; susp. f. ind. coil, r. coil; 2-door; 2/4-seat; servo brks., disc front; max. 110 m.p.h.; cruise 95; m.p.g. 28-30; whl. base 8ft. 0½in.; track f. and r. 4ft. 3½in.; lgth. 14ft. 5½in.; wdth. 5ft. 7in.; ht. 4ft. 2½in.; g.c. 6in.; turng. cir. 31ft.; kerb wt. 24 cwt.; tank, 10 gals.; 12-volt.
£1,335+£613.2.3 p.t.=£1,948.2.3

Abbreviations—g.c.—ground clearance; susp.—suspension; f.—front; r.—rear; comp.—compression; s.v.—side-valves; o.h.v.—overhead valves; o.h.c.—overhead camshaft; hyd.—hydraulic.

WOLSELEY HORNET

REMEMBER the original Hornet? With its fast-revving little six-cylinder engine, it won a reputation for high performance either as saloon or open sports car. The new one has the same character, but its engine is a four-cylinder, riding side-saddle, borrowed from the Mini-minor and driving the front wheels. Interior trim is more luxurious and an extended tail provides more luggage space.

CLOSE-UP

Four-cyl.; o.h.v.; 62.94 × 68.26 mm.; 848 c.c.; 37 b.h.p.; 8.3 to 1 comp.; coil ign.; S.U. carb.: 4-speed, 13.657, 8.176, 5.317, 3.765 to 1; cen. lvr.; susp., f. and r. ind. rubber; 2-door; 4-seat; hyd. brks.; max. 73 m.p.h.; cruise, 65; m.p.g. 42-45; whl. base, 6ft. $8\frac{5}{32}$in.; track f. 3ft. $11\frac{3}{4}$in., r. 3ft. $9\frac{7}{8}$in.; lgth., 10ft. $8\frac{3}{4}$in.; wdth., 4ft. $7\frac{1}{2}$in.; ht. 4ft. 5in.; g.c. $6\frac{3}{8}$in.; turng. circ., 31 ft.; kerb wt., $11\frac{3}{4}$ cwt.; tank, $5\frac{1}{2}$ gals.; 12-volt.

£460 + £212.1.5 p.t. = £672.1.5

WOLSELEY 16/60

LATEST development of a popular medium-range quality car brings some practical modifications and some new features. The larger engine gives extra torque for top-gear performance, and the new Borg Warner automatic transmission is an optional extra. A wider wheel-track improves stability and leaves extra space in the interior. Most noticeable exterior changes are the toned-down tail fins.

CLOSE-UP

Four-cyl.; o.h.v.; 76.2 × 88.9 mm.; 1,622 c.c.; 55 b.h.p.; 8.3 to 1 comp.; coil ign.; S.U. carb.; 4-speed, 15.64, 9.52, 5.91, 4.3 to 1; cen. lvr. auto. opt.; susp., f. ind. coil, r. half-elliptic; 4-door; 4-seat; hyd. brks.; max. 80 m.p.h.; cruise, 70; m.p.g. 26-33; whl. base, 8ft. $4\frac{1}{4}$in.; track f. 4ft. $2\frac{5}{8}$in., r. 4ft. $3\frac{3}{8}$in.; lgth., 14ft. $6\frac{1}{2}$in.; wdth., 5ft. $3\frac{1}{2}$in.; ht. 4ft. $10\frac{7}{8}$in.; g.c. $5\frac{7}{8}$in.; turng. cir., 37 ft.; kerb wt., $22\frac{1}{2}$ cwt.; tank, 10 gals.; 12-volt.

£680 + £312.18.1 p.t. = £992.18.1

WOLSELEY 6/110

LONGER wheelbase and new rear springs are incorporated in this latest Wolseley model. It also has increased power output from engine modifications, with twin exhausts. There is more leg room inside, both front and back, and a centre floor change is now available. The car comes out in new colours, too. One of the bigger models in the B.M.C. range, this car combines sturdiness with grace.

CLOSE-UP

Six-cyl.; o.h.v.; 83.34 × 88.9 mm.; 2,912 c.c.; 120 b.h.p.; 8.23 to 1 comp.; coil ign.; 2 S.U. carbs.; 3-speed, 12.09, 6.45, 3.9 to 1 overdrive; cen. lvr. BW. auto. opt.; susp. f. ind. coil, r. half-elliptic; 4-door; 5-seat; hyd. servo brks. disc front; max. 104 m.p.h.; cruise, 85; m.p.g. 22-24; whl. base, 9ft. 2in.; track f. 4ft. $5\frac{13}{16}$in., r. 4ft. $5\frac{1}{4}$in.; lgth., 15ft. $7\frac{1}{2}$in.; wdth., 5ft. $8\frac{1}{2}$in.; ht. 5ft. $0\frac{1}{2}$in.; g.c. $6\frac{1}{4}$in.; turng. cir., 41ft.; kerb wt., 31 cwt.; tank, 16 gals.; 12-volt.

[illegible]

ZAPOROGIETS

RUSSIA'S latest baby car with unique air-cooled V4 engine at the rear. Smooth running is assured by the counter-rotating balance shaft inside the camshaft. Front suspension by transverse torsion bars; rear by coil springs. For Russian winters, a petrol-burning heater blows hot air inside. Room for small bags under the bonnet; rear backrest folds down for larger loads.

CLOSE-UP

Four-cyl.; o.h.v.; 66 × 54.5 mm.; 748 c.c.; 23 b.h.p.; 6.5 to 1 comp.; coil ign.; Ouroveni carb.; 4-speed; cen. lvr.; susp. f. ind. torsion bar, r. ind. coil; 2-door; 4-seat; hyd. brks.; max. 56 m.p.h.; cruise 50; m.p.g. 40-45; whl. base 6ft. $7\frac{1}{2}$in.; track f. 3ft. 9in., r. 3ft. $9\frac{1}{2}$in.; lgth. 10ft. 11in.; wdth. 4ft. $7\frac{1}{8}$in.; ht. 4ft. $6\frac{1}{2}$in.; g.c. 7in.; turng. cir. 31ft. 4in.; kerb wt. $11\frac{3}{4}$ cwt.; tank, $6\frac{1}{2}$ gals.; 12-volt.

Abbreviations—g.c.—ground clearance; susp.—suspension; f.—front; r.—rear; comp.—compression; s.v.—side-valves; o.h.v.—overhead valves; o.h.c.—overhead camshaft; hyd.—hydraulic.

MORRIS
put
'QUALITY FIRST'
into every part of every car

Minor 1000 Traveller

Minor 1000 Saloon

Minor 1000 Convertible

New Oxford (Series VI) Saloon

New Oxford (Series VI) Traveller

Mini-Minor Saloon

Mini-Traveller

That's why Morris is today's best motoring buy!

Morris quality really shows! Finer Morris styling and finish, better features—all have the stamp of quality. But it's out on the road you really appreciate what quality means. Morris performance, Morris comfort and economy, Morris value... each, in each model, is outstanding. *Prove it—at your Morris dealer.*

All Morris cars carry a Twelve Months' Warranty and are backed by B.M.C. Service.

MORRIS MOTORS LIMITED · COWLEY · OXFORD · ENGLAND
OVERSEAS BUSINESS: NUFFIELD EXPORTS LIMITED · OXFORD *and at* **41-46 PICCADILLY · LONDON · W.1**

How to pick the Standard-Triumph that's right for you

Choose the two qualities you most want in a car—one from the three below, and one from the left-hand column. Where they meet, you'll find a Standard-Triumph car *outstanding* for these qualities. ('Outstanding' because *every* car here has something of all six.) So shop around on this page. And see the Standard-Triumph range at the Motor Show.

	HIGH PERFORMANCE	EASE OF DRIVING	LOW OUTLAY

STYLING

New Triumph TR4 New and beautiful. All the classic Triumph verve plus built-in luxury—winding windows, full-height doors.
ENGINE: 2138 cc, 105 bhp (gross). PERFORMANCE: 0-50 7½ secs. 110 mph max. WEIGHT: 18½ cwt. GEARS: 4-speed, all synchro.

Triumph Herald 1200 Saloon
A beautiful, drivable mechanical marvel. Independent suspension all round. 25-ft turning circle. Needs servicing once in 3,000 miles. Big new 1147 cc engine. Front-wheel disc brakes available.

Triumph Herald Model 'S'
All the mechanical marvels of the Herald, at a bargain price. 948 cc engine makes petrol last and last. Front-wheel disc brakes available.

LUXURY

Vanguard Luxury Six Saloon
New 6-cylinder 2-litre engine gives 85 bhp (gross). Smoothest 6-cylinder car in its class, and the most luxurious. Compact overall dimensions for ease of handling.

Triumph Herald 1200 Convertible
Gives you the freedom of the air. Room for four adults, and a 13 cu. ft. boot. Front-wheel disc brakes are available on all Herald models.

Triumph Herald 1200 Coupé
A honeymoon car for two. Fitted with walnut facia, pile carpets, 72-position seats, screenwashers. As for performance, the new 1147 cc engine stands comparison with 1½-litre cars.

CARRYING CAPACITY

Vanguard Luxury Six Estate Car
An estate car under 'High Performance'? By all means—the Vanguard Estate with the new 6-cylinder engine is a pace-keeper in any company, even with 57 cu. ft. to boot.

Triumph Herald 1200 Estate
For the greatest load length of any estate car under £870. Packs anything up to 5 ft 4 ins long—even a mini-piano.

Standard Companion
The four-door light estate car. Carries up to 50 cubic feet, gives 42-47 mpg, depending on conditions.

A member of the Leyland Motors Group **MOTOR SHOW** STANDARD STAND NO. 118 TRIUMPH STAND NO. 109

UNDER TEST

BASIL CARDEW, man at the wheel, explains what that phrase means

THERE is time for a lot of water to pass under the bridge before the glossy, spick-and-span cars you see on the luxurious stands at Earls Court have grown up from designs on the drawing board to practical models to catch the customer's eye.

Take for instance, a big selling car before it is put on the market. At least 50 prototypes for the new model will have been produced, tested, built on and then discarded.

At least three years—and more often five years—have been spent in bringing the original design to the final appealing showpiece.

At least half a million miles have been dedicated to testing all the prototypes before the plant executives decide on the ultimate model.

At least 2,000 planners, designers and engineers have worked on the blueprints, many of them burning midnight oil for months.

At last, when all is ready the debutant vehicle is probably submitted to me for testing—for an appraisal which the public will understand.

What do I look for?

First, I inspect the car from the front bumper to the rear end.

I take a look at its line. Is it modern? Is it too square, too short, too long? Does it please the eye?

Then I sit in the car. Is there reasonable comfort? Are the seats too low or too high?

Is the passenger room adequate? Is the driving position as it should be—with ease of controls, of manipulation of throttle, brakes and clutch?

Next I survey the appointments of the car. Has it soft and comfortable seating? Are the interior refinements adequate? Is the interior lighting sound? Are the locks safe? Is the boot, whether at the front or the back, large enough to take a useful load of luggage?

Then the controls. Is the dashboard properly laid out, equipped with meters, gauges, speedometer and on some models, revolutions counter? Can the driver see them without effort?

These points and a host of minor details complete my inspection of the car as it stands by the kerbside.

I next examine the vehicle's mechanical features—the engine under the bonnet (fitted fore or aft), the brakes, the suspension, the steering unit and the transmission. This usually takes some time.

Now for road performance.

First I have a test-run on a side road near Hammersmith which the courtesy police use. They calibrate the accuracy of the speedometers by driving along a pre-determined line of green palings, a quarter of a mile long.

The last paling, marking the end of the quarter mile, is painted white. Few would notice it but I have been out with the police cars and I know where to find it.

With careful eye I do the distance test, and often decide that the meter is just a bit optimistic.

Now, having dealt with the distance reading of the speedometer I take the car to an airfield near London where there are electric timing-strips.

Between these strips I make my own run and automatically the car's true speed is recorded. Thus I check the accuracy of the speed recording of the speedometer. Again the readings are often optimistic, especially at higher speeds. So I make allowances for them on my next series of tests.

On the straight 73-mile M1 motorway I drive at high speed, checking the maximum and cruising speeds of the car and its general behaviour under full throttle.

Then I motor across country to a favourite 10-mile road stretch spanning Salisbury Plain. Here I know the traffic will be light and I shall be able to see along the undulating road ahead of me for miles. Here I put the car through its acceleration or pick-up tests and its braking tests.

On the way back to London, along the rolling roads I test the car's general road behaviour, its road holding, and its reaction to sudden turns and awkward bumps.

And so, after this long trial and experiment, the report is made and the new model comes to you—and to the plush stands of this year's brilliant Motor Show.

Cardew checks the external points of a Vauxhall Victor under test. . .

CARS
OF THE EARLY 60'S
BRITISH AND IMPORTED MODELS 1960-1964

MOTOR SHOW REVIEW GUIDE
1962

A - Z
SECTION

VITALITY

That's the keynote

A Message from Mr. L. G. T. Farmer, President of the Society of Motor Manufacturers and Traders and Executive Vice-Chairman of the Rover Company.

¶ Welcome once again to what is recognised as one of London's most exciting annual exhibitions—the International Motor Show. On display will be the latest designs of more than 60 car manufacturers from nine countries, and an impressive array of accessories and components, tyres, and servicing equipment.

¶ More than ever before, the British exhibits will highlight the ability of our manufacturers to produce cars of international appeal, combining good looks with high standards of mechanical engineering and reliability. Behind all the glamour and publicity lies a story of up-to-the-minute resourcefulness and vitality—the story of the British Motor Industry, the largest export industry in Britain.

¶ The number of cars on our roads has increased substantially since the 1961 Show and there is no doubt that there is a far greater recognition of the motor car as an essential part of modern life. It is this integration of the car as an inherent part of our society which has added much to the appeal of the Motor Show.

¶ As a background to the October Show, the Daily Express Review is a most valuable source of information for visitors, and even for those who are in the position of being generally well-informed about the industry and its products. The high-quality photographs and interesting features on less familiar aspects of the motoring scene will surely add to the pleasure of your visit to Earls Court.

All this—with you in mind . . .

I PREDICT that the biggest battle at the Motor Show this year will be between the manufacturers seeking to bridge the gap between small cars and medium-priced models.

The big guns were first fired by the British Motor Corporation which recently produced the Morris 1,100 with its revolutionary suspension.

Then the giant Ford company of America entered this 1,100 to 1,200 c.c. class battle in a fascinating way.

It asked Fords of Dagenham to produce a new 1,200 c.c. car which was code-named "The Archbishop." At the same time it asked its Cologne factory to produce another 1,200 c.c. model, code-named "The Cardinal."

We now know that the Archbishop is the recently announced Cortina with its orthodox backwheel drive, and the Cardinal emerges as the front-wheel drive Taunus 12M, built entirely in Germany for world markets.

I would say that these three cars are outstanding in their own way, and in their class there is further savage competition from the car-makers of Italy and France.

This all adds up to a big business jungle war which can only result in the average motorist being given more and more at a lower price. Good for the motorist who, as the customer, is really the only one who counts.

Along the plush gangways at Earls Court many other new models, or face-lifted models, appear for the first time. All have been constructed with four ideas in mind: They must be dependable, low-priced in the sales list, low-priced to run, and they must have a good performance—snappy getaway, fairly high top-gear speed and good road-holding.

Every year there are improvements in these four basic requirements, for the motor industry is run by tough, combative business men. They have to plan years ahead, and it is true to say that many of the newest models on the glittering stands were first shown to me a year or two ago.

That, however, was when these new cars were in an embryonic stage, before they had been subjected—every one of them—to at least half a million miles of road tests.

The car makers realise that world markets

by
BASIL CARDEW

Daily Express motoring expert who edits this Motor Show Review

are changing, that in Europe alone the yearly output of motor vehicles has risen from less than 2,000,000 in 1952 to nearly 6,000,000 last year.

In that year nearly 4,000,000 cars were sold in Europe and 6,000,000 in the United States. Africa, too, is a new market with almost unlimited potentialities.

At Earls Court you will see the latest models of cars made to capture world markets—cars from nine countries. Apart from the exhibits of more than 34 British manufacturers, the latest products from the United States, Canada, France, Germany, Italy, the Netherlands, Sweden and Czechoslovakia will be on view. More than 400 other stands in the hall will demonstrate coachwork, motorised caravans, accessories and components, tyres and transport service equipment.

I believe that the 600,000 home visitors (578,000 last year) will mingle with the 22,000 overseas visitors and, after touring the stands, will decide that the British cars are as good as, and many of them better than their foreign rivals.

It is admitted that car manufacturers are not having too good a time this year because of the incessant credit squeezes, purchase-tax changes and changes in the Bank Rate.

It is time our rulers faced facts and permitted the British manufacturer a chance to sell a cheaper car in Britain, for without a flourishing home trade there is no possibility of making big headway overseas.

Now for the trend at the Show: the accent is

on providing a car as maintenance-free as is possible within its price. Sealed-engine cooling systems and self-adjusting brakes come into this category for the do-it-yourself motorist, who will now have more time to mow the lawn.

New, almost wear-proof tyres are at the Show, and so are the new wonder plugs that do not need to be examined for 10,000 to 20,000 miles.

Then there is the new sealed suspension unit, which operates with water as its fluid. Improved and more automatic transmissions are displayed, and there has been a swing to fitting synchromesh on first gear. Many more overdrives will be seen. These usually add to the top speed of the car and reduce the petrol thirst of the engine by a third.

There is a growing tendency to fit functional aids such as heaters, windscreen washers and mirrors as standard equipment, but I still consider that some manufacturers make too many of these components an extra for which the motorist has extra to pay.

During the 10 days of the 47th International Motor Show I understand that more than 75 countries are sending their buyers and top brass to inspect the British motor industry's new products—models that are as exciting mechanically as are their good looks externally.

A last word: the wooing of women motorists is still at its height. It takes the form of providing plenty of shopping space in the cars and offering gorgeously blended modern fashion hues on the coachwork.

With nearly one-third of the cars on the roads today being driven by women, it is sound psychology to cater for them, though the man usually foots the bill.

Perhaps you will drive to the Exhibition in one of the 9,000,000 vehicles now on our roads. To those who come to the Show this Daily Express Motor Show Review is intended to be an abridged guide to assist you in the fascinating hours ahead.

There will be many less fortunate who will not be able to visit Earls Court. For them I hope this Review will capture some of the glamour of the gleaming stands.

Don't laugh too soon —these made the Show

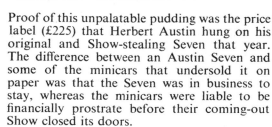

They came, they were seen, they vanished . . . Three models from the 1919 Motor Show: above left, the 12 h.p. Butterosi; top, the Dort; above, the 14 h.p. Hurtu.

"ITS engine can neither be seen, felt, smelt nor heard . . . the car takes up very little more room than a cab without a horse".

Take three guesses at the identity of this vibrationless, odourless, noiseless paragon. Right—it was a Rolls, and not merely the Best Car in the World but also the Slowest.

The sloth of the famous Legalimit, to give the model its second name, was intentional. It worried designer Royce to see his clientele in constant hot water for overshooting the 20 m.p.h.-everywhere speed limit then in force. So he built in a governor that made it physically impossible for his brain-child to beat twenty-per, even downhill, down-wind and with the driver's cap on backwards.

From the dawn of the exhibition's history, almost every Show has had its shock, or anyway its sensation, and in 1905, the year the London Show abandoned here-today-and-there-tomorrow status and adopted Olympia as its fixed abode, this Rolls was IT.

Intended as a rival for the vibrationless, odourless, noiseless electric brougham, reigning queen of London's dowagerwagen, the Legalimit did not vibrate because its big V8 engine was never allowed to exert or excite itself (the governor saw to that). It did not smell because the oil supply to the pistons and cylinders was deliberately and stringently rationed. It was virtually noiseless because R.R. engineering standards were just naturally din-proof. Its engine was invisible because Royce had buried it under the floorboards.

Another 1905 exhibitor, anxious to give you *time* to savour his product's wonders, offered to send a car and a "man" (meaning a mechanic-instructor) to your home for a week. "If the car is not satisfactory, send it back and your liability will be nil". And the man? Send him back too? Keep him?

In 1919, 105 separate and distinct makes, including such long-forgottens as Butterosi, Chiribiri, Dort, Hurtu, Meteorite and Palladium, darkened Olympia's door, and the crowding was such that houseroom could only be found for the big Farman tourer by taking off its wings.

Failing any other formula for standing Olympia on its ear, designers would settle for something new in the way of cylinder multiples and configurations. Two such odd-men-out were Enfield-Allday and C.A.R., both pinning faith, or anyway hope, on air-cooled radial engines, the former with five cylinders, the latter with three.

Italy's contribution to this let's-be-different movement was the narrow-angle Lancia Trikappa power unit, with its twelve pots in two banks and sharply offset to each other.

The real headliners at the Shows of the 'twenties tended to fall mostly into two contrasting classes, at opposite extremes—low-priced cars and prestige models. Representative of the cheap cars were such ruthlessly cheese-pared offerings as the £100 Waverley, with its flat-twin engine at the back, and the similarly priced Gillet, with four cylinders and a normal position for the power unit.

But the fact was that the £100 motor-car was an economic mirage in the climate of 1922.

Proof of this unpalatable pudding was the price label (£225) that Herbert Austin hung on his original and Show-stealing Seven that year. The difference between an Austin Seven and some of the minicars that undersold it on paper was that the Seven was in business to stay, whereas the minicars were liable to be financially prostrate before their coming-out Show closed its doors.

Two more of the period's big newsmakers in the marginal-motoring category were the putter putt Trojan, offshoot of Leyland, and the stark and unlovely Stoneleigh, sired by Armstrong-Siddeley.

The Trojan, which still survives and thrives in a van version, featured a 4-cylinder, 2-stroke engine (located under the floor, like Royce's crawlabout of 17 years earlier), final transmission by chain, and springs of such suppleness that the car's solid tyres were an acceptable substitute for *pneus*.

by DENNIS MAY

Running a Trojan, it used to be said, was cheaper than walking. Shoe-soles wore out, the Trojan's solid tyres did not, or only at an unmeasurably slow rate.

The Stoneleigh seated its driver centrally, with his passengers alongside and behind him, like a gangster's bodyguard.

If your taste in automobiles ran to sheer size and ostentation, the Show never let you down. A world away from the humble Stoneleigh was the same factory's sumptuous Leyland straight-eight, a technical triumph for its racing-driver designer, Parry Thomas (torsional suspension, anti-roll bars, eccentric-driven camshaft of a type that would later give W. O. Bentley ideas).

Eight cylinders were chicken-feed, though. Equalling the Lancia Trikappa's multiple, Daimler came out with a V-12—the truck-length Double Six—at the 1926 Show, only to be out-cylindered by Detroit's huge V-16 Marmon and Cadillac a few Olympias later.

Transmissions aimed at simpler motoring, right up to the point of two-pedal control, sprinkle the pages of Show history.

As far back as 1921, a car called the Crown Magnetic had Olympia a-boggle with a form of drive in which there was "no mechanical connection between the engine and the back axle. There are no gears to change—the whole operation is carried out by a lever on the steering wheel."

Seven years later the cult of the foolproof shift took another bound, or rather two simultaneous and divergent bounds, when Cadillac and La Salle gave Britain its first experience of synchromesh, and Armstrong-Siddeley pioneered the pre-selector gear-box. About the same time—1928—freewheels, enabling the shift lever to be chopped from notch to notch without the driver doing a thing with his feet, were giving a talking point to the Show salesmen of a dozen makes of car.

Like synchromesh, hydraulic brakes were an import from the United States. In 1924, Triumph's new 14 h.p. model featured the first

Lockheeds to be standardised on a British car. Perhaps for the same reason that B.M.C. fills the new Morris 1100's suspension-coupling pipework with an unboozeable fluid, Triumph charged their brake lines with a castor-oil-*cum*-methylated-spirit mixture. Try drinking *that*!

In the coachwork field, stunning the customer with novelty was ever a favourite pastime. Lancia's Airway model of 1927 had such a crazily falling roofline that an outcropping conning-tower had to be built above the rear compartment to add some afterthought headroom. This one, incidentally, featured radio, a compass, an altimeter, an electric fan, an air-speed recorder and a free-gift Kodak among its equipment.

Not to be outdone, the coachbuilding firm of Hill and Boll exhibited a Talbot-based "observation car". The back-seat passengers, who presumably did not care where they were going so long as they could see where they had been, faced astern and were surrounded on three sides by unimpeded glass.

Time marched on and the aerodynamicists moved in on the act. An appropriate "Cor!" chorus greeted the Crossley rear-engined streamliner, a way-out saloon based on the revolutionary Burney.

A year later it was Chrysler's turn with the Airflow line. Then the English bodybuilding house of Lancefield sprang the even more *outre* Transcontinental Hudson, going one better than Crossley and Chrysler by swelling the entire *carrosserie* out to the frontier normally formed by the edge of the running-boards.

This treatment left several cubic yards of lateral *lebensraum* going to waste, so Lancefield used it for suitcase cupboards that in effect transposed the "boot" from the rump to the sides of the car.

"Shocks", by definition, do not have to be aback-taking, and the flutters created at successive Shows by the advent of the grandfather Morris Minor (1928), the first-ever Hillman Minx (1931), and the Fiat 500 (1936), were nothing if not salutary.

The same could be said for the jewelled-in-every-hole Phantom III Rolls that scaled the Olympian heights in 1935. This one had 12 cylinders, and, Royces of divers dates and types having already rung changes on two, three, four, six and eight-cylinder permutations, it looked like having the last word.

It did not quite, of course, because just a year or two ago Rolls switched back to the V8 configuration, repeating history that the vibrationless, odourless, noiseless, invisible-engined Legalimit had made more than half a century earlier. That, I think, is where we came in.

103

Mobil Economy Run gives proof– in cars like yours!

In the 1962 Mobil Economy Run, a Morris Mini-Minor, driven by D. H. F. Keen, averaged 54.53 m.p.g.

54 m.p.g.? In a Mini-Minor like mine?

YES, ON MOBIL SPECIAL!

In the 1962 Mobil Economy Run, an Austin A40 (Mk II), driven by N. J. Milne, averaged 49.58 m.p.g.

49 m.p.g.? In an Austin A40 like mine?

YES, ON MOBIL SPECIAL!

In the 1962 Mobil Economy Run, a Ford Classic, driven by G. Keys, averaged 43.19 m.p.g.

43 m.p.g.? In a Ford Classic like mine?

YES, ON MOBIL SPECIAL!

In the 1962 Mobil Economy Run, a Triumph Herald 1200, driven by P. R. Giles, averaged 44.16 m.p.g.

44 m.p.g.? In a Triumph Herald like mine?

YES, ON MOBIL SPECIAL!

In the 1962 Mobil Economy Run, a Jaguar 2.4 (overdrive), driven by Lt-Col. J. F. May, averaged 26.94 m.p.g.

26 m.p.g.? In a Jaguar like mine?

YES, ON MOBIL SPECIAL!

For perfectly standard family cars like yours to achieve the remarkable petrol milages they do achieve in the long, arduous Mobil Economy Run each year, three things are needed: expert driving; perfect lubrication and tune throughout; and absolutely first-class petrol. Mobil Economy Service offers help in all three. Your Mobil dealer will give you our free leaflet PROOF OF ECONOMY, containing practical advice on economy driving (and all the 1962 Run results); he will keep your car at its 'performance peak' with Mobilubrication and superb, all-season Mobiloil Special; and he'll fill your tank with Mobil Special—the petrol that *proves* its economy in the Mobil Economy Run each year!

MOBIL SPECIAL
MOBILOIL SPECIAL

Mobil

ECONOMY SERVICE
GIVES YOU MORE FROM THE MOBIL GALLON

ZEPHYRS
OOM MORE
ESTFULLY ON
UPER NATIONAL

Artist ROBB in a swift impression captures the bustle, the expectancy, the admiration that makes the Show UNIQUE each year

ABARTH FIAT 1000

LIKE the Scorpion, this one has the sting in the tail. It comes from a splendid little twin-cam twin-carburettor engine that has shot these tiny streamlined coupes rasping to success in races all over the world. All-independent suspension based on Fiat parts, and disc brakes from Britain. Abarth's range extends up to front-engined 2,300 c.c. cars with special coachwork.

CLOSE-UP

Four-cyl.; o.h.c.; 65×74 mm.; 982 c.c.; 105 b.h.p.; 10.4 to 1 comp.; coil ign.; 2 Weber carbs.; 4-speed, 16.44, 9.95, 6.45, 4.33 to 1; cen. lvr.; susp., f. ind. trans. leaf, r. ind. coil; 2-door; 2-seat; disc brks.; max 130 m.p.h.; cruise 90; m.p.g. 30-32; whl. base 6ft. 6¾in.; track f. 3ft. 9¼in., r. 3ft. 9¼in.; lgth. 11ft. 3¼in.; wdth. 4ft. 7in.; ht. 3ft. 11in.; g.c. 6¼in.; turng. cir. 28ft. 8in.; kerb wt. 11¼ cwt.; tank, 6½ gals.; 12-volt.
£2,538 + £1,056.3 p.t. = £3,594.3

A.C. ACE 2.6

FORD'S latest Zephyr engine provides power at moderate cost for this latest edition of a long-lived sporting model. Tubular chassis and all-independent suspension give the key to its road-holding. Alternative engines are the 2-litre Bristol or A.C.'s own light alloy six. Aceca coupe on the same chassis offers high performance with the comfort of roof, windows and heater.

CLOSE-UP

Six-cyl.; o.h.v.; 82.55×79.50 mm.; 2,553 c.c.; 170 b.h.p.; 9 to 1 comp.; coil ign.; 3 S.U. carbs.; 4-speed, 10.81, 6.352, 4.386, 3.64 to 1; cen. lvr.; susp., f. and r. ind. transv. leaf; 2-door; 2-seat; hy brks., disc front; max. 130 m.p.h.; cruise, 100; m.p.g. 24; whl. base 7ft. 6in.; track, f. 4ft. 2in.; r. 4ft. 2in.; lgth. 12 ft. 9in.; wdth. 4ft. 11in.; ht. 4ft. 1in.; g.c. 7in.; turng. cir., 36ft.; kerb wt. 15½ cwt.; tank, 12 gals.; 12-volt.
£1,220 + £458.10.3 p.t. = £1,678.10.3

A.C. GREYHOUND
THIS is a high performance, grand touring car built by craftsmen who have jealously guarded A.C.'s hand-made reputation for the last 50 years. Its sleek lines have been preserved, though this grand tourer has accommodation for back-seat passengers. Interesting features are unique four-wheel independent suspension and rigid steel chassis. Car for the owner who wants high speed and good looks.

CLOSE-UP
Six-cyl.; o.h.v.; 66×96 mm.; 1,971 c.c.; 125 b.h.p.; 9 to 1 comp.; coil ign.; 3 Solex carbs.; 4-speed, 11.97, 7.48, 5.29, 4.1 to 1; cen. lvr.; susp., f. and r. ind. coil; 2-door; 4-seat; hyd. brks., disc front; max. 120 m.p.h.; cruise 90; m.p.g. 24; whl. base 8ft. 4in.; track f. and r. 4ft. 6in.; lgth. 15ft.; wdth. 5ft. 5½in.; ht. 4ft. 4½in.; g.c. 7in.; turng. cir. 37ft.; kerb wt. 20 cwt.; tank, 12 gals.; 12-volt.
£2,116+£794.10.3 p.t. = £2,910.10.3

ALFA GIULIETTA SPRINT
ONE of the most famous sporting cars of the post-war era; the Giulietta has been made in many variations—saloon, TI sports saloon, Sprint coupe by Bertone, Super Sprint roadster and hardtop by Pininfarina, SS. coupe by Bertone, SZ racing coupe by Zagato—and so on. All true Alfas with a crisp note from the twin-cam engine, fine road-holding and exciting performance.

CLOSE-UP
Four-cyl.; o.h.c.; 74×75 mm.; 1,290 c.c.; 90 b.h.p.; 9.5 to 1 comp.; coil ign.; Twin Weber carbs.; 4-speed, 13.58, 8.03, 5.55, 4.1 to 1; cen. lvr.; susp., f. ind. coil, r. coil; 2-door; 2/4-seat; hyd. brks.; max. 112 m.p.h.; cruise 80; m.p.g. 24-26; whl. base 7ft. 10in.; track f. 4ft. 2½in., r. 4ft. 2in.; lgth. 12ft. 10½in.; wdth. 5ft.; ht. 4ft. 4in.; g.c. 5½in.; turng. cir. 36ft. 1in.; kerb wt. 17½ cwt.; tank, 18 gals.; 12-volt.
£1,392+£523.0.3 p.t. = £1,915.0.3

ALFA ROMEO GIULIA T.I.
BIG sister for the Giulietta, with more ample curves. A fast worker, with twin-cam 1,570 c.c. engine to give a 100-plus maximum. Bench seats front and rear for maximum passenger capacity and a big rear trunk. Interesting rear end with radius arms and central link to locate the axle. Drum brakes, finned in front. Sprint coupe and Spider have similar bodywork to Giulietta.

CLOSE-UP
Four-cyl.; o.h.c.; 78×82 mm.; 1,570 c.c.; 106 b.h.p.; 9 to 1 comp.; coil ign.; Solex carb.; 5-speed, 16.93, 10.18, 6.94, 5.12, 4.05 to 1; cen. lvr.; susp., f. ind. coil, r. coil; 4-door; 4/5-seat; hyd. brks.; max. 103 m.p.h.; cruise 85; m.p.g. 30; whl. base 8ft. 2⅞in.; track f. 4ft. 3⅓in., r. 4ft. 2in.; lgth. 13ft. 9⅝in.; wdth. 5ft. 1⅓in.; ht. 4ft. 8¼in.; g.c. 6in.; turng. cir. 36ft.; kerb wt. 21 cwt.; tank, 10 gals.; 12-volt.

ALFA ROMEO 2600 SPIDER
SUCCESSOR to the four-cylinder 2000. Powered by a new high-efficiency twin-cam six-cylinder unit, coupled to a fine five-speed fully synchronised gearbox. Fast and roomy convertible in the Italian tradition, with disc front brakes. Coil spring front suspension and coil springs with rigid rear axle and radius arms at rear. Also available are a roomy six-seater saloon and four-seater streamlined coupe. Picture shows saloon.

CLOSE-UP
Six-cyl.; o.h.c.; 83×79.6 mm.; 2,584 c.c.; 165 b.h.p.; 8.5 to 1 comp.; coil ign.; 3 Solex carbs.; 5-speed, 9.496, 6.496, 4.77, 3.77 to 1; cen. lvr.; susp., f. ind. coil, r. coil; 2-door; 2-4 seat; hyd. servo brks., disc front; max. 125 m.p.h.; cruise 100; m.p.g. 20; whl. base 8ft. 2in.; track f. 4ft. 7in., r. 4ft. 6in.; lgth. 14ft. 4in.; wdth. 5ft. 5in.; ht. 4ft. 8⅝in.; g.c. 5¾in.; turng. cir. 34ft. 1½in.; kerb wt. 22½ cwt.; tank, 13¼ gals.; 12-volt.
£1,996+£749.10.3 p.t. = £2,745.10.3

Abbreviations—g.c.—ground clearance; susp.—suspension; f.—front; r.—rear; comp.—compression; s.v.—side-valves; o.h.v.—overhead valves; o h.c.—overhead camshaft; hyd.—hydraulic.

ALVIS 3-LITRE

AN optional 5-speed gearbox is now available in next year's 3-litre Alvis, giving higher speed and less engine wear. It is a fast, graceful car, combining the clever Continental styling by the Swiss with chassis and engine built by a British firm famed for many years. It will easily exceed 100 m.p.h. with ultra-safe disc braking. A saloon or convertible this is one of the most sumptuous cars in the Show.

CLOSE-UP
Six-cyl.; o.h.v.; 84×90 mm.; 2,993 c.c.; 115 b.h.p.; 8.5 to 1 comp.; coil ign.; 2 S.U. carbs.; 5-speed, 11.38, 6.97, 4.86, 3.77, 3.07 to 1; cen. lvr.; BW auto. opt.; susp., f. ind. coil, r. half-elliptic; 2-door; 4-seat; disc brks.; max. 100 m.p.h.; cruise, 80; m.p.g. 18-22; whl. base 9ft. 3½in.; track f. 4ft. 7½in., r. 4ft. 6 5/16 in.; lgth. 15ft. 8½in.; wdth. 5ft. 6in.; ht. 5ft.; g.c. 7in.; turng. cir. 39ft. 6in.; kerb wt. 30 cwt.; tank, 14½ gals.; 12-volt.
£2,095+£786.12.9 p.t. = £2,881.12.9

ASTON MARTIN DB4 VANTAGE

SUPER-POWERED version of a famous four-seater. Three carburettors and higher compression boost its aluminium twin-cam engine to give 260 h.p., and faired-in headlamps reduce the wind resistance. Servo-operated Dunlop discs provide the fade-free stopping power. Body panels are aluminium on steel tube frame. Same mechanical modifications apply to the convertible.

CLOSE-UP
Six-cyl.; o.h.c.; 92×92 mm.; 3,670 c.c.; 266 b.h.p.; 9 to 1 comp.; coil ign.; 3 S.U. carbs.; 4-speed, 9.67, 6.14, 4.14, 3.31 to 1; cen. lvr.; susp., f. ind. coil, r. coil; 2-door; 4-seat; disc servo brks.; max. 145 m.p.h.; cruise 120; m.p.g. 17-20; whl. base 8ft. 2in.; track f. 4ft. 6in., r. 4ft. 5½in.; lgth. 14ft. 8⅜in.; wdth. 5ft. 6in.; ht. 4ft. 4in.; g.c. 6⅛in.; turng. cir. 34ft.; kerb wt. 27 cwt.; tank, 19 gals.; 12-volt.
£2,950+£1,107.5.3 p.t. = £4,057.5.3

ASTON MARTIN DB4

BASIC model of a famous line; inheriting a tradition of quality, craftsmanship and high performance that goes back to the nineteen-twenties. Race-proved twin-cam engine, twin-plate clutch and disc servo brakes take care of the performance. Styling by Canozzeria Touring gives it beautiful lines that don't date; Superleggera construction with light alloy body panels on steel tube frame ensures strength without excess weight.

CLOSE-UP
Six-cyl.; o.h.c.; 92×92 mm.; 3,670 c.c.; 240 b.h.p.; 8.25 to 1 comp; coil ign.; 2 S.U. carbs.; 4-speed, 8.82, 6.16, 4.42, 3.54 to 1; cen. lvr.; susp., f. ind. coil, r. coil; 2-door; 4-seat; disc servo brks.; max. 140 m.p.h.; cruise 115; m.p.g. 16-20; whl. base 8ft. 2in.; track f. 4ft. 6in., r. 4ft. 5½in.; lgth. 14ft. 8⅜in.; wdth. 5ft. 6in.; ht. 4ft. 4in.; g.c. 6⅛in.; turng. cir. 34ft.; kerb wt. 26¾ cwt.; tank, 19 gals.; 12-volt.
£2,900+£1,088.10.3 p.t. = £3,988.10.3

AUSTIN MINI-COOPER

BABY bomb that leaves puzzled faces in larger cars as it sets high averages in safety. Twin-carburettor, high-powered engine with special crankshaft and vibration damper. Disc front brakes and fully waterproof ignition system. Special quality interior trim as on Mini Super plus remote control gear lever. Special instrument panel, interior door handles, roof lamp and fully carpeted luggage locker.

CLOSE-UP
Four-cyl.; o.h.v.; 62.43×81.28 mm.; 997 c.c.; 55 b.h.p.; 9 to 1 comp.; coil ign.; 2 S.U. carbs.; 4-speed, 12.05, 7.213, 5.11, 3.765 to 1; cen. lvr.; susp., f. and r. ind. rubber; 2-door; 4-seat; hyd. brks., disc front; max. 88 m.p.h.; cruise, 75; m.p.g. 36-40; whl. base, 6ft. 8 5/32 in.; track f. 3ft. 11 7/16 in., r. 3ft. 9⅞in.; lgth. 10ft. 0¼in.; wdth. 4ft. 7¾in.; ht. 4ft. 5in.; g.c. 6½in.; turng. cir. 31ft.; kerb wt. 11½ cwt.; tank, 5½ gals.; 12-volt.
£465+£175.7.9 p.t. = £640.7.9

AUSTIN MINI COUNTRYMAN

IF you want to get about nippily and cheaply, sometimes with a load, then this is the car for you. Slightly longer than its precocious relative, the Austin Seven, it loses a little in speed, but certainly nothing in road holding. The kind of car that is at home in town as well as in the country. It is gaining popularity from week to week.

CLOSE-UP
Four-cyl.; o.h.v.; 62.9 × 68.26 mm.; 848 c.c.; 34 b.h.p.; 8.3 to 1 comp.; coil ign.; S.U. carb.; 4-speed, 13.65, 8.17, 5.31, 3.76 to 1; cen. lvr.; susp., f. and r. ind. rubber; 2-door; 4-seat; hyd. brks.; max. 74 m.p.h.; cruise, 60; m.p.g. 40; whl base 7ft. $0\frac{5}{32}$in.; track f. 3ft. $11\frac{7}{16}$in., r. 3ft. $9\frac{7}{8}$in.; lgth. 10ft. $9\frac{7}{8}$in.; width 4ft. $7\frac{1}{2}$in.; ht. 4ft. $5\frac{1}{2}$in.; g.c. $6\frac{3}{8}$in.; turng. cir. 32ft. 9in.; kerb wt. $12\frac{3}{4}$ cwt. tank $5\frac{3}{4}$ gals.; 12-volt.
£439 + £166.12.9 p.t. = £605.12.9

AUSTIN A40 MARK II

ONLY slight modifications have been made to this shapely forerunner of the famous Pininfarina styling from Italy. It is a robust little car in two versions, saloon with fixed rear window, and station wagon with accessible lift-up rear door. It is proving to be a best seller in Europe since Innocenti began building it under licence in Italy.

CLOSE-UP
Four-cyl.; o.h.v.; 62.9 × 76.2 mm.; 948 c.c.; 37 b.h.p.; 8.3 to 1 comp.; coil ign.; S.U. carb.; 4-speed, 16.52, 10.8, 6.43, 4.55 to 1; cen. lvr.; susp., f. ind. coil, r. half-elliptic; 2-door; 4-seat; hyd. brks.; max. 75 m.p.h.; cruise, 60; m.p.g. 40; whl. base 7ft. $3\frac{1}{16}$in.; track f. 3ft. $11\frac{1}{2}$in., r. 3ft. 11in.; lgth. 12ft. $0\frac{1}{4}$in.; wdth. 4ft. $11\frac{3}{8}$in.; ht. 4ft. $9\frac{3}{4}$in.; g.c. 6in.; turng. cir. 36ft.; kerb wt. 15 cwt.; tank, 7 gals.; 12-volt.
£450 + £169.10.3 p.t. = £619.15.3

AUSTIN A60 CAMBRIDGE

THIS was the first mass-produced medium-sized family saloon to come on the market with the torque-converter type of fully automatic transmission. The car has a smartly designed tail with subdued fins, rear-lamp clusters and an eye-catching radiator grille. These combine to give the car a neat appearance. It has the famous 1.6 litre B.M.C. engine. These A.60's are well thought of and freely bought.

CLOSE-UP
Four-cyl.; o.h.v.; 76.2 × 88.9 mm.; 1,622 c.c.; 61 b.h.p.; 8.3 to 1 comp.; coil ign.; S.U. carb.; 4-speed, 15.63, 9.52, 5.91, 4.3 to 1; cen. or col. lvr.; auto. opt.; susp., f. ind. coil, r. half-elliptic; 4-door; 4/5-seat; hyd. brks.; max. 80 m.p.h.; cruise 70; m.p.g. 30-32; whl. base, 8ft. $4\frac{1}{2}$in.; track f. 4ft. $2\frac{5}{8}$in., r. 4ft. $3\frac{3}{8}$in.; lgth. 14ft. $6\frac{1}{2}$in.; wdth., 5ft. 3in.; ht. 4ft. 10in.; g.c. $5\frac{7}{8}$in.; turng. cir. 37ft.; kerb wt. $21\frac{1}{2}$ cwt.; tank 10 gals.; 12-volt.
£585 + £220.7.9 p.t. = £805.7.9

AUSTIN A/110

FEW changes have been made to this ideal family car which, since the last Motor Show, has sold well. Its good looks include snazzy-styled radiator grille and headlamp and side-lamp mountings. Power of the 3-litre engine raised to 120 brake horse power gives the car plenty of urge. It is the car for the family man who has a sizeable garage and wants plenty of room inside his car for passengers. A new highlift camshaft gives better pick-up at speed.

CLOSE-UP
Six-cyl.; o.h.v.; 83 × 89 mm.; 2,912 c.c.; 120 b.h.p; 8.2 to 1 comp.; coil ign.; 2 S.U. carbs.; 3-speed, 12.1, 6.45, 3.91 to 1; cen. lvr. BW overdrive auto. opt.; susp., f. ind. coil, r. half-elliptic; 4-door; 5/6 seat; servo brakes, disc front; max. 104 m.p.h.; cruise, 80; m.p.g. 22-26; whl. base, 9ft. 2in.; track, f. 4ft. 6 in., r. 4ft. $5\frac{1}{2}$in.; lgth. 15ft. $7\frac{1}{2}$in.; wdth. 5ft. $8\frac{1}{2}$in.; ht. 5ft. $0\frac{1}{2}$in.; g.c. $6\frac{1}{2}$in.; turng. cir. 38ft. 9in.; kerb wt. $30\frac{1}{2}$ cwt.; tank 16 gals.; 12-volt.
£870 + £327.5.3 p.t. = £1,197.5.3

Abbreviations—g.c.—ground clearance; susp.—suspension; f.—front; r.—rear; comp.—compression; s.v.—side-valves; o.h.v.—overhead valves; o.h.c.—overhead camshaft; hyd.—hydraulic.

AUSTIN HEALEY SPRITE MARK II
A FAVOURITE with the younger generation, the Sprite continues its career as a top-selling sports car. Lines are simple. Headlamps are mounted in the wings, and there is external access to luggage boot through lockable lid. Tireless cruising at 72 m.p.h. and more than 33 m.p.g. Bucket seats with space for packages behind. Light steering, zippy performance and good brakes make this an outstanding low-priced sports car.

CLOSE-UP

Four-cyl.; o.h.v.; 62.94 × 76.2 mm.; 948 c.c.; 50 b.h.p.; 9 to 1 comp.; coil ign.; 2 S.U. carbs.; 4-speed, 13.50, 8.08, 5.73, 4.22 to 1; cen. lvr.; susp., f. ind. coil, r. quarter-elliptic; 2-door; 2-seat; hyd. brks.; max. 86 m.p.h.; cruise, 70; m.p.g. 33-38; whl. base, 6ft. 8in.; track, f. 3ft. 9¾in., r. 3ft. 8⅝in.; lgth., 11ft. 5⅝in.; wdth., 4ft. 5in.; ht. 4ft. 1¾in.; g.c. 7in.; turng. cir., 29ft. 3in.; kerb wt., 12½ cwt.; tank, 6 gals.; 12-volt.

£452 + £170.10.3 p.t. = £622.10.3

AUSTIN HEALEY 3000
ALL-WEATHER comfort for sporting motorists in the latest versions of a long-established 115 m.p.h. speedster. Curved windscreen, winding side windows and new quick-action folding top. Plastic rear window drops down for extra ventilation. Engine reverts from three carburettors to two, gaining torque without significant loss of power. Gear lever is now centrally mounted, front springs are stiffer to improve road-holding. Overdrive is optional.

CLOSE-UP

Six-cyl.; o.h.v.; 83.34 × 88.9 mm.; 2,912 c.c.; 132 b.h.p.; 9.03 to 1 comp.; coil ign.; 2 S.U. carbs.; 4-speed, 10.209, 7.302, 4.743, 3.545 to 1; de Normanville overdrive opt.; cen. lvr.; susp., f. ind. coil, r. half-elliptic; 2-door; 2/3 seat; hyd. brks., disc front; max. 116 m.p.h.; cruise, 95; m.p.g. 20; whl. base 7ft. 8in.; track f. 4ft. 0¾in., r. 4ft. 2in.; lgth. 13ft. 1⅛in.; wdth. 5ft.; ht. 4ft. 1in.; g.c. 4¾in.; turng. cir. 32ft. 7in.; kerb wt. 21¾ cwt.; tank, 12 gals.; 12-volt.

£865 + £325 p.t. = £1,190

AUTO UNION 1000SP
DISC front brakes and a pump lubrication system drawing oil from an under-bonnet tank are the latest advances available on this high-performance three-cylinder two-stroke sports car. Front wheel drive through four-speed all-synchro gearbox. Choice of coupe or roadster bodywork. The range also includes two- and four-door saloons, four-seater coupe and station wagon with lower compression ratio.

CLOSE-UP

Three-cyl.; two-stroke; 74 × 76 mm.; 981 c.c.; 62 b.h.p.; 8 to 1 comp.; coil ign.; Zenith carb.; 4-speed, 16.65, 9.6, 6.1, 4.0 to 1.; col. lvr.; susp., f. ind. transv. leaf, r. transv. leaf; 2-door; 2/4-seat; hyd. brks.; max. 93 m.p.h.; cruise, 87; m.p.g. 28-31; whl. base, 7ft. 8½in.; track, f. 4ft. 2in., r. 4ft. 5in.; lgth., 13ft. 8in.; wdth., 5ft. 6in.; ht. 4ft. 4¾in.; g.c. 7in.; turng. cir., 36ft.; kerb wt., 18¾ cwt.; tank, 11 gals.; 6-volt.

£1,364.7.1 + £512.12.11 p.t. = £1,877

BENTLEY S.3 CONTINENTAL
MOST desirable property for the rich prospector who has struck oil, gold or uranium. Pools winners might qualify—anyone with the means to maintain it in the style to which it is accustomed. Large and luxurious, but with plenty of urge from the V8 engine now with higher compression. Swift and silent, it rushes along at 120 m.p.h. without strain to itself or its occupants.

CLOSE-UP

Eight-cyl.; o.h.v.; 104.14 × 91.44 mm.; 6,230 c.c.; 9 to 1 comp.; coil ign.; 2 S.U. carbs.; 4-speed auto.; 11.75, 8.10, 4.46, 3.08 to 1; col. lvr.; susp., f. ind. coil, r. half-elliptic; 2/4-door; 4-seat; hyd. servo brks.; max. 120 m.p.h.; cruise 90-100; m.p.g. 14-16; whl. base 10ft. 3in.; track f. 4ft. 10½in., r. 5ft.; lgth. 17ft. 8in.; wdth. 6ft.; ht. 5ft. 2in.; g.c. 7in.; turng. cir. 41ft. 8in.; kerb wt. 39¾ cwt.; tank, 18 gals.; 12-volt.

£6,505 + £2,440.7.9 p.t. = £8,945.7.9

Abbreviations—g.c.—ground clearance; susp.—suspension; f.—front; r.—rear; comp.—compression; s.v.—side-valves; o.h.v.—overhead valves; o h.c.—overhead camshaft; hyd.—hydraulic.

BENTLEY S3

FAMOUS car with a completely re-designed front-end to incorporate two twin headlights to give owner driver (or chauffeur) much better visibility at night. The side-lights have been taken off the top of the wings to join the group of lights below. Raising the power of the eight-cylinder engine by a 9 to 1 compression ratio calls for 100 octane petrol for better performance all round. The bonnet line of this almost matchless car has been lowered.

CLOSE-UP

Eight-cyl.; o.h.v.; 104.14 × 91.44 mm.; 6,230 c.c.; 9 to 1 comp.; coil ign.; 2 S.U. carbs.; 4-speed auto., 11.75, 8.10, 4.46, 3.08 to 1; col. lvr.; susp., f. ind. coil, r. half-elliptic; 4-door; 5/6-seat; hyd. servo brks.; max. 110 m.p.h.; cruise 90; m.p.g. 12-15; whl. base 10ft. 3in.; track. f. 4ft. 10in., r. 5ft.; lgth. 17ft. 7¾in.; wdth. 6ft. 2¾in.; ht. 5ft. 4in.; g.c. 7in.; turng. cir. 41ft. 8in.; kerb wt. 41½ cwt.; tank, 18 gals.; 12-volt.

£4,455 + £1,671.12.9 p.t. = £6,126.12.9

B.M.W. 700 LS

GOOD thing that comes in a small package, but the parcel is longer in this new, long wheelbase model, that gives extra rear-seat leg-room. Zips along with a top speed of 78 m.p.h. which satisfies a large number of buyers. Good all round vision, two wide doors with seats for four in 'reasonable comfort. There is good luggage space under the bonnet. Engine is an air-cooled flat twin at the rear.

CLOSE-UP

Two-cyl.; air-cooled, o.h.v.; 73 × 78 mm.; 697 c.c.; 30 b.h.p.; 7.5 to 1 comp.; coil ign.; Solex carb.; 4-speed, 19.22, 10.53, 6.89, 4.55 to 1; cen. lvr.; susp., f. ind. coil, r. ind. coil/rubber; 2-door; 4/5-seat; hyd brks.; max. 75 m.p.h.; cruise, 65; m.p.g. 48; whl. base 7ft. 8in.; track, f. 4ft. 2in.; r. 3ft. 11in.; lgth. 12ft. 8¼in.; wdth. 4ft. 10in.; ht. 4ft. 5½in.; g.c. 7¼in.; turng. cir., 32ft. 2in.; kerb wt., 13½ cwt.; tank, 7 gals.; 12-volt.

£567.19.10 + £214.0.2 p.t. = £782

B.M.W. 1500

TECHNICALLY and aesthetically one of the Show's most interesting newcomers. Overhead cam engine canted sideways to reduce height, four-speed all-synchro gearbox, all-independent suspension (trailing wishbones at rear with coil springs and air cushions). Dunlop disc brakes in front. Michelotti was the consultant for the body-styling, which retains the BMW identity in a clear-cut modern form that gives plenty of space for passengers and luggage.

CLOSE-UP

Four cyl.; o.h.c.; 82 × 71 mm.; 1,499 c.c.; 80 b.h.p.; 8.2 to 1 comp.; coil ign.; Solex carb.; 4-speed, 16.676, 9.483, 5.921, 4.375 to 1; cen. lvr.; susp., f. and r. ind. coil; 4-door; 4/5-seat; hyd. brks, disc front; max. 94 m.p.h.; cruise 84; m.p.g. 28; whl. base 8ft. 4in.; track, f. 4ft. 4in.; r. 4ft. 6in.; lgth., 14ft. 6in.; wdth. 5ft. 5in.; ht. 4ft. 8in.; g.c. 6¼in.; turng. cir., 31ft.; kerb wt. 18¾ cwt.; tank, 12 gals.; 6-volt.

£1,175 + £441.12.9 p.t. = £1,616.12.9

BRISTOL 407

WITH background of aircraft engineering, the car is naturally given a number. Body is elegant without being ultra, and is appreciated by connoisseurs of timelessness. Packing 5.2 litre V8 engine under the bonnet, it swishes along at more than 120. Comfortable four-seater with two doors. Assured stopping power of Dunlop disc brakes. Certainly the best from the West.

CLOSE-UP

Eight-cyl.; o.h.v.; 98.55 × 84.07 mm.; 5,130 c.c.; 250 b.h.p; 9 to 1 comp.; coil ign.; Carter carb.; 3-speed auto., 8.10, 4.80, 3.31 to 1; push button control; susp., f. ind. coil, r. torsion bar; 2-door; 4-seat; disc servo brks.; max 122 m.p.h.; cruise, 100; m.p.g. 18-20; whl. base, 9ft. 6in.; track f. 4ft. 5in.; r. 4ft. 6½in.; lgth., 16ft. 7in.; wdth., 5ft. 8in.; ht. 5ft.; g.c. 6½in.; turng. cir., 39ft. 6in.; kerb wt., 32 cwt.; tank, 18 gals.; 12-volt.

£3,525 + £1,322.17.10 p.t. = £4,847.17.10

Abbreviations—g.c.—ground clearance; susp.—suspension; f.—front; r.—rear; comp.—compresssion; s.v.—side-valves; o.h.v.—overhead valves; o.h.c.—overhead camshaft; hyd.—hydraulic

111

BUICK RIVIERA

RIVIERA is Buick's big news for 1963: a four-seater sports coupe of terrific performance with four separate seats flanking a big centre console. A universally jointed steering-wheel that can be tilted at any angle to suit the driver is an optional extra. Parking lamps and direction indicators are concealed behind grilles in front wings. Engine is a 6½-litre V8. Electra—see specification below—is a luxury saloon model.

CLOSE-UP

Eight-cyl.; o.h.v.; 101.36 × 92.45 mm.; 6,571 c.c.; 312 b.h.p.; 10.25 to 1 comp.; coil ign.; Stromberg carb.; 2-speed auto., 5.88, 3.23 to 1; col. lvr.; susp., f. ind. coil, r. coil; 4-door; 6-seat; hyd. servo brks.; max. 112 m.p.h.; cruise 80; m.p.g. 14-17; whl. base 10ft. 3in.; track f. 5ft. 2⅜in.; r. 5ft.; lgth. 18ft. 1½in.; wdth. 6ft. 8⅜in.; ht. 4ft. 9in.; g.c. 6⅝in.; turng. cir. 44ft.; kerb wt. 41 cwt.; tank, 16¾ gals.; 12-volt.

£2,465 + £925.4.1 p.t. = £3,390.4.1

BUICK SPECIAL

BUICK'S new compact with V6 engine was given the 1962 Car of the Year award by a leading American motor magazine as "most outstanding example of progress in design." Lines are smooth and wide door openings give ease of entry and exit. Tall guys have ample leg-room in rear seat and there is a big choice of upholstery materials. Luxury travel with more than 110 m.p.h. on tap.

CLOSE-UP

Eight-cyl.; o.h.v.; 88.97 × 71 mm.; 3,532 c.c.; 150 b.h.p.; 8.8 to 1 comp.; coil ign.; Rochester carb.; 3-speed, 8.6, 5.2, 3.4 to 1; col. lvr.; susp., f. ind. coil, r. coil; 4-door; 6-seat; hyd. brks.; max. 92 m.p.h.; cruise 80; m.p.g. 18-22; whl. base 9ft. 4in.; track f. and r. 4ft. 8in.; lgth. 15ft. 8⅜in.; wdth. 5ft. 11¼in.; ht. 4ft. 4⅜in.; g.c. 6⅛in.; turng. cir. 36ft.; kerb wt. 23¾ cwt.; tank, 16½ gals.; 12-volt.

£1,716 + £644 p.t. = £2,360

CADILLAC ELDORADO

STATUS seekers the world over have at the top of their shopping lists this auto with the mostest from the U.S.A. All home comforts available, super soft seats, silent automatic transmission, air conditioning, special cornering lights, radio and power assisted steering and brakes. If there is anything else you need, you name it, they have it.

CLOSE-UP

Eight-cyl.; o.h.v.; 101.6 × 98.42 mm.; 6,384 c.c.; 345 b.h.p.; 10.5 to 1 comp.; coil ign.; Carter carb.; 4-speed auto., 11.66, 7.49, 4.55, 2.94 to 1; col. lvr.; susp., f. ind. coil, r. coil; 4-door; 6-seat; hyd. servo brks.; max. 110 m.p.h.; cruise 85; m.p.g. 13-15; whl. base 10ft. 9½in.; track f. and r. 5ft. 1in.; lgth. 18ft. 6in.; wdth. 6ft. 7in.; ht. 4ft. 8⅛in.; g.c. 5in.; turng. cir. 45ft.; kerb wt. 42¾ cwt.; tank, 20 gals.; 12-volt.

CADILLAC FLEETWOOD

A CAR that is just the job for those with money to burn, for this low and opulent automobile gobbles gas at the rate of 9-13 m.p.g., but gives a handy 118 m.p.h. in return. Luckily the fuel tank holds 17 gallons. Elegant, refined interior with new trim designs. Air conditioning, heater and automatic trunk lock are among the amenities. Gracious living, American style, on wheels.

CLOSE-UP

Eight-cyl.; o.h.v.; 101.6 × 98.42 mm.; 6,384 c.c.; 330 b.h.p.; 10.5 to 1 comp.; coil ign.; Carter carb.; 4-speed auto., 13.31, 8.57, 5.21, 3.36 to 1; col. lvr.; susp., f. ind. coil, r. coil; 4-door; 9-seat; hyd. servo brks.; max. 118 m.p.h.; cruise 90; m.p.g. 9-13; whl. base 12ft. 5½in.; track f. and r. 5ft. 1in.; lgth. 20ft. 4¾in.; wdth. 6ft. 8in.; ht. 4ft. 11in.; g.c. 6⅝in.; turng. cir. 52ft.; kerb wt. 50½ cwt.; tank, 17½ gals.; 12-volt.

　Abbreviations—g.c.—ground clearance; susp.—suspension; f.—front; r.—rear; comp.—compression; s.v.—side-valves; o.h.v.—overhead valves; o.h.c.—overhead camshaft; hyd.—hydraulic.

CHEVROLET CORVAIR

STILL a big car by English standards, the neat and clean-cut Corvair compact is changing its character. Planned as a family car to beat the Volkswagen it is now developing into an American sporting model. Unfinned, little chromed, the lines have been widely copied in Europe. Cruising at 75 m.p.h. and moderate fuel consumption of 18-24 m.p.g. As well as four-door model there is a two-door coupe. A convertible is the newest addition.

CLOSE-UP
Six-cyl.; o.h.v.; air-cooled 87.3×66 mm.; 2,372 c.c.; 80 b.h.p.; 8 to 1 comp.; coil ign.; 2 Rochester carbs.; 3-speed, 11.44, 6.50, 3.27 to 1, 4-speed or auto. opt.; cen. lvr.; susp., f. and r. ind. coil.; 4-door; 5/6-seat; hyd. brks.; max. 84 m.p.h.; cruise 75; m.p.g. 18-24; whl. base 9ft.; track f. and r. 4ft. 6in.; lgth. 15ft.; wdth. 5ft. 6⅔in.; ht. 4ft. 3in.; g.c. 6in.; turng. cir. 39ft. 11in.; kerb wt. 22 cwt.; tank, 9¼ gals.; 12-volt.

£1,610+£492 p.t. = £2,102

CHEVROLET CORVETTE

BRIGHT and breezy is this slick streamlined sports model with plastic body. Brisk cruising at 90 m.p.h. from the 5.3 litre engine. Automatic transmission an optional extra. Ideal car for a honeymoon with two-doors, two-seater body, luggage stowed in the boot and a good bumper for affixing the good-luck horseshoe. Fuel tank holds 16 gals. and drivers should get 15 m.p.g.

CLOSE-UP
Eight-cyl.; o.h.v.; 5,358 c.c.; 250 b.h.p.; coil ign.; 4-speed, 8.14, 6.14, 4.84, 3.7 to 1, auto opt.; cen. lvr.; susp., f. ind. coil, r. coil; 2-door; 2-seat; hyd. brks.; max. 114 m.p.h.; cruise 90; m.p.g. 15; whl. base 8ft. 6in.; track f. 4ft. 9in., r. 4ft. 11in.; lgth. 14ft. 9in.; wdth. 6ft.; ht. 4ft. 3in.; g.c. 8in.; turng. cir. 37ft.; kerb wt. 26 cwt.; tank, 16 gals.; 12-volt.

£2,700+£991 p.t. = £3,691

CHEVROLET CHEVY II

SIMPLE, smart and right up to date is the Chevy II. Low-priced, too, in the U.S.A. Models include convertible, coupe and a four-door station wagon. Nice cruising at 75 with low engine noise. Brakes reasonable, steering manual or powered. Chevrolet has reputation for high quality finish, and there are 14 exterior colours to choose from. Space for up to six people and lots of luggage.

CLOSE-UP
Four-cyl.; o.h.v.; 98.5×82.5 mm.; 2,519 c.c.; 90 b.h.p.; 8.5 to 1 comp.; coil ign.; Rochester carb.; 3-speed, 9.05, 5.17, 3.08 to 1; col. lvr., auto. opt.; susp., f. ind. coil, r. half-elliptic; 2 or 4-door; 6-seat; hyd. brks.; max. 86 m.p.h.; cruise, 70; m.p.g. 22-25; whl. base, 9ft. 2in.; track f. 4ft. 8⅜in.; r. 4ft. 6⅜in.; lgth. 15ft. 3in.; wdth. 5ft. 10⅜in.; ht. 4ft. 7in.; g.c. 6in.; turng. cir., 39ft.; kerb wt., 22½ cwt.; tank, 12½ gals.; 12-volt.

CHRYSLER NEW YORKER

FIVE years or 50,000 miles is the sensational guarantee period on 1963 Chrysler Corporation products. Next year's Chrysler models are slightly smaller. New Yorker remains as the luxury line, Windsor the medium-priced model and Newport the lowest-priced. Top performer is 300-I series with more than 400 horse-power. High-charge alternators replace dynamos and chassis lubrication intervals are extended to 32,000 miles. Manual or automatic transmission.

CLOSE-UP
Eight-cyl.; o.h.v.; 106.3×95.3 mm.; 6,767 c.c.; 350 b.h.p.; 10 to 1 comp.; coil ign.; downdraught carb.; 3-speed auto., 8.11, 4.79, 3.31 to 1; push button control; susp., f. ind. torsion bar, r. half-elliptic; 4-door; 6-seat; hyd. servo brks.; max. 115 m.p.h.; cruise 80; m.p.g. 13-16; whl. base 10ft. 6in.; track f. 5ft. 1⅛in.; r. 5ft.; lgth. 18ft. 3in.; wdth. 6ft. 7⅜in.; ht. 4ft. 7⅜in.; g.c. 6in.; turng. cir. 47ft.; kerb wt. 37½ cwt.; tank, 19½ gals.; 12-volt.

Abbreviations—g.c.—ground clearance; susp.—suspension; f.—front; r.—rear; comp.—compression; s.v.—side-valves; o.h.v.—overhead valves; o.h.c.—overhead camshaft; hyd.—hydraulic.

CITROEN DS

STILL the most advanced car of its time, with its hydro-pneumatic self-levelling suspension, disc brakes compensated for weight distribution, automatic clutch and servo gear change. A single nut holds each wheel, all external body panels are quickly removable for repair. New nose for 1963 raises maximum speed, new trim improves the interior. Spare wheel in the nose leaves maximum luggage space in the tail.

CLOSE-UP

Four-cyl.; o.h.v.; 78×100 mm.; 1,911 c.c.; 83 b.h.p.; 8.5 to 1 comp.; coil ign.; Weber carb.; 4-speed, 13.79, 6.96, 4.77, 3.31 to 1; dash lvr.; susp., f. and r. ind. hyd. pneu.; 4-door; 5/6 seat; hyd. servo brks., disc front; max. 100 m.p.h.; cruise 80; m.p.g. 25-30; whl. base 10ft. 3in.; track f. 4ft. 11in., r. 4ft. 3½in.; lgth. 15ft. 9in.; wdth. 5ft. 10½in.; ht. 4ft. 11⅞in., g.c. 6¼in.; turng. cir. 36ft.; kerb wt. 23 cwt.; tank, 14 gals.; 12-volt.
£1,263+£474.12.9 p.t. = £1,737.12.9

CITROEN SAFARI (ESTATE CAR)

THE latest model has the new aerodynamic front for higher speed and better fuel consumption. It is a good all-rounder that can be used for passengers or heavy loads. Its top speed is now 90 m.p.h., and power-assisted steering is an optional extra. Engine and disc brake cooling have been improved. Small rubber buffers have been added to the front and rear bumpers for better protection of this eight-seater estate car.

CLOSE-UP

Four-cyl.; o.h.v.; 78×100 mm.; 1,911 c.c.; 69 b.h.p.; 7.5 to 1 comp.; coil ign.; Solex carb.; 4-speed, 13.79, 7.35, 4.77, 3.31 to 1; col. lvr.; susp., f. and r. hyd. pneu.; 4-door; 8-seat; hyd. servo brks., disc front; max. 90 m.p.h.; cruise 70; m.p.g. 25-30; whl. base 10ft. 3in.; track f. 4ft. 11in., r. 4ft. 3½in.; lgth. 16ft. 5in.; wdth. 5ft. 10½in.; ht. 4ft. 11⅞in., g.c. 6¼in.; turng. cir. 36ft. 1in.; kerb wt. 25¾ cwt.; tank, 14 gals.; 12-volt.
£1,298+£487.15.3 p.t. = £1,785.15.3

CITROEN AMI 6

ODDEST of current styles but easy to identify, the Ami 6 matches appearance with far-out technical features—flat-twin air-cooled engine, front wheel drive and ultra-soft springing interconnected front to rear. It cruises at 60-65 m.p.h. in extraordinary comfort, does 45 miles to the gallon and has very good brakes. Seats are among the softest. Wings unbolt for quick repair.

CLOSE-UP

Two-cyl.; o.h.v.; 74×70 mm.; 602 c.c.; 22 b.h.p.; 7.25 to 1 comp.; coil ign.; Solex carb.; 4-speed, 20.365, 10.505, 6.97, 4.77 to 1; dash lvr.; susp., f. and r. ind. coil; 4-door; 4-seat; hyd. brks.; max. 65 m.p.h.; cruise 50; m.p.g. 38-45; whl. base 7ft. 10½in.; track f. 4ft. 1⅜in., r. 4ft.; lgth. 12ft. 8⅜in.; wdth. 4ft. 11⅞in.; ht. 4ft. 10½in.; g.c. 7½in.; turng. cir. 36ft.; kerb wt. 12 cwt.; tank, 5½ gals.; 12-volt.
£564+£212.10.3 p.t. = £776.10.3

DAF DAFFODIL

A BREATH of the bulb fields lingers in the name of this new luxury version of Holland's unique family car; smallest car in the Show to have automatic transmission. Flat-twin air-cooled o.h.v. engine at the front drives through twin belts on variable pulleys, which automatically adjust the speed for acceleration, hillclimbing or effortless motorway cruising. More elaborate grille and finish marks Daffodil from standard DAF.

CLOSE-UP

Two-cyl.; o.h.v. air cooled; 85.5×65 mm.; 746 c.c.; 30 b.h.p.; 7.1 to 1 comp.; coil ign.; BCI carb.; auto. belt drive 16.4 to 3.9 to 1; cen. lvr.; susp., f. ind. trans. leaf; r. ind. coil; 2-door; 4-seat; hyd. brks.; max. 65 m.p.h.; cruise 65; m.p.g. 38-48; whl. base 6ft. 9in.; track f. and r. 3ft. 10½in.; lgth. 12ft. 1in.; wdth. 4ft. 9in.; ht. 4ft. 6½in.; g.c. 6¾in.; turng. cir. 31ft.; kerb wt. 13 cwt.; tank, 6¼ gals.; 6-volt.
£590+£222.5.3 p.t. = £812.5.3

Abbreviations—g.c.—ground clearance; susp.—suspension; f.—front; r.—rear; comp.—compression; s.v.—side-valves; o.h.v.—overhead valves; o h.c.—overhead camshaft; hyd.—hydraulic.

DAIMLER SP250

AN eight-cylinder sports car that is so tough that it is used by many police forces around the country. It has two big advantages: fade-free disc brakes all round, and, in a crash following a chase, its convertible body is cheaply repaired with plastic mouldings. Its handling, since Jaguars bought up Daimlers, is greatly improved.

CLOSE-UP

Eight-cyl.; o.h.v.; 76.2×62.85 mm.; 2,548 c.c.; 140 b.h.p.; 8.2 to 1 comp.; coil ign.; 2 S.U. carbs.; 4-speed, 10.5, 6.236, 4.41, 3.58 to 1; cen. lvr.; susp., f. ind. coil, r. half-elliptic; 2-door; 2/3-seat; disc brks.; max 120 m.p.h.; cruise, 90; m.p.g. 28; whl. base, 7ft. 8in.; track f. 4ft. 2in., r. 4ft.; lgth. 14ft. 0½in.; wdth. 5ft. 0½in.; ht. 4ft. 2¼in.; g.c. 6in.; turng. cir., 33ft.; kerb wt. 19½ cwt.; tank, 12 gals.; 12-volt.
£1,054.10+£396.9 p.t. = £1,450.19

DAIMLER 2½-LITRE V8

BORG-WARNER automatic transmission is fitted to this exciting newcomer. The body trim has been modified to suit the new image, and much of the Jaguar 2.4 mark II model has been Daimlerised, including the fluted front. Internally there are new front seats of the split bench type, which can be converted easily to carry three abreast. Power-assisted steering is an extra.

CLOSE-UP

Eight-cyl.; o.h.v.; 76.2/69.85 mm.; 2,548 c.c.; 140 b.h.p.; 8.2 to 1 comp.; coil ign.; 2 S.U. carbs.; 3-speed, BW auto., 10.2, 6.19, 4.27 to 1; col. lvr.; susp., f. ind. coil, r. cantilever leaf; 4-door; 5-seat; disc servo brks.; max. 110 m.p.h.; cruise 80-90; m.p.g. 20-22; whl. base 8ft. 11⅜in.; track f. 4ft. 7in., r. 4ft. 5⅜in.; lgth. 15ft. 0¾in.; wdth. 5ft. 6⅞in.; ht. 4ft. 9½in.; g.c. 7in.; turng. cir. 33ft. 6in.; kerb wt. 28 cwt.; tank, 12 gals.; 12-volt.
£1,298+£487 p.t. = £1,785

DAIMLER LIMOUSINE

A GREAT town carriage which makes kings and queens out of all on board. Stout steel body with feather-bed comfort. Each compartment has its individually controlled heating system. Sliding glasses between front and rear. Power unit is a 4½-litre V8 developing 220 b.h.p. Reaches 110 m.p.h. smoothly and quietly to the astonishment of sports-car drivers. Automatic transmission, power-assisted steering and Dunlop disc brakes, servo assisted.

CLOSE-UP

Eight-cyl.; o.h.v.; 95.25×80.01 mm.; 4,561 c.c.; 220 b.h.p.; 8 to 1 comp.; coil ign.; 2 S.U. carbs.; 3-speed, auto 8.7, 5.4, 3.77 to 1; col. lvr.; susp., f. ind. coil, r. half-elliptic; 4-door; 8-seat; disc servo brks.; max. 110 m.p.h.; cruise, 90; m.p.g. 17-20; whl. base, 11ft. 6in.; track f. and r. 4ft. 9in.; lgth., 18ft. 10in.; wdth., 6ft. 1⅛in.; ht., 5ft. 5½in.; g.c. 7in.; turng. cir., 44ft.; kerb wt., 40 cwt.; tank, 16 gals.; 12-volt.
£2,738.11.7+£1,027.19.7 p.t. = £3,766.11.2

D.K.W. 800S

IMPOSING new grille and sidelamps, dual colour schemes and ventilating panes in the doors distinguish this de luxe version of the popular three-cylinder front drive DKW. Engine capacity is raised to 796 c.c., giving higher torque, and lubrication is by belt-driven Lubrimat pump. No more mixing oil with the petrol. Among the optional extras are automatic clutch and a sunshine roof.

CLOSE-UP

Three-cyl.; two-stroke; 68×70.5 mm.; 796 c.c.; 39 b.h.p.; 7.25 to 1 comp.; coil ign.; Solex carb.; 4-speed, 15.47, 9.20, 5.86, 3.88 to 1; col. lvr.; susp., f. ind. torsion bar, r. torsion bar; 2-door; 4-seat; hyd. brks.; max. 75 m.p.h.; cruise, 75; m.p.g. 34-38; whl. base 6ft. 3⅛in.; track f. 3ft. 10⅜in., r. 3ft. 11¼in.; lgth. 13ft.; wdth. 5ft. 2in.; ht. 4ft. 7in.; g.c. 6⅛in.; turng. cir. 32ft.; kerb wt. 13¾ cwt.; tank, 7½ gals.; 6-volt.
£634.3.6+£238.16.6 p.t. = £873

DODGE DART 440

NEARLY 17ft. long, this automobile is no aftful dodger for easy parking in small spaces but it is almost compact by American standards. Power comes from a 5.1 litre V8 giving 230 b.h.p. Split front seat backs, individual bolsters, folding centre armrest provide style and comfort of bucket seats while keeping bench advantages. Full chassis lubrication needed only every 32,000 miles. Available as saloon, hardtop, convertible and station wagon.

CLOSE-UP
Eight-cyl.; o.h.v.; 98.55×84.07; 5,130 c.c.; 230 b.h.p.; 9 to 1 comp.; coil ign.; Carter carb.; 3-speed auto., 6.76, 3.0, 2.76 to 1; push button control; susp., f. ind. torsion bar, r. half-elliptic; 4-door; 6-seat; hyd. servo brks.; max. 108 m.p.h.; cruise 90; m.p.g. 16-21; whl. base 9ft. 8in.; track f. 4ft. 11½in., r. 4ft. 9in.; lgth. 16ft. 10in.; wdth., 6ft. 4½in.; ht. 4ft. 6in.; g.c. 5in.; turng. cir. 42ft. 9in.; kerb wt. 30 cwt.; tank, 17 gals.; 12-volt.
£1,841 + £691.7.8 p.t. = £2,532.7.8

FACEL VEGA II

CELEBRITIES of show business like France's opulent Facel. 6.2 litre Chrysler-built V8 engine with choice of one or two quadruple-choke carburettors give it a maximum anywhere between 130 and 150, with breath-snatching acceleration. Brakes are Dunlop discs. Transmission is Torque-Flite automatic or four-speed all-synchro. Latest body has lower, slimmer roof. The larger four-door Excellence tempts tycoons.

CLOSE-UP
Eight-cyl.; o.h.v.; 107.95 × 85.85 mm.; 6,286 c.c.; 355 b.h.p.; 10 to 1 comp.; coil ign.; Carter carb.; 3-speed auto., 8.10, 4.79, 3.31 to 1; press buttons; 4-speed synchro opt.; susp., f. ind. coil, r. half-elliptic; 2-door; 4-seat; disc servo brks.; max. 135 m.p.h.; cruise 120; m.p.g. 14; whl. base, 8 ft. 8½in.; track f. and r. 4ft. 8in.; lgth. 15ft. 7in.; wdth. 5ft. 10in.; ht. 4ft. 2in.; g.c. 7in.; turng. cir. 38ft.; kerb wt. 34½ cwt.; tank, 22 gals.; 12-volt.
£4,050 + £1,520.13.3 p.t. = £5,570.13.3

FACEL VEGA FACELLIA

CLASS distinction. Class in the lean uncluttered line. Distinction in the sober luxury of its upholstery and instrument lay-out. Three body styles are available for this junior Facel—convertible, two-seater coupe and 2/4 seater saloon. Twin-cam engine with four-speed all-synchro gearbox and Dunlop disc brakes, servo assisted. For still higher performance the F2S has two twin-choke carburettors and choice of axle ratios.

CLOSE-UP
Four-cyl.; o.h.c.; 82 × 78 mm.; 1,600 c.c.; 115 b.h.p.; 9.4 to 1 comp.; coil ign.; Solex carb.; 4-speed, 14.1, 8.0, 5.2, 4.1 to 1; cen. lvr.; susp. f. ind. coil, r. half-elliptic; 2-door; 2-seat; disc brks.; max. 115 m.p.h.; cruise 95; m.p.g. 25; whl. base 8ft. 0½in.; track f. and r. 4ft. 3½in.; lgth. 13ft. 7½in.; wdth. 5ft. 4in.; ht. 4ft. 1½in.; g.c. 7in.; turng. cir. 32ft.; kerb wt. 19¼ cwt.; tank, 12½ gals.; 12-volt.
£1,770 + £664.11.9 p.t. = £2,434.11.9

FAIRTHORPE ELECTRINA

AIR VICE-MARSHAL Donald Bennett produces a whole series of highly individual designs for those who want a sports car that is not a mass-produced machine. Small plastic-bodied Electrina and Electron Minor have similar specifications with Triumph four-cylinder engines. Rockette is the new speedster with Triumph Vitesse six-cylinder engine. Front suspension is coil spring independent: rear suspension is by trailing wishbones and links with coil springs.

CLOSE-UP
Four-cyl.; o.h.v.; 63 × 76 mm.; 948 c.c.; 50 b.h.p.; 8.5 to 1 comp.; coil ign.; twin S.U. carb.; 4-speed, 15.52, 8.88, 5.74, 4.11 to 1; cen. lvr.; susp., f. ind. coil, r. coil; 2-door; 2/4 seat; hyd. brks.; max. 90 m.p.h.; cruise 70; m.p.g. 38-50; whl base 6ft. 10 in.; track f. and r. 4ft.; lgth. 12ft. 3in.; wdth. 4ft. 10in.; ht. 4ft. 4in.; g.c. 7½in.; turng. cir. 23ft.; kerb wt. 9 cwt.; tank, 10 gals.; 12-volt.
£594 + £223.15.3 p.t. = £817.15.3

FERRARI 250GT

BEARING the prancing-horse badge, the 250 GT fascinates sportsmen of all ages and races. Engine is well-known V-12 with three twin choke carburettors giving 235 b.h.p. in normal production form, or 300 in the Scaglietti Berlinetta so familiar on British race tracks. Four-speed all-synchromesh gearbox, Dunlop disc brakes on all wheels, and utterly accurate steering make it a dream to drive.

CLOSE-UP

Twelve-cyl.; o.h.c.; 73×58.8 mm.; 2,953 c.c.; 280 b.h.p.; 9.2 to 1 comp.; coil ign.; 3 Weber carbs.; 4-speed, 10.59, 7.76, 5.73, 4.57 to 1; cen. lvr.; susp., f. ind. coil, r. half-elliptic; 2-door; 2-seat; disc-servo brks.; max. 150-167 m.p.h.; cruise 130; m.p.g. 15-18; wh. base 7ft. $10\frac{1}{2}$in.; track f. 4ft. $5\frac{1}{4}$in., r. 4ft. 5in.; lgth. 13ft. 8in.; wdth. 5ft.; ht. 4ft.; g.c. 6in.; turng. cir. 30ft. 3in.; kerb wt. $19\frac{3}{4}$ cwt.; tank, $19\frac{1}{2}$ gals.; 12-volt.

£4,500 + £1,772.17.9 p.t. = £6,272.17.9

FIAT 500 GIARDINIERA

MINIATURE station wagon from Italy with surprising carrying capacity. Two-cylinder, air-cooled engine lies on its side under the floor, fed with air from grilles in the corner panels. Unusual but popular feature is a folding roof, which also figures on the cosy little 500D-saloon. Fuel tank and spare wheel are in the front. Minimum-cost motoring with good road-holding.

CLOSE-UP

Two-cyl.; o.h.v.; air-cooled; 67.4×70 mm.; 499.5 c.c.; 21.5 b.h.p.; 7.1 to 1 comp.; coil ign.; Weber carb.; 4-speed, 18.96, 10.59, 6.66, 4.48 to 1; cen. lvr.; susp., f. ind. transv. leaf, r. ind. coil; 3-door; 4-seat; hyd. brks.; max. 60 m.p.h.; cruise 55; m.p.g. 55; whl base 6ft. $4\frac{3}{8}$in.; track f. 3ft. $8\frac{1}{8}$in., r. 3ft. $8\frac{1}{2}$in.; lgth. 10ft. $5\frac{1}{4}$in.; wdth. 4ft. $4\frac{1}{4}$in.; ht. 4ft. $5\frac{1}{4}$in.; g.c. $5\frac{1}{4}$in.; turng. cir. 28ft. $2\frac{1}{2}$in.; kerb wt. 11 cwt.; tank, $4\frac{1}{2}$ gals.; 12-volt.

£400 + £151.0.3 p.t. = £551.0.3

FIAT 600 D

YEARS of development have brought Italy's most popular small car to its present state of refinement. Engine enlarged to 770 c.c. gives it the needed urge and climbing power and a centrifugal filter built into the fan pulley keeps the oil clean. A neat folding top is available. Another 600D model is the forward-control six-seater Multipla, used as station wagon or taxi.

CLOSE-UP

Four-cyl.; o.h.v.; 62×63.5 mm.; 767 c.c.; 32 b.h.p.; 7.5 to 1 comp.; coil ign.; Weber carb.; 4-speed, 14.47, 8.78, 5.69, 4.4 to 1; cen. lvr.; susp., f. ind. trans. leaf, r. ind. coil; 2-door; 4-seat; hyd. brks.; max. 69 m.p.h.; cruise 60; m.p.g. 45; whl. base 6ft. $6\frac{3}{4}$in.; track f., 3ft. $9\frac{1}{4}$in., r. 3ft. $9\frac{3}{8}$in.; lgth. 10ft. $9\frac{3}{8}$in.; wdth. 4ft. $6\frac{3}{8}$in.; g.c. $6\frac{1}{4}$in.; turng. cir. 28ft. $6\frac{1}{4}$in.; kerb wt. $11\frac{3}{4}$ cwt.; tank, $6\frac{1}{4}$ gals.; 12-volt.

£408 + £154.0.3 p.t. = £562.0.3

FIAT 1300/1500

CHOOSE your engine for thrift or performance. The 1300 has sparkle enough for the week-end pleasure driver; the 1500 has the extra acceleration for the all-week business driver with appointments to keep. Driving hard, there is little difference in fuel consumption. Each has disc front brakes and a host of practical features like roof grab handles, head-lamp flasher, adjustable back rests, fuel reserve.

CLOSE-UP

Four-cyl.; o.h.v.; 72×79.5 mm.; 1,295 c.c.; 72 b.h.p.; 8.8 to 1 comp.; or 77×79.5 mm.; 1,481 c.c.; 80 b.h.p.; coil ign.; Weber carb. or Solex; 4-speed, 15.37, 9.43, 6.12, 4.1 to 1; col. lvr.; susp., f. ind. coil, r. half-elliptic; 4-door; 4-seat; hyd. brks., disc front; max. 86-93 m.p.h.; cruise 80-85; m.p.g. 30-35; whl. base, 7ft. $11\frac{1}{4}$in.; track f. 4ft. 3in., r. 4ft. 2in.; lgth. 13ft. $2\frac{3}{8}$in.; wdth. 5ft. $0\frac{3}{8}$in.; ht. 4ft. $5\frac{3}{8}$in.; g.c. 5in.; turng. cir. 33ft. 5in.; kerb wt. $18\frac{1}{2}$ cwt.; tank, 10 gals.; 12-volt.

1300: £753 + £283.7.10 p.t. = £1,036.7.10

1500: £785 + £295.7.9 p.t. = £1,080.7.9

Abbreviations—g.c.—ground clearance; susp.—suspension; f.—front; r.—rear; comp.—compression; s.v.—side-valves; o.h.v.—overhead valves; o.h.c.—overhead camshaft; hyd.—hydraulic.

FIAT 2300

IRRESISTIBLE Italian styling by Ghia, engine development by Lampredi, the former Ferrari wizard, chassis in the best Fiat tradition complemented by British disc brakes. A practical four-seater with immense luggage space, finish to charm the connoisseur and performance to challenge cars costing a thousand or two more. 2300S has higher compression and twin Weber carburettors, 2300 has lower compression and one twin-choke carburettor.

CLOSE-UP
Six-cyl.; o.h.v.; 78×79.5 mm.; 2,279 c.c.; 117 b.h.p.; 8.8 to 1 comp.; coil ign.; twin choke Weber carb.; 4-speed, 13,82, 8.15, 6.03, 4.30 to 1; coil. lvr.; susp., f. ind. coil, r. half-elliptic; 4-door; 4-seat; disc brks.; max. 110 m.p.h.; cruise 90; m.p.g. 22; whl. base 8¾ft.; track f. 4ft. 4⅜in., r. 4ft. 3⅜in.; lgth. 15ft. 2in.; width 5ft. 3⅛in.; ht. 4ft. 5¾in.; g.c. 5¾in.; turning cir. 37ft. 8¾in.; kerb wt. 24 cwt.; tank, 13¼ gals.; 12-volt.

FORD ANGLIA

COLOURED flash enclosed in bright metal and special wheel discs distinguish the Super Anglia. Its 1,200 c.c. engine is the same as in the Cortina, also its 4-speed all-synchro gearbox and larger brakes. More luxury inside completes up-to-the-minute transformation. Many people still go for the regular model, which is being poured out faster than any other British car.

CLOSE-UP
Four-cyl.; o.h.v.; 80.96×48.41 mm.; 997 c.c.; 41 b.h.p.; 8.9 to 1 comp.; Super: 80.96×58.17 mm.; 1,198 c.c.; 53 b.h.p.; 8.7 to 1 comp.; coil ign.; Solex carb.; 4-speed, 16.987, 9.884, 5.826, 4.125 to 1; Super: 14.615, 9.883, 5.824, 4.125 to 1; cen. lvr.; susp., f. ind. coil, r. half-elliptic; 2-door; 4-seat; hyd. brks.; max. 75 m.p.h.; cruise 65; Super: 80 and 70; m.p.g. 35-42; whl. base 7ft. 6½in.; track f. 3ft. 10in.; r. 3ft. 9¾in.; lgth. 12ft. 11½in.; wdth. 4ft. 9½in.; ht. 4ft. 7in.; g.c. 6½in.; turng cir. 32ft.; kerb wt. 14¾ cwt.; Super 15 cwt.; tank, 7 gals.; 12-volt.

Anglia: £425+£160.7.9 p.t. = £585.7.9
Super: £445+£167.17.9 p.t. = £612.17.9

FORD CONSUL CLASSIC

FIRST British car to have a five-bearing crankshaft on a four-cylinder engine. Livelier performance. Owners are finding that the engines are retaining their youth with a new smoothness of running, now the Classic has the new 1½ litre engine in place of the discarded 1,340 c.c. unit, and a new gearbox with synchromesh on all four gears. An outstanding car for its size and price.

CLOSE-UP
Four-cyl.; o.h.v.; 80.97×72.75 mm.; 1,499 c.c.; 64 b.h.p.; 8.3 to 1 comp.; coil ign.; Zenith carb.; 4-speed, 14.615, 9.883, 5.824, 4.125 to 1; col. or cen. lvr.; susp., f. ind. coil, r. half-elliptic; 2 or 4-door; 4/5 seat; hyd. brks., disc front; max. 82 m.p.h.; cruise 75; m.p.g. 26-32; whl. base 8ft. 3in.; track f. and r. 4ft. 1⅛in.; lgth. 14ft. 2⅜in.; wdth. 5ft. 5⅛in.; ht. 4ft. 6⅛in.; g.c. 6½in.; turng. cir. 34ft.; kerb wt., 2-door, 18½ cwt.; tank, 9 gals.; 12-volt.

£545+£205.7.9 p.t. = £750.7.9

FORD CONSUL CORTINA

PLANNED to give big-car comfort at a small-car price, the Cortina comes between Anglia and Classic to complete Ford's British range. Choice includes two or four doors, centre or steering-column gear lever, attractive new colours and upholstery materials. Engine developed from the race-proved Anglia. Gearbox with synchromesh on all four speeds. Body is the strongest Ford has ever made, and one of the lightest.

CLOSE-UP
Four-cyl.; o.h.v.; 80.96×58.17 mm.; 1,198 c.c.; 53 b.h.p.; 8.7 to 1 comp.; coil ign.; Solex carb.; 4-speed, 14.615, 9.883, 5.824, 4.125 to 1; cen. lvr.; col. opt.; susp., f. ind. coil, r. half-elliptic; 2 or 4-door; 4/5 seat; hyd. brks.; max. 78 m.p.h.; cruise 65; m.p.g. 38-40; whl base 8ft. 2in.; track f. and r. 4ft. 1⅛in.; lgth. 14ft. ½in.; wdth. 5ft. 2⅛in.; ht. 4ft. 8½in.; g.c. 6½in.; turng. cir. 34ft. 8in.; kerb wt. 11½ cwt.; tank, 8 gals.; 12-volt.

£464+£175.0.3 p.t. = £639.0.3

FORD CONSUL CAPRI

AWAITED urge arrives in the form of the new five-bearing 1½-litre engine to give this pretty two/four-seater coupe performance to match its looks. With it comes the new four-speed all-synchro gearbox to complete a power pack with much increased performance potential. Maintenance is reduced by new sealed-for-life ball joint steering pivots. Engine oil changes are only needed at 5,000-mile intervals.

CLOSE-UP

Four-cyl.; o.h.v.; 80.97 × 72.75 mm.; 1,499 c.c.; 64 b.h.p.; 8.3 to 1 comp.; coil ign.; Zenith carb.; 4-speed, 14.615, 9.883, 5.824, 4.125 to 1; col. or cen. lvr.; susp., f. ind. coil, r. half-elliptic; 2-door; 2-seat; hyd. brks., disc front; max. 83 m.p.h.; cruise 75; m.p.g. 26-33; whl. base 8ft. 3in.; track f. and r. 4ft. 1½in.; lgth. 14ft. 2¾in.; wdth. 5ft. 5¼in.; ht. 4ft. 4½in.; g.c. 6½in.; turng. cir. 34ft.; kerb wt. 18½ cwt.; tank, 9 gals.; 12-volt.
£627+£236.2.9 p.t. = £863.2.9

FORD ZEPHYR FOUR

THE secret of this car is the similarity of many of its structural features and mechanical components to the new top-class luxury Zodiac. This has kept down tooling costs, and it makes this new Zephyr a sound buy. It is a roomy six-seater, with disc brakes, all synchromesh gearbox and a 1,703 c.c. engine developing 73.5 brake horse power. A fine successor to the reliable Consul 375.

CLOSE-UP

Four-cyl.; o.h.v.; 82.55 × 79.50 mm.; 1,703 c.c.; 73.5 b.h.p.; 8.3 to 1 comp.; coil ign.; Zenith carb.; 4-speed, 17.207, 9.167, 5.869, 3.9 to 1; col. lvr., BW overdrive or auto. opt.; susp., f. ind. coil, r. half-elliptic; 4-door; 5/6-seat; hyd. brks., disc front; max. 76 m.p.h.; cruise 70; m.p.g. 23-27; whl. base 8ft. 11in.; track f. 4ft. 5in. r. 4ft. 5½in.; lgth. 15ft. ½in.; wdth. 5ft. 9in.; ht. 4ft. 7¼in.; g.c. 6¾in.; turng. cir. 36ft. 6in.; kerb wt. 23 cwt.; tank, 12½ gals.; 12-volt.
£615+£231.12.9 p.t. = £846.12.9

FORD ZEPHYR SIX/& ZODIAC

TWO new six-cylinder cars, Zodiac III, Zephyr Six. Basic structure same for both. Zodiac the luxury job with four headlamps, twin exhaust system, choice of hide, Bedford cord or new synthetic weaves. Zephyr has two headlamps. Curved side glass gives maximum body width. Trunk holds 22 cu. ft. of luggage. Front brakes are discs. Greasing and oil changes at 5,000 mile intervals only.

Six cyl.; o.h.v.; 82.55 × 79.50 mm.; 2,553 c.c.; 106 b.h.p., Zod. 114 b.h.p.; 8.3 to 1 comp.; coil ign.; Zenith carb.; 4-speed, 11.213, 7.849, 5.005, 3.545 to 1; col. lvr., BW overdrive or auto. opt.; susp., f. ind. coil, r. half-elliptic; 4-door; 5/6 seat; hyd. brks., disc front; max. 96-100 m.p.h.; cruise 85; m.p.g. 19-24; whl. base 8ft. 11in.; track f. 4ft. 5in., r. 4ft. 5½in.; lgth. 15ft. ½in., Zod. 15ft. 1¾in.; wdth. 5ft. 9in.; ht. 4ft. 7in.; g.c. 6¾in.; turng. cir. 36ft. 6in.; kerb wt. 24 cwt., Zod. 25½ cwt.; tank, 12½ gals.; 12-volt.
Zephyr: £675+£254.2.9 p.t. = £929.2.9
Zodiac: £778+£292.15.3 p.t. = £1,070.15.3

FORD TAUNUS 12M

DECISIONS about exhibiting this, the first front-wheel drive Ford were pending as we went to press. Originally designed as the Cardinal for manufacture in U.S.A. with German-built power plant, it has engine, four-speed all-synchro gearbox, differential and front drive in one unit. Suspension wishbones are bolted to transmission casing. Now made entirely in Germany, it will compete with Dagenham's Cortina in export markets.

CLOSE-UP

Four-cyl.; o.h.v.; 80 × 58.8 mm.; 1,183 c.c.; 50 b.h.p.; 7.8 to 1 comp.; coil ign.; Solex carb.; 4-speed, 15,23, 8.80, 5.59, 3.78 to 1; col. lvr.; susp., f. ind. transv. leaf, r. half-elliptic; 2-door; 4/5-seat; hyd. brks.; max. 78 m.p.h.; cruise 78; m.p.g. 37; whl. base 8ft. 3½in.; track f. and r. 4ft. 1in.; lgth. 13ft. 11¼in.; wdth. 5ft. 2¾in.; ht. 4ft. 9¾in.; g.c. 6⅛in.; turng. cir. 35ft. 2in.; kerb wt. 16⅜ cwt.; tank, 8⅓ gals.; 6-volt.
£850+£319.15.3 p.t. = £1,169.15.3

Abbreviations—g.c.—ground clearance; susp.—suspension; f.—front; r.—rear; comp.—compresssion; s.v.—side-valves; o.h.v.—overhead valves; o.h.c.—overhead camshaft; hyd.—hydraulic

FORD TAUNUS 17M

LITHE and lissom lines set people talking about this elegant 1.7 litre German saloon. There is a 1.5 litre engine as well for the thrifty. It comes with two or four doors and in standard and de luxe versions. Top speed of the 1.7 is 84 m.p.h. and of the 1.5 speed is 80 m.p.h. There is a station wagon with similar lines to carry lots of people and luggage. A car that rates a second look anywhere.

CLOSE-UP

Four-cyl.; o.h.v.; 84 × 76.7 mm.; 1,698 c.c.; 67 b.h.p.; 7 to 1 comp.; coil ign.; Solex carb.; 4-speed, 13.34, 7.66, 5.32, 3.89 to 1; col. lvr.; susp., f. ind. coil, r. half-elliptic; 2-door; 6-seat; hyd. brks.; max. 86 m.p.h.; cruise 75; m.p.g. 28-35; whl. base 8ft. 7½in.; track f. 4ft. 3in., r. 4ft. 2¾in.; lgth. 14ft. 7½in.; wdth. 5ft. 5in.; ht. 4ft. 10½in.; g.c. 7in.; turng. cir. 35ft.; kerb wt. 19¼ cwt.; tank, 10 gals.; 6-volt.
£815 + £306.12.9 p.t. = £1,121.12.9

FORD FALCON

RIDING the tide of success in the compact car market, Ford's American Falcon has a six-cylinder engine giving more than 100 h.p. and will do 23 m.p.g. Bench or bucket front seats; bench at rear. Wide doors let occupants in or out easily. On de luxe Futura, centre armrest is ideal storage for cigarettes, sun glasses or maps; white steering-wheel and door panels in washable vinyl add interest.

CLOSE-UP

Six-cyl.; o.h.v.; 88.9 × 74.64 mm.; 2,786 c.c.; 85 b.h.p.; 8.7 to 1 comp.; coil ign.; Ford carb.; 2-speed auto., 6.6, 3.2 to 1; col. lvr.; susp., f. ind. coil, r. half-elliptic; 2 or 4-door; 6-seat; hyd. brks.; max. 75 m.p.h.; cruise 65; m.p.g. 22-24; whl. base 9ft. 1½in.; track f. 4ft. 7in., r. 4ft. 6½in.; lgth. 15ft. 1in.; wdth. 5ft. 10½in.; ht. 4ft. 7in.; g.c. 6½in.; turng. cir. 38ft.; kerb wt. 21 cwt.; tank, 11½ gals.; 12-volt.
£1,075 + £404.3.7 p.t. = £1,479.3.7

FORD THUNDERBIRD

AMERICA'S luxury performance model built for four passengers and based on luxury car standards. Almost unique among American cars by offering one type of engine, a 6.3 litre V8, one transmission, and one rear axle ratio. Optional swinging steering wheel moves 10 inches sideways for easier entry and exit. Bucket seats at front. Large luggage compartment. Convertible T-Bird top folds into trunk giving unusually sleek lines.

CLOSE-UP

Eight-cyl.; o.h.v.; 102.8 × 96 mm.; 6,392 c.c.; 300 b.h.p.; 9.6 to 1 comp.; coil ign.; Ford carb.; 3-speed auto., 7.2, 4.41, 3.0 to 1; col. lvr.; susp., f. ind. coil, r. half-elliptic; 2-door; 4-seat; hyd. servo brks.; max. 120 m.p.h.; cruise 90; m.p.g. 12-16; whl. base 9ft. 5in.; track f. 5ft. 1in., r. 5ft.; lgth. 17ft. 1in.; wdth. 6ft. 4⅛in.; ht. 4ft. 4½in.; g.c. 5¼in.; turng. cir. 41ft. 6in.; kerb wt. 38¼ cwt.; tank, 16 gals.; 12-volt.

FORD GALAXIE 500

ONE of America's low-priced cars (but not after British import duty) the Galaxie offers choice of engines giving 175 to 300 h.p. Borg Warner automatic transmission with torque converter coupled to a planetary gearbox or three-speed manual and overdrive are the transmission options. Car has seats for six in high style and comfort. Slight reduction in length makes parking easier, and there is a galaxy of colour combinations.

CLOSE-UP

Eight-cyl.; o.h.v.; 101.6 × 88.9 mm.; 5,769 c.c.; 220 b.h.p.; 8.9 to 1 comp.; coil ign.; Holley carb.; 3-speed auto., 7.2, 4.41, 3.0 to 1; col. lvr.; susp., f. ind. coil, r. half-elliptic; 4-door; 6-seat; hyd. servo brks.; max. 114 m.p.h.; cruise 85; m.p.g. 17-20; whl. base 9ft. 11in.; track f. 5ft. 1in., r. 5ft.; lgth. 17ft. 5¼in.; wdth. 6ft. 7¼in.; ht. 4ft. 6¼in.; g.c. 7in.; turng. cir. 41ft.; kerb wt. 33½ cwt.; tank, 16½ gals.; 12-volt.

Abbreviations—g.c.—ground clearance; susp.—suspension; f.—front; r.—rear; comp.—compression; s.v.—side-valves; o.h.v.—overhead valves; o.h.c.—overhead camshaft; hyd.—hydraulic.

FRAZER NASH

AN individualist's car, built and finished by hand. The seats, steering rake, length of steering column and the layout of the control pedals are tailor-made for personal tastes. Even the colour schemes are entirely to choice, with upholstery of first quality leather. Its maximum speed is more than two miles a minute, and it cruises at 100 m.p.h. A very rare car that inherits a great tradition. Engine is by B.M.W.

CLOSE-UP
Eight-cyl.; o.h.v.; 82×75 mm.; 3,168 c.c.; 173 b.h.p.; 8.2 to 1 comp.; coil ign.; 2 downdraught carbs.; 4-speed, 11.6, 7.1, 4.6, 3.4 to 1; cen. lvr.; susp., f. ind. trans. leaf, r. de Dion; 2-door; 2-seat; disc brks.; max. 135 m.p.h.; cruise 100; m.p.g. 28; whl. base 8ft. 3in.; track f. 4ft. 2in., r. 4ft. 5½in.; lgth. 13ft. 5in.; wdth. 7ft.; ht. 4ft. 4in.; g.c. 6½in.; turng. cir. 27ft.; kerb wt. 16½ cwt.; tank, 17 gals; 12-volt.
£2,500 + £938.10.2 p.t. = £3,438.10.2

GLAS FLEETWING S1004

ANGULAR and appealing, the Glas small car made its debut at the Frankfurt motor show last year. It is available either as coupe or convertible. The 1,000 c.c. engine is canted sideways and gives 42 b.h.p. The camshaft is driven by a silent ribbed plastic cog-driven belt which adjusts itself to the expansion of the engine. Front engine rear-drive from the company that makes the rear-engined Goggomobil.

CLOSE-UP
Four-cyl.; o.h.c.; 72×61 mm.; 992 c.c.; 42 b.h.p.; 8.5 to 1 comp.; coil ign.; Solex carb.; 4-speed, 16.68, 8.466, 5.64, 4.25 to 1; cen. lvr.; susp., f. ind. coil, r. half-elliptic; 2-door; 2-seat; hyd. brks.; max. 84 m.p.h.; cruise 75; m.p.g. 40; whl. base 6ft. 10¾in.; track f. 4ft., r. 3ft. 11¼in.; lgth. 12ft. 6¾in.; wdth. 4ft. 11in.; ht. 4ft. 5¼in.; g.c. 7in.; turng. cir. 31ft. 3in.; kerb wt. 14¾ cwt.; tank, 8¼ gals.; 6-volt.

GOGGOMOBIL ROYAL

GROWING up gracefully. The Goggomobil began as a rampaging bug-eyed rear-engined baby which stormed across country tracks like a small tank but the Royal has front engine and rear drive, plus bigger body, more luggage space and a well finished interior. Seats for four and a top speed of 69 m.p.h.—with fuel consumption an economical 55-60 m.p.g. A pleasant small car easy on the eye.

CLOSE-UP
Two-cyl.; o.h.v. air-cooled; 78×72 mm.; 688 c.c.; 30 b.h.p.; 7.2 to 1 comp.; coil ign.; Solex carb.; 4-speed, 22.4, 11.35, 6.65, 5.0 to 1; cen. lvr.; susp., f. ind. coil, r. half-elliptic; 2-door; 4-seat; hyd. brks.; max. 69 m.p.h.; cruise 55-60; m.p.g. 50; whl. base 6ft. 7in.; track f. 3ft. 11¼in., r. 3ft. 10in.; lgth. 11ft. 4in.; wdth. 4ft. 10in.; ht. 4ft. 6in.; g.c. 7½in.; turng. cir. 29ft. 6in.; kerb wt. 14½ cwt.; tank, 8¼ gals.; 12-volt.
£473 + £217.16.1 p.t. = £690.16.1

HILLMAN HUSKY

A RELIABLE all-purpose car which has been in service for some time, yet is still in high demand. It is a town or country runabout. With the driver only, there is full capacity for a 750 lb. load. It is sturdy and has the advantage of a rear door which opens sideways. Interior is sealed against damp and dust, wings and bonnet are treated against rust and corrosion.

CLOSE-UP
Four-cyl.; o.h.v.; 76.2×76.2 mm.; 1,390 c.c.; 43.5 b.h.p. 8 to 1 comp.; coil ign.; Zenith carb.; 4-speed, 15.816, 9.038, 5.877, 4.22 to 1; cen. lvr.; susp., f. ind. coil, r. half-elliptic; 3-door; 4-seat; hyd. brks.; max. 75 m.p.h.; cruise 60; m.p.g. 30; whl. base 7ft. 2in.; track f. 4ft. 1in., r. 4ft. 0½in.; lgth. 12ft. 5½in.; wdth. 5ft. 0½in.; ht. 4ft. 11½in.; g.c. 6½in.; turng. cir. 33ft. 6in.; kerb wt. 18¾ cwt.; tank, 6¼ gals.; 12-volt.
£475 + £179.2.9 p.t. = £654.2.9

Abbreviations—g.c.—ground clearance; susp.—suspension; f.—front; r.—rear; comp.—compression; s.v.—side-valves; o.h.v.—overhead valves; o.h.c.—overhead camshaft; hyd.—hydraulic.

HILLMAN MINX DE LUXE

THIS is a car that has stood the test of time and now, with its 1.6 litre engine, it is still highly popular. It has strong brakes with a total lining area of 121 square inches, and these cope well when the Minx is travelling at more than 80 m.p.h. Women are particularly attracted to it as it has a good shape, easy driving and sound road-holding.

CLOSE-UP
Four-cyl.; o.h.v.; 81.5 × 76.2 mm.; 1,592 c.c.; 56.5 b.h.p.; 8.3 to 1 comp.; coil ign.; Zenith carb.; 4-speed, 15.816, 9.038, 5.877, 4.22 to 1; cen. lvr.; BW auto. opt.; susp., f. ind. coil, r. half-elliptic; 4-door; 5-seat; hyd. brks.; max. 82 m.p.h.; cruise 70; m.p.g. 30-35; whl. base 8ft.; track f. 4ft. 1in., r. 4ft. 0⅛in.; lgth. 13ft. 6in.; wdth. 5ft. 0¾in.; ht. 4ft. 11½in.; g.c. 7in.; turng. cir. 36ft.; kerb wt. 20 cwt.; tank, 7¼ gals.; 12-volt.
£510 + £192.5.3 p.t. = £702.5.3

HILLMAN SUPER MINX

THIS handsome 1½ litre Rootes Group model offers disc front brakes for 1963. Torque goes up and axle ratio is higher for easy cruising at lower revs. There are now no chassis greasing points. Standard equipment includes headlamp flasher, two-speed heater fan, individual adjustable front seats. Increased luggage space is obtained by moving petrol tank into the left rear wing. BW automatic transmission is an optional extra.

CLOSE-UP
Four-cyl.; o.h.v.; 81.5 × 76.2 mm.; 1,592 c.c.; 62 b.h.p.; 8.3 to 1 comp.; Solex carb.; 4-speed, 13.013, 8.324, 5.413, 3.889 to 1; cen. lvr.; BW auto. opt.; susp., f. ind. coil, r. half-elliptic; 4-door; 4/5-seat; hyd. brks., disc front; max. 84 m.p.h.; cruise 70; m.p.g. 28-32; whl. base 8ft. 5in.; track f. 4ft. 3½in., r. 4ft. 0½in.; lgth., 13ft. 9in.; wdth. 5ft. 3¼in.; ht. 4ft. 10¼in.; g.c. 6½in.; turng. cir. 36ft.; kerb wt. 21 cwt.; tank, 11 gals.; 12-volt.
£585 + £220.7.9 p.t. = £805.7.9

HUMBER HAWK

THIS is the Rootes Group's 2¼ litre, six-seater luxury car in their 1963 range. It is the kind of car that takes you on long journeys smoothly with its four-cylinder engine (78 b.h.p.) topping 80 m.p.h. The overdrive, as an extra, now operates on third as well as on top gear. So the driver has the choice of six forward speeds and greater flexibility of performance.

CLOSE-UP
Four-cyl.; o.h.v.; 81 × 110 mm.; 2,267 c.c.; 78 b.h.p.; 7.5 to 1 comp.; coil ign.; Zenith carb.; 4-speed, 14.128, 9.038, 5.877, 4.22 to 1; de Normanville overdrive opt.; col. lvr.; susp., f. ind. coil, r. half-elliptic; 4-door; 6-seat; servo brks., disc front; max. 85 m.p.h.; cruise 70-75; m.p.g. 20-25; whl. base 9ft. 2in.; track f. 4ft. 9in., r. 4ft. 7⅛in.; lgth. 15ft. 4¾in.; wdth. 5ft. 9½in.; ht. 5ft. 1in.; g.c. 7in.; turng. cir. 38ft.; kerb wt. 28¼ cwt.; tank, 16 gals.; 12-volt.
£875 + £329.2.9 p.t. = £1,204.2.9

HUMBER SUPER SNIPE

IT looks much the same but there are differences like the better-shaped rear window. Engine power is increased from 129.5 to 132.5 h.p., clutch is new and a higher top gear appears on manual gearchange models. Borg Warner automatic transmission is an extra. Fuel tank increased to 16 gallons. Handbrake and fluid level warning light on facia. There is a headlamp flasher switch, in the trafficator too.

CLOSE-UP
Six-cyl.; o.h.v.; 87.3 × 82.55 mm.; 2,965 c.c.; 132.5 b.h.p.; 8 to 1 comp.; coil ign.; Zenith carb.; 3-speed, 11.835, 6.129, 4.22 to 1; col. lvr.; de Normanville overdrive or BW auto. opt.; susp., f. ind. coil, r. half-elliptic; 4-door; 6-seat; servo brks., disc front; max. 100 m.p.h.; cruise 80; m.p.g. 20-25; whl. base 9ft. 2in.; track f. 4ft. 9in., r. 4ft. 7½in.; lgth. 15ft. 8in.; wdth. 5ft. 9½in.; ht. 5ft. 1in.; g.c. 7in.; turng. cir. 38ft.; kerb wt. 29½ cwt.; tank, 16 gals.; 12-volt.
£1,120 + £421.0.3 p.t. = £1,541.0.3

JAGUAR E-TYPE

FORGET the map reading; when you have found the place you've passed it. A new conception of motoring is born with this 150 m.p.h. two-seater. Speed in safety with excellent brakes and race-bred all-independent suspension that allows them to be used. 3.8-litre 265 b.h.p. engine gives its best in this scientifically streamlined shell. Convertible has room for week-end luggage; coupe holds as much luggage as many saloons.

CLOSE-UP
Six-cyl.; o.h.c.; 87 × 106 mm.; 3,781 c.c.; 265 b.h.p.; 9 to 1 comp.; coil ign.; 3 S.U. carbs.; 4-speed, 11.18, 6.16, 4.25, 3.31 to 1; cen. lvr.; susp., f. ind. torsion bar, r. ind. coil; 2-door; 2-seat; servo disc brks.; max. 150 m.p.h.; cruise, 130; m.p.g. 18-22; whl. base, 8ft.; track f. and r. 4ft. 2in.; lgth., 14ft. 7⅜in.; wdth., 5ft. 5¼in.; ht. 4ft. 0⅛in.; g.c. 5½in.; turng. cir., 37ft.; kerb wt. 24 cwt.; tank, 14 gals.; 12-volt.

£1,480+£556.0.3 p.t. = £2,036.0.3

JAGUAR 2.4 LITRE MARK 2

WHEN this car came out along with the larger 3.4-litre Jaguar saloons, the demand was so heavy that the makers had to double their output. It is typically a car for enthusiastic owners, and gives them just what they want. This means that they want a model with a moderate engine thirst and one that will travel, on occasion, at more than 100 miles an hour. It is sleek, well finished and extraordinarily simple to drive.

CLOSE-UP
Six-cyl.; o.h.c.; 83 × 76.5 mm.; 2,483 c.c.; 120 b.h.p., 8 to 1 comp.; coil ign.; 2 Solex carbs.; 4-speed, 14.42, 7.94, 5.48, 4.27 to 1; cen. lvr. de Normanville overdrive or BW auto. opt.; susp., f. ind. coil, r. cantilever leaf; 4-door; 5-seat; servo disc brks.; max. 105 m.p.h.; cruise, 70-75; m.p.g. 23; whl. base 8ft. 11¾in.; track, f. 4ft. 7in., r. 4ft. 5⅜in.; wdth. 5ft. 6¾in.; ht. 4ft. 9½in.; g.c. 7in.; turng. cir. 33ft. 6in.; kerb wt. 28¼ cwt.; tank, 12 gals.; 12-volt.

£1,082+£406.15.3 p.t. = £1,488.15.3

JAGUAR 3.4/3.8 LITRE MARK 2

STATUS symbol and swift, comfortable transport combined, the best-selling Jaguar 3.4 and 3.8 continue as before. Choice of engines; manual gearbox with optional overdrive or Borg Warner auto transmission. The 3.8 gives top speed of 125, the 3.4 120 m.p.h. 3.8 has spin-controlling differential. Both have 4 doors, and fitted with servo assisted disc brakes.

CLOSE-UP
Six-cyl.; o.h.c.; 83 × 106 mm.; 3,442 c.c.; 210 b.h.p; 8 to 1 comp. or 87 × 106 mm.; 3,781 c.c.; 220 b.h.p.; coil ign.; 2 S.U. carbs.; 4-speed, 11.95, 6.58, 4.54, 3.54 to 1; cen. lvr.; BW auto. or de Normanville overdrive opt.; susp., f. ind. coil; r. cantilever leaf; 4-door; 5-seat; servo disc brks.; max. 120 m.p.h. (3.4), 125 m.p.h. (3.8); cruise 90-100; m.p.g. 16-23; whl. base 8ft. 11⅜in.; track, f. 4ft. 7in., r. 4ft. 5⅜in.; lgth. 15ft. 0⅜in.; wdth. 5ft. 6¾in.; ht. 4ft. 9½in.; g.c. 7in.; turng. cir. 33ft. 6.in; kerb wt. 29¼ cwt.; tank, 12 gals.; 12-volt.

3.4 — £1,177+£442. 7.9 p.t. = £1,619. 7.9
3.8 — £1,255+£471.12.9 p.t. = £1,726.12.9

JAGUAR MARK X

IT is doubtful whether any car made is better value than this relatively new saloon which is selling like hot chestnuts on a freezing night. It is certainly the best-looking car built by Jaguars and it stems from the Mark IX and 'E' type models, which are pretty good parents. It is a 4/5-seater of unit construction and its six-cylinder engine develops as much as 265 b.h.p. Add to this independent suspension and disc brakes fitted all round.

CLOSE-UP
Six-cyl.; o.h.c.; 87 × 106 mm.; 3,781 c.c.; 265 b.h.p.; 9 to 1 comp.; coil ign.; 3 S.U. carbs.; 4-speed, 11.95, 6.58, 4.54, 3.54 to 1; cen. lvr.; overdrive or auto. opt.; susp., f. and r. ind. coil; 4-door; 5-seat; servo disc brks.; max. 120 m.p.h.; cruise 90; m.p.g. 15-20; whl. base 10ft.; track f. and r. 4ft. 10in.; lgth. 16ft. 10in.; wdth. 6ft. 4¼in.; ht. 4ft. 6½in.; g.c. 6½in.; turng. cir. 37ft.; kerb wt. 35 cwt.; tank, 20 gals.; 12-volt.

£1,640+£616.0.3 p.t. = £2,256.0.3

IMPERIAL

OPULENT prestige car from Chrysler Corporation; the only model retaining a separate body bolted to a chassis frame. Engine of 6.7 litres is teamed with Torqueflite automatic transmission; one of the smoothest currently available. Parking this near-19ft. automobile is largely intuitive. Interior appointments are luxurious and complete. Air conditioning unit is redesigned and there is Electroluminescent lighting for instruments and switches at night.

CLOSE-UP

Eight-cyl.; o.h.v.; 106.2 × 95.25 mm.; 6,768 c.c.; 350 b.h.p.; 10 to 1 comp.; coil ign.; downdraught carb.; 3-speed auto., 7.18, 4.25, 2.93 to 1; press button control; susp., f. ind. torsion bar., r. half-elliptic; 2 or 4-door; 6-seat; hyd. brks.; max. 120 m.p.h.; cruise 100; m.p.g. 18-22; whl. base 10ft. 9in.; track f. 5ft. 1¾in., r. 5ft. 2½in.; lgth. 18ft. 11in.; wdth. 6ft. 9¾in.; ht. 4ft. 9in.; g.c. 5½in.; turng. cir. 48 ft.9in.; kerb wt. 43½ cwt.; tank, 17 gals.; 12-volt.

JENSEN C-V8

A CHRYSLER V8 engine is fitted to this newcomer, a four-seater grand touring saloon whose top speed exceeds 140 m.p.h. Generous use of glass fibre and a new centre twin tube chassis gives the car a lightness and an urge which calls for only 4,460 engine revolutions at 120 m.p.h. It accelerates from 0 to 100 m.p.h. in 19 seconds and gives 20 miles to the gallon at a steady 60 m.p.h.

CLOSE-UP

Eight-cyl.; o.h.v.; 105 × 86 mm.; 5,916 c.c.; 305 b.h.p.; 9 to 1 comp.; coil ign.; Carter carb.; 3-speed auto, 7.52, 4.45, 3.07 to 1; col. lvr.; susp., f. ind. coil, r. half-elliptic; 2-door; 4-seat; disc servo brks.; max. 142 m.p.h.; cruise 110; m.p.g. 17-20; whl. base 8ft. 9in.; track f. 4ft. 7⅞in., r. 4ft. 8⅞in.; lgth. 15ft. 4½in.; wdth. 5ft. 7½in.; ht. 4ft. 6in.; g.c. 6in.; turng. cir. 38ft.; kerb wt. 29 cwt.; tank, 16 gals.; 12-volt.
£2,255 + £846.12.9 p.t. = £3,101.12.9

LAGONDA RAPIDE

STYLED by Carrozzeria Touring the handsome Lagonda 5-seater body is panelled in aluminium on a steel-tube frame. The 4-litre engine gives a top speed of 125 m.p.h. Body-chassis structure is rust proofed, insulated and undersealed. Front seats have adjustable reclining backrests. Equipment includes electrically operated radio aerial and windows, courtesy lamps, reading lamps in the rear, heater-demister and fresh air ventilation system.

CLOSE-UP

Six-cyl.; o.h.c.; 96 × 92 mm.; 3,995 c.c.; 236 b.h.p.; 8.25 to 1 comp.; coil ign.; 2 Solex carbs.; 3-speed auto., 8.7, 5.41, 3.77 to 1; col. lvr.; susp., f. ind. coil, r. de Dion, torsion bar; 4-door; 5-seat; disc servo brks.; max. 125 m.p.h.; cruise 100; m.p.g. 16-18; whl. base 9ft. 6in.; track f. 4ft. 6in., r. 4ft. 7½in.; lgth. 16ft. 3½in.; wdth. 5ft. 9½in.; ht. 4ft. 8in.; g.c. 6in.; turng. cir. 40ft. 6in.; kerb wt. 33¾ cwt.; tank, 16½ gals.; 12-volt.
£3,600 + £1,351 p.t. = £4,951

LANCIA FLAMINIA

PROUD, pretty and powerful—a delightful car from the House of Lancia with unique features: V6 2½-litre engine; four-speed all-synchro gearbox in unit with de Dion rear axle. Will take six people, too, and give high performance with good fuel economy. Luxury finish, and disc brakes all round. Pininfarina, Zagato and Carrozzeria Touring have designed a variety of body styles, convertibles and coupes.

CLOSE-UP

Six-cyl.; o.h.v; 80 × 81.5 mm.; 2,458 c.c.; 102 b.h.p.; 8 to 1 comp.; coil ign.; Solex carb.; 4-speed, 12.3, 7.6, 5.6, 3.75 to 1; col. lvr.; susp., f. ind. coil, r. de Dion half-elliptic; 4-door; 6-seat; disc brks.; max .105 m.p.h.; cruise 90; m.p.g. 24-28; whl. base 9ft. 9in.; lgth. 15ft. 11in.; wdth. 5ft. 9in.; ht. 4ft. 9½in.; g.c. 5½in.; turng. cir. 40ft.; kerb wt. 29½ cwt.; tank, 12¾ gals.; 12-volt.
£2,469 + £926.17.9 p.t. = £3,395.17.9

Abbreviations—g.c.—ground clearance; susp.—suspension: f.—front; r.—rear; comp.—compression; s.v.—side-valves; o.h.v.—overhead valves; o.h.c.—overhead camshaft; hyd.—hydraulic.

LANCIA FLAVIA

HIGH-GRADE 1½-litre front-drive family saloon with a big interior and a large luggage trunk. Handles like a sports car. A true Lancia, beautifully built to last a long time, cruising at up to 80 m.p.h. Red warning lamps in door edges light up when door is opened. Headlamps number four, and main beams are automatically extinguished when the engine is switched off.

CLOSE-UP

Four-cyl.; o.h.v.; 82×71 mm.; 1,500 c.c.; 78 b.h.p.; 8.3 to 1 comp.; coil ign.; Solex carb.; 4-speed, 16.16, 9.53, 6.71, 4.09 to 1; col. lvr.; susp., f. ind. trans. leaf, r. half-elliptic; 4-door; 5/6-seat; disc brks.; max. 95 m.p.h.; cruise 85; m.p.g. 26-32; whl. base 8ft. 8½in.; track f. 4ft. 3in., r. 4ft. 2in.; lgth. 15ft. 0¼in.; wdth. 5ft. 3in.; ht. 4ft. 11in.; g.c. 5in.; turng. cir. 36ft. kerb wt. 24 cwt.; tank, 10½ gals.; 12-volt.

£1,453+£545.17.9 p.t. = £1,998.17.9

LINCOLN CONTINENTAL

PRIME offering of the Lincoln Mercury Division of Ford, the Continental continues to attract lovers of luxury and quality cars. With seven litres under the bonnet, maximum speed is around 110 m.p.h. Innovations include unglamorous but important details, such as an improved automatic choke and freedom from chassis maintenance. The Continental comes in two styles—a four-door saloon and a convertible.

CLOSE-UP

Eight-cyl.; o.h.v.; 109.2×93.9 mm.; 7,045 c.c.; 300 b.h.p.; 10 to 1 comp.; coil ign.; Carter carb.; 3-speed auto, 6.85, 4.04, 2.89 to 1; col. lvr.; susp., f. ind. coil, r. half-elliptic; 4-door; 5-seat; hyd. servo brks.; max. 110 m.p.h.; cruise 90; m.p.g. 11-15; whl. base 10ft. 3in.; track f. and r. 5ft. 2in.; lgth. 17ft. 9in.; wdth. 6ft. 6in.; ht. 4ft. 5¾in. g.c. 5⅜in.; turng. cir. 48ft.; kerb wt. 44½ cwt.; tank, 17½ gals.; 12-volt.

£3,515+£1,319 p.t. = £4,834

LOTUS ELAN 1500

SUCCESSOR to the all-plastic Elite, the Elan has plastic body with an added metal chassis. There is more room—two bucket adjustable seats with an occasional seat at the rear and separate luggage locker. Headlamps are retractable to improve the streamlining. Power unit is the five-bearing Ford 1,498 c.c. unit with Lotus twin overhead camshaft conversion. Suspension is all-independent and disc brakes are used on all wheels.

CLOSE-UP

Four-cyl.; o.h.c.; 80.96×72.75 mm.; 1,498 c.c.; 100 b.h.p.; 9.5 to 1 comp.; coil ign.; 2 Weber carbs.; 4-speed, 16.04, 9.31, 6.50, 3.89 to 1; cen. lvr.; susp., f. and r. ind. coil; 2-door; 2/3-seat; disc brks.; max. 130 m.p.h.; cruise, 100; m.p.g. 30; whl. base, 7ft.; track f. and r. 3ft. 11½in.; lgth., 12ft. 1⅓in.; wdth., 4ft. 8in.; ht. 3ft. 5in.; g.c. 6in.; turng. cir., 29ft. 3in.; tank, 10 gals.; 12-volt.

LOTUS SUPER SEVEN 1500

BUILD-IT-YOURSELF kit car with acceleration to rival an E-Type Jaguar when fitted with a race-tuned Ford Classic 1,498 c.c. engine. Body has tubular space frame with glass fibre wing and nose panels. Equipment includes rev. counter, speedometer, hood and frame, side screens, dipping headlights, and washable plastic interior trim. There are disc brakes at front, drums at rear. Top speed is about 110 m.p.h., or more than 100 with standard engine.

CLOSE-UP

Four-cyl.; o.h.v.; 80.96×72.75 mm.; 1,498 c.c.; 75 b.h.p.; 8 to 1 comp.; coil ign.; Weber carb.; 4-speed, 17.32, 10.05, 5.93, 4.2 to 1; cen. lvr.; susp., f. ind. coil, r. coil; no doors; 2-seat; hyd. brks., disc front; max. 102 m.p.h.; cruise, 85; m.p.g. 30-35; whl. base, 7ft. 4in.; track f. and r. 3ft. 11in.; lgth., 12ft.; wdth., 4ft. 8in.; ht. 2ft. 4in.; g.c. 6in.; turng. cir., 28ft. 4in.; tank, 8 gals.; 12-volt.

Abbreviations—g.c.—ground clearance; susp.—suspension; f.—front; r.—rear; comp.—compression; s.v.—side-valves; o.h.v.—overhead valves; o.h.c.—overhead camshaft; hyd.—hydraulic.

MASERATI 3500 G.T.

MACCHINA Bellissima—and Veloce with it. Superlatives are in order to welcome back to the London Show this fast Gran Turismo coupe after a year's absence. Britain supplies the Lucas fuel injection and Girling disc brakes, but the character is essentially Italian, with bodies by Touring and Vignale. ZF gearbox with five speeds, all synchro. Option of Salisbury limited slip differential to tame wheelspin on full-bore take-offs.

CLOSE-UP

Six-cyl.; o.h.c.; 86 ╳ 100 mm.; 3,485 c.c.; 235 b.h.p.; 8.8 to 1 comp.; dual ign.; Lucas injection; 5-speed, 11.38, 6.97, 4.86, 3.77, 3.20 to 1; cen. lvr.; susp., f. ind. coil, r. half-elliptic; 2-door; 4-seat; disc servo brks.; max. 146 m.p.h.; cruise 125; m.p.g. 18-20; whl. base 8ft. 6¼in.; track f. 4ft. 6⅝in., r. 4ft. 5⅛in.; lgth. 15ft. 4in.; wdth. 5ft. 9in.; ht. 4ft. 3in.; g.c. 7in.; turng. cir. 40ft.; kerb wt. 26 cwt.; tank, 18 gals.; 12-volt.

£4,449.14 + £1,668.12 p.t. = £6,118.6

MERCEDES BENZ 220SE

SLEEK, spacious, swift and stylish, that is the Mercedes 220SE. A 2,195 c.c. fuel injection engine gives top speed of 105. Choice of 4-door 5-seat saloon or coupe and convertible. 220 and 220S saloons have carburettor engines and simpler trim. Automatic transmission is now optional. Equipment includes heating-ventilation system, padded steering wheel, grab handles in roof. Coupe and convertible have disc front brakes.

CLOSE-UP

Six-cyl.; o.h.c.; 80×72.8 mm.; 2,195 c.c.; 134 b.h.p.; 8.7 to 1 comp.; coil ign.; Bosch injection; 4-speed, 14.92, 9.34, 6.27, 4.1 to 1; cen. lvr., auto. opt.; susp., f. and r. ind. coil; 2-door; 4-seat; disc servo brks.; max. 105 m.p.h.; cruise 90; m.p.g. 22-25; whl. base 9ft. 0½in.; track f. and r. 4ft. 10½in.; lgth. 16ft. 0½in.; wdth. 6ft. 0½in.; ht. 4ft. 8½in.; g.c. 6⅛in.; turng. cir. 37ft. 7in.; kerb wt. 29¾ cwt.; tank, 14¼ gals.; 12-volt.

£2,033 + £763 p.t. = £2,796

MERCEDES BENZ 300SE

MAGNIFICENCE in the Mercedes tradition. Features are light metal fuel injection engine, four-speed automatic transmission, power-assisted steering, air suspension and Dunlop disc brakes with a unique anti-dive device. Impeccable finish, with cool air outlets to refresh the face, adjustable backrests, grab handles in roof. Safety measures include padded steering wheel and instrument panel, cushioned sunvisors, special locks that resist impact. Saloon, coupe and convertible bodies.

CLOSE-UP

Six-cyl.; o.h.c.; 85 × 88 mm.; 2,996 c.c.; 185 b.h.p.; 9 to 1 comp.; coil ign.; Bosch injection; 4-speed auto, 16.31, 10.33, 6.47, 4.1 to 1; col. levr.; susp., f. and r. ind. pneumatic; 4-door; 5/6-seat; disc servo brks.; max. 109 m.p.h.; cruise 90; m.p.g. 19-20; whl. base 9ft. 0⅛in.; track f. 4ft. 10⅜in., r. 4ft. 10½in.; lgth. 16ft.; wdth. 5ft. 10⅝in.; ht. 4ft. 9½in.; g.c. 7¼in.; turng. cir. 38ft. 5in.; kerb wt. 30½cwt.; tank, 14¼ gals.; 12-volt.

£4,370 + £1,639 p.t. = £6,009

MERCEDES BENZ 300SL

MOST powerful sports cars of the Mercedes range, the 300SL has 215 horses under the bonnet produced by a 2,996 c.c. fuel injection engine. After years of testing by Daimler-Benz and Dunlop, disc brakes are fitted on all four wheels. There is power to spare with anything up to 155 m.p.h. on tap, according to axle ratio. Mercedes sold in England are now guaranteed for a year.

CLOSE-UP

Six-cyl.; o.h.c.; 85×88 mm.; 2,996 c.c.; 240 b.h.p.; 8.55 to 1 comp.; coil ign.; Bosch injection; 4-speed, 12.16, 7.17, 5.06, 3.64 to 1; cen. lever; susp., f. and r. ind. coil; 2-door; 2-seat; disc servo brks.; max. 146 m.p.h.; cruise 130; m.p.g. 18-22; whl. base 7ft. 10½in.; track f. 4ft. 7in., r. 4ft. 9in.; lgth. 15ft.; wdth. 5ft. 10½in.; ht. 4ft. 3½in.; g.c. 5in.; turng. cir. 37ft.; kerb wt. 26¼ cwt.; tank, 22 gals.; 12-volt.

£3,939 + £1,478.2.9 p.t. = £5,417.2.9

Abbreviations—g.c.—ground clearance; susp.—suspension; f.—front; r.—rear; comp.—compresssion; s.v.—side-valves; o.h.v.—overhead valves; o.h.c.—overhead camshaft; hyd.—hydraulic

MERCURY COMET

COMET with 2.3 litre engine, the compact car of the Mercury stable. There is a new grille and four tail-lights. Rear is higher and squared off to give better luggage trunk capacity. Changes include improved starter to cut down noise level on engagement. Body styles come in nine different varieties. Oil change and chassis greasing every 6,000 miles only. Radiator filled with two-year anti-freeze. Valves need no adjustment.

CLOSE-UP
Six-cyl.; o.h.v.; 88.9 × 74.64 mm.; 2,786 c.c.; 101 b.h.p.; 8.7 to 1 comp.; coil ign.; Ford carb.; 2-speed auto., 6.6, 3.2 to 1; col. lvr.; susp., f. ind. coil, r. half-elliptic; 4-door; 6-seat; hyd. brks.; max. 85 m.p.h.; cruise 70; m.p.g. 22; whl. base 9ft. 1½in.; track f. 4ft. 7in., r. 4ft. 6½in.; lgth. 16ft. 3in.; wdth. 5ft. 10in.; ht. 4ft. 6½in.; g.c. 6¾in.; turng. cir. 39ft. 10in.; kerb wt. 21¾ cwt.; tank, 11 gals.; 12-volt.

MERCURY MONTEREY

REVERSE-ANGLED like that of the Anglia, the rear window on some '63 Mercurys also drops. The cheapest V8 Monterey packs a 4.7-litre engine under its broad snout and reaches a maximum speed of more than 100. The new grille is now convex and circular tail-lights replace canted fins. There are five different engines available to Mercury buyers, plus usual options of power steering and brakes, auto or manual transmission.

CLOSE-UP
Eight-cyl.; o.h.v.; 95.25 × 83.82 mm.; 4,785 c.c.; 170 b.h.p.; 8.8 to 1 comp.; coil ign.; Ford carb.; 2-speed auto., 5.25, 3.00 to 1; col. lvr.; susp., f. ind. coil, r. half-elliptic; 4-door; 6-seat; hyd. brks., servo opt.; max. 105 m.p.h.; cruise 85; m.p.g. 14-17; whl. base 10ft.; track f. 5ft. 1in., r. 5ft.; lgth. 17ft. 1½in.; wdth. 6ft. 7½in.; ht. 4ft. 7in.; g.c. 7in.; turng. cir. 41ft. 6in.; kerb wt. 35 cwt.; tank, 16½ gals.; 12-volt.
£1,916 + £719 p.t. = £2,635

M.G. MIDGET

IT is said that this M.G. has a sporting tradition dating back 33 years—the vast resources of the British Motor Corporation and the craftsmanship of the "hand-made" experts in the factory at Abingdon, Berkshire. Together they have produced an attractive body style, exceptional elbow-room for driver and passengers, a robust engine and smooth cornering. Suspension is independent at the front controlled by hydraulic shock absorbers, and the rear suspension is by leaf springs.

CLOSE-UP
Four-cyl.; o.h.v.; 62.9 × 76.2 mm.; 948 c.c.; 50 b.h.p.; 9 to 1 comp.; coil ign.; 2 S.U. carbs.; 4-speed, 13.50, 8.08, 5.73, 4.22 to 1; cen. lvr.; susp., f. ind. coil, r. quarter-elliptic; 2-door; 2/3-seat; hyd. brks.; max. 86 m.p.h.; cruise 70; m.p.g. 33-38; whl. base 6ft. 8in.; track f. 3ft. 9¾in., r. 3ft. 8¾in.; lgth. 11ft. 4½in.; wdth. 4ft. 5in.; ht. 4ft. 1¾in.; g.c. 5in.; turng. cir. 31ft. 2½in.; kerb wt. 13¾ cwt.; tank, 6 gals.; 12-volt.
£472 + £178.0.2 p.t. = £650.0.2

M.G. MGB

LOGICAL next step for the sports-car owner who uses his car daily. More space, more comfort, better weather protection, higher performance. Unit body-chassis, winding windows, room for an occasional seat or a load of luggage behind the bucket seats. More space in the tail. Bigger engine. Oil cooler optional on home-market cars. Heater and space for radio. Disc front brakes. Disc or wire wheels.

CLOSE-UP
Four-cyl.; o.h.v.; 80.26 × 89 mm.; 1,798 c.c.; 94 b.h.p.; 8.8 to 1 comp.; coil ign.; 2 S.U. carbs.; 4-speed, 14.21, 8.65, 5.37, 3.90 to 1; cen. lvr.; susp., f. ind. coil, r. half-elliptic; 2-door; 2/3-seat; hyd. brks., disc front; max. 108 m.p.h.; cruise 85; m.p.g. 26-28; whl. base 7ft. 9in.; track f. 4ft. 1in., r. 4ft. 1¼in.; lgth. 12ft. 9¼in.; wdth. 4ft. 11¾in.; ht. 4ft. 1¾in.; g.c. 5in.; turng. cir. 32 ft.10in.; kerb wt. 17¾ cwt.; tank, 10 gals.; 12-volt.
£690 + £259.15.3 p.t. = £949.15.3

M.G. 1100

CECIL KIMBER, who created the first MG, would be surprised at this one—but would applaud the efficient use of space—with its transverse engine, and front-wheel drive and the uncanny road-holding of its Hydrolastic suspension. Twin carburettors give its 1,100 c.c. engine the M.G. edge in performance and disc front brakes complete the Safety Fast specifications. Timber touches add the quality air. Two or four-door bodies are available.

CLOSE-UP
Four-cyl.; o.h.v.; 64.57 × 83.72 mm.; 1,098 c.c.; 55 b.h.p.; 8.9 to 1 comp.; coil ign.; 2 S.U. carbs.; 4-speed, 14.99, 8.98, 5.83, 4.133 to 1; cen. lvr.; susp., f. and r. ind. rubber-hydraulic; 2 or 4-door; 4-seat; hyd. brks., disc front; max. 85 m.p.h.; cruise 75; m.p.g. 35-38; whl. base 7ft. 9½in.; track f. 4ft. 3½in., r. 4ft. 2⅞in.; lgth. 12ft. 2¾in.; wdth. 5ft. 0¾in.; ht. 4ft. 4¾in.; g.c. 6in.; turng. cir. 34ft.; kerb wt. 17¼ cwt.; tank, 8½ gals.; 12-volt.

£590+ £222 p.t. = £812

MORGAN PLUS 4 SUPER SPORTS

FITTED with Standard Lawrence Tune engine with an 8.9 to 1 compression ratio, the body-work of this new car is aluminium. Two of the models of this famous West of England car manufacturer raced at Le Mans this year. They went there and back by road, and the fastest lap they put up in the race was 99.5 m.p.h., and in practice 102 m.p.h. These figures speak for themselves. An extremely tough sportsman's car.

CLOSE-UP
Four-cyl.; o.h.v.; 83 × 92 mm.; 1,991 c.c.; 117 b.h.p.; 9.2 to 1 comp.; coil ign.; 2 Weber carbs.; 4-speed, 12.85, 7.38, 5.24, 3.73 to 1; cen. lvr.; susp., f. ind. coil, r. half-elliptic; 2-door; 2-seat; hyd. brks., disc front; max. 120 m.p.h.; cruise, 105; m.p.g. 24; whl. base 8ft.; track f. 4ft., r. 4ft. 1in.; lgth. 12ft.; wdth. 4ft. 8in.; ht. 4ft. 1in.; g.c. 6⅛in.; turng. cir. 32ft.; kerb wt. 15½ cwt.; tank, 11 gals.; 12-volt.

£900+ £338.10.3 p.t. = £1,238.10.3

MORRIS MINI MINOR SUPER

BASICALLY the well-known nimble Mini that darts through the thickest traffic, but with a better interior finish and dual colour scheme. It is still the little car with the large heart, seen everywhere, passing everything. Special instrument panel, bigger seats, interior light, proper inside door handles, carpeted luggage trunk, plus full-width parcel shelf, seemingly bottomless door pockets, space in rear armrests and under rear seats.

CLOSE-UP
Four-cyl.; o.h.v.; 63 × 68.26 mm.; 848 c.c.; 34 b.h.p.; 8.3 to 1 comp.; coil ign.; S.U. carb.; 4-speed, 13.657, 8.176, 5.317, 3.765 to 1; cen. lvr.; susp., f. and r. ind. rubber; 2-door; 4-seat; hyd. brks.; max. 73 m.p.h.; cruise 60; m.p.g. 45; whl. base 6ft. 8in.; track f. 3ft. 11 7/16 in., r. 3ft. 9⅞in.; lgth. 10ft.; wdth. 4ft. 7in.; ht. 4ft. 5in.; g.c. 6⅜in.; turng. cir. 31ft.; kerb wt. 11¾ cwt.; tank, 5½ gals.; 12-volt.

£405+ £152.17.9 p.t. = £557.17.9

MORRIS MINOR 1000

THEY say that old soldiers never die—and this is certainly true of the brilliantly inspired Morris Minor 1000. First of the B.M.C. cars to be styled by Alec Issigonis (Mini car fame) the Minor 1000 still continues to sell splendidly, and it is understood that the makers have no intention of withdrawing it. It has been a family favourite for more than 14 years. Among its attractions are exceptional luggage capacity, and economical running.

CLOSE-UP
Four-cyl.; o.h.v.; 62.9 × 76 mm.; 948 c.c.; 37 b.h.p.; 8.3 to 1 comp.; coil ign.; S.U. carb.; 4-speed, 16.507, 10.802, 6.425, 4.555 to 1; cen. lvr.; susp., f. ind. torsion bar, r. half-elliptic; 2-door; 4-seat; hyd. brks.; max. 75 m.p.h.; cruise 55; m.p.g. 36-48; whl. base 7ft. 2in.; track f. 4ft. 2⅝in., r. 4ft. 2½in.; lgth. 12ft. 4in.; wdth. 5ft. 1in.; ht. 5ft.; g.c. 6⅜in.; turng. cir. 33ft.; kerb wt. 14¾ cwt.; tank, 6½ gals.; 12-volt.

£416+ £157.0.3 p.t. = £573.0.3

Abbreviations— g.c.—ground clearance; susp.—suspension; f.—front; r.—rear; comp.—compression; s.v.—side-valves; o.h.v.—overhead valves; o.h.c.—overhead camshaft; hyd.—hydraulic.

MORRIS 1100

SENSATIONAL new front-drive car developed by the B.M.C. design team under Alex Issigonis. Crosswise engine of 1,089 c.c. giving 48 b.h.p. with 70 m.p.h. cruising. Wonderful ride and road holding are obtained from new Hydrolastic suspension system which prevents pitch and roll. The brakes (disc in front) are powerful and safe on wet or dry roads. Body styling was by Pininfarina. Two or four doors. Takes five people and luggage.

CLOSE-UP

Four-cyl.; o.h.v.; 64.58×83.72 mm.; 1,098 c.c.; 50 b.h.p.; 8.5 to 1 comp.; coil ign.; S.U. carb.; 4-speed, 14.99, 8.98, 5.83, 4.133 to 1; cen. lvr.; susp., f. and r. ind. rubber/water; 2 or 4-door; 5-seat; hyd. brks., disc front; max. 78 m.p.h.; cruise 70; m.p.g. 36-38; whl. base 7ft. 9½in.; track f. 4ft. 3½in., r. 4ft. 2⅞in.; lgth. 12ft. 3in.; wdth. 5ft.; ht. 4ft. 5in.; g.c. 6in.; turng. cir. 34ft. 9in.; kerb wt. 16⅓ cwt.; tank, 8½ gals.; 12-volt.

£490+£184.15.3 p.t.=£674.15.3

MORRIS OXFORD VI

ONLY very minor modifications have been made on this car, which last year had a first-class face-lift with improvements to the bodywork. It was given a larger 1,622 c.c. engine. Result is a well-balanced, four-door saloon that pulls away with delightful power and cruises comfortably at more than 60 miles an hour. It is a good road-holder, too, with its broad track and its longer wheelbase.

CLOSE-UP

Four-cyl.; o.h.v.; 76.2×88.9 mm.; 1,622 c.c.; 55 b.h.p.; 8.3 to 1 comp.; coil ign.; S.U. carb.; 4-speed, 15.64, 9.52, 5.91, 4.3 to 1; col. or cen. lvr.; susp., f. ind. coil, r. half-elliptic; 4-door; 4-seat; hyd. brks.; max. 80 m.p.h.; cruise 65; m.p.g. 25-33; whl. base 8ft. 4¼in.; track f. 4ft. 2⅝in., r. 4ft. 3⅜in.; lgth. 14ft. 6½in.; wdth. 5ft. 3½in.; ht. 4ft. 10⅞in.; g.c. 5⅞in.; turng. cir. 37ft.; kerb wt. 21¾ cwt.; tank, 10 gals.; 12-volt.

£595+£224.2.9 p.t.=£819.2.9

MOSKVITCH

RUSSIAN utility model now offered on the Continent with a British Perkins diesel engine, making it the smallest diesel car on the market. A low-compression petrol engine able to run on cheap fuel is alternative in this strongly-built Slav. The tool-kit is exceptionally comprehensive, the heater is dimensioned with Siberian winters in mind, and a radiator blind helps to control engine temperature.

CLOSE-UP

Four-cyl.; o.h.v.; 76×75 mm.; 1,360 c.c.; 45 b.h.p.; 7 to 1 comp.; coil ign.; downdraught carb.; 4-speed, 17.89, 11.39, 7.83, 4.71 to 1; col. lvr.; susp., f. ind. coil, r. half-elliptic; 4-door; 4-seat; hyd. brks.; max. 72 m.p.h.; cruise 50; m.p.g. 35; whl. base 7ft. 9in.; track f. and r. 4ft.; lgth. 13ft. 4in.; wdth. 5ft. 1in.; ht. 5ft. 1¼in.; g.c. 7¾in.; turng. cir. 39½ft.; kerb wt. 18¾ cwt.; tank, 7¾ gals.; 12-volt.

£440+£166.0.3 p.t.=£606.0.3

NECKAR FIAT 500

ONLY recently introduced to Britain, these are Fiats built in Germany in a former NSU factory with local differences in appearance, and Bosch electrical equipment. Smallest is the 500, with re-styled body. The Jagst 770 based on the 600D comes as a two-door saloon or Riviera sports coupe and convertible, and the Neckar 1100 is a luxuriously finished four-door saloon.

CLOSE-UP

Two-cyl.; o.h.v., air-cooled; 67.4×70 mm.; 499 c.c.; 22 b.h.p.; 7 to 1 comp.; coil ign.; Weber carb.; 4-speed, 19.0, 10.6, 6.7, 4.5 to 1; cen. lvr.; susp., f. ind. transv. leaf, r. ind. coil; 2-door; 2/4-seat; hyd. brks.; max. 60 m.p.h.; cruise 50; m.p.g. 50; whl. base 6ft. 0½in.; track f. 3ft. 8⅛in., r. 3ft. 8½in.; lgth. 10ft. 1¾in.; wdth. 4ft. 5¼in.; ht. 4ft. 3½in.; g.c. 5⅛in.; turng. cir. 28ft. 3in.; kerb wt. 10 cwt.; tank, 4⅝ gals.; 12-volt.

£408+£154.0.3 p.t.=£562.0.3

Abbreviations—g.c.—ground clearance; susp.—suspension; f.—front; r.—rear; comp.—compression; s.v.—side-valves; o.h.v.—overhead valves; o.h.c.—overhead camshaft; hyd.—hydraulic.

NSU PRINZ 4

LIKE a Corvair in miniature, this latest and quickest NSU saloon has chunky lines that enclose four full seats and useful luggage space. High efficiency vertical twin engine with overhead camshaft and air cooling is mounted transversely at rear. Suspension is independent all round by coil springs with added air cushions at rear. Prinz III has smaller engine, occasional four-seater body, lower price.

CLOSE-UP

Two-cyl.; o.h.c. air-cooled; 76×66 mm.; 598 c.c.; 36 b.h.p.; 7.5 to 1 comp.; coil ign.; Solex carb.; 4-speed, 19.89, 10.61, 6.77, 4.80 to 1; cen. lvr.; susp., f. ind. coil, r. ind coil/air; 2-door; 4-seat; hyd. brks.; max. 74 m.p.h.; cruise, 65; m.p.g. 50; whl. base, 6ft. 8in.; track f. 4ft. 0¼in., r. 3ft. 11¼in.; lgth. 11ft. 6in.; wdth. 4ft. 10½in.; ht. 4ft. 5½in.; g.c. 7in.; turng. cir. 28ft.; kerb wt. 11 cwt.; tank, 8 gals.; 12-volt.
£499.5.9 + £188.4.10 p.t. = £687.10.7

OLDSMOBILE F-85

ALUMINIUM V8 engine continues in a roomier car for 1963 with more luggage space. Cutlass convertible is a peppy sports coupe with a showy interior and semi-bucket seats. Roof line is shortened and crisper with a rectangular rear window. All models have well-engineered rear suspension, with axle located on radius arms and centre pivot. Choice of three-speed manual or auto transmission.

CLOSE-UP

Eight-cyl.; o.h.v.; 88.9×71.12 mm.; 3,531 c.c.; 155 b.h.p.; 8.75 to 1 comp.; coil ign.; twin-choke carb.; 3-speed, 7.91, 4.77, 3.08 to 1, auto opt.; col. lvr.; susp., f. ind. coil, r. coil; 4-door; 5-seat; hyd. brks.; max. 93 m.p.h.; cruise 80; m.p.g. 17-23; whl. base 9ft. 4in.; track f. and r. 4ft. 8in.; lgth. 15ft. 8½in.; wdth. 5ft. 11½in.; ht. 4ft. 2½in.; g.c. 5in.; turng. cir. 37ft.; kerb wt. 22¾ cwt.; tank, 13 gals.; 12-volt.
£1,718 + £645.5.3 p.t. = £2,363.5.3

OLDSMOBILE SUPER 88

THE big 88 and 98 Oldsmobiles emphasize a squared off look and have practical benefit of offering more usable luggage space. Engines give 250 to 325 h.p. Grille has been redesigned. Roof lines are sportier and air conditioning outlet ducts are in the centre of the dashboard. Hydramatic transmission has been modified to give better performance. Interior trim is lavish and passenger comfort sumptuous.

CLOSE-UP

Eight-cyl.; o.h.v.; 104.7×93.7 mm.; 6,456 c.c.; 330 b.h.p.; 10.25 to 1 comp.; coil ign.; Rochester carb.; 3-speed, 6.94, 3.97, 3.23 to 1; col. lvr.; auto. opt.; susp., f. ind. coil, r. coil; 4-door; 6-seat; hyd. brks.; max. 115 m.p.h.; cruise 90; m.p.g. 14; whl. base 10ft. 3in.; track f. and r. 5ft. 1in.; lgth. 17ft. 9¾in.; wdth. 6ft. 5⅞in.; ht. 4ft. 7¾in.; g.c. 5½in.; turng. cir. 46ft. 3in.; kerb wt. 37½ cwt.; tank, 17 gals.; 12-volt.
£3,299 + £900 p.t. = £4,199

PANHARD P.L.17

FLAT-TWIN air-cooled engine with torsion bars for valve springs driving the front wheels gives this roomy car its individual character. High gearing means easy 70 m.p.h. cruising, though with vigorous use of gear lever to get there, for this full-five seater with cavernous luggage trunk relies on only 850 c.c. Monte-Carlo Rally winning Tiger has tuned engine giving 50 h.p. Panhard is now controlled by Citroen.

CLOSE-UP

Two-cyl.; o.h.v.; air-cooled; 85×75 mm.; 850 c.c.; 50 b.h.p.; 7.2 to 1 comp.; coil ign.; Zenith carb.; 4-speed, 16.495, 9.277, 6.148, 4.525 to 1; col. lvr.; susp., f. transv. ind., r. torsion bar; 4-door; 5-seat; hyd. brks.; max. 80 m.p.h.; cruise 70; m.p.g. 47; whl. base 8ft. 10⅛in.; track f. and r. 4ft. 3¼in.; lgth. 15ft. 0¾in.; wdth. 5ft. 5⅛in.; ht. 4ft. 9½in.; g.c. 6¼in.; turng. cir. 31ft.; kerb wt. 15¾ cwt.; tank, 9½ gals.; 12-volt.
£710 + £267.5.3 p.t. = £977.5.3

Abbreviations—g.c.—ground clearance; susp.—suspension; f.—front; r.—rear; comp.—compression; s.v.—side-valves; o.h.v.—overhead valves; o.h.c.—overhead camshaft; hyd.—hydraulic.

PEUGEOT 404
RENOWNED for well-built, reliable cars, Peugeot are now concentrating their efforts on the 404, available as saloon, coupe, convertible or station wagon, all styled by Pininfarina. The four-cylinder engine is tilted to one side, front suspension is strut-type with coil springs, and coils are used with a rigid axle at the rear. Gearbox has synchromesh on all four speeds.

CLOSE-UP
Four-cyl.; o.h.v.; 84×73 mm.; 1,618 c.c.; 72 b.h.p.; 7.4 to 1 comp.; coil ign.; Solex carb.; 4-speed, 16.80, 9.42, 6.05, 4.2 to 1; col. lvr.; susp., f. ind. coil, r. coil; 4-door; 5/6-seat; hyd. brks.; max. 90 m.p.h.; cruise 75-80; m.p.g. 30; whl. base 8ft. 8¼in.; track f. 4ft. 4¾in., r. 4ft. 2¼in.; lgth. 14ft. 6in.; width 5ft. 5¼in.; ht. 4ft. 9¼in.; g.c. 6in.; turng. cir. 30ft.; kerb wt. 20½ cwt.; tank, 11 gals.; 12-volt.

£915 + £344.2.9 p.t. = £1,259.2.9

PLYMOUTH FURY
LOWEST-PRICED of Chrysler's large cars, the Plymouth is offered in a range to suit every taste—two or four-door saloons, coupes, convertibles, station wagons, with a bewildering choice of six or eight-cylinder engines and manual or automatic transmissions, each with three speeds. Fury is the fiery high performer with more than 300 horse-power to give a top speed around 130 m.p.h.

CLOSE-UP
Eight-cyl.; o.h.v.; 98.55×84.07 mm.; 5,130 c.c.; 305 b.h.p.; 9 to 1 comp.; coil ign.; Carter carb.; 3-speed auto., 6.76, 3.0, 2.76 to 1; press button control; susp., f. ind. torsion bar, r. half-elliptic; 4-door; 6-seat; hyd. servo brks.; max. 130 m.p.h.; cruise 100; m.p.g. 13-18; whl. base 9ft. 8in.; track f. 4ft. 11½in., r. 4ft. 9in.; lgth. 16ft. 10in.; wdth. 6ft. 3in.; ht. 4ft. 6in.; g.c. 7¼in.; turng. cir. 40ft. 3in.; kerb wt. 30 cwt.; tank, 16½ gals.; 12-volt.

£1,811 + £680.2.9 p.t. = £2,491.2.9

PONTIAC CATALINA
DARING design is a feature of the Pontiac range. A big four-cylinder engine, curved propeller shaft to reduce tunnel height and rear-mounted gearbox make news on the Tempest. Le Mans Tempest convertible has a V8 engine. Strato-Chief, Laurentian and Parisienne are Canadian-built six-cylinder models. Catalina is the big American with V8 engine giving up to 350 horse-power and choice of saloon, convertible or station wagon bodies.

CLOSE-UP
Eight-cyl.; o.h.v.; 106×95.25 mm.; 6,374 c.c.; 267 b.h.p.; 8.6 to 1 comp.; coil ign.; Rochester carb.; 4-speed auto., 12.8, 8.23, 5.0, 3.23 to 1; col. lvr.; susp., f. ind. coil, r. coil; 4-door; 6-seat; hyd. servo brks.; max. 105 m.p.h.; cruise 80; m.p.g. 14-17; whl. base 10ft.; track f. 5ft. 3¼in., r. 5ft. 4in.; lgth. 17ft. 7⅝in.; wdth. 6ft. 6¾in.; ht. 4ft. 10⅝in.; g.c. 6¼in.; turng. cir. 42ft. 9in.; kerb wt. 42½ cwt.; tank, 17½ gals.; 12-volt.

£1,665 + £624 p.t. = £2,289

PORSCHE 356B/1600
NOW the basic Porsche model, the 1600 is sold in three stages of tune, giving 60, 75 or 90 horsepower. Variations in carburettors and gear ratios give maximum speeds between 100 and 115 m.p.h., coupled with startling fuel economy to prove that streamlining saves money. Reliability and excellent finish have won it a faithful following wherever fine fast cars are appreciated.

CLOSE-UP
Four-cyl.; o.h.v.; air-cooled; 82.5×74 mm.; 1,582 c.c.; 60 b.h.p.; 7.5 to 1 comp.; coil ign.; 2 Zenith carbs.; 4-speed, 13.7, 7.82, 5.0, 3.62 to 1; cen. lever; susp., f. and r. ind. torsion bar; 2-door; 2/4-seat; hyd. brks.; max. 100 m.p.h.; cruise 90; m.p.g. 33; whl. base 6ft. 10¾in.; track f. 4ft. 2¾in., r. 4ft. 2in.; lgth 13ft. 2in.; wdth. 5ft. 5¾in.; ht. 4ft. 4½in.; g.c. 6in.; turng. cir. 33ft. 6in.; kerb wt. 18½ cwt.; tank, 10¼ gals.; 6-volt.

Abbreviations—g.c.—ground clearance; susp.—suspension; f.—front; r.—rear; comp.—compression; s.v.—side-valves; o.h.v.—overhead valves; o.h.c.—overhead camshaft; hyd.—hydraulic.

131

PORSCHE 356B/2000GS

FASTEST of all the production Porsches, with a flat-four four-camshaft air-cooled engine, this is the car for the sportsman who wants maximum performance, allied to Porsche finish and care for detail, in a comfortable closed car that will hold enough luggage for a longish trip. Twin grilles, under an enlarged rear window, ventilate the engine compartment. Gearbox has the famous Porsche synchromesh.

CLOSE-UP
Four-cyl.; o.h.c.; air-cooled; 92 × 74 mm.; 1,966 c.c.; 130 b.h.p.; 9.5 to 1 comp.; coil ign.; 2 Solex carbs.; 4-speed, 13.7, 7.82, 5.45, 3.92 to 1; cen. lvr.; susp., f. and r. ind. torsion bar; 2-door; 2/4-seat; hyd. brks.; max. 125 m.p.h.; cruise 110; m.p.g. 24; whl. base 6ft. 10¾in.; track f. 4ft. 2¾in., r. 4ft. 2in.; lgth. 13ft. 2in.; wdth. 5ft. 5¾in.; ht. 4ft. 4¾in.; g.c. 6in.; turng. cir. 33ft. 6in.; kerb wt. 20 cwt.; tank, 10¼ gals.; 12-volt.

RAMBLER CLASSIC 6

CONCENTRATING on improvement of their big cars and letting the small American continue its successful career, the engineers have introduced bold new engineering changes and much sleeker styling. Rambler Classic and Rambler Ambassador have same overall dimensions. Classic has a 3.2-litre six-cylinder engine, Ambassador has a V8 of 5.7 litres producing 250 horse-power. Both have automatic transmission and a big choice of colours and trim details.

CLOSE-UP
Six-cyl.; o.h.v.; 79.37 × 107.95 mm.; 3,205 c.c.; 127 b.h.p.; 8.7 to 1 comp.; coil ign.; Holley carb.; 3-speed; col. lvr.; susp., f. and r. ind. coil; 2 or 4-door; 5-6 seat; hyd. brks.; max. 85 m.p.h.; cruise 70; m.p.g. 25-27; whl. base 9ft.; track f. 4ft. 10¾in.; r. 4ft. 10in.; lgth. 15ft. 10in.; wdth. 6ft. 0½in.; ht. 4ft. 9½in.; g.c. 7in.; turng. cir. 37ft. 3in.; kerb wt. 26½ cwt.; tank, 16 gals.; 12-volt.

RELIANT SABRE

NEW sports model from a company which previously specialised in three-wheeler utility vehicles. A Ford Zephyr 4 engine in a light chassis gives it high performance with low running costs. The gearbox has synchromesh on all speeds; front brakes are discs. Front suspension is by coil struts; rear axle is located by Watt linkage. Equipment includes cigarette-lighter, windscreen washers. Body is moulded plastic.

CLOSE-UP
Four-cyl.; o.h.v.; 82.6 × 79.5 mm.; 1,703 c.c.; 90 b.h.p.; 8.8 to 1 comp.; coil ign.; 2 S.U. carbs.; 4-speed, 9.0, 6.0, 4.37, 3.55 to 1; cen. lvr.; susp., f. ind. coil strut, r. coil; 2-door; 2-seat; hyd. brks., disc front; max. 105 m.p.h.; cruise, 85; m.p.g. 25-28; whl. base, 7ft. 6in.; track f. and r. 4ft.; lgth., 13ft. 9in.; wdth. 5ft. 1in.; ht. 4ft. 2in.; g.c. 6in.; turng. cir. 30ft.; kerb wt. 15¾ cwt.; tank, 8 gals.; 12-volt.
£800.10 + £301.4 p.t. = £1,101.14

RENAULT R4

USEFUL as a fleet of cars. Commuting or shopping, local delivery, exploring, camping or moving house—it is all the same to this versatile new Renault. There is a big lift-up door at the back, plus four at the sides. Seats lift out in seconds. All-independent suspension takes it sailing over gullies and hummocks. Front engine with sealed cooling system drives the front wheels.

CLOSE-UP
Four-cyl.; o.h.v.; 54.5 × 80 mm.; 747 c.c.; 26.5 b.h.p.; 8.5 to 1 comp.; coil ign.; Solex carb.; 3-speed, 15.675, 7.598, 4.282 to 1; dash lvr.; susp., f. and r. ind. torsion bar; 5-door; 4-seat; hyd. brks.; max. 65 m.p.h.; cruise 50; m.p.g. 45-50; whl. base 8ft.; track f. 4ft. 1in., r. 3ft. 11½in.; lgth. 11ft. 11½in.; wdth. 4ft. 10½in.; ht. 5ft. 4in.; g.c. 7½in.; turng. cir. 28ft.; kerb wt. 11¼ cwt.; tank, 5¾ gals.; 6-volt.
£399 + £150.12.9 p.t. = £549.12.9

RENAULT DAUPHINE

MATURED by years of development, France's popular rear-engined family model offers comfort and refinement, lively performance and economy. Better seats, improved heater, parking lamps, and option of three or four speeds are points to note. Roomy luggage trunk in front with spare wheel slung underneath. Dauphine Gordini has 40 h.p. engine, special luxury trim and wheel discs. There is a super-performance rally model, too.

CLOSE-UP

Four-cyl.; o.h.v.; 58×80 mm.; 845 c.c.; 30 b.h.p.; 8.0 to 1 comp.; coil ign.; Solex carb.; 3-speed, 16.1, 7.88, 4.52 to 1; cen. lvr., 4-speed opt.; susp., f. ind. coil, r. ind. coil and pneu.; 4-door; 4-seat; hyd. brks.; max. 75 m.p.h.; cruise 60; m.p.g. 42-48; whl. base 7ft. 5¼in.; track f. 4ft. 1¼in.; r. 4ft.; lgth. 12ft. 11¼in.; wdth. 5ft.; ht. 4ft. 9in.; g.c. 6in.; turng. cir. 29ft. 10in.; kerb wt. 12⅜ cwt.; tank, 7 gals.; 12-volt.

£479 + £180.12.9 p.t. = £659.12.9

RENAULT FLORIDE CARAVELLE

FIXED-HEAD, four-seater coupe to accompany the much-improved Floride S convertible. No more air intakes in the sides. The radiator is at the extreme rear to increase passenger space, and receives air through top of engine cover. New five-bearing 956 c.c. engine for higher performance. New front suspension with ball joint steering pivots. Rear swing axles have added radius arms and disc brakes are used all round.

CLOSE-UP

Four-cyl.; o.h.v.; 65×72 mm.; 956 c.c.; 51 b.h.p.; 9.5 to 1 comp.; coil ign.; Solex or Zenith carb.; 4-speed, 16.10, 9.17, 6.65, 4.50 to 1; cen. lvr.; susp., f. and r. ind. coil; 2-door; 4-seat; disc. brks.; max. 85 m.p.h.; cruise 78; m.p.g. 38; whl. base 7ft. 5¼in.; track f. 4ft. 1¼in., r. 4ft.; lgth. 14ft.; wdth. 5ft. 2in.; ht. 4ft. 3in.; g.c. 5¾in.; turng. cir. 31ft. 6in.; kerb wt. 15½ cwt.; tank, 6½ gals.; 12-volt.

£849 + £319.7.9 p.t. = £1,168.7.9

RENAULT R8

EXCITING companion for the Dauphine giving more power and space without venturing into engine sizes that are heavily taxed in France. Roomy four-door body with big square trunk in front. New free-revving five-bearing engine, sealed radiator, improved ball-joint front suspension. Rear radius arms to absorb braking effort and take the shake out of the gear lever. Ultra-light disc brakes on all wheels.

CLOSE-UP

Four-cyl.; o.h.v.; 65×72 mm.; 956 c.c.; 48 b.h.p.; 8.5 to 1 comp.; coil ign.; Solex or Zenith carb.; 4-speed, 16.10, 9.17, 6.65, 4.50 to 1; cen. lvr.; susp., f. and r. ind. coil; 4-door; 4/5-seat; disc. brks.; max. 75 m.p.h.; cruise 70; m.p.g. 38-42; whl. base 7ft. 5¼in.; track f. 4ft. 1¼in., r. 4ft.; lgth. 13ft. 1in.; wdth. 4ft. 10½in.; ht. 4ft. 7½in.; g.c. 5¾in.; turng. cir. 30ft. 3in.; kerb wt. 14½ cwt.; tank, 6¾ gals.; 12-volt.

£555 + £209.2.9 p.t. = £764.2.9

RILEY ELF

STEMMING from the famous gaggle of the B.M.C.'s Mini cars, this one has the same small engine, but it has the Riley radiator treatment and many additional comforts inside the car compared with the ordinary Morris Mini. For those whose appreciate the speed nippiness and minimum-sized parking spaces for their cars, this is the model, especially if they want to have a slight social status over the rugged Austin and Morris babies.

CLOSE-UP

Four-cyl.; o.h.v.; 62.94×68.26 mm.; 848 c.c.; 37 b.h.p.; 8.3 to 1 comp.; coil ign.; S.U. carb.; 4-speed, 13.657, 8.176, 5.31, 3.765 to 1; cen. lvr.; susp., f. and r. ind. rubber; 2-door; 4-seat; hyd. brks.; max. 73 m.p.h.; cruise 65; m.p.g. 42-45; whl. base 6ft. 8⅛in.; track f. 3ft. 11⅞in.; r. 3ft. 9⅞in.; lgth. 10ft. 8⅜in.; wdth. 4ft. 7½in.; ht. 4ft. 5in.; g.c. 6⅜in.; turng. cir. 31ft.; kerb wt. 11¾ cwt.; tank, 5½ gals.; 12-volt.

£475 + £179.2.9 p.t. = £654.2.9

Abbreviations—g.c.—ground clearance; susp.—suspension; f.—front; r.—rear; comp.—compression; s.v.—side-valves; o.h.v.—overhead valves; o.h.c.—overhead camshaft; hyd.—hydraulic.

133

RILEY ONE-POINT-FIVE

RILEY owners go for this model in a big way because it has two interesting characteristics—it can be a lively small family car and it can be a stern challenger in sporting competition. Its performance is increased by its twin-carburettor engine, matched with a specially high top gear for fast cruising with the engine running well within its limits. Inside the car are just those refinements that a Riley owner likes, including leather upholstery, walnut instrument panel.

CLOSE-UP
Four-cyl.; o.h.v.; 73.025×88.9 mm.; 1,489 c.c.; 60 b.h.p.; 8.3 to 1 comp.; coil ign.; 2 S.U. carbs.; 4-speed, 13.56, 8.25, 5.12, 3.73 to 1; cen. lvr.; susp., f. ind. torsion bar, r. half-elliptic; 4-door; 4-seat; hyd. brks.; max. 85 m.p.h.; cruise 70; m.p.g. 25-35; whl. base 7ft. 2in.; track f. 4ft. 2⅞in., r. 4ft. 2¼in.; lgth. 12ft. 9in.; wdth. 5ft. 1in.; ht. 4ft. 11¾in.; g.c. 6½in.; turng. cir. 34ft. 3in.; kerb wt. 18½ cwt.; tank, 7 gals.; 12-volt.

£580+£218.10.3 p.t. = £798.10.3

RILEY 4/72

BIG-BORE engine of 1,622 c.c. with twin carburettors gives this aristocrat of the B.M.C. middle range a near-90 maximum and brisk acceleration. Lighter steering, roomier rear seat and stabiliser bar are recent improvements. Standard transmission is four-speed gearbox with remote-control centre lever, but Borg Warner automatic is an optional extra. A well-established model with quality finish, and enough space for most families.

CLOSE-UP
Four-cyl.; o.h.v.; 76.2×88.9 mm.; 1,622 c.c.; 65 b.h.p.; 8.3 to 1 comp.; coil ign.; 2 S.U. carbs., 15.64, 9.52, 5.91, 4.3 to 1; cen. lvr.; susp., f. ind. coil, r. half-elliptic; 4-door; 4-seat; hyd. brks.; max. 88 m.p.h.; cruise 75; m.p.g. 23-29; whl. base 8ft. 4¼in.; track f. 4ft. 2⅝in., r. 4ft. 3⅜in.; lgth. 14ft. 6½in.; wdth. 5ft. 3in.; ht. 4ft. 10⅞in.; g.c. 5⅞in.; turng. cir.; 37ft.; kerb wt. 22¾ cwt.; tank, 10 gals.; 12-volt.

£745+£280.7.9 p.t. = £1,025.7.9

ROLLS-ROYCE SILVER CLOUD III

FOUR headlamps are the obvious change on the 1963 series of the world's best cars. Side lamps and direction-indicator lamps are grouped together, the bonnet line has been lowered slightly to improve forward vision, and bumper overriders are of a neater design. Engine power is increased by higher compression and bigger carburettors but exact figures remain a Rolls-Royce secret. New front seats, too, and more leg-room.

CLOSE-UP
Eight-cyl.; o.h.v.; 104.14×91.44 mm.; 6,230 c.c.; 9 to 1 comp.; coil ign.; 2 S.U. carbs.; 4-speed auto. 11.75, 8.10, 4.46, 3.08 to 1; col. lvr.; susp., f. ind. coil, r. half-elliptic; 4-door; 5/6-seat; hyd. servo brks.; max. 110 m.p.h.; cruise 90; m.p.g. 12-15; whl. base 10ft. 3in.; track f. 4ft. 10in., r. 5ft.; lgth. 17ft. 7⅜in.; wdth. 6ft. 2¾in.; ht. 5ft. 4in.; g.c. 7in.; turng. cir. 41ft. 8in.; kerb wt. 41½ cwt.; tank, 18 gals.; 12-volt.

£4,565+£1,712.17.9 p.t. = £6,277.17.9

ROLLS-ROYCE PHANTOM V

REGAL magnificence, with performance, comfort and silence. Seats for any number up to nine, and speeds up to 100 m.p.h. Cocktail cabinet, electric division, pigskin companion fittings and dual heater. Options of electric window lifts and air conditioning with refrigerator. Bodies include limousines by Park Ward and James Young, and a sedanca de ville by Young. Engine power is increased by higher compression and bigger carburettors.

CLOSE-UP
Eight-cyl.; o.h.v.; 104.14×91.44 mm.; 6,230 c.c.; 9 to 1 comp.; coil ign.; 2 S.U. carbs.; 4-speed auto., 14.86, 10.23, 5.64, 3.89 to 1; col. lvr.; susp., f. ind. coil, r. half-elliptic; 4-door; 7-seat; hyd. servo brks.; max. 100 m.p.h.; cruise 85; m.p.g. 12; whl. base 12ft.; track f. 5ft. 0⅞in., r. 5ft. 4in.; lgth. 19ft. 10in.; wdth. 6ft. 7in.; ht. 5ft. 9in.; g.c. 7¼in.; turng. cir. 48ft. 9in.; tank, 23 gals.; 12-volt.

£7,305+£2,740.7.9 p.t. = £10,045.7.9

ROVER 95

THIS new model has the luxury of quality car motoring at relatively low cost. It replaces the "80" and has what was formerly the "100" engine. This power unit has a seven bearing crankshaft and the six-cylinder engine produces 102 brake horse power. It has disc brakes in front and is built for the family (and the doctor) for swift and comfortable motoring.

CLOSE-UP

Six-cyl.; o.h. inlet, side exhaust; 77.8×92.07 mm.; 2.625 c.c.; 102 b.h.p.; 8.8 to 1 comp.; coil ign.; S.U. carb.; 4-speed, 13.16, 7.96, 5.37, 3.9 to 1; cen. lvr.; susp., f. ind. coil, r. half-elliptic; 4-door; 4/5-seat; hyd. servo brks., disc front; max. 95 m.p.h.; cruise 75; m.p.g. 19-25; whl. base 9ft. 3in.; track f. 4ft. 4½in., r. 4ft. 3½in.; lgth. 14ft. 10⅝in.; wdth. 5ft. 5⅝in.; ht. 5ft. 3¾in.; g.c. 7in.; turng. cir. 37ft.; kerb wt. 29¼ cwt.; tank, 11½ gals.; 12-volt.

£998+£375.5.3 p.t. = £1,373.5.3

ROVER 110

FAMILIAR exterior conceals many worthwhile improvements for 1963. Most important, the more powerful engine with new manifold and improved head. De Normanville overdrive. Revised instrument panel, new wheel discs, electric screen-washer, and Dunlop or Avon speed tyres are now standard. Leather-covered bench front seat is standard, with separate seats and adjustable backrests as options. Only one grease point to attend to every 3,000 miles.

CLOSE-UP

Six-cyl.; o.h. inlet, side exhaust; 77.8×92.07 mm.; 2.625 c.c.; 123 b.h.p.; 8.8 to 1 comp.; coil ign.; S.U. carb.; 4-speed, 14.41, 8.78, 5.82, 4.3 to 1, de Normanville overdrive; cen. lvr.; susp., f. ind. coil, r. half-elliptic; 4-door; 4/5-seat; hyd. servo brks.; max. 100 m.p.h.; cruise 80; m.p.g. 18-25; whl. base 9ft. 3in.; track f. 4ft. 4½in., r. 4ft. 3½in.; lgth. 14ft. 10⅝in.; wdth. 5ft. 5⅝in.; ht. 5ft. 3¾in.; g.c. 7in.; turng. cir. 37ft.; kerb wt. 29½ cwt.; tank, 11½ gals.; 12-volt.

£1,115+£419.2.9 p.t. = £1,534.2.9

ROVER 3-LITRE COUPE

LOWER, leaner lines allied to Rover's traditional quality finish. New model with front seats adjustable for reach, height and rake. Separate rear seats with ashtray and lighter between. Latest engine (also available on saloon) gains extra horse-power from improved head design and new water-jacketed inlet manifold. New remote-control gear lever on strengthened gearbox with de Normanville overdrive.

CLOSE-UP

Six-cyl.; o.h. inlet, side exhaust; 77.8×105 mm.; 2.995 c.c.; 134 b.h.p.; 8.75 to 1 comp.; coil ign.; S.U. carb.; 4 speed, 14.41, 8.07, 5.47, 4.3 to 1, de Normanville overdrive; cen. lvr., BW auto. opt.; susp., f. ind. torsion bar, r. half-elliptic; 4-door; 4-seat; hyd. servo brks., disc front; max. 105 m.p.h.; cruise 85; m.p.g. 18-25; whl. base 9ft. 2½in.; track f. 4ft. 7½in., r. 4ft. 8in.; lgth. 15ft. 6½in.; wdth. 5ft. 10in.; ht. 4ft. 9¼in.; g.c. 7¾in.; turng. cir. 40ft.; kerb wt. 32½ cwt.; tank, 14 gals.; 12-volt.

£1,499+£563.2.9 p.t. = £2,062.2.9

SAAB 96

VICTOR in this year's Monte Carlo and two successive RAC rallies, plus countless others. Sweden's small family car with solid build and fine road-holding. Three-cylinder two-stroke engine, front-wheel drive and refinements such as radiator blind, thermostatically controlled heater, rear window demister slots. 90 m.p.h. Sports SAAB has three-carburettor engine, pump instead of petroil lubrication, four speeds, disc front brakes. Station wagon has a third seat facing rearwards.

CLOSE-UP

Three-cyl.; two-stroke; 70×72.9 mm.; 841 c.c.; 42 b.h.p.; 7.3 to 1 comp.; coil ign.; Zenith carb.; 3-speed, 17.19, 8.53, 5.23 to 1; col. lvr.; susp., f. ind. coil, r. coil; 2-door; 4/5-seat; hyd. brks.; max. 75 m.p.h.; cruise, 70; m.p.g. 34; whl base 8ft. 2in.; track f. and r. 4ft.; lgth. 13ft. 2in.; wdth. 5ft. 2in.; ht. 4ft. 10in.; g.c. 7½in.; turng. cir. 36ft.; kerb wt. 16⅛ cwt.; tank, 8½ gals.; 12-volt.

£600+£226.0.3 p.t. = £826.0.3

Abbreviations—g.c.—ground clearance; susp.—suspension; f.—front; r.—rear; comp.—compression; s.v.—side-valves; o.h.v.—overhead valves; o h.c.—overhead camshaft; hyd.—hydraulic.

SIMCA 1000

LIVELY new French baby with five-bearing four-cylinder engine at the rear canted to one side to leave room for the radiator alongside. Rear-mounted battery and fuel tank leave a lot of luggage space in the square nose. Four doors, four seats, all-independent suspension and synchromesh on all four speeds. Fun to drive, light to handle and very economical.

CLOSE-UP

Four-cyl.; o.h.v.; 68 × 65 mm.; 944 c.c.; 45 b.h.p.; 7.8 to 1 comp.; coil ign.; Solex carb.; 4-speed, 15.51, 9.26, 6.16, 4.21 to 1; cen. lvr.; susp., f. ind. trans. leaf, r. ind. coil; 4-door; 4-seat; hyd. brks.; max. 75 m.p.h.; cruise, 70; m.p.g. 35-44; whl. base 7ft. 3½in.; track. f. 4ft. 5in., r. 4ft. 0⅜in.; lgth. 12ft. 5½in.; wdth. 4ft. 10½in.; ht. 4ft. 4½in.; g.c. 5½in.; turng. cir. 30ft.; kerb wt. 14 cwt.; tank, 6⅝ gals.; 12-volt.

£550.10.8 + £207.9.4 p.t. = £758

SIMCA ARONDE ELYSEE

ONE basic design with many variations: Etoile saloon, Monaco hardtop, Oceane coupe, Plein Ciel convertible, Castel station wagon and Montlhery sports saloon with 70 h.p. engine. Reclining seats promote comfort on long journeys and a sliding roof is an optional extra. Finished in typical French style the Aronde has been steadily improved through the years. The engine now has five main bearings for extra smoothness and durability.

CLOSE-UP

Four-cyl.; o.h.v.; 74 × 75 mm.; 1,290 c.c.; 52 b.h.p.; 7.5 to 1 comp.; coil ign.; Solex carb.; 4-speed, 16.4, 10.43, 6.53, 4.44 to 1; col. lvr.; susp., f. ind. coil, r. coil and half-elliptic; 4-door; 4-seat; hyd. brks.; max. 82 m.p.h.; cruise, 70; m.p.g. 32-35; whl. base 8ft. 0½in.; track, f. 4ft. 1½in., r. 4ft. 1½in.; lgth 13ft. 9½in.; wdth. 5ft. 1½in.; ht. 4ft. 8½in.; g.c. 5½in.; turng. cir. 35ft. 4in.; kerb wt. 18½ cwt.; tank, 9⅝ gals.; 12-volt.

£598.15 + £224.19.4 p.t. = £823.14.4

SIMCA ARIANE

BIG French cars are very few. Ariane combines six-seater body space and a really roomy luggage trunk with the operating economy of the latest five-bearing Aronde engine. It provides thrifty transport for the man with a large family, and has enough performance to hold its own in the cut and thrust of traffic in Paris or on France's long Routes Nationales.

CLOSE-UP

Four-cyl.; o.h.v.; 74 × 75 mm.; 1,290 c.c.; 62 b.h.p.; 8.5 to 1 comp.; coil ign.; Solex carb.; 4-speed, 17.8, 11.2, 7.0, 4.77 to 1; col. lvr.; susp., f. ind. coil, r. half-elliptic; 4-door; 5/6-seat; hyd. brks.; max. 78 m.p.h.; cruise, 65; m.p.g. 25-30; whl. base 8ft. 10in.; track, f. 4ft. 6in.; r. 4ft. 5in.; lgth. 14ft. 10in.; wdth. 5ft. 9in.; ht. 4ft. 10½in.; g.c. 6in.; turng. cir. 35ft. 6in.; kerb wt. 21¾cwt.; tank, 13 gals.; 12-volt.

£789.18.2 + £297.4.7 p.t. = £1,087.2.9

SINGER GAZELLE

LOW-COST luxury in a well-developed model from the Rootes stable. A year's experience has shown the value of the bigger 1.6-litre engine, and it can now be coupled with the Borg Warner automatic transmission which has been adopted in place of Easidrive. It uses a fluid torque converter instead of magnetic powder clutches. Heater is standard equipment. Big range of options includes radio, white wall tyres.

CLOSE-UP

Four-cyl.; o.h.v.; 81.5 × 76.2 mm.; 1,592 c.c.; 56.5 b.h.p.; 8.3 to 1 comp.; coil ign.; Zenith carb.; 4-speed, 15.816, 9.038, 5.877, 4.22 to 1; cen. lvr., de Normanville overdrive or BW auto. opt.; susp. f. ind. coil, r. half-elliptic; 4-door; 4/5 seat; hyd. brks.; max. 82 m.p.h.; cruise 70; m.p.g. 30-35; whl. base 8ft.; track f. 4ft. 1in., r. 4ft. 0½in.; lgth. 13ft. 7½in.; wdth. 5ft. 0½in.; ht. 4ft. 11½in.; g.c. 7in.; turng. cir. 36ft.; kerb wt. 20¾ cwt.; tank, 10 gals.; 12-volt.

£585 + £220.7.9 p.t. = £805.7.9

Abbreviations—g.c.—ground clearance; susp.—suspension; f.—front; r.—rear; comp.—compression; s.v.—side-valves; o.h.v.—overhead valves; o.h.c.—overhead camshaft; hyd.—hydraulic.

SINGER VOGUE

DISC brakes in front are the main change in the 1963 Singer Vogue. One of the first British cars to break away from the old styling and incorporate two twin headlights for more night-driving safety. Changes are also made in the interior, where the trim and upholstery are even more luxurious than before. The kind of car for buyers interested in the 1.6 litre class, a category gaining favour rapidly.

CLOSE-UP

Four-cyl.; o.h.v.; 81.5×76.2 mm.; 1,592 c.c.; 62 b.h.p.; 8.3 to 1 comp.; coil ign.; Solex carb.; 4-speed, 13.013, 8.324, 5.413, 3.889 to 1; de Normanville overdrive or BW auto. opt.; cen. lvr.; susp., f. ind. coil, r. half-elliptic; 4-door; 4/5-seat; hyd. brks., disc front; max. 84 m.p.h.; cruise 70; m.p.g. 28-32; whl. base 8ft. 5in.; track f. 4ft. 3½in., r. 4ft. 0½in.; lgth. 13ft. 9½in.; wdth. 5ft. 2½in.; ht. 4ft. 10½in.; g.c. 6½in.; turng. cir. 36ft.; kerb wt. 21½ cwt.; tank, 11 gals.; 12-volt.

£655 + £246.12.9 p.t. = £901.12.9

SKODA OCTAVIA

CZECH mate for those who like a lively, thrifty small car with highly individual character. Tubular backbone chassis with all-independent suspension; coil springs at front, transverse leaf spring at rear. Choice of 1,089 or 1,221 c.c. engines with saloon, convertible or station wagon bodies. Touring Sport saloon has two carburettors giving 53 h.p. Reclining seats are among the optional extras. The price is interesting, too.

CLOSE-UP

Four-cyl.; o.h.v.; 68×75 mm.; 1,089 c.c.; 43 b.h.p.; 7.5 to 1 comp.; coil ign.; Jikov carb.; 4-speed, 20.4, 11.8, 7.6, 4.78 to 1; col. lvr.; susp., f. ind. coil, r. ind. transv. leaf; 2-door; 4-seat; hyd. brks.; max. 77 m.p.h.; cruise, 65; m.p.g. 35-40; whl. base 7ft. 10½in.; track f. 3ft. 11½in., r. 4ft. 1in.; lgth. 13ft. 4in.; wdth. 5ft. 3in.; ht. 4ft. 8½in.; g.c. 6½in.; turng. cir. 32ft. 9in.; kerb wt. 17¾ cwt.; tank, 6½ gals.; 12-volt.

£430.16 + £162.11.3 p.t. = £593.7.3

STANDARD ENSIGN

DURABLE 2.1-litre engine with replaceable cylinder liners gives a performance boost to this spacious family model. Trim and finish are improved, window frames are polished aluminium, facia is padded, floor is carpeted and head lining is washable. Saloon has 14 cubic feet trunk capacity: station wagon takes 57 cubic feet of freight with rear seat folded flat. Among the extras are disc front brakes, duo-tone paintwork, heater, de Normanville overdrive.

CLOSE-UP

Four-cyl.; o.h.v.; 86×92 mm.; 2,138 c.c.; 75 b.h.p.; 8.5 to 1 comp.; coil ign.; Solex carb.; 4-speed, 14.50, 8.61, 5.68, 4.10 to 1; cen. lvr., de Normanville overdrive opt.; susp., f. ind. coil, r. half-elliptic; 4-door; 5/6-seat; hyd. brks.; max. 80 m.p.h.; cruise 65-70; m.p.g. 30-38; track f. and r. 4ft. 3½in.; lgth. 14ft. 3½in.; wdth. 5ft. 7½in.; ht. 5ft.; g.c. 7½in.; turng. cir. 39ft.; kerb wt. 23¾ cwt.; tank, 12 gals.; 12-volt.

£616 + £232.0.3 p.t. = £848.0.3

STANDARD VANGUARD VI

ONE of the best tried models at the Show, this Vanguard is sturdy, has good characteristics and comes in saloon and estate-car versions. You can choose from two types of gearbox—a four-speed, with floor-mounted lever, or a three-speed with steering-column gear-change lever. Its 2-litre engine developing 85 b.h.p. is as good as the rest of the car.

CLOSE-UP

Six-cyl.; o.h.v.; 74.7×76 mm.; 1,998 c.c.; 85 b.h.p.; 8 to 1 comp.; col. ign.; 2 Solex carbs.; 4-speed, 14.5, 8.61, 5.66, 4.1 to 1, 3-speed opt.; cen. lvr.; susp., f. ind. coil, r. half-elliptic; 4-door; 5/6-seat; hyd. brks.; max. 90 m.p.h.; cruise, 70; m.p.g. 25-35; whl. base, 8ft. 6in.; track f. and r. 4ft. 3in.; lgth. 14ft. 3½in.; ht. 5ft.; g.c. 7½in.; turng. cir. 39ft.; kerb wt. 23½ cwt.; tank, 12 gals.; 12-volt.

STUDEBAKER AVANTI

RAYMOND LOEWY resumes styling for Studebaker with this unusual glass-fibre bodied sports coupe. It has the Hawk V8 engine tuned to produce 220 h.p. and there is an optional supercharger to boost it to 280. First American car to use British disc brakes (Dunlops) it has a limited-slip differential for spin-free getaways. Choice of three transmissions—three-speed manual, three-speed or four-speed automatic.

CLOSE-UP
Eight-cyl.; o.h.v.; 90.4×92 mm.; 4,737 c.c.; 220 b.h.p.; 10 to 1 comp.; coil ign.; downdraught carb.; 3-speed, 8.94, 5.48, 3.73 to 1; cen. lvr.; susp., f. ind. coil, r. half-elliptic and radius arms; 2-door; 4/5-seat; hyd. servo brks. disc front; max. 112 m.p.h.; cruise 95; m.p.g. 17-20; whl. base 9ft. 1in.; track f. 4ft. 9⅜in., r. 4ft. 8⅝in.; lgth. 16ft. 0⅜in.; kerb wt. 28½ cwt.; 12-volt.

STUDEBAKER LARK

GRILLE and panel changes are limited on Studebaker's successful economy model which helped to start the American swing to smaller cars. With six-and eight-cylinder engines to choose from the buyer can fix his own balance between performance and economy. The same goes for transmissions; the basic three-speed gearbox can be supplemented by overdrive, or a fully automatic torque converter rig.

CLOSE-UP
Six-cyl.; o.h.v.; 76.2×101.6 mm.; 2,785 c.c.; 112 b.h.p.; 8.25 to 1 comp.; coil ign.; Stromberg carb.; 3-speed, 9.58, 5.78, 3.73 to 1 auto. opt.; col. lvr.; susp. f. ind. coil, r. half-elliptic; 4-door; 5-seat; hyd. brks., servo opt.; max. 88 m.p.h.; cruise 75; m.p.g. 20-24; whl. base 9ft. 5in.; track f. 4ft. 9in., r. 4ft. 8½in.; lgth. 15ft. 8in.; wdth. 5ft. 11in.; ht. 4ft. 8½in.; g.c. 6in.; turng. cir. 41ft.; kerb wt. 28 cwt.; tank, 14¾ gals.; 12-volt.
£1,150+£432.5.3 p.t. = £1,582.5.3

SUNBEAM ALPINE

WINDING side windows and coupe comfort began a trend which has been widely followed—the trend towards more comfort and better weather protection in sports cars. Die-hards may deplore it, but the girls who occupy the passenger seat are in favour. The optional de Normanville gives the transmission a total of seven forward speeds, and disc front brakes provide the safety margins a 100 m.p.h. car needs.

CLOSE-UP
Four-cyl.; o.h.v.; 81.5×76.2 mm.; 1,592 c.c.; 85.5 b.h.p.; 9.1 to 1 comp.; coil ign.; 2 Zenith carbs.; 4-speed, 13.013, 8.324, 5.413, 3.89 to 1; cen. lvr.; de Normanville overdrive opt.; susp. f. ind. coil, r. half-elliptic; 2-door; 2-seat; hyd. brks. disc front; max. 100 m.p.h.; cruise 80; m.p.g. 25; whl. base 7ft. 2in.; track f. 4ft. 3in., r. 4ft. 0½in.; lgth. 12ft. 11¼in.; wdth. 5ft. 0½in.; ht. 4ft. 3½in.; g.c. 5in.; turng. cir. 34ft.; kerb wt. 19¼ cwt.; tank, 9 gals.; 12-volt.
£695+£261.12.9 p.t. = £956.12.9

SUNBEAM RAPIER

THIS car has probably had the toughest upbringing of any in its range. An instant success when it first appeared on the market, it has since won many awards in both motor rallies and high-speed races. The Rapier has glamour too, as a sports saloon, with or without the hardtop. A splendid champion for Britain. Latest triumphs include class win and Ladies' Award in Tour de France.

CLOSE-UP
Four-cyl.; o.h.v.; 81.5×76.2 mm.; 1,592 c.c.; 80.25 b.h.p.; 9.1 to 1 comp.; coil ign.; 2 Zenith carbs.; 4-speed, 14.128, 9.038, 5.877, 4.22 to 1; cen. lvr.; de Normanville overdrive opt.; susp. f. ind. coil, r. half-elliptic; 2-door; 4-seat; hyd. brks., disc front.; max. 93 m.p.h.; cruise 80; m.p.g. 25-30; whl. base 8ft.; track f. 4ft. 1½in., r. 4ft. 0½in.; lgth. 13ft. 6½in.; wdth. 5ft. 1in.; ht. 4ft. 10½in.; g.c. 5¾in.; turng. cir. 36ft.; kerb wt. 21 cwt.; tank 10 gals.; 12-volt.
£705+£265.7.9 p.t. = £970.7.9

Abbreviations—g.c.—ground clearance; susp.—suspension; f.—front; r.—rear; comp.—compression; s.v.—side-valves; o.h.v.—overhead valves; o h.c.—overhead camshaft; hyd.—hydraulic.

TRIUMPH VITESSE

FLASHING six-cylinder power in a chassis developed from the Triumph Herald plus extra features such as new front-end styling with four headlamps, lamp-flasher switch and disc front brakes. All-independent suspension, 25-foot turning circle, detachable body panels, telescopic safety steering column. No chassis greasing. Herald four-cylinder models continue, with choice of saloon, convertible or estate car.

CLOSE-UP

Six-cyl.; o.h.v.; 66.75 × 76 mm.; 1,596 c.c.; 70 b.h.p.; 8.75 to 1 comp.; coil ign.; 2 Solex carbs.; 4-speed, 12.06, 7.31, 5.16, 4.11 to 1; cen. lvr. de Normanville overdrive opt.; susp., f. ind. coil, r. ind. transv. leaf; 2-door; 4-seat; hyd. brks. disc front; max. 88 m.p.h.; cruise 75-80; m.p.g. 28-35; whl. base 7ft. 7½in.; track f. 4ft. 1in., r. 4ft.; lgth. 12ft. 9in.; wdth. 5ft.; ht. 4ft. 4⅓in.; g.c. 6¾in.; turng. cir. 25ft.; kerb wt. 18¼ cwt.; tank, 8¾ gals.; 12-volt.

£649 + £244.7.9 p.t. = £893.7.9

TRIUMPH SPITFIRE 4

EAGERLY awaited by those in the know, the sprightly Spitfire has a chassis like the Herald but with shorter wheelbase. Its twin-carburettor engine produces 63 h.p. and the maximum speed is comfortably more than 90. Winding windows fit into current conceptions of comfort and there is a luggage trunk in the tail with room for more baggage behind the seats. Bonnet tips forward to give free access to engine and accessories.

CLOSE-UP

Four-cyl.; o.h.v.; 69.3 × 76 mm.; 1,147 c.c.; 63 b.h.p.; 9 to 1 comp.; coil ign.; 2 S.U. carbs; 4-speed; 15.40, 8.87, 5.73, 4.11 to 1; cen. lvr.; susp., f. ind. coil, r. ind. transv. leaf; 2-door; 2-seat; hyd. brks.; max. 93 m.p.h.; cruise 80; m.p.g. 35-40; whl. base 6ft. 11in.; track f. 4ft. 1in.; r. 4ft.; lgth. 12ft. 1in.; wdth. 4ft. 9in.; ht. 3ft. 11½in.; g.c. 5in.; turng. cir. 24ft.; kerb wt. 14 cwt.; tank, 9 gals.; 12-volt.

TRIUMPH T.R.4

FULL-HEIGHT doors, winding windows and snug convertible top give passengers in the TR4 comfort they never knew on the TR3. Yet continuing demand for the TR3 has forced the factory to re-start production. TR4 has roomier body, wider track, synchromesh on all four speeds. The hardtop has a bright idea for sunny climates—a removable roof panel which stows away, leaving the rear window standing to eliminate back draughts.

CLOSE-UP

Four-cyl.; o.h.v.; 86 × 92 mm.; 2,138 c.c.; 105 b.h.p.; 9 to 1 comp.; coil ign.; 2 S.U. carbs.; 4-speed, 11.61, 7.44, 4.9, 3.7 to 1; cen. lvr.; susp., f. ind. coil, r. half-elliptic; 2-door; 2/3-seat; hyd. brks. disc front; max. 110 m.p.h.; cruise 95; m.p.g. 25; whl. base 7ft. 4in.; track f. 4ft. 1in., r. 4ft.; lgth. 13ft.; wdth. 4ft. 9½in.; ht. 4ft. 2in.; g.c. 6in.; turng. cir. 33ft.; kerb wt. 20 cwt.; tank, 11¾ gals.; 12-volt.

TVR MARK III

NEWCOMER to the Motor Show is this Blackpool-built Gran Turismo speed model which has already made its name in racing at home and abroad. Latest model, the Mark III has MG engine with special HRG cylinder head to order. Redesigned tubular space-frame chassis has new independent rear suspension by wishbones and coil springs. Body is in glass fibre bonded to the chassis. Front brakes are discs.

CLOSE-UP

Four-cyl.; o.h.v.; 76.2 × 88.9 mm.; 1,622 c.c.; 90 b.h.p.; 8.9 to 1 comp.; coil ign.; 2 S.U. carbs.; 4-speed, 15.65, 9.52, 5.91, 4.3 to 1; cen. lvr.; susp., f. and r. ind. coil; 2-door; 2-seat; hyd. brks. disc front; max. 105 m.p.h.; cruise 85-90; m.p.g. 23-26; whl. base 7ft. 1½in.; track f. 4ft. 2⅓in. r. 4ft. 3in.; lgth. 11ft. 8in.; wdth. 5ft. 4in.; ht. 4ft.; g.c. 6in.; turng. cir. 29ft. 6in.; kerb wt. 14½ cwt.; tank, 10 gals.; 12-volt.

VALIANT

AFTER a three-year run, Chrysler have completely re-styled their compact Valiant for 1963, and given it a guarantee for 5 years or 50,000 miles. It is slightly longer and reverts to two headlamps instead of four. Will this start a new trend? Convertibles will be introduced in November, with power-operated top as optional equipment. The heater-ventilation system has increased capacity.

CLOSE-UP

Six-cyl.; o.h.v.; 86×79 mm.; 2,786 c.c.; 101 b.h.p.; 8.2 to 1 comp.; coil ign.; Ball-Ball or Holley carb.; 3-speed auto., 9.53, 5.85, 3.23 to 1; press button control; susp., f. ind. torsion bar, r. half-elliptic; 4-door; 6-seat; hyd. brks.; max. 101 m.p.h.; cruise 85; m.p.g. 18-22; whl. base 8ft. 10½in.; track f. 4ft. 8in.; r. 4ft. 7½in.; lgth. 15ft. 4½in.; wdth. 5ft. 10½in.; ht. 4ft. 6½in.; g.c. 6½in.; turng. cir. 36ft. 4in.; kerb wt. 24 cwt.; tank, 11 gals.; 12-volt.

£1,460+£548 p.t. = £2,008

VANDEN PLAS PRINCESS 4-LITRE

A NINE-SEATER luxury limousine that is highly competitive in the big-car market. It is mostly used as a prestige car, with chauffeur, and there are incredibly numerous fittings in the interior to suit individual tastes. The biggest model produced by the go-ahead British Motor Corporation, it is one of the cheapest limousines and first-class value for money.

CLOSE-UP

Six-cyl.; o.h.v.; 87.3×111 mm.; 3,993 c.c.; 6.8 to 1 comp.; coil ign.; Stromberg carb.; 4-speed, 15.1, 10.3, 6.4, 4.4 to 1; col. lvr., auto. opt.; susp., f. ind. coil, r. half-elliptic; 4-door; 8-seat; hyd. brks.; max. 100 m.p.h.; cruise, 80; m.p.g. 16-19; whl. base, 11ft. 0⅞in.; track f. 4ft. 10½in.; r. 5ft. 2⅜in.; lgth. 17ft. 11in.; wdth. 6ft. 2½in.; ht. 5ft. 10in.; g.c. 6½in.; turng. cir. 45ft. 6in.; kerb wt. 41¾ cwt.; tank, 16 gals.; 12-volt.

£2,150+£807.5.3 p.t. = £2,957.5.3

VAUXHALL CRESTA

HEATER, screenwasher, electric clock, fog-lamps, reversing lights, lighter, headlamp flasher, leather or nylon upholstery and two-tone colour schemes—all these things, so often optional extras, figure in the standard specification of Vauxhall's handsome new six-cylinder Cresta. Overdrive may be added or the General Motors automatic transmission. Only grease points are on front suspension and once every 30,000 miles will do.

CLOSE-UP

Six-cyl.; o.h.v.; 82.55×82.55 mm.; 2,651 c.c.; 113 b.h.p.; 8.5 to 1comp.; coil ign.; Zenith carb.; 3-speed, 11.2, 6.4, 3.9 to 1; col. lvr. overdrive or auto. opt.; susp. f. ind. coil, r. half-elliptic; 4-door; 6-seat; hyd. brks. disc. front; max. 96 m.p.h.; cruise 80; m.p.g. 20-25; whl. base 8ft. 11½in.; track f. 4ft. 6¾in., r. 4ft. 8¼in.; lgth. 15ft. 1½in.; wdth. 5ft. 10¾in.; ht. 4ft. 8¾in.; g.c. 6½in.; turng. cir. 36ft. 6in.; kerb wt. 23¾ cwt.; tank, 10¾ gals.; 12-volt.

£760+£286 p.t. = £1,046

VAUXHALL VELOX

FAMILY resemblance to the latest Victor is obvious in the new Velox which offers more leg, head and shoulder room than before. Interior features are padded walnut dash, safety-padded steering wheel, safety-zone windscreen to help the driver stop safely if it is broken. Engine and transmission are developed from those of previous models. Axle ratio is higher for silent cruising. Brakes are discs in front, servo-assisted.

CLOSE-UP

Six-cyl.; o.h.v.; 82.55×82.55 mm.; 2,651 c.c.; 113 b.h.p.; 8.5 to 1 comp.; coil ign.; Zenith carb.; 3-speed, 11.2, 6.4, 3.9 to 1; col. lvr. overdrive or auto. opt.; susp., f. ind. coil, r. half-elliptic; 4-door; 6-seat; hyd. brks. disc front; max. 96 m.p.h.; cruise 80; m.p.g. 20-25; whl. base 8ft. 11½in.; track f. 4ft. 6¾in., r. 4ft. 8¼in.; lgth. 15ft. 1½in.; wdth. 5ft. 10¾in.; ht. 4ft. 8¾in.; g.c. 6½in.; turng. cir. 36ft. 6in.; kerb wt. 23½ cwt.; tank, 10¾ gals.; 12-volt.

£680+£256 p.t. = £936

Abbreviations—g.c.—ground clearance; susp.—suspension; f.—front; r.—rear; comp.—compression; s.v.—side-valves; o.h.v.—overhead valves; o h.c.—overhead camshaft; hyd.—hydraulic.

VAUXHALL VICTOR ESTATE CAR DE LUXE

A GOOD-LOOKING, well-styled estate car, ideal for the man who wants to carry his passengers in comfort, or a big payload. Externally, the new car has a thin chrome bead along the waist line. Within, it has the equipment corresponding to that of the Victor de luxe saloon: individual front seats trimmed in leather, carpets on all floors, and a screen cleaner and heater which are also standard. A sumptuous car for all work.

CLOSE-UP

Four-cyl.; o.h.v.; 79.4×76.2 mm.; 1,508 c.c.; 56.3 b.h.p.; 8 to I comp.; coil ign.; Zenith carb.; 3-speed, 13.2, 6.74, 4.125 to I, 4-speed opt.; col. lvr.; susp., f. ind. coil, r. half-elliptic; 5-door; 5-seat; hyd. brks.; max. 80 m.p.h.; cruise 70; m.p.g. 28-34; whl. base 8ft. 4in.; track f. 4ft. 2⅜in., r. 4ft. 4½in.; lgth. 14ft. 5¼in.; wdth. 5ft. 4in.; ht. 4ft. 8in.; g.c. 7in.; turng. cir. 33ft. 6in.; kerb wt. 19¾ cwt.; tank, 10 gals.; 12-volt.

£655 + £247 p.t. = £902

VAUXHALL VX4/90

SUNDAY-SUIT Victor with a Sunday punch. Twin carburettors and higher compression produce an extra 25 h.p. to give this roomy five-seater 90 m.p.h. performance. The central gear-lever controls four speeds, all synchronised. Front brakes are disc with vacuum servo to lighten the pedal pressure. Special trim, seating and instrument panel with tachometer. It is identified externally by special grille, coloured side flash, new tail lamps.

CLOSE-UP

Four-cyl.; o.h.v.; 79.4×76.2 mm.; 1,508 c.c.; 81 b.h.p.; 9.3 to I comp.; coil ign.; 2 Zenith carbs.; 4-speed, 12.58, 8.79, 5.59, 4.125 to I; cen. lvr.; susp., f. ind. coil, r. half-elliptic; 4-door; 5-seat; hyd. brks. disc front.; max. 88 m.p.h.; cruise 75; m.p.g. 28-33; whl. base 8ft. 4in.; track f. 4ft. 3⅛in.; r. 4ft. 2⅜in.; lgth. 14ft. 5¼in.; wdth. 5ft. 4in.; ht. 4ft. 7⅜in.; g.c. 6¾in.; turng. cir. 33ft. 6in.; kerb wt. 18¾ cwt.; tank, 10 gals; 12-volt.

£674 + £253.15.3 p.t. = £927.15.3

VOLGA

BALL of fire it may not be, but the Volga offers solid construction and relaxing comfort on reclining seats for those who have to face the moujik. Lusty heater keeps passengers comfortable in the Siberian winter, a radiator blind conserves engine heat. The tool-kit can cope with extensive repair work, and even a pot of paint is provided. Automatic transmission is now available as an extra.

CLOSE-UP

Four-cyl.; o.h.v.; 92×92 mm.; 2,445 c.c.; 80 b.h.p.; 7.5 to I comp.; coil ign.; downdraught carb.; 3-speed, 14.911, 8.072, 4.556 to I; col. lvr.; susp., f. ind. coil, r. half-elliptic; 4-door; 6-seat; hyd. brks.; max. 84 m.p.h.; cruise 60; m.p.g. 31; whl. base 8ft. 10in.; track f. 4ft. 7½in., r. 4ft. 8in.; lgth. 15ft. 10in.; wdth. 5ft. 11in.; ht. 5ft. 4in.; g.c. 7½in.; turng. cir. 42ft.; kerb wt. 27¾ cwt.; tank, 13 gals.; 12-volt.

£668 + £251.10.3 p.t. = £919.10.3

VOLKSWAGEN DE LUXE

TANTALISING its competitors, the VW goes on increasing its sales. Odd and obsolete to those who do not understand it, this is a very different car from Dr. Porsche's original conception. Innumerable improvements have advanced performance, comfort, road-holding and reliability. There is a plastic headlining, at last, instead of cloth. Sliding-roof control handles are recessed. Convertibles have bigger rear windows. Heater output is increased.

CLOSE-UP

Four-cyl.; o.h.v.; air-cooled; 77×64 mm.; 1,192 c.c.; 40 b.h.p.; 7 to I comp.; coil ign.; Solex carb.; 4-speed, 16.63, 9.01, 5.77, 3.89 to I; cen. lvr.; susp., f. and r. ind. torsion bars; 2-door; 4-seat; hyd. brks.; max. 72 m.p.h.; cruise 72; m.p.g. 38; whl. base 7ft. 10½in.; track f. 4ft. 3in., r. 4ft. 2⅜in.; lgth. 13ft. 4½in.; width 5ft. 0½in.; ht. 4ft. 11in.; g.c. 6in.; turng. cir. 36ft.; kerb wt. 14½ cwt.; tank, 8¾ gals.; 6-volt.

£521 + £196.7.9 p.t. = £717.7.9

Abbreviations—g.c.—ground clearance; susp.—suspension; f.—front; r.—rear; comp.—compression; s.v.—side-valves; o.h.v.—overhead valves; o.h.c.—overhead camshaft; hyd.—hydraulic.

141

VOLKSWAGEN 1500

LUGGAGE trunks at front and rear? Then where is the engine? Neatly concealed under the rear boot floor. You can check and replenish oil without opening up and it is air cooled, so there are no worries about water. Some people find the body a little small for a 1½ litre. VW enthusiasts like its easy, fast cruising, fine finish and reliable service. Stronger clutch, bigger brakes for 1963.

CLOSE-UP
Four-cyl.; o.h.v. air cooled; 83×69 mm.; 1,493 c.c.; 53 b.h.p.; 7.8 to 1 comp.; coil ign.; Solex carb.; 4-speed, 15.67, 8.50, 5.44, 3.67 to 1; cen. lvr.; susp., f. and r. ind. torsion bar; 2-door; 4-seat; hyd. brks.; max. 81 m.p.h.; cruise 81; m.p.g. 30; whl. base 7ft. 10½in.; track f. 4ft. 3½in.; r. 4ft. 5in.; lgth. 13ft. 10½in.; wdth. 5ft. 3¼in.; ht. 4ft. 10in.; g.c. 6in.; turng. cir. 36ft.; kerb wt. 17¼ cwt.; tank, 8¾ gals.; 6-volt.
£752.10.0 + £283.4.0 p.t. = £1,035.14.0

VOLKSWAGEN KARMANN-GHIA

ITALIAN styling and Karmann's conscientious craftsmanship unite to produce the beautiful coupes and convertibles which cater for people who want something different from the standard VW saloons. Flowing curves of the 1200 styles contrast with the strongly sculptured mouldings on the 1500 models which have space for luggage at front and rear. Front-seat back-rests are adjustable. Mechanically these cars are the same as the saloons.

CLOSE-UP
Four-cyl.; o.h.v. air-cooled; 77×64 mm.; 1,192 c.c.; 40 b.h.p.; 7 to 1 comp.; coil ign.; Solex carb.; 4-speed, 16.63, 9.01, 5.77, 3.89 to 1; cen. lvr.; susp., f. and r. ind. torsion bars; 2-door; 2/4 seat; hyd. brks.; max. 75 m.p.h.; cruise 75; m.p.g. 38; whl. base 7ft. 10½in.; track f. 4ft. 3in., r. 4ft. 2¾in.; lgth. 13ft. 7in.; wdth. 5ft. 4¼in.; ht. 4ft. 4½in.; g.c. 6in.; turng. cir. 37ft.; kerb wt. 16 cwt.; tank, 8¾ gals.; 6-volt.
£820 + £308.10.3 p.t. = £1,128.10.3

VOLVO 122S

SWEDISH as smorgasbord, Volvo's fast family model exhibits Scandinavian taste and care for detail—qualities which are winning it friends in many export markets. New 1,780 c.c. engine boosts the performance, Girling disc brakes in front ensure ample safety factors and the de Normanville overdrive is an optional supplement to the all-synchro gearbox. New to the range are a two-door saloon and a station wagon.

CLOSE-UP
Four-cyl.; o.h.v.; 84.14×80 mm.; 1,780 c.c.; 90 b.h.p.; 8.5 to 1 comp.; coil ign.; 2 S.U. carbs.; 4-speed 12.8, 8.16, 5.58, 4.1 to 1; cen. lvr.; overdrive opt., susp., f. ind. coil, r. coil; 4-door; 5-seat; hyd. brks., disc front.; max. 100 m.p.h.; cruise 85; m.p.g. 28-36; whl. base 8ft. 6½in.; track f. and r. 4ft. 3¾in.; lgth. 14ft. 7½in.; wdth. 5ft. 3¾in.; ht. 4ft. 11½in.; g.c. 7⅛in.; turng. cir. 32ft.; kerb wt. 22 cwt.; tank, 10 gals.; 12-volt.
£940 + £353.10.3 p.t. = £1,293.10.3

VOLVO P.1800

E.F.T.A. in action—a Swedish sports coupe of outstanding performance with British-built body and Swedish mechanical parts. High performance 1,780 c.c. twin-carburettor four-cylinder engine, 4-speed all-synchro gearbox with optional de Normanville overdrive and Girling disc brakes in front, servo assisted, added to a body of individual style, create a model of international appeal which holds the hundred with disarming ease.

CLOSE-UP
Four-cyl.; o.h.v.; 84.14×80 mm.; 1,780 c.c.; 100 b.h.p.; 9.5 to 1 comp.; coil ign.; 2 S.U. carbs.; 4-speed, 14.27, 9.07, 6.2, 4.5 to 1; cen. lvr. overdrive; susp.; f. ind. coil, r. coil; 2-door; 2/4-seat; servo brks.; disc front; max. 110 m.p.h.; cruise 95; m.p.g. 28-30; whl. base 8ft. 0½in.; track f. and r. 4ft. 3¾in.; lgth. 14ft. 5¼in.; wdth. 5ft. 7in.; ht. 4ft. 2½in.; g.c. 6in.; turng. cir. 31ft.; kerb wt. 24 cwt.; tank, 10 gals.; 12-volt.
£1,335 + £501.12.9 p.t. = £1,836.12.9

Abbreviations—g.c.—ground clearance; susp.—suspension; f.—front; r.—rear; comp.—compression; s.v.—side-valves; o.h.v.—overhead valves; o h.c.—overhead camshaft; hyd.—hydraulic.

WOLSELEY HORNET

ONE of the infinite variations on the Mini theme, with the same transverse engine, front-wheel drive and all-independent suspension using rubber cones. Equipment and interior trim are to luxury car standards—there is even walnut on the instrument panel—and the extended tail encloses a larger luggage trunk. The bigger body means more weight. Some people would prefer this car with a Cooper engine.

CLOSE-UP
Four-cyl.; o.h.v.; 62.94×68.26 mm.; 848 c.c.; 37 b.h.p.; 8.3 to 1 comp.; coil ign.; S.U. carb.; 4-speed, 13.657· 8.176, 5.317, 3.765 to 1; cen. lvr.; susp., f. and r. ind· rubber; 2-door; 4-seat; hyd. brks.; max. 73 m.p.h.; cruise 65; m.p.g. 42-45; whl. base 6ft. 8½in.; track f. 3ft. 11¾in., r. 3ft. 9⅞in.; lgth. 10ft. 8¾in.; wdth. 4ft· 7½in.; ht. 4ft. 5in.; g.c. 6⅜in.; turng. circ. 31ft.; kerb wt. 11¾ cwt.; tank, 5½ gals.; 12-volt.
£460+£173.10.2 p.t. = £633.10.2

WOLSELEY 16/60

THIS is one of the upper-class family cars which has loads of power, with its 1,622 c.c. overhead valve engine and its good looks all round. In the indirect gears, pick-up is really brisk. On long runs the higher rear axle ratio of 4.3 to 1 is complementary to the extra power available. Result: high cruising speed at an economical running cost. The Borg-Warner automatic transmission is an optional extra.

CLOSE-UP
Four-cyl.; o.h.v.; 76.2×88.9 mm.; 1,622 c.c.; 55 b.h.p.; 8.3 to 1 comp.; coil ign.; S.U. carb.; 4-speed, 15.64, 9.52, 5.91, 4.3 to 1; cen. lvr. auto. opt.; susp., f. ind. coil, r. half-elliptic; 4-door; 4-seat; hyd. brks.; max. 80; m.p.h.; cruise 70; m.p.g. 26-33; whl. base 8ft. 4½in.; track f. 4ft. 2⅝in., 4ft. 3⅜in.; lgth. 14ft. 6½in.; wdth. 5ft. 3½in.; ht. 4ft. 10⅞in.; g.c. 5⅞in.; turng. cir. 37ft.; kerb wt. 22½ cwt.; tank, 10 gals.; 12-volt.
£680+£256.0.3 p.t. = £936.0.3

WOLSELEY 6/110

EXECUTIVE transport combining spacious comfort, quality finish and silent running at a strictly moderate price. Its attraction has been enhanced by last year's increase in wheelbase which added to rear-seat comfort and leg-room, and by the extra engine power, with twin exhaust system. The all-synchro three-speed gearbox now has a centre change. You can have Borg Warner automatic as alternative. Front brakes are discs, with vacuum servo.

CLOSE-UP
Six-cyl.; o.h.v.; 83.34×88.9 mm.; 2,912 c.c.; 120 b.h.p.; 8.23 to 1 comp.; coil ign.; 2 S.U. carbs.; 3-speed, 12.09, 6.45, 3.9 to 1 overdrive; cen. lvr., BW. auto. opt.; susp., f. ind. coil, r. half-elliptic; 4-door; 5-seat; hyd. servo brks. disc front; max. 104 m.p.h.; cruise 85; m.p.g. 22-24; whl. base 9ft. 2in.; track f. 4ft. 5¾in., r. 4ft. 5⅛in.; lgth. 15ft. 7½in.; wdth. 5ft. 8½in.; ht. 5ft. 0½in.; g.c. 6⅛in.; turng. cir. 41ft.; ker bwt., 31 cwt.; tank, 16 gals.; 12-volt.
£920+£346 p.t. = £1,266

ZAPOROGIETS

INGENIOUS design makes the rear-mounted V4 engine of Russia's small car worth a closer look. It is air-cooled and, to combat vibration problems, it has a counter-rotating shaft carrying balance weights, running inside the hollow camshaft. The car's four seats are simply finished, but the back-rests are adjustable. A petrol-burning heater provides the searing blast needed to counter sub-arctic winters.

CLOSE-UP
Four-cyl.; o.h.v.; 66×54.5 mm.; 748 c.c.; 23 b.h.p.; 6.5 to 1 comp.; coil ign.; Ouroveni carb.; 4-speed; cen. lvr.; susp.; f. ind. torsion bar, r. ind. coil; 2-door; 4-seat; hyd. brks.; max. 56 m.p.h.; cruise 50; m.p.g. 40-45; whl. base 6ft. 7½in.; track f. 3ft. 9in., r. 3ft. 9½in.; lgth. 10ft. 11in.; wdth. 4ft. 7½in.; ht. 4ft. 6½in.; g.c. 7in.; turng. cir. 31ft. 4in.; kerb wt. 11¾ cwt.; tank, 6½ gals.; 12-volt.

Abbreviations—g.c.—ground clearance; susp.—suspension; f.—front; r.—rear; comp.—compression; s.v.—side-valves; o.h.v.—overhead valves; o.h.c.—overhead camshaft; hyd.—hydraulic.

JAGUAR

Grace . . . Space . . . Pace

A special kind of motoring

which no other car in the

world can offer

**SEE THE
JAGUAR RANGE ON STAND 108 EARLS COURT**

LONDON SHOWROOMS 88 PICCADILLY W.1

144

Take a girl like you

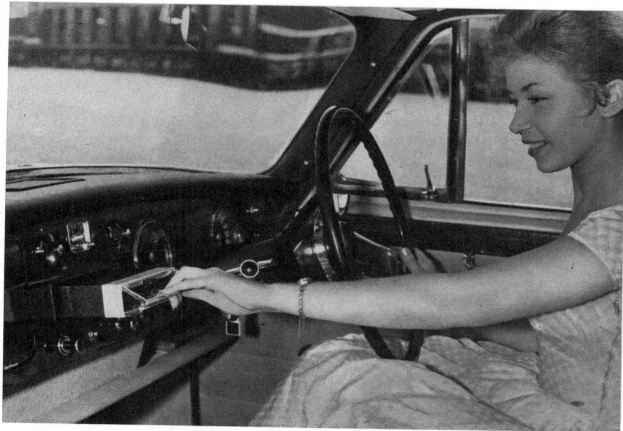

Well, it's true she is not one of the hundreds of accessories on show, but there are plenty of eye-catchers among the gadgets

by Dennis May

The new EKCO Twin-Set is one of the radios on show which can be used either as a built-in car radio or a self-contained transistor portable. In the car it operates a powerful 3-watt amplifier. Out of the car, a dry battery takes over.

OMITTING the accessories and components section from a tour of Earls Court would be like missing the leaning tower on a trip to Pisa, or the Gorge when visiting Cheddar, or the buns while sojourning in Bath.

This year, for instance, if you kept away from bits-and-pieces-ville you would miss a development that promises to banish the skidding hazard from emergency braking on slippery surfaces.

The Anti-Lock Braking Device, as Lockheed, its inventors, call it, has a built-in "brain" that pre-senses skids and tramples them to death before they have time to do their dirty work. See it on Stand 331, junction of Avenues H and L.

Disc brakes, unlike drums, have no inherent self-servo action. True or false? True in the past, false today, at least so far as one disc brake system in particular is concerned. "Integral with the individual brake, it consists of a pair of angled and opposed pistons which press the pads against the disc. Each pad is in contact with an angled thrust face: the rotation of the disc tends to pull the pads on by a wedging action". Nicely put, Dunlop! Stand 200, Av. O.

Of course, the efficiency, longevity and fade-resistance of any braking system depends largely on its friction material, and this is where such products as Ferodo, Don and Mintex come into their own. One reason why, in all probability, you never set eyes on your own brake linings, and need not give them a thought from one year's end to another (almost), is that competition-conscious people like Ferodo use the Grands Prix and international rallying as a forcing-house for development.

Ferodo's photo-montage displays on Stand 257, Av. C, drive home the racing-improves-the-breed-of-brakes lesson.

Preventing accidents is one thing. Taking the sting out of the unavoidable ones is another. For that you need safety harness and, among other things, a windscreen that can still be seen through when impact has robbed its main areas of all trace of transparency.

The belt vendors are present in force, as usual, at Earls Court—Lexington, Desmo, Romac, Britax, more besides. A food-for-thought Lexington line is their rear-seat lap belt—timely reminder that is is not only the up-fronters who need restraining in a bad shunt.

Newest Britax product is an inertia belt allowing full freedom of movement yet designed to lock instantly on impact or sudden shock. It is self-adjusting and, when not in use, stows itself neatly out of the way.

Triplex, to revert to see-out ability in crashes or other misadventures involving a beaten-up screen, makes a feature of zone-toughened safety glass. Quote: "Should the zone-toughened screen shatter on being struck by a stone or pointed object, the area in front of the driver's eyes crazes into larger fragments than the rest of the screen, so that his vision is still sufficiently good to enable him to retain full control of the vehicle". Stand 304, Av. F.

Security of a different kind is the common aim of the MM Automatic Immobiliser* and a device known as the Melguard*, by Coventry and Jeffs Ltd. and Johnson Carguard Ltd. respectively. Both are in business to make life difficult for the car thief, a highly essential service in view of the fact that more than 30,000 cars are stolen or "borrowed" every

(continued on Page 60)

Neatness is all for those with the sort of car wardrobe offered by Conway.

Still in Gadgetville

with everything from a spark to a light

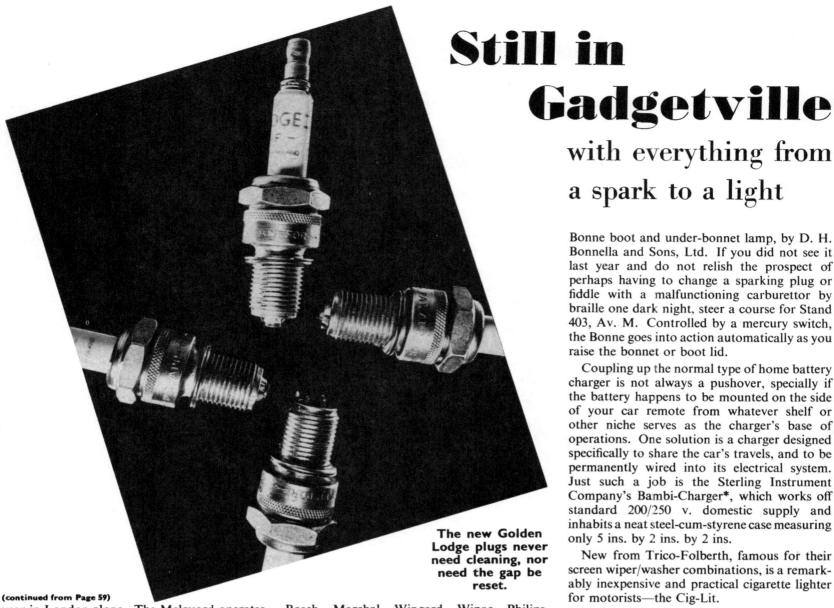

The new Golden Lodge plugs never need cleaning, nor need the gap be reset.

Bonne boot and under-bonnet lamp, by D. H. Bonnella and Sons, Ltd. If you did not see it last year and do not relish the prospect of perhaps having to change a sparking plug or fiddle with a malfunctioning carburettor by braille one dark night, steer a course for Stand 403, Av. M. Controlled by a mercury switch, the Bonne goes into action automatically as you raise the bonnet or boot lid.

Coupling up the normal type of home battery charger is not always a pushover, specially if the battery happens to be mounted on the side of your car remote from whatever shelf or other niche serves as the charger's base of operations. One solution is a charger designed specifically to share the car's travels, and to be permanently wired into its electrical system. Just such a job is the Sterling Instrument Company's Bambi-Charger*, which works off standard 200/250 v. domestic supply and inhabits a neat steel-cum-styrene case measuring only 5 ins. by 2 ins. by 2 ins.

New from Trico-Folberth, famous for their screen wiper/washer combinations, is a remarkably inexpensive and practical cigarette lighter for motorists—the Cig-Lit.

Designed for attachment to the facia or at some convenient lower level, the gadget takes the form of a chrome-rimmed socket into which the cigarette is inserted. You then depress the rim for a few seconds and presto! your weed is asmoulder. No hot element to handle, no need to take your eyes off the road. The Cig-Lit costs 12s. 6d.

Three words, "Look—no hands," tell the story of Marchal's Portablast, a portable warning device combining an efficient horn with a container of non-toxic, low-pressure gas. Squeeze the trigger once and the gas does the rest, giving up to 300 two-second blasts, or extended blasts lasting about 10 minutes.

(continued on Page 61)

(continued from Page 59)
year in London alone. The Melguard operates on a combination principle and dispenses with all keys and hidden switches. If the thief can outwit, he *deserves* any car he hijacks.

What is cooking in the car-radio world? Well, there is the Pye Two-in-One receiver (Stand 27, ground floor). Cast for a dual role, as its name implies, this neat package functions either as a car radio or as a self-contained portable, using its own battery, aerial and speaker.

Similar in concept to the Two-in-One is the Transmobil 2, by Lee Products Ltd. (Stand 388, Av. N). Completely transistorised, the Transmobil is notably compact at 7 ins. × 6 ins. × 2⅛ ins. and in its portable capacity is powered by four low-cost and universally obtainable 1.5 v. batteries.

Yet another variation on the same theme is the Ekco Twin-Set, for which its makers market a range of kits and speakers permitting "tailored" fitting in more than a hundred current car models. To use the Twin-Set as a portable, assuming it to be rigged into your car, you just turn a key in a thief-proof lock, and slide the receiver from its facia housing.

While you are in the listen-as-you-motor mood, make a point of seeing the wares of World Radio (242, B), Smiths Radiomobile (244, B), Philips Electrical (23, ground). They all have something new, something to pin your ears back.

With days seasonally shortening and nights equivalently lengthening, car illumination, a hundred-faceted subject, demands attention whether we like after-dark driving or not. All the established specialists in this field—Lucas,

Bosch, Marchal, Wingard, Wipac, Philips, Butlers, to mention a few—are at their Show action stations, wooing the avenue-prowler with varied and fascinating lines in headlamps, foglamps, driving lamps, reversing lamps, inspection lamps, dash lamps, every imaginable kind of candle-power dispenser.

Taking one out of the hat, we come up with a new, shown-for-the-first-time fog and driving-lamp set by L. E. Perei Auto Devices Ltd. (377, junction of N and O). We illustrate one of these on page 61. Of an attractive rectangular shape, these lamps measure 6½ ins. by 4 ins., cost a reasonable 65s. and 68s. for the driving and fog units respectively.

Making its second Show appearance is the

This Motor Maid Kettle boils 1¼ pints of picnic water in less than 15 minutes. Its element never needs replacing.

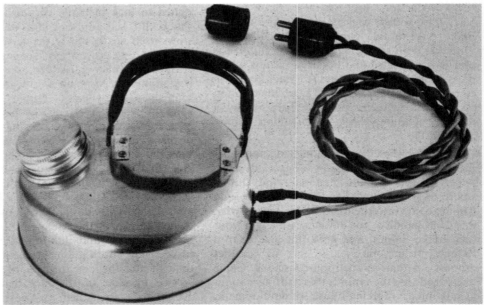

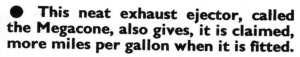 This neat exhaust ejector, called the Megacone, also gives, it is claimed, more miles per gallon when it is fitted.

A little more quiet, please

(continued from Page 60)

Primarily a fog signal, the Portablast's secondary uses include giving warning of road accidents or hazards obscured from oncoming drivers.

If quelling din, rather than making it, is your idea of happiness, the Q.L.M. sound-insulating kits shown by the Exhaust Ejector Co. Ltd. on Stand 364, L-M, should be on your list of objectives. Q.L.M. treatment—the initials denote Quiet Luxury Motoring—involves the application of special p.v.c.-coated felt sheets to the interior surfaces of otherwise resonant body panels, parcel shelves, roofs, etc.

Sets are made up, packaged and marketed for a wide variety of makes and models. If your particular car is not on the Q.L.M. list, you can buy the stuff by the yard and do your own tailoring job.

The Exhaust Ejector people, not too surprisingly, also busy themselves with exhaust ejection. See their venturied Megacone, which not only speeds the parting gas but, with its chrome finish and elegant shape, looks good as well. More power, better fuel economy, are among the claims made for it.

"A brilliant idea that puts an end to the messy, time-wasting job of dealing with punctures on the road." Recognise it? Redi-Spare is the name—Lexington Products' brainwave. Not unlike a greasegun in appearance, though perhaps a bit bigger, the Redi-Spare contains a gas propellent and a chemical sealant.

Stuck with a puncture, instead of going through the normal jack-her-up-and-get-the-wheel-off routine, you simply screw this gadget's nozzle to the valve and in a matter of moments the puncture is mended and the tyre re-inflated. Lexington (238, A-B) have recently introduced a new small Redi-Spare for Mini-sized tyres.

Talking of the Mini in its Morris and Austin forms, Key-Leather, at Stand 362 (L-M), show a well-made replacement bonnet lock for the B.M.C. babe. Remotely controlled from the facia, it not only enables the lid to be lifted without dirtying your hands, it also denies unauthorised persons access to the engine and its auxiliaries. Fitting involves no drilling. The kit costs only 19s. 6d.

What do you do when your child is suddenly car-sick? The ancient Romans had their vomitória (no, it is not a pretty subject, is it?), and the modern motoring parent has his K-L Car Bin. Not that protecting carpets and upholstery from sickly infants is this versatile receptacle's primary purpose, but you *can* use it for that, K-L point out.

In the normal course of duty the Car Bin serves most usefully as a far-from-unsightly dump for the odds and ends of rubbish that so easily accumulate in and spoil the look of a car's interior. Not even the Romans had high-density polythene vomitoria with "smart gold rim design".

Also smartly golden in appearance—though this, as it happens is the least of its merits—is the new H.F. Lodge plug, making its first Earls Court appearance. The makers describe it as revolutionary, and that is scarcely an overstatement; the design characteristics that make it so are a story in themselves. Suffice it to say that the Golden Lodge plug needs no cleaning, servicing or adjustment during its whole working life, and this anyway, is at least twice the normal span. Why? Ask for yourself at Stand 203, O.

(continued on Page 63)

● This anti-skid device (below) is by Lockheed. The small sensing unit, not so very much bigger than a matchbox, signals the servo when the wheels are about to lock. Below, right, is the new half shielded fog or driving lamp by Perei Auto Devices.

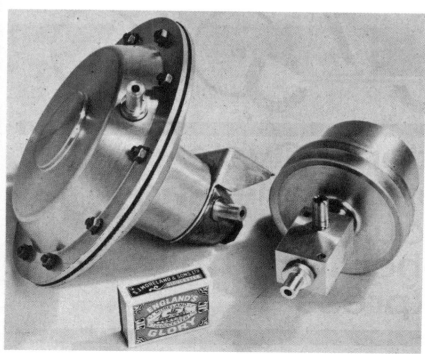

Guess what?

(continued from Page 61)

For the last lap of our tour of the avenues, let us make a lucky-dip selection from the scores of eligibles:—

Conway's latest is the Car Wardrobe, made in hide-simulating plastic, an on-tour protection for the suit you will not be wearing until you arrive. It is hung from the roof, so it is anti-crease as well as anti-soiling. Stand 237, A-B.

Barnacle say it with badges on Stand 338, H. Subjects depicted include veteran cars. For the badge connoisseur, real 18 carat gold finish is available. Other Barnacle lines include switches, facia instrument, panels.

Philbar and Co. Ltd. bring car valeting up to date with the Whirl-a-Way* washer. Conveniently long handle eliminates reaching and groping. Rotary brush dispenses water-borne suds. You connect up the Whirl-a-Way to your domestic hose.

Armstrong Patents Co. Ltd. (181, O) introduce a new idler-bearing steering damper. Overcomes kicks and vibrations in the steering system.

Cox of Watford Ltd. look ahead to holiday time with a new folding roof-rack. When not in use it stows away tidily and compactly in a box measuring only 25 ins. by 7 ins. by 9 ins. Stand 386, N.

Trufits Ltd. cater for a nation of tea-drinkers with the Motor Maid* electric kettle. For compactness its handle is designed to fold, for lightness it is made of aluminium. Complete kit, 39s. 11d.

Tyre Products Ltd. (350, J-M) again enlarge their range of car mats. Full sets for a saloon (front and rear compartments) cost as little as £3.10s., and save at least that sum in terms of lengthened carpet life.

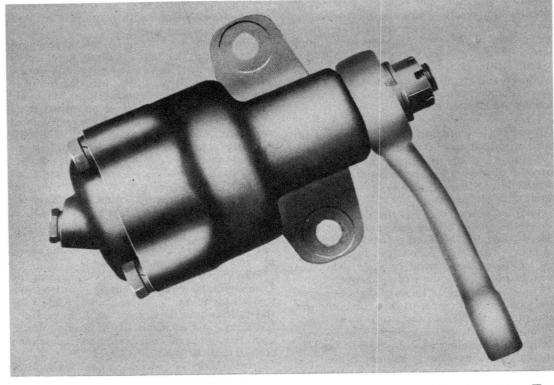

ANSWER Both the pictures above are steering dampers. Top picture shows the GT5 telescopic version; immediately above is the Armstrong Idler bearing damper.

Tudor Accessories Ltd. develop the gentle art of self-defence (for cars) with their new Deefenders—shock absorbers in a non-standard sense of the word. Moulded from resilient white rubber, they fit to normal bumpers and take care of nudges and scrapes that could otherwise cause expensive-to-remedy dents and scratches.

Makers of products marked with an asterisk are not themselves at Earls Court, but the articles will probably be seen on other exhibitors' stands.

The shampoo sachet contains wax for a wash-and-polish finish, and (below) the Peco free flow exhaust system for the smaller Ford engine.

Below is shown an automatic repair outfit for mini-size tyres.

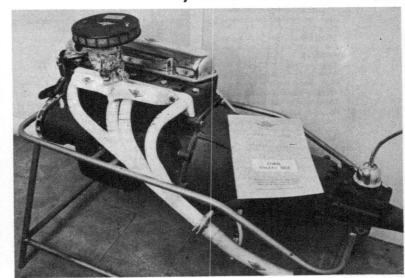

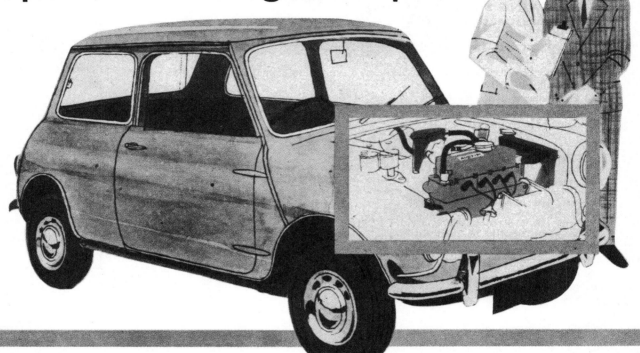

CARS
OF THE EARLY 60'S
BRITISH AND IMPORTED MODELS 1960-1964

MOTOR SHOW REVIEW GUIDE
1963

A - Z
SECTION

OCTOBER 1963

Bright BRIGHTER Brightest!

Message from Mr. L. G. T. Farmer, President of the Society of Motor Manufacturers and Traders; Executive Chairman of the Rover Company.

❡ I am pleased to contribute to this *Daily Express* Review which once again performs successfully the difficult task of giving a clear picture of trends in design and engineering to be found at this year's Motor Show. In doing this it enables the reader to appreciate better the exhibits of over sixty-five car manufacturers from all parts of the world, as well as the wealth of accessories, tyres, and transport service equipment, when he comes to Earls Court to see them for himself.

❡ The background to the 1963 Motor Show is brighter than it has been for three years. Every car on show is within reach of a far greater number of people, thanks to the substantial cut in Purchase Tax last November.

❡ As a result, production of British cars has leapt ahead of the 1962 figures, and exports, too, have been increasing.

❡ The challenge of Continental motor manufacturers has been a strong incentive. Despite fierce competition and the tariff barriers of the Common Market countries of Europe, more British cars are being exported to these thriving and expanding markets than ever before, a very creditable achievement. In the first six months of this year, 70,000 cars were shipped to these countries—14,600 more than in the same period of 1962. At Earls Court and in the pages of this Review you will see the reasons for this success: advanced engineering, up-to-date styling, safer motoring, cars that give the motorist economic driving—this is what the British motor industry is offering the public both at home and abroad.

I believe that this year's Motor Show is the best and most comprehensive held since the war.

Apart from the latest models from sixty-five world-wide manufacturers—including East Germany, Russia and Israel—the British car makers have swept into Earls Court with products that cater for every individual need and every whim of the motoring public.

For the first time at the Show you will see the fabulous Scottish-built Hillman Imp, of which Rootes plan to turn out 150,000 every year. It has a 875 c.c. engine with all major castings made completely of light aluminium—the first aluminium ever to be fitted to a mass-production British car.

Slightly up the price class is the brilliant new Vauxhall Viva, the smallest car this powerful Luton organisation has produced for more than 20 years.

The great record-breaking British Motor Corporation produces the latest Austin 1100 with its *new* sealed suspension unit, which operates with water.

Higher up the scale is Rover's exciting 2,000 c.c. model. Jaguars add to their list of well-proven cars with a new S-type.

These are only a few of the new models you will see as you tour the plush gangways at Earls Court—and many more have been given fascinating face-lifts.

This year the results of the British motor industry on the crest of its success are apparent. When, at the last budget, the Chancellor of the Exchequer halved the purchase tax on cars, he gave the British manufacturer a chance to sell a cheaper car in Britain.

Now, with record sales reported from many of the biggest factories, executives have discovered that a flourishing home trade improves the opportunities for making big headway overseas. So home sales and export sales have risen and everybody is happy.

What is the main trend this year? I would say without doubt that it is a movement to encourage the do-it-yourself motorist so that he will be

Good ... BETTER BEST!

says **BASIL CARDEW**

Editor of the Daily Express Motor Show Review for 1963

able to cut his costs in the car dealer's workshops.

For instance, most manufacturers have concentrated on producing a car as maintenance-free as is possible within its price. Their efforts include supplying fool-proof suspension that is sealed and never requires servicing.

There is, too, a drive to sell cars with sealed-engine cooling systems and self-adjusting brakes.

The experts are also showing new long-life tyres which more than double the working span of those they replace. There are, too, new super plugs that can be used for 10,000 to 20,000 miles without being checked.

All this adds up to cheaper motoring for the car owner who, at the same time, gets more and more at a lower price.

Makers have also fitted more disc brakes and more powerful drum brakes with the idea of increasing the safety of cars in a period when the Black Charter automatically excludes a driver from the road for six months if he incurs three offences—many of them minor—such as earning

three endorsements in a period of three years.

Part of this safety campaign also includes the fitting of interior housings for safety belts.

The public is still slow to adopt these belts, but their proved high value in saving the occupants of cars from serious injury is bound in time to increase their popularity.

Under the bright lights and soft carpeting at Earls Court you will see not only the car exhibits but more than 400 other stands showing svelt bodywork by specialised coach builders; motorised caravans; accessories and components; tyres and transport service equipment. Even the hire purchase and finance houses have not been forgotten.

Most of the components, ranging from a split pin to a full-sized cutaway engine ticking over, are being displayed in the myriad-stand gallery circling the main body of the hall below.

The woman's angle is well looked after in two ways: the cars are easy to drive, with more automatic transmission and petrol-saving overdrives, and many new models have synchromesh on all forward gears—including first gear.

The makers also make a set at women not only by providing plenty of shopping space in the interiors of cars, but by beautifully blended modern fashion hues on the coach work, and new straight lines allowing a maximum of window light.

During the ten days of the 48th International Motor Show, I expect more than 500,000 home visitors will mingle with the 22,000 overseas representatives. Main interest, I believe, will be centered in the smaller cars such as the ubiquitous Minis, the Imp and the new Vauxhall.

For those who drive to the Exhibition in one of the near 10,000,000 vehicles (paying more than £700,000,000 a year in taxes) on our roads, this Daily Express Motor Show Review is intended as a guide.

To those who, for one reason or another, will not be able to visit Earls Court, I hope this Review will bring some of the glamour, fascination and excitement of the exhibits on the brightly-lit gangways and stands.

152

When stepping on the GAS . . .

YOUR motoring future may be bound up with the Rover-B.R.M. gas-turbine car—Earls Court guest exhibit that stole a different kind of show at Le Mans last June—more closely than you think.

Apart from its limited passenger space, lack of weather protection, and pugnacious, combat-hungry looks, this mobile blowlamp almost synthesises the everyman ideal of prosaic family automobilism.

It has no gears to change, no clutch to pump. It suffers fools gladly, or anyway unprotestingly, being impossible to over-rev or stall. It never needs warming up. It uses no cooling water, so it can't freeze or boil. It has no valves or contact-breaker and its solitary sparking plug probably won't need adjusting or cleaning in its entire lifetime.

All this . . . and a 107.84 m.p.h. average for twenty-four consecutive hours at Le Mans.

WAITING

So what are Rover waiting for? Seven years ago they were at the Show with a habitable and apparently well-developed turbocar (remember the T3 coupe, boasting all-round disc brakes, four-wheel drive, a de Dion back axle and fibreglass bodywork?). Over six years before that, their famous JET1, the World's first gas turbine car, inaugurated a new class of speed record with 150 m.p.h. bursts at Jabbeke, Belgium. This success marked the end of a beginning dating, in embryo, from as far back as 1945.

"Be not too lengthy in preparing the banquet, lest you die of hunger", was Walter Pater's verbal accelerator for slow-motion cooks.

Is eighteen years unreasonably lengthy for the preparation of this particular banquet, and how much longer do our stomachs have to rumble in anticipation of it?

TALKING

Mr. Maurice Wilks, chairman of the Rover Co. Ltd., is better qualified than most people to read the gas turbine's future, so let's tap him.

The passenger turbocar, he says, can be a production reality less than two years hence—if the public is ready for it. Bearing significantly on this estimate is the fact that Rover's current T4 saloon is the company's first gas-turbine prototype to be designed with future production in mind. Indeed, apart from its front-wheel drive and slightly modified nose shape, it's hardly distinguishable from the news-making 2000 (piston-engined, of course) which Rover are launching at Earls Court.

"In the final analysis", Mr. Wilks adds, "the question to be answered is: 'When will the market be ready for the gas turbine car, which is nearly ready for the market?' ". He leaves that one unanswered (stop *rumbling*, stomach) but lobs us some clues to factors that might tend to retard the fledgling's acceptance. Weighed in the balance against the pros we listed earlier, these cons don't look too formidable, but to ignore them would be stupid. Here they are:—

Cost. Initially, assuming equal manufacturing volumes, the g/t car would cost up to 25% more to produce than a normal vehicle of comparable performance.

Fuel consumption. By the use of a heat exchanger, which, briefly, uses surplus heat from the exhaust efflux to boost the temperature of the ingoing air charge, Rover are winning their long battle with the g/t powerplant's inherently lively thirst.

Consumption range for the T4, which I have ridden in but not driven, is given as 16-20 m.p.g.; and this, we are told, is "approximately the same

means a big step into your future

by DENNIS MAY

as that of a conventional car having the same carrying capacity and the same performance". (The 3.4 Jaguar averages 18 m.p.g., which suggests that the T4's top speed and acceleration is roughly equal to this beefy Jag's).

Add it all up, therefore, and the conclusion is that the gas turbine, while no longer soberingly extravagant, isn't outstandingly economical to run, and is unlikely to be in the forseeable future.

Unfortunately, the well-known fact that gas-turbines are just as happy on low-grade fuels as high—Rover normally use kerosene—has little bearing on actual operating costs, in the U.K. anyway. Why? Because fuel tax in Britain accounts for a large proportion of the price of whatever you feed your engine; if somebody discovered that old army socks went well in gas turbines, the government would assuredly slap a leveller tax on them, fast.

But "in many European countries," to quote Mr. Wilks again, "diesel fuel is much cheaper than petrol, and in these countries the gas turbine will take advantage of this lower cost".

Acceleration. A lag in initial pick-up, admittedly of only split-second duration, is characteristic of the gas turbine in its present form. While this may be frustrating to a generation that has made "instant" its favourite adjective, it is fortunately offset by the rate of acceleration once the car *is* on the move. For instance, the T3 Rover coupe of 1956—which the current T4 would undoubtedly out-grasshopper—went from zero to 80 m.p.h. in 18 seconds—a stunning 11 secs. faster than today's piston-packing 3-litre Rover.

The Rover engineers, incidentally, aren't turning their backs on this problem of initial lag. An automatic two-speed transmission, which ought to see it off, is under development at the Solihull factory.

Engine braking. There isn't much, but the Rover view is that modern disc brakes make it dispensible. A counter-argument, if you were looking for one, might be that you don't miss the piston engine's free-gift braking until you lose it; in countless situations where, without your consciously registering the fact, a normal engine supplies the whole whoa-back requirement, a turbiner will have to rouse his left foot from a light doze (or swivel the right one across from the accelerator) and plant it on the brake pedal.

That about completes the debit entries, unless you include the inescapable bulkiness of the gas turbine's exhaust system. There are two ways round this problem, though, and Rover have used them both. JET1 and T3 had their engines at the back (so too, of course, has the Rover-B.R.M.), thus minimising exhaust tract length and incidentally uncluttering the whole underbelly space between the axle planes. The T4, on the other hand, has a front-mounted engine driving the front wheels; so again the midships/nether area is disencumbered of transmission,

leaving room for the massive trunking through which the spent gases escape astern.

QUIET

Reared on piston engines, with their rubbing contacts between moving and static surfaces, and destructive inertia stresses, we tend to associate sky-high revolutions per minute with a short life and an anxious one. So it's difficult to assimilate the idea that a unit like Rover's 2S/150, operating at compressor and power turbine speeds of 65,000 and 40,000 r.p.m. respectively, can be, and indeed is, outstandingly reliable and quite reasonably quiet. Also, despite its gargantuan throughput of air, it doesn't snatch hats off the heads of passers-by nor scorch them with its efflux.

Autocar's technical editor, my learned friend Harry Mundy, reported his findings after examining the Rover-B.R.M.'s dismantled 2S/150 engine in the state in which it finished its Le Mans stint (in all essentials, this unit was identical with the production-destined T4's). The sole deterioration capable of affecting performance was slight and local erosion of the compressor guide vanes and (even slighter) of the turbine blades. The cause in each case, Mundy deduced, was the entry of abrasive dust from the atmosphere. On a passenger car application, of course, there would be a stronger incentive to prevent such infiltrations. Both erosion colonies were removable by simple polishing, after which the unit was ready for reassembly—and another Le Mans.

CLEAN

Rover's industrial gas turbines, approximating to those that will power the mobile blowlamps of tomorrow, commonly run 3,000 hours without needing major attention. This, by Rover translation, equals 60,000 to 90,000 road miles.

No hats snatched off heads. No, because, surprising as it seems, air velocity is low at its point of entry to the compressor.

No scorched, blasted or fume-choked populace? No. The exhaust gases are actually "cleaner" than a piston engine's, and also, moreover, cooler. Their actual mass, of course, is greater, but judicious positioning and directing of the final exits eliminate all danger and nuisance elements.

Chrysler, in America, who entered the turbo-car race years after Rover, have taken a seemingly decisive step towards series production by releasing a substantial fleet of gas turbine cars to John Doe motorists, on the understanding that they will report their laymanlike reactions to Chrysler in due course.

Think you could sell Rover on a similar proposition, involving *a* T4, in the singular? It might, just might, be worth trying it on that big-I-am gent with the cigar and the Savile-Row suit on. Stand No.

Visor mirrors, lighters, hoods, windows, wipers and garages
—over such things does
SUSAN BARNES
let her hair down

I'M TELLING YOU NOW!

ONE of the most brilliant strokes of genius shown by a motor car manufacturer was the simple thought of glueing a small mirror on the upper side of the non-driver's sun visor. (If the woman is behind the wheel—I am assuming, absurdly, that only women want to check their appearance—she can see her own reflection in the rearview mirror easily enough by leaning two inches to one side.)

There are two fascinating things about this bit of genius: with thousands of men having bellowed for years about the rearview mirror being twisted out of position in order that their companion put on her lipstick, why has the solution to the problem been only recently discovered? And—more relevant—why, now that it *has* been discovered, doesn't every motor car have one? So far as I know, it is virtually impossible for a woman to buy the cheapest handbag without finding therein a mirror. Why can't this small item—at non-existent cost to the manufacturer—be installed in each and every car? Is there really a class system operating in Britain that regards free comfort as the prerogative of the well-to-do?

Equally baffling is the absence of cigarette lighters in every car. (Most of the trade calls them "cigar lighters". The subtleties of snobbery are infinite, it seems.) This cannot be put off on the campaign against smoking. Cheaper cars have been without lighters long before the Royal College of Physicians' report scared the wits out of us. If only because a motor car manufacturer may have some interest in making money, why on earth doesn't he invest a few extra shillings per car and provide them all with a cigarette lighter? If car A and car B have roughly the same attractions, surely the presence of a lighter in one of them is going to influence prospective buyers. Or am I really the only human being who likes small luxuries in this world?

If snobbery blinds some British manufacturers to providing obvious small services to the masses, is it the stiff-upper-lip tradition that makes them determined that the well-to-do aren't allowed to be *too* comfortable? While for years American convertibles of all grades have been operated mechanically, in Britain they still are not. "What makes you think there is any demand for this in Britain?" I was asked by the sales representative of one of the largest groups. Anyhow, he added, even if the British *were* so demanding as to want to put their hoods up and down simply by pressing a button, they

wouldn't want to pay the extra £50 that such a device, mass-produced, would cost them. Really?

He may be right. But I should have thought that the man who has the money to pay £50 extra for overdrive and who has the temperament to want a convertible in the first place would be happy to pay another £50 to make the thing work automatically. When more and more British motor car manufacturers announce that they are discontinuing convertibles because there is no demand for them in Britain, should they not consider whether the demand is for convertibles to work with the ease of the thousands and thousands and thousands produced in America for the last decade?

Other mildly puzzling things in my experience with $1\frac{1}{2}$ litre convertibles is that whoever has designed them has apparently suffered from a disordered retina of the eye: at least, something must account for why the windows are not made to wind up high enough to meet the roof. Or perhaps the designer is a sadist. Why else on a £900 car should the windshield wiper knob fall off within a week of purchase, should both doorhandles break within a month, should

the driver's window get stuck three inches from the bottom, should the boot's trigger jam so that even a garage is reduced to looking for a giant tin-opener to prise the thing open so he can at least put some water and oil in.

And finally garages. Because really, what I want even more than certain small obvious items in a car is the large obvious item to put the car in—namely, a garage.

Are the British so affluent that garages have no need any longer to worry about losing customers? Or is it the British consumer's fault for not sueing for shortening-of-life-apoplexy when he goes to collect his car after a general overhaul and discovers when he starts the motor that the muffler has mysteriously disappeared in the course of the overhaul (and that there are none in stock to replace it). Quite apart from what became of the muffler, why didn't anyone notice? Are garage mechanics deaf?

And are garage managers actually trained to aggravate motorists quite capriciously? If I am told I cannot have my car back for two days, all right. I adjust. But if I am told I can have it back in one, and I go to collect it only to have the manager say with an indifferent shrug, "So sorry, Moddum, your car's not ready. You know how it is. Can you call back tomorrow?"—then to this I cannot adjust. Can you?

Surely the British motorist should be able to find decent garage service without emigrating. Shouldn't he?

THE MOTORING MUSE

The jealous poet overtaken by an E-type

**Your wit's too hot, it speeds too fast,
  'twill tire**

—Shakespeare (Love's Labour's Lost)

The poet negotiating Hyde Park underpass

**The grave itself is but a covered bridge
Leading from light to light, through a
            brief darkness**

—Longfellow

The poet trying to sleep in a room overlooking any Continental square

**Did ye not hear it? No! 'twas but the wind
Or the car rattling o'er the stony street**

—Byron

The poet held up in a Strand traffic jam and about to miss an appointment

**Upon thy so sore loss
Shall shine the traffic of Jacob's ladder
Pitched betwixt Heaven and Charing
                                Cross**

—Francis Thompson

The misdirected poet bumping over an endless country lane

**Oh Life! thou art a galling load
Along a rough, a weary road
        To wretches such as I!**

—Burns

BMC MAKES A CAR FOR YOU

(designed, sized, powered and priced for your kind of motoring)

Made-to-measure BMC caters for individuality . . . with a range of 38 cars. Within this range you will see twelve Minis, but each with a personality all of its own. You'll find several versions of the trend-setting 1100, each produced to meet a specific need. The same goes for BMC sports cars, estate cars and luxury family cars . . . it's like getting made-to-measure service off the peg.

Unscrimping care Although BMC cars are all different, certain basic qualities are common to each : like 4-speed synchromesh gearboxes, ohv engines, robust, mono-construction bodies, wide colour range. All BMC high-performance cars—and many of the family cars—have disc brakes. All are superbly styled, craftsman-engineered, and manufactured with unscrimping care.

ALL PRICES INCLUDE PURCHASE TAX

TWENTY CARS BETWEEN £447 and £600 *including the* **NEW AUSTIN 1100**

Austin and Morris Mini Saloons £447.12.11
Austin and Morris Mini Super de Luxe Saloons £492.19.2

Morris Minor '1000' 2-door Saloon
Basic £515.6.3 De Luxe £539.9.7
Morris Minor '1000' 4-door Saloon
Basic £545.10.5 De Luxe £573.18.4

Morris Minor '1000' Convertible
Basic £515.6.3
De Luxe £539.9.7

Austin Mini Countryman and Morris Mini Traveller with wood embellishment £550.19.2

£556 TO £600

Wolseley Hornet £556.7.11
Riley Elf £574.10.5

Austin A40 Saloon Basic £556.7.11
Super de Luxe £598.13.9
A40 Countryman Basic £575.14.7
Super de Luxe £616.16.3

Austin and Morris Mini Cooper Saloons £567.17.6

Morris Minor '1000' Traveller
Basic £581.15.5
De Luxe £605.18.9

Austin '1100' 4-door Saloon
Basic £592.12.11
De Luxe £610.15.5
The latest addition to the Austin range

Morris '1100' 4-door Saloon
Basic £592.12.11
De Luxe £610.15.5

Austin-Healey Sprite £586.12.1
M.G. Midget £598.13.9

SIXTEEN MORE BETWEEN £640 and £1112

Wolseley '1500'
Fleet model £640.19.7
Family model £665.2.11
Riley One-Point-Five £701.7.11

Austin and Morris Mini Coopers, 'S' type £695.7.1

M.G. '1100' 4-door Saloon £713.9.7

£720 TO £840

Austin A60 Saloon
Basic £720.14.7. De Luxe £755.15.5
Morris Oxford Saloon
Basic £730.7.11. De Luxe £765.8.9
Wolseley 16/60 Saloon £837.6.8

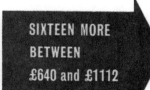

Austin A60 Countryman £828.5.5
Morris Oxford Traveller £837.18.9

M.G. Series M.G.B. £834.6.3

£890 TO £1112

M.G. Magnette Saloon £891.14.2
Riley 4/Seventy Two Saloon £915.17.6

Austin-Healey '3000' Sports Convertible £1045.15.4

Austin A110 Westminster de Luxe
Saloon with overdrive £1051.16.3
Automatic transmission £1112.4.7
Wolseley 6/110 Saloon
With overdrive £1112.4.7
Automatic transmission £1172.12.11

TWO LUXURY CARS *with outstanding appointments* **£1346 £2840**

Vanden Plas Princess 3-litre Saloon
With overdrive £1346.12.11
Automatic transmission £1407.1.3

Vanden Plas Princess 4-litre Saloon
or limousine £2840.2.11

THE BRITISH MOTOR CORPORATION LIMITED

BIRMINGHAM AND OXFORD

BUY BRITISH

155

THE Show . . . .

and artist ROBB puts into streamline the essential modernity of the Earls Court spectacle

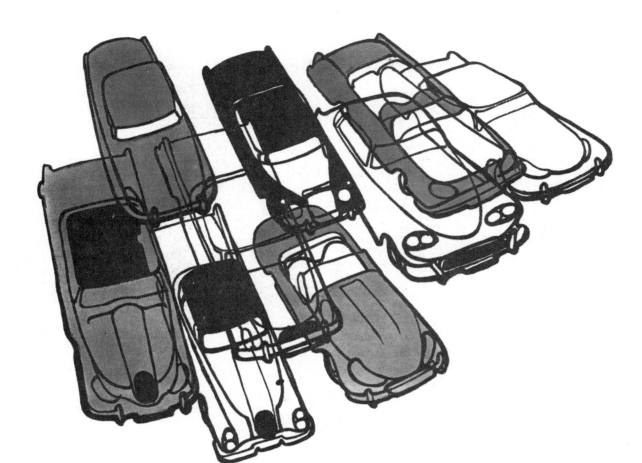

ABARTH FIAT 1000

CARLO ABARTH goes on producing new engines and new cars like a conjurer producing rabbits from a hat. And they win countless victories in international speed events. He enlarges and breathes upon the Fiat 500. Next come the fast 850 c.c., and this Fiat-Abarth 1000 Berlina, with special ohc engine. There's a Simca 2000 too, with twin ohc and top speed around 140 m.p.h.

CLOSE-UP
Four-cyl.; o.h.c.; 65×74 mm.; 982 c.c.; 97 b.h.p.; 10.1 to 1 comp.; coil ign.; 2 Weber carbs.; 4-speed, 14.7, 8.8, 5.3, 4.33 to 1; cen. lvr.; susp., f. ind. trans. leaf, r. ind. coil; 2-door; 2-seat; disc brks.; max. 130 m.p.h.; cruise 100; m.p.g. 30-32; whl. base 6ft. 6¾in.; track f. 3ft. 9¼in., r. 3ft. 9¾in.; lgth. 11ft. 3¾in.; wdth. 4ft. 7in.; ht. 3ft. 11in.; g.c. 6¼in.; turng. cir. 28ft. 8in.; kerb wt. 11¼ cwt.; tank, 6½ gals.; 12-volt.

A.C. COBRA

AMERICAN racing driver Carroll Shelby had the idea of mating a powerful Ford V8 engine with the chassis and body by A.C. to produce the Cobra, a new sports car of terrific performance which is already familiar in international race tracks. Car and body are built at Thames Ditton. Engines are fitted in Los Angeles and each car is test driven by Shelby before delivery.

CLOSE-UP
Eight-cyl.; o.h.v.; 96.5×72.9 mm.; 4,262 c.c.; 320 b.h.p.; 9.2 to 1 comp.; coil ign.; Ford carb.; 4-speed, 8.36, 6.30, 4.99, 3.54 to 1; cen. lvr.; susp., f. and r. ind. trans leaf; 2-door; 2-seat; disc brks.; max. 150 m.p.h.; cruise 130; m.p.g. 20; whl. base 7ft. 6in.; track f. 4ft. 3½in., r. 4ft. 4½in.; lgth. 12ft. 7in.; wdth. 5ft. 1in.; ht. 4ft. 1in.; g.c. 7in.; turng. cir. 36ft.; kerb wt. 18 cwt.; tank, 15 gals.; 12-volt.

ALFA ROMEO GIULIA T.I.

THIS medium sized sports saloon made its debut in 1962. Built in a factory world famed for sports and racing cars it has space for four people and a large luggage boot. Five speed fully synchronised gearbox makes gear changing a pleasure and sophisticated suspension ensures a stable ride even when hitting the top speed of over 100 m.p.h. There's also a 1600 2-seater Spider for sports car fans.

CLOSE-UP

Four-cyl.; o.h.c.; 78×82 mm.; 1,570 c.c.; 106 b.h.p.; 9 to 1 comp.; coil ign.; Solex carb.; 5-speed, 16.93, 10.18, 6.94, 4.05 to 1; cen. lvr.; susp., f. ind. coil, r. coil; 4-door; 4/5-seat; hyd. brks.; max. 103 m.p.h.; cruise 85; m.p.g. 30; whl. base 8ft. 2⅞in.; track f. 4ft. 3½in., r. 4ft. 2in.; lgth. 13ft. 9⅝in.; wdth. 5ft. 1½in.; ht. 4ft. 8½in.; g.c. 6in.; turng. cir. 36ft.; kerb wt. 21 cwt.; tank, 10 gals.; 12-volt.

£1,144 + £238.17.11 p.t. = £1,382.17.11

ALFA ROMEO 2600 SPRINT

THIS desirable thoroughbred with six-cylinder twin-cam engine and super-smooth five-speed gearbox comes in three versions, the Berlina, Sprint and Spider. Berlina is a handsome 6-seater saloon with servo-assisted Girling disc brakes on the front for high stopping power. Sprint coupe by Bertone and Spider by Touring are faster with a maximum speed of over 120 m.p.h. A pleasure to see and to drive.

CLOSE-UP

Six-cyl.; o.h.c.; 83×79.6 mm.; 2,582 c.c.; 160 b.h.p.; 9 to 1 comp.; coil ign.; 3 Solex carbs.; 5-speed, 16.93, 10.19, 6.94, 5.12, 5.04 to 1; cen. lvr.; susp., f. ind. coil, r. coil; 4-door; 4/5-seat; hyd. servo brks, disc front; max. 120 m.p.h.; cruise 100; m.p.g. 20; whl. base 8ft. 5⅝in.; track f. 4ft. 7in., r. 4ft. 6in.; lgth. 15ft. 0½in.; wdth. 5ft. 7in.; ht. 4ft. 6½in.; g.c. 8in.; turng. cir. 36ft. 5in.; kerb wt. 27¾ cwt.; tank, 13½ gals. 12-volt.

£2,399 + £500.7.2 p.t. = £2,899.7.2

ASTON MARTIN DB5 CONVERTIBLE

THE open-car man's all-weather mount with the new big engine. Fully adjustable seats and luxurious fittings add to the pleasure of being wafted about at high cruising speeds. Disc brakes all round with servo assistance make stopping smooth and easy. Aston Martins are a familiar sight on the world's race tracks and race-proved design features quickly find their way into production models.

CLOSE-UP

Six-cyl.; o.h.c.; 96×92 mm.; 3,995 c.c.; 282 b.h.p.; 8.75 to 1 comp.; coil ign.; 3 S.U. carbs.; 5-speed, 10.18, 6.64, 4.64, 3.77, 3.14 to 1; cen. lvr., auto. opt.; susp., f. ind. coil, r. coil; 2-door; 4-seat; disc servo brks.; max. 148 m.p.h.; cruise 120; m.p.g. 15-18; whl. base 8ft. 2in.; track f. 4ft. 6in., r. 4ft. 5½in.; lgth. 14ft. 8⅜in.; wdth. 5ft. 6in.; ht. 4ft. 4in.; g.c. 6½in.; turng. cir. 34ft.; kerb wt. 29½ cwt.; tank, 19 gals.; 12-volt.

ASTON MARTIN DB5

AN engine increased from 3.6 to 4 litres gives commanding new power and flexibility to this latest version of a famous luxury sports model. For the first time an automatic transmission is offered as alternative to the all-synchromesh five-speed gearbox. New AC generator keeps the battery fully charged at low engine speeds: but with motorways beckoning and a top speed of over 150 m.p.h. who wants to drive slowly?

CLOSE-UP

Six-cyl.; o.h.c.; 96×92 mm.; 3,995 c.c.; 282 b.h.p.; 8.75 to 1 comp.; coil ign.; 3 S.U. carbs.; 5-speed, 10.18, 6.64, 4.64, 3.77, 3.14 to 1; cen. lvr., auto opt.; susp. f. ind. coil, r. coil; 2-door; 4-seat; disc servo brks.; max. 150 m.p.h.; cruise 125; m.p.g. 15-18; whl. base 8ft. 2in.; track f. 4ft. 6in., r. 4ft. 5½in.; lgth. 14ft. 8⅜in.; wdth. 5ft. 6in.; ht. 4ft. 4in.; g.c. 6½in.; turng. cir. 34ft.; kerb wt. 29 cwt.; tank, 19 gals.; 12-volt.

£3,455 + £720.7.1 p.t. = £4,175.7.1

ALVIS 3-LITRE.

THIS car is made in two versions, as a saloon and a coupe. Both reach standards of luxury usually found only in individually-built cars. Gracefully styled by Graber from abroad, its main feature is in its precision engineering in the true Alvis tradition. The motorist in a hurry can glide along at more than 100 miles an hour in real comfort.

CLOSE-UP

Six-cyl.; o.h.v.; 84×90 mm.; 2,993 c.c.; 115 b.h.p.; 8.5 to 1 comp.; coil ign.; 2 S.U. carbs.; 5-speed, 11.38, 6.97, 4.86, 3.77, 3.07 to 1; cen. lvr.; BW auto. opt.; susp., f. ind. coil, r. half-elliptic; 2-door; 4-seat; disc brks.; max. 100 m.p.h.; cruise, 80; m.p.g. 18-22; whl. base 9ft. 3½in.; track f. 4ft. 7½in., r. 4ft. 6 9/16 in.; lgth. 15ft. 8½in.; wdth. 5ft. 6in.; ht. 5ft.; g.c. 7in.; turng. cir. 39ft. 6in.; kerb wt. 30½ cwt.; tank, 14½ gals.; 12-volt.
£2,095+£437.0.5 p.t. = £2,532.0.5

AUSTIN MINI COOPER S

SINCE its introduction in 1959 the BMC Mini has appeared in many versions, production and tuned. The Mini Cooper S has engine increased to 1,071 c.c. It takes off like a rocket and zooms up to 80 in third; top speed is 90. Larger front discs with vacuum servo give extra stopping power and special broad-based tyres add high speed stability. Originally intended as a competition machine, it goes into regular production by popular demand.

CLOSE-UP

Four-cyl.; o.h.v.; 70.6×68.26 mm.; 1,071 c.c.; 70 b.h.p.; 9 to 1 comp.; coil ign.; S.U. carb.; 4-speed, 12.04, 7.21, 5.10, 3.77 to 1; cen. lvr.; susp., f. and r. ind. rubber; 2-door; 4-seat; brks. hyd. servo disc front; max. 90 m.p.h.; cruise 80; m.p.g. 35; whl. base 6ft. 8in.; track f. 4ft. 0½in., r. 3ft. 10¾in.; lgth. 10ft. 0½in.; wdth. 4ft. 7½in.; ht. 4ft. 5in.; g.c. 6in.; turng. cir. 31ft. 10in.; kerb wt. 12¾ cwt.; tank, 5½ gals.; 12-volt.
£575+£120.7.1 p.t. = £695.7.1

AUSTIN MINI COUNTRYMAN

IT is one of the most popular utility cars on the market. Reasons: cheap to run; easy to park; very functional in carrying passengers or cargo; at home both in town and in the country. It is a little longer than its sister standard mini and not quite so fast, but it certainly loses nothing in road holding, and is here to stay for a long time.

CLOSE-UP

Four-cyl.; o.h.v.; 62.9×68.26 mm.; 848 c.c.; 34 b.h.p.; 8.3 to 1 comp.; coil ign.; S.U. carb.; 4-speed, 13.65, 8.17, 5.31, 3.76 to 1; cen. lvr.; susp., f. and r. ind. rubber; 2-door; 4-seat; hyd. brks.; max. 74 m.p.h.; cruise, 60; m.p.g. 40; whl. base 7ft. 0 5/32 in.; track f. 3ft. 11 7/16 in., r. 3ft. 9⅞in.; lgth. 10ft. 9¾in.; width 4ft. 7½in.; ht. 4ft. 5⅛in.; g.c. 6⅜in.; turng. cir. 32ft. 9in.; kerb wt. 12¾ cwt.; tank 5½ gals.; 12-volt.
£439.10+£92.2.6 p.t. = £531.12.6

AUSTIN 1100

FOURTH version of an original and successful design. (First three were Morris 1100, and two twin-carburetter models, MG 1100 and Italian-built Innocenti IM3.) Besides distinctive scalloped Austin grille it has new rectangular facia treatment and rubber floor mats for durability. Space-saving transverse engine and front-wheel drive, plus revolutionary Hydrolastic suspension for a smooth pitch-free ride over the roughest tracks. Sealed cooling system.

CLOSE-UP

Four-cyl.; o.h.v.; 64.58×83.72 mm.; 1,098 c.c.; 55 b.h.p.; 8.5 to 1 comp.; coil ign.; S.U. carb.; 4-speed; 14.99, 8.98, 5.83, 4.133 to 1; cen. lvr.; susp., f. and r. ind. rubber-hyd.; 2- or 4-door; 4-seat; hyd. brks., disc front; max. 76 m.p.h.; cruise 60; m.p.g. 36-38; whl. base 7ft. 9½in.; track f. 4ft. 3½in., r. 4ft. 2⅞in.; lgth. 12ft. 2¾in.; wdth. 5ft. 0⅜in.; ht. 4ft. 4½in.; g.c. 6in.; turng. cir. 32ft.; kerb wt. 16½ cwt.; tank, 8½ gals.; 12-volt.

Abbreviations—g.c.—ground clearance; susp.—suspension; f.—front; r.—rear; comp.—compression; s.v.—side-valves; o.h.v.—overhead valves; o.h.c.—overhead camshaft; hyd.—hydraulic.

AUSTIN A60 CAMBRIDGE

MEDIUM sized, spacious family saloon designed by Pininfarina combines Italian design flair with British practicality. Smart appearance, good luggage trunk, moderate fuel consumption and good performance attract many buyers. Automatic transmission is optional alternative to the 4-speed manual gearbox. A diesel engine can now be supplied and is proving popular especially for export to countries where diesels receive tax concessions.

CLOSE-UP
Four-cyl.; o.h.v.; 76.2×88.9 mm.; 1,622 c.c.; 61 b.h.p.; 8.3 to 1 comp.; coil ign.; S.U. carb.; 4-speed, 15.63, 9.52, 5.91, 4.3 to 1; cen. or col. lvr.; auto. opt.; susp., f. ind. coil, r. half-elliptic; 4-door; 4/5-seat; hyd. brks.; max. 80 m.p.h.; cruise 70; m.p.g. 30-32; whl. base, 8ft. 4½in.; track f. 4ft. 2⅞in., r. 4ft. 3⅜in.; lgth. 14ft. 6½in.; wdth., 5ft. 3in.; ht. 4ft. 10in.; g.c. 5⅝in.; turng. cir. 37ft.; kerb wt. 21½ cwt.; tank 10 gals.; 12-volt.
£596 + £124.14.7 p.t. = £720.14.7

AUSTIN A/110

BIGGEST of the B.M.C. Farina-designed saloons, this six-seater with 3-litre engine offers 100 m.p.h. motoring at moderate cost. Standard transmission is three-speed all-synchro. Borg Warner automatic transmission is optional and there are Lockheed disc brakes at the front. On a long run the A 110 gives a pleasant cruising at 80 m.p.h. Well appointed and upholstered with a big trunk, it is a lot for the money.

CLOSE-UP
Six-cyl.; o.h.v.; 83×89 mm.; 2,912 c.c.; 126 b.h.p.; 8.3 to 1 comp.; coil ign.; 2 S.U. carbs.; 3-speed, 12.1, 6.45, 3.91 to 1; cen. lvr. BW overdrive auto. opt.; susp., f. ind. coil, r. half-elliptic; 4-door; 5/6 seat; servo brakes, disc front; max. 104 m.p.h.; cruise, 80; m.p.g. 16-23; whl. base, 9ft. 2in.; track, f. 4ft. 6in., r. 4ft. 5½in.; lgth. 15ft. 7½in.; wdth. 5ft. 8½in.; ht. 5ft. 0½in.; g.c. 6½in.; turng. cir. 41ft.; kerb wt. 30½ cwt.; tank, 16 gals.; 12-volt.
£870 + £181.16.3. p.t. = £1,051.16.3.

AUSTIN HEALEY SPRITE MARK II

A CAR that is sporting and cheap to run. Since the last Motor Show it has been fitted with a bigger engine of 1,098 c.c. In twin-carburettor form it develops 55 h.p. Women motorists like it especially as it has a sports car glamour yet can be parked in towns in a minimum of space. To cope with the higher performance the Sprite now has 8¼in. diameter disc brakes in front.

CLOSE-UP
Four-cyl.; o.h.v.; 64.58×83.72 mm.; 1,098 c.c.; 55 b.h.p.; 8.9 to 1 comp.; coil ign.; 2 S.U. carbs.; 4-speed, 13.50, 8.08, 5.73, 4.22 to 1; cen. lvr.; susp., f. ind. coil, r. quarter-elliptic; 2-door; 2-seat; hyd. brks. disc front; max. 90 m.p.h.; cruise, 75; m.p.g. 32-35; whl. base, 6ft. 8in.; track, f. 3ft. 9¾in., r. 3ft. 8¾in.; lgth., 11ft. 5⅜in.; wdth., 4ft. 5in.; ht. 4ft. 1⅜in.; g.c. 7in.; turng. cir. 29ft. 3in.; kerb wt., 13½ cwt.; tank, 6 gals.; 12-volt.
£485 + £101.12.1 p.t. = £586.12.1

AUSTIN HEALEY 3000

THIS is a top-selling thoroughbred sports car, brought up the hard way through rallies and races. It is built to give real comfort in high-speed, all-weather motoring. With improved aerodynamics and a sleeker appearance, normal consumption under fast driving conditions averages 20-25 miles to the gallon. In overdrive it can return 34 m.p.g. at a steady 40, and 23 m.p.g. at a fast 80. An exciting car that will continue for a long time.

CLOSE-UP
Six-cyl.; o.h.v.; 83.34×88.9 mm.; 2,912 c.c.; 132 b.h.p.; 9.03 to 1 comp.; coil ign.; 2 S.U. carbs.; 4-speed, 10.209, 7.302, 4.743, 3.545 to 1; de Normanville overdrive opt.; cen. lvr.; susp., f. ind. coil, r. half-elliptic; 2-door; 2/3 seat; hyd. brks., disc front; max. 116 m.p.h.; cruise, 95; m.p.g. 22; whl. base 7ft. 8in.; track f. 4ft. 0¾in., r. 4ft. 2in.; lgth. 13ft. 1½in.; wdth. 5ft.; ht. 4ft. 1in.; g.c. 4⅜in.; turng. cir. 32ft. 7in.; kerb wt. 21¾ cwt.; tank, 12 gals.; 12-volt.
£865 + £180.15.4 P.t. = £1,045.15.4

Abbreviations—g.c.—ground clearance; susp.—suspension; f.—front; r.—rear; comp.—compression; s.v.—side-valves; o.h.v.—overhead valves; o.h.c.—overhead camshaft; hyd.—hydraulic.

159

AUTO UNION DKW F102

REPLACING the Auto Union 1000 series, this new front-drive model with longer smoother lines and a larger engine is called the DKW F.102. Its three-cylinder two-stroke engine enlarged to 1175 c.c. gives 69 h.p. gross, enough for 85 m.p.h. cruising with fuel consumption around 30 m.p.g. Metered oil feed replaces the old oil-in-petrol system. Cooling system is sealed, front brakes are discs. No grease points; service checks every 6,000 miles.

CLOSE-UP

Three-cyl.; two-stroke; 81 × 76 mm.; 1,175 c.c.; 60 b.h.p.; 7.5 to 1 comp.; coil ign.; Solex carb.; 4-speed, 14.91, 7.79, 4.80, 3.64 to 1; col. lvr.; susp., f. ind. torsion bar, r. torsion bar; 2/4-door; 5-seat; hyd. brks., disc front; max. 81 m.p.h.; cruise 75; m.p.g. 30-33; whl. base 8ft. 5in.; track f. 4ft. 4in., r. 4ft. 3½in.; lgth. 14ft. 5in.; wdth. 5ft. 3⅜in.; ht. 4ft. 9½in.; g.c. 6½in.; turng. cir. 37ft. 10in.; kerb wt. 17¼ cwt.; tank, 11 gals.; 6-volt.

BENTLEY S.3 CONTINENTAL

THIS is a queen of the road—graceful, powerful, swift. It is the car for the sporty rich with not a detail in luxury lacking. If its V8 engine gives you only 16 miles to the gallon, you know you will be the envy of everyone on the road, and be able to travel at a speed of two miles a minute. Britain's top coachbuilders produce coupe and convertible bodies for this fine chassis.

CLOSE-UP

Eight-cyl.; o.h.v.; 104.14 × 91.44 mm.; 6,230 c.c.; 9 to 1 comp.; coil ign.; 2 S.U. carbs.; 4-speed auto., 11.75, 8.10, 4.46, 3.08 to 1; col. lvr.; susp., f. ind. coil, r. half-elliptic; 2/4-door; 4-seat; hyd. servo brks.; max. 120 m.p.h.; cruise 90-100; m.p.g. 14-16; whl. base 10ft. 3in.; track f. 4ft. 10½in., r. 5ft.; lgth. 17ft. 8in.; wdth. 6ft.; ht. 5ft. 2in.; g.c. 7in.; turng. cir. 41ft. 8in.; kerb wt. 39¾ cwt.; tank, 18 gals.; 12-volt.

£6,505 + £1,355.15 p.t. = £7,860.15

BENTLEY S3

SIX litres of light alloy V8 ensure there's plenty of power and four headlamps illuminate the roads for high after-dark cruising speeds. 21 points on the chassis need greasing every 12,000 miles and you remove a front wheel to change a plug, so this is not a car for those who have to practise economy, but it combines power, prestige and luxurious comfort.

CLOSE-UP

Eight-cyl.; o.h.v.; 104.14 × 91.44 mm.; 6,230 c.c.; 9 to 1 comp.; coil ign.; 2 S.U. carbs.; 4-speed auto., 11.75, 8.10, 4.46, 3.08 to 1; col. lvr.; susp., f. ind. coil, r. half-elliptic; 4-door; 5/6 seat; hyd. servo brks.; max. 110 m.p.h.; cruise 90; m.p.g. 12-15; whl. base 10ft. 3in.; track, f. 4ft. 10in., r. 5ft.; lgth. 17ft. 7¾in.; wdth. 6ft. 2¾in.; ht. 5ft. 4in.; g.c. 7in.; turng. cir. 41ft. 8in.; kerb wt. 41½ cwt.; tank, 18 gals.; 12-volt.

£4,455 + £928.13.5 p.t. = £5,383.13.5

B.M.W. 700

ONE of a family of 700 models, nimble little four-seater rear-engined two-cylinder cars from a German house previously famed for sports cars. There is the little standard 700 which gives 32 h.p. and two high performance sports versions, the 700CS and the 700 Cabrio which develop 40 h.p. and then there's the luxury five-seater with 32 h.p. and longer, higher and wider bodywork.

CLOSE-UP

Two-cyl.; o.h.v. air-cooled; 73 × 78 mm.; 697 c.c.; 35 b.h.p.; 7.5 to 1 comp.; coil ign.; Solex carb.; 4-speed, 19.2, 10.5, 6.9, 4.5 to 1; cen. lvr.; susp., f. and r. ind. coil; 2-door; 4/5-seat; hyd. brks.; max. 70 m.p.h.; cruise 60; m.p.g. 31-40; whl. base 6ft. 11½in.; track f. 4ft. 2in., r. 3ft. 11in.; lgth. 11ft. 7½in.; wdth. 4ft. 10½in.; ht. 4ft. 5in.; g.c. 5⅛in.; turng. cir. 33ft.; kerb wt. 12½ cwt.; tank, 7 gals.; 12-volt.

£565.2.6 + £118.3.10 p.t. = £683.6.4

BOND EQUIPE G.T.

TAKE a Triumph Herald 1200 chassis with all-independent suspension and disc front brakes. Fit a 1,147 c.c. Spitfire engine with two carburetters giving 64 b.h.p., and a coupe body with two seats, using scuttle, windscreen and doors of the Herald and you have the recipe for a low-cost Grand Touring car. The Bond Equipe is a new model from well-known makers of three-wheelers.

CLOSE-UP
Four-cyl.; o.h.v.; 69.3×76 mm.; 1,147 c.c.; 64 b.h.p.; 9 to 1 comp.; coil ign.; S.U. carb.; 4-speed, 15.40, 8.87, 5.73, 4.11 to 1; cen. lvr.; susp., f. ind. coil, r. ind. trans. leaf; 2-door; 2/3-seat; hyd. brks., disc front; max. 93 m.p.h.; cruise 80; m.p.g. 35-40; whl. base 7ft. 7½in.; track f. and r. 4ft.; lgth. 12ft. 11in.; wdth. 5ft.; ht. 4ft. 4in.; g.c. 6⅜in.; turng. cir. 25ft.; kerb wt. 14¾ cwt.; tank, 10 gals.; 12-volt.
£680+£142.4.7 p.t. = £822.4.7

BRISTOL 408

A BRISTOL car owner is usually a tremendous enthusiast and the car he likes is this semi-streamlined model. It certainly has tremendous urge, with its 5.2-litre engine which quietly swishes the car along at more than 120 m.p.h. The product of speed enthusiasts, it has all the advantages of their know-how in building an immaculately turned-out and well-finished model.

CLOSE-UP
Eight-cyl.; o.h.v.; 98.55×84.07 mm.; 5,130 c.c.; 250 b.h.p.; 9 to 1 comp.; coil ign.; Carter carb.; 3-speed auto., 8.10, 4.80, 3.31 to 1; push button control; susp., f. ind. coil, r. torsion bar; 2-door; 4-seat; disc servo brks.; max. 122 m.p.h.; cruise, 100; m.p.g. 18-20; whl. base, 9 ft. 6 in.; track, f. 4ft. 5in., r. 4ft. 6½in.; lgth., 16ft. 7in.; wdth., 5ft. 8in.; ht. 5ft.; g.c. 6½in.; turng. cir. 39ft. 6in.; kerb wt., 32 cwt.; tank, 18 gals.; 12-volt.
£3,690+£769 p.t. = £4,459

BUICK RIVIERA

LARGE and luxurious coupe in Italian-American style to appeal to the man who likes a sporty looking car with terrific performance but all home comforts too. Engine of 6½ litres gives power to spare, big servo assisted brakes handle the stopping and Turbine Drive automatic transmission make this a very pleasurable machine for town and country driving. Four separate seats give armchair comfort. Engines range up to 6,964 c.c.

CLOSE-UP
Eight-cyl.; o.h.v.; 106.36×92.45 mm.; 6.572 c.c.; 325 b.h.p.; 10.25 to 1 comp.; coil ign.; Stromberg carb.; 2-speed auto., 5.88, 3.23 to 1; col. lvr.; susp., f. ind. coil, r. coil; 2-door; 4-seat; hyd. servo brks.; max. 122 m.p.h.; cruise 100; m.p.g. 13-18; whl. base 9ft. 9in.; track f. 5ft., r. 4ft. 11in.; lgth. 17ft. 4in.; wdth. 6ft. 2⅝in.; ht. 4ft. 5½in.; g.c. 5½in.; turng. cir. 43ft. 6in.; kerb wt. 38 cwt.; tank, 16¾ gals.; 12-volt.
£2,725+£568 p.t. = £3,293

BUICK SPECIAL

LENGTH, power and performance are increased on Buicks for 1964. The Special, modest model of the range has V6 engines ranging up to 3,686 c.c. Optional on Special and standard on Wildcat and Electra is a new V8 of 6,571 c.c. Wildcat and Electra can have a bigger V8 of 6,964 c.c. Cast iron replaces the former aluminium block. A tilting steering wheel for easy entry is optional.

CLOSE-UP
Six-cyl.; o.h.v.; 92×81 mm.; 3,247 c.c.; 135 b.h.p.; 8.8 to 1 comp.; coil ign.; Rochester carb.; 3-speed, 8.6, 5.2, 3.4 to 1; col. lvr., auto. opt.; susp., f. ind. coil, r. coil; 4-door; 6-seat; hyd. brks.; max. 96 m.p.h.; cruise 80; m.p.g. 18-22; whl. base 9ft. 7in.; track f. and r. 4ft. 8in.; lgth. 16ft. 10in.; wdth. 5ft. 10¼in.; ht. 4ft. 6in.; g.c. 6in.; turng. cir. 36ft.; kerb wt. 26 cwt.; tank, 13½ gals.; 12-volt.
£1,716+£358 p.t. = £2,074

Abbreviations—g.c.—ground clearance; susp.—suspension; f.—front; r.—rear; comp.—compression; s.v.—side-valves; o.h.v.—overhead valves; o.h.c.—overhead camshaft; hyd.—hydraulic.

CADILLAC ELDORADO

BELOVED of potentates and presidents, film stars and financiers, the vast high-powered Cadillac, top price make in the General Motors range, personifies high life and good living standards. Engine is a V8 of 6.4 litres. Hydra-Matic automatic transmission, servo brakes and power steering make driving easy. Sedan, Sedan de ville, Coupe de ville or convertible provide seats for six with two or four doors. Enormous trunks swallow VIP luggage.

CLOSE-UP
Eight-cyl.; o.h.v.; 101.6 × 98.42 mm.; 6,384 c.c.; 325 b.h.p.; 10.5 to 1 comp.; coil ign.; Carter carb.; 4-speed auto., 11.66, 7.49, 4.55, 2.94 to 1; col. lvr.; susp., f. ind. coil, r. coil; 4-door; 6-seat; hyd. servo brks.; max. 120 m.p.h.; cruise 100; m.p.g. 13-15; whl. base 10ft. 9½in.; track f. and r. 5ft. 1in.; lgth. 18ft. 7in.; wdth. 6ft. 7¾in.; ht. 4ft. 7in.; g.c. 5½in.; turng. cir. 45ft.; kerb. wt. 42¾ cwt.; tank, 21 gals.; 12-volt.

£3,052 + £636 p.t. = £3,688

CHEVROLET CORVAIR

SPORTS version of the rear-engined air-cooled Corvair with coupe or cabriolet body-work. Long, low and lively, it features engines of increased size for 1964. Three or four-speed gearbox, with option of Powerglide automatic transmission. There are three versions of the Corvair Monza, the saloon, coupe and convertible, with two or four doors and five to six seats. Its styling has been widely copied.

CLOSE-UP
Six-cyl.; o.h.v.; air-cooled 87.3 × 66 mm.; 2,372 c.c.; 80 b.h.p.; 8 to 1 comp.; coil ign.; 2 Rochester carbs.; 3-speed, 11.44, 6.50, 3.27 to 1, 4-speed or auto. opt.; cen. lvr.; susp., f. and r. ind. coil; 4-door; 5/6-seat; hyd. brks.; max. 84 m.p.h.; cruise 75; m.p.g. 18-24; whl. base 9ft.; track f. and r. 4ft. 6in.; lgth. 15ft.; wdth. 5ft. 6⅞in.; ht. 4ft. 3in.; g.c. 6in.; turng. cir. 39ft. 11in.; kerb wt. 22 cwt.; tank, 9¼ gals.; 12-volt.

£1,742 + £363 p.t. = £2,105

CHEVROLET CORVETTE STINGRAY

RIDE, handling and performance are all improved on America's own sports special for 1964, and the coupe now has a one-piece rear window. Bodies are quantity-produced in glass fibre by costly double dies. Sound insulation is improved to combine sports car handling with the luxury feel that American car buyers demand. Suspension is all-independent, by coil springs in front and transverse leaf at the rear.

CLOSE-UP
Eight-cyl.; o.h.v.; 101.2 × 82.6 mm.; 5,360 c.c.; 300 b.h.p.; 10.5 to 1 comp.; coil ign.; Carter 4-choke carb.; 4-speed, 8.53, 6.35, 4.07, 3.36 to 1; cen. lvr.; susp., f. ind. coil, r. ind. trans. leaf; 2-door; 2-seat; hyd. brks., servo opt.; max. 150 m.p.h.; cruise 125; m.p.g. 13-16; whl. base 8ft. 2in.; track f. 4ft. 8½in., r. 4ft. 9in.; lgth. 14ft. 7⅜in.; wdth. 5ft. 9¼in.; ht. 4ft. 1½in.; g.c. 5in.; turng. cir. 38ft. 6in.; kerb wt. 26¼ cwt.; tank, 16¾ gals.; 12-volt.

CHEVROLET CHEVY II

AMERICA'S top-selling make, heading for record sales in 1963, plans to do better in 1964 with 43 models in five sizes; or ten more models than this year.

Engines range from 90 to 155 horsepower. Chevy II is the low-priced popular line with front engine and rear drive. Between it and the big Chevrolets comes a new range, the Chevelle, with coil spring rear suspension.

CLOSE-UP
Four-cyl.; o.h.v.; 98.5 × 82.5 mm.; 2,512 c.c.; 90 b.h.p.; 8.5 to 1 comp.; coil ign.; Rochester carb.; 3-speed, 9.05, 5.17, 3.08 to 1; col. lvr.; auto. opt.; susp., f. ind. coil, r. half-elliptic; 2 or 4-door; 6-seat; hyd. brks.; max. 84 m.p.h.; cruise 70; m.p.g. 22-25; whl. base 9ft. 2in.; track f. 4ft. 8⅜in., r. 4ft. 6⅜in.; lgth. 15ft. 3in.; wdth. 5ft. 10⅞in.; ht. 4ft. 7in.; g.c. 6in.; turng. cir. 39ft.; kerb wt. 22½ cwt.; tank, 12½ gals.; 12-volt.

Abbreviations g.c.—ground clearance, susp.—suspension; f.—front; r.—rear; comp.—compression; s.v.—side-valves; o.h.v.—overhead valves; o.h.c.—overhead camshaft; hyd.—hydraulic.

CHRYSLER TURBO DART

FIFTY favoured motorists are getting this pioneer turbine model on loan to help in evaluating its potential in everyday use before Chrysler make decisions on production. Twin rotary heat exchangers promote fuel economy but help to prove that the turbine, with its accessories is not a space-saving power unit. Piston-engined Chryslers now have engines and transmissions guaranteed for five years or 50,000 miles.

CLOSE-UP

Gas turbine with regenerator. Power turbine with 9.8 to 1 reduction gear; 130 b.h.p.; 3-speed auto., 7.91, 4.68, 3.23 to 1; cen. lvr.; susp., f. ind. coil, r. half-elliptic; 2-door; 4-seat; hyd. servo brks.; max. 100 m.p.h.; cruise 90; m.p.g. 15; whl. base 9ft. 2in.; track f. 4ft. 11in., r. 4ft. 8¾in.; lgth. 16ft. 9⅝in.; wdth. 6ft. 0⅞in.; ht. 4ft. 5½in.; g.c. 5½in.; turng. cir. 38ft. 9in.; kerb wt. 35½ cwt.; tank, 17 gals.; 24-volt.

CITROEN AMI 6

EASILY identified with its off-beat styling and rearward-sloping back window, the Ami 6 is the medium sized car in the Citroen range. Good all round vision, all-synchronised four-speed gearbox and independent suspension on all four wheels interconnected between front and rear are some of the features of this little family car. Since its Paris debut in 1961 it is now seen on all French highways.

CLOSE-UP

Two-cyl.; o.h.v., air-cooled; 74×70 mm.; 602 c.c.; 22 b.h.p.; 7.25 to 1 comp.; coil ign.; Solex carb.; 4-speed, 20.365, 10.505, 6.97, 4.77 to 1; dash lvr.; susp., f. and r. ind. coil; 4-door; 4-seat; hyd. brks.; max. 65 m.p.h.; cruise 50; m.p.g. 38-45; whl. base 7ft. 10¼in.; track f. 4ft. 1⅝in., r. 4ft.; lgth. 12ft. 8 3/16 in.; wdth. 4ft. 11⅞in.; ht. 4ft. 10½in.; g.c. 7½in.; turng. cir. 36ft.; kerb wt. 12 cwt.; tank, 5½ gals.; 12-volt.

£580 + £121.7.11 p.t. = £701.7.11

CITROEN DS

A CAR that made history with 20th Century styling that was new and functional. Sensational self-levelling, air-hydraulic suspension that adjusts itself according to load. Servo brakes that match their effort to the weight distribution; servo clutch and gear change too. The ID 19 is the economy version with simpler mechanical features. There is a super de luxe DS 19 and in France a custom-built cabriolet by Chapron.

CLOSE-UP

Four-cyl.; o.h.v.; 78×100 mm.; 1,911 c.c.; 83 b.h.p.; 8.5 to 1 comp.; coil ign.; Weber carb.; 4-speed, 13.79, 6.96, 4.77, 3.31 to 1; dash lvr.; susp., f. and r. ind. hyd. pneu.; 4-door; 5/6 seat; hyd. servo brks., disc front.; max. 100 m.p.h.; cruise 80; m.p.g. 25-30; whl. base 10ft. 3in.; track f. 4ft. 11in., r. 4ft. 3¼in.; lgth. 15ft. 9in.; wdth. 5ft. 10½in.; ht. 4ft. 11⅞in.; g.c. 6¼in.; turng. cir. 36ft.; kerb wt. 23 cwt.; tank, 14 gals.; 12-volt.

£1,298 + £270.19.7 p.t. = £1,568.19.7

CITROEN SAFARI ESTATE CAR

THIS high-performance 8-seater estate car now has a more powerful 1,911 c.c. engine giving it speeds in excess of 95 m.p.h. Power steering is added, as well as a new anti-dazzle rear-view mirror, outside door mirror, courtesy switches on all five doors and foam rubber underlay. One of the most luxurious estate cars available, with a large built-in luggage rack on the roof.

CLOSE-UP

Four-cyl.; o.h.v.; 78×100 mm.; 1,911 c.c.; 69 b.h.p.; 7.5 to 1 comp.; coil ign.; Solex carb.; 4-speed, 13.79, 7.35, 4.77, 3.31 to 1; col. lvr.; susp., f. and r. hyd. pneu.; 5-door; 8-seat; hyd. servo brks., disc front; max. 90 m.p.h.; cruise 70; m.p.g. 25-30; whl. base 10ft. 3in.; track f. 4ft. 11in., r. 4ft. 3¼in.; lgth. 16ft. 5in.; wdth. 5ft. 10½in.; ht. 4ft. 11⅞in.; g.c. 6¼in.; turng. cir. 36ft. 1in.; kerb wt. 25¾ cwt.; tank, 14 gals.; 12-volt.

£1,405 + £293.5.5 p.t. = £1,698.5.5

Abbreviations—g.c.—ground clearance; susp.—suspension; f.—front; r.—rear; comp.—compression; s.v.—side-valves; o.h.v.—overhead valves; o.h.c.—overhead camshaft; hyd.—hydraulic.

DAF DAFFODIL

ONLY car made in Holland but a good one and the only car with small engine of 750 c.c. to have fully automatic transmission. Twin-cylinder air-cooled engine gives over 60 m.p.h. and fuel consumption is a useful 42 m.p.g. Nicely appointed and with two doors, this Dutch baby has faithful supporters on the Continent. There is also a station wagon. New roof line and 40 detail improvements for 1964.

CLOSE-UP
Two-cyl.; o.h.v. air cooled; 85.5×65 mm.; 746 c.c.; 30 b.h.p.; 7.5 to 1 comp.; coil ign.; BCI carb.; auto. belt drive 16.4 to 3.9 to 1; cen. lvr.; susp., f. ind. trans. leaf; r. ind. coil; 2-door; 4-seat; hyd. brks.; max. 65 m.p.h.; cruise 65; m.p.g. 38-48; whl. base 6ft. 9in.; track f. and r. 3ft. 10½in.; lgth. 12ft. 1in.; wdth. 4ft. 9in.; ht. 4ft. 6½in.; g.c. 6¾in.; turng. cir. 31ft.; kerb wt. 13 cwt.; tank, 7 gals.; 6-volt.

£578+£120.19.7 p.t. = £698.19.7

DAIMLER SP250

DAIMLER surprised many motoring people when they brought out this fast—but safe—sports car. Now, with its Jaguar sponsorship, its versatility is quite outstanding. With an eight-cylinder engine, plastic mouldings (for cheapness of repair) and disc brakes all round, many police forces have adopted it after trying and discarding other sports cars. An exciting model that appeals to the man who likes to drive fast.

CLOSE-UP
Eight-cyl.; o.h.v.; 76.2×69.85 mm.; 2,548 c.c.; 140 b.h.p.; 8.2 to 1 comp.; coil ign.; 2 S.U. carbs.; 4-speed, 10.5, 6.236, 4.41, 3.58 to 1; cen. lvr.; susp., f. ind. coil, r. half-elliptic; 2-door; 2/3-seat; disc brks.; max. 120 m.p.h.; cruise, 90; m.p.g. 28; whl. base 7ft. 8in.; track f. 4ft. 2in., r. 4ft.; lgth. 14ft. 0½in.; wdth. 5ft. 0½in.; ht. 4ft. 2½in.; g.c. 6in.; turng. cir. 33ft.; kerb wt. 19½ cwt.; tank, 12 gals.; 12-volt.

£1,121+£234.2.1 p.t. = £1,355.2.1

DAIMLER 2½-LITRE V8

THE marriage of a Jaguar body and Daimler engine in this 2½-litre car has proved worthy of its traditional name. A newish car, it carries the well-known radiator grille and a "D" emblem on the wheels, although in other respects it resembles the Mark 2 Jaguar. Filling the gap at the lower end of the Daimler range, the car should continue to be a success.

CLOSE-UP
Eight-cyl.; o.h.v.; 76.2×69.85 mm.; 2,548 c.c.; 140 b.h.p.; 8.2 to 1 comp.; coil ign.; 2 S.U. carbs.; 3-speed, BW auto., 10.2, 6.19, 4.27 to 1; col. lvr.; susp., f. ind. coil, r. cantilever leaf; 4-door; 5-seat; disc servo brks.; max. 110 m.p.h.; cruise 80-90; m.p.g. 20-22; whl. base 8ft. 11⅜in.; track f. 4ft. 7in., r. 4ft. 5⅜in.; lgth. 15ft. 0¾in.; wdth. 5ft. 6¾in.; ht. 4ft. 9½in.; g.c. 7in.; turng. cir. 33ft. 6in.; kerb wt. 28 cwt.; tank, 12 gals.; 12-volt.

£1,298+£270.19.7 p.t. = £1,568.19.7

DAIMLER LIMOUSINE

POWERED by one of Britain's few V8 engines, this great seven-seater has 220 h.p. on tap to give it a maximum of 110 mph. Silent but swift, it is a worthy successor to a long line of chauffeur-driven luxury limousines at a price that is decidedly reasonable for a carriage of this size, performance and finish. Sliding glass division, automatic transmission, power-assisted steering and servo disc brakes are standard items.

CLOSE-UP
Eight-cyl.; o.h.v.; 95.25×80.01 mm.; 4,561 c.c.; 220 b.h.p.; 8 to 1 comp.; coil ign.; 2 S.U. carbs.; 3-speed, auto. 8.7, 5.4, 3.77 to 1; col. lvr.; susp., f. ind. coil, r. half-elliptic; 4-door; 8-seat; disc servo brks.; max. 110 m.p.h.; cruise, 90; m.p.g. 17-20; whl. base 11ft. 6in.; track f. and r. 4ft. 9in.; lgth. 18ft. 10in.; wdth. 6ft. 1½in.; ht. 5ft. 5½in.; g.c. 7in.; turng. cir. 44ft.; kerb wt. 40 cwt.; tank, 16 gals.; 12-volt.

£2,809+£585.15.5 p.t. = £3,394.15.5

Abbreviations—g.c.—ground clearance; susp.—suspension; f.—front; r.—rear; comp.—compression; s.v.—side-valves; o.h.v.—overhead valves; o.h.c.—overhead camshaft; hyd.—hydraulic.

D.K.W. F.12

LATEST model derived from the DKW Junior but with two-stroke engine increased to 889 c.c. and power increased to 40 h.p. Front brakes are discs made under Dunlop licence and wheelbase is increased to 7ft. 4½in. There is soon to be a roadster with F.12 chassis and body pressings to the waistline, and a hood that disappears into the body when folded. Power is increased by five h.p.

CLOSE-UP

Three-cyl.; two-stroke; 74.5×68 mm.; 889 c.c.; 40 b.h.p.; 7 to 1 comp.; coil ign.; Solex carb.; 4-speed, 15.47, 9.20, 5.86, 3.88 to 1; col. lvr.; susp., f. ind. torsion bar, r. torsion bar; 4-door; 4-seat; hyd. brks.; max. 78 m.p.h.; cruise 72; m.p.g. 33-36; whl. base 7ft. 4½in.; track f. 3ft. 11½in., r. 4ft. 2¼in.; lgth. 13ft 0½in.; wdth. 5ft. 2in.; ht. 4ft. 9½in.; g.c. 6⅜in.; turng. cir. 32ft. 9in.; kerb wt. 14½ cwt.; tank, 7⅞ gals.; 6-volt.
£661.10 + £138.7.6 p.t. = £799.17.6

DODGE DART 440

THIS clean-cut car from the Chrysler group offers good looks and getaway power. Its 5.2 litre V8 engine drives through a three-speed gearbox but Torqueflite automatic gearbox with hydraulic torque converter is an optional extra and is specified by many buyers. Hardtop coupe and estate car version as well as the normal saloons complete a colourful range. Dodge buyers can choose from six engines between 145 and 425 horsepower.

CLOSE-UP

Eight-cyl.; o.h.v.; 99.3×84.07; 5,199 c.c.; 230 b.h.p.; 9 to 1 comp.; coil ign.; Carter carb.; 3-speed auto., 9.15, 5.15, 2.93 to 1; push button control; susp., f. ind. torsion bar, r. half-elliptic; 4-door; 6-seat; hyd. servo brks.; max. 108 m.p.h.; cruise 90; m.p.g. 16-21; whl. base 9ft. 11in.; track f. 4ft. 11½in., r. 4ft. 9½in.; lgth. 17ft. 4in.; wdth. 6ft. 4½in.; ht. 4ft. 6in.; g.c. 5in.; turng. cir. 42ft. 9in.; kerb wt. 30½ cwt.; tank, 17 gals.; 12-volt.
£1,841 + £384.2.1 p.t. = £2,225.2.1

ELVA COURIER

DEVELOPED by Frank Nichols who named the car from the French "Elle va!" and it really does go. The car is now made by Trojan Ltd. who also sell scooters. The Courier comes in roadster and coupe versions with plastic bodywork, MGA 1622 c.c. engine, and Lockheed disc brakes at the front. The MGB 1798 c.c. engine will be available too. Mark VI coupe has independent rear suspension.

CLOSE-UP

Four-cyl.; o.h.v.; 76.2×88.9 mm.; 1,622 c.c.; 90 b.h.p.; 9 to 1 comp.; coil ign.; 2 S.U. carbs.; 4-speed, 13.56, 8.25, 5.12, 3.73 to 1; cen. lvr.; susp., f. ind. coil, r. coil; 2-door; 2-seat; hyd. brks., disc front; max. 104 m.p.h.; cruise 90; m.p.g. 28; whl. base 7ft. 6in.; track f. and r. 4ft. 1in.; lgth. 12ft. 10in.; wdth. 4ft. 11in.; ht. 4ft. 1½in.; g.c. 5in.; turng. cir. 35ft.; kerb wt. 12¾ cwt.; tank, 9 gals.; 12-volt.
£701.10 + £146.13.2 p.t. = £848.3.2

FACEL VEGA II

FRANCE'S fastest and most luxurious car, with terrific performance from a Chrysler V8 of 6.3 litres producing 355 h.p. on one carburetter or 385 on two. Transmission is four-speed fully synchronised or Chrysler 3-speed automatic. Tubular chassis and steel body, lavishly equipped. Electric windows, two-speaker radio, variable-speed wipers. Option of power steering and air conditioning. Facel is now associated with Sud Aviation, builders of the Caravelle.

CLOSE-UP

Eight-cyl.; o.h.v.; 107.95×85.85mm.; 6,286 c.c.; 355 b.h.p.; 10 to 1 comp.; coil ign.; Carter carb.; 3-speed auto., 10.1, 5.74, 2.93 to 1; press buttons; 4-speed synchro opt.; susp., f. ind. coil, r. half-elliptic; 2-door; 4-seat; disc servo brks.; max. 135 m.p.h.; cruise 120; m.p.g. 14; whl. base 8ft. 8¼in.; track f. and r. 4ft. 8in.; lgth. 15ft. 7in.; wdth. 5ft. 10in.; ht. 4ft. 2in.; g.c. 7in.; turng. cir. 38ft.; kerb wt. 34½ cwt.; tank, 22 gals.; 12-volt.
£4,050 + £844.15.5 p.t. = £4,894.15.5

Abbreviations—g.c.—ground clearance; susp.—suspension; f.—front; r.—rear; comp.—compression; s.v.—side-valves; o.h.v.—overhead valves; o.h.c.—overhead camshaft; hyd.—hydraulic.

165

FACEL VEGA FACEL III

CHIC and superb finish of France's Facellia, allied to the lusty and durable Volvo 1.8-litre five-bearing engine. Transmission by four-speed all-synchro gearbox with de Normanville overdrive. Servo-assisted disc brakes by Dunlop. Two body styles, 2-4 seater coupe and 2-3 seater convertible with optional hard top. The original Facellia, with the ambitious twin-cam engine that did not fulfil expectations, is no longer shown.

CLOSE-UP
Four-cyl.; o.h.v.; 84.1×80 mm.; 1,780 c.c.; 108 b.h.p.; 10 to 1 comp.; coil ign.; 2 S.U. carbs.; 4-speed, 12.83, 8.16, 5.57, 4.1 to 1; cen. lvr., de Normanville overdrive opt.; susp. f. ind. coil, r. half-elliptic; 2-door; 2-seat; disc servo brks.; max. 112 m.p.h.; cruise 95; m.p.g. 25; whl. base 8ft. 0½in.; track f. and r. 4ft. 3½in.; lgth. 13ft. 7½in.; wdth. 5ft. 4in.; ht. 4ft. 1½in.; g.c. 7in.; turng. cir. 32ft.; kerb wt. 27 cwt.; tank, 12½ gals.; 12-volt.

FAIRTHORPE EM THREE

AIR VICE-MARSHAL Donald Bennett produces a new light grand touring car which will replace the Electron Minor. It is powered by a Triumph four-cylinder engine of 1143 c.c. Present plans are to market the car with a hard top with the alternative of a sports soft top. Accommodation is for two, occasional three, persons and there is generous baggage space in the boot.

CLOSE-UP
Four-cyl.; o.h.v.; 69.3×76 mm.; 1,143 c.c.; 63 b.h.p.; 9 to 1 comp.; coil ign.; 2 S.U. carbs.; 4-speed, 15.41, 8.87, 5.71, 4.11 to 1; cen. lvr.; susp., f. and r. ind. coil; 2-door; 2-seat; hyd. brks., disc front opt.; max. 95 m.p.h.; cruise 85; m.p.g. 43-48; whl. base, 7ft.; track, f. and r. 4ft.; lgth., 11ft. 11in.; wdth., 4ft. 10in.; ht. 3ft. 10in.; g.c. 7in.; turng. cir., 23ft.; kerb wt., 9¼ cwt.; tank, 10 gals.; 12-volt.

FERRARI 250GT

NO selection of the world's great cars could omit this classic design with the silky-smooth twelve-cylinder engine. Built in various models from the road-going occasional four-seater by Pininfarina pictured here, to the race-winning Berlinetta built by Scaglietti that has won top awards on countless famous tracks. Top personalities in all walks of life make the pilgrimage to Maranello to try and to buy.

CLOSE-UP
Twelve-cyl.; o.h.c.; 73×58.8 mm.; 2,953 c.c.; 280 b.h.p.; 9.2 to 1 comp.; coil ign.; 3 Weber carbs.; 4-speed, 10.59, 7.76, 5.73, 4.57 to 1; cen. lvr.; susp., f. ind. coil, r. half-elliptic; 2-door; 2-seat; disc servo brks.; max. 150-167 m.p.h.; cruise 130; m.p.g. 15-18; wh. base 7ft. 10½in.; track f. 4ft. 5½in., r. 4ft. 5in.; lgth. 13ft. 8in.; wdth. 5ft.; ht. 4ft.; g.c. 6in.; turng. cir. 30ft. 3in.; kerb wt. 19¾ cwt.; tank, 19½ gals.; 12-volt.
£4,800+£1,006.16.3 p.t. = £5,606.16.3

FIAT 500D

BABY of the immense Fiat range, the 500D has survived a shaky start to become a steady seller. Its front-opening doors exclude it from some markets where these are banned, but its economical air-cooled engine, easy gear change and good road holding win it friends among the thrifty. Its neat folding top is a popular feature which is found also on the little 500D station wagon.

CLOSE-UP
Two-cyl.; o.h.v.; air-cooled; 67.4×70 mm.; 499 c.c.; 21.5 b.h.p.; 7.1 to 1 comp.; coil ign.; Weber carb.; 4-speed, 18.96, 10.59, 6.66, 4.48 to 1; cen. lvr.; susp., f. ind. transv. leaf, r. ind. coil; 2-door; 2/4-seat; hyd. brks.; max. 60 m.p.h.; cruise 55; m.p.g. 55; whl. base 6ft. 0½in.; track f. 3ft. 8½in., r. 3ft. 8½in.; lgth. 9ft. 9in.; wdth. 4ft. 4in.; ht. 4ft. 4½in.; g.c. 5½in.; turng. cir. 28ft. 2½in.; kerb wt. 9⅞ cwt.; tank, 4½ gals.; 12-volt.
£340+£71.7.11 p.t. = £411.7.11

Abbreviations—g.c.—ground clearance; susp.—suspension; f.—front; r.—rear; comp.—compression; s.v.—side-valves; o.h.v.—overhead valves; o.h.c.—overhead camshaft; hyd.—hydraulic.

FIAT 600 D

CUTE little Italian bambino, this small four-seater from Turin is still produced in greater numbers than Britain's Minis. The 767 c.c. engine gives a useful top speed of 68 m.p.h. with fuel consumption of 48 m.p.g. A turning circle of only 28½ft. makes this an ideal car for expeditions into town for business or shopping. Luggage goes in front or behind the seats. For extra passengers or cargo there's the forward-drive six-seater 600D Multipla.

CLOSE-UP

Four-cyl.; o.h.v.; 62×63.5 mm.; 767 c.c.; 32 b.h.p.; 7.5 to 1 comp.; coil ign.; Weber carb.; 4-speed, 14.47, 8.78, 5.69, 4.4 to 1; cen. lvr.; susp., f. ind. trans. leaf, r. ind. coil; 2-door; 4-seat; hyd. brks.; max. 68 m.p.h.; cruise 60; m.p.g. 48; whl. base 6ft. 6¾in.; track f. 3ft. 9¼in., r. 3ft. 9⅝in.; lgth. 10ft. 9⅜in.; wdth. 4ft. 6⅜in.; g.c. 6¼in.; turng. cir. 28ft. 6½in.; kerb wt. 11¾ cwt.; tank, 6¼ gals.; 12-volt.

£408+£85.11.3 p.t.=£493.11.3

FIAT 1300/1500

FAST family car with performance and fine road holding in the Italian tradition Choice of two engines: 1300 for lively performance with economy, 1500 for the hard-driving long distance man who rides the motorways. Adjustable backrests and grab handles in the roof appeal to experienced owners. Detail equipment includes fuel reserve, headlamp flasher and numerous reminders for the driver. Front brakes are discs.

CLOSE-UP

Four-cyl.; o.h.v.; 72×79.5 mm.; 1,295 c.c.; 72 b.h.p.; 8.8 to 1 comp.; or 77×79.5 mm.; 1,481 c.c.; 80 b.h.p.; coil ign.; Weber carb. or Solex; 4-speed, 15.37, 9.43, 6.12. 4.1 to 1; col. lvr.; susp., f. ind. coil, r. half-elliptic; 4-door; 4-seat; hyd. brks., disc front; max. 86-93 m.p.h.; cruise 80-85; m.p.g. 30-35; whl. base, 7ft. 11¼in.; track f. 4ft. 3in., r. 4ft. 2in.; lgth. 13ft. 2⅝in.; wdth. 5ft. 0⅞in.; ht. 4ft. 5¾in.; g.c. 5in.; turng. cir. 33ft. 5in.; kerb wt. 18⅛ cwt.; tank, 10 gals.; 12-volt.

1300: £753+£157.8.9 p.t.=£910.8.9
1500: £785+£164.2.1 p.t.=£949.2.1

FIAT 2300

LARGEST in the Fiat family this handsome vehicle appears as saloon or estate car with 105 h.p. engine to give a top speed of 100 m.p.h. All models have four headlamps, adjustable back rests and vacuum servo with disc brakes. Optional extras include de Normanville overdrive or Smith electromagnetic transmission and sunshine roof. See the sleek 2300S Ghia coupe too with four comfortable seats and 136 h.p. engine.

CLOSE-UP

Six-cyl.; o.h.v.; 78×79.5 mm.; 2,279 c.c.; 117 b.h.p.; 8.8 to 1 comp.; coil ign.; twin choke Weber carb.; 4-speed, 13.82, 8.15, 6.03, 4.30 to 1, de Normanville overdrive opt.; coil lvr.; susp., f. ind. torsion bar, r. half-elliptic; 4-door; 5-seat; disc servo brks.; max. 100 m.p.h.; cruise 90; m.p.g. 22; whl. base 8ft. 8¾in.; track f. 4ft. 4¾in.; r. 4ft. 3½in., lgth. 15ft. 2in.; wdth. 5ft. 3¼in.; ht. 4ft. 5¾in.; g.c. 5¾in.; turng. cir. 37ft. 8¾in.; kerb wt. 24 cwt.; tank, 13¼ gals.; 12-volt.

£1,100+£229.11.3 p.t.=£1,329.11.3

FORD ANGLIA

THIS car has been with us for a long time but its popularity never seems to diminish. It has the distinctive swept-back rear window which allows generous luggage space. Its highspots include a 4-speed all-synchro gearbox, large brake drums and a degree of luxury inside. Probably the most popular car in the Ford range, it is now available with choice of two engine sizes.

CLOSE-UP

Four-cyl.; o.h.v.; 80.96×48.41 mm.; 997 c.c.; 41 b.h.p.; 8.9 to 1 comp.; Super: 80.96×58.17 mm.; 1,198 c.c.; 53 b.h.p.; 8.7 to 1 comp.; coil ign.; Solex carb.; 4-speed, 16.987, 9.884, 5.826, 4.125 to 1; Super; 14.615, 9.883, 5.824, 4.125 to 1; cen. lvr.; susp., f. ind. coil, r. half-elliptic; 2-door; 4-seat; hyd. brks.; max. 75 m.p.h.; cruise 65; Super: 80 and 70; m.p.g. 35-42; whl. base 7ft. 6½in.; track f. 3ft. 10in., r. 3ft. 9¾in.; lgth. 12ft. 11½in.; wdth. 4ft. 9½in.; ht. 4ft. 7in.; g.c. 6½in.; turng. cir. 32ft.; kerb wt. 14¾ cwt.; Super 15 cwt.; tank, 7 gals.; 12-volt.

Anglia: £425+£89.2.1 p.t.=£514.2.1
Super: £495+£103.13.9 p.t.=£598.13.9

Abbreviations—g.c.—ground clearance; susp.—suspension; f.—front; r.—rear; comp.—compression; s.v.—side-valves; o.h.v.—overhead valves; o.h.c.—overhead camshaft; hyd.—hydraulic.

FORD CONSUL CORSAIR

ROOMIER than the Cortina, Ford's new Corsair has almost as much space inside as the old Mark II Consul. Styling raises echoes of Lincoln and Thunderbird. Bodies have two or four doors. High performance G.T. version features servo brakes, bucket front seats, tachometer and centre console with additional instruments. Central or steering column gear levers are available. Four speeds, all synchromesh and an automatic transmission to come later.　　　　　CLOSE-UP

Four-cyl.; o.h.v.; 80.97 × 72.75 mm.; 1,498 c.c.; 64 b.h.p.; 8.3 to 1 comp.; coil ign.; Solex carb. (GT. 83.5 b.h.p.; Weber 2-choke carb.); 4-speed, 13.818, 9.344, 5.507, 3.90 to 1; cen. or col. lvr.; susp., f. ind. coil, r. half-elliptic; 2 or 4-door; 5-seat; hyd. brks., disc front; max. 80 (GT. 90) m.p.h.; cruise 75; m.p.g. 30; whl. base 8ft. 5in.; track f. 4ft. 2in.; r. 4ft. 1½in.; lgth. 14ft. 8½in.; width 5ft. 3⅜in.; ht. 4ft. 9½in.; g.c. 6¾in.; turng. cir. 33ft. 9in.; kerb wt. 17½ cwt.; tank, 8 gals.; 12-volt.

£540 + £113.1.3 p.t. = £653.1.3

FORD CONSUL CORTINA

THIS comes as a first-class saloon with a 1200 c.c. engine, and as the Cortina Super with a 1500 c.c. five-bearing crankshaft engine. Both cars have become immediate successes. Their sturdiness and good looks match their performance. Deliberately the Cortina has been planned to fill the gap in the extensive Ford range. A reliable and durable car, it will continue to be a best-seller for a long time.

Four-cyl.; o.h.v.; 80.96 × 58.17 mm.; 1,198 c.c.; 53 b.h.p.; 8.7 to 1 comp.; or 80.96 × 72.75 mm.; 1,498 c.c.; 64 b.h.p.; coil ign.; Solex carb.; 4-speed, 14.615, 9.883, 5.824, 4.125 to 1; or 13.76, 9.32, 5.49, 3.9; cen. lvr.; col. opt.; susp., f. ind. coil, r. half-elliptic; 2 or 4-door; 4/5 seat; hyd. brks.; max. 78-85 m.p.h.; cruise 65-75; m.p.g. 35-40; whl. base 8ft. 2in.; track f. and r. 4ft. 1½in.; lgth. 14ft. 0½in.; wdth. 5ft. 2½in.; ht. 4ft. 8½in.; g.c. 6½in.; turng. cir. 34ft. 8in.; kerb wt. 16-16¾ cwt.; tank, 8 gals.; 12-volt.

1200—£489 + £102.8.9 p.t. = £591.8.9
1500—£544 + £125.19.7 p.t. = £669.19.7

FORD CONSUL CAPRI G.T.

EXTRA acceleration for today's difficult traffic conditions is provided by the G.T. engine with twin-choke Weber carburetter. Thus equipped the pretty Capri has performance to please the sportsman plus glamorous interior appointments to please his girl friends. Disc front brakes and a four-speed all-synchro gearbox with short central lever add to the pleasure of fast driving and the trunk holds enough luggage for long holiday trips.　CLOSE-UP

Four-cyl.; o.h.v.; 80.97 × 72.75 mm.; 1,498 c.c.; 84 b.h.p.; 9.3 to 1 comp.; coil ign.; Weber 2-choke carb.; 4-speed, 14.615, 9.883, 5.824, 4.125 to 1; col. or cen. lvr.; susp., f. ind. coil, r. half-elliptic; 2-door; 2-seat; hyd. servo brks., disc front; max. 93 m.p.h.; cruise 80; m.p.g. 25-32; whl. base 8ft. 3in.; track f. and r. 4ft. 1½in.; lgth. 14ft. 2½in.; wdth. 5ft. 5¼in.; ht. 4ft. 4½in.; g.c. 6½in.; turng. cir. 34ft.; kerb wt. 18¾ cwt.; tank, 9 gals.; 12-volt.

£745 + £155.15.5 p.t. = £900.15.5

FORD ZEPHYR SIX/& ZODIAC

LARGEST and most expensive of the British Fords, the Zodiac offers armchair comfort for six people and luggage space to match. Good vision, padded facia and visors for extra safety. Four headlamps and disc brakes in front. Heater is standard and overdrive or automatic gearbox are optional extras. Zephyr is basically similar but with two headlamps, less powerful engine, lower price.

Six cyl.; o.h.v.; 82.55 × 79.50 mm.; 2,553 c.c.; 106 b.h.p., Zod. 114 b.h.p.; 8.3 to 1 comp.; coil ign.; Zenith carb.; 4-speed, 11.213, 7.849, 5.005, 3.545 to 1; col. lvr., BW overdrive or auto. opt.; susp., f. ind. coil, r. half-elliptic; 4-door; 5/6 seat; hyd. brks., disc front; max. 96-100 m.p.h.; cruise 85; m.p.g. 19-24; whl. base 8ft. 11in.; track f. 4ft. 5in., r. 4ft. 5½in.; lgth 15ft. 0½in., Zod. 15ft. 1½in.; wdth. 5ft. 9in.; ht. 4ft. 7in.; g.c. 6½in.; turng. cir. 36ft. 6in.; kerb. wt. 24 cwt., Zod. 25¼ cwt.; tank, 12½ gals.; 12-volt.

Zephyr: £692 + £144.14.7 p.t. = £836.14.7
Zodiac: £803 + £167.17.1 p.t. = £970.17.1

Abbreviations—g.c.—ground clearance; susp.—suspension; f.—front; r.—rear; comp.—compression; s.v.—side-valves; o.h.v.—overhead valves; o.h.c.—overhead camshaft; hyd.—hydraulic.

FORD TAUNUS 12M

FRONT-WHEEL drive German Ford that competes directly with Britain's Cortina. Unusual V4 engine is now available in 1500 cc. TI version for extra performance and a four-door saloon is a recent addition to the range. Engine, four-speed all-synchromesh gearbox and differential are in one unit with front suspension wishbones bolted to it instead of to car frame. So far, Dagenham leads the sales race, but Cologne is working hard.

CLOSE-UP

Four-cyl.; o.h.v.; 80 × 58.8 mm.; 1,183 c.c.; 50 b.h.p.; 7.8 to 1 comp.; coil ign.; Solex carb.; 4-speed, 15.23, 8.80, 5.59, 3.78 to 1; col. lvr.; susp., f. ind. transv. leaf, r. half-elliptic; 2-door; 4/5 seat; hyd. brks.; max. 78 m.p.h.; cruise 75; m.p.g. 35; whl. base 8ft. 3½in.; track f. and r. 4ft. 1in.; lgth. 13ft. 11½in.; wdth. 5ft. 8¾in.; ht. 4ft. 9⅜in.; g.c. 6½in.; turng. cir. 35ft. 2in.; kerb wt. 16⅝ cwt.; tank, 8⅝ gals.; 6-volt.

FORD FALCON

AGGRESSIVE new lines change the appearance of Detroit's Compact Ford after a four-year run. Better seats, softer ride, more fuel economy are sales points. There are 17 models to choose from: two and four-door saloons, hard tops, sports coupes, station wagons, convertibles, light buses, with engines ranging from a 2,360 c.c. six giving 85 h.p. to a hefty V8 of 4,260 c.c. producing 164 h.p.

CLOSE-UP

Six-cyl.; o.h.v.; 88.9 × 63.5 mm.; 2,360 c.c.; 85 b.h.p.; 8.7 to 1 comp.; coil ign.; Ford carb.; 3-speed, 10.2, 5.67, 3.1 to 1; col. lvr., 4-speed or auto. opt.; susp., f. ind. coil, r. half-elliptic; 2- or 4-door; 5-seat; hyd. brks., servo opt.; max. 82 m.p.h.; cruise 75; m.p.g. 23-25; whl. base 9ft. 1½in.; track f. 4ft. 7in., r. 4ft. 8in.; lgth. 15ft. 1⅝in.; wdth. 5ft. 11⅝in.; ht. 4ft. 6½in.; g.c. 5¾in.; turng. cir. 38ft. 9in.; kerb wt. 22 cwt.; tank, 11½ gals.; 12-volt.

FORD THUNDERBIRD

LUXURY family-sized sports car for young Americans to cruise round the sun-drenched playgrounds of Florida and California. Four types of body, Hardtop, Landau Hardtop, Convertible and Sports Roadster. All models have Cruise-o-Matic automatic transmission. Power varies from 304 to 345 h.p. 1964 cars have a squarer silhouette, strip tail lights cross the rear, headlamps deeply recessed and changed interior. Steering wheel swings sideways for ease of entry.

CLOSE-UP

Eight-cyl.; o.h.v.; 102.8 × 96 mm.; 6,384 c.c.; 300 b.h.p.; 9.6 to 1 comp.; coil ign.; Ford carb.; 3-speed auto., 7.2, 4.41, 3.0 to 1; col. lvr.; susp., f. ind. coil, r. half-elliptic; 2-door; 4-seat; hyd. servo brks.; max. 120 m.p.h.; cruise 90; m.p.g. 12-16; whl. base 9ft. 5in.; track f. 5ft. 1in., r. 5ft.; lgth. 17ft. 1in.; wdth. 6ft. 4½in.; ht. 4ft. 4½in.; g.c. 5½in.; turng. cir. 41ft. 6in.; kerb wt. 38½ cwt.; tank, 16 gals.; 12-volt.

£2,832 + £590.11.3 p.t. = £3,422.11.3

FORD GALAXIE 500

TRULY a bewildering galaxy of these imposing cars with six versions to choose from in a dazzling array of colour schemes. Engines are powerful sixes or V8s from 3.6 to 6.3 litres. Power assisted steering and brakes and automatic transmission are optional extras. All cars are about 17½ft. long and the station wagons can carry enough equipment for long hunting trips or Trans-Continental tours.

CLOSE-UP

Eight-cyl.; o.h.v.; 101.6 × 88.9 mm.; 5,766 c.c.; 220 b.h.p.; 8.9 to 1 comp.; coil ign.; Holley carb.; 3-speed auto., 7.2, 4.41, 3.0 to 1; col. lvr.; susp., f. ind. coil, r. half-elliptic; 4-door; 6-seat; hyd. servo brks.; max. 114 m.p.h.; cruise 85; m.p.g. 17-20; whl. base 9ft. 11in.; track f. 5ft. 1in., r. 5ft.; lgth. 17ft. 5½in.; wdth. 6ft. 7½in.; ht. 4ft. 6½in.; g.c. 7in.; turng. cir. 41ft.; kerb wt. 33½ cwt.; tank, 16½ gals.; 12-volt.

£1,700 + £354.14.5 p.t. = £2,054.14.5

Abbreviations—g.c.—ground clearance; susp.—suspension; f.—front; r.—rear; comp.—compression; s.v.—side-valves; o.h.v.—overhead valves; o.h.c.—overhead camshaft; hyd.—hydraulic.

169

HILLMAN SUPER MINX

STEPPING up from the normal Minx, with more power and roomier bodywork, the Super is easily identified by the half-moon sidelamps above its headlamps. Well finished, fully equipped, with slim pillars for good all-round vision, it started the trend to smaller wheels that has since spread to other Rootes models. Chassis greasing is eliminated. BW automatic transmission can be supplied and the range includes a convertible.

CLOSE-UP
Four-cyl.; o.h.v.; 81.5 × 76.2 mm.; 1,592 c.c.; 62 b.h.p.; 8.3 to 1 comp.; coil ign.; Solex carb.; 4-speed, 13.013, 8.324, 5.413, 3.889 to 1; cen. lvr.; BW auto. opt.; susp., f. ind. coil, r. half-elliptic; 4-door; 4/5-seat; hyd. brks., disc front; max. 84 m.p.h.; cruise 70; m.p.g. 28-32; whl. base 8ft. 5in.; track f. 4ft. 3½in., r. 4ft. 0½in.; lgth. 13ft. 9in.; wdth. 5ft. 3½in.; ht. 4ft. 10½in.; g.c. 6½in.; turng. cir. 36ft.; kerb wt. 21 cwt.; tank, 11 gals.; 12-volt.
£615 + £128.13.9 p.t. = £743.13.9

HILLMAN MINX DE LUXE

COUPLED with crisp new styling of this car comes a range of detailed improvements—for instance, front disc brakes, lighter steering, better suspension, wider rear doors, individual front seats, redesigned dashboard and a bigger fuel tank. Optional is Borg Warner automatic transmission. One of Britain's most popular family cars, the changes bring the Rootes Group's 1600 c.c. face-lifted model bang up to date.

CLOSE-UP
Four-cyl.; o.h.v.; 81.5 × 76.2 mm.; 1,592 c.c.; 56.5 b.h.p.; 8.3 to 1 comp.; coil ign.; Zenith carb.; 4-speed, 14.567, 8.324, 5.413, 3.89 to 1; cen. lvr.; BW auto. opt.; susp., f. ind. coil, r. half-elliptic; 4-door; 5-seat; hyd. brks., disc front; max. 82 m.p.h.; cruise 70; m.p.g. 30-35; whl. base 8ft.; track f. 4ft. 1½in., r. 4ft. 0½in.; lgth. 13ft. 5½in.; wdth. 5ft. 0½in.; ht. 4ft. 10in.; g.c. 6in.; turng. cir. 36ft.; kerb wt. 20 cwt.; tank, 10 gals.; 12-volt.
£525 + £109.18.9 p.t. = £634.18.9

HILLMAN IMP DE LUXE

IMP Impels Impartial critics to Impassioned praise. Road holding almost Impeccable. Engine in fast cruising almost Imperceptible. Performance Impressive. Waiting buyers Impatient. Best handling rear-engined car yet built, Rootes Group's Scottish-built baby shows advanced design with light alloy overhead camshaft engine, pneumatic throttle control, all-synchromesh gearbox, logical controls, no greasing points. Rear window opens to assist loading of luggage.

CLOSE-UP
Four-cyl.; o.h.c.; 68 × 60.4 mm.; 875 c.c.; 39 b.h.p.; 10 to 1 comp.; coil ign.; Solex carb.; 4-speed, 16.59, 8.91, 5.70, 4.14 to 1; cen. lvr.; susp., f. and r. ind. coil; 2-door; 4-seat; hyd. brks.; max. 80 m.p.h.; cruise 75; m.p.g. 40; whl. base 6ft. 10in.; track. f. 4ft. 1in., r. 3ft. 11½in.; lgth. 11ft. 9in.; wdth. 5ft. 0½in.; ht. 4ft. 6½in.; g.c. 6½in.; turng. cir. 28ft.; kerb wt. 14 cwt.; tank, 6 gals.; 12-volt.
£440 + £92.4.7 p.t. = £532.4.7

HUMBER HAWK

THIS is a big favourite with the motorist who has to make long business trips and also likes to take out his family on extensive pleasure jaunts. It is a robust 2¼-litre, six-seater luxury car with the sound tradition of the Rootes Group behind it. Smoothness is matched with strength and its long-established popularity is likely to continue.

CLOSE-UP
Four-cyl.; o.h.v.; 81 × 110 mm.; 2,267 c.c.; 78 b.h.p.; 7.5 to 1 comp.; coil ign.; Zenith carb.; 4-speed, 14.128, 9.038, 5.877, 4.22 to 1; de Normanville over-drive opt.; col. lvr.; susp., f. ind. coil, r. half-elliptic; 4-door; 6-seat; servo brks., disc front; max. 85 m.p.h.; cruise 70-75; m.p.g. 20-25; whl. base 9ft. 2in.; track f. 4ft. 9in., r. 4ft. 7½in.; lgth 15ft. 4½in.; wdth. 5ft. 9½in.; ht. 5ft. 1in.; g.c. 7in.; turng. cir. 38ft.; kerb wt. 28½ cwt.; tank, 16 gals.; 12-volt.
£875 + £182.17.1 p.t. = £1,057.17.1

HUMBER SCEPTRE

HERE is a fast and elegant 1.6-litre sports saloon. With a top speed of more than 90 and servo-assisted front disc brakes, it offers a carefree ride with delightful smoothness. Standard fittings include a heating and ventilating system, screen washers, reversing lamp, padded sun visors, rev. counter and cigarette lighter, in addition to a full range of instruments including fuel, oil and water gauges, ammeter and speedometer.

CLOSE-UP

Four-cyl.; o.h.v.; 81.5×76.2 mm.; 1,592 c.c.; 80 b.h.p.; 9 to 1 comp.; coil ign.; 2 Zenith carbs.; 4-speed, 14.13, 9.04, 5.88, 4.22 to 1; cen. lvr.; susp., f. ind. coil, r. half-elliptic; 4-door; 4/5-seat; hyd. servo brks., disc front; max.90 m.p.h.; cruise 80; m.p.g. 25; whl. base 8ft. 5in.; track f. 4ft. 3½in., r. 4ft. 0½in.; lgth. 13ft. 9½in.; wdth. 5ft. 2½in.; ht. 4ft. 9in.; g.c. 6½in.; turng. cir. 36ft.; kerb wt. 21⅞ cwt.; tank, 10½ gals.; 12-volt.

£825 + £172.8.9 p.t. = £997.8.9

HUMBER SUPER SNIPE

EVERYTHING happens in threes on this luxurious and spacious model, the biggest now built by the Rootes Group. There are three kinds of body, an engine of three litres and three variations on the transmission, gearbox is manual all-synchronised, with de Normanville overdrive or Borg Warner automatic as options. The buyers can choose from four-door saloon, limousine with glass division or four-door station wagon.

CLOSE-UP

Six-cyl.; o.h.v.; 87.3×82.55 mm.; 2,965 c.c.; 132.5 b.h.p.; 8 to 1 comp.; coil ign.; Zenith carb.; 3-speed, 11.835, 6.129, 4.22 to 1; de Normanville overdrive or BW auto. opt.; susp., f. ind. coil, r. half-elliptic; 4-door; 6-seat; servo brks., disc front; max. 100 m.p.h.; cruise 85; m.p.g. 20-25; whl. base 9ft. 2in.; track f. 4ft. 9in., r. 4ft. 7½in.; lgth. 15ft. 8in.; wdth. 5ft. 9½in.; ht. 5ft. 1in.; g.c. 7in.; turng. cir. 38ft.; kerb wt. 29½ cwt.; tank, 16 gals.; 12-volt.

£1,120 + £233.17.11 p.t. = £1,353.17.11

ISO-RIVOLTA

GLAMOROUS new competitor to Ferrari and Maserati, with 300 h.p. 5.3-litre Chevrolet Corvette engine in a light pressed steel Italian chassis with coupe body by Bertone. Front suspension is by coil springs; rear axle is de Dion with coil springs. Brakes are Dunlop discs and it has the superb Chevrolet all-synchro gearbox. A hotter model for those who like plenty of power has 11.25 to 1 compression and produces 340 horsepower.

CLOSE-UP

Eight-cyl.; o.h.v.; 101.6×82.55 mm.; 5,354 c.c.; 300 b.h.p.; 10.5 to 1 comp.; coil ign.; Carter carb.; 4-speed, 7.44, 5.62, 4.42, 2.93 to 1; cen. lvr.; susp., f. ind. coil, r. de Dion coil; 2-door; 4-seat; disc servo brks.; max. 135 m.p.h.; cruise 120; m.p.g. 14-18; whl. base 8ft. 10⅜in.; track f. and r. 4ft. 7½in.; lgth. 15ft. 8⅜in.; wdth. 5ft. 10in.; ht. 4ft. 4½in.; g.c. 4¼in.; turng. cir. 40ft. 3in.; kerb wt. 30 cwt.; tank, 23 gals.; 12-volt.

IMPERIAL

WITH model names like Custom, Crown and Le Baron, the Imperial presents a really regal range and has a high price to match. It is the super de luxe model from the Chrysler Group. Choose from a variety of two and four-door hardtops and two-door cabriolets, all with 345 h.p. to give a useful 120-125 m.p.h. top speed. Power assistance for brakes, steering, windows and seat adjustment. Adjustable head rests, too.

CLOSE-UP

Eight-cyl.; o.h.v.; 106.2×95.25 mm.; 6,746 c.c.; 340 b.h.p.; 10 to 1 comp.; coil ign.; Carter 4-choke carb.; 3-speed auto, 7.18, 4.25, 2.93 to 1; press button control; susp., f. ind. torsion bar, r. half-elliptic; 2 or 4-door; 6-seat; hyd. servo brks.; max. 125 m.p.h.; cruise 100; m.p.g. 18-22; whl. base 10ft. 9in.; track f. 5ft. 1¼in., r. 5ft. 2¼in.; lgth. 18ft. 11in.; wdth. 6ft. 9¾in.; ht. 4ft. 9in.; g.c. 5½in.; turng. cir. 48ft. 9in.; kerb wt. 43¼ cwt.; tank, 17 gals.; 12-volt.

Abbreviations—g.c.—ground clearance; susp.—suspension; f.—front; r.—rear; comp.—compression; s.v.—side-valves; o.h.v.—overhead valves; o.h.c.—overhead camshaft; hyd.—hydraulic.

171

JAGUAR E-TYPE

WITH the power packed punch of its name-sake, this potent machine streaks ahead of the traffic with nonchalant ease. Bucket seats keep the driver and passenger in place and in the coupe, the flat platform in the tail leaves room for a good amount of luggage. Powerful 3.8 litre engine rushes it up to 100 in 16 seconds. The open two-seater can now be supplied with a neat detachable hard top.

CLOSE-UP

Six-cyl.; o.h.c.; 87×106 mm.; 3,781 c.c.; 265 b.h.p.; 9 to 1 comp.; coil ign.; 3 S.U. carbs.; 4-speed, 11.18, 6.16, 4.25, 3.31 to 1; cen. lvr.; susp., f. ind. torsion bar, r. ind. coil; 2-door; 2-seat; servo disc brks.; max. 150 m.p.h.; cruise, 130; m.p.g. 18-22; whl. base, 8 ft.; track f. and r. 4ft. 2in.; lgth., 14ft. 7⅜in.; wdth. 5ft. 5½in.; ht. 4ft. 0½in.; g.c. 5½in., turng. cir.. 37ft.; kerb wt. 24 cwt.; tank, 14 gals.; 12-volt.

£1,583+£330.6.10 p.t.=£1,913.6.10

JAGUAR 2.4 LITRE MARK 2

THIS is the small brother of a brilliant family of cars. Less powerful, it is cheaper to run than the 3.4 and 3.8-litre models, yet it still supplies the high speed and excitement of a sports car with a saloon body. It is one of the most popular cars in the Jaguar range, smooth, sleek-lined and full of urge. Mark 2 is also continued with 3.4 engine, but not 3.8.

CLOSE-UP

Six-cyl.; o.h.c.; 83×76.5 mm.; 2,483 c.c.; 120 b.h.p.; 8 to 1 comp.; coil ign.; 2 Solex carbs.; 4-speed, 14.42, 7.94, 5.48, 4.27 to 1; cen. lvr., de Normanville overdrive or BW auto. opt.; susp., f. ind. coil, r. cantilever leaf; 4-door; 5-seat; servo disc brks.; max. 105 m.p.h.; cruise, 70-75; m.p.g. 23; whl. base 8ft. 11¾in.; track, f. 4ft. 7in., r. 4ft. 5⅜in.; lgth. 15ft. 0¾in.; wdth. 5ft. 6¾in.; ht. 4ft. 9½in.; g.c. 7in.; turng. cir. 33ft. 6in.; kerb wt. 28¼ cwt.; tank, 12 gals.; 12-volt.

£1,115+£232.16.10 p.t. = £1,347.16.10

JAGUAR S TYPE

DEVELOPED from the still-popular Mark 2 saloons, the S type is an additional model with a Mark X flavour. The longer higher tail modernises the line and encloses more luggage space: the modified roof line allows more space for rear seat passengers. Ride and road holding are improved by the independent rear suspension with double wishbones and coil springs, replacing the former rigid axle with cantilever leaf springs.

CLOSE-UP

Six-cyl.; o.h.c.; 83×106 mm.; 3,442 c.c.; 210 b.h.p.; 8 to 1 comp.; or 87×106 mm.; 3,781 c.c.; 220 b.h.p.; coil ign.; 2 S.U. carbs.; 4-speed, 11.95, 6.58, 4.54, 3.54 to 1; cen. lvr.; de Normanville overdrive or BW auto. opt.; susp., f. and r. ind. coil; 4-door; 4-seat; disc servo brks.; max. 118 m.p.h. (3.4), 123 m.p.h. (3.8); cruise 90-100; m.p.g. 16-23; whl. base, 8ft. 11⅜in.; track f. 4ft. 7in., r. 4ft. 5½in.; lgth. 15ft. 7⅜in.; wdth. 5ft. 6¾in.; ht. 4ft. 9½in.; g.c. 7in.; turng. cir. 33ft. 6in.; kerb wt. 31¼ cwt.; tank, 14 gals.; 12-volt.

JAGUAR MARK X

THIS is the finest car yet to be produced in the Jaguar big-saloon tradition. Producing 265 horse power, the engine, save for minor details, is identical with that of the "E" type grand touring model. Independent suspension front and rear and disc brakes on all four wheels give safety to high speed. An outstanding car stemming from an illustrious line.

CLOSE-UP

Six-cyl.; o.h.c.; 87×106 mm.; 3,781 c.c.; 265 b.h.p.; 9 to 1 comp.; coil ign.; 3 S.U. carbs.; 4-speed, 11.95, 6.58, 4.54, 3.54 to 1; cen. lvr.; overdrive or BW auto. opt.; susp., f. and r. ind. coil; 4-door; 5-seat; servo disc brks.; max. 120 m.p.h.; cruise 90; m.p.g. 15-20; whl. base 10 ft.; track, f. and r. 4ft. 10in.; lgth. 16ft. 10in.; wdth. 6ft. 4½in.; ht. 4ft. 6½in.; g.c. 6½in.; turng. cir. 37ft.; kerb wt. 35 cwt.; tank, 20 gals.; 12-volt.

£1,673+£349.1.10 p.t.=£2,022.1.10

Abbreviations—g.c.—ground clearance; susp.—suspension; f.—front; r.—rear; comp.—compression; s.v.—side-valves; o.h.v.—overhead valves; o.h.c.—overhead camshaft; hyd.—hydraulic.

JENSEN C-V8

HERE is a four-seater grand touring saloon for the connoisseur. Its Chrysler V8 engine gives the car a speed well in excess of two miles a minute and acceleration from 0-100 m.p.h. in 19 seconds. The body is of resin-bonded fibrous glass built with a high standard of craftsmanship. Just the car for a fast, luxurious holiday. Of special appeal to North American markets.

CLOSE-UP
Eight-cyl.; o.h.v.; 105×86 mm.; 5,916 c.c.; 305 b.h.p.; 9 to 1 comp.; coil ign.; Carter carb.; 3-speed auto, 7.52, 4.45, 3.07 to 1; col. lvr.; susp., f. ind. coil, r. half-elliptic; 2-door; 4-seat; disc servo brks.; max. 134 m.p.h.; cruise, 110; m.p.g. 17-20; whl. base 8ft. 9in.; track f. 4ft. 7½in., r. 4ft. 8⅜in.; lgth. 15ft. 4½in.; wdth. 5ft. 7½in.; ht. 4ft. 6in.; g.c. 6in.; turng. cir. 38ft.; kerb wt. 29 cwt.; tank, 16 gals.; 12-volt.

£2,807 + £585.6.10 p.t. = £3,392.6.10

LAGONDA RAPIDE

THIS is a luxury car built by David Brown in the highest Lagonda tradition. It is ideal for really fast touring with almost every comfort inside and out. Example: the front seats have adjustable reclining back-rests. The 4-litre engine gives a smooth and easily held top speed of 125 m.p.h. A car for the true connoisseur who appreciates all that is best in motoring.

CLOSE-UP
Six-cyl.; o.h.c.; 96×92 mm.; 3,995 c.c.; 236 b.h.p.; 8.25 to 1 comp.; coil ign.; 2 Solex carbs.; 3-speed auto., 8.7, 5.41, 3.77 to 1; col. lvr.; susp., f. ind. coil, r. de Dion, torsion bar; 4-door; 5-seat; disc servo brks.; max. 125 m.p.h.; cruise 100; m.p.g. 16-18; whl. base 9ft. 6in.; track f. 4ft. 6in., r. 4ft. 7½in.; lgth. 16ft. 3½in.; wdth. 5ft. 9½in.; ht. 4ft. 8in.; g.c. 6in.; turng. cir. 40ft. 6in.; kerb wt. 33¾ cwt.; tank, 16½ gals.; 12-volt.

£3,600 + £750.11 p.t. = £4,350.11

LANCIA FLAMINIA

CHOICE of two engine sizes for 1964 on this advanced Italian car with V6 engine and rear-mounted gearbox. 2,458 c.c. 102 h.p. or 2,775 c.c. 129 h.p. (nett). The standard saloon body by Pininfarina is famed for its elegance. The coupe has 2.8-litre engine tuned to give 140 h.p. nett and does 113 m.p.h. The convertible by Touring and sports coupe by Zagato have 150 h.p. and do 120 m.p.h.

CLOSE-UP
Six-cyl.; o.h.v.; 80×81.5 mm.; 2,458 c.c.; 102 b.h.p.; 8 to 1 comp.; coil ign.; Solex carb.; 4-speed, 12.3, 7.6, 5.6, 3.75 to 1; col. lvr.; susp., f. ind. coil, r. de Dion half-elliptic; 4-door; 6-seat; disc brks.; max. 105 m.p.h.; cruise 90; m.p.g. 24-28; whl. base 9ft. 5in.; track f. and r. 4ft. 6in.; lgth. 15ft. 11in.; wdth. 5ft. 9in.; ht. 4ft. 9½in.; g.c. 5½in.; turng. cir. 40ft.; kerb wt. 29½ cwt.; tank, 12¾ gals.; 12-volt.

£2,356 + £491.1.3 p.t. = £2,847.1.3

LANCIA FLAVIA

THE 1½-litre saloon with flat-four engine and front-wheel drive is joined by a new range with engines of 1.8-litres. The new engine with 92 h.p. nett pushes saloon maximum up to 100 m.p.h. The coupe by Pininfarina and convertible by Vignale have different exhausts, do 107 m.p.h. The Zagato sports coupe with 100 h.p. does 111. There is also a new gearbox permitting higher speed in the first three gears.

CLOSE-UP
Four-cyl.; o.h.v.; 82×71 mm.; 1,500 c.c.; 78 b.h.p.; 8.3 to 1 comp.; coil ign.; Solex carb.; 4-speed, 16.16, 9.53, 6.71, 4.09 to 1; col. lvr.; susp., f. ind. trans. leaf, r. half-elliptic; 4-door; 5/6-seat; disc brks.; max. 95 m.p.h.; cruise 85; m.p.g. 26-32; whl. base 8ft. 8½in.; track f. 4ft. 3in., r. 4ft. 2in.; lgth. 15ft. 0½in.; wdth. 5ft. 3in.; ht. 4ft. 11in.; g.c. 5in.; turng. cir. 36ft.; kerb wt. 24 cwt.; tank, 10½ gals.; 12-volt.

£1,456 + £303.17.11 p.t. = £1,759.17.11

LANCIA FULVIA

NEWEST arrival in the Lancia stable, this star of the 1,100 c.c. class is a worthy successor to the likeable Appia and emerged for our approval earlier this year. It offers popular features such as front wheel drive, disc brakes on all four wheels, and four headlamps. Eleven points need greasing every 1800 miles. Unusual V4 engine gives it a top speed of 85 m.p.h.

CLOSE-UP
Four-cyl.; o.h.v.; 72×67 mm.; 1,091 c.c.; 58 b.h.p.; 7.8 to 1 comp.; coil ign.; Solex carb.; 4-speed, 21.18, 12.16, 7.36, 4.78 to 1; cen. lvr.; susp., f. ind. trans. leaf, r. half-elliptic; 4-door; 4/5-seat; disc brks.; max. 85 m.p.h.; cruise 75; m.p.g. 31-34; whl. base 9ft. 9¼in.; track f. 4ft. 3⅛in., r. 4ft. 2½in.; lgth. 13ft. 7in.; wdth. 5ft. 2½in.; ht. 4ft. 7in.; g.c. 5in.; turng. cir. 34ft.; kerb wt. 20 cwt.; tank, 8½ gals.; 12-volt.

LINCOLN CONTINENTAL

WITH its handsome classic lines and lavish equipment there is little change to report for Ford's prestige model. Grille treatment is slightly modified. V8 engine of seven litres pushes sedan or convertible along at a racing pace. Need to protect expensive cars from depreciation may be the reason why Lincoln management has decided against radical changes. One of the few American cars with unit body-chassis.

CLOSE-UP
Eight-cyl.; o.h.v.; 109.2×93.9 mm.; 7,045 c.c.; 320 b.h.p.; 10 to 1 comp.; coil ign.; Carter carb.; 3-speed auto, 6.85, 4.04, 2.89 to 1; col. lvr.; susp., f. ind. coil, r. half-elliptic; 4-door; 5-seat; hyd. servo brks.; max. 115 m.p.h.; cruise 90; m.p.g. 11-15; whl. base 10ft. 3in.; track f. and r. 5ft. 2in.; lgth. 17ft. 9in.; wdth. 6ft. 6in.; ht. 4ft. 5½in.; g.c. 5½in.; turng. cir. 48ft.; kerb wt. 44½ cwt.; tank, 17½ gals.; 12-volt.
£3,658+£762.12.10 p.t. = £4,420.12.10

LOTUS CORTINA

SPORTS special developed by Lotus has many characteristics the same as the Consul Cortina but modified with two carburetters, 9.5 compression, Lotus cylinder head with twin camshafts to give 106 h.p., front disc brakes, different axle ratio. Rear suspension is new, with coil springs, and axle located by radius arms. With this kind of potential it is bound to find favour with rallyists and production car racers after homologation.

CLOSE-UP
Four-cyl.; o.h.c.; 82.5×72.7 mm.; 1,558 c.c.; 106 b.h.p.; 9.5 to 1 comp.; coil ign.; 2 Weber carbs.; 4-speed, 9.75, 6.39, 4.79, 3.9 to 1; cen. lvr.; susp., f. ind. coil, r. coil; 2-door; 4/5-seat; hyd. servo brks., disc front; max. 115 m.p.h.; cruise 100; m.p.g. 20-25; whl. base 7ft. 10⅞in.; track f. 4ft. 3⅜in., r. 4ft. 1⅛in.; lgth. 14ft. 0⅜in.; wdth. 5ft. 2½in.; ht. 4ft. 5½in.; g.c. 5⅜in.; turng. cir. 35ft.; kerb wt. 17½ cwt.; tank, 8½ gals.; 12-volt.
£910+£190.2.11 p.t. = £1,100.2.11

LOTUS ELAN 1500

SMOOTH, swift two-seater with plastic body on deep back-bone chassis. Twin-cam engine derived from the 1.5-litre Consul Classic with special head and valve gear. The gearbox is fully synchronised on all four speeds. All wheels have disc brakes. Elite coupe which has been around since 1957, retains its unique all-plastic unit structure. Engine is Coventry Climax 1.2 litres and most highly tuned versions give 130 m.p.h.

CLOSE-UP
Four-cyl.; o.h.c.; 80.96×72.75 mm.; 1,498 c.c.; 100 b.h.p.; 9.5 to 1 comp.; coil ign.; 2 Weber carbs.; 4-speed, 16.04, 9.31, 6.50, 3.89 to 1; cen. lvr.; susp., f. and r. ind. coil; 2-door; 2/3-seat; disc brks.; max. 125 m.p.h.; cruise, 100; m.p.g. 30; whl. base 7ft.; track f. and r. 3ft. 11½in.; lgth. 12ft. 1½in.; wdth. 4ft. 8in.; ht. 3ft. 5in.; g.c. 6in.; turng. cir. 29ft. 3in.; tank, 10 gals.; 12-volt.
£1,090+£227.4.5 p.t. = £1,317.4.5

LOTUS SUPER SEVEN 1500

ONE of the originators of the kit car, Lotus still offer one model in this form for build-it-yourself enthusiasts but it can be bought ready to drive too. Construction is simple and ultra light. A tuned 1.5-litre Ford engine is used for reliability. Much favoured by aspiring racing drivers, it has had many successes on the track and hits 100 m.p.h. despite its un-streamlined shape.

CLOSE-UP
Four-cyl.; o.h.v.; 80.63×72.75 mm.; 1,498 c.c.; 75 b.h.p.; 8 to 1 comp.; coil ign.; Weber carb.; 4-speed, 10.31, 6.98, 5.79, 4.1 to 1; cen. lvr.; susp., f. ind. coil, r. coil; no doors; 2-seat; hyd. brks., disc front; max. 102 m.p.h.; cruise 85; m.p.g. 25-32; whl. base 7ft. 4in.; track f. and r. 4ft. 1in.; lgth. 10ft. 11½in.; wdth. 4ft. 9½in.; ht. 3ft. 7in.; g.c. 4in.; turng. cir. 26ft.; kerb wt. 9½ cwt.; tank, 8 gals.; 12-volt.
£695+£173.15 p.t. = £868.15

MASERATI 3500 G.T.

MASERATIS have made history on the world's race tracks; now production models reflect racing experience. 3.5 litres with fuel injection. Twin-cam six-cylinders give a maximum of 146 m.p.h. to the Coupe by Touring or the cabriolet by Vignale. Luxury Gran Turismo coupe of five litres by Allemano is newest addition to the range with Lucas fuel injection, disc brakes and speeds around 170 miles an hour.

CLOSE-UP
Six-cyl.; o.h.c.; 86×100 mm.; 3,485 c.c.; 235 b.h.p.; 8.8 to 1 comp.; dual ign.; Lucas injection; 5-speed, 11.38, 6.97, 4.86, 3.77, 3.20 to 1; cen. lvr.; susp., f. ind. coil, r. half-elliptic; 2-door; 4-seat; disc servo brks.; max. 146 m.p.h.; cruise 125; m.p.g. 18-20; whl. base 8ft. 6½in.; track f. 4ft. 6½in., r. 4ft. 5½in.; lgth. 15ft. 4in.; wdth. 5ft. 9in.; ht. 4ft. 3in.; g.c. 7in.; turng. cir. 40ft.; kerb wt. 26 cwt.; tank, 18 gals.; 12-volt.
£3,874+£807.12.11 p.t. = £4,681.12.11

MERCEDES-BENZ 190

PETROL or diesel engines are offered in the lowest-priced model of the Mercedes-Benz range and the diesel is so quiet that few passengers ever spot it. Disc front brakes with servo assistance are standard equipment for 1964 and the smooth acting DB four-speed automatic transmission is now optional. Typical Mercedes style and finish and a well-planned interior make this a very popular model.

CLOSE-UP
Four-cyl.; o.h.c.; 85×83.6 mm.; 1,897 c.c.; 80 b.h.p.; 8.7 to 1 comp.; coil ign.; Solex carb.; 4-speed, 16.6, 9.75, 6.27, 4.1 to 1; col. lvr., auto. opt.; susp., f. and r. ind. coil; 4-door; 5-seat; hyd. servo brks., disc front; max. 90 m.p.h.; cruise 76; m.p.g. 28; whl. base 8ft. 8in.; track f. 4ft. 9½in., r. 4ft. 10½in.; length 15ft. 6½in.; wdth. 5ft. 10⅝in.; ht. 4ft. 10⅞in.; g.c. 7⅛in.; turng. cir. 37ft. 5in.; kerb wt. 23¾ cwt.; tank, 12½ gals.; 12-volt.
£1,400+£292.4.7 p.t. = £1,692.4.7

MERCEDES-BENZ 220SE

DISC front brakes, twin servo, twin master cylinders are new safety features on the beautifully finished Mercedes-Benz six cylinder range; the comfortable 220, the 220S with higher performance from new compound carburetters, and the fuel injection 220 SE. Power steering and the DB four-speed automatic transmission with instant manual over-ride are optional extras. Race-proved rear suspension has swing axles with single pivot.

CLOSE-UP
Six-cyl.; o.h.c.; 80×72.8 mm.; 2,195 c.c.; 134 b.h.p.; 8.7 to 1 comp.; coil ign.; Bosch injection; 4-speed, 14.92, 9.34, 6.27, 4.1 to 1; cen. lvr., auto opt.; f. and r. ind. coil; 2-door; 4-seat; servo brks., disc front; max. 105 m.p.h.; cruise 90; m.p.g. 22-25; whl. base 9ft. 0½in.; track f. and r. 4ft. 10½in.; lgth. 16ft. 0½in.; wdth. 6ft. 0½in.; ht. 4ft. 8½in.; g.c. 7½in.; turng. cir. 36ft.; kerb wt. 27½ cwt.; tank, 14½ gals.; 12-volt.
£2,033+£424.2.1 p.t. = £2,457.2.1

MERCEDES 230 SL

BRILLIANT new sporting model to replace 190SL and 300SL. Concave "pagoda" top is coupe's distinguishing style feature. Convertible available with option of removable hard top. Smooth six-cylinder fuel injection engine developed from 220SE with bigger bores, higher compression, new camshaft giving an extra 30 h.p. Disc front brakes, drum rear, with separate master cylinders and vacuum servo. All-synchro gearbox. Option of automatic transmission and power steering.

CLOSE-UP
Six-cyl.; o.h.c.; 82×72 mm.; 2,306 c.c.; 170 b.h.p.; 9.3 to 1 comp.; coil ign.; Bosch injection; 4-speed, 16.57, 8.55, 5.83, 3.75 to 1; cen. lvr.; susp., f. and r. ind. coil; 2-door; 2-seat; hyd. servo brks., disc front; max. 125 m.p.h.; cruise 110; m.p.g. 20-24; whl. base 7ft. 10in.; track f. and r. 4ft. 10½in.; lgth. 14ft. 1½in.; wdth. 5ft. 9¼in.; ht. 4ft. 3½in.; g.c 5in.; turng. cir. 33ft. 4in.; kerb wt. 25½ cwt.; tank, 14½ gals.; 12-volt.
£2,825+£637.8.9 p.t. = £3,462.8.9

MERCEDES-BENZ 600

FANTASTIC new peak of motoring luxury. Doors close hydraulically at finger pressure. One key locks all doors, trunk and fuel filler by vacuum servo. Rear lounge has two rows of seats facing, hydraulically adjustable. Finger-touch controls work windows, chauffeur division, sliding roof, raise and lower trunk lid. V8 engine, automatic transmission, self-levelling pneumatic suspension, adjustable dampers, compressed air brakes, power steering.

CLOSE-UP
Eight-cyl.; o.h.c.; 103.1×95 mm.; 6,330 c.c.; 300 b.h.p.; 9.0 to 1 comp.; coil ign.; Bosch injection; 4-speed auto., 12.85, 8.14, 5.10, 3.23 to 1; col. lvr.; susp., f. and r. ind. pneu.; 4-door; 7/8-seat; disc compressed air brks.; max. 125 m.p.h.; cruise 100; m.p.g. 18; whl. base 12ft. 9½in.; track, f. 5ft. 2½in., r. 5ft. 2in.; lgth. 20ft. 6in.; wdth., 6ft. 6¾in.; ht. 4ft. 11½in.; g.c. 8in.; turng. cir. 47ft. 9in.; kerb wt. 51¾ cwt.; tank 24½ gals.; 12-volt.

MERCURY COMET

COMPACT model of the Mercury range. Choose from sedan, hardtop and station-wagon with V6 2.3 litre engines or a cabriolet with 2.7 litres. There is a choice of three- or four-speed gearboxes or Merc-O-Matic automatic transmission. Features on the 1964 range include sharp-edge front-to-rear wing line, big round tail lights, new grille and front wing line that give it a Lincoln look.

CLOSE-UP
Six-cyl.; o.h.v.; 88.9×74.68 mm.; 2,781 c.c.; 100 b.h.p.; 8.7 to 1 comp.; coil ign.; Ford carb.; 2-speed auto., 6.6, 3.2 to 1; col. lvr.; susp., f. ind. coil, r. half-elliptic; 4-door; 6-seat; hyd. brks.; max. 85 m.p.h.; cruise 70; m.p.g. 22; whl. base 9ft. 6in.; track f. 4ft. 7in., r. 4ft. 6½in.; lgth. 16ft. 3in.; wdth. 5ft. 10⅜in.; ht. 4ft. 6½in.; g.c. 6in.; turng. cir. 39ft. 10in.; kerb wt. 24½ cwt.; tank, 11½ gals.; 12-volt.

MERCURY MONTEREY

PRESTIGE cars from the Mercury stable with V8 engines of 6.3 to 6.6 litres. There are saloons, convertibles, hardtops and station-wagons with six to nine seats and five doors. Gearboxes are three or four-speed manual or automatic. Top speed varies from 105 to 140 m.p.h. Bumpers merge into the wing line, six tail lamps are arranged across the rear, four headlamps across the front.

CLOSE-UP
Eight-cyl.; o.h.v.; 102.9×96 mm.; 6,380 c.c.; 250 b.h.p.; 8.9 to 1 comp.; coil ign.; Ford carb.; 3-speed auto., 7.20, 4.41, 3.0 to 1; col. lvr.; susp., f. ind. coil, r. half-elliptic; 4-door; 6-seat; hyd. brks., servo opt.; max. 105 m.p.h.; cruise 85; m.p.g. 14-17; whl. base 10ft.; track f. 5ft. 1in., r. 5ft. 1in.; lgth. 17ft. 11½in.; wdth. 6ft. 6½in.; ht. 4ft. 6½in.; g.c. 7in.; turng. cir. 41ft. 6in.; kerb wt. 36 cwt.; tank, 16½ gals.; 12-volt.
£1,916+£399.8.10 p.t. = £2,315.8.10

Abbreviations—g.c.—ground clearance; susp.—suspension; f.—front; r.—rear; comp.—compression; s.v.—side-valves; o.h.v.—overhead valves; o.h.c.—overhead camshaft; hyd.—hydraulic.

M.G. MIDGET

PROVING that good things come in small packages, the Midget is a big-hearted performer. The 1,098 c.c. engine introduced at last year's Show gives fast motoring at modest cost. The dream car of young men who want speed and sporty lines at a price they can afford. Girl friends appreciate the weather protection of a sound hood and sliding plastic side windows. Disc front brakes give extra security.

CLOSE-UP

Four-cyl.; o.h.v.; 64.58 × 83.72 mm.; 1,098 c.c.; 55 b.h.p.; 8.9 to 1 comp.; coil ign.; 2 S.U. carbs.; 4-speed, 13.50, 8.08, 5.73, 4.22 to 1; cen. lvr.; susp., f. ind. coil, r. quarter elliptic; 2-door; 2/3-seat; hyd. brks. disc front; max. 90 m.p.h.; cruise 75; m.p.g. 31-36; whl. base 6ft. 8in.; track f. 3ft. 9⅞in., r. 3ft. 8¾in.; lgth. 11ft. 4¼in.; wdth. 4ft. 5in.; ht. 4ft. 1⅜in.; g.c. 5in.; turng. cir. 31ft. 2½in.; kerb wt. 13½ cwt.; tank, 6 gals.; 12-volt.

£495 + £103.13.9 p.t. = £598.13.9

M.G. MGB

CRISPLY styled successor to the MGA, this two-seater of 1.7 litres is a fast mover from the Abingdon factory long famed for value for money in sports cars. It has a unit body-chassis and disc front brakes. Good space for luggage in the boot and space for more behind the front seats. Glass side windows with pivoted ventilating panes; choice of folding or pack-away hoods.

CLOSE-UP

Four-cyl.; o.h.v.; 80.26 × 89 mm.; 1,798 c.c.; 94 b.h.p.; 8.8 to 1 comp.; coil ign.; 2 S.U. carbs.; 4-speed, 14.21, 8.65, 5.37, 3.90 to 1; cen. lvr.; susp., f. ind. coil, r. half-elliptic; 2-door; 2/3 seat; hyd. brks., disc front; max. 108 m.p.h.; cruise 85; m.p.g. 26-28; whl. base 7ft. 9in.; track f. 4ft. 1in., r. 4ft. 1¼in.; lgth. 12ft. 9¼in.; wdth. 4ft. 11⅞in.; ht. 4ft. 1⅜in.; g.c. 5in.; turng. cir. 32ft. 10in.; kerb wt. 17¾ cwt.; tank, 10 gals.; 12-volt.

£690 + £144.6.3 p.t. = £834.6.3

M.G. 1100

FASTER development of the Morris and Austin 1100 cars. With two carburettors it gives much more getaway speed in the lower gears. On motorway test between Brussels and Ostend easily averaged 72 m.p.h. without ever putting the foot full down on the throttle. The car has plenty of power and zest, and takes four people in absolute comfort. Unique Hydrolastic suspension and disc front brakes.

CLOSE-UP

Four-cyl.; o.h.v.; 64.57 × 83.72 mm.; 1,098 c.c.; 55 b.h.p.; 8.9 to 1 comp.; coil ign.; 2 S.U. carbs.; 4-speed, 14.99, 8.98, 5.83, 4.133 to 1; cen. lvr.; susp., f. and r. ind. rubber-hydraulic; 2 or 4-door; 4-seat; hyd. brks., disc front; max. 85 m.p.h.; cruise 75; m.p.g. 35-38; whl. base 7ft. 9½in.; track f. 4ft. 3½in., r. 4ft. 2⅝in.; lgth. 12ft. 2⅞in.; wdth. 5ft. 0⅞in.; ht. 4ft. 4½in.; g.c. 6in.; turning. cir. 34ft.; kerb wt. 17½ cwt.; tank, 8½ gals.; 12-volt.

£590 + £123.9.7 p.t. = £713.9.7

MORGAN PLUS 4 SUPER SPORTS

THIS model is made in at least four versions —as a 2-seater, 4-seater, drop-head coupe and super sports car. The cars are built by a small West of England manufacturer and have a coterie of enthusiasts who compete in them in races, rallies and hill-climbs. A thoroughly tested and reliable car, likely to be with us for some time to come.

CLOSE-UP

Four-cyl.; o.h.v.; 83 × 92 mm.; 1,991 c.c.; 117 b.h.p.; 9.2 to 1 comp.; coil ign.; 2 Weber carbs.; 4-speed, 12.85, 7.38, 5.24, 3.73 to 1; cen. lvr.; susp., f. ind. coil, r. half-elliptic; 2-door; 2-seat; hyd. brks., disc front; max. 120 m.p.h.; cruise 105; m.p.g. 24; whl. base 8ft.; track f. 4ft., r. 4ft. 1in.; lgth. 12ft.; wdth. 4ft. 8in.; ht. 4ft. 1in.; g.c. 6½in.; turng. cir. 32ft.; kerb wt. 15½ cwt.; tank, 11 gals.; 12-volt.

£925 + £193.5.2 p.t. = £1,118.5.2

MORRIS MINI SUPER

PEERS and Princesses grace it, M.Ps and councillors vote for it, all parties agree about it and the public love it. It's BMC's unique front drive crosswise-engined Mini. Super de luxe form has special interior trim similar to the Cooper models but retains 848 c.c. engine with single carburetter. Seats for four, a surprising amount of space for parcels and luggage, and a top speed of over 73 m.p.h.

CLOSE-UP
Four-cyl; o.h.v.; 63×68.26 mm.; 848 c.c.; 34 b.h.p.; 8.3 to 1 comp.; coil ign.; S.U. carb.; 4-speed, 13.657, 8.176, 5.317, 3.765 to 1; cen. lvr.; susp., f. and r. ind. rubber; 2-door; 4-seat; hyd. brks.; max. 73 m.p.h.; cruise 60; m.p.g. 45; whl. base 6ft. 8in.; track f. 3ft. 11 7/16 in., r. 3ft. 9⅞in.; lgth. 10ft.; wdth. 4ft. 7in.; ht. 4ft 5in.; g.c. 6⅛in.; turng. cir. 31 ft.; kerb wt. 11½ cwt.; tank, 5½ gals.; 12-volt.
£407.10 + £85.9.2 p.t. = £492.19.2

MORRIS 1100

RARELY has a new model received such unanimous acclaim from the world's press as that which greeted this compact but incredibly roomy saloon with the transverse engine, front-wheel drive and all-independent self damping Hydrolastic suspension. Water pumped continuously between front and rear by the movement of the wheels gives a unique flat, level ride over the worst bumps. Road holding is magnificent.

CLOSE-UP
Four-cyl.; o.h.v.; 64.58×83.72 mm.; 1,098 c.c.; 50 b.h.p.; 8.5 to 1 comp.; coil ign.; S.U. carb.; 4-speed, 14.99, 8.98, 5.83, 4.133 to 1; cen. lvr.; susp. f. and r. ind. rubber-hydraulic; 2 or 4-door; 5-seat; hyd. brks., disc front; max. 78 m.p.h.; cruise 70; m.p.g. 36-38; whl. base 7ft. 9½in.; track f. 4ft. 3½in., r. 4ft. 2⅜in.; lgth. 12ft. 3in.; wdth. 5ft.; ht. 4ft. 5in.; g.c. 6in.; turng. cir. 34ft. 9in.; kerb wt. 16¼ cwt.; tank, 8½ gals.; 12-volt.
£490 + £102.12.11 p.t. = £592.12.11

MORRIS OXFORD TRAVELLER

TRAVELLERS' tales are happy ones with either version of the Morris Traveller. The 850 model has the same specification as the Mini except that it has a longer wheelbase. The Morris Oxford is the 1.6-litre Pininfarina-styled wagon which seats five. Rear seat folded flat frees a large freight space. Top speed around 80 m.p.h. BMC diesel engine available for economy-minded big-mileage users.

CLOSE-UP
Four-cyl.; o.h.v.; 76.2×88.9 mm.; 1,622 c.c.; 55 b.h.p.; 8.3 to 1 comp.; coil ign.: S.U. carb.; 4-speed, 15.64, 9.52, 5.91, 4.3 to 1; col. or cen. lvr.; susp., f. ind. coil, r. half-elliptic; 4-door; 4-seat; hyd brks.; max. 80; m.p.h.; cruise 65; m.p.g. 25-33; whl base 8ft. 4⅛in.; track f. 4ft. 2⅜in., r. 4ft. 3⅜in.; lgth. 14ft. 6⅛in.; wdth. 5ft. 3⅜in.; ht. 4ft. 10⅞in.; g.c. 5⅞in.; turng. cir. 37ft.; kerb wt. 21¾ cwt.; tank, 10 gals.; 12-volt.
£693 + £144.18.9 p.t. = £837.18.9

MOSKVITCH

RUSSIAN small car from factories in Moscow now being assembled in Brussels with British Perkins 1.6-litre diesel engine for the European market. Show models have the standard 1.3-litre petrol engine for the British market. Fully reclining front seats and a good heater spell comfortable long distance travel. Four-door saloon and station wagon are available. Construction is conventional, with unit structure, coil spring front suspension, semi-elliptic rear.

CLOSE-UP
Four-cyl.; o.h.v.; 76×75 mm.; 1,360 c.c.; 45 b.h.p.; 7 to 1 comp.; coil ign.; downdraught carb.; 4-speed, 17.89, 11.39, 7.83, 4.71 to 1; col. lvr.; susp., f. ind. coil, r. half-elliptic; 4-door; 4-seat; hyd. brks.; max. 72 m.p.h.; cruise 50; m.p.g. 35; whl base 7ft. 9in.; track f. and r. 4ft.; lgth. 13ft. 4in.; wdth 5ft. 1in.; ht 5ft. 1¼in.; g.c. 7¼in.; turng. cir. 39½ft.; kerb wt. 18¾ cwt.; tank, 7¾ gals.; 12-volt.
£520 + £108.17.11 p.t. = £628.17.11

Abbreviations—g.c.—ground clearance; susp.—suspension; f.—front; r.—rear; comp.—compression; s.v.—side-valves; o.h.v.—overhead valves; o.h.c.—overhead camshaft; hyd.—hydraulic.

N.S.U. PRINZ WANKEL

EAGERLY awaited, Fritz Wankel's rotating piston engine invades the car market in this neat two-seater Bertone-styled convertible. Almost hidden by gearbox, clutch, dynamo, starter and carburettor, the tiny circular engine is tucked under the floor of the rear luggage trunk. More luggage goes in front, above fuel tank and radiator. Lighter, smaller, smoother than ordinary engines, the Wankel may also be cheaper when in full production.

CLOSE-UP
Wankel rotating piston engine; 500 c.c.; 50 b.h.p.; coil ign., single plug; Solex carb.; 4-speed, 13.65, 7.87, 5.20, 3.77 to 1; cen. lvr.; susp., f. and r. ind. coil; 2-door; 2-seat; hyd. brks., disc front; max. 95 m.p.h.; cruise 85; m.p.g. 35; whl. base 6ft. 7⅞in.; track f. 4ft. 2in., r. 4ft. 0⅛in.; lgth. 11ft. 8½in.; wdth. 4ft. 11⅞in.; ht. 4ft. 0⅝in.; g.c. 7in.; turng. cir. 30ft.; kerb wt. 13½ cwt.; tank, 7¾ gals.; 12-volt.

N.S.U. PRINZ 1000

BACKING both horses, N.S.U. announce a longer, more powerful piston-engined saloon to supplement the Wankel convertible. Adopting the transverse engine layout already popular in Britain and Japan, it has a rear-mounted air-cooled four-cylinder unit of 996 c.c. with chain-driven overhead camshaft. Cooling air passes through a grille in the left rear wing. Suspension is all-independent by coil springs; disc front brakes are optional.

CLOSE-UP
Four-cyl.; o.h.c., air-cooled; 69×66.9 mm.; 996 c.c.; 43 b.h.p.; 8 to 1 comp.; coil ign.; Solex carb.; 4-speed, cen. lvr.; susp., f. and r. ind. coil; 2-door; 4-seat; hyd. brks., disc opt.; max. 84 m.p.h.; cruise 80; m.p.g. 37-45; whl. base 7ft. 4⅜in.; track f. 4ft. 2in., r. 4ft. 0⅞in.; lgth. 12ft. 6in.; wdth. 4ft. 10⅝in.; ht. 4ft. 5½in.; g.c. 7in.; turng. cir. 30ft. 9in.; kerb wt. 12¼ cwt.; tank, 8 gals.; 6-volt.

OGLE SX 1000

ZIPPY Ogle SX 1000 has transverse BMC-Cooper engine, tuned by Alexander, with front-wheel drive and disc front brakes. Moulded in resin-bonded glass fibre, its smooth low-drag shape gives this luxuriously finished little two-seater maximum speeds up to 100 m.p.h. according to engine tune. Product of a house with a growing reputation for industrial design in motoring and other fields.

CLOSE-UP
Four-cyl.; o.h.v.; 62.4×81.2 mm.; 997 c.c.; 55 b.h.p.; 9 to 1 comp.; coil ign.; 2 SU carbs.; 4-speed, 12.05, 7.213, 5.11, 3.765 to 1; cen. lvr.; susp., f and r. ind. rubber; 2-door; 2-seat; hyd. servo brks., disc front; max. 92 m.p.h.; cruise 80; m.p.g. 30; whl. base 6ft. 7⅞in.; track f. 3ft. 11⅜in., r. 3ft. 9⅞in.; lgth. 11ft. 2in.; wdth. 4ft. 10in.; ht. 3ft. 10½in.; g.c. 6⅜in.; turng. cir. 31ft. 3in.; kerb wt. 12¼ cwt.; tank, 10½ gals.; 12-volt.
£873+£196.16.9 p.t. = £1,069.16.9

OLDSMOBILE F-85

RE-STYLED, on a longer wheelbase, the smallest Oldsmobile now has curved side windows. Options include air conditioning, tilt-away adjustable steering wheel and electric four-way adjustment for seats. Engines now include a choice of a V6 of 3,686 c.c. giving 155 h.p. and a 5,408 c.c. V8 developing 330 h.p. Another option is the Jetaway automatic transmission with variable-vane torque converter. There are 15 colours to choose from.

CLOSE-UP
Eight-cyl.; o.h.v.; 88.9×71.12 mm.; 3,515 c.c.; 155 b.h.p.; 8.75 to 1 comp.; coil ign.; Rochester twin-choke carb.; 3-speed, 7.91, 4.77, 3.08 to 1, auto. opt.; col. lvr.; susp., f. ind. coil, r. coil; 4-door; 5-seat; hyd. brks.; max. 93 m.p.h.; cruise 80; m.p.g. 17-23; whl. base 9ft. 7in.; track f. and r. 4ft. 8in.; lgth. 15ft. 8½in.; wdth. 5ft. 11½in.; ht. 4ft. 2½in.; g.c. 5in.; turng. cir. 37ft.; kerb wt. 23 cwt.; tank, 13 gals.; 12-volt.
£1,718+£358.9.5 p.t. = £2,076.9.5

Abbreviations—g.c.—ground clearance; susp.—suspension; f.—front; r.—rear; comp.—compression; s.v.—side-valves; o.h.v.—overhead valves; o.h.c.—overhead camshaft; hyd.—hydraulic.

OLDSMOBILE SUPER 98

TOP class car in the Oldsmobile range, the Ninety-Eight is offered as Town sedan, Luxury sedan, Holiday Sports sedan, Custom Sports coupe, and Convertible. Three- or four-speed gearboxes are offered. Hydra-Matic automatic transmission is available to order and the V8 engines are 6.4-litres developing 330 h.p. Lavish interiors with space to spare, and concave rear windows are 1964 features.

CLOSE-UP

Eight-cyl.; o.h.v.; 104.7×93.7 mm.; 6,442 c.c.; 330 b.h.p.; 10.25 to 1 comp.; coil ign.; Rochester 4-choke carb.; 3-speed auto, 9.02, 4.80, 3.08 to 1; col. lvr.; susp.: f. ind. coil, r. coil; 4-door; 6-seat; hyd. brks.; max. 115 m.p.h.; cruise 90; m.p.g. 14; whl. base 10ft. 6in.; track f. 5ft. 2¼in., r. 5ft. 1in.; lgth. 18ft. 5in.; wdth. 6ft. 5⅞in.; ht. 4ft. 9in.; g.c. 6in.; turng. cir. 46ft. 3in.; kerb wt. 40¼ cwt.; tank, 17 gals.; 12-volt.

PANHARD 24 C.T.

OLD wine; new bottle. Indisputably elegant, this latest model from France's oldest manufacturer, allies new bodywork to the familiar flat twin engine and front-wheel drive system developed from previous Dynas. It obtains 50 hp. from 843 cc. in standard form or 60 in G.T. version. Front seats are adjustable for legroom, height and slope. The heater system feeds warm air to feet, windscreen and rear window. Panhard is now in the Citroen group.

CLOSE-UP

Two-cyl.; o.h.v., air-cooled; 84.9×75 mm.; 843 c.c.; 50 b.h.p.; 8.3 to 1 comp.; coil ign.; Zenith 2-choke carb.; 4-speed, 16.495, 9.277, 6.148, 4.525 to 1; cen. lvr.; susp., f. ind. transv. leaf, r. torsion bar; 2-door; 2/4 seat; hyd. brks.; max. 93 m.p.h.; cruise 85; m.p.g. 34-36; whl. base 7ft. 6in.; track f. and r. 4ft. 3in.; lgth. 14ft.; wdth. 5ft. 4in.; ht. 4ft.; g.c. 6¼in.; turng. cir. 30ft.; kerb wt. 15½ cwt.; tank, 9¼ gals.; 12-volt.

PEUGEOT 404

FIRST introduced in 1960, with its Pininfarina styling, the Peugeot 404 is now a firm favourite in France. Engine has hemispherical heads, the four-speed gearbox is fully synchronised. Independent front suspension and rigid rear axle with radius arms give good ride and road holding. Range includes Berline, GT Super de Luxe, Cabriolet, Coupe and two station wagons. The saloon does 87 m.p.h. Convertible with fuel injection does 98 m.p.h.

CLOSE-UP

Four-cyl.; o.h.v.; 84×73 mm.; 1,618 c.c.; 72 b.h.p.; 7.4 to 1 comp.; coil ign.; Solex carb.; 4-speed, 16.80, 9.42, 6.05, 4.2 to 1; col. lvr.; susp., f. ind. coil, r. coil; 4-door; 5/6-seat; hyd. brks.; max. 90 m.p.h.; cruise 75-80; m.p.g. 30; whl base 8ft. 8½in.; track f. 4ft. 4¾in., r. 4ft. 2½in.; lgth. 14ft. 6in.; wdth 5ft. 5½in.; ht. 4ft. 9½in.; g.c. 6in.; turng. cir. 30ft.; kerb wt. 20½ cwt.; tank, 11 gals.; 12-volt.

£890 + £185.19.7 p.t. = £1,075.19.7

PLYMOUTH FURY

THE Furies come in four types, all with V8 engines; the two-door Sports Hardtop, two-door Convertible, five-door Estate Car and four-door Hardtop. Front grille is changed for 1964 but otherwise the mixture is as before, with the long, lean look continued. Five litres of engine give a top speed of 110 m.p.h. Transmission is three-speed manual or Torque-Flite Eight automatic.

CLOSE-UP

Eight-cyl.; o.h.v.; 96.3×84 mm.; 5,199 c.c.; 230 b.h.p.; 9 to 1 comp.; coil ign.; Carter carb.; 3-speed auto., 6.76, 3.0, 2.76 to 1; press button control; susp., f. ind. torsion bar, r. half-elliptic; 4-door; 6-seat; hyd. servo brks.; max. 110 m.p.h.; cruise 90; m.p.g. 15-18; whl. base 9ft. 8in.; track f. 4ft. 11½in., r. 4ft. 9in.; lgth. 17ft. 1in.; wdth. 6ft. 3in.; ht. 4ft. 6in.; g.c. 6in.; turng. cir. 40ft. 3in.; kerb wt. 29¼ cwt.; tank, 16¼ gals.; 12-volt.

£1,740 + £363.1.3 p.t. = £2,103.1.3

Abbreviations—g.c.—ground clearance; susp.—suspension; f.—front; r.—rear; comp.—compression; s.v.—side-valves; o.h.v.—overhead valves; o.h.c.—overhead camshaft; hyd.—hydraulic

PONTIAC CATALINA

EXTRAS available on the opulent Pontiacs for 1964 include Electro-cruise automatic speed control for driving on America's speed-limited motorways, six-way power-operated rising and tilting front seat, special wheel discs. New styling kick; walnut spokes for the steering wheel. Engines cover a range from 215 to 370 horsepower. Models marketed in Britain include the Parisienne assembled in Canada.

CLOSE-UP
Eight-cyl.; o.h.v.; 101.5×82.55 mm.; 5,354 c.c.; 250 b.h.p.; 10 to 1 comp.; coil ign.; Carter carb.; 2-speed auto., 5.60, 3.08 to 1; col. lvr.; susp., f. ind. coil, r. coil; 4-door; 6-seat; hyd. servo brks.; max. 105 m.p.h.; cruise 80; m.p.g. 14-17; whl. base 10ft.; track f. 5ft. 3¾in., r. 5ft. 4in.; lgth. 17ft. 7in.; wdth. 6ft. 6¾in.; ht. 4ft. 10⅝in.; g.c. 6½in.; turng. cir. 42ft. 9in.; kerb wt. 42½ cwt.; tank, 17½ gals.; 12-volt.

PORSCHE 356C/1600

DISC brakes made under Dunlop licence are featured on all 1600 cc. Porsches for 1964. Neat and new is the efficient drum-type parking brake built into rear discs. The 60 hp. model is dropped. New cylinder heads give higher power and torque for the other models, now rated as 75 and 95 hp. Heater controls are easier to use; jet airflow assists rear window de-misting. Front seats have deeper cushions.

CLOSE-UP
Four-cyl.; o.h.v.; air-cooled; 82.5×74 mm.; 1,582 c.c.; 75 b.h.p.; 8.5 to 1 comp.; coil ign.; 2 Zenith carbs.; 4-speed, 13.68, 7.81, 4.43, 3.61 to 1; cen. lvr.; susp., f. and r. ind. torsion bar; 2-door; 2/4-seat; disc brks.; max. 110 m.p.h.; cruise 95; m.p.g. 32; whl. base 6ft. 10¾in.; track f. 4ft. 2¾in., r. 4ft. 2in.; lgth. 13ft. 2in.; wdth. 5ft.-5¾in.; ht. 4ft. 4¾in.; g.c. 6in.; turng. cir. 33ft. 6in.; kerb wt. 18½ cwt.; tank, 10¼ gals.; 6-volt.
£1,707+£356.3.9 p.t. = £2,063.3.9

PORSCHE Type 901

A NEW, larger Porsche in the same tradition. Even better streamlined, slimmer outside to suit today's traffic, but wider inside. Flat-six overhead camshaft air-cooled engine at the rear, and five-speed fully-synchronised gearbox. Torsion bar all-independent suspension and disc brakes. A 120 m.p.h. beauty, built to last, that is loafing at a hundred. Equipped with every comfort for transcontinental travel.

CLOSE-UP
Six-cyl.; o.h.c.; air-cooled; 80×66 mm.; 1,991 c.c.; 130 b.h.p.; 9 to 1 comp.; coil ign.; 4 carbs.; 5-speed, 13.68, 8.36, 5.84, 4.43, 3.35 to 1; cen. lvr.; susp., f. and r. ind. torsion bar; 2-door; 2/4-seat; hyd. disc brks.; max. 130 m.p.h.; cruise 120; m.p.g. 25; whl. base 7ft. 2¾in.; track f. 4ft. 4½in., r. 4ft. 3½in.; lgth. 13ft. 6½in.; wdth. 5ft. 3in.; ht. 4ft. 4in.; g.c. 6in.; turng. cir. 32ft. 9in.; kerb wt. 19¾cwt.; tank, 16¼ gals.; 12-volt.

RAMBLER CLASSIC 6

SPEARHEAD of the American Motors drive to win back the place in the British Market once held by Hudson and Essex. Three versions all with 3-litre six-cylinder engines giving top speed of about 96 m.p.h. 1964 brings extensive face lifting, with a new grille, four recessed headlamps, and a new treatment for side panels. Luxurious Rambler American V8 range is re-styled with a rounder look.

CLOSE-UP
Six-cyl.; o.h.v.; 79.37×107.95 mm.; 3,205 c.c.; 127 b.h.p.; 8.7 to 1 comp.; coil ign.; Holley carb.; 3-speed; 8.63, 5.39, 3.31 to 1; col. lvr., overdrive or auto. opt.; susp., f. ind. coil, r. coil; 2 or 4-door; 5-6 seat; hyd. brks.; max. 96 m.p.h.; cruise 70; m.p.g. 25; whl. base 9ft. 4in.; track f. 4ft. 10¾in., r. 4ft. 9½in.; lgth. 15ft. 10in.; wdth. 6ft.; ht. 4ft. 6½in.; g.c. 6in.; turng. cir. 37ft. 3in.; kerb wt. 26½ cwt.; tank, 16 gals.; 12-volt.
£1,253+£261.12.1 p.t. = £1,514.12.1

RELIANT SABRE

THE Romans never saw anything like this bowling down Watling Street, but since Reliant Engineering live there these fast two seaters are now a familiar sight. So, incidentally are the economical three-wheelers from the same factory. The two-seater cabriolet or coupe with plastic body has a modified four-cylinder Ford Zephyr engine, four speed fully synchronised gearbox and disc brakes. Sabre Six has a 2.5-litre Zephyr engine.

CLOSE-UP
Four-cyl.; o.h.v.; 82.6×79.5 mm.; 1,703 c.c.; 90 b.h.p.; 8.8 to 1 comp.; coil ign.; 2 SU carbs.; 4-speed, 9.0, 6.0, 4.37, 3.55 to 1; cen. lvr.; susp., f. ind. coil strut, r. coil; 2-door; 2-seat; hyd. brks., disc front; max. 105 m.p.h.; cruise 85; m.p.g. 25-28; whl. base, 7ft. 6in.; track f. and r. 4ft.; lgth., 13ft. 6in.; wdth. 5ft. 1in.; ht. 4ft. 2in.; g.c. 6in.; turng. cir. 30ft.; kerb wt. 15¾ cwt.; tank, 8 gals.; 12-volt.

£799+£167.0.5 p.t. = £966.0.5

RENAULT DAUPHINE

MORE than 2,000,000 of these French rear-engined cars have been built on a reputation of long-life, economy and comfort. A 4-door saloon with child-proof safety locks on the rear doors, this car has a roomy luggage boot in front with the spare wheel slung underneath. It is said that 50,000 Frenchmen can't be wrong—and they all like the Dauphine. Disc brakes for 1964.

CLOSE-UP
Four-cyl.; o.h.v.; 58×80 mm.; 845 c.c.; 30 b.h.p.; 8.0 to 1 comp.; coil ign.; Solex carb.; 3-speed, 16.1, 7.88, 4.52 to 1; cen. lvr., 4-speed opt.; susp., f. ind. coil, r. ind. coil; 4-door; 4-seat; disc brks.; max. 75 m.p.h.; cruise 60; m.p.g. 42-48; whl. base 7ft. 5¼in.; track f. 4ft. 1¼in.; r. 4ft.; lgth. 12ft. 11¼in.; wdth. 5ft.; ht. 4ft. 9in.; g.c. 6in.; turng. cir. 29ft. 10in.; kerb wt. 12⅝ cwt.; tank, 7 gals.; 12-volt.

£479+£100.7.1 p.t. = £579.7.1

RENAULT FLORIDE CARAVELLE

PRESTIGE model from Renault available as convertible or four-seater fixed-head coupe. Extra speed and flexibility for 1964 with enlarged engine of 1108 c.c. and greater driving pleasure with a new four-speed all-synchronised gearbox. There is a larger fuel tank. Well finished and comfortable, Caravelle offers luxury travel in a moderate size. A neat clip-on hardtop is available for the convertible. Brakes are discs.

CLOSE-UP
Four-cyl.; o.n.v.; 70×72 mm.; 1,108 c.c.; 55 b.h.p.; 8.5 to 1 comp.; coil ign.; Solex or Zenith carb.; 4-speed, 14.93, 9.28, 6.10, 4.25 to 1; cen. lvr.; susp., f. and r. ind. coil; 2-door; 4-seat; disc brks.; max 88 m.p.h.; cruise 80; m.p.g. 36; whl. base 7ft. 5½in.; track f. 4ft. 1½in.; r. 4ft.; lgth. 14ft.; wdth. 5ft. 2in.; ht. 4ft. 3in.; g.c. 5¾in.; turng. cir. 31ft. 6in.; kerb wt. 15½ cwt.; tank, 8½ gals.; 12-volt.

£849+£177.8.9 p.t. = £1,026.8.9

RENAULT R4L

R4 made headlines as Renault's front-wheel drive car, very different from the rear-engined 4 CV which it replaced. Original model, for French market only, had 747 c.c., and four side windows. R4L has station wagon body with six windows and engine of 845 c.c. Soft independent torsion bar suspension for riding over rocks and rutted cow tracks. Seats with foam overlay on rubber bands for comfort and lightness. Super model has more luxury.

CLOSE-UP
Four-cyl.; o.h.v.; 58×80 mm.; 845 c.c.; 34 b.h.p.; 8 to 1 comp.; coil ign.; Solex carb.; 3-speed, 15.675, 7.598, 4.282 to 1; dash lvr.; susp., f. and r. ind. torsion bar; 5-door; 4-seat; hyd. brks.; max. 68 m.p.h.; cruise 55; m.p.g. 45-50; whl. base 8ft.; track f. 4ft. 1in., r. 3ft. 11½in.; lgth. 12ft.; wdth. 4ft. 10½in.; ht. 5ft. 4in.; g.c. 7⅛in.; turng. cir. 28ft.; kerb wt. 11½ cwt.; tank, 5½ gals.; 6-volt.

£446+£93.9.7 p.t. = £539.9.7

Abbreviations—g.c.—ground clearance; susp.—suspension; f.—front; r.—rear; comp.—compression; s.v.—side-valves; o.h.v.—overhead valves; o.h.c.—overhead camshaft; hyd.—hydraulic.

RENAULT R8

CHIC Parisienne, introduced last year after extensive trials over rough Spanish and African roads. A comfortable saloon with excellent seats and a rear engine of 956 c.c. which gives a maximum speed of approaching 80 m.p.h. Suspension is all-independent and there is a choice of four-speed all-synchro or three-speed automatic gearbox. There are disc brakes on all four wheels.

CLOSE-UP

Four-cyl.; o.h.v.; 65×72 mm.; 956 c.c.; 48 b.h.p.; 8.5 to 1 comp.; coil ign.; Solex or Zenith carb.; 4-speed 16.10, 9.17, 6.65, 4.50 to 1; cen. lvr.; susp., f. and r. ind. coil; 4-door; 4/5 seat; disc brks.; max. 75 m.p.h.; cruise 70; m.p.g. 38-42; whl. base 7ft. 5½in.; track f. 4ft. 1½in., r. 4ft.; lgth. 13ft. 1in.; wdth. 4ft. 10½in.; ht. 4ft. 7½in.; g.c. 5¾in.; turng. cir. 30ft. 3in.; kerb wt. 14½ cwt.; tank, 6¾ gals.; 12-volt.

£555+£116.3.9 p.t. = £671.3.9

RILEY ELF

SINCE the last Motor Show extra pep has been given this car by increasing the engine size to 998 c.c. This improves its acceleration by 6 per cent and slightly raises its top speed to about 75. To match this extra urge the brakes have been enlarged. The car handles on the straight and through the corners with the usual brilliance of the Mini series, but retains its Riley characteristics.

CLOSE-UP

Four-cyl.; o.h.v.; 64.58×76.2 mm.; 998 c.c.; 38 b.h.p.; 8.3 to 1 comp.; coil ign.; S.U. carb.; 4-speed, 13.657, 8.176, 5.317, 3.765 to 1; cen. lvr.; susp. f. and r. ind. rubber; 2-door; 4-seat; hyd. brks.; max. 75 m.p.h.; cruise 62; m.p.g. 40; whl. base 6 ft. 8in.; track f. 4ft, r. 3ft. 10in.; lgth. 10ft. 10in.; wdth. 4ft. 7½in.; ht. 4ft. 5in.; g.c. 5½in.; turng. cir. 31ft.; kerb wt. 12½ cwt.; tank, 5½ gals.; 12-volt.

£475+£99.10.5 p.t. = £574.10.5

RILEY ONE-POINT-FIVE

TRUE to the Riley tradition for quick, reliable machines, the 1.5 has had many successes in rallies and in production car races. But sporting aspects aside, it is a solid family car with four seats, reasonable luggage space, a moderate thirst and a creditable top speed. A broader base to the grille and more prominent tail lamps in rounded fairings are additions which have improved the appearance.

CLOSE-UP

Four-cyl.; o.h.v.; 73.025×88.9 mm.; 1,489 c.c.; 60 b.h.p.; 8.3 to 1 comp.; coil ign.; 2 S.U. carbs.; 4-speed; 13.56, 8.25, 5.12, 3.73 to 1; cen. lvr.; susp. f. ind. torsion bar, r. half-elliptic; 4-door; 4-seat; hyd. brks.. max. 85 m.p.h.; cruise 70; m.p.g. 25-35; whl. base 7ft. 2in.; track f. 4ft. 2½in.; r. 4ft. 2½in., lgth. 12ft. 9in.; wdth. 5ft. 1in.; ht. 4ft. 11¾in.; g.c. 6½in.; turng. cir. 34ft. 3in.; kerb wt. 18½ cwt.; tank, 7 gals.; 12-volt.

£580+£121.7.11 p.t. = £701.7.11

RILEY 4/72

THIS is the car for the motorist who likes a sporting shape but plenty of luggage room for the family. The boot has 19 cubic feet capacity yet the car looks low and slender in the true Riley tradition. It has luxury and craftsmanship and performs well on the road. A car for the individualist wanting a nice turn of speed with roominess.

CLOSE-UP

Four-cyl.; o.h.v.; 76.2×88.9 mm.; 1,622 c.c.; 65 b.h.p.; 8.3 to 1 comp.; coil ign.; 2 S.U. carbs.; 4-speed, 15.64, 9.52, 5.91, 4.3 to 1; cen. lvr.; susp., f. ind. coil, r. half-elliptic; 4-door; 4-seat; hyd. brks.; max. 88 m.p.h.; cruise 75; m.p.g. 23-29; whl. base 8ft. 4½in.; track f. 4ft. 2½in., r. 4ft. 3½in.; lgth. 14ft. 6½in.; wdth. 5ft. 3in.; ht. 4ft. 10½in.; g.c. 5½in.; turng. cir. 37ft.; kerb wt. 22¾ cwt.; tank, 10 gals.; 12 volt.

£757.10+£158.7. p.t. = £915.17.

ROLLS-ROYCE SILVER CLOUD III

SALOON bodies in two lengths of wheelbase, for owner-driver or chauffeur operation are the standard body styles, but this Mulliner drophead coupe, and a James Young saloon are among the alternatives available to the discriminating buyer with money to spend. Four headlamps and a fractionally lower bonnet line are the most recent changes in a make which never changes radically or suddenly.

CLOSE-UP
Eight-cyl.; o.h.v.; 104.14×91.44 mm.; 6,230 c.c.; 9 to 1 comp.; coil ign.; 2 S.U. carbs.; 4-speed auto. 11.75, 8.10, 4.46, 3.08 to 1; col. lvr.; susp., f. ind. coil, r. half-elliptic; 4-door; 5/6-seat; hyd. servo brks.; max. 110 m.p.h.; cruise 90; m.p.g. 12-15; whl. base 10ft. 3in.; track f. 4ft. 10in., r. 5ft.; lgth. 17ft. 7¾in.; wdth. 6ft. 2⅞in.; ht. 5ft. 4in.; g.c. 7in.; turng. cir. 41ft. 8in.; kerb wt. 41½ cwt.; tank, 18 gals.; 12-volt.

£4,565+£951.11.10 p.t. = £5,516.11.10

ROLLS-ROYCE PHANTOM V

HIGHEST expression of luxury in the inimitable Rolls-Royce manner, with coachwork by Mulliner and Park Ward craftsmen so beautifully proportioned that its size is not at first obvious. An alternative model is built by James Young, a subsidiary of the Jack Barclay organisation. Electric control for windows and division, and full air conditioning are among the items that contribute to motoring enjoyment for top people.

CLOSE-UP
Eight-cyl.; o.h.v.; 104.14×91.44 mm.; 6,230 c.c.; 9 to 1 comp.; coil ign.; 2 S.U. carbs.; 4-speed auto., 14.86, 10.23, 5.64, 3.89 to 1; col. lvr.; susp., f. ind. coil, r. half-elliptic; 4-door; 7-seat; hyd. servo brks.; max. 100 m.p.h.; cruise 85; m.p.g. 12; whl. base 12ft.; track f. 5ft. 0⅛in., r. 5ft. 4in.; lgth. 19ft. 10in.; wdth. 6ft. 7in.; ht. 5ft. 9in.; g.c. 7½in.; turng. cir. 48ft. 9in.; tank, 23 gals.; 12-volt.

£7,305+£1,522.8.5 p.t. = £8,827.8.5

ROVER 110

THE flowed cylinder head in this car's six-cylinder engine allows it to attain quietly and in comfort the 100-mile-an-hour mark. A model that is particularly popular with professional men, the Rover 110 is what is known as a "hand-built" car, engineered to the highest degree. One of the first cars to reduce maintenance worries, it has only one grease point to be checked every 3,000 miles.

CLOSE-UP
Six-cyl.; o.h. inlet, side exhaust; 77.8×92.07 mm.; 2,625 c.c.; 123 b.h.p.; 8.8 to 1 comp.; coil ign.; S.U. carb.; 4-speed, 14.41, 8.78, 5.82, 4.3 to 1, de Normanville overdrive; cen. lvr.; susp., f. ind. coil, r. half-elliptic; 4-door; 4/5-seat; hyd. servo brks.; max. 100 m.p.h.; cruise 80; m.p.g. 18-25; whl. base 9ft. 3in.; track f. 4ft. 4½in., r. 4ft. 3½in.; lgth 14ft. 10⅝in.; wdth. 5ft. 5⅞in.; ht. 5ft. 3¼in.; g.c. 7in.; turng. cir. 37ft.; kerb wt. 29½ cwt.; tank, 11½ gals.; 12-volt.

£1,143+£238.13.9 p.t. = £1,381.13.9

ROVER 2000

ENTIRELY new from front bumper to rear and packed with good ideas for safe, fast motoring, this compact 100 m.p.h. saloon puts Rover ownership within reach of many more buyers. All body panels are removable for repair, steering column and backrest angles are adjustable, capacious lockers for personal possessions act as crash protection for front-seat occupants. Highlights are o.h.c. five-bearing engine, servo disc brakes, de Dion rear axle.

CLOSE-UP
Four-cyl.; o.h.c.; 85.7×85.7 mm.; 1,978 c.c.; 99 b.h.p.; 9 to 1 comp.; coil ign.; SU carb.; 4-speed, 12.83, 7.55, 4.92, 3.54 to 1; cen. lvr.; susp., f. ind. coil, r. de Dion coil; 4-door; 4-seat; disc servo brks.; max. 105 m.p.h.; cruise 95; m.p.g. 32; whl. base 8ft. 7¾in.; track, f. 4ft. 5¾in.; r. 4ft. 4½in.; lgth., 14ft. 10½in.; wdth., 5ft. 6¼in.; ht. 4ft. 6¾in.; g.c. 8½in.; turng. cir. 31ft. 6in.; kerb wt. 24¾ cwt.; tank, 12 gals.; 12-volt.

£1,046+£218.9.7. p.t. = £1,264.9.7

   Abbreviations—g.c.—ground clearance; susp.—suspension; f.—front; r.—rear; comp.—compression; s.v.—side-valves; o.h.v.—overhead valves; o.h.c.—overhead camshaft; hyd.—hydraulic.

ROVER 3-LITRE

THIS is one of the finest 3-litre maid-of-all-work cars built anywhere in the world. It has a reputation not only for splendid performance, but for its magnificent road-holding and luxury finish. Its owner-enthusiasts are always impressed by the immaculate condition in which it is delivered, and by its long life with miniscule maintenance. A British car of which to be truly proud.

CLOSE-UP

Six-cyl.; o.h. inlet, side exhaust; 77.8×105 mm.; 2,995 c.c.; 134 b.h.p.; 8.75 to 1 comp.; coil ign.; S.U. carb.; 4-speed, 14.41, 8.07, 5.47, 4.3 to 1, de Normanville overdrive; cen. lvr., BW auto. opt; susp., f. ind. torsion bar, r. half-elliptic; 4-door; 4-seat; hyd. servo brks., disc front; max. 105 m.p.h.; cruise 85; m.p.g. 18-25; whl. base 9ft. 2½in.; track f. 4ft. 7½in., r. 4ft. 8in.; lgth. 15ft. 6½in.; wdth. 5ft. 10in.; ht. 4ft. 11½in.; g.c. 7⅞in.; turng. cir. 40ft.; kerb wt. 32½ cwt.; tank, 14 gals.; 12-volt.

£1,358+£273.9.7 p.t. = £1,641.9.7

SAAB 96

RALLY winner from a famous Swedish aircraft manufacturer who makes fast transport for earth and sky. Assembly line at Trollhattan is efficient and inspection thorough. Saab Sport has fully synchronised gearbox, more power and disc brakes. Saab have gained many rally successes, especially in the hands of ace rallyist and compatriot Erik Carlsson. New feature: brakes linked diagonally front-to-rear with dual master cylinder.

CLOSE-UP

Three-cyl.; two-stroke; 70×72.9 mm.; 841 c.c.; 42 b.h.p.; 7.3 to 1 comp.; coil ign.; Zenith carb;. 3-speed, 17.19, 8.53, 5.23 to 1; col. lvr.; susp, f. ind. coil, r. coil; 2-door; 4/5-seat; hyd. brks.; max. 75 m.p.h.; cruise, 70; m.p.g. 34; whl. base 8ft. 2in.; track f. and r. 4ft.; lgth 13ft. 2in.; wdth. 5ft. 2in.; ht 4ft. 10in.; g.c. 7½in.; turng. cir. 36ft.; kerb wt. 16¼ cwt.; tank, 8½ gals.; 12-volt.

£600+£125.11.2 p.t. = £725.11.2

SABRA SUSSITA

STRUGGLING to become self-supporting, Israel has started a motor industry building three models with Ford engines and plastic bodywork. The Sussita station wagon and Carmel saloon have Anglia engines: the Sabra sports car the Consul 1.7-litre. Reliant helped with body and chassis designs for the latter two. The Carmel uses the Anglia Super engine of 1.2-litres. Carmel and Sabra have independent rear suspension.

CLOSE-UP

Four-cyl.; o.h.v.; 80.97×48.4 mm.; 997 c.c.; 37 b.h.p.; 8.9 to 1 comp.; coil ign.; Solex carb.; 4-speed, 16.98, 9.88, 5.81, 5.41 to 1; cen. lvr.; susp., f. ind. coil, r. half-elliptic; 2-door; 4-seat; hyd. brks.; max. 72 m.p.h.; cruise 62; m.p.g. 38-42; lgth. 12ft. 6in.; wdth. 4ft. 11½in.; ht. 5ft. 5in.; turng. cir. 30ft.; tank, 6 gals.; 12-volt.

SIMCA 1000

INCREASINGLY familiar on British roads, this roomy little rear-engined four-seater has re-established Simca's position in the small car market. Chunky lines enclose a big luggage trunk up front. Four-cylinder engine has five bearings for smoothness at high revs. Tilting it sideways leaves room for the radiator alongside. Fuel tank and battery are also at the rear. Design shows Fiat influence, but Simca is now under Chrysler control.

CLOSE-UP

Four-cyl.; o.h.v.; 68×65 mm.; 944 c.c.; 45 b.h.p.; 7.8 to 1 speed; coil ign.; Solex carb.; 4-speed, 15.51, 9.26, 6.16, 4.21 to 1; cen. lvr.; susp, f. ind. trans. leaf, r. ind. coil; 4-door; 4-seat; hyd. brks.; max. 75 m.p.h.; cruise 70; m.p.g. 35-44; whl. base 7ft. 3½in.; track, f. 4ft. 5in., r. 4ft. 0⅞in.; lgth. 12ft. 5½in.; wdth. 4ft. 10½in.; ht. 4ft. 4½in.; g.c. 5½in.; turng. cir. 30ft.; kerb wt. 14 cwt.; tank, 6½ gals.; 12-volt.

£495+£103.13.9 p.t. = £598.13.9

SIMCA 1300/1500

WELL-PLANNED new family model from a famous French factory, offered with choice of two engines, distinguished by variations in the radiator grille. Photo shows 1300; the 1500 has no vertical bars. Seating comfort and outstanding road holding are the main attractions, apart from the clean uncluttered modern body lines. Rear suspension is by rigid axle on radius arms and coil springs and it works well.

CLOSE-UP
Four-cyl.; o.h.v.; 74×75 mm.; 1,290 c.c.; 62 b.h.p.; or 75.4×83 mm.; 1,482 c.c.; 81 b.h.p.; 8.5/9.5 to I comp.; coil ign.; Solex carb.; 4-speed, 16.22, 9.14, 6.15, 4.45 to I; cen. lvr.; susp., f. ind. coil, r. coil; 4-door; 4-seat; hyd. brks., disc front 1500; max. 85/93 m.p.h.; cruise 70-80; m.p.g. 28-32; whl. base 8ft. 3½in.; track f. 4ft. 4in.; r. 4ft. 3½in.; lgth. 13ft. 11½in.; wdth. 5ft. 2in.; ht. 4ft. 7½in.; g.c. 6in.; turng. cir. 32ft.; kerb wt. 19½-20 cwt.; tank, 12 gals.; 12-volt.

SINGER GAZELLE

EXTENSIVE panel changes modernise the appearance of this moderately priced quality model. Rear doors are larger, headroom is increased. Smaller wheels, disc front brakes, improved suspension and steering, no greasing points. Option of Borg Warner fully automatic transmission. Standard equipment includes heater, screen washers, headlamp flasher, twin sun visors, lockable glove box, overriders and wheel trim discs. Individual front seats.

CLOSE-UP
Four-cyl.; o.h.v.; 81.5×76.2 mm.; 1,592 c.c.; 56.5 b.h.p.; 8.3 to I comp.; coil ign.; Zenith carb.; 4-speed, 14.56, 8.32, 5.41, 3.89 to I; cen. lvr., de Normanville overdrive or BW auto opt.; susp., f. ind. coil, r. half-elliptic; 4-door; 4/5 seat; hyd. brks., disc front; max. 82 m.p.h.; cruise 70; m.p.g. 30-35; whl. base 8ft.; track f. 4ft. 1½in., r. 4ft. 0½in.; lgth. 13ft. 7½in.; wdth. 5ft. 0½in.; ht. 4ft. 10in.; g.c. 6in.; turng. cir. 36ft.; kerb wt. 20¾ cwt.; tank, 10 gals.; 12-volt.

£598+£125.2.11 p.t. = £723.2.11

SINGER VOGUE

PERHAPS the most outstanding safety feature of this car is the superb strength of its all-steel unitary construction. That, and its reputation for being one of the most inexpensive luxury cars on the market. The efficiency of its well-proven 1.6-litre engine and front disc brakes matches the lushness of its interior and seating. All greasing points are eliminated so servicing is necessary only at every 3,000 miles.

CLOSE-UP
Four-cyl.; o.h.v.; 81.5×76.2 mm.; 1,592 c.c.; 62 b.h.p.; 8.3 to I comp.; coil ign.; Solex carb.; 4-speed, 13.013, 8.324, 5.413, 3.889 to I; de Normanville overdrive or BW auto. opt.; cen. lvr.; susp., f. ind. coil, r. half-elliptic; 4-door; 4/5-seat; hyd. brks., disc front; max. 84 m.p.h.; cruise 70; m.p.g. 28-32; whl. base 8ft. 5in.; track f. 4ft. 3½in., r. 4ft. 0½in.; lgth. 13ft. 9½in.; wdth. 5ft. 2½in.; ht. 4ft. 10½in.; g.c. 6½in.; turng cir. 36ft.; kerb wt. 21½ cwt.; tank, 11 gals.; 12-volt.

£685+£143.5.5 p.t. = £828.5.5

SKODA OCTAVIA

CZECHOSLOVAKIAN light car at a low price that has won it a place on British roads. Backbone chassis and all-independent suspension. Standard engine is 1,089 c.c. and gives about 77 m.p.h. maximum. There is a faster model, the Super with 1,221 c.c. which does 80, and the twin-carburetter Touring Sport model which does 85. The latter is available with convertible bodywork. There are station wagons too.

CLOSE-UP
Four-cyl.; o.h.v.; 68×75 mm.; 1,089 c.c.; 43 b.h.p.; 7.5 to I comp.; coil ign.; Jikov carb.; 4-speed, 20.4, 11.8, 7.6, 4.78 to I; col. lvr.; susp., f. ind. coil, r. ind. transv. leaf; 2-door; 4-seat; hyd. brks.; max. 77 m.p.h.; cruise 65; m.p.g. 35-40; whl. base 7ft. 10½in.; track, f. 3ft. 11½in., r. 4ft. 1in.; lgth. 13ft. 4in.; wdth. 5ft. 3in.; ht 4ft. 8½in.; g.c. 6½in.; turng. cir. 32ft. 9in.; kerb wt. 17¾ cwt.; tank, 6½ gals.; 12-volt.

£430.15+£90.7.3 p.t. = £521.2.3

Abbreviations—g.c.—ground clearance; susp.—suspension; f.—front; r.—rear; comp.—compression; s.v.—side-valves; o.h.v.—overhead valves; o.h.c.—overhead camshaft; hyd.—hydraulic.

STUDEBAKER AVANTI

SOME like it hot and this ultra modern Raymond Loewy styled sports car can certainly go. With V8 engine of 4.7-litres and the optional Paxton supercharger, it will reach a maximum of 140 m.p.h. Body is plastic and brakes are discs. Choice of three- or four-speed gearbox or Borg Warner automatic. Headlamps are enclosed in squared-off bezels for 1964.

CLOSE-UP

Eight-cyl.; o.h.v.; 90.4×92 mm.; 4,737 c.c.; 220 b.h.p.; 10 to 1 comp.; coil ign.; downdraught carb., supercharger opt.; 3-speed, 8.94, 5.48, 3.73 to 1; cen. lvr.; susp., f. ind. coil, r. half elliptic and radius arms; 2-door; 4/5-seat; hyd. servo brks., disc front; max. 112 m.p.h.; cruise 95; m.p.g. 17-20; whl. base 9ft. 1in.; track f. 4ft. $9\frac{3}{8}$in., r. 4ft. $8\frac{5}{8}$in.; lgth. 16ft. $0\frac{3}{8}$in.; wdth. 5ft. $10\frac{3}{8}$in.; ht. 4ft. $5\frac{7}{8}$in.; g.c. 7in.; kerb wt. $28\frac{1}{2}$ cwt.; 12-volt.

£2,119+£484 p.t.=£2,603

STUDEBAKER LARK

CHALLENGER is the new name attached to this model, one of the pioneers in the American move to compact cars, to emphasise that it has grown longer and isn't campact any more. The United States industry is launched on another longer-lower-wider cycle. Studebaker offers seven engines and six transmissions for 1964 and on sports models a dash-mounted exhaust gas analyser which ought to start sports fans talking.

CLOSE-UP

Six-cyl.; o.h.v.; 76.2×101.6 mm.; 2,785 c.c.; 112 b.h.p.; 8.25 to 1 comp.; coil ign.; Stromberg carb.; 3-speed, 9.58, 5.78, 3.73 to 1; col. lvr., auto. opt.; susp., f. ind. coil, r. half-elliptic; 4-door; 5-seat; hyd. brks., servo opt.; max. 88 m.p.h.; cruise 75; m.p.g. 20-24; whl. base 9ft. 1in.; track f. 4ft. $9\frac{3}{8}$in., r. 4ft. $8\frac{7}{8}$in.; lgth. 15ft. 10in.; wdth. 5ft. $11\frac{1}{2}$in.; ht. 4ft. $6\frac{7}{8}$in.; g.c. 6in.; turng. cir. 37ft. 6in.; kerb wt. $25\frac{1}{4}$ cwt.; tank, $14\frac{3}{4}$ gals.; 12-volt.

£1,168.7.6+£265.19.9 p.t.=£1,434.7.3

SUNBEAM ALPINE

HERE is an exciting model that comes in two versions—as a sports tourer and a grand touring model. The seat and foot controls alone offer a range of 64 different adjustments. It has servo-assisted front disc brakes, a capacious luggage compartment and a top speed of 100 miles an hour. Rootes engineers have drawn liberally on Sunbeam's racing and rally experience to produce this fine car.

CLOSE-UP

Four-cyl.; o.h.v.; 81.5×76.2 mm.; 1,592 c.c.; 85.5 b.h.p.; 9.1 to 1 comp.; coil ign.; Solex 2-choke carb.; 4-speed, 13.013, 8.324, 5.413, 3.89 to 1; cen. lvr.; de Normanville overdrive opt.; susp., f. ind. coil, r. half-elliptic; 2-door; 2-seat; hyd. brks., disc front; max. 100 m.p.h.; cruise 80; m.p.g. 25; whl. base 7ft. 2in.; track f. 4ft. 3in., r. 4ft. $0\frac{1}{2}$in.; lgth. 12ft. $11\frac{1}{4}$in.; wdth. 5ft. $0\frac{1}{2}$in.; ht. 4ft. $3\frac{1}{2}$in.; g.c. 5in.; turng. cir. 34ft.; kerb wt. $19\frac{1}{4}$ cwt.; tank, 9 gals.; 12-volt.

£695+£145.7.1 p.t.=£840.7.1

SUNBEAM RAPIER

RE-STYLED, with lower lines and smaller wheels, the Rapier now features a top covered in synthetic hide in a choice of four colours. New front suspension adds comfort, eliminates greasing. Front seats are new with increased legroom and backrest adjustment. Engine, with new compound carburetter instead of previous twins, gains $3\frac{3}{4}$ horsepower. Brakes are now servo-assisted. Steering column is adjustable, tyres are nylon cord.

CLOSE-UP

Four-cyl.; o.h.v.; 81.5×76.2 mm.; 1,592 c.c.; 84 b.h.p.; 9.1 to 1 comp.; coil ign.; Solex carb.; 4-speed, 13.013, 8.324, 5.413, 3.89 to 1; cen lvr.; de Normanville overdrive opt.; susp., f. ind. coil, r. half-elliptic; 2-door; 4-seat; hyd. servo brks., disc front.; max. 95 m.p.h.; cruise 80; m.p.g. 25-30; whl. base 8ft.; track f. 4ft. $1\frac{3}{4}$in., r. 4ft. $0\frac{1}{2}$in.; lgth. 13ft. $6\frac{1}{2}$in.; wdth. 5ft. 1in.; ht. 4ft. $10\frac{1}{2}$in.; g.c. $5\frac{3}{4}$in.; turng. cir. 36ft.; kerb wt. 21 cwt.; tank 10 gals.; 12-volt.

£725+£151.12.1 p.t.=£876.12.1

Abbreviations—g.c.—ground clearance; susp.—suspension; f.—front; r.—rear; comp.—compression; s.v.—side-valves; o.h.v.—overhead valves; o.h.c.—overhead camshaft; hyd.—hydraulic.

TRABANT

FIRST appearance in Britain of an East German small car built in a state-controlled factory at Zwickau, once owned by Auto Union. Engine is an air-cooled two-cylinder two-stroke of 594 c.c., driving the front wheels. A more powerful model with bigger engine is on the way. The gearbox has synchromesh on all four speeds. Steering is by rack and pinion. Suspension is all-independent, using transverse leaf springs.

CLOSE-UP
Two-cyl.; two stroke air-cooled; 72×73 mm.; 594 c.c.; 23 b.h.p.; 7.6 to 1 comp.; coil ign.; BVF carb.; 4-speed, 17.66, 10.04, 6.58, 4.45 to 1; dash lvr.; susp., f. and r. ind. transv. leaf; 2-door; 4-seat; hyd. brks.; max. 62 m.p.h.; cruise 58; m.p.g. 40; whl. base, 6ft. 7⅝in.; track f. 3ft. 11 11/16 in., r. 4ft. 1 7/16 in.; lgth. 11ft. 0 6/16 in.; wdth. 4ft. 10¾in.; ht. 4ft. 7½in.; g.c. 6in.; turng. cir. 31ft.; kerb wt. 12½ cwt.; tank, 5¼ gals.; 6-volt.

TRIUMPH 2000

STANDARD'S Vanguard, first British post-war car, has reached the end of the line. Its successor is this Michelotti-styled Triumph with a six-cylinder 2-litre engine already proved in service, four-speed fully synchronised gearbox and disc brakes. Like the Herald, it has all-independent suspension for riding comfort over poor roads, but the system is different, with semi-trailing wishbones at the rear.

CLOSE-UP
Six-cyl.; o.h.v.; 74.7×76 mm.; 1,998 c.c.; 90 b.h.p.; 8.5 to 1 comp.; coil ign.; 2 Stromberg carbs.; 4-speed, 13.45, 8.61, 5.68, 4.1 to 1; cen. lvr.; susp., f. and r. ind. coil; 4-door; 5-seat; hyd. servo brks., disc front; max. 95 m.p.h.; cruise 85; m.p.g. 23-25; whl. base 8ft. 10in.; track f. 4ft. 6in., r. 4ft. 2⅜in.; lgth. 14ft. 5¾in.; wdth. 5ft. 5in.; ht. 4ft. 6½in.; g.c. 7in.; turng. cir. 31ft.; kerb wt. 23¾ cwt.; tank, 14 gals.; 12-volt.
£905+£189.2 p.t. = £1,094.2

TRIUMPH HERALD 12/50

HIGHLY original engineering and Michelotti styling formed the recipe for this Standard-Triumph best-seller. Latest version is the 12-50 with extra engine power, disc front brakes, folding roof. Heralds led the way to minimum maintenance; are noted for their excellent driving position and taxi-like turning ability. Range includes saloon, convertible and station wagon, all with backbone chassis and body panels removable for repair.

CLOSE-UP
Four-cyl.; o.h.v.; 69.3×76 mm.; 1,147 c.c.; 51 b.h.p.; 8.5 to 1 comp.; coil ign.; Solex carb.; 4-speed, 15.40, 8.87, 5.73, 4.11 to 1; cen. lvr.; susp., f. ind. coil, r. ind. transv. leaf; 2-door; 4-seat; hyd. brks., disc front; max. 77 m.p.h.; cruise 70; m.p.g. 30-32; whl. base 7ft. 7½in.; track f. 4ft., r. 4ft.; lgth. 12ft. 9in.; wdth. 5ft.; ht. 4ft. 4in.; g.c. 6¾in.; turng. cir. 26ft. 3in.; kerb wt. 16½ cwt.; tank, 6¼ gals.; 12-volt.
£525+£109.18.9 p.t. = £634.18.9

TRIUMPH T.R.4

ONE of the best-known, and a well-tried British sports car, this model continues to rank among the best sellers, both here and abroad. It is compact, available as a hard-top, and is a favourite with all sports car enthusiasts. Top speed exceeds 110 m.p.h., yet in traffic it is as docile as a pekingese on a lead. Its roomier body, wider track and synchromesh on all four speeds have proved a great success.

CLOSE-UP
Four-cyl.; o.h.v.; 86×92 mm.; 2,138 c.c.; 105 b.h.p.; 9 to 1 comp.; coil ign.; 2 S.U. carbs.; 4-speed, 11.61, 7.44, 4.9, 3.7 to 1; cen. lvr.; susp., f. ind. coil, r. half-elliptic; 2-door; 2/3-seat; hyd. brks., disc front; max. 110 m.p.h.; cruise 95; m.p.g. 25; whl. base 7ft. 4in.; track f. 4ft. 1in., r. 4ft.; lgth. 13ft.; width 4ft. 9½in.; ht. 4ft. 2in.; g.c. 6in.; turng. cir. 33ft.; kerb wt. 20 cwt.; tank, 11¾ gals.; 12-volt.
£750+£156.16.3 p.t. = £906.16.3

Abbreviations—g.c.—ground clearance; susp.—suspension; f.—front; r.—rear; comp.—compression; s.v.—side-valves; o.h.v.—overhead valves; o.h.c.—overhead camshaft; hyd.—hydraulic.

TRIUMPH SPITFIRE 4

USING main components of the Herald 1200 chassis but with shorter wheelbase and power raised to 63 h.p., Triumph have scored a success in the low-priced sports car market. Two carburetters and disc brakes are extra amenities and as on 1200 there is little greasing to bother about. Bucket type seats, adjustable fore and aft, winding glass windows and a heater for snug winter motoring.

CLOSE-UP
Four-cyl.; o.h.v.; 69.3×76 mm.; 1,147 c.c.; 63 b.h.p.; 9 to 1 comp.; coil ign.; 2 S.U. carbs; 4-speed; 15.40, 8.87, 5.73, 4.11 to 1; cen. lvr.; susp., f. ind. coil, r. ind. transv. leaf; 2-door; 2-seat; hyd. brks.; max. 93 m.p.h.; cruise 80; m.p.g. 35-40; whl. base 6ft. 11in.; track f. 4ft. 1in., r. 4ft.; lgth. 12ft. 1in.; wdth. 4ft. 9in.; ht. 3ft. 11½in.; g.c. 5in.; turng. cir. 24ft.; kerb wt. 14 cwt.; tank, 9 gals.; 12-volt.

£530 + £110.19.7 p.t. = £640.19.7

TRIUMPH VITESSE

SMOOTHNESS of a small six-cylinder engine in a chassis with all-independent suspension like the Herald. Four headlamps for fast night driving and disc front brakes. Detachable body panels for easy repair, and collapsible steering column to protect the driver in the event of a crash. Wings and bonnet tip forward for easy access to the engine; chassis greasing is almost eliminated.

CLOSE-UP
Six-cyl.; o.h.v.; 66.75×76 mm.; 1,596 c.c.; 70 b.h.p.; 8.75 to 1 comp.; coil ign.; 2 Solex carbs.; 4-speed, 12.06, 7.31, 5.16, 4.11 to 1; cen. lvr., de Normanville overdrive opt.; susp., f. ind. coil, r. ind. transv. leaf; 2-door; 4-seat; hyd. brks., disc front; max. 88 m.p.h.; cruise 75-80; m.p.g. 28-35; whl. base 7ft. 7½in.; track f. 4ft. 1in., r. 4ft.; lgth. 12ft. 9in.; wdth. 5ft.; ht. 4ft. 4½in. g.c. 6¾in.; turng. cir. 25ft.; kerb wt. 18¼ cwt.; tank, 8¾ gals.; 12-volt.

£608 + £127.4.7 p.t. = £735.4.7

VALIANT

SMALLEST car from the Chrysler group but massive by British standards, Valiant has a six-cylinder engine of 2.7 litres which gives over 90 m.p.h. Three-speed or automatic gearbox and hydraulic brakes with option of servo assistance. Choice of hardtop coupe, saloon, convertible and estate car. Changes for 1964 include more horizontal grille and higher tail lights.

CLOSE-UP
Six-cyl.; o.h.v.; 86×79 mm.; 2,789 c.c.; 100 b.h.p.; 8.2 to 1 comp.; coil ign.; Ball-Ball or Holley carb.; 3-speed auto., 9.53, 5.85, 3.23 to 1; press button control; susp., f. ind. torsion bar, r. half-elliptic; 4-door; 6-seat; hyd. brks.; max. 100 m.p.h.; cruise 85; m.p.g. 18-22; whl. base 8ft. 10½in.; track f. 4ft. 8in., r. 4ft. 7½in.; lgth. 15ft. 6½in.; wdth. 5ft. 9½in.; ht. 4ft. 5½in.; g.c. 6½in.; turng. cir. 36ft. 4in.; kerb wt. 24cwt.; tank, 11 gals.; 12-volt.

VANDEN PLAS PRINCESS 4-LITRE

HERE is a big luxury car selling at a most reasonable cost. Either chauffeur or owner-driven the model has all the plush majesty of a long established coachbuilding company allied to the tremendous know-how of the British Motor Corporation. It is, in fact, the largest model the Corporation builds, combining a powerful 4-litre engine with all-round sumptuousness inside.

CLOSE-UP
Six-cyl.; o.h.v.; 87.3×111 mm.; 3,993 c.c.; 6.8 to 1 comp.; coil ign.; Stromberg carb.; 4-speed, 15.1, 10.3, 6.4, 4.4 to 1; col. lvr., RR Hydra-matic auto. opt.; susp., f. ind. coil, r. half-elliptic; 4-door; 8-seat; hyd. brks.; max. 100 m.p.h.; cruise, 80; m.p.g. 16-19; whl. base, 11ft. 0⅜in.; track f. 4ft. 10½in., r. 5ft. 2¼in.; lgth. 17ft. 11in.; wdth. 6ft. 2½in.; ht. 5ft. 10in.; g.c. 6½in.; turng. cir. 45ft. 6in.; kerb wt. 41¾ cwt.; tank, 16 gals.; 12-volt.

£2,350 + £496.2.11 p.t. = £2,846.2.11

Abbreviations—g.c.—ground clearance; susp.—suspension; f.—front; r.—rear; comp.—compression; s.v.—side-valves; o.h.v.—overhead valves; o.h.c.—overhead camshaft; hyd.—hydraulic.

VAUXHALL VIVA

LUTON'S long-awaited baby is born at last. Designed to one better than its competitors, the Viva offers more body length, width, luggage space, performance, fuel economy with low maintenance costs. Four points to grease at 30,000 miles. First British model to have acrylic lacquer high-gloss finish. Safety features include drop-centre steering wheel, anti-burst door locks, safety-zone windscreen.

CLOSE-UP

Four-cyl.; o.h.v.; 74.3×60.9 mm.; 1,057 c.c.; 44.2 b.h.p.; 8.5 to 1 comp.; coil ign.; Zenith carb.; 4-speed, 15.53, 9.12, 5.79, 4.125 to 1; cen. lvr.; susp., f. ind. transv. leaf, r. half-elliptic; 2-door; 4-seat; hyd. brks., disc opt.; max. 80 m.p.h.; cruise 70; m.p.g. 40-45; whl. base 7ft. 7½in.; track f. 3ft. 11⅜in.; r. 4ft. 0¼in.; lgth. 12ft. 11⅛in.; wdth. 4ft. 11⅜in.; ht. 4ft. 5⅜in.; g.c. 5in.; turng. cir. 27ft. 4in.; kerb wt. 14 cwt.; tank, 7 gals.; 12-volt.

£436+£91.7.11 p.t.=£527.7.11

VAUXHALL CRESTA

CRESTA, the biggest and most expensive Vauxhall model, has axle ratio changed from 3.7 to 3.9 to 1 for smoother top gear performance in traffic and better hill climbing. The optional Hydra-Matic transmission now costs only £115 extra tax paid. Interior trim of Cresta is in leather or a new nylon-suede material. Entire underbody gets a treatment of bituminous sealing against winter salt, mud and gravel.

CLOSE-UP

Six-cyl.; o.h.v.; 82.55×82.55 mm.; 2,651 c.c.; 113 b.h.p.; 8.5 to 1 comp.; coil ign.; Zenith carb.; 3-speed, 11.2, 6.4, 3.9 to 1; col. lvr. overdrive or Hydra-matic auto. opt.; susp., f. ind. coil, r. half-elliptic; 4-door; 6-seat; hyd. brks. disc front; max. 96 m.p.h.; cruise 80; m.p.g. 20-25; whl. base 8ft. 11½in.; track f. 4ft. 6¾in., r. 4ft. 8⅛in.; lgth. 15ft. 1¾in.; wdth. 5ft. 10⅜in.; ht. 4ft. 8⅝in.; g.c. 6½in.; turng. cir. 36ft. 6in.; kerb wt. 23¾ cwt.; tank, 10¾ gals.; 12-volt.

£780+£163.1.3 p.t.=£943.1.3

VAUXHALL VELOX

FOR smoother top-gear performance in traffic and more urge to top-gear hill-climbing this robust family car has its standard axle ratio changed from 3.7 to 1 to 3.9 to 1. It has also been given new and distinctive trim styles. With a well-proven engine it will motor docilely in town and with dash in the country. First class for family and business needs.

CLOSE-UP

Six-cyl.; o.h.v.; 82.55×82.55 mm.; 2,651 c.c.; 113 b.h.p.; 8.5 to 1 comp.; coil ign.; Zenith carb.; 3-speed, 11.2, 6.4, 3.9 to 1; col. lvr. overdrive or Hydra-matic auto. opt.; susp., f. ind. coil, r. half-elliptic; 4-door; 6-seat; hyd. brks. disc front; max. 96 m.p.h.; cruise 80; m.p.g. 20-25; whl. base 8ft. 11½in.; track f. 4ft. 6¾in., r. 4ft. 8⅛in.; lgth. 15ft. 1¾in.; wdth. 5ft. 10⅜in.; ht. 4ft. 8⅝in.; g.c. 6½in.; turng. cir. 36ft. 6in.; kerb wt. 23½ cwt.; tank, 10¾ gals.; 12-volt.

£695+£145.7.1 p.t.=£840.7.1

VAUXHALL VICTOR

THIS best-seller now has more punch with a bigger engine and more stopping-power with larger brakes. It has 69 b.h.p. against 56.3 h.p.; engine size is increased from 1,508 c.c. to 1,594 c.c. The stroke is unchanged, the bore is larger. Additions also include a new aluminium grille, a smart new rear number-plate, easier-to-handle controls and more inviting trim styles. Estate Car is shown.

CLOSE-UP

Four-cyl.; o.h.v.; 81.63×76.2 mm.; 1,594 c.c.; 69 b.h.p.; 8.5 to 1 comp.; coil ign.; Zenith carb.; 3-speed, 13.2, 6.74, 4.125 to 1, 4-speed opt.; col. lvr.; susp., f. ind. coil, r. half-elliptic; 5-door; 5-seat; hyd. brks., disc opt.; max. 80 m.p.h.; cruise 70; m.p.g. 28-34; whl. base 8ft. 4in.; track f. 4ft. 2¾in., r. 4ft. 4⅜in.; lgth. 14ft. 5¼in.; wdth. 5ft. 4in.; ht. 4ft. 8in.; g.c. 7in.; turng. cir. 33ft. 6in.; kerb wt. 19¾ cwt.; tank, 10 gals.; 12-volt.

£525+£109.18.9 p.t.=£634.18.9

Abbreviations—g.c.—ground clearance; susp.—suspension; f.—front; r.—rear; comp.—compression; s.v.—side-valves; o.h.v.—overhead valves; o.h.c.—overhead camshaft; hyd.—hydraulic.

VAUXHALL VX4/90

ON this twin-carburetter luxury version of the Victor, engine goes up to 1,594, which gives 90 plus m.p.h. Recognise it by new grille and rear number plate grouping, increased front bumper height and new emblem on the side. Facia panel is grained veneer and full width parcel shelf with padded edge is standard. Front passenger has sturdy grab handle to hold on to when motoring fast.

CLOSE-UP

Four-cyl.; o.h.v.; 81.63×76.2 mm.; 1,594 c.c.; 85 b.h.p.; 9.3 to 1 comp.; coil ign.; 2 Zenith carbs; 4-speed, 12.83, 8.30, 5.28, 3.9 to 1; cen. lvr.; susp., f. ind. coil, r. half-elliptic; 4-door; 5-seat; hyd. servo brks., disc front; max. 91 m.p.h.; cruise 80; m.p.g. 28-32; whl. base 8ft. 4in.; track f. 4ft. 3½in., r. 4ft. 2½in.; lgth. 14ft. 5½in.; wdth. 5ft. 4in.; ht. 4ft. 7½in.; g.c. 7in.; turng. cir. 33ft. 6in.; kerb wt. 19⅞ cwt.; tank, 10 gals.; 12-volt.

£695+£145.7.1 p.t. = £840.7.1

VOLGA

CARBURETTER changes give an extra 5 h.p. and a central gear lever is now fitted on this solidly built Russian model. Telescopic dampers are fitted all round, the reclining backrests are simplified; interior trim is improved, bumpers and grille redesigned. Heater, radio, electric clock, two-speed wipers, cigar lighter, remote-control radiator shutters, handbrake warning light, starting handle and full toolkit are standard equipment.

CLOSE-UP

Four-cyl.; o.h.v.; 92×92 mm.; 2,445 c.c.; 85 b.h.p.; 7.5 to 1 comp.; coil ign.; downdraught carb.; 3-speed, 14.911, 8.072, 4.556 to 1; cen. lvr.; susp., f. ind. coil, r. half-elliptic; 4-door; 6-seat; hyd. brks.; max. 84 m.p.h.; cruise 60; m.p.g. 30; whl. base 8ft. 10in.; track f. 4ft. 7½in., r. 4ft. 8in.; lgth. 15ft. 10in.; wdth. 5ft. 11in.; ht. 5ft. 4in.; g.c. 7½in.; turng. cir. 42ft.; kerb wt. 27¾ cwt.; tank, 13 gals.; 12-volt.

£742+£155.2.11 p.t. = £897.2.11

VOLKSWAGEN DE LUXE

FOR the first time, sales of Europe's most successful car are levelling off in Germany, but its position as No. 1 is not yet challenged. Changes for 1964 include new number plate lamp and door handles, levers instead of horn ring, and option of metal sun roof instead of fabric. Fine finish, durability, good service and its "unbreakable" feel on motorways will keep it in demand for a long time yet.

CLOSE-UP

Four-cyl.; o.h.v.; air-cooled; 77×64 mm.; 1,192 c.c.; 40 b.h.p.; 7 to 1 comp.; coil ign.; Solex carb.; 4-speed, 16.63, 9.01, 5.77, 3.89 to 1; cen. lvr.; susp., f. and r. ind. torsion bars; 2-door; 4-seat; hyd. brks.; max. 72 m.p.h.; cruise 72; m.p.g. 38; whl. base 7ft. 10½in.; track f. 4ft. 3in., r. 4ft. 2½in.; lgth. 13ft. 4½in.; width 5ft. 0½in.; ht. 4ft. 11in.; g.c. 6in.; turng. cir. 36ft.; kerb wt. 14½ cwt.; tank, 8¾ gals.; 6-volt.

£517+£108.5.5 p.t. = £625.5.5

VOLKSWAGEN 1500

CONTINUATION of the single carburetter 45 h.p. model or a new twin-carburetter 54 h.p. model at a higher price are options on this 1½-litre from Europe's biggest manufacturer. Braking area is increased, improved thermostatic control for cooling air should give better heater output on short runs and interior heat distribution is by levers instead of turn-knobs. Chromium strips along the sides identify the twin-carb 1500S.

CLOSE-UP

Four-cyl.; o.h.v. air cooled; 83×69 mm.; 1,493 c.c.; 45 b.h.p.; 7.8 to 1 comp.; coil ign.; Solex carb. (1500S 2 carbs., 54 b.h.p.); 4-speed, 15.67, 8.50, 5.44, 3.67 to 1; cen. lvr.; susp., f. and r. ind. torsion bar; 2-door; 4-seat; hyd. brks.; max. 81-84 m.p.h.; cruise 81; m.p.g. 30; whl. base 7ft. 10½in.; track f. 4ft. 3½in., r. 4ft. 5in.; lgth. 13ft. 10½in.; wdth. 5ft. 3½in.; ht. 4ft. 10in.; g.c. 6in.; turng. cir. 36ft.; kerb wt. 17¼ cwt.; tank, 8¾ gals.; 6-volt.

£747.10+£156.5.10 p.t. = £903.15.10

VOLKSWAGEN KARMANN-GHIA

TWIN carburetters give a boost in power which is said to raise maximum speed of the distinctive Italian-styled 1500 cc. models to 90 mph. Improved brakes match the extra speed and the four-speed all-synchromesh gearbox is famous for precision of control. There are two models, coupe and convertible, with space for luggage at front and rear. Karmann also builds the shapely 1200 coupe and convertible styled by Ghia.

CLOSE-UP
Four-cyl.; o.h.v.; air-cooled; 83×69 mm.; 1,493 c.c.; 54 b.h.p.; 8.5 to 1 comp.; coil ign.; 2 Solex carbs.; 4-speed, 15.67, 8.50, 5.44, 3.67 to 1; cen. lvr.; susp., f. and r. ind. torsion bar; 2-door; 2/4-seat; hyd. brks.; max. 90 m.p.h.; cruise 90; m.p.g. 34; whl. base 7ft. 10½in.; track f. 4ft. 3½in., r. 4ft. 5in.; lgth. 14ft. 0⅜in.; wdth. 5ft. 3⅞in.; ht. 4ft. 5⅜in.; g.c. 5¼in.; turng. cir. 36ft. 4in.; kerb wt. 18½ cwt.; tank, 8¼ gals.; 6-volt.
£835+£174.10.5 p.t. = £1,009.10.5

VOLVO 122S

ROBUST contender from Sweden, the Volvo 122S offers stylish Scandinavian design with superfine finish and quick acceleration. Twin carburetter engine of 1.8-litres gives top speed of about 100 m.p.h. Front brakes are Girling discs, gearbox has four speeds synchronised—de Normanville overdrive is optional. Volvo range now includes saloons and station wagons with two or four doors, built to stand up to northern winters.

CLOSE-UP
Four-cyl.; o.h.v.; 84.14×80 mm.; 1,780 c.c.; 90 b.h.p.; 8.5 to 1 comp.; coil ign.; 2 S.U. carbs.; 4-speed 12.8, 8.16, 5.58, 4.1 to 1; cen. lvr.; overdrive opt., susp., f. ind. coil, r. coil; 4-door; 5-seat; hyd. brks., disc front; max. 100 m.p.h.; cruise 85; m.p.g. 28-36; whl. base 8ft. 6½in.; track f. and r. 4ft. 3½in.; lgth. 14ft. 7¼in.; wdth. 5ft. 3⅜in.; ht. 4ft. 11½in.; g.c. 7¼in.; turng. cir. 32ft.; kerb wt. 22 cwt.; tank, 10 gals.; 12-volt.
£940+£196.7.11 p.t. = £1,136.7.11

VOLVO P.1800

VERVE and virile styling mark out this potent Swedish coupe with stout engine of 1.8 litres under the bonnet. Brakes in front are discs, rear are drums, all with servo assistance and the gearbox has four speeds all synchronised. Seats for two with adjustable backrests, plus two occasional seats for children. P.1800 is built in England by Pressed Steel and Jensen with Swedish mechanical parts.

CLOSE-UP
Four-cyl.; o.h.v.; 84.14×80 mm.; 1,780 c.c.; 100 b.h.p.; 9.5 to 1 comp.; coil ign.; 2 S.U. carbs.; 4-speed, 14.27, 9.07, 6.2, 4.5 to 1; cen. lvr. overdrive; susp., f. ind. coil, r. coil; 2-door; 2/4-seat; servo brks., disc front; max. 110 m.p.h.; cruise 95; m.p.g. 28-30; whl. base 8ft. 0½in.; track f. and r. 4ft. 3½in.; lgth. 14ft. 5¼in.; wdth. 5ft. 7in.; ht. 4ft. 2½in.; g.c. 6in.; turng. cir. 31ft.; kerb wt. 24 cwt.; tank, 10 gals.; 12-volt.
£1,366+£285.2.11 p.t. = £1,651.2.11

WARTBURG

KNOWN in Northern Europe but new to Britain, East Germany's Wartburg is built in a former Auto Union factory at Eisenach. It has a water-cooled three-cylinder two-stroke engine driving the front wheels. Body styles are 4-door saloon, 2-door coupe, 2-door station wagon and a 4-door "camping wagon" with folding top, and side windows curving into the roof. An automatic clutch is optional.

CLOSE-UP
Three-cyl.; two-stroke; 73.5×78 mm.; 991 c.c.; 50 b.h.p.; 7.3 to 1 comp.; coil ign.; BVF carb.; 4-speed, 15.89, 10.35, 6.55, 4.62 to 1; col. lvr.; susp., f. ind. transv. leaf, r. transv. leaf; 4-door; 4/5-seat; hyd. brks.; max. 77 m.p.h.; cruise 70; m.p.g. 30-32; whl. base 8ft. 0½in.; track f. 3ft. 10½in., r. 4ft. 1½in.; lgth. 14ft. 1½in.; wdth. 5ft. 1⅜in.; ht. 4ft. 9in.; g.c. 7½in.; turng. cir. 39ft. 9in.; kerb wt. 18½ cwt.; tank, 9⅝ gals.; 6-volt.

WOLSELEY HORNET

UNDERPOWERED in its original form, the Hornet now buzzes along faster with a larger 998 c.c. engine which gives an extra four horse-power. Front brakes are larger too. Same side-ways engine and front-drive system as the Mini and the same excellent rubber suspension. The front end has a scaled down traditional Wolseley radiator grille. A good-sized boot is obtained with the extended tail and the wings house tail and stop lights.

CLOSE-UP

Four-cyl.; o.h.v.; 64.58×76.2 mm.; 998 c.c.; 38 b.h.p.; 8.3 to 1 comp.; coil ign.; S.U. carb.; 4-speed, 13.657, 8.176, 5.317, 3.765 to 1; cen. lvr.; susp., f. and r. ind. rubber; 2-door; 4-seat; hyd. brks.; max. 74 m.p.h.; cruise 65; m.p.g. 42-45; whl. base 6ft. 8⅛in.; track f. 3ft. 11¾in., r. 3ft. 9⅞in.; lgth. 10ft. 8¾in.; wdth. 4ft. 7½in.; ht. 4ft. 5in.; g.c. 6⅜in.; turng. cir. 31ft.; kerb wt. 11¾ cwt.; tank, 5½ gals.; 12-volt.

£460+£96.7.11 p.t.=£556.7.11

WOLSELEY 16/60

HERE is a car for the motorist who likes the tradition of Wolseleys and the forward thinking of the record-breaking British Motor Corporation. It is stylish and sturdy. Luxuries include leather over foam-rubber cushions, and pile carpet with underfelt covering the entire floor. Driving motions are reduced by as much as 70 per cent with the optional fitting of the Borg-Warner automatic transmission.

CLOSE-UP

Four-cyl.; o.h.v.; 76.2×88.9 mm.; 1,622 c.c.; 55 b.h.p.; 8.3 to 1 comp.; coil ign.; S.U. carb.; 4-speed, 15.64, 9.52, 5.91, 4.3 to 1; cen. lvr. BW auto. opt.; susp., f. ind. coil, r. half-elliptic; 4-door; 4-seat; hyd. brks.; max. 80; m.p.h.; cruise 70; m.p.g. 26-33; whl. base 8ft. 4½in.; track f. 4ft. 2⅝in., r. 4ft. 3⅜in.; lgth. 14ft. 6½in.; wdth. 5ft. 3½in.; ht. 4ft. 10⅞in.; g.c. 5⅞in.; turng. cir. 37ft.; kerb wt. 22½ cwt.; tank, 10 gals.; 12-volt.

£692.10+£134.16.8.p.t.=£837.6. 8.

WOLSELEY 6/110

LARGEST of the Wolseleys is this capacious six-seater with 3-litre engine. Styled by Pininfarina, it has been on the market since 1959 but power has been increased to 128 h.p. giving top speed of 104 m.p.h. Gearbox is three-speed with Borg Warner overdrive or buyers can order the Borg Warner automatic. Brakes are discs at the front with vacuum servo. Interior offers armchair comfort for four passengers and driver.

CLOSE-UP

Six-cyl.; o.h.v.; 83.34×88.9 mm.; 2,912 c.c.; 120 b.h.p.; 8.23 to 1 comp.; coil ign.; 2 S.U. carbs.; 3-speed, 12.09, 6.45, 3.9 to 1 overdrive; cen. lvr., BW. auto. opt.; susp., f. ind. coil, r. half-elliptic; 4-door; 5-seat; hyd. servo brks., disc front; max. 104 m.p.h.; cruise 85; m.p.g. 22-24; whl. base 9ft. 2in.; track f. 4ft. 5¾in., r. 4ft. 5¼in.; lgth. 15ft. 7½in.; wdth. 5ft. 8½in.; ht. 5ft. 0½in.; g.c. 6¼in.; turng. cir. 41ft.; kerb wt., 31 cwt.; tank, 16 gals.; 12-volt.

£920+£192.4.7.p.t.=£1,112.4.7.

WOLSELEY 1500

COMPACT and sturdily built, this is a real family favourite. Extra large windows, interior finished in leather and walnut veneer—these are part of the Wolseley craftsmanship. Good performance comes from 1½-litre overhead-valve engine and four-speed gearbox. It is a car that has proved its worth beyond doubt. An individualistic car, snappy and easy on the eye.

CLOSE-UP

Four-cyl.; o.h.v.; 73×88.9 mm.; 1,489 c.c.; 53 b.h.p.; 8.3 to 1 comp.; coil ign.; S.U. carb.; 4-speed, 13.56, 8.25, 5.12, 3.73 to 1; cen. lvr.; susp., f. ind. torsion bar, r. half-elliptic; 4-door; 4/5-seat; hyd. brks.; max. 78 m.p.h.; cruise 70; m.p.g. 30-35; whl. base 7ft. 2in.; track f. 4ft. 2⅞in., r. 4ft. 2¼in.; lgth. 12ft. 9¼in.; wdth. 5ft. 1in.; ht. 4ft. 11in.; g.c. 6½in.; turng. cir. 34ft.; kerb wt. 17¾ cwt.; tank, 7 gals.; 12-volt.

£550+£95.2.11 p.t.=£665.2.11

Abbreviations—g.c.—ground clearance; susp.—suspension; f.—front; r.—rear; comp.—compression; s.v.—side-valves; o.h.v.—overhead valves; o.h.c.—overhead camshaft; hyd.—hydraulic.

ALVIS THREE LITRE SERIES III

Improved performance and re-styling, are features of the new Alvis Series III Saloon and Drophead Coupe which are being shown for the first time at Earls Court this year. The Graber styled body has been given a new frontal design, incorporating a twin headlamp system. Steering and front suspension have been modified to give better handling, and engine power has been increased to 130 B.H.P. at 5,000 R.P.M., giving improved top speed and acceleration characteristics.

SERIES III SALOON
£2,773 · 13 · 9 inc. P.T.

SERIES III
DROPHEAD COUPE
£3,015 · 7 · 1 inc. P.T.

ALVIS OF COVENTRY · SOLE LONDON DISTRIBUTORS : BROOKLANDS OF BOND STREET · TELEPHONE : MAYFAIR 8351

And this isn't all!

What is an Acadian? A car built by General Motors in Canada with a strong Chevy II flavour. Choice of 90 h.p. four-cylinder engine or 120 h.p. six. It has an alternator instead of a dynamo.

GORDON WILKINS talking

Earls Court is one of the great international motor shows, with cars from England, Scotland, France, Italy, East and West Germany, Holland, Sweden, Israel, Czechoslovakia, Canada, United States and Soviet Russia . . . but there are many more that you don't see.

IT would take several halls like Earls Court to hold a complete collection of the varied makes and models that are now being turned out by the world's motor industries. Italy is well represented at the London Show but we shall not see the Innocenti IM3, most luxurious of all the variations upon the Morris 1100, with its specially angled steering wheel, reclining seats, extra instruments and lockable fuel filler. Nor the beautiful little Innocenti 1100 bodied by Ghia, the Italian-built version of the Austin Healey Sprite. Rootes have co-operated with Carrozzeria Touring to produce the beautiful Sunbeam Venezia which is exciting the international set but it is being kept out of Britain by the tax collector.

German cars are prominent in the Earls Court aisles but Opel, one of the top German makes has not been seen in Britain since thousands of pre-war models were dumped here at give-away prices as a means of getting money out of the grip of the Nazis.

Opel and Vauxhall both belong to General Motors and don't compete on each other's home ground, which saves confusion, for only an expert could tell an Opel Kadett from a Vauxhall Viva. The Rekord range, roughly equivalent to the Victor, features some beautifully finished coupes.

The rear-engined miniature Goggomobils and their successors, the front-engined Glas coupe and convertible have been seen in London but Glas are now launching out in a much more ambitious way with a handsome 1500 saloon styled in Italy by Frua.

If you want to keep track of the new trend towards engines-behind-the-seats for high performance cars, you may have glimpsed the Ford V8-engined Lola on the race tracks, but you should also see Italy's A.T.S., built with the financial support of Jaime Ortiz-Patino.

East German cars are coming to London for the first time, and the Skoda from Czechoslovakia has been selling fairly well but we don't see the impressive rear-engined Tatra, with its air-cooled V8 engine apart from the occasional visitor on diplomatic plates. After the Nazis conquered Czechoslovakia so many German officers were killed in oversteering V8 Tatras that the High Command must have thought it was a secret weapon, but the current model is reported to be more docile.

Soviet Russia is exhibiting two makes but keeps at home the little rear-engined Zaporo-

zhets which has recently been completely re-designed and the V.I.P. Zil 111G with the new rounder front that is a big improvement over the gaudy 111 which was merely an exact copy of the last Packard. Also reserved for Soviets and Satellites is the Tschaika 5½-litre V8, the successor to the Zim. Remoter still are the prospects of seeing the products of Communist China's new motor industry; the Dong-Feng (East Wind) a highly conventional 1½-litre saloon, or the 2½-litre four-cylinder four-headlamp Phoenix limousine.

In Spain, where a Fiat is a Seat, you lift the bonnet of what looks like a six-cylinder 1800 saloon to find a 1395 c.c. four-cylinder engine doing the work and doing it so well that Fiat have now marketed an Italian economy model with the big body and their 1500 engine. The Fiat 600 built in Spain still has its original 633 c.c. engine but a Fiat 600 assembled in Austria has an air-cooled Steyr flat twin at the rear (and if you look at the prototype in the Turin motor museum, you will find that this is what Fiat had in mind in the beginning). An air-cooled flat twin also provides the power for Austria's miniature four-wheel drive cross-country model, the Steyr Haflinger which looks like a magnificent toy but does a serious job of work in Central Europe's mountains and forests.

Switzerland, as one of the world's great car importers gets special attention from motor industry export directors but there are a few specialist firms on the spot, like Enzmann who make a most unorthodox rear-engined

Built in Brazil. The Aero Willys 260 is a re-styled and modernised version of one of the pioneer "compact" cars that was marketed in the United States just too early to catch on.

South Africa's latest; the Flamingo sports car with plastic body. It has the German Ford Taunus 17M engine but a faster version may be produced with Chevrolet engine.

Continued on next page

This beautifully finished coupe is the latest addition to the range of 1.7-litre Opel Rekords produced by G.M. in Germany. Top speed is over 90 m.p.h.

Smallest car available with automatic transmission; Japan's Mazda with Vee-twin air-cooled engine at the rear. 356 c.c.

Hino Contessa, a sleek new Japanese sports coupe with engine at the rear. Body styling was done in Italy by Michelotti.

about some of the cars you won't be seeing

sports car with VW mechanical parts and a plastic body. Getting in is rather like entering a fighter aircraft. You tilt back the plastic canopy and climb in by foot holds recessed in the side. Switzerland has its own builder of Formula Junior racing cars, Peter Monteverdi who also builds the MBM sports coupe with Ford Anglia engine and plastic bodywork. Israeli cars are now becoming regular visitors to the London Show but Earls Court has not yet seen anything from their bitter rivals, the Egyptians who produce the Phoenix, designed in England, with NSU mechanical parts from Germany and a soap box body built in Cairo.

Further East, India soldiers on building the old-style Morris Oxford under the name of Hindustan and assembling the Standard Pennant.

Perhaps the greatest number of old cars looking for a pleasant climate to retire to have chosen to end their days in South America. The Aero-Willys restyled by Brooks Stevens, has taken on a new lease of life in Brazil. Its six-cylinder engine has overhead inlet and side exhaust valves, a distinction it once shared with both Rolls-Royce and Rover. Another Brazilian model which is by no means obsolete in its country of origin is the fast little Renault-engined Alpine designed by rally driver Jean Redele.

In the Argentine, the car that looks like an old type Alfa Romeo 1900 will probably turn out to be a Bergantin with a jeep engine. The ungraceful Graciela has an East German Wartburg two-stroke engine and the Carabela turns out to be the old American Kaiser of bygone days.

The Holden, built by General Motors still holds top place in the Australian market but efforts by other manufacturers to compete with it can produce some surprises for visitors who think they know about motor cars. A car that looks like an Austin A.60 with Pininfarina body styling will probably turn out to be a locally built B.M.C. model with a 2-litre six cylinder engine and automatic transmission. Among the smaller saloons, any resemblance to a Wolseley 1500 will probably put you on the track of an Austin Lancer or a Morris Major.

Way across the southern hemisphere, South Africa struggles to make her motor industry self-supporting. B.M.C. has a big plant there and many other manufacturers are assembling cars with a growing content of locally produced components. The G.S.M. Delta sports car found its way to the English market and now the Flamingo shows that South Africans have a flair for individual styling.

But perhaps the most noticeable absentee from Earls Court is Japan and after the terrific

success scored on the British market by Japanese motor cycles, this situation is not likely to continue indefinitely. With an assembly plant already started in Belgium and a team of cars competing in the tough Liege-Sophia-Liege rally, Honda obviously mean business. The export version of their sports car has a four-cylinder o.h.c. engine of 531 c.c. canted over at the front. The body is all steel and all wheels have independent suspension. We shall be hearing more of Mr. Honda, now that he is switching his big competition budget from motor cycle to car racing.

We sometimes accuse the British motor industry of dispersing its efforts over too many different models but Japan, with far smaller total production, seems to produce an infinite variety of cars, most of them tiny, to fit the narrow twisty Japanese roads. Some of the bigger ones like the Nissan, Cedric and the Prince Skyline would look good in any company and Italian stylists have been called in to produce some smaller beauties like the Michelotti-styled Hino Contessa Sprint coupe.

There are some engineering surprises too. The Mazda P.600 has a four-cylinder mounted cross-wise at the rear like a Mini in reverse, and only the Japanese would dare to mate an automatic transmission with an engine of a mere 360 c.c. as they do on the rear-engined Mazda R360.

Needless to say, Earls Court brings us only a minute selection of the hundreds of glittering colourful high-powered cars produced by the world's greatest motor industry, that of the United States; cars that look gaudy and sometimes downright ugly to our eyes but which on their own home market represent incomparable value for money. For Americans the "compact" kick is over. It's back to the long wide, silent monsters that spell prestige to the Transatlantic buyer. And there isn't room for very many of them in Earls Court.

MBM G.T. coupe (top left) built in Switzerland by Peter Monteverdi. It uses a tuned Ford Anglia engine in a locally built chassis with glass fibre bodywork.

This (centre left) is the Siata sports convertible. Designed in Italy, but most of them are sold in Spain.

BMC in Italian dress (bottom left). The Innocenti 1100 with body by Ghia; built in Italy, using chassis of the Austin-Healey Sprite.

More Anglo-Italian collaboration (right). The Sunbeam Venezia is a beautiful new 1.6-litre sports saloon built by Carrozzeria Touring with Rootes mechanical parts. But import duty and purchase tax will keep it off the British market.

Get a new car and before you have even driven it home you will be thinking of all the new gadgets that will make it just that much superior . . .

DON'T look now but thieves *could* be testing your car's getaway, downstairs and outside, while you're upstairs and inside, dreaming dreams of avarice in the Show's accessory and component warren. So if it isn't too late already, get on the track of the Auto Lock, which simultaneously "immobilises the fuel supply, cuts off the current to the starter motor, locks the braking system, secures the bonnet and boot, and connects an aural warning to the door locks" (Is that *all*?).

This is a mechanical combination device, operated from a dashboard selector dial, which controls certain electrical circuits. London's wonderful police recently spent two fruitless hours trying to remove an Auto Locked car that a director of the company that markets the apparatus (Auto Securities Ltd.) had left o'er long in a Mayfair side street. Red faces all round.

Cars of marked character attract accessory designers as millionaires magnetise chorus girls. If you loaded a Mini, for instance, with all the exclusive-to-the-species gooks that Earls Court has to offer, it wouldn't *have* a power/weight ratio. Selective buying is another matter, however, so here are some Mini bits at random:—

(1) K. F. Ward's special wheel discs, hub spinners, mudflaps, anti-vibration mirrors,

clear-view panels, spotlamps, frontal grilles, tyre trims, all familiarly hallmarked Styla.

(2) Desmo's spare wheel carrier, increasing effective boot capacity by 20%, and the same exhibitor's aluminium roof rack.

(3) Cosmic's mechanical door stay, which clicks in more senses than one at 7/6 a time.

Key-Leather's facia-operated bonnet lock for Minis is an established seller, and now K-L follow up with a counterpart for the Morris 1100. ("Secure against anything but a heavy attack with large crowbars", so malefactors contemplating light attacks with small crowbars had better think again).

If you're more concerned with your own security than your possessions', see the safety-belt makers' latest lines. Britax bring their new automatic harness, featuring the ingenious Auto-Lok reel, to the Show for the first time; and if nature didn't equip you or your front-seat passenger with gorilla-length arms, take a look too at the Britax Windo-Lift, enabling strapped travellers to open or close opposite

● The Kangol "universal" three-point pillar fitting safety belt—shown in use on the left—has a magnet in the top half of the re-designed buckle (below).

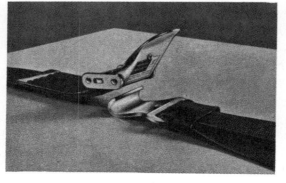

● This coy-seeming cover has many purposes, say the purveyors, Conway Car Accessories. Apart from keeping the car windows free from dirt, rain, frost or snow, it conserves interior heat in winter and keeps the car cool in summer, if ever we have a summer. And if you have anything to hide, it "will conceal contents of car from public view". Nobody suggests you should drive in this shrouded fashion, but the cover—made to fit all popular models at prices from £3 19s. 6d. to £4 9s. 6d.—is considered ideal for "holidays, camping and on the beach". So let it rain. . . .

side windows by just pressing a button. First, though, they have to press £25 into their Britax dealer's palm.

Kangol Magnet Ltd. beat the bugbear of belts which jangle and tangle annoyingly when not in use with an improved version of their magnetic buckle, applicable to all three types of harness they market. "Both sections of the belt . . . . can be parked against any metal part of the vehicle".

Let winter fall-out from the atmosphere do its worst to your windscreen and windows and you don't spy with your little eye any longer. Two obvious defences against this dangerous nuisance are (a) to protect the glass surfaces before the climate gets a chance to foul them up; and (b) to accept a *fait accompli*, then disaccomplish it. For the (a) line, what you need ideally is Conway's Sun-and-Wetha Cover, which is the car's equivalent to the upper half of a Bikini and, as the name implies, is equally effective in heatwaves for protection against roasting after long parking spells in the open. Made from tough but soft-lined material,

continued on Page 60

197

continued from Page 59

Going on about Gadgets

it envelops the whole upperstructure of the body from waistline to roof inclusive. "Fixed and removed in seconds. Individually tailored for all popular models".

For the (b) strategy, The thing to have is Trico's double-acting Squeegee. This clear-vision aid has two wiping edges, one made from hard rubber and shaped like a blade for scraping, the other soft and moisture absorbent to deal the *coup de grace* to water, ice, snow and frost when it's lost its toehold on your Triplex.

Talking of accessories that pay one dividend in winter and another in summer, Romac point out that their steering wheel gloves, shown in a variety of colours, cool the palms in hot weather just as comfortingly as they warm them when there is an 'r' in the month.

Music, maestro? Why not? Ekco fill a gap with a new 6-volt version of their popular CR921 all-transistor car radio, designed with an eye to such continental cars as the DAF, Ford Taunus, Opel, Kapitan, Olympia and Rekord, Porsche 90 and 1600, VW, Renault R4 and Dauphine, Saab 86, Volvo PV544. This neat number is planned for installation behind the facia without modifying the standard continental-car radio aperture.

World Radio's up-to-the-minute portable, the Playmate, incorporates aerial-matched tuning, claimed to overcome the problems of interference, poor sensitivity and directional fading experienced with some portables when used inside the car. A push-button selects one of two tuning circuits, which suit either an external aerial for car use or the built-in ferrite rod aerial for operation in a state of divorcement.

Lee Products (Elpico) exhibit their new CR575 car radio, with press-button wave band selection and attractive black and chromium finish. Elpico specialise in car aerials and show a wide selection from a range of models said to be the U.K.'s biggest.

Now back to haphazardry—an excusable formula for a feature with a built-in space famine that annually crowds out nineteen stands out of twenty anyway . . . .

If you are one of those motorists who like to *see* fresh air, with nothing between you and it, except perhaps in arctic temperatures, Cyplas Industries' Galemaster composite weather shield will be up your street. Tailored for the 105E Ford Anglia and the A40 Austin, it fits into the void left by a wound-down window in the driver's door. Eliminates misting, prevents headaches and drowsiness, doesn't hinder vision, admits fresh air without draughts. Reasonable too at 59/6.

Partial clogging of the carburetter by dirt and

continued on next page

with a note about tuning-in to transistors . . .

Like sex, they reckon transistors are here to stay. Mostly they come with purchase tax, but for the lucky ones they come with feminine attachments as well. The girl in the picture above appears to have got on to the right wave-length with the Playmate, a set made by World Radio. It incorporates "aerial-matched" tuning which is said to overcome interference and directional fading when the portable is used in a car. Complete with a car fixing bracket, it costs 16½ guineas including tax—but not the girl.

Virtually any car can have a "tailored" fitting for Ekco's new "super-performance" radio—conceived, as the makers claim, with motorway speeds in mind. Wind and road noise does not spoil reception from this de-luxe receiver—pictured in a Jaguar 3.8 Mark II (above) and in its natural state (on the left). Cost: 24½ guineas.

continued from Page 60

gum deposits is blamed by the Pennsylvania Refining Company for rough idling, stalling and high fuel consumption. The answer, P.R.C. claim, is a preparation of theirs called Gumout, recently launched on the British Market. You can either add it to your petrol or introduce it directly through the carburetter, using the makers' specially designed clean-out kit.

Performance liveners in great variety, many of them in the bolt-on category, are again all over the Show. The Exhaust Ejector Company display their well-known lines in tail-pipe trumpetry for ushering the spent gases out and away, with beneficial effect on back pressure. The Performance Equipment Co. makes a similar appeal to go-faster folk with a wide range of goodies starting at free-flow exhaust plumbing and ending up with the Peco-Judson belt driven supercharger; blowers suitable for MGAs and TR Triumphs retail at £98, and a competent amateur mechanic should be capable of doing the installation job himself.

Tapley, whose larger brake testing meters enjoy official M.o.T. approval for use in compulsory car testing, are making a strong feature of the much lower priced and less elaborate Tapley brake efficiency indicator at Earls Court, where it appears for the first time. This little instrument, adapted for facia fitting and selling for only 50/-, is a real aid to safety inasmuch as it brings to light insidiously gradual deteriorations in the braking system of the car that sports it.

When you consider the wide range of impacts your car's suspension takes, depending on the passenger/luggage load and the state of the roads, it's remarkable that the great majority of vehicles go through life on a single damper setting—because there just isn't provision for varying it. Adjustable shock-absorbers are nothing new, however, and the Armstrong Patents Co., among others, show both lever-arm and telescopic types with this valuable feature. Some Armstrong models really go the whole hog with no less than twenty-two different degrees of damping.

Even in these days of cavernous boots, holidaying tourist drivers with a full complement of fellow-travellers sometimes find their luggage capacity is taxed to the limit. One

continued on Page 63

You don't HAVE to have a pretty girl to sell gadgets, but it's been known to help

Sealed beam headlight units by Lucas are being demonstrated at the Show floating in a pool of water. There are fish in the pool too—which goes to prove that there are other eye-catching gimmicks than girls.

The lady on the left is finger-pointing to two Smith's car heaters—the F.260 Fresh Air version (£15 a kit) and the Universal Recirculatory heater, R.201, at £10.

199

A final light on Gadget Corner

continued from Page 61

solution, suitable for any car that doesn't have a markedly sloped "fast back" tail, is a type of luggage harness made by Hornbush Ltd. of Luton. Overflow suitcases—two big ones or three of lesser size—are bedded on the boot lid after the rest of the cargo has been stowed within, and made fast there by a complex of strong, interlinked straps whose ends attach to the outer sections of the rear bumper and special wheel-arch grapnels.

"Would anyone dream of driving forwards without a light at night?" asks a Joseph Lucas bulletin rhetorically. Of course he wouldn't, yet his eyes are in the front of his head. This makes it all the odder that despite the lack of eyes in the *back* of his head, only one motorist in ten in Britain uses a reversing lamp. Even granting that one motors forward farther and faster than in reverse, Lucas regard this as a situation ripe for redress, and accordingly are putting a big effort into popularising a stream-lined, easy-to-fit reversing lamp, Model L.661, that they introduced last year. If *you* do your nocturnal reversing by guess and instinct, get a look at this one.

Did you know that within seconds from starting from cold, your engine's speed can rise to 60 revolutions per second, giving a rubbing speed between working parts of over a quarter of a mile per minute? We didn't either, but that's no reason to disbelieve Stack Engineering and Manufacturing Co. Ltd., of Swindon, makers of a device called the pre-start oil-pressure unit. Purpose of this quencher is to reinforce the gravity-depleted oil film during the period of greatest need. The unit consists of a steel reservoir which stores about 16 fluid ounces of oil at a pressure of 40 p.s.i. When the engine is switched on, but before it starts, a solenoid is momentarily energised which opens a valve through which oil is injected into the motor.

And while Stack bend their brains to avoiding harmful dry-out's in engines, one of Les Leston's specialities is saving the sporting motorist from an equally unwelcome wetting. Assuming you have the heart to put up a pretence at gaiety in the kind of deluges we have had all summer and can certainly expect all winter, Leston's special polychromatic umbrellas, "exclusively for golfers, horse racing and motor racing enthusiasts", are just the accessory you need.

NOTE.—*Not all the manufacturers mentioned in this article are themselves exhibiting at Earls Court, but most of their products will be found on factors' stands.*

and a P.S. on braking

Easy now. . . . A new reversing lamp by Lucas—the L661 to give it a prosaic number—gives a wide distribution of light to aid driver backing in or up.
Easy now. . . . Tapley Meters are introducing their Brake Efficiency Indicator, a tiny instrument no more than 2¼in. by 1⅝in. which by means of coloured shuttles tells the driver at once the state of his brakes. It costs 50s.

 ROVER engineering takes motoring years ahead

ROVER 2000

The new light 2-litre saloon with Grand Touring specification

Meet the car that demonstrates what creative engineering really means—the ROVER 2000. This new O.H.C. 2-litre saloon combines independent front and de Dion rear suspension—base unit construction—4-speed, all-synchromesh gearbox—disc brakes all round—and a lavish, 4-seat, continental-style G.T. interior. Brilliantly designed, impeccably finished, the ROVER 2000 is as safe as it's fast, as economical as it's luxurious. This is the car that's "years ahead" in every way. Price: £1,264.9.7 (including tax). Meet this superb new light saloon at the Motor Show—together with the rest of the swift, silent Rover range—the 95, the 110, the 3-Litre and the Coupé which will continue unchanged.

ROVER—ONE OF THE WORLD'S BEST ENGINEERED CARS

The Rover Company Ltd., Solihull, Warwickshire. London offices and showrooms: Devonshire House, Piccadilly. Makers of fine cars and the world-famous Land-Rover.

The masterly new 6-cylinder Triumph 2000 introduces
grand luxe motoring at a medium price

IT IS FAST (nudging 100 mph). It is beautiful (the long low look, interpreted by Michelotti). It is very quiet (two litres shared among six cylinders). It is luxurious, and a delight to drive. So far, so good. You can say the same of many fine cars. But what puts the Triumph 2000 in a completely new class?

Simply, its over-all refinement. The Triumph 2000 is no larger than other cars in the same price bracket but it has a sumptuousness of appointment and quality of finish that you associate with big luxury cars. It is built with thoroughness and care, with one thought in mind. To make motoring the pleasure it should be for the driver and his passengers. This quality of detail puts the Triumph 2000 in a class all its own.

The Triumph cachet Every car in the Triumph range has been designed to fill a particular niche of its own. The Herald 1200: still the most advanced light car on the market. The Herald 12/50: 51 bhp, front discs, and the open-and-shut skylight roof. The Vitesse: only 1.6-litre car with a silky 6-cylinder engine. The Spitfire: low-price sports car with all the home comforts (now offered with a hardtop). The TR4: high-performance sports car at the price of a moderate roadster. And now the Triumph 2000. (£1095 tax paid)

Triumph Herald 1200 (From £579 tax paid)

Triumph TR4 (£907 tax paid)

Triumph Vitesse (£735 tax paid)

Triumph Spitfire (£641 tax paid, hard top £34 extra)

STANDARD TRIUMPH

A member of the Leyland Motor Corporation

CARS
OF THE EARLY 60'S
BRITISH AND IMPORTED MODELS 1960-1964

MOTOR SHOW REVIEW GUIDE
1964

A - Z
SECTION

This is why our sports cars amaze the world

by

ALAN BRINTON

It's a double Triumph—two of the reasons why the range of sports cars from British makers is the biggest in the world, as explained here by Alan Brinton. That's him, above, at the wheel of a Spitfire. On the left, the familiar TR4.

BRITAIN is the world's most prolific and successful producer of sports cars—machines that bring all the zest of pace and thoroughbred handling to the enthusiastic driver.

Behind this success story is a unique British tradition of building sports cars within the reach of the pockets of the younger driver, a policy which developed in the 1930s and which after the war brought an ever-mushrooming demand from overseas, and particularly from the United States.

Looking at our nippy little value-for-money sports two-seaters, such as the Austin Healey Sprite, its BMC sister the MG Midget, and Triumph Spitfire, foreigners are amazed that we can build them so well and sell them so cheaply.

When it first appeared six years ago, the Sprite—brainchild of dynamic Donald Healey—was an instant hit with the younger enthusiast who had been starved of a low-cost sports car since the earlier MG Midgets had gradually grown up into refined, medium-sized machines. Since then, the Sprite has been joined by the MG Midget, with similar mechanical components, and in their latest form with 1,098 c.c. engine these lively and compact cars offer zippy performance, a maximum speed of around 90 miles an hour, economical running, and a precise handling bred from competition experience.

The Triumph Spitfire is another machine with the attraction of high performance (a little over 90 m.p.h.) in relation to its reasonable price of £641. Attractively styled by that Italian genius, Giovanni Michelotti, the Spitfire pioneered such items as wind-up windows and all-independent suspension on this class of car. You can get the Spitfire in several stages of tune, depending on the performance you want; in stage 2 form it will top 105 m.p.h.

Our medium-sized sports cars, of which the MGB and the Triumph TR4 are the outstanding examples, give the customer well over the 'ton-up' performance, and this is linked to refined equipment and top quality finish. Each of these models has a tremendous following among fans abroad, especially in the West coast region of the United States, where the earlier MGs gave the post-war generation its first real taste of British sports cars and established a trend which is earning millions of valuable dollars today.

The MGB is noted especially for the delightful way in which it can be controlled under all sorts of driving conditions, with precise steering, a pleasant gearbox and lots of urge. The bigger engine of the TR4 gives a slightly higher acceleration and top speed; this is a rugged, very masculine car, still retaining some of the traditional beefiness of earlier sports cars with their firm springing, and with a power unit which has achieved an enviable reputation for durability.

Slotted between these two in price is the Sunbeam Alpine Sports Tourer which, as its name suggests, puts the accent on comfort and refinement (and which is also available with automatic transmission). This is the sort of car with manners which will not frighten off your wife if she wants to drive it herself.

If you feel that you can cope with around two miles a minute, and still want a car as docile in traffic as a family saloon, then the Austin Healey 3000 is a real tiger-and-lamb machine which costs only a little over £1,100. One of the big virtues of this model is that it is powered by a muscular 3 litre engine which does not have to work really hard, and so high-speed cruising is possible without fatiguing the car or the driver.

Further up the scale, we have one of the prides of the British motor industry—the Jaguar 'E' Type—which for less than £2,000 provides breathtaking performance in a sleek body of superb lines. It is baffling how Sir William Lyons manages to produce his magnificent cars for the money, and with the six cylinder twin overhead camshaft XK engine under the bonnet the 'E' Type is one of the most desirable pieces of machinery on the roads of the world.

Jaguar, of course, are based on a firm foundation of racing experience—remember they won Le Mans five times—and so are Aston Martin, whose DB5 is one of the world's most prized models in the luxury Grand Touring class.

Racing *does* improve the breed, and Colin Chapman, whose Lotus designs have brought this young company world honours in the Grand Prix field, has put all his know-how into a series of high-performance production sports cars with handling qualities that set a new standard for road machines. The Lotus Elite and Elan have become status symbols for the discerning driver who appreciates the value of cars with top responsiveness and precision.

Though the general conception of sports cars has changed in recent years, there is still a market for the stark, functional, open two-seater which eschews modern styling and all-in comfort. Lotus built their production success on the Lotus Seven, and this simple yet extremely effective design is still attracting the affections of practically-minded enthusiasts who can assemble the components in just a few hours to produce one of the most eager little sports cars on the road. (The Lotus Super Seven with 1½ litre Ford engine is a 100 m.p.h. car.)

While the Lotus Seven incorporates much modern thinking, the Morgan 4/4 is what it appears—virtually the only 'traditional' sports car now being made. The basic Morgan design dates back to before the war, but there are still many customers for a new Morgan echoing what some keen types consider the Golden Age of sports cars.

Many a sporting driver who also has family obligations is well catered for by British manufacturers, who produce high-performance versions of their bread-and-butter saloons. In the forefront of this approach are our two major car firms—BMC and Ford—who offer an enticing range of comfortable saloons with sports car performance.

The original Austin and Morris Minis have gone much further than designer Alec Issigonis originally envisaged, and in various Cooper versions these little transverse-engined rubber-sprung runabouts with a surprising amount of interior room have been turned into very exciting cars which in some cases will 'see off' some large-engined sports cars.

Ford, too, have realised the growing market for 'saloon sports cars,' and their GT versions of the Cortina and Corsair bridge most effectively the gap between the standard models and the race-bred Lotus-Cortina which has won this year's British Saloon Car Championship. Then there is the Vauxhall VX 4/90, the added performance model of the Victor, with which father can enjoy his urge for lively motoring while at the same time giving his family refined and comfortable transport.

The range of sports and high-performance cars from British manufacturers is easily the biggest in the world. If your interests lie in this direction, you have only one problem—how to choose your model from such an enticing array.

A woman behind the wheel

EVERYONE SAYS IT—

I'm really rather a good driver

BUT HOW TRUE IS IT?

by DENISE McCANN
Chairman and Managing Director of the world's largest driving school

DRIVING today is a pretty serious business. Once, it was virtually a sport for the enthusiast who found miles of traffic-free roads at his disposal in which to manoeuvre his vehicle.

Now there are more cars to the square mile on Britain's roads than those of any other country in the world. A sobering thought. And one which underlines the absolute necessity for us, who are motorists, and all who are potentially so, to be able to drive safely and well.

For, whether it is for pleasure, business or just convenience, driving is a matter of life and death which affects everyone who takes as much as one step on the public highway.

Driving standards are not as high as they should be, I am afraid. Undoubtedly there are many contributory causes to, this state of affairs but it all boils down to the same basic reason—lack of the proper sort of education in driving techniques and road sense.

People's road behaviour causes me a great deal of concern. As a driver, because it affects my own considerable journeys by car; and, not unnaturally, as Chairman of the largest driving school in the world, I, with my colleagues feel a tremendous responsibility towards the public as well as towards our pupils in aiming at general higher driving standards.

It is easy to be termed a killjoy, or some such expression, and I hope people who know me personally never think of me in that way. But I am often disappointed in other people's apparent attitude towards driving and learning to drive.

Many people are prepared to invest money running into three figures in a leisure pursuit such as golf, but when it comes to learning to drive they want to do it on the cheap. Yet golf—which, incidentally I consider a great game—is played fairly infrequently by the average participant; they drive every day.

Not only that, but their driving affects their families, passengers and the millions of people who use the roads, as well as themselves. Good driving is also a protection for one of the biggest capital investments in many people's lives—their motor car!

Yet, as I know from personal experience, the suggestion to an experienced motorist that his or her driving could be improved frequently provokes a most heated response. And many drivers' opinions of the skill of other drivers are often equally pungent!

Personally, after the hundreds of thousands of miles both here and on the Continent that I must have driven both for business and pleasure, I still know there are times when my own driving could be improved. Just as our golfing friends will revisit the pro regularly to freshen up their game, so I feel no shame in returning to an expert driving instructor from time to time for a "refresher course".

As a driver I know this is of benefit. As someone involved in all forms of driving instruction—from family cars to high performance "giants" of the various types that can be seen here at the Motor Show, and even articulated trucks—I try at least to make sure the facilities to do this are available to the public.

That is why I have instituted the High Performance Course, the GT Course, Continental driving courses for both private and commercial vehicle operators, specialised anti-skid training on a new type of skid-road, and, in conjunction with a national motoring magazine, an A-Level Course. But it does come down to people in the end, of course. It is up to them to decide to do something positive in maintaining an accident-free driving career.

I love motoring and, where it is safe to do so, driving fast. I use a powerful motor car myself and have not been on a train more than a dozen times since the war. Speed in itself is not dangerous—we all know, in fact, what a menace the fellow is who hogs the middle of the road at 35 miles an hour and will not move over—but a fast car which is not handled properly does become a lethal weapon. Motoring is now within the range of almost everybody. At our schools throughout the country, which train something like a quarter of a million new pupils a year, 45 per cent are now women. I am glad to see it, not just because it is good business but as a woman driver myself I really do believe that the hoary old music-hall-type joke about women motorists has now been scotched. And 1,500 *male* **driving instructors** in my organisation agree that on average pupils of both sexes stand an equally good chance of reaching an equally high standard.

But the accident rate really must stop increasing. I sincerely believe that qualified professional instruction—and more of it—will go a long way towards achieving this. It is just basically wrong in today's traffic conditions to take lessons from relatives, friends and other unqualified people. All their bad driving habits are picked up, the atmosphere is frequently not calm, and there are no dual-controls for the safety of other road-users.

The future of the motor car is tremendous. The manufacturers are doing a wonderful job in producing exciting, good-looking and often revolutionary developments in their new models.

I hope every motorist who attends the Show to see these thrilling cars and accessories will do at least one thing to play his part in ensuring that these developments will be, in due course, a benefit to everyone. Take a few moments to give a fresh look to your driving; don't be antagonised by others perhaps less capable than yourself—and, please, go carefully.

THE MOTORING MUSE Second series

On the other driver, after an "incident":
. . . *"Perjur'd, murderous, bloody, full of blame,*
Savage, extreme, rude, cruel, not to trust"
—Shakespeare

★ ★ ★

Anywhere in London (1)
We are all driven one road
—Horace

Anywhere in London (2)
There was once a man who said "Damn!
It is borne in upon me I am
An engine that moves
In predestinate grooves
I'm not even a bus—I'm a train"
—Maurice Hare

Why doesn't he dip?
. . . *blasted with excess of light*
Closed his eyes in endless night
—Milton

★ ★ ★

On the M1 (1)
Where the beetle winds
His small but sullen horn
— William Collins

On the M1 (2)
What is this that roareth thus
Can it be a Motor Bus?
—A. D. Godley

205

The Regent
work team

produces positive **team work** between you and your car

 Team up with **REGENT** - *for results!*

THE 1965 $\mathcal{D}$aimler MODELS

**THE 2½ LITRE
V.8 SALOON**

2½ litre V-8 engine.
Automatic transmission
with dual drive.
Disc brakes on all four wheels

Every model in the current Daimler range faithfully preserves the Daimler reputation for fine engineering and superb quality. Moreover, each offers the highest degree of modern performance combined with exceptional road safety under all conditions. Whatever your individual requirements you will find a demonstration run in any Daimler model a most rewarding experience.

Stand No. 127, Earls Court

THE MAJESTIC MAJOR 4½ LITRE SALOON
4½ litre V-8 engine. Automatic transmission. Disc brakes
on all four wheels. 20 cubic ft. capacity luggage boot

THE EIGHT SEATER LIMOUSINE
4½ litre V-8 engine. Automatic transmission.
Disc brakes on all four wheels.
Power assisted steering

PRESTIGE MOTORING IN THE MODERN MANNER

LONDON SHOWROOMS: 40 BERKELEY STREET W.1

207

1964

Drawing by ROBB

ABARTH MONOMILLE

ASTROLOGERS say those born under the sign Scorpio, which Carlo Abarth adopted as his emblem, combine changeable character with tenacity of purpose. Constant change is evident in the Abarth stable of highly tuned thoroughbreds and he shows extreme tenacity in bringing them home to win their class year in and year out in the world's speed events. Small Abarths have rear engines with Fiat or Simca chassis parts.

CLOSE-UP

Four-cyl.; o.h.v.; 65×74 mm.; 982 c.c.; 60 b.h.p.; 9.6 to I comp.; coil ign.; Solex carb.; 4-speed, 15.07, 8.90, 6.77, 4.33 to 1; cen. lvr. 5-speed opt.; susp., f. ind. transv. leaf, r. ind. coil; 2-door; 2-seat; disc brks.; max. 110 m.p.h.; cruise, 95; m.p.g. 30-34; whl. base, 6ft. 6¾in.; track f. and r. 3ft. 9⅞in.; lgth., 11ft. 9¼in.; width, 4ft. 7⅞in.; ht. 3ft. 9⅝in.; g.c. 5¼in.; turng. cir., 29ft.; kerb wt., 12½ cwt.; tank, 10 gals.; 12-volt.

£1,991 + £440 p.t. = £2,431

ABARTH 2000

THE sting in the tail of this Scorpion-branded coupe is a light alloy twin-cam four-cylinder engine of 1948 c.c., with two twin-choke Weber carburetters, and five-bearing crankshaft, giving 190 h.p. nett at 7,000 r.p.m. To achieve the ultimate in competition performance, it can be mated with a six-speed gearbox as alternative to the normal four-speed. The disc brakes have twin master cylinders.

CLOSE-UP

Four-cyl.; o.h.c.; 88×80 mm.; 1,948 c.c.; 190 b.h.p.; 9.8 to 1 comp.; coil ign.; 2 Weber carbs; 4-speed, 13.82, 8.25, 5.75, 4.71 to 1; cen. lvr.; susp., f. ind. transv. leaf, r. ind. coil; 2-door; 3-seat; disc brks.; max. 150 m.p.h.; cruise 130; m.p.g. 19-21; whl. base 6ft. 10½in.; track f. 4ft. 1½in., r. 4ft. 0¾in.; lgth. 11ft. 8½in.; wdth. 4ft. 10½in.; ht. 3ft. 8½in.; g.c. 5in.; turng. cir. 29ft. 6in.; kerb wt. 11¾ cwt.; tank, 12 gals.; 12-volt.

A.C. COBRA

ANGLO-AMERICAN effort with Ford V8 engine sponsored by Carroll Shelby who has raced them triumphantly on the world's circuits this year. A crushing victory in the GT class of the TT was included and they won the GT class at Le Mans. A.C. production is geared to make only this model at present and it is mainly for export but a few are being released on the home market.

CLOSE-UP

Eight-cyl.; o.h.v.; 96.5×72.9 mm.; 4,262 c.c.; 320 b.h.p.; 9.2 to 1 comp.; coil ign.; Ford carb.; 4-speed, 8.36, 6.30, 4.99, 3.54 to 1; cen. lvr.; susp., f. and r. ind. trans. leaf; 2-door; 2-seat; disc brks.; max. 150 m.p.h.; cruise 130; m.p.g. 20; whl. base 7ft. 6in.; track f. 4ft. 3½in., r. 4ft. 4½in.; lgth. 12ft. 7in.; wdth. 5ft. 1in.; ht. 4ft. 1in.; g.c. 7in.; turng. cir. 36ft.; kerb wt. 18 cwt.; tank, 15 gals.; 12-volt.

£2,030+£424 p.t. = £2,454

ALFA ROMEO GIULIA SPIDER

NOW fast selling Italian sports car, the Giulia Spider offers good value for money to the driver who likes to enjoy fresh air and sunshine. For the bad days it has a good hood and glass windows to keep out rain and diesel smoke. Four cylinder twin-cam engine and disc front brakes to ensure good stopping power. Immaculately finished Pininfarina interior makes it a possession to prize.

CLOSE-UP

Four-cyl.; o.h.c; 78×82 mm.; 1,570 c.c.; 92 b.h.p.; 9 to 1 comp.; coil ign.; Solex carb.; 5-speed, 16.93, 10.19, 6.94, 5.12, 4.05 to 1; cen. lvr.; susp., f. ind. coil, r. coil; 2-door; 2-seat; hyd. brks., disc front; max. 108 m.p.h.; cruise 90; m.p.g. 27-29; whl. base 7ft. 5in.; track f. 4ft. 3in., r. 4ft. 2in.; lgth. 13ft.; width 5ft. 1in.; ht. 4ft. 3in.; g.c. 5½in.; turng. cir. 34ft. 6in.; kerb wt. 18½ cwt.; tank, 11¾ gals.; 12-volt.

£1,155+£242 p.t. = £1,397

ALFA ROMEO 2600

POPULAR with Continental long-distance drivers are the 2600 convertible and coupe on a shorter wheelbase than the saloon. Choice of coachwork from either Bertone or Carrozzeria Touring, two doors and seats for four. Like the saloon, they have the excellent five-speed all-synchromesh gearbox and disc front brakes with servo assistance. Top speed is around 124 m.p.h. against 110 m.p.h. from the saloon.

CLOSE-UP

Six-cyl.; o.h.c.; 83×79.6 mm.; 2,584 c.c.; 130 b.h.p.; 8.5 to 1 comp.; coil ign.; 2 Solex carbs.; 5-speed, 16.93, 10.19, 6.94, 5.12, 4.05 to 1; cen. lvr.; susp., f. ind. coil, r. coil; 4-door; 5-seat; hyd. servo brks., disc front; max. 110 m.p.h.; cruise, 95; m.p.g. 18-20; whl. base, 8ft. 11in.; track f. 4ft. 7in., r. 4ft. 6in.; lgth., 15ft. 6in.; width., 5ft. 7in.; ht. 4ft. 10½in.; g.c. 4¾in.; turng. cir., 34ft.; kerb wt., 25½ cwt.; tank, 13½ gals.; 12-volt.

£1,879+£393 p.t. = £2,272

ASTON MARTIN DB5

THIS is one of the greatest thoroughbreds of the motor racing world. New items last year include twin-plate diaphragm clutch, an alternator, Girling instead of Dunlop disc brakes having twin hydraulic circuits and servos. Electrically operated windows are standard. Four-speed gearbox, or ZF box with five speeds all synchronised as option. Engine 6-cylinder, 3,995 c.c. It is a model for the wealthy motoring enthusiast.

CLOSE-UP

Six-cyl.; o.h.c.; 96×92 mm.; 3,995 c.c.; 282 b.h.p.; 8.75 to 1 comp.; coil ign.; 3 S.U. carbs.; 5-speed, 10.18, 6.64, 4.64, 3.77, 3.14 to 1; cen. lvr., auto opt.; susp. f. ind. coil, r. coil; 2-door; 4-seat; disc servo brks.; max. 150 m.p.h.; cruise 125; m.p.g. 15-18; whl. base 8ft. 2in.; track f. 4ft. 6in., r. 4ft. 5½in.; lgth. 14ft. 8½in.; wdth. 5ft. 6in.; ht. 4ft. 4in.; g.c. 6½in.; turng. cir. 34ft.; kerb wt. 29 cwt.; tank, 19 gals.; 12-volt.

£3,515+£734 p.t. = £4,249

ASTON MARTIN DB5 CONVERTIBLE

OPEN-CAR motoring with speed and comfort. The neat hood is claimed to be wind and weather-proof and easy to stow and erect. There is also a hard-top model. The light-alloy 4-litre engine develops 282 b.h.p. at 5,500 r.p.m. and there is a wide choice of transmissions; four or five-speed gearbox, with option of overdrive, or automatic torque converter and three-speed gear.

CLOSE-UP

Six-cyl.; o.h.c.; 96×92 mm.; 3,995 c.c.; 282 b.h.p.; 8.75 to 1 comp.; coil ign.; 3 S.U. carbs.; 5-speed, 10.18, 6.64, 4.64, 3.77, 3.14 to 1; cen. lvr., auto. opt.; susp., f. ind. coil, r. coil; 2-door; 4-seat; disc servo brks.; max. 148 m.p.h.; cruise 120; m.p.g. 15-18; whl. base 8ft. 2in.; track f. 4ft. 6in., r. 4ft. 5½in.; lgth. 14ft. 8⅜in.; wdth. 5ft. 6in.; ht. 4ft. 4in.; g.c. 6¼in.; turng. cir. 34ft.; kerb wt. 29½ cwt.; tank, 19 gals.; 12-volt.

£3,775 + £788 p.t. = £4,563

ALVIS 3-LITRE

STYLED by Graber of Switzerland, this plush convertible has all the luxury and refinements you would expect in a hand-built car. It will travel at well over 100 miles an hour silently and powerfully. This year power-assisted steering is offered as a £120 optional extra. It is a car for the individualist with caviare tastes for motoring—and it is beautifully engineered.

CLOSE-UP

Six-cyl.; o.h.v.; 84×90 mm.; 2,993 c.c.; 115 b.h.p.; 8.5 to 1 comp.; coil ign.; 2 S.U. carbs.; 5-speed, 11.38, 6.97, 4.86, 3.77, 3.07 to 1; cen. lvr.; BW auto. opt.; susp., f. ind. coil, r. half-elliptic; 2-door; 4-seat; disc brks.; max. 100 m.p.h.; cruise 80; m.p.g. 18-22; whl. base 9ft. 3½in.; track f. 4ft. 7⅜in., r. 4ft. 6⅛in.; lgth. 15ft. 8½in.; wdth. 5ft. 6in.; ht. 5ft.; g.c. 7in.; turng. cir. 39ft. 6in.; kerb wt. 30½ cwt.; tank, 14¼ gals.; 12-volt.

£2,295 + £480 p.t. = £2,775

AUSTIN MINI

YOU see these roomy, magnificently efficient little cars everywhere, including most countries on the Continent. For 1965 they will have some useful improvements including the famous hydrolastic suspension (water through pipes) on all saloons. Other additions include two leading shoe brakes; a diaphragm spring clutch; key starting; courtesy light; crushable sun visors and safety driving mirror. A winner car that goes on winning.

CLOSE-UP

Four-cyl.; o.h.v.; 63×68.26 mm.; 848 c.c.; 34 b.h.p.; 8.3 to 1 comp.; coil ign.; S.U. carb.; 4-speed, 13.657, 8.176, 5.317, 3.765 to 1; cen. lvr.; susp., f. and r. ind. rubber-hydraulic; 2-door; 4-seat; hyd. brks.; max. 73 m.p.h.; cruise 60; m.p.g. 45; whl. base 6ft. 8in.; track f. 3ft. 11⅞in., r. 3ft. 9⅞in.; lgth. 10ft.; width 4ft. 7in.; ht. 4ft. 5in.; g.c. 6⅛in.; turng. cir. 31ft.; kerb wt. 11¾ cwt.; tank, 5½ gals.; 12-volt.

£388 + £82 p.t. = £470

AUSTIN A40 MARK II

FIRST of the Pininfarina styles from the BMC, still going strong, though it has been running since 1958. The engine increased to 1098 c.c. in 1963 gives a sprightly performance. Good looking compact lines enclose plenty of space for family and luggage. The price is right too for those who must watch their budget. Countryman version has a one-piece lift-up rear panel for bulky loads.

CLOSE-UP

Four-cyl.; o.h.v.; 64.6×83.7 mm.; 1,098 c.c.; 48 b.h.p.; 8.5 to 1 comp.; coil ign.; S.U. carb.; 4-speed, 16.52, 10.82, 6.43, 4.56 to 1; cen. lvr.; susp., f. ind. coil, r. half-elliptic; 2-door; 4-seat; hyd. brks.; max. 83 m.p.h.; cruise 70; m.p.g. 31-33; whl. base 7ft. 3in.; track f. and r. 3ft. 11in.; lgth. 12ft. 1½in.; wdth. 4ft. 11½in.; ht. 4ft. 8⅜in.; g.c. 7⅛in.; turng. cir. 36ft.; tank, 7 gals.; 12-volt.; kerb wt. 15⅝ cwt.

£460 + £97 p.t. = £557

Abbreviations—g.c.—ground clearance; susp.—suspension; f.—front; r.—rear; comp.—compression; s.v.—side-valves; o.h.v.—overhead valves; o.h.c.—overhead camshaft; hyd.—hydraulic.

AUSTIN 1100

BROTHER to the Mini, the 1100 with its Hydrolastic rubber-water suspension will take on any kind of surface. The Austin version has a neat strip-type speedometer, fluted grille, number plate lamp on rear bumper instead of on boot lid. Ample space with good parcel shelf and door bins. Low-built with a road-hugging look, this is one of today's most stable family cars.

CLOSE-UP

Four-cyl.; o.h.v.; 64.58×83.72 mm.; 1,098 c.c.; 55 b.h.p.; 8.5 to 1 comp.; coil ign.; S.U. carb.; 4-speed, 14.99, 8.98, 5.83, 4.133 to 1; cen. lvr.; susp., f. and r. ind. rubber-hyd.; 2- or 4-door; 4-seat; hyd. brks., disc front; max. 76 m.p.h.; cruise 60; m.p.g. 36-38; whl. base 7ft. 9½in.; track f. 4ft. 3½in.; r. 4ft. 2⅞in.; lgth. 12ft. 2⅞in.; wdth. 5ft. 0⅜in.; ht. 4ft. 4½in.; g.c. 6in.; turng. cir. 32ft.; kerb wt. 16½ cwt.; tank, 8½ gals.; 12-volt.

£490+£104 p.t. = £594

AUSTIN 1800

MINI formula brilliantly stretched to medium size. Crosswise engine and front wheel drive for compactness. Hydrolastic suspension for that pitch-free flat ride. A car that offers lounging space for five but parks in less space than an average 1200 c.c. model. Five-bearing crankshaft for smoothness, synchromesh on all four speeds, servo assistance for the brakes. Wheels at the corners for stability and a luggage boot of surprising size.

CLOSE-UP

Four-cyl.; o.h.v.; 80.26×88.9 mm.; 1,798 c.c.; 84 b.h.p.; 8.2 to 1 comp.; coil ign.; S.U. carb.; 4-speed, 13.78, 9.28, 5.79, 4.19 to 1; cen. lvr.; susp., f. and r. ind. rubber hydraulic; 4-door; 5-seat; hyd. servo brks., disc front; max. 90 m.p.h.; cruise 80; m.p.g. 28-30; whl. base 8ft. 10in.; track f. 4ft. 8½in., r. 4ft. 7½in.; lgth. 13ft. 8¼in.; width 5ft. 7in.; ht. 4ft. 7½in.; g.c. 6½in.; turng. cir. 34ft. 6in.; kerb wt. 23½ cwt.; tank, 10¾ gals.; 12-volt.

AUSTIN A/110 MARK II

BETTER brakes and springing, new transmissions, smaller wheels and fatter tyres—these are key improvements to a car that is externally unchanged. Front brake discs are thicker, the servo is bigger and a new ball valve regulates rear brake pressure in panic stops to prevent skids. New dampers and longer rear springs increase the comfort, three silencers reduce noise to a whisper. Four speeds now, instead of three, or a better type of BW automatic.

CLOSE-UP

Six-cyl.; o.h.v.; 83×89 mm.; 2,912 c.c.; 120 b.h.p.; 8.3 to 1 comp.; coil ign.; 2 S.U. carbs.; 4-speed, 10.31, 8.1, 5.11, 3.92 to 1; cen. lvr. BW overdrive or auto. opt.; susp., f. ind. coil, r. half-elliptic; 4-door; 5/6-seat; servo brks., disc front; max. 102 m.p.h.; cruise 80; m.p.g. 18-23; whl. base 9ft. 2in.; track f. 4ft. 6in., r. 4ft. 5½in.; lgth. 15ft. 7½in.; width 5ft. 8½in.; ht. 5ft. 0½in.; g.c. 6½in.; turng. cir. 41ft.; kerb wt. 28½ cwt.; tank, 16 gals.; 12-volt.

£825+£173 p.t. = £998

AUSTIN HEALEY SPRITE MARK III

TWIN small sports cars from BMC, the Sprite and the MG Midget have been vastly improved. New doors that can be locked, curved windscreen, winding glass windows and revised instrument layout; new semi-elliptic rear suspension for better ride and road-holding; improved engine with higher compression, larger inlet valves, stronger crankshaft, new exhaust manifold to give an extra 3 h.p. Cheap speed in civilised surroundings.

CLOSE-UP

Four-cyl.; o.h.v.; 64.6×83.7 mm.; 1,098 c.c.; 59 b.h.p.; 8.9 to 1 comp.; coil ign.; 2 S.U. carbs.; 4-speed, 13.5, 8.09, 5.73, 4.22 to 1; cen. lvr.; susp., f. ind. coil, r. half-elliptic; 2-door; 2-seat; hyd. brks., disc front; max. 90 m.p.h.; cruise 75; m.p.g. 29-32; whl. base 6ft. 8in.; track f. 3ft. 9¾in., r. 3ft. 8¾in.; lgth. 11ft. 5¼in.; width 4ft. 5in.; ht. 4ft. 1¾in.; g.c. 5in.; turng. cir. 32ft.; kerb wt. 14 cwt.; tank, 6 gals.; 12-volt.

£505+£107 p.t. = £612

Abbreviations—g.c.—ground clearance; susp.—suspension; f.—front; r.—rear; comp.—compression; s.v.—side-valves; o.h.v.—overhead valves; o.h.c.—overhead camshaft; hyd.—hydraulic.

AUSTIN HEALEY 3000 MARK III

APPEARANCES are deceptive. The Austin Healey 3000 looks the same, but it's different. Power is up from 132 to 149 hp. and it is much quieter. Driving compartment is improved with a central console and lockable glove box. Main instruments are in a polished wood facia in front of the driver. Rear backrest can be folded flat to form luggage platform; the vinyl upholstery is modified for greater comfort.

CLOSE-UP
Six-cyl.; o.h.v.; 83.4×88.9 mm.; 2 912 c.c.; 149 b.h.p.; 9 to 1 comp.; coil ign.; 2 S.U. carbs.; 4-speed, 10.209, 7.302, 4.743, 3.545 to 1; cen. lvr., de Normanville overdrive opt.; susp., f. ind. coil, r. half-elliptic; 2-door; 2/3-seat; hyd. servo brks., disc front; max. 120 m.p.h.; cruise 100; m.p.g. 20-23; whl. base 7ft. 7½in.; track f. 4ft. 0¾in., r. 4ft. 2in.; lgth. 13ft. 1½in.; width 5ft.; ht. 4ft. 1in.; g.c. 4½in.; turng. cir. 35ft.; kerb wt. 23 cwt.; tank, 12 gals.; 12-volt.

£915+£192 p.t. = £1,107

BENTLEY S.3 CONTINENTAL

A BRILLIANT beauty of the Motor Show, this is not the car for the economist. It has the hall-marks of good breeding—grace, power and speed. It is available with coachwork by H. J. Mulliner with four doors, as a James Young 4-door saloon, or as a coupe by Park Ward with two doors. The man who drives a Continental really gets the best out of motoring. And it has Rolls-Royce automatic transmission.

CLOSE-UP
Eight-cyl.; o.h.v.; 104.14×91.44 mm.; 6,230 c.c.; 9 to 1 comp.; coil ign.; 2 S.U. carbs.; 4-speed auto., 11.75, 8.10, 4.46, 3.08 to 1; col. lvr.; susp., f. ind. coil, r. half-elliptic, 2/4-door; 4-seat; hyd. servo brks.; max. 120 m.p.h.; cruise 90-100; m.p.g. 14-16; whl. base 10ft. 3in.; track f. 4ft. 10½in., r. 5ft.; lgth. 17ft. 8in.; wdth. 6ft.; ht. 5ft. 2in.; g.c. 7in.; turng. cir. 41ft. 8in.; kerb wt. 39¾ cwt.; tank, 18 gals.; 12-volt.

£6,505+£1,357 p.t. = £7,862

BENTLEY S3

POSSIBLY disturbed by buyers who have the money but feel they are "not old enough" for a Rolls-Royce or Bentley, the makers have been running a campaign to emphasise that this is something to be enjoyed in your prime, not merely a refuge for opulent old age. If you appreciate instantly responsive but feather-light controls, commanding performance and whispering quiet, impeccable finish and time-less elegance, place your order now.

CLOSE-UP
Eight-cyl.; o.h.v.; 104.14×91.44 mm.; 6,230 c.c.; 9 to 1 comp.; coil ign.; 2 S.U. carbs.; 4-speed auto., 11.75, 8.10, 4.46, 3.08 to 1; col. lvr.; susp., f. ind. coil, r. half-elliptic; 4-door; 5/6-seat; hyd. servo brks.; max. 110 m.p.h.; cruise 90; m.p.g. 12-15; whl. base 10ft. 3in.; track, f. 4ft. 10in., r. 5ft.; lgth. 17ft. 7½in.; wdth. 6ft. 2¾in.; ht. 5ft. 4in.; g.c. 7in.; turng. cir. 41ft. 8in.; kerb wt. 41½ cwt.; tank, 18 gals.; 12-volt.

£4,455+£930 p.t. = £5,385

B.M.W. 700

BAYERISCHE Motorenwerke, the full name of the makers is quite a mouthful and this zippy little car has gone past before you could say it. The B.M.W. 700 with 697 c.c. two-cylinder air-cooled engine at the rear has a maximum speed of 70 m.p.h. For sporting drivers, there's the 700 CS with twin-carburetter 40 hp. engine and family men can have the LS Luxus with longer wheelbase and roomier body.

CLOSE-UP
Two-cyl.; o.h.v. air-cooled; 73×78 mm.; 697 c.c.; 37 b.h.p.; 7.5 to 1 comp.; coil ign.; Solex carb.; 4-speed, 19.2, 10.5, 6.9, 4.5 to 1; cen. lvr.; susp., f. and r. ind. coil; 2-door; 4/5-seat; hyd. brks.; max. 70 m.p.h.; cruise 60; m.p.g. 31-40; whl. base 6ft. 11½in.; track f. 4ft. 2in., r. 3ft. 11in.; lgth. 11ft. 7½in.; wdth. 4ft. 0½in.; ht. 4ft. 5in.; g.c. 5½in.; turng. cir. 33ft.; kerb wt. 12½ cwt.; tank, 7 gals.; 12-volt.

£577+£122 p.t. = £699

Abbreviations—g.c.—ground clearance; susp.—suspension; f.—front; r.—rear; comp.—compression; s.v.—side-valves; o.h.v.—overhead valves; o.h.c.—overhead camshaft; hyd.—hydraulic.

B.M.W. 1800 TI

STARTLING performances in this year's production car races set people talking about this super-quick version of an established model. Its canted light alloy engine with overhead camshaft and two twin-choke carburetters gives 110 h.p.: can be tuned for more. Steering column lock, headlamp flasher, electric screen washer and grab handles for all passengers are standard equipment. Same basic car also available with 1500 or single-carb 1800 engines.

CLOSE-UP

Four-cyl.; o.h.c.; 84×80 mm.; 1,773 c.c.; 110 b.h.p.; 9.5 to 1 comp.; coil ign.; 2 Solex carbs.; 4-speed, 15.69, 8.50, 5.46, 4.11 to 1; cen. lvr.; susp., f. and r. ind. coil; 4-door; 4-seat; hyd. servo brks., disc front; max. 106 m.p.h.; cruise 90; m.p.g. 20; whl. base 8ft. 4½in.; track f. 4ft. 4½in., r. 4ft. 6½in.; lgth., 14ft. 9in.; width 5ft. 7½in.; ht. 4ft. 8¾in.; g.c. 5½in.; turng. cir. 31ft. 6in.; kerb wt. 21¼ cwt.; tank, 12 gals.; 12-volt.

£1,274 + £267 p.t. = £1,541

BOND EQUIPE G.T.

WELL known makers of economy three-wheelers in Preston, Lancashire, produce this popular priced GT coupe. It owes much to Triumph, having a Spitfire engine in a Triumph Herald chassis and uses Herald doors. Body shell, in glass fibre, offers seats for two and two occasionals with a backrest which folds flat for extra luggage space. Lockable glove box, padded facia, carpets throughout and winding windows. There's a new four-seater, too.

CLOSE-UP

Four-cyl.; o.h.v.; 69.3×76 mm.; 1,147 c.c.; 64 b.h.p.; 9 to 1 comp.; coil ign.; S.U. carb.; 4-speed, 15.40, 8.87, 5.73, 4.11 to 1; cen. lvr.; susp., f. ind. coil, r. ind. trans. leaf; 2-door; 2/4-seat; hyd. brks., disc front; max. 93 m.p.h.; cruise 80; m.p.g. 35–40; whl. base 7ft. 7½in.; track f. and r. 4ft.; lgth. 12ft. 11in.; wdth. 5ft.; ht. 4ft. 4in.; g.c. 6½in.; turng. cir. 25ft.; kerb wt. 14¾ cwt.; tank, 10 gals.; 12-volt.

£650 + £137 p.t. = £787

BRISTOL 408

AIRCRAFT techniques adapted to car manufacture, Bristol fashion, produced this 125 m.p.h. fast touring car which is as pleasing on the eye as it is to drive. Chrysler supply the V8 engine and Torqueflite automatic transmission; Dunlop the disc brakes, servo-assisted on all four wheels. Bodywork is aluminium, floor is soundproofed, upholstery is in leather and front seats are fully reclining. Rear suspension is by torsion bars.

CLOSE-UP

Eight-cyl.; o.h.v.; 98.55×84.07 mm.; 5,130 c.c.; 250 b.h.p.; 9 to 1 comp.; coil ign.; Carter carb.; 3-speed auto., 8.10, 4.80, 3.31 to 1; push button control; susp., f. ind. coil, r. torsion bar; 2-door; 4-seat; disc servo brks.; max. 125 m.p.h.; cruise 100; m.p.g. 18–20; whl. base, 9ft. 6in.; track, f. 4ft. 5in., r. 4ft. 6½in.; lgth. 16ft. 7in.; wdth. 5ft. 8in.; ht. 5ft.; g.c. 6½in.; turng. cir. 39ft. 6in.; kerb wt. 32 cwt.; tank, 18 gals.; 12-volt.

£3,690 + £770 p.t. = £4,460

BUICK RIVIERA

UNCLUTTERED body lines, which were widely acclaimed when they first appeared, are further simplified for 1965. Headlamps are behind grilles which automatically swing aside when they are switched on. Tail lamps are now within the bumper. Instrument dials are new and a wood-grain steering wheel is an option. Only one model is produced, a two-door hard top coupe with a 6½-litre V8 engine which gives 340 horsepower.

CLOSE-UP

Eight-cyl.; o.h.v.; 106.36×92.45 mm.; 6,572 c.c.; 340 b.h.p.; 10.25 to 1 comp.; coil ign.; Stromberg carb.; 2-speed auto., 5.88, 3.23 to 1; col. lvr.; susp., f. ind. coil, r. coil; 2-door; 4-seat; hyd. servo brks.; max. 122 m.p.h.; cruise 100; m.p.g. 13–18; whl. base 9ft. 9in.; track f. 5ft., r. 4ft. 11in.; lgth. 17ft. 5in.; width 6ft. 2⅜in.; ht. 4ft. 5½in.; g.c. 5½in.; turng. cir. 43ft. 6in.; kerb wt. 38 cwt.; tank, 16¾ gals.; 12-volt.

£2,830 + £591 p.t. = £3,421

Abbreviations—g.c.—ground clearance; susp.—suspension; f.—front; r.—rear; comp.—compression; s.v.—side-valves; o.h.v.—overhead valves; o.h.c.—overhead camshaft; hyd.—hydraulic.

213

BUICK SKYLARK

V6 ENGINES in the Skylark saloons, sports saloons, convertibles and sports station wagons have modified cylinder heads for still more power. Buick's new Super Turbine automatic transmission has two low ranges, a straight second gear hold and another hold which will shift straight to first gear below 40 m.p.h. Manual transmission controls have been improved for smoother operation. New grilles and side mouldings identify the 1965 models and interior styling is revised.

CLOSE-UP
Six-cyl.; o.h.v.; 95.2 × 86.3 mm.; 3,685 c.c.; 160 b.h.p.; 9 to 1 comp.; coil ign.; Rochester carb.; 3-speed, 8.07, 4.78, 3.23 to 1; col. lvr., 4-speed or auto opt.; susp., f. ind. coil, r. coil; 2- or 4-door; 5/6-seat; hyd. brks., servo opt.; max. 98 m.p.h.; cruise 85; m.p.g. 18-20; whl. base 9ft. 7in.; track f. and r. 4ft. 9¾in.; lgth. 16ft. 11½in.; width 6ft. 1⅜in.; ht. 4ft. 6⅜in.; g.c. 5½in.; turng. cir. 40ft. 3in.; kerb wt. 28½ cwt.; tank, 16½ gals.; 12-volt.

£2,145 + £448 p.t. = £2,593

CADILLAC FLEETWOOD 60

VERTICAL grouping of headlamps permits a still wider grille, revised side panels and frameless windows of curved glass identify the 1965 series. A six-way power-operated seat and a tilt and telescope steering wheel are options to please the fastidious driver. Power-operated door locks, compressor-controlled rear dampers to maintain a constant height and full air conditioning and cruise control for motorway driving, are available to order.

CLOSE-UP
Eight-cyl.; o.h.v.; 104.9 × 101.6 mm.; 7,031 c.c.; 340 b.h.p.; 10.5 to 1 comp.; coil ign.; Carter carb.; 3-speed auto, 7.49, 4.55, 2.94 to 1; col. lvr.; susp., f. ind. coil, r. coil; 4-door; 6-seat; hyd.-servo brks.; max. 120 m.p.h.; cruise 100; m.p.g. 12-15; whl. base 11ft. 1in.; track f. and r. 5ft. 2½in.; lgth. 18ft. 11½in.; width 6ft. 7¾in.; ht. 4ft. 7⅞in.; g.c. 5¾in.; turng. cir. 45ft. 9in.; kerb wt. 43¼ cwt.; tank, 21 gals.; 12-volt.

£3,516 + £734 p.t. = £4,250

CHEVROLET IMPALA STATION WAGON

TYPICAL of the big American station wagons, this one is available with two or three rows of seats to carry up to nine people and choice of six- or eight-cylinder engines. Still bigger interiors, flush-mounted windscreen, curved side windows and 19½-gallon fuel tank are featured for 1965. The new perimeter-type chassis frame has side members swept out wide for maximum body support.

CLOSE-UP
Eight-cyl.; o.h.v.; 97.8 × 76.2 mm.; 4,638 c.c.; 198 b.h.p.; 9.25 to 1 comp.; coil ign.; Rochester carb.; 3-speed, 8.66, 4.97, 3.36 to 1; col. lvr. 4-speed, overdrive or auto opt.; susp., f. ind. coil, r. coil; 3 or 5-door; 6/8-seat; hyd. brks. servo opt.; max. 105 m.p.h.; cruise 90; m.p.g. 15-18; whl. base 9ft. 11in.; track f. 5ft. 1½in., r. 5ft. 3¼in.; lgth. 17ft. 9½in.; wdth. 6ft. 7⅛in.; ht. 4ft. 8⅛in.; g.c. 7½in.; turng. cir. 39ft. 6in.; kerb wt. 36 cwt.; tank, 19½ gals.; 12-volt.

£1,950 + £408 p.t. = £2,358

CHEVROLET IMPALA SPORTS SEDAN

MOST sweeping changes for years are incorporated in the 1965 models of the world's best-selling make. New bonnet and grille, longer tail, curved side windows, flush-mounted windscreen and rear window are features. The new wide-spaced perimeter frame design is combined with new coil-spring suspension nuts all-round. Optional extras include power steering, translucent floor mats! compass and transistor ignition.

CLOSE-UP
Eight-cyl.; o.h.v.; 97.8 × 76.2 mm.; 4,638 c.c.; 198 b.h.p.; 9.25 to 1 comp.; coil ign.; Rochester carb.; 2-speed auto; 6.11, 3.36 to 1; col. lvr.; susp., f. ind. coil, r. coil; 2 or 4-door; 6-seat; hyd. brks. servo opt.; max. 108 m.p.h.; cruise 90; m.p.g. 15-18; whl. base 9ft. 11in.; track f. 5ft. 1⅛in., r. 5ft. 3¼in.; lgth. 17ft. 9in.; wdth. 6ft. 7⅛in.; ht. 4ft. 8⅛in.; g.c. 7½in.; turng. cir. 39ft. 6in.; kerb wt. 33 cwt.; tank, 16¾ gals.; 12-volt.

£1,646 + £344 p.t. = £1,990

Abbreviations—g.c.—ground clearance; susp.—suspension; f.—front; r.—rear; comp.—compression; s.v.—side-valves; o.h.v.—overhead valves; o.h.c.—overhead camshaft; hyd.—hydraulic.

CHEVROLET IMPALA CONVERTIBLE

WORLD'S best selling make, Chevrolet is represented by the Impalas in a small selection of the big range available with six- or eight-cylinder engines and manual or automatic transmissions. Chevrolet also make the Corvair with flat-six air-cooled rear engine, the Chevy II with conventional four- or six-cylinder engines, the Chevelle, with six or eight cylinders and the Corvette sports coupe. Their range would make a show in itself.

CLOSE-UP
Eight-cyl.; o.h.v.; 101.6×82.5 mm.; 5,354 c.c.; 250 b.h.p.; 10.5 to 1 comp.; coil ign.; Carter carb.; 3-speed, 8.66, 4.97, 3.36 to 1; col. lvr. 4-speed, overdrive or auto opt.; susp., f. ind. coil, r. coil; 2-door; 5/6-seat; hyd. brks. servo opt.; max. 106 m.p.h.; cruise 90; m.p.g. 15-18; whl. base 9ft. 11in.; track f. 5ft. 1⅝in., r. 5ft. 3⅛in.; lgth. 17ft. 9in.; wdth. 6ft. 7½in.; ht. 4ft. 8in.; g.c. 7½in.; turng. cir. 39ft. 6in.; kerb wt. 33 cwt.; tank, 16¾ gals.; 12-volt.

£1,765+£369 p.t. = £2,134

CHRYSLER NEW YORKER

SEVENTEEN models now comprise the Chrysler range. The New Yorker four-door town sedan is matched by another one in the Newport series. Six side windows instead of four make a change from recent American convention, but there is also the two-door hardtop with windows and frames which disappear completely. 1965 models will have longer wheelbase, roomier bodies, more powerful engines; specification below covers 1964.

CLOSE-UP
Eight-cyl.; o.h.v.; 106.1×95.2 mm.; 6,746 c.c.; 340 b.h.p.; 10 to 1 comp.; coil ign.; Carter carb.; 3-speed auto., 6.76, 4.0, 2.76 to 1; push-button control; susp., f. ind. torsion bar, r. half-elliptic; 2 or 4-door; 6-seat; hyd. servo brks.; max. 118 m.p.h.; cruise 95; m.p.g. 12-15; whl. base 10ft. 2in.; track f. 5ft. 1in., r. 4ft. 11¾in.; lgth. 17ft. 11⅜in.; wdth. 6ft. 7¼in.; ht. 4ft. 7½in.; g.c. 5½in.; turng. cir. 46ft. 3in.; kerb wt. 38 cwt.; tank, 19 gals.; 12-volt.

CITROEN SAFARI ESTATE CAR

RUMOURED new models with Wankel engines won't displace this big practical station wagon yet awhile. Going over rough country, the self-levelling hydraulic-pneumatic suspension gives you extra ground clearance at a touch on a lever. And it gives you the same ride, not too choppy, not too soft, whether the car is fully laden or nearly empty. A pioneer design that is still among the engineering leaders.

CLOSE-UP
Four-cyl.; o.h.v.; 78×100 mm.; 1,911 c.c.; 69 b.h.p.; 7.5 to 1 comp.; coil ign.; Solex carb.; 4-speed, 13.79, 7.35, 4.77, 3.31 to 1; col. lvr.; susp., f. and r. hyd. pneu.; 5-door; 8-seat; hyd. servo brks., disc front; max. 90 m.p.h.; cruise 70; m.p.g. 25-30; whl. base 10ft. 3in.; track f. 4ft. 11in., r. 4ft. 3½in.; lgth. 16ft. 5in.; wdth. 5ft. 10⅜in.; ht. 4ft. 11¾in.; g.c. 6⅛in.; turng. cir. 36ft. 1in.; kerb wt. 25¾ cwt.; tank, 14 gals.; 12-volt.

£1,405+£294 p.t. = £1,699

CITROEN DS 19

STILL waiting for the others to catch up after nine years, the Citroen DS 19 remains unique with its combination of front wheel drive, self-levelling hydraulic-pneumatic suspension, servo action for clutch, gear shift and the disc/drum brakes, which distribute their effort according to the load on board. All body panels are detachable for easy repair. Puzzle for new-comers—where does the radiator get its air?

CLOSE-UP
Four-cyl.; o.h.v.; 78×100 mm.; 1,911 c.c.; 83 b.h.p.; 8.5 to 1 comp.; coil ign.; Weber carb.; 4-speed, 13.79, 6.96, 4.77, 3.31 to 1; dash lvr.; susp., f. and r. ind. hyd. pneu.; 4-door; 5/6-seat; hyd. servo brks., disc front; max. 100 m.p.h.; cruise 80; m.p.g. 25-30; whl. base 10ft. 3in.; track f. 4ft. 11in., r. 4ft. 3½in.; lgth. 15ft. 9in.; wdth. 5ft. 10½in.; ht. 4ft. 11¾in.; g.c. 6⅛in.; turng. cir. 36ft.; kerb wt. 23 cwt.; tank, 14 gals.; 12-volt.

£1,298+£272 p.t. = £1,570

Abbreviations—g.c.—ground clearance; susp.—suspension; f.—front; r.—rear; comp.—compression; s.v.—side-valves; o.h.v.—overhead valves; o.h.c.—overhead camshaft; hyd.—hydraulic.

215

CITROEN DW

CHIC addition to the Citroen front-drive range is a new convertible by Paris coach-builder Chapron, which keeps the family resemblance but has a shorter wheelbase. Power steering and brakes and an all-synchromesh four-speed gearbox. There are separate heating systems for front and rear passengers and fully reclining seats. Fast open-air motoring with a relaxing ride and a Gallic air. But good weather protection too.

CLOSE-UP
Four-cyl.; o.h.v.; 78×100 mm.; 1,911 c.c.; 83 b.h.p.; 8.5 to 1 comp.; coil ign.; Weber carb.; 4-speed, 13.79, 7.35, 4.77, 3.31 to 1; dash lvr.; susp., f. and r. ind. hyd. pneu.; 4-door; 5-seat; hyd. servo brks., disc front; max. 100 m.p.h.; cruise 90; m.p.g. 28-32; whl. base 10ft. 3in.; track f. 4ft. 11¼in., r. 4ft. 3½in.; lgth. 15ft. 10½in.; width 5ft. 10½in.; ht. 4ft. 11⅝in.; g.c. 6½in.; turng. cir. 37ft.; kerb wt. 22½ cwt.; tank, 14 gals.; 12-volt.

£1,298 + £272 p.t. = £1,570

DAF DAFFODIL

DUTCH treat for those who dislike gear shifting. Europe's smallest automatic-transmission car with the famous silent belt drive. As a demonstration of faith in its reliability, the Concessionaires give an unconditional 12-months guarantee which includes parts and labour. Since its introduction, it has been given more power, larger windows. Facia and instruments have been re-arranged and the glove compartment has a magnetic lock.

CLOSE-UP
Two-cyl.; o.h.v. air cooled; 85.5×65 mm.; 746 c.c.; 30 b.h.p.; 7.5 to 1 comp.; coil ign. BCI carb.; auto. belt drive 16.4 to 3.9 to 1; cen. lvr.; susp., f. ind. trans. leaf; r. ind. coil; 2-door; 4-seat; hyd. brks.; max. 65 m.p.h.; cruise 65; m.p.g. 38-48; whl. base 6ft. 9in.; track f. and r. 3ft. 10½in.; lgth. 12ft. 1in.; wdth. 4ft. 9in.; ht. 4ft. 6¼in.; g.c. 6¾in.; turng. cir. 31ft.; kerb wt. 13 cwt.; tank, 7 gals.; 6-volt.

£456 + £97 p.t. = £553

DKW F12

THREE cylinders giving the power impulses of six because they're two-strokes. It's still a popular formula in West and East Germany and in Sweden, when combined with front wheel drive. DKW also offers disc front brakes and there's now a sporty looking convertible as alternative to the clean-cut saloon body. Old messy oil-in-petrol lubrication is replaced by pump feed.

CLOSE-UP
Three-cyl.; two-stroke; 74.5×68 mm.; 889 c.c.; 40 b.h.p.; 7 to 1 comp.; coil ign.; Solex carb.; 4-speed, 15.47, 9.20, 5.86, 3.88 to 1; col. lvr.; susp., f. ind. torsion bar, r. torsion bar; 4-door; 4-seat; hyd. brks.; max. 78 m.p.h.; cruise 72; m.p.g. 33-36; whl. base 7ft. 4¼in.; track f. 3ft. 11¼in., r. 4ft. 2¼in.; lgth. 13ft. 0¼in.; wdth. 5ft. 2in.; ht. 4ft. 9¼in.; g.c. 6⅜in.; turng. cir. 32ft. 9in.; kerb wt. 14½ cwt.; tank, 7⅜ gals.; 6-volt.

£661 + £140 p.t. = £801

DKW F102

DESIGNED to replace the old Auto Union 1000 range, the DKW F102 is an impressive new front-drive saloon. The bodywork has bolt-on wings for easy repair. Three-cylinder two-stroke engine, sealed cooling system, disc brakes on the front wheels are highlights. No greasing is necessary and service is required at 6,000 mile intervals. The 1,175 c.c. engine develops 69 b.h.p. and the makers claim 84 m.p.h. maximum with 30 m.p.g.

CLOSE-UP
Three-cyl.; two-stroke; 81×76 mm.; 1,175 c.c.; 60 b.h.p.; 7.5 to 1 comp.; coil ign.; Solex carb.; 4-speed, 14.91, 7.79, 4.80, 3.64 to 1; col. lvr.; susp., f. ind. torsion bar, r. torsion bar; 2/4-door; 5-seat; hyd. brks., disc front; max. 81 m.p.h.; cruise 75; m.p.g. 30-33; whl. base 8ft. 5in.; track f. 4ft. 4in., r. 4ft. 3½in.; lgth. 14ft. 5in.; wdth. 5ft. 3⅝in.; ht. 4ft. 9½in.; g.c. 6¼in.; turng. cir. 37ft. 10in.; kerb wt. 17¼ cwt.; tank, 11 gals.; 6-volt.

£806 + £170 p.t. = £976

Abbreviations—g.c.—ground clearance; susp.—suspension; f.—front; r.—rear; comp.—compression; s.v.—side-valves; o.h.v.—overhead valves; o.h.c.—overhead camshaft; hyd.—hydraulic.

DAIMLER LIMOUSINE

HERE is a long plush car that offers discreet luxury to VIPs and visiting film stars. It can carry eight people in comfort including chaffeur and bodyguards. All steel body has four large doors. Vast luggage space. Separate heating systems for front and rear, and fresh-air heater for front compartment. Borg Warner automatic transmission is standard. It is, oddly enough, feather-light to drive with power-assisted steering and servo disc brakes.

CLOSE-UP

Eight-cyl.; o.h.v.; 95.25×80.01 mm.; 4,561 c.c.; 220 b.h.p.; 8 to 1 comp.; coil ign.; 2 S.U. carbs.; 3-speed, auto. 8.7, 5.4, 3.77 to 1; col. lvr.; susp., f. ind. coil, r. half-elliptic; 4-door; 8-seat; disc servo brks.; max. 110 m.p.h.; cruise, 90; m.p.g. 17-20; whl. base 11ft. 6in.; track f. and r. 4ft. 9in.; lgth. 18ft. 10in.; wdth. 6ft. 1¼in.; ht. 5ft. 5½in.; g.c. 7in.; turng. cir. 44ft.; kerb wt. 40 cwt.; tank, 16 gals.; 12-volt.

£2,809 + £586 p.t. = £3,395

DAIMLER SP250

NOW made under the Jaguar banner, Daimler SP250 is as popular with the police as with the public. This is because it is docile in traffic yet has the fast getaway of a greyhound. The sleek-lined car packs a 2,548 c.c. eight-cylinder engine, and has a maximum speed of 120 miles an hour. So it is built for the motorway as much as for the town centre. And this Daimler can now be bought with a detachable hardtop.

CLOSE-UP

Eight-cyl.; o.h.v.; 76.2×69.85 mm.; 2,548 c.c.; 140 b.h.p.; 8.2 to 1 comp.; coil ign.; 2 S.U. carbs.; 4-speed, 10.5, 6.236, 4.41, 3.58 to 1; cen. lvr.; susp., f. ind. coil, r. half-elliptic; 2-door; 2/3-seat; disc brks.; max. 120 m.p.h.; cruise 90; m.p.g. 28; whl. base 7ft. 8in.; track f. 4ft. 2in., r. 4ft.; lgth. 14ft. 0¾in.; wdth. 5ft. 0½in.; ht. 4ft. 2½in.; g.c. 6in.; turng. cir. 33ft.; kerb wt. 19½ cwt.; tank, 12 gals.; 12-volt.

£1,121 + £235 p.t. = £1,356

DAIMLER 2½-LITRE V8

LOOKS like a Jaguar but isn't. Body shell is Jaguar but radiator grille and interior furnishing are in typical Daimler style and the 2½-litre V8 engine purrs at 80-90. Transmission is BW automatic. Power assisted steering is optional. Dunlop disc brakes have vacuum servo. Equipment includes twin fog lamps, headlamp flasher, two speed wipers, electric windscreen washer, electric clock, leather upholstery, figured walnut instrument panel.

CLOSE-UP

Eight-cyl.; o.h.v.; 76.2 / 69.85 mm.; 2,548 c.c.; 140 b.h.p.; 8.2 to 1 comp.; coil ign.; 2 S.U. carbs.; 3-speed, BW auto., 10.2, 6.19, 4.27 to 1; col. lvr.; susp., f. ind. coil, r. cantilever leaf; 4-door; 5-seat; disc servo brks.; max. 110 m.p.h.; cruise 80-90; m.p.g. 20-22; whl. base 8ft. 11¾in.; track f. 4ft. 7in., r. 4ft. 5⅜in.; lgth. 15ft. 0¾in.; wdth. 5ft. 6¾in.; ht. 4ft. 9½in.; g.c. 7in.; turng. cir. 33ft. 6in.; kerb wt. 28 cwt.; tank, 12 gals.; 12-volt.

£1,322 + £277 p.t. = £1,599

DODGE DART

BEARING the name of one of the pioneers of the American industry, Dodge has long formed part of the Chrysler group and produces a big range of cars covering a large section of the market. The Dart is the lowest priced model, with six or eight cylinder engines, then come Dodge Six and Polara, in many variants, with many engine options, and finally the luxurious Dodge Custom.

CLOSE-UP

Six-cyl.; o.h.v.; 86.3×104.8 mm.; 3,690 c.c.; 145 b.h.p.; 8.4 to 1 comp.; coil ign.; Holley carb.; 3-speed, 9.59, 6.05, 3.31 to 1; col. lvr., auto opt.; susp., f. ind. torsion bar, r. half-elliptic; 2 or 4-door; 5/6-seat; hyd. servo brks.; max. 90 m.p.h.; cruise 80; m.p.g. 16-20; whl. base 9ft. 3in.; track f. 4ft. 8in., r. 4ft. 7½in.; lgth. 16ft. 4¼in.; wdth. 5ft. 9¾in.; ht. 4ft. 5½in.; g.c. 5½in.; turng. cir. 38ft. 6in.; kerb wt. 23 cwt.; tank, 15 gals.; 12-volt.

£1,650 + £345 p.t. = £1,995

Abbreviations—g.c.—ground clearance; susp.—suspension; f.—front; r.—rear; comp.—compression; s.v.—side-valves; o.h.v.—overhead valves; o.h.c.—overhead camshaft; hyd.—hydraulic.

ELVA COURIER

FLEXIBLE specifications offer choice of engines from MGB to 1½-litre Ford Cortina or Cortina GT. Doors are wide, with winding windows and body is glass fibre reinforced with steel. Extras include Laycock de Normanville overdrive, wood facia panel, two-speed windscreen wipers. Independent wishbone rear suspension is now appearing as alternative to rigid rear axle and half elliptics. Trojan now control the rear-engined racing Elvas too.

CLOSE-UP
Four-cyl.; o.h.v.; 76.2×88.9 mm.; 1,622 c.c.; 90 b.h.p.; 9 to 1 comp.; coil ign.; 2 S.U. carbs; 4-speed, 13.56, 8.25, 5.12, 3.73 to 1; cen. lvr.; susp., f. ind. coil, r. coil; 2-door; 2-seat; hyd. brks., disc front; max. 104 m.p.h.; cruise 90; m.p.g. 28; whl. base 7ft. 6in.; track f. and r. 4ft. 1in.; lgth. 12ft. 10in.; width 4ft. 11in.; ht. 4ft. 1½in.; g.c. 5in.; turng. cir. 35ft.; kerb wt. 12¾ cwt.; tank, 9 gals.; 12-volt.

£823 + £173 p.t. = £996

FACEL 6

BETWEEN the opulent 150 m.p.h. Facel II with Chrysler Typhoon V8 engine and the smaller Facel III with Swedish Volvo four-cylinder engine, comes the new Facel 6 with British BMC six-cylinder unit. Wheel base and body panels are the same as for Facel III. The BMC 2.9-litre engine is that used on the Austin Healey 3000. Front seats with adjustable backrests, two-speed electric wipers and disc servo brakes are standard.

CLOSE-UP
Six-cyl.; o.h.v.; 82.5×89 mm.; 2,860 c.c.; 150 b.h.p.; 9 to 1 comp.; coil ign.; 2 SU carbs.; 4-speed; 10.59, 6.02, 4.2, 3.07 to 1; cen. lvr.; susp., f. ind. coil, r. half elliptic; 2-door; 2-3 seat; disc servo brks.; max. 120 m.p.h.; cruise, 100; m.p.g. 18; whl. base, 8ft. 0½in.; track f. 4ft. 3½in., r. 4ft. 2⅜in.; lgth., 13ft. 8⅛in.; width, 5ft. 2½in.; ht. 4ft. 2in.; g.c. 5⅛in.; turng. cir., 32ft. 3in.; kerb wt., 23¼ cwt.; tank, 22 gals.; 12-volt.

FERRARI 330 GT

MERE 3-litre engines no longer guarantee the casual superiority Ferrari buyers expect, so the power-seeking plutocrat is now offered a V-12 of 4-litres in this GT coupe by Pininfarina. Basic design similar to that of the 250 GT, with single overhead camshafts to each bank of cylinders, tubular chassis with coil spring suspension at front and rigid rear axle on half-elliptic springs with twin radius arms at rear.

CLOSE-UP
Twelve-cyl.; o.h.c.; 77×71 mm.; 3,967 c.c.; 340 b.h.p.; 8.8 to 1 comp.; coil ign.; 3 Weber carbs.; 4-speed with overdrive, 9.58, 6.42, 4.64, 3.78, 2.94 to 1; cen. lvr.; susp., f. ind. coil, r. half-elliptic; 2-door; 2-seat; disc servo brks.; max. 152 m.p.h.; cruise 130; m.p.g. 12-16; whl. base 8ft. 8⅜in.; track f. 4ft. 7½in., r. 4ft. 6⅜in.; lgth. 15ft. 10⅓in.; width 5ft. 5⅓in.; ht. 4ft. 5¾in.; g.c. 4¾in.; turng. cir. 45ft.; kerb wt. 25¾ cwt.; tank, 22 gals.; 12-volt.

£5,100 + £1,118 p.t. = £6,218

FERRARI 500 SUPERFAST

PEGASUS the flying horse would need strong wings to keep ahead of the little prancing horse from the Ferrari stable. The acme of all that is fast and elegant is seen in this fabulous Farina-styled coupe. Its 4.9-litre V-12 engine has six twin-choke carburettors; the four-speed gearbox is fully synchronised and overdrive is standard. The chassis is tubular, the disc brakes have twin circuits and twin servos.

CLOSE-UP
Twelve-cyl.; o.h.c.; 68×68 mm.; 4,963 c.c.; 400 b.h.p.; 8.8 to 1 comp.; coil ign.; 6 Weber carbs.; 4-speed with overdrive, 9.58, 6.42, 4.64, 3.78, 2.94 to 1; cen. lvr.; susp., f. ind. coil, r. half-elliptic; 2-door; 2-seat; disc servo brks.; max. 174 m.p.h.; cruise 150; m.p.g. 10; whl. base 8ft. 8⅛in.; track f. 4ft. 7½in., r. 4ft. 6⅜in.; lgth. 15ft. 9½in.; width 5ft. 8in.; ht. 4ft. 2⅜in.; g.c. 4½in.; turng. cir. 45ft.; kerb wt. 30 cwt.; tank, 22 gals.; 12-volt.

£8,970 + £1,963 p.t. = £10,933

FIAT 500D

CHEAPEST four-wheel on the British market. If it's a nippy little runabout you seek—neatly equipped, which parks in small spaces, needs little fuel and no water, this is the car for you. Simple maintenance with only two greasing points. Power unit is rear mounted and suspension independent on all four wheels. The folding top attracts sun lovers, and it's an ideal second car. There's also a 500D station wagon.

CLOSE-UP

Two-cyl.; o.h.v.; air cooled; 67.4×70 mm.; 499 c.c.; 21.5 b.h.p.; 7.1 to 1 comp.; coil ign.; Weber carb.; 4-speed, 18.96, 10.59, 6.66, 4.48 to 1; cen. lvr.; susp., f. ind. transv. leaf, r. ind. coil; 2-door; 2/4-seat; hyd. brks.; max. 60 m.p.h.; cruise 55; m.p.g. 55; whl. base 6ft. 0½in.; track f. 3ft. 8⅛in., r. 3ft. 8½in.; lgth. 9ft. 9in.; wdth. 4ft. 4in.; ht. 4ft. 4⅛in.; g.c. 5⅛in.; turng. cir. 28ft. 2½in.; kerb wt. 9⅞ cwt.; tank, 4½ gals.; 12-volt.

£330+£70 p.t.=£400

FIAT 850

NEWEST addition to the Fiat family circle is this colourful two-door four-seater. Mechanically similar to the 600D but with longer wheelbase, increased seating space and more room for luggage which is carried under the bonnet and behind the rear seat. Engine is rear-mounted, all synchro gearbox is delightful and drum brakes powerful. Headlamp dipper and flasher on steering column. Screen washer standard. Sealed cooling system.

CLOSE-UP

Four-cyl.; o.h.v.; 65×63.5 mm.; 843 c.c.; 42 b.h.p.; 8.8. to 1 comp.; coil ign.; Weber carb.; 4-speed, 16.82, 9.27, 6.51, 4.16 to 1; cen. lvr.; susp., f. ind. transv. leaf, r. ind. coil; 2-door; 4-seat; hyd. brks.; max. 76 m.p.h.; cruise 65; m.p.g. 40; whl. base 6ft. 7¾in.; track f. 3ft. 9⅛in., r. 3ft. 11⅝in.; lgth. 11ft. 8¾in.; width 4ft. 8⅛in.; ht. 4ft. 6½in.; g.c. 7½in.; turng. cir. 29ft. 2in.; kerb wt. 13¼ cwt.; tank 6½ gals.; 12-volt.

FIAT 1600 S

ENGINE based on a Maserati design and coachwork by Pininfarina; sounds like a perfect recipe for a fast GT car. The 1600S is getting 112 m.p.h. on 1568 cc. There are bucket seats, facia is padded, anti-theft lock is standard. Disc brakes on all four wheels with servo assistance and steering linkage lubricated for life. Similar in style, the 1500 has pushrods instead of overhead camshafts.

CLOSE-UP

Four-cyl.; o.h.c.; 80×78 mm.; 1,568 c c.; 100 b.h.p.; 8.5 to 1 comp.; coil ign.; 2 Weber carbs.; 4-speed, 14.53, 8.98, 5.93, 4.3 to 1; cen. lvr.; susp., f. ind. coil, r. half-elliptic; 2-door; 2-seat; disc servo brks.; max. 108 m.p.h.; cruise 95; m.p.g. 26-29; whl. base 7ft. 8⅛in.; track f. 4ft. 0⅞in., r. 3ft. 11⅞in.; lgth 13ft. 4⅞in.; width 4ft. 11⅞in.; ht. 4ft. 3⅛in.; g.c. 4¾in.; turng. cir. 34ft. 5in.; kerb wt. 20¾ cwt.; tank, 8½ gals.; 12-volt.

FIAT 2300

SALOON, station wagon and a high speed coupe styled by Ghia comprise the Fiat 2300 range. They have disc brakes on all four wheels and no greasing required for steering or suspension. An alternator replaces the dynamo to give high charge at town speeds. All offer the high class finish of the thoroughbred car with thoughtful touches like reminder lamp for handbrake, grab handles in the roof for passengers.

CLOSE-UP

Six-cyl.; o.h.v.; 78×79.5 mm.; 2,279 c.c.; 117 b.h.p.; 8.8 to 1 comp.; coil ign.; twin choke Weber carb.; 4-speed, 13.82, 8.15, 6.03, 4.30 to 1; de Normanville overdrive opt.; col lvr.; susp., f. ind. torsion bar, r. half-elliptic; 4-door; 5-seat; disc servo brks.; max. 100 m.p.h.; cruise 90; m.p.g. 22; whl. base 8ft. 8¾in.; track f. 4ft. 4¾in.; r. 4ft. 3½in.; lgth. 15ft. 2in.; wdth. 5ft. 3¼in.; ht. 4ft. 5¾in.; g.c. 5¾in.; turng. cir. 37ft. 8¾in.; kerb wt. 24 cwt.; tank, 13¼ gals.; 12-volt.

£2,160+£451 p.t.=£2,611

Abbreviations—g.c.—ground clearance; susp.—suspension; f.—front; r.—rear; comp.—compression; s.v.—side-valves; o.h.v.—overhead valves; o.h.c.—overhead camshaft; hyd.—hydraulic.

FORD ANGLIA

THREE years old and already a mature member of the Ford family tree, the Anglia Super has a 1.2 litre engine, all synchronised gearbox, bigger brakes, to give it the edge on the other Anglias. Normal Anglias still in strong demand come as saloon, station wagon and in de luxe versions all with 997 c.c. engines. This is motoring at a modest price.

CLOSE-UP

Four-cyl.; o.h.v.; 80.96 × 48.41 mm.; 997 c.c.; 41 b.h.p.; 8.9 to 1 comp.; Super: 80.96 × 58.17 mm.; 1,198 c.c.; 53 b.h.p.; 8.7 to 1 comp.; coil ign.; Solex carb.; 4-speed, 16.987, 9.884, 5.826, 4.125 to 1; Super: 14.615, 9.883, 5.824, 4.125 to 1; cen. lvr.; susp., f. ind. coil, r. half-elliptic; 2-door; 4-seat; hyd. brks.; max. 75 m.p.h.; cruise 65; Super: 80 and 70; m.p.g. 35-42; whl. base 7ft. 6½in.; track f. 3ft. 10in., r. 3ft. 9¾in.; lgth. 12ft. 11½in.; wdth. 4ft. 9½in.; ht. 4ft. 7in.; g.c. 6½in.; turng. cir. 32ft.; kerb wt. 14¾ cwt.; Super: 15 cwt.; tank, 7 gals.; 12-volt.

Anglia: £395 + £84 p.t. = £479
Super: £475 + £101 p.t. = £576

FORD CONSUL CORSAIR

BUILT in Ford's new factory near Liverpool, the Corsair fills the gap between the Cortina and the Zephyr-Zodiac series. Four-speed all-synchro gearbox with centre or column lever; big boot and roomy body with carefully matched trim and accessories. BW 35 automatic transmission is an optional extra. GT version has nearly 20 more horsepower, servo brakes, bucket front seats, extra instruments on centre console.

CLOSE-UP

Four-cyl.; o.h.v.; 80.97 × 72.75 mm.; 1,498 c.c.; 64 b.h.p.; 8.3 to 1 comp.; coil ign.; Solex carb. (GT.83.5 b.h.p.; Weber 2-choke carb.); 4-speed, 13.818, 9.344, 5.507, 3.90 to 1; cen. or col. lvr.; susp., f. ind. coil, r. half-elliptic; 2 or 4-door; 5-seat; hyd. brks., disc front; max. 80 (GT. 90) m.p.h.; cruise 75; m.p.g. 30; whl. base 8ft. 5in.; track f. 4ft. 2in., r. 4ft. 1½in.; lgth. 14ft. 8⅝in.; wdth. 5ft. 3⅜in.; ht. 4ft. 9½in.; g.c. 6¾in.; turng. cir. 33ft. 9in.; kerb wt. 17¼ cwt.; tank, 8 gals.; 12-volt.

£560 + £118 p.t. = £678

FORD CORTINA

THIS car comes in many versions and all are top favourites. The range last year had a redesigned instrument panel on the lines of the Lotus Cortina, with gauges and warning lamps clustered in a convenient cowl over the steering column. The 1.2 litre engine models include saloon and station wagons. Then there are the faster Cortina Super and GT 1500.

CLOSE-UP

Four-cyl.; o.h.v.; 80.96 × 58.17 mm.; 1,198 c.c.; 53 b.h.p.; 8.7 to 1 comp.; or 80.96 × 72.75 mm.; 1,498 c.c.; 64 b.h.p.; coil ign.; Solex carb.; 4-speed, 14.615, 9.883, 5.824, 4.125 to 1; or 13.76, 9.32, 5.49, 3.9; cen. lvr., col. opt.; susp., f. ind. coil, r. half-elliptic; 2 or 4-door; 4/5-seat; hyd. brks.; max. 78-85 m.p.h.; cruise 65-75; m.p.g. 35-40; whl. base 8ft. 2in.; track f. and r. 4ft. 1½in.; lgth. 14ft. 0½in.; wdth. 5ft. 2½in.; ht. 4ft. 8½in.; g.c. 6½in.; turng. cir. 34ft. 8in.; kerb wt. 16-16¾ cwt.; tank, 8 gals.; 12-volt.

1200—£489 + £103 p.t. = £592
1500—£569 + £120 p.t. = £689

FORD ZEPHYR FOUR

YOUR money buys a lot of space in this boldly styled comfortable saloon. It buys even more in the Ford Zephyr station wagon. The big four-cylinder engine combines performance with economy. Four-speed gearbox is all-synchronised and Borg Warner overdrive or automatic transmission are optional. And there are disc front brakes. A car for hard work with a finish that is simple and practical.

CLOSE-UP

Four-cyl.; o.h.v.; 82.55 × 79.50 mm.; 1,703 c.c.; 73.5 b.h.p.; 8.3 to 1 comp.; coil ign.; Zenith carb.; 4-speed, 17.207, 9.167, 5.869, 3.9 to 1; col. lvr., BW overdrive or auto. opt.; susp., f. ind. coil, r. half-elliptic; 5/6-seat; hyd. brks., disc front; max. 76 m.p.h.; cruise 70; m.p.g. 23-27; whl. base 8ft. 11in.; track f. 4ft. 5in., r. 4ft. 5½in.; lgth. 15ft. ½in.; width 5ft. 9in.; ht. 4ft. 7½in.; g.c. 6½in.; turng. cir. 36ft. 6in.; kerb wt. 23 cwt.; tank, 12½ gals.; 12-volt.

£639 + £135 p.t. = £774

Abbreviations—g.c.—ground clearance; susp.—suspension; f.—front; r.—rear; comp.—compression; s.v.—side-valves; o.h.v.—overhead valves; o.h.c.—overhead camshaft; hyd.—hydraulic.

FORD ZEPHYR SIX & ZODIAC

100 M.P.H. and six seats for under £1,000. That's the Zodiac story. Still lower-priced, the Zephyr Six has 106 h.p. engine, two head-lamps, does over 90. The Zodiac, most luxurious British Ford, has more power, four headlamps, reversing lamps built into the rear bumpers. A central floor gear change originally used on police cars is now optional.

CLOSE-UP

Six-cyl.; o.h.v.; 82.55 × 79.50 mm.; 2,553 c.c.; 106 b.h.p., Zod. 114 b.h.p.; 8.3 to 1 comp.; coil ign.; Zenith carb.; 4-speed, 11.213, 7.849, 5.005, 3.545 to 1; col. lvr., BW overdrive or auto. opt.; susp., f. ind. coil, r. half-elliptic; 4-door; 5/6 seat; hyd. brks., disc front; max. 96-100 m.p.h.; cruise 85; m.p.g. 19-24; whl. base 8ft. 11in.; track f. 4ft. 5in., r. 4ft. 5½in., lgth. 15ft. 0½in., Zod. 15ft. 1¾in.; wdth. 5ft. 9in.; ht. 4ft. 7in.; g.c. 6¾in.; turng. cir. 36ft. 6in.; kerb wt. 24 cwt., Zod. 25½ cwt.; tank, 12½ gals.; 12-volt.

Zephyr: £692 + £146 p.t. = £838
Zodiac: £813 + £171 p.t. = £984

FORD TAUNUS 12M

THE German-built Ford 12M now comes with the option of 1.5 litre engine developing 57 h.p. at 5,000 or the 1.2 litre producing 50 h.p. The 1.5 litre version has a maximum speed of over 80 m.p.h. and the increase in power and torque have made this family saloon much more lively. Though they resemble Cortinas in style, the small Taunus models have front-wheel drive and V4 engines.

CLOSE-UP

Four-cyl.; o.h.v.; 80 × 58.8 mm.; 1,183 c.c.; 50 b.h.p.; 7.8 to 1 comp.; coil ign.; Solex carb.; 4-speed, 15.23, 8.80, 5.59, 3.78 to 1; col. lvr.; susp., f. ind. transv. leaf, r. half-elliptic; 2-door; 4/5 seat; hyd. brks.; max. 78 m.p.h.; cruise 75; m.p.g. 35; whl. base 8ft. 3½in.; track f. and r. 4ft. 1in.; lgth. 13ft. 11½in.; width 5ft. 8½in.; ht. 4ft. 9¾in.; g.c. 6¼in.; turng. cir. 35ft. 2in.; kerb wt. 16⅝ cwt.; tank, 8⅜ gals.; 6-volt.

FORD FALCON

GRILLE, interior trim and instrument panel are new for 1965. Low-profile tyres give better handling and performance is increased by three engine options; 2,785 c.c. six-cylinder giving 105 h.p., 3,277 c.c. six-cylinder with new seven-bearing crankshaft giving 120 h.p. or 4,735 c.c. V8 of 200 h.p. Body styles include two- or four-door saloons. Station wagons, station bus, club wagon.

CLOSE-UP

Six-cyl.; o.h.v.; 88.9 × 74.67 mm.; 2,785 c.c.; 105 b.h.p.; 9 to 1 comp.; coil ign.; Ford carb.; 3-speed, 9.3, 5.17, 2.83 to 1; col. lvr. 4-speed or auto opt.; susp., f. ind. coil, r. half-elliptic; 2- or 4-door; 5-seat; hyd. brks., servo opt.; max. 90 m.p.h.; cruise, 80; m.p.g. 20-23; whl. base, 9ft. 1⅜in.; track f. 4ft. 7in.; r. 4ft. 8in.; lgth. 15ft. 1⅜in.; width, 5ft. 11½in.; ht. 4ft. 6½in.; g.c. 5⅞in.; turng. cir., 38ft. 9in.; kerb wt., 22½ cwt.; tank, 13 gals.; 12-volt.

£1,703 + £318 p.t. = £2,021

FORD THUNDERBIRD

SEGMENTAL turn signals, in which a line of lights forms a moving strip, make clear the driver's intention on the 1965 version of these popular sporting coupes and convertibles. Disc front brakes now provide sustained stopping power. Power steering, power brakes and swing-away steering wheel for corpulent sportsmen are standard. Limited slip differential, vacuum controlled boot lock, air conditioning and reclining passenger seat are among the options.

CLOSE-UP

Eight-cyl.; o.h.v.; 101.7 × 96 mm.; 6,391 c.c.; 300 b.h.p.; 10.8 to 1 comp.; coil ign.; Ford carb.; 3-speed auto, 7.20, 4.41, 3.0 to 1; col. lvr.; susp., f. ind. coil, r. half elliptic; 2-door; 5-seat; hyd. servo brks. disc front; max. 118 m.p.h.; cruise 95; m.p.g. 12-16; whl. base 9ft. 5in.; track f. 5ft. 1in., r. 5ft.; lgth. 17ft. 1in.; wdth. 6ft. 5½in.; ht. 4ft. 4½in.; g.c. 5½in.; turng. cir. 43ft.; kerb wt. 41½ cwt.; tank, 18 gals.; 12-volt.

£2,832 + £592 p.t. = £3,424

FORD GALAXIE 500
WHETHER they are racing wheel to wheel at 150 m.p.h. round the big American stock car tracks, or streaking away from the field on British circuits like Brands Hatch and Silverstone, the big Galaxies have brought colour and variety into motor racing. But basically these are American family saloons structurally strengthened to protect the pilot and beefed up engines. And don't miss the Mustangs.

CLOSE-UP
Eight-cyl.; o.h.v.; 101.6 × 88.9 mm.; 5,766 c.c.; 253 b.h.p.; 9.3 to 1 comp.; coil ign.; Ford 4-choke carb.; 3-speed auto., 7.2, 4.41, 3.0 to 1; col. lvr.; susp., f. ind. coil, r. half-elliptic; 4-door; 6-seat; hyd. servo brks.; max. 120 m.p.h.; cruise 100; m.p.g. 15-18; whl. base 9ft. 11in.; track f. 5ft. 1in., r. 5ft. 1in.; lgth. 17ft. 5½in.; width 6ft. 7½in.; ht. 4ft. 6¾in.; g.c. 7in.; turng. cir. 41ft.; kerb wt. 33½ cwt.; tank, 16½ gals.; 12-volt.

£1,601 + £335 p.t. = £1,936

HILLMAN SUPER MINX
LATEST model has a squared-off back, a new roofline and a deeper windscreen. The car now has a snappy appearance with overriders and wheel disc trims and a lockable petrol-filler cap as standard. Inside there are reclining adjustable front seats, and a new panel of wood veneer. Chassis greasing is abolished and much more sound-deadening material has been added to the car. One of the finest models Rootes produce.

CLOSE-UP
Four-cyl.; o.h.v; 81.5 × 76.2 mm.; 1,592 c.c.; 62 b.h.p.; 8.3 to 1 comp.; coil ign.; Solex carb.; 4-speed, 13.013, 8.324, 5.413, 3.889 to 1; cen. lvr.; BW auto. opt.; susp. f. ind. coil, r. half-elliptic; 4-door; 4/5 seat; hyd. brks., disc front; max. 84 m.p.h.; cruise 70; m.p.g. 28-32; whl. base 8ft. 5in.; track f. 4ft. 3½in., r. 4ft. 0½in.; lgth. 13ft. 9in.; width 5ft. 3½in.; ht. 4ft. 10½in.; g.c. 6½in.; turng. cir. 36ft.; kerb wt. 21 cwt.; tank, 11 gals.; 12-volt.

£615 + £130 p.t. = £745

HILLMAN MINX DE LUXE
ONE of Britain's most popular family cars, the big improvements made to it last year have paid off well. Enthusiasts appreciate the front disc brakes, lighter steering, wider rear doors and bump-resisting suspension. The 1965 model now has synchromesh on all four forward gears and there are dashboard meter improvements. Optional is Borg Warner automatic transmission. An ideal car for the man with a medium-sized pocket.

CLOSE-UP
Four-cyl.; o.h.v.; 81.5 × 76.2 mm.; 1,592 c.c.; 53 b.h.p.; 8.3 to 1 comp.; coil ign.; Zenith carb.; 4-speed, 14.567, 8.324, 5.413, 3.89 to 1; cen. lvr.; BW auto. opt.; susp., f. ind. coil, r. half-elliptic; 4-door; 5-seat; hyd. brks., disc front; max. 80 m.p.h.; cruise 70; m.p.g. 27-33; whl. base 8ft.; track f. 4ft. 1½in., r. 4ft. 0½in.; lgth. 13ft. 5½in.; width 5ft. 0½in.; ht. 4ft. 10in.; g.c. 6in.; turng. cir. 34ft.; kerb wt. 19¼ cwt.; tank, 10 gals.; 12-volt.

£525 + £111 p.t. = £636

HILLMAN IMP DE LUXE
THE lively, likeable baby that brought the motor industry back to Scotland. Britain's first rear-engined car in large scale production. Compact four-seater, with small luggage trunk in the front, space behind the rear seats for more. For extra cargo space rear backrest folds flat and rear window opens for easy loading. Extra body stiffness, detail improvements to power unit and accessories are incorporated for 1965.

CLOSE-UP
Four-cyl.; o.h.c.; 68 × 60.4 mm.; 875 c.c.; 39 b.h.p.; 10 to 1 comp.; coil ign.; Solex carb.; 4-speed, 16.59, 8.91, 5.70, 4.14 to 1; cen. lvr.; susp., f. and r. ind. coil; 2-door; 4-seat; hyd. brks.; max. 80 m.p.h.; cruise 75; m.p.g. 40; whl. base 6ft. 10in.; track f. 4ft. 1in., r. 3ft. 11½in.; lgth. 11ft. 9in.; wdth. 5ft. 0½in.; ht. 4ft. 6½in.; g.c. 6½in.; turng. cir. 28ft.; kerb wt. 14 cwt.; tank, 6 gals.; 12-volt.

£440 + £93 p.t. = £533

Abbreviations—g.c.—ground clearance; susp.—suspension; f.—front; r.—rear; comp.—compression; s.v.—side-valves; o.h.v.—overhead valves; o.h.c.—overhead camshaft; hyd.—hydraulic.

HUMBER HAWK

SHARPER roof lines rejuvenate the big four-cylinder Humber and better all-round vision is obtained through the deeper windscreen and rear window. Chief of the mechanical improvements is the new gearbox with synchromesh on all four forward speeds. Saloon and station wagon models are roomy cars with moderate operating costs, fully equipped and finished with the attention to detail that always distinguishes cars bearing the Humber name.

CLOSE-UP
Four-cyl.; o.h.v.; 81 × 110 mm.; 2,267 c.c.; 78 b.h.p.; 7.5 to 1 comp.; coil ign.; Zenith carb.; 4-speed, 14.128, 9.038, 5,877, 4.22 to 1; de Normanville overdrive opt.; col. lvr.; susp., f. ind. coil, r. half-elliptic; 4-door; 6-seat; servo brks., disc front; max. 85 m.p.h.; cruise, 70-75; m.p.g. 20-25; whl. base, 9ft. 2in.; track f. 4ft. 9in., r. 4ft. 7½in.; lgth., 15ft. 4½in.; width, 5ft. 9½in.; ht. 5ft. 1in.; g.c. 7in.; turng. cir., 38ft.; kerb wt., 28¼ cwt.; tank, 16 gals.; 12-volt.

HUMBER SCEPTRE

DOMED windscreen gives a highbrow look to this fast well-equipped luxury sports saloon. Efficient 1.6-litre engine gives a top speed of over 90. Four speeds with overdrive and servo-assisted brakes with discs at front are standard. Included in the price are heating and ventilating system, screen washers, reversing lamp, wheel discs, four headlamps, padded sun visors, rev counter and cigarette lighter.

CLOSE-UP
Four-cyl.; o.h.v.; 81.5 × 76.2 mm.; 1,592 c.c.; 80 b.h.p.; 9 to 1 comp.; coil ign.; 2 Zenith carbs.; 4-speed, 14.13, 9.04, 5.88, 4.22 to 1; cen. lvr.; susp., f. ind. coil, r. half-elliptic; 4-door; 4/5-seat; hyd. servo brks., disc front; max. 90 m.p.h.; cruise 80; m.p.g. 25; whl. base 8ft. 5in.; track f. 4ft. 3½in., r. 4ft. 0½in.; lgth. 13ft. 9½in.; wdth. 5ft. 2½in.; ht. 4ft. 9in.; g.c. 6½in.; turng. cir. 36ft.; kerb wt. 21⅛ cwt.; tank, 10½ gals.; 12-volt.

£825 + £173 p.t. = £998

HUMBER SUPER SNIPE

OBVIOUS styling changes making for sleeker lines and better vision, are accompanied by engine modifications giving an extra five horsepower, two Stromberg carburetters, new manifolds and a larger air cleaner. The name of a luxurious pre-war Humber is revived in the Imperial, which has automatic transmission, power assisted steering, Selectaride adjustable dampers. The brakes have servo assistance and a glass division for chauffeur drive is an extra.

CLOSE-UP
Six-cyl.; o.h.v.; 87.3 × 82.55 mm.; 2,965 c.c.; 137 b.h.p.; 8 to 1 comp.; coil ign.; 2 Stromberg carbs.; 3-speed, 11.835, 6.129, 4.22 to 1; col. lvr.; de Normanville overdrive or BW auto. opt.; susp., f. ind. coil, r. half-elliptic; 4-door; 6-seat; servo brks., disc front; max. 105 m.p.h.; cruise, 90; m.p.g. 20-25; whl. base, 9ft. 2in.; track f. 4ft. 9in., r. 4ft. 7½in.; lgth., 15ft. 8in.; width, 5ft. 9½in.; ht. 5ft. 1in.; g.c. 7in.; turng. cir., 38ft.; kerb wt., 29½ cwt.; tank, 16 gals.; 12-volt.

ISO-RIVOLTA

CHEVROLET Corvette engine in a light sports chassis makes Italy's Rivolta an exciting contender in the exclusive 130 m.p.h. plus class. Four-seater body by Bertone, Borg Warner all-synchromesh gear box, Salisbury limited slip differential. If it's not fast enough, the 325 hp. High Performance version does 147 m.p.h.; the Iso Grifo A3L, two-seater coupe with four twin-choke carburetters hits 170 or the Grifo A3C with riveted light alloy body should do over 180.

CLOSE-UP
Eight-cyl.; o.h.v.; 101.6 × 82.55 mm.; 5,354 c.c.; 300 b.h.p.; 10.5 to 1 comp.; coil ign.; Carter carb.; 4-speed, 7.44, 5.62, 4.42, 2.93 to 1; cen. lvr.; susp., f. ind. coil, r. de Dion coil; 2-door; 4-seat; disc servo brks.; max. 135 m.p.h.; cruise 120; m.p.g. 14-18; whl. base 8ft. 10¾in.; track f. and r. 4ft. 7½in.; lgth. 15ft. 8¾in.; wdth. 5ft. 10in.; ht. 4ft. 4½in.; g.c. 4½in.; turng. cir. 40ft. 3in.; kerb wt. 30 cwt.; tank, 23 gals.; 12-volt.

£3,309 + £691 p.t. = £4,000

IMPERIAL

CHRYSLER'S luxurious prestige model with simple flowing lines. It is available as convertible or hard top coupe, each with seats for six and every aid to easy driving: self adjusting servo brakes, power assisted steering, pedal-operated parking brake, automatic transmission. Full air conditioning is optional. The Chrysler Corporation, which now has a big European stake in Simca and the Rootes Group, has also had a successful year in the United States.

CLOSE-UP
Eight-cyl.; o.h.v.; 106.2×95.25 mm.; 6,746 c.c.; 3.45 b.h.p.; 10 to 1 comp.; coil ign.; Carter 4-choke carb.; 3-speed auto., 7.18, 4.25, 2.93 to 1; press button control; susp., f. ind. torsion bar, r. half elliptic; 2-door; 6-seat; hyd. servo brks.; max. 125 m.p.h.; cruise, 100; m.p.g. 17-21; whl. base, 10ft. 9⅛in.; track f. 5ft. 1⅜in.; r. 5ft. 1⅝in.; lgth., 19ft.; width, 6ft. 8in.; ht. 4ft. 9½in.; g.c. 5½in.; turng. cir., 46ft. 6in.; kerb wt., 46¼ cwt.; tank, 19 gals.; 12-volt.

JAGUAR E-TYPE

GOOD news for E-type enthusiasts. An enlarged engine of 4.2 litres and all-synchromesh four-speed gearbox make this streamlined speedster an even more exciting car. Seats now have variable angle backrests. New Dunlop discs with suspended vacuum booster give better braking response. Modernised electrical system with high-output alternator instead of dynamo and new starter with pre-engaged pinion.

CLOSE-UP
Six-cyl.; o.h.c.; 92×106 mm.; 4,235 c.c.; 265 b.h.p.; 9 to 1 comp.; coil ign.; 3 S.U. carbs.; 4-speed, 11.18, 6.16, 4.25, 3.31 to 1; cen. lvr.; susp., f. ind. torsion bar, r. ind. coil; 2-door; 2-seat; servo disc brks.; max. 150 m.p.h.; cruise, 130; m.p.g. 18-22; whl. base, 8 ft.; track f. and r. 4ft. 2in.; lgth., 14ft. 7⅞in.; wdth. 5ft. 5¼in.; ht. 4ft. 0½in.; g.c. 5½in.; turng. cir., 37ft.; kerb wt. 24 cwt.; tank, 14 gals.; 12-volt.
£1,648+£345 p.t. = £1,993

JAGUAR 2.4 LITRE MARK 2

STILL one of the best-selling cars in the brilliant Jaguar range, this car is cheaper to run than its bigger brothers and gives lusty high performance. Its appeal is to those who want a sleek, well-shaped car that can offer speed and comfort. Its engine was, of course, derived from the 3.4 litre Jaguar.

CLOSE-UP
Six-cyl.; o.h.c.; 83×76.5 mm.; 2,483 c.c.; 120 b.h.p.; 8 to 1 comp.; coil ign.; 2 Solex carbs.; 4-speed, 14.42, 7.94, 5.48, 4.27 to 1; cen. lvr., de Normanville overdrive or BW auto. opt.; susp., f. ind. coil, r. cantilever leaf; 4-door; 5-seat; servo disc brks.; max. 105 m.p.h.; cruise, 70-75; m.p.g. 23; whl. base 8ft. 11¾in.; track, f. 4ft. 7in., r. 4ft. 5⅜in.; lgth. 15ft. 0¾in.; wdth. 5ft. 6¾in.; ht. 4ft. 9½in.; g.c. 7in.; turng. cir. 33ft. 6in.; kerb wt. 28¼ cwt.; tank, 12 gals.; 12-volt.
£1,115+£234 p.t. = £1,349

JAGUAR S-TYPE

DEVELOPED from the still popular Mark 2 range, it is bigger, roomier and has independent suspension on all four wheels. Disc brakes all round and the longer higher tail give it exceptional luggage space. Complementary to all other models turned out by this famous firm, you can have 3.4 or 3.8 litre engines and choice of a normal four-speed gearbox, with overdrive and Borg Warner automatic optional.

CLOSE-UP
Six-cyl.; o.h.c.; 83×106 mm.; 3,442 c.c.; 210 b.h.p.; 8 to 1 comp.; or 87×106 mm.; 3,781 c.c.; 220 b.h.p.; coil ign.; 2 S.U. carbs.; 4-speed, 11.95, 6.58, 4.54, 3.54 to 1; cen. lvr., de Normanville overdrive or BW auto. opt.; susp., f. and r. ind. coil; 4-door; 4-seat; disc servo brks.; max. 118 m.p.h. (3.4), 123 m.p.h. (3.8); cruise 90-100; m.p.g. 16-23; whl. base, 8ft. 11⅛in.; track f. 4ft. 7in., r. 4ft. 5⅛in.; lgth. 15ft. 7⅞in.; wdth. 5ft. 6¾in.; ht. 4ft. 9½in.; g.c. 7in.; turng. cir. 33ft. 6in.; kerb wt. 31¼ cwt.; tank, 14 gals.; 12-volt.
£1,381+£289 p.t. = £1,670

JAGUAR MARK X

EXTERNALLY unchanged, but with bigger engine to give high performance with less effort. As transmissions there are a new four-speed all-synchromesh gearbox and the BW Type 8 automatic. Viscous fan coupling to reduce noise at speed, an alternator for fast battery charging, a pre-engaged starter pinion for positive quiet starting and improved power steering add extra luxury to this elegant and spacious car.

CLOSE-UP
Six-cyl.; o.h.c.; 92×106 mm.; 4,235 c.c.; 265 b.h.p.; 8 to 1 comp.; coil ign.; 3 S.U. carbs.; 4-speed, 10.76, 6.98, 4.70, 3.54 to 1; cen. lvr.; overdrive or BW auto. opt.; susp., f. and r. ind. coil; 4-door; 5-seat; disc servo brks.; max. 120 m.p.h.; cruise 90; m.p.g. 15-20; whl. base 10ft.; track, f. and r. 4ft. 10in.; lgth. 16ft. 10in.; width 6ft. 4½in.; ht. 4ft. 6½in.; g.c. 6½in.; turng. cir. 37ft.; kerb wt. 35 cwt.; tank, 20 gals.; 12-volt.
£1,783+£373 p.t. = £2,156

JENSEN C-V8

A HAPPY Anglo-American marriage produces a car lavishly equipped with loads of power and speed from its U.S. built Chrysler V8 engine. Automatic transmission is standard. Body in fibre glass with a very good finish. Armstrong Selectaride rear dampers are also a standard fitting. Two of the most recent changes are a flatter boot panel and the replacement of a chrome bonnet handle by a recessed one. A car for fast luxury motoring.

CLOSE-UP
Eight-cyl.; o.h.v.; 105×86 mm.; 5,916 c.c.; 305 b.h.p.; 9 to 1 comp.; coil ign.; Carter carb.; 3-speed auto, 7.52, 4.45, 3.07 to 1; col. lvr.; susp., f. ind. coil, r. half-elliptic; 2-door; 4-seat; disc servo brks.; max. 134 m.p.h.; cruise 110; m.p.g. 17-20; whl. base 8ft. 9in.; track f. 4ft. 7⅞in., r. 4ft. 8⅞in.; lgth. 15ft. 4½in.; wdth. 5ft. 7½in.; ht. 4ft. 6in.; g.c. 6in.; turng. cir. 38ft.; kerb wt. 29 cwt.; tank, 16 gals.; 12-volt.
£2,888+£603 p.t. = £3,491

LANCIA FLAMINIA

RARE, but now catching on in other makes, the compact V6 engine is a Lancia speciality. The Flaminia has its engine at the front, clutch, gearbox and differential at the rear. Brakes are discs, servo-assisted and mounted inboard at the rear. Coachwork includes saloon or coupe by Pininfarina, convertible GT coupe by Touring, sports coupe by Zagato. With the latest 2.8-litre engine they do from 105 to 120 m.p.h.

CLOSE-UP
Six-cyl.; o.h.v.; 80×81.5 mm.; 2,458 c.c.; 102 b.h.p.; 8 to 1 comp.; coil ign.; Solex carb.; 4-speed, 12.3, 7.6, 5.6, 3.75 to 1; col. lvr.; susp., f. ind. coil, r. de Dion half-elliptic; 4-door; 6-seat; disc brks.; max. 105 m.p.h.; cruise 90; m.p.g. 24-28; whl. base 9ft. 5in.; track f. and r. 4ft. 6in.; lgth. 15ft. 11in.; wdth. 5ft. 9in.; ht. 4ft. 9½in.; g.c. 5½in.; turng. cir. 40ft.; kerb wt. 29½ cwt.; tank, 12¾ gals.; 12-volt.
£2,356+£492 p.t. = £2,848

LANCIA FLAMINIA 3B 2800 COUPE

SLIM, simple but superbly proportioned, this Pininfarina coupe is on a short wheelbase version of the Flaminia. Engine power is increased to 140 h.p. and the braking system has twin master cylinders for maximum security. The rear axle is de Dion with half-elliptic springs. Buyers seeking maximum performance have the option of 150 h.p. engines in the Vignale Convertible and Zagato light alloy coupe.

CLOSE-UP
Six-cyl.; o.h.v.; 85×81.5 mm.; 2,775 c.c.; 140 b.h.p.; 9 to 1 comp.; coil ign.; Solex carb.; 4-speed, 11.64, 7.76, 5.35, 3.77 to 1; cen. lvr.; susp., f. ind. coil, r. de Dion half-elliptic; 2-door; 4-seat; disc servo brks.; max. 112 m.p.h.; cruise 95; m.p.g. 20; whl. base 9ft. 0½in.; track f. and r. 4ft. 6in.; lgth. 15ft. 4½in.; width 5ft. 8½in.; ht. 4ft. 7½in.; g.c. 4½in.; turng. cir. 39ft.; kerb wt. 30¼ cwt.; tank, 12¾ gals.; 12-volt.
£2,803+£586 p.t. = £3,389

Abbreviations—g.c.—ground clearance; susp.—suspension; f.—front; r.—rear; comp.—compression; s.v.—side-valves; o.h.v.—overhead valves; o.h.c.—overhead camshaft; hyd.—hydraulic.

225

LANCIA FLAVIA

ADJOINING the Turin-Milan autostrada at Chivasso, Lancia's ultra-modern factory is busy producing front-drive Flavias. An alternative flat-four light alloy engine of 1.8 litres gives the needed top-gear flexibility and there are disc brakes on all four wheels. Pininfarina makes a coupe, Vignale a convertible and Zagato a sports coupe that does 112 m.p.h., so there is something to suit a wide range of tastes and pockets.

CLOSE-UP

Four-cyl.; o.h.v.; 82×71 mm.; 1,500 c.c.; 78 b.h.p.; 8.3 to 1 comp.; coil ign.; Solex carb.; 4-speed, 16.16, 9.53, 6.71, 4.09 to 1; col. lvr.; susp., f. ind. trans. leaf, r. half-elliptic; 4-door; 5/6-seat; disc brks.; max. 95 m.p.h.; cruise 85; m.p.g. 26-32; whl. base 8ft. 8½in.; track f. 4ft. 3in., r. 4ft. 2in.; lgth. 15ft. 0½in.; wdth. 5ft. 3in.; ht. 4ft. 11in.; g.c. 5in.; turng. cir. 36ft.; kerb wt. 24 cwt.; tank, 10½ gals.; 12-volt.

£1,882 + £394 p.t. = £2,276

LANCIA FULVIA

V-TYPE engines are now spreading from the United States to Europe, but they are no novelty to Lancia, who pioneered the V6 and the narrow V4. It's the latter that's used on the Fulvia, smallest car in the Lancia range, which is one of the aristocrats of the 1100 c.c. class. Front wheel drive, fully synchronised gearbox and disc brakes with twin fluid circuits for extra safety.

CLOSE-UP

Four-cyl.; o.h.v.; 72×67 mm.; 1,091 c.c.; 58 b.h.p.; 7.8 to 1 comp.; coil ign.; Solex carb.; 4-speed, 21.18, 12.16, 7.36, 4.78 to 1; cen. lvr.; susp., f. ind. trans. leaf, r. half-elliptic, 4-door; 4/5-seat; disc brks.; max. 85 m.p.h.; cruise 75; m.p.g. 31-34; whl. base 9ft. 9½in.; track f. 4ft. 3½in., r. 4ft. 2½in.; lgth. 13ft. 7in.; wdth. 5ft. 2½in.; ht. 4ft. 7in.; g.c. 5in.; turng. cir. 34ft.; kerb wt. 20 cwt.; tank, 8½ gals.; 12-volt.

£1,149 + £240 p.t. = £1,389

LINCOLN CONTINENTAL

DISC front brakes are standard for 1965, a major step for an American motor manufacturer. Specification also includes automatic transmission, power steering and power brakes, six-way power-operated seat adjustment, power operation for side windows and ventilating panes, seat belts with retractors and whitewall tyres. An alternator is now used and transistor ignition is an option. The Lincoln guarantee extends for two years or 24,000 miles.

CLOSE-UP

Eight-cyl.; o.h.v.; 109.2×94 mm.; 7,046 c.c.; 320 b.h.p.; 10 to 1 comp.; coil ign.; Carter carb.; 3-speed auto, 6.84, 4.27, 2.89 to 1; col. lvr.; susp., f. ind. coil, r. half-elliptic; 2 or 4-door; 6-seat; hyd. servo brks.; max. 120 m.p.h.; cruise 100; m.p.g. 11-15; whl. base 10ft. 6in.; track f. 5ft. 2in., r. 5ft. 1in.; lgth. 18ft. 0½in.; wdth. 6ft. 6⅜in.; ht. 4ft. 6½in.; g.c. 5⅜in.; turng. cir. 47ft. 6in.; kerb wt. 46¾ cwt.; tank, 17½ gals.; 12-volt.

£3,658 + £764 p.t. = £4,422

LOTUS CORTINA

WHEN Ford and Lotus get together you may expect a pretty potent motor car. This speedy saloon is the outcome and really it is a full brother of the highly successful Consul Cortina GT. Modified for competition work by Cosworth Engineering, the Lotus Cortina is a favourite with rallyists and production-car racers. It is one of Britain's fastest saloon cars, and it has a splendid record of victories.

CLOSE-UP

Four-cyl.; o.h.c.; 82.5×72.7 mm.; 1,558 c.c.; 106 b.h.p.; 9.5 to 1 comp.; coil ign.; 2 Weber carbs.; 4-speed, 9.75, 6.39, 4.79, 3.9 to 1; cen. lvr.; susp., f. ind. coil, r. coil; 2-door; 4/5-seat; hyd. servo brks., disc front; max. 115 m.p.h.; cruise 100; m.p.g. 20-25; whl. base 7ft. 10⅜in.; track f. 4ft. 3⅜in., r. 4ft. 1⅛in.; lgth. 14ft. 0⅜in.; wdth. 5ft. 2½in.; ht. 4ft. 5⅜in.; g.c. 5⅜in.; turng. cir. 35ft.; kerb wt. 17½ cwt.; tank, 8½ gals.; 12-volt.

£820 + £172 p.t. = £992

Abbreviations—g.c.—ground clearance; susp.—suspension; f.—front; r.—rear; comp.—compression; s.v.—side-valves; o.h.v.—overhead valves; o.h.c.—overhead camshaft; hyd.—hydraulic.

LOTUS ELAN 1500

ROAD car with a Grand Prix pedigree. The Elan has glass fibre bodywork on a sheet-steel backbone chassis with all-independent suspension. Engine is the Lotus-Ford with twin-cam head and two twin-choke carburetters. To improve streamlining, headlamps are retractable. The two front seats are adjustable for reach and height and a small occasional seat behind accommodates the children. Luggage goes in the tail. Regular chassis greasing has been eliminated.

CLOSE-UP
Four-cyl.; o.h.c.; 80.96 × 72.75 mm.; 1,498 c.c.; 100 b.h.p.; 9.5 to 1 comp.; coil ign.; 2 Weber carbs.; 4-speed, 16.04, 9.31, 6.50, 3.89 to 1; cen. lvr.; susp., f. and r. ind. coil; 2-door; 2/3-seat; disc brks.; max. 125 m.p.h.; cruise, 100; m.p.g. 30; whl. base 7ft.; track f. and r. 3ft. 11½in.; lgth. 12ft. 1½in.; wdth. 4ft. 8in.; ht. 3ft. 5in.; g.c. 6in.; turng. cir. 29ft. 3in.; tank, 10 gals.; 12-volt.

£1,148 + £241 p.t. = £1,389

LOTUS SUPER SEVEN 1500

LOTUS complain that their Super Seven 1500 was banned from production car events in the USA because it was too fast for the opposition. The Cosworth-Ford engine gives it terrific performance and classic handling qualities make it a fine car for the apprentice race driver. Designed as a built-it-yourself car it is easy to maintain and will zip from standstill to 60 m.p.h. in 6½ seconds.

CLOSE-UP
Four-cyl.; o.h.v.; 80.63 × 72.75 mm.; 1,498 c.c.; 75 b.h.p.; 8 to 1 comp.; coil ign.; Weber carb.; 4-speed, 10.31, 6.98, 5.79, 4.1 to 1; cen. lvr.; susp., f. ind. coil, r. coil; no doors; 2-seat; hyd. brks., disc front; max. 102 m.p.h.; cruise 85; m.p.g. 25-32; whl. base 7ft. 4in.; track f. and r. 4ft. 1in.; lgth. 10ft. 11½in.; wdth. 4ft. 9½in.; ht. 3ft. 7in.; g.c. 4in.; turng. cir. 26ft.; kerb wt. 9½ cwt.; tank, 8 gals.; 12-volt.

£695 + £173 p.t. = £868

MASERATI V8

MANY-SPLENDOURED motoring is the reward of those who can afford this powerful new V8 saloon with svelte sophisticated styling by Frua. Probably the world's fastest four-door saloon it is credited with a top speed of 143 m.p.h. Its V8 light alloy engine has four overhead camshafts and four twin-choke carburetters. It has disc brakes with servo and twin master cylinders. Choice of five-speed ZF gearbox or automatic transmission.

CLOSE-UP
Eight-cyl.; o.h.c.; 88 × 85 mm.; 4,136 c.c.; 260 b.h.p.; 8.5 to 1 comp.; coil ign.; 4 Weber carbs.; 5-speed, 9.66, 6.22, 4.35, 3.54, 2.91 to 1; cen. lvr., BW auto. opt.; susp., f. ind. coil, r. de Dion coil; 4-door; 5-seat; disc servo brks.; max. 143 m.p.h.; cruise 110; m.p.g. 17-18; whl. base 8ft. 10½in.; track f. 4ft. 6¾in.; r. 4ft. 7⁷⁄₁₆in.; lgth. 16ft. 5in.; width 5ft. 6½in.; ht. 4ft. 5½in.; g.c. 7in.; turng. cir. 42ft. 9in.; kerb wt. 33 cwt.; tank, 20 gals.; 12-volt.

MERCURY COMET

NEW grille, bonnet and roof line go along with many mechanical changes for 1965. The wide choice of power units comprises six-cylinder 120 h.p. engine, V8 of 200 h.p. running on normal grade fuel, or V8s of 225 and 271 h.p. designed to use premium fuel. Power steering, power brakes, air conditioning are optional extras and on V8 models a four-speed manual gearbox is available.

CLOSE-UP
Eight-cyl.; o.h.v.; 101.6 × 72.9 mm.; 4,736 c.c.; 220 b.h.p.; 9.3 to 1 comp.; coil ign.; Ford carb.; 3-speed, 8.37, 5.1, 3.0 to 1; col. lvr. auto opt.; susp., f. ind. coil, r. half-elliptic; 2 or 4-door; 5/6 seat; hyd. brks.; max. 100 m.p.h.; cruise 90; m.p.g. 14-17; whl. base 9ft. 6in.; track f. 4ft. 7⅝in., r. 4ft. 8in.; lgth. 16ft. 3½in.; wdth. 6ft. 1in.; ht. 4ft. 7½in.; g.c. 5½in.; turng. cir. 40ft.; kerb wt. 27½ cwt.; tank, 16 gals.; 12-volt.

Abbreviations—g.c.—ground clearance; susp.—suspension; f.—front; r.—rear; comp.—compression; s.v.—side-valves; o.h.v.—overhead valves; o.h.c.—overhead camshaft; hyd.—hydraulic.

MERCURY MONTEREY

WINDSCREEN wiping gets a new twist with Mercury's optional interval selector for 1965. It gives intermittent action for light drizzle or a continuous sweep for downpours. An alternator now replaces the dynamo, and for breakdowns or accidents an optional emergency switch sets all flashers operating simultaneously. Brakes are self adjusting and intervals between major lubrication have been extended to 36,000 miles, so most owners will never need one.

CLOSE-UP

Eight-cyl.; o.h.v.; 101.6 × 96 mm.; 6,384 c.c.; 253 b.h.p.; 9.4 to 1 comp.; coil ign.; Ford carb.; 3-speed, 7.26, 4.83, 3.0 to 1; col. lvr. auto opt.; susp., f. ind. coil, r. half-elliptic; 2 or 4-door; 6-seat; hyd. servo brks.; max. 108 m.p.h.; cruise 90; m.p.g. 15-19; whl. base 10ft.; track f. 5ft. 1in., r. 5ft.; lgth. 17ft. 11¾in.; wdth. 6ft. 7⅞in.; ht. 4ft. 8⅝in.; g.c. 5¼in.; turng. cir. 45ft. 6in.; kerb wt. 36¾ cwt.; tank, 16½ gals.; 12-volt.

M.G. MGB

BEST all-British performance at Le Mans and victory in the GT class of the Monte Carlo Rally are two of this year's successes for the popular MGB. Body and structure form one sheet steel unit. Windows wind up and down. There's good space for luggage in the tail and behind the leather-trimmed seats there's more luggage space or an occasional seat for the children. Five bearing crankshaft for 1965.

CLOSE-UP

Four-cyl.; o.h.v.; 80.26 × 89 mm.; 1,798 c.c.; 94 b.h.p.; 8.8 to 1 comp.; coil ign.; 2 S.U. carbs.; 4-speed, 14.21, 8.65, 5.37, 3.90 to 1; cen. lvr.; susp., f. ind. coil, r. half-elliptic; 2-door; 2/3 seat; hyd. brks., disc front; max. 108 m.p.h.; cruise 85; m.p.g. 26-28; whl. base 7ft. 9in.; track f. 4ft. 1in., r. 4ft. 1¼in.; lgth. 12ft. 9¼in.; wdth. 4ft. 11¾in.; ht. 4ft. 1⅜in.; g.c. 5in.; turng. cir. 32ft. 10in.; kerb wt. 17¼ cwt.; tank, 10 gals.; 12-volt.

£690 + £144 p.t. = £834

M.G. 1100

FASTEST production model of the now famous B.M.C. 1,100 c.c. cars, this snappy good-looking version has become a firm favourite here and abroad. It has synchromesh on second, third and top gears; an 8.9 engine compression ratio, with disc brakes in front and drum brakes at the back. Big point is the relatively new Hydrolastic suspension which uses anti-freeze and water in pipes connecting front and rear wheels.

CLOSE-UP

Four-cyl.; o.h.v.; 64.57 × 83.72 mm.; 1,098 c.c.; 55 b.h.p.; 8.9 to 1 comp.; coil ign.; 2 S.U. carbs.; 4-speed, 14.99, 8.98, 5.83, 4.133 to 1; cen. lvr.; susp., f. and r. ind. rubber-hydraulic; 2 or 4-door; 4-seat; hyd. brks., disc front; max. 85 m.p.h.; cruise 75; m.p.g. 35-38; whl. base 7ft. 9½in.; track f. 4ft. 3½in., r. 4ft. 2⅞in.; lgth. 12ft. 2¾in.; wdth. 5ft. 0⅜in.; ht. 4ft. 4⅞in.; g.c. 6in.; turng. cir. 34ft.; kerb wt. 17¼ cwt.; tank, 8½ gals.; 12-volt.

£590 + £124 p.t. = £714

MORGAN PLUS 4 SUPER SPORTS

NEVER a company that believes in making frequent changes, but rather one that prefers to go on refining existing models. Ford-engined 4/4 comes in two versions; with 8.3 compression and 64 h.p. or 9.1 compression and 83.5 h.p. Plus 4 has TR4 engine and is supplied as roadster, convertible or hardtop coupe. There's also Plus 4 Plus with coupe body, Triumph 2.2-litre engine and a top speed of 110 m.p.h.

CLOSE-UP

Four-cyl.; o.h.v.; 83 × 92 mm.; 1,991 c.c.; 117 b.h.p.; 9.2 to 1 comp.; coil ign.; 2 Weber carbs.; 4-speed, 12.85, 7.38, 5.24, 3.73 to 1; cen. lvr.; susp., f. ind. coil, r. half-elliptic; 2-door; 2-seat; hyd. brks., disc front; max. 120 m.p.h.; cruise, 105; m.p.g. 24; whl. base 8ft.; track f. 4ft., r. 4ft. 1in.; lgth. 12ft.; wdth. 4ft. 8in.; ht. 4ft. 1in.; g.c. 6½in.; turng. cir. 32ft.; kerb wt. 15½ cwt.; tank, 11 gals.; 12-volt.

£925 + £194 p.t. = £1,119

MERCEDES-BENZ 220SE

AT last a six-cylinder Mercedes is available at under £2,000 and if you have £1,994 6s. 3d. burning a hole in your pocket you'll find a lot to admire in the performance, equipment and finish of the 220. Advancing up the price scale, there are the faster and more powerful 220S, the fuel-injection 220SE and the beautiful 220SE coupe and convertible. The excellent Mercedes automatic transmission is optional on all models.

CLOSE-UP
Six-cyl.; o.h.c.; 80×72.8 mm.; 2,195 c.c.; 134 b.h.p.; 8.7 to 1 comp.; coil ign.; Bosch injection; 4-speed, 14.92, 9.34, 6.27, 4.1 to 1; cen. lvr., auto opt.; susp. f. and r. ind. coil; 2-door; 4-seat; servo brks., disc front; max. 105 m.p.h.; cruise 90; m.p.g. 22-25; whl. base 9ft. 0½in.; track f. and r. 4ft. 10½in.; lgth. 16ft. 0½in.; wdth. 6ft. 0½in.; ht. 4ft. 8½in.; g.c. 7½in.; turng. cir. 36ft.; kerb wt. 27¾ cwt.; tank, 14¼ gals.; 12-volt.

£2,033 + £425 p.t. = £2,458

MERCEDES 230 SL

GUYS and dolls alike go for this dual personality car which is both town and sports model. Magnificent road-holding and riding comfort. Option of power steering and automatic transmission. Adjustable backrests in soft leather, perforated for ventilation. Separate controls distribute cool or warm air to face, windscreen and side windows. Safety features include padded centre to steering wheel, recessed finger grips for door latches and strong grab handles.

CLOSE-UP
Six-cyl.; o.h.c.; 82×72 mm.; 2,306 c.c.; 170 b.h.p.; 9.3 to 1 comp.; coil ign.; Bosch injection; 4-speed, 16.57, 8.55, 5.83, 3.75 to 1; cen. lvr.; susp., f. and r. ind. coil; 2-door; 2-seat; hyd. servo brks., disc front; max. 125 m.p.h.; cruise 110; m.p.g. 20-24; whl. base 7ft. 10in.; track f. and r. 4ft. 10½in.; lgth. 14ft. 1½in.; wdth. 5ft. 9½in.; ht. 4ft. 3½in.; g.c. 5in.; turng. cir. 33ft. 4in.; kerb wt. 25½ cwt.; tank, 14¼ gals.; 12-volt.

£2,865 + £598 p.t. = £3,463

MERCEDES-BENZ 600

MOST completely automated car ever offered. Prestige car of the German industry. Self-levelling hydraulic-pneumatic suspension, compressed-air brakes. Hydraulically operated doors close with finger pressure, vacuum servos lock doors, trunk and fuel filler. At a touch the seat slides, is raised or lowered or changes the backrest angle. Self-erecting aerial, electric windows and silent sliding roof are other features. Full air conditioning with refrigerator on request.

CLOSE-UP
Eight-cyl.; o.h.c.; 103.1×95 mm.; 6,330 c.c.; 300 b.h.p.; 9.0 to 1 comp.; coil ign.; Bosch injection; 4-speed auto., 12.85, 8.14, 5.10, 3.23 to 1; col. lvr.; susp., f. and r. ind. pneu.; 4-door; 7/8-seat; disc compressed air brks.; max. 125 m.p.h.; cruise 100; m.p.g. 18; whl. base 12ft. 9½in.; track, f. 5ft. 2½in., r. 5ft. 2in.; lgth. 20ft. 6in.; wdth. 6ft. 6¾in.; ht. 4ft. 11½in.; g.c. 8in.; turng. cir. 47ft. 9in.; kerb wt. 51¾ cwt.; tank, 24½ gals.; 12-volt.

£7,242 + £1,510 p.t. = £8,752

MERCEDES-BENZ 190D

THIS well-established saloon with a four-cylinder diesel engine is a favourite on the Continent and is gaining ground in favour in Britain. It has roomy coachwork and disc brakes. Automatic transmission is optional. Diesel cars are usually dearer to buy but make up for it in the economy of running. The car is a worthy product of a famous car maker.

CLOSE-UP
Four-cyl.; o.h.c.; 85×83.6 mm.; 1,897 c.c.; 80 b.h.p.; 8.7 to 1 comp.; coil ign.; Solex carb.; 4-speed, 16.6, 9.75, 6.27, 4.1 to 1; col. lvr., auto. opt.; susp., f. and r. ind. coil; 4-door; 5-seat; hyd. servo brks., disc front; max. 90 m.p.h.; cruise 76; m.p.g. 28; whl. base 8ft. 10⅜in.; track f. 4ft. 9⅞in., r. 4ft. 10½in.; lgth. 15ft. 6½in.; wdth. 5ft. 10⅞in.; ht. 4ft. 10¾in.; g.c. 7½in.; turng. cir. 37ft. 5in.; kerb wt. 23⅞ cwt.; tank, 12½ gals.; 12-volt.

£1,514 + £317 p.t. = £1,831

MORRIS MINI COOPER S

GIANT-KILLING achievements in races and rallies established the fame of the Cooper S overnight. Choice of two engine sizes, 970 or 1,275 c.c. to suit competition classes, with special crankshaft, pistons, connecting rods, valves, guides and camshafts. Vacuum servo brakes (discs in front). Hydrolastic suspension for 1965.

CLOSE-UP

Four-cyl.; o.h.v.; 70.64×61.91 mm., 970 c.c.; 68 b.h.p.; 70.64\81.33 mm., 1,275 c.c.; 78 b.h.p.; 9 to 9.75 to 1 comp.; coil ign.; 2 SU carbs.; 4-speed; 12.05, 7.21, 5.11, 3.77 to 1 etc.; cen. lvr.; susp., f. and r. ind. rubber-hydraulic; 2-door; 4-seat; hyd. servo brks., disc front; max. 90–95 m.p.h.; cruise, 80–85; m.p.g. 28–32; whl. base, 6ft. 8in.; track f. 4ft. 0⅜in., r. 3ft. 10⅞in.; lgth., 10ft. 0½in.; width, 4ft. 7½in.; ht. 4ft. 5in.; g.c. 6in.; turng. cir., 32ft. 10in.; kerb wt., 15⅝ cwt.; tank, 5½ gals.; 12-volt.

970 c.c., £555+£117 p.t. = £672
1,275 c.c., £625+£132 p.t. = £757

MORRIS MINOR 1000

STILL popular—"age cannot wither nor custom stale". This car has been around for a long, long time, and has been exhibited at 16 London Motor Shows. Its cheapest form is the Minor 1,000 two-door saloon, but it comes in a range of eight variants, including estate car and traveller de luxe. It has a wonderfully sturdy 1,098 c.c engine, hydraulic brakes, and synchromesh on second, third and top gear.

CLOSE-UP

Four-cyl.; o.h.v.; 62.9×76 mm.; 948 c.c.; 37 b.h.p.; 8.3 to 1 comp.; coil ign.; S.U. carb.; 4-speed, 16.507, 10,802, 6.425, 4.555 to 1; cen. lvr.; susp., f. ind. torsion bar, r. half-elliptic; 2- or 4-door; 4-seat; hyd. brks.; max. 75 m.p.h.; cruise 55; m.p.g. 36–48; whl. base 7ft. 2in.; track f. 4ft. 2⅝in., r. 4ft. 2⅛in.; lgth. 12ft. 4in.; width 5ft. 1in.; ht. 5ft.; g.c. 6⅛in.; turng. cir. 33ft.; kerb wt. 14¾ cwt.; tank, 6½ gals.; 12-volt.

£426+£90 p.t. = £516

MORRIS OXFORD VI

ONE of the real favourites among family motorists, the Oxford saloon is roomy, comfortable and a pleasure to drive. Its elegance stems from the Italian Pininfarina design. Add to this the choice of two robust engines of 1.6 litres, with an option of 7.2 or 8.3 compression ratios. It has a four-speed gearbox with synchromesh on second, third and fourth. Borg Warner automatic transmission is optional. Just the car for the business man who likes to take out his family at week-ends.

CLOSE-UP

Four-cyl.; o.h.v.; 76.2×88.9 mm.; 1,622 c.c.; 55 b.h.p.; 8.3 to 1 comp.; coil ign.; S.U. carb.; 4-speed, 15.64, 9.52, 5.91, 4.3 to 1; col. or cen. lvr.; BW auto. opt.; susp., f. ind. coil, r. half-elliptic; 4-door; 4-seat; hyd. brks.; max. 80 m.p.h.; cruise 65; m.p.g. 25–33; whl. base 8ft. 4¼in.; track f. 4ft. 2⅜in., r. 4ft. 3⅜in.; lgth. 14ft. 6½in.; width 5ft. 3½in.; ht. 4ft. 10⅝in.; g.c. 5⅞in.; turng. cir. 37ft.; kerb wt. 21¾ cwt.; tank, 10 gals.; 12-volt.

£604+£128 p.t. = £732

MOSKVITCH

LIKE Vodka, the Moskvitch is proving palatable to a lot of people. Made in Russia, it is now assembled in Belgium where it is known as the Moskvitch Scaldia. 1.4-litre engine gives it a top speed of over 70 m.p.h. There is also a diesel version with British Perkins 1.6-litre engine. Designed for lands where service stations may be scarce, the Moskvitch is solid and well equipped with tools.

CLOSE-UP

Four-cyl.; o.h.v.; 76×75 mm.; 1,360 c.c.; 45 b.h.p.; 7 to 1 comp.; coil ign.; downdraught carb.; 4-speed, 17.89, 11.39, 7.83, 4.71, to 1; col. lvr.; susp., f. ind. coil, r. half-elliptic; 4-door; 4-seat; hyd. brks.; max. 72 m.p.h.; cruise 50; m.p.g. 35; whl. base 7ft. 9in.; track f. and r. 4ft.; lgth. 13ft. 4in.; wdth 5ft. 1in.; ht. 5ft. 1⅛in.; g.c. 7⅜in.; turng. cir. 39½ft.; kerb wt. 18¾ cwt.; tank, 7½ gals.; 12-volt.

£520+£110 p.t. = £630

Abbreviations—g.c.—ground clearance; susp.—suspension; f.—front; r.—rear; comp.—compression; s.v.—side-valves; o.h.v.—overhead valves; o.h.c.—overhead camshaft; hyd.—hydraulic.

N.S.U. PRINZ WANKEL

ENJOY a new motoring sensation and move a step ahead, in the first car with the Wankel rotating-piston engine. The two-seater convertible body styled by Bertone is based on the Sport Prinz. It is low built and light in weight. After much fiscal argument, its tiny engine with three-point rotor is rated as 1,500 c.c. and gives it a maximum around 95 m.p.h.

CLOSE-UP
Wankel rotating-piston engine; 500 c.c.; 50 b.h.p.; coil ign., single plug; Solex carb.; 4-speed, 13.65, 7.87, 5.20, 3.77 to 1; cen. lvr.; susp., f. and r. ind. coil; 2-door; 2-seat; hyd. brks., disc-front; max. 95 m.p.h.; cruise 85; m.p.g. 35; whl. base 6ft. 7⅛in.; track f. 4ft. 2in., r. 4ft. 0⅝in.; lgth. 11ft. 8½in.; wdth. 4ft. 11½in.; ht. 4ft. 0⅝in.; g.c. 7in.; turng. cir. 30 ft.; kerb wt. 13½ cwt.; tank, 7¾ gals.; 12-volt.
£984 + £206 p.t. = £1,190

N.S.U. PRINZ 1000

NOW available with right-hand drive, this lively new model is powered by a four-cylinder overhead camshaft air-cooled engine of 996 c.c. mounted crosswise at the rear. Top speed is said to be 85 and fuel consumption 40 m.p.g. Front backrests are adjustable. Included in the price are four-speed all-synchromesh gearbox, two-speed windscreen wipers, headlamp dipper and flasher, steering column anti-theft lock, separate heater controls for front and rear passengers.

CLOSE-UP
Four-cyl.; o.h.c.; air-cooled; 69×66.9 mm.; 996 c.c.; 43 b.h.p.; 8 to 1 comp.; coil ign.; Solex carb.; 4-speed, cen. lvr.; susp., f. and r. ind. coil; 2-door; 4-seat; hyd. brks., disc opt.; max. 85 m.p.h.; cruise 80; m.p.g. 37-45; whl. base 7ft. 4⅛in.; track f. 4ft. 2in., r. 4ft. 0⅝in.; lgth. 12ft. 6in.; wdth. 4ft. 10⅝in.; ht. 4ft. 5½in.; g.c. 7in.; turng. cir. 30ft. 9in.; kerb wt. 12½ cwt.; tank, 8 gals.; 6-volt.
£572 + £121 p.t. = £693

OLDSMOBILE F85

RARE bird in a world of straight sixes and V-eights, Oldsmobile's V-six engine continues as the economy power unit for the F85, but buyers wanting faster acceleration can have eight cylinders to order. Styling changes for 1965 affect grille front wings, bumpers and tail lamps. Body mountings, front springs and rear suspension have been modified in search of a smoother ride and better handling.

CLOSE-UP
Six-cyl.; o.h.v.; 95.25 × 86.3 mm.; 3,692 c.c.; 155 b.h.p.; 9 to 1 comp.; coil ign.; Rochester carb.; 3-speed, 8.34, 4.78, 3.23 to 1; col. lvr. auto opt.; susp., f. inf. coil, r. coil; 2- or 4-door; 5-seat; hyd. brks.; max. 95 m.p.h.; cruise 85; m.p.g. 17-22; whl. base 9ft. 7in.; track f. and r. 4ft. 10in.; lgth. 17ft.; wdth. 6ft. 1⅜in.; ht. 5ft. 5¾in.; g.c. 6in.; turng. cir. 44ft.; kerb wt. 27½ cwt.; tank, 16½ gals.; 12-volt.
£2,096 + £438 p.t. = £2,534

OLDSMOBILE DYNAMIC 88

CHASSIS and body are new for next year and the 6.9-litre V8 engine is teamed with a new Turbo Hydra-matic transmission. Curved side windows are used, and the convertible now has a glass rear window. Brushed aluminium is used for 88 instrument panels and simulated walnut for the 98, which also offers mirror, vanity lights and a tissue dispenser. Luggage capacity has been increased and the tank now holds over 20 gallons.

CLOSE-UP
Eight-cyl.; o.h.v.; 104.7 × 100.9 mm.; 6,965 c.c.; 300 b.h.p.; 10.25 to 1 comp.; coil ign.; Rochester carb.; 3-speed, 8.75, 4.69, 3.23 to 1; col. lvr. auto opt.; susp., f. ind. coil, r. coil; 2- or 4-door; 6-seat; hyd. brks.; max. 115 m.p.h.; cruise 95; m.p.g. 13-14; whl. base 10ft. 3in.; track f. 5ft. 2⅜in., r. 5ft. 1in.; lgth. 18ft. 8½in.; wdth. 6ft. 5¾in.; ht. 4ft. 8½in.; g.c. 6in.; turng. cir. 46ft.; kerb wt. 37½ cwt.; tank, 20¾ gals.; 12-volt.
£2,399 + £501 p.t. = £2,900

PANHARD 24 C.T.

HIGH performance with economy is the aim on the shapely Panhard 24. The Parisian body style is available in two forms, a Sports Coupe with Tiger engine, seating two with two occasional seats and a saloon seating four. They have a lusty air-cooled flat-twin engine, floor gear change, fully synchronised four-speed gearbox, two-speed wipers, four headlamps, fresh air ventilation. Seats have height and slope adjustments.

CLOSE-UP

Two-cyl.; o.h.v.; air-cooled; 84.9×75 mm.; 843 c.c.; 50 b.h.p.; 8.3 to 1 comp.; coil ign.; Zenith 2-choke carb.; 4-speed, 16.495, 9.277, 6.148, 4.525 to 1; cen. lvr.; susp., f. ind. transv. leaf, r. torsion bar; 2-door; 2/4 seat; hyd. brks.; max. 93 m.p.h.; cruise 85; m.p.g. 34-36; whl. base 7ft. 6in.; track f. and r. 4ft. 3in.; lgth. 14ft.; wdth. 5ft. 4in.; ht. 4ft.; g.c. 6¼in.; turng. cir. 30ft.; kerb wt. 15½ cwt.; tank, 9¼ gals.; 12-volt.

£1,046+£219 p.t. = £1,265

PANHARD TIGER

FRANCE'S oldest car manufacturer and frequent winner of the Index of Performance at Le Mans combines speed and economy in this 80 m.p.h. saloon propelled by a two-cylinder engine of only 848 c.c. It is a front-wheel drive 4/5 seater with a large boot and the specification includes battery master switch, steering column lock, and a really powerful hand brake operating on the front wheels.

CLOSE-UP

Two-cyl.; o.h.v., air-cooled; 85×75 mm.; 848 c.c.; 50 b.h.p.; 8.3 to 1 comp.; coil ign.; Zenith carb.; 4-speed, 18.38, 9.28, 6.15, 4.52 to 1; col. lvr.; susp., f. ind. transv. leaf, r. torsion bar; 4-door; 4-seat; hyd. brks.; max. 80 m.p.h.; cruise 75; m.p.g. 28-35; whl. base 8ft. 5in.; track f. and r. 4ft. 3in.; lgth. 15ft. width 5ft. 5in.; ht. 4ft. 9½in.; g.c. 6in.; turng. cir. 37ft. 5in.; kerb wt. 16¾ cwt.; tank, 9 gals.; 12-volt.

£826+£174 p.t. = £1,000

PEUGEOT 403

THIS is one of the most popular French-built cars, and it has been with us for a long time. It has a well-engineered and robust 1.5-litre engine capable of carrying five people in moderate comfort. For those who want to save on running costs there is a diesel engine available. One of France's good bread-and-butter cars, it holds its own among many keen competitors.

CLOSE-UP

Four-cyl.; o.h.v.; 80×73 mm.; 1,468 c.c.; 65 b.h.p.; 7.2 to 1 comp.; coil ign.; Solex carb.; 4-speed, 16.8, 9.42, 6.05, 4.20 to 1; col. lvr.; susp., f. ind. transv. leaf, r. coil; 4-door; 5-seat; hyd. brks.; max. 85 m.p.h.; cruise 78; m.p.g. 26-30; whl. base 8ft. 9in.; track f. 4ft. 5½in., r. 4ft. 4½in.; lgth. 14ft. 8in.; width 5ft. 6in.; ht. 5ft. 5¾in.; g.c. 6in.; turng. cir. 30ft.; kerb wt. 21¾ cwt.; tank, 11 gals.; 12-volt.

£719+£151 p.t. = £870

PEUGEOT 404

PININFARINA was styling consultant on this clean cut saloon which is building up a reputation for quality and durability in the Peugeot tradition. The gearbox is fully synchronised. The fan is driven by a thermostatically controlled magnetic clutch which disconnects when not required, saving power and reducing engine noise. Included in the range are a station wagon and a fast convertible with fuel injection engine.

CLOSE-UP

Four-cyl.; o.h.v.; 84×73 mm.; 1,618 c.c.; 72 b.h.p.; 7.4 to 1 comp.; coil ign.; Solex carb.; 4-speed, 16.80, 9.42, 6.05, 4.2 to 1; col. lvr.; susp., f. ind. coil, r. coil; 4-door; 5/6-seat; hyd. brks.; max. 90 m.p.h.; cruise 75-80; m.p.g. 30; whl. base 8ft. 8½in.; track f. 4ft. 4½in., r. 4ft. 2¼in.; lgth. 14ft. 6in.; wdth. 5ft. 5½in.; ht. 4ft. 9½in.; g.c. 6in.; turng. cir. 30ft.; kerb wt. 20½ cwt.; tank, 11 gals.; 12-volt.

£903+£190 p.t. = £1,093

PLYMOUTH BARRACUDA

FAST-BACK styling returns for this high-performance coupe designed for the new market for American compact sporting cars where Ford's Mustang is its major competitor. Based on the Valiant chassis, it has a 3.7-litre six-cylinder engine and Torqueflite automatic transmission. V8 engines are available and four-speed manual transmissions. The rear backrest folds flat for extra luggage-carrying capacity.

CLOSE-UP

6 cyl.; o.h.v.; 86.4×104.8 mm.; 3,682 c.c.; 145 b.h.p.; 8 to 1 comp.; coil ign.; Carter carb.; 3-speed auto., 7.913, 4.68, 3.23 to 1; cen. lvr.; susp., f. ind. torsion bar, r. half-elliptic; 2-door; 4-seat; hyd. brks.; max. 100 m.p.h.; cruise 90; m.p.g. 20; whl. base 8ft. 10ins.; track, f. 4ft. 7$\frac{7}{8}$in., r. 4ft. 7$\frac{5}{8}$in.; lgth 15ft. 8$\frac{1}{4}$in.; wdth. 5ft. 10in.; ht. 4ft. 5in.; g.c. 6$\frac{1}{4}$in.; turng. cir. 36ft. 4in.; kerb wt. 22 cwt.; tank, 15 gals.; 12-volt.

PONTIAC PARISIENNE

ACADIAN and Parisienne are two exclusively Canadian models, produced by General Motors at their factory in Ontario and now exported to Britain. In style and specification they contain elements of Chevy II, Chevelle and Pontiac and as usual, there is a range of six-in-line or V-eight engines to choose from, with normal synchromesh gearboxes or the option of automatic transmissions.

CLOSE-UP

Six-cyl.; o.h.v.; 98.4×82.5 mm.; 3.768 c.c.; 140 b.h.p.; 8.5 to 1 comp.; coil ign.; Rochester carb.; 3-speed, 9.05, 5.17, 3.08 to 1; col. lvr. auto opt.; susp., f. ind. coil, r. coil; 2- or 4-door; 5-seat; hyd. brks.; max. 94 m.p.h.; cruise 80; m.p.g. 16-20; whl. base 9ft. 11in.; track f. 5ft. 0$\frac{1}{4}$in., r. 4ft. 11$\frac{1}{4}$in.; lgth. 17ft. 9in.; wdth. 6ft. 7$\frac{1}{8}$in.; ht. 4ft. 6$\frac{3}{4}$in.; g.c. 6in.; turng. cir. 44ft.; tank, 16$\frac{1}{2}$ gals.; 12-volt.

£1,780+£372 p.t.=£2,152

PORSCHE Type 901

ROAD-HOLDING and handling of a thoroughbred sports car with Grand Touring comfort; that was the aim of Porsche engineers in the 901. Flat-six engine in light alloy, with five-speed all-synchro gearbox. Suspension breaks away from Porsche tradition; McPherson struts at front; trailing wishbones at rear, all with torsion bars. For racing there's the streamlined 904 with flat-four four-cam engine ahead of the rear axle.

CLOSE-UP

Six-cyl.; o.h.c.; air-cooled; 80×66 mm.; 1,991 c.c.; 130 b.h.p.; 9 to 1 comp.; coil ign.; 4 carbs.; 5-speed, 13.68, 8.36, 5.84, 4.43, 3.35 to 1; cen. lvr.; susp., f. and r. ind. torsion bar; 2-door; 2/4-seat; hyd. disc brks.; max. 130 m.p.h.; cruise 120; m.p.g. 25; whl. base 7ft. 2$\frac{3}{4}$in.; track f. 4ft. 4$\frac{1}{2}$in., r. 4ft. 3$\frac{1}{2}$in.; lgth. 13ft. 6$\frac{3}{4}$in.; wdth. 5ft. 3in.; ht. 4ft. 4in.; g.c. 6in.; turng. cir. 32ft. 9in.; kerb wt. 19$\frac{3}{4}$ cwt.; tank, 16$\frac{1}{4}$ gals.; 12-volt.

PORSCHE 356C/1600

CONSTANT improvement has produced a high degree of refinement and reliability in the 1600 series, which come in fixed-head coupe or convertible form with option of detachable hardtop. Riding comfort and road holding have been improved by the transverse rear compensator spring. The light alloy engine is air cooled and the gearbox has the famous Porsche servo-ring synchromesh. There's jet air flow for rear window demisting.

CLOSE-UP

Four-cyl.; o.h.v.; air-cooled; 82.5×74 mm.; 1,582 c.c.; 75 b.h.p.; 8.5 to 1 comp.; coil ign.; 2 Zenith carbs.; 4-speed, 13.68, 7.81, 4.43, 3.61 to 1; cen. lvr.; susp., f. and r. ind. torsion bar; 2-door; 2/4-seat; disc brks.; max. 110 m.p.h.; cruise 95; m.p.g. 32; whl. base 6ft. 10$\frac{3}{4}$in.; track f. 4ft. 2$\frac{3}{4}$in., r. 4ft. 2in.; lgth. 13ft. 2in.; wdth. 5ft. 5$\frac{3}{4}$in.; ht. 4ft. 4$\frac{3}{8}$in.; g.c. 6in.; turng. cir. 33ft. 6in.; kerb wt. 18$\frac{1}{2}$ cwt.; tank, 10$\frac{1}{4}$ gals.; 6-volt.

£1,915+£399 p.t.=£2,314

Abbreviations—g.c.—ground clearance; susp.—suspension; f.—front; r.—rear; comp.—compression; s.v.—side-valves; o.h.v.—overhead valves; o.h.c.—overhead camshaft; hyd.—hydraulic.

RAMBLER CLASSIC SIX

REVISED styling and a longer luggage boot, an alternator for high current output and twin-circuit brakes with option of discs in front are innovations on the Classic for 1965. There are two- and four-door saloons, station wagons, convertibles and hard top coupes. Engine options are 3,262 c.c. and 3,802 c.c. sixes and V8s of 4,704 or 5,360 c.c. Servo brakes, overdrive and automatic transmission are among the optional extras.

CLOSE-UP

Six-cyl.; o.h.v.; 95.25 × 101.6 mm.; 3,262 c.c.; 128 b.h.p.; 8.5 to 1 comp.; coil ign.; Carter carb.; 3-speed, 8.63, 5.39, 3.31 to 1; col. lvr., overdrive or auto. opt.; susp., f. ind. coil, r. coil; 2- or 4-door; 5/6-seat; dual hyd. brks., disc front opt.; max. 95 m.p.h.; cruise 85; m.p.g. 23; whl. base 9ft. 4in.; track f. 4ft. 10½in., r. 4ft. 9⅜in.; lgth. 16ft. 3in.; width 6ft. 2⅜in.; ht. 4ft. 6⅜in.; g.c. 6in.; turng. cir. 37ft. 3in.; kerb wt. 27 cwt.; tank, 15¾ gals.; 12-volt.

£1,298 + £272 p.t. = £1,570

RELIANT SCIMITAR

CLEAN-CUT in style to match a swash-buckling name. Reliant's new 120 m.p.h. GT car provides comfort as well as speed. The body was styled by David Ogle Associates. Front seats rise as they move forward, adjusting the driver's vision to his height. Safety padded steering wheel, padded gear lever knob and door lock handles are added touches of luxury. The engine is a Ford Zephyr.

CLOSE-UP

Six-cyl.; o.h.v.; 82.6 × 79.5 mm.; 2,553 c.c.; 120 b.h.p.; 8.3 to 1 comp.; coil ign.; 3 S.U. carbs.; 4-speed, 12.24, 8.56, 5.46, 3.875 to 1, de Normanville overdrive opt.; cen. lvr.; susp., f. ind. coil, r. coil; 2-door; 2/3-seat; hyd. brks., disc front; max. 122 m.p.h.; cruise 100; m.p.g. 22-26; whl. base 7ft. 6in.; track f. and r. 4ft. 2in.; lgth. 14ft.; width 5ft. 2¾in.; ht. 4ft. 2½in.; g.c. 6in.; turng. cir. 35ft.; kerb wt. cwt.; tank, 20 gals.; 12-volt.

£1,068 + £224 p.t. = £1,292

RELIANT REBEL

CHALLENGING the big groups with a new popular-priced family car for the first time since World War II, Reliant Motor Co., makers of three wheelers, present the Rebel, a neat two-door saloon. Body in glass fibre designed by David Ogle Associates. Water-cooled four-cylinder light alloy engine, said to give 60 m.p.g. and 65 m.p.h. cruising. Spare wheel mounted in front, leaving rear trunk free for luggage.

CLOSE-UP

Four-cyl.; o.h.v.; 55.88 × 60.96 mm.; 600 c.c.; 28 b.h.p.; 8.45 to 1 comp.; coil ign.; Solex carb.; 4-speed, 21.94, 12.69, 7.45, 5.14 to 1; cen. lvr.; susp., f. ind. coil, r. half-elliptic; 2-door; 4-seat; hyd. brks.; max. 68 m.p.h.; cruise 60; m.p.g. 55-60; whl. base 7ft. 5in.; track f. 4ft. r. 3ft. 10⅝in.; lgth. 11ft. 5in.; width 4ft. 10in.; ht. 4ft. 8½in.; g.c. 5⅛in.; turng. cir. 27ft.; kerb wt. 9 cwt.; tank, 6 gals.; 12-volt.

£433 + £92 p.t. = £525

RENAULT DAUPHINE

STILL popular in France and made under licence by Alfa Romeo in Italy, the Dauphine is a lively economical four-door car. Developed and refined over a number of years, it offers choice of 3 or 4-speed all-synchromesh gearbox. It now has disc brakes on all four wheels. Equipment includes anti-theft steering lock, town and country horns and an efficient heater. The front luggage trunk is surprisingly roomy.

CLOSE-UP

Four-cyl.; o.h.v.; 58 × 80 mm.; 845 c.c.; 30 b.h.p.; 8.0 to 1 comp.; coil ign.; Solex or Zenith carb.; 3-speed, 16.1, 7.88, 4.52 to 1; cen. lvr., 4-speed opt.; susp., f. and r. ind. coil; 4-door; 4-seat; disc brks.; max. 75 m.p.h.; cruise 60; m.p.g. 40-44; whl. base 7ft. 5½in.; track f. 4ft. 1½in., r. 4ft.; lgth. 12ft. 11½in.; width 5ft.; ht. 4ft. 9in.; g.c. 6in.; turng. cir. 29ft. 10in.; kerb wt. 12¾ cwt.; tank, 7 gals.; 12-volt.

£479 + £101 p.t. = £580

Abbreviations—g.c.—ground clearance; susp.—suspension; f.—front; r.—rear; comp.—compression; s.v.—side-valves; o.h.v.—overhead valves; o.h.c.—overhead camshaft; hyd.—hydraulic.

RENAULT CARAVELLE

THIS is the prestige model of the famous Renault firm that appeals specially to the sports-car minded public. Its larger engine of 1,108 c.c. producing 55 brake horse power now makes this semi-sports car as snappy as its smooth-lined appearance. It has a four-speed all synchromesh gearbox and is a delight to drive. Available as a coupe and a drophead convertible.

CLOSE-UP
Four-cyl.; o.h.v.; 70×72 mm.; 1,108 c.c.; 55 b.h.p.; 8.5 to 1 comp.; coil ign.; Solex or Zenith carb.; 4-speed, 14.93, 9.28, 6.10, 4.25 to 1; cen. lvr.; susp. f. and r. ind. coil; 2-door; 4-seat; disc brks.; max. 88 m.p.h.; cruise 80; m.p.g. 36; whl. base 7ft. 5½in.; track f. 4ft. 1⅛in., r. 4ft.; lgth. 14ft.; width 5ft. 2in.; ht. 4ft. 3in.; g.c. 5⅜in.; turng. cir. 31ft. 6in.; kerb wt. 15½ cwt.; tank, 8½ gals.; 12-volt.

£849+£178 p.t. = £1,027

RENAULT R4L

A COSY little estate car, the Renault 4L first sprinted into public favour as a front-wheel driven car. This version has six windows and a sturdy 845 c.c. engine. It is particularly suited to semi-farm work, with soft independent torsion bar suspension for riding over rough terrain. Continental farmers are addicted to it, and the model is now gaining favour on our roads.

CLOSE-UP
Four-cyl.; o.h.v.; 58×80 mm.; 845 c.c.; 34 b.h.p.; 8 to 1 comp.; coil ign.; Solex carb.; 3-speed, 15.675, 7.598, 4.282 to 1; dash lvr.; susp., f. and r. ind. torsion bar; 5-door; 4-seat; hyd. brks.; max. 68 m.p.h.; cruise 55; m.p.g. 45-50; whl. base 8ft.; track f. 4ft. 1in., r. 3ft. 11½in.; lgth. 12ft.; wdth. 4ft. 10½in.; ht. 5ft. 4in.; g.c. 7⅞in.; turng. cir. 28ft.; kerb wt. 11½ cwt.; tank, 5¾ gals.; 6-volt.

£446+£94 p.t. = £540

RENAULT R8 1100

EXTRA performance and flexibility has been obtained by expanding the engine from 956 to 1,108 c.c. It has a five-bearing crankshaft for long life and a sealed cooling system. Disc brakes on all four wheels are a rare advantage on this class of car. Standard equipment includes full fresh air heating and ventilation, interior courtesy light, town and country horns, anti-theft steering lock, twin sun visors, windscreen washers, leather grab handles, recessed safety door latches.

CLOSE-UP
Four-cyl.; o.h.v.; 70×72 mm.; 1,108 c.c.; 44.5 b.h.p.; 8.5 to 1 comp.; coil ign.; Solex or Zenith carb.; 4-speed, 14.93, 9.28, 6.11, 4.25 to 1; cen. lvr.; susp., f. and r. ind. coil; 4-door; 4-seat; hyd. disc brks.; max. 83 m.p.h.; cruise 70; m.p.g. 37-39; whl. base 7ft. 5in.; track f. 4ft. 1in., r. 4ft.; lgth. 13ft. 1in.; width 4ft. 11in.; ht. 4ft. 6½in.; g.c. 5⅜in.; turng. cir. 32ft. 10in.; kerb wt. 14¾ cwt.; tank, 8½ gals.; 12-volt.

£558+£118 p.t. = £676

RILEY ELF

LOOK lively when the Elf is around. Basically a Mini in party dress, it now has a 998 c.c. engine giving a top speed of nearly 75 m.p.h. The Riley grille is bordered by chromium side grilles and the boot flanked by discreet fins which house rear and stop lights and flashing indicators. Wood veneer instrument panel contains speedometer, fuel gauge, oil gauge, thermometer. Heater and windscreen washers are standard.

CLOSE-UP
Four-cyl.; o.h.v.; 64.58×76.2 mm.; 998 c.c.; 38 b.h.p.; 8.3 to 1 comp.; coil ign.; S.U. carb.; 4-speed, 13.657, 8.176, 5.317, 2.765 to 1; cen. lvr.; susp., f. and r. ind. rubber; 2-door; 4-seat; hyd. brks.; max. 75 m.p.h.; cruise 62; m.p.g. 40; whl. base 6ft. 8in.; track f. 4ft., r. 3ft. 10in.; lgth. 10ft. 10in.; wdth. 4ft. 7½in.; ht. 4ft. 5in.; g.c. 5½in.; turng. cir. 31ft.; kerb wt. 12½ cwt.; tank, 5½ gals.; 12-volt.

£475+£101 p.t. = £576

Abbreviations—g.c.—ground clearance; susp.—suspension; f.—front; r.—rear; comp.—compression; s.v.—side-valves; o.h.v.—overhead valves; o.h.c.—overhead camshaft; hyd.—hydraulic.

RILEY ONE-POINT-FIVE

ALTHOUGH this is one of the most popular family cars, it has the breeding of a true Riley and continues to register many successes in rallies and production-car races. Its appeal is mostly for the home-cum-sporting type, who appreciates the speedy reliability of its 1,489 c.c., 8.3 compression ratio engine and four-speed gearbox. It pulls up well with its Girling hydraulic brakes.

CLOSE-UP

Four-cyl.; o.h.v.; 73.025 × 88.9 mm.; 1,489 c.c.; 60 b.h.p.; 8.3 to 1 comp.; coil ign.; 2 S.U. carbs.; 4-speed; 13.56, 8.25, 5.12, 3.73 to 1; cen. lvr.; susp. f. ind. torsion bar, r. half-elliptic; 4-door; 4-seat; hyd. brks. max. 85 m.p.h.; cruise 70; m.p.g. 25-35; whl. base 7ft. 2in.; track f. 4ft. 2⅜in., r. 4ft. 2½in.; lgth. 12ft. 9in.; wdth. 5ft. 1in.; ht. 4ft. 11¾in.; g.c. 6½in.; turng. cir. 34ft. 3in.; kerb wt. 18½ cwt.; tank, 7 gals.; 12-volt.

£580 + £122 p.t. = £702

RILEY 4/72

MIXTURE as before for Riley enthusiasts who find the qualities they like in this elegant Farina-styled 1.6-litre model. Two carburetters and the option of Borg Warner 35 automatic transmission. Mono-construction four-door saloon body incorporates floor, bulkhead, frame members and wing valances. Leather upholstery, with wood veneer facia and door cappings. Windscreen washer, carpets, four ashtrays and two sun visors. Lockable glove box and large parcel tray.

CLOSE-UP

Four-cyl.; o.h.v.; 76.2 × 88.9 mm.; 1,622 c.c.; 65 b.h.p.; 8.3 to 1 comp.; coil ign.; 2 S.U. carbs.; 4-speed, 15.64, 9.52, 5.91, 4.3 to 1; cen. lvr.; susp., f. ind. coil, r. half-elliptic; 4-door; 4-seat; hyd. brks.; max. 88 m.p.h.; cruise 75; m.p.g. 23-29; whl. base 8ft. 4½in.; track f. 4ft. 2⅜in., r. 4ft. 3⅜in.; lgth. 14ft. 6½in.; wdth. 5ft. 3in.; ht. 4ft. 10⅞in.; g.c. 5⅝in.; turng. cir. 37ft.; kerb wt. 22¾ cwt.; tank, 10 gals.; 12-volt.

£757 + £160 p.t. = £917

ROLLS-ROYCE SILVER CLOUD III

ROLLS know they have a winner in this plush and powerful dream car, so they make no mechanical changes this year. Some chromium-plate parts of the trim, however, are now in the more expensive stainless steel. Its perfectly engineered 6.2 litre engine silently operates through a fluid coupling transmission. It has an automatic four-speed gearbox and special inimitable Rolls Royce drum brakes, servo-assisted.

CLOSE-UP

Eight-cyl.; o.h.v.; 104.14 × 91.44 mm.; 6,230 c.c.; 9 to 1 comp.; coil ign.; 2 S.U. carbs.; 4-speed auto. 11.75, 8.10, 4.46, 3.08 to 1; col. lvr.; susp., f. ind. coil, r. half-elliptic; 4-door; 5/6-seat; hyd. servo brks.; max. 110 m.p.h.; cruise 90; m.p.g. 12-15; whl. base 10ft. 3in.; track f. 4ft. 10in., r. 5ft. 5in.; lgth. 17ft. 7¾in.; wdth. 6ft. 2⅞in.; ht. 5ft. 4in.; g.c. 7in.; turng. cir. 41ft. 8in.; kerb wt. 41½ cwt.; tank, 18 gals.; 12-volt.

£4,565 + £953 p.t. = £5,518

ROLLS-ROYCE PHANTOM V

BRITAIN'S most exclusive car, used by the Queen and the Royal Family. Graceful despite its size, with space for five people in the rear compartment. West of England cloth upholstery, thick pile carpets, adjustable foot-rests and a sliding roof if required. Cocktail cabinet, cigarette case, notebook and mirror, lighters, ashtrays; finger-tip controls for the heater and electrically operated glass division. Top speed of this 2½-ton limousine is over 100 m.p.h.

CLOSE-UP

Eight-cyl.; o.h.v.; 104.14 × 91.44 mm.; 6,230 c.c.; 9 to 1 comp.; coil ign.; 2 S.U. carbs.; 4-speed auto., 14.86, 10.23, 5.64, 3.89 to 1; col. lvr.; susp., f. ind. coil, r. half-elliptic; 4-door; 7-seat; hyd. servo brks.; max. 100 m.p.h.; cruise 85; m.p.g. 12; whl. base 12ft.; track f. 5ft. 0⅞in., r. 5ft. 4in.; lgth. 19ft. 10in.; wdth. 6ft. 7in.; ht. 5ft. 9in.; g.c. 7⅛in.; turng. cir. 48ft. 9in.; tank, 23 gals.; 12-volt.

£7,305 + £1,523 p.t. = £8,828

Abbreviations—g.c.—ground clearance; susp.—suspension; f.—front; r.—rear; comp.—compression; s.v.—side-valves; o.h.v.—overhead valves; o.h.c.—overhead camshaft; hyd.—hydraulic.

ROVER 2000

CELEBRATING its first anniversary, this attractive 2-litre model from Rover has been improved in many details during the year. Smoother clutch, stronger synchromesh, quieter exhaust, improved ventilating panes. It is fast, comfortable and economical, with good road-holding and many safety features. Large drop down parcel lockers hinged above the ankles are padded to protect legs in an accident. All body panels are easily replaceable if damaged.

CLOSE-UP

Four-cyl.; o.h.c.; 85.7×85.7 mm.; 1,978 c.c.; 99 b.h.p.; 9 to 1 comp.; coil ign.; S.U. carb.; 4-speed, 12.83, 7.55, 4.92, 3.54 to 1; cen. lvr.; susp., f. ind. coil, r. de Dion coil; 4-door; 4-seat; disc servo brks.; max. 105 m.p.h.; cruise 95; m.p.g. 32; whl. base 8ft. 7⅜in.; track, f. 4ft. 5⅜in., r. 4ft. 4½in.; lgth. 14ft. 10½in.; wdth., 5ft. 6½in.; ht. 4ft. 6⅜in.; g.c. 8⅛in.; turng. cir., 31ft. 6in.; kerb wt. 24¾ cwt.; tank, 12 gals.; 12-volt.

£1,046+£219 p.t. = £1,265

ROVER 3-LITRE COUPE

LOWERING the roof gives a racier line than on the saloon and the seats are shaped to permit fast touring for four in maximum comfort. Power steering is standard and automatic transmission is optional. Facia and door cappings are in African cherry wood. A fully lined tool tray slides out beneath parcel shelf and the armrests on the two front doors are adjustable for height.

CLOSE-UP

Six-cyl.; o.h. inlet, side exhaust; 77.8×105 mm.; 2.995 c.c.; 134 b.h.p.; 8.75 to 1 comp.; coil ign.; S.U. carb.; 4-speed, 14.41, 8.07, 5.47, 4.3 to 1; de Normanville overdrive; cen. lvr., BW auto opt.; susp., f. ind. torsion bar, r. half-elliptic; 4-door; 4-seat; hyd. servo brks., disc front; max. 105 m.p.h.; cruise 85; m.p.g. 18-22; whl. base 9ft. 2½in.; track f. 4ft. 7½in., r. 4ft. 8in.; lgth. 15ft. 6½in.; width 5ft. 10in.; ht. 4ft. 9½in.; g.c. 7⅞; turng. cir. 37ft.; kerb wt. 33 cwt.; tank, 14 gals.; 12-volt.

£1,537+£321 p.t. = £1,858

ROVER 3-LITRE

MANY Rover enthusiasts contend that this three-litre car is the best model produced by this "hand-made" car manufacturer. Its popularity among professional men—doctors and barristers for instance—is well known, and these are discerning people. The three-litre engine, with automatic transmission, continues to please so many that the car is bound to be with us for a long time. It deserves its popularity.

CLOSE-UP

Six-cyl.; o.h. inlet, side exhaust; 77.8×105 mm.; 2,995 c.c.; 134 b.h.p.; 8.75 to 1 comp.; coil ign.; S.U. carb.; 4-speed, 14.41, 8.07, 5.47, 4.3 to 1, de Normanville overdrive; cen. lvr., BW auto. opt.; susp., f. ind. torsion bar, r. half-elliptic; 4-door; 4-seat; hyd. servo brks., disc front; max. 105 m.p.h.; cruise 85; m.p.g. 18-25; whl. base 9ft. 2½in.; track f. 4ft. 7½in., r. 4ft. 8in.; lgth. 15ft. 6½in.; wdth. 5ft. 10in.; ht. 4ft. 11¼in.; g.c. 7⅞in.; turng. cir. 40ft.; kerb wt. 32¼ cwt.; tank, 14 gals.; 12-volt.

£1,358+£284 p.t. = £1,642

SAAB 96

AGGRESSIVE new front conceals an engine with higher compression giving an extra 2 h.p. and 3 m.p.h., but still running happily on commercial fuel. Mounting the radiator ahead of the engine instead of behind gives quicker warm up. The heater is hotter, the exhaust quieter; the fuel pump now works by crankcase pressure and Rzeppa universal joints reduce the turning circle. The 55 h.p. sports model is now available with right hand drive.

CLOSE-UP

Two-cyl.; two-stroke; 70×72.9 mm.; 841 c.c.; 44 b.h.p.; 8 to 1 comp.; coil ign.; Zenith carb.; 3-speed, 17.19, 8.53, 5.23 to 1; col. lvr.; susp., f. ind. coil, r. coil; 2-door; 4-seat; hyd. brks.; max. 78 m.p.h.; cruise 72; m.p.g. 32-34; whl base 8ft. 2in.; track f. and r. 4ft.; lgth. 13ft. 8in.; width 5ft. 2in.; ht. 4ft. 10in.; g.c. 7½in.; turng. cir. 35ft.; kerb wt. 16¼ cwt.; tank, 8½ gals.; 12-volt.

£875+£184 p.t. = £1,059

SABRA SUSSITA

ANGLO-ISRAELI collaboration produced this international effort, designed in England by the Reliant Company and built in Haifa with many British components. It is a dual purpose vehicle used by commercial concerns and private motorists. Also available as a van and pick-up. Tough and easily mended glass fibre body, four-cylinder 997 c.c. engine, four-speed gearbox. Sealed beam headlamps, interior light and twin windscreen wipers are included.

CLOSE-UP
Four-cyl.; o.h.v.; 80.97 × 48.4 mm.; 997 c.c.; 37 b.h.p. 8.9 to 1 comp.; coil ign.; Solex carb.; 4-speed, 16.98, 9.88, 5.81, 5.41 to 1; cen. lvr.; susp., f. ind. coil, r. half-elliptic; 2-door; 4-seat; hyd. brks.; max. 72 m.p.h.; cruise 62; m.p.g. 38–42; lgth. 12ft. 6in.; wdth. 4ft. 11½in.; ht. 5ft. 5in.; turng. cir. 30ft.; tank, 6 gals.; 12-volt.

SIMCA 1000

LIVELY, well mannered French car that thrives on being driven fast (maximum is 82). Four doors and four seats. Rear-mounted 944 c.c. engine, all-round independent suspension for good road holding and comfortable ride. Standard equipment includes heater/demister, underseal, windscreen washer and headlight flasher. Trim is simple and practical, floor is covered with rubber and facia is in black crackle to provide a non-reflecting surface.

CLOSE-UP
Four-cyl.; o.h.v.; 68 × 65 mm.; 944 c.c.; 45 b.h.p.; 7.8 to 1 comp.; coil ign.; Solex carb.; 4-speed, 15.51, 9.26, 6.16, 4.21 to 1; cen. lvr.; susp., f. ind. trans. leaf, r. ind. coil; 4-door; 4-seat; hyd. brks.; max. 82 m.p.h.; cruise 70; m.p.g. 35–44; whl. base 7ft. 3½in.; track, f. 4ft. 5in., r. 4ft. 0⅜in.; lgth. 12ft. 5½in.; wdth. 4ft. 10½in.; ht. 4ft. 4½in.; g.c. 5½in.; turng. cir. 30ft.; kerb wt. 14 cwt.; tank, 6⅝ gals.; 12-volt.

£495 + £105 p.t. = £600

SIMCA 1300/1500

TWO new 1500 station wagons now supplement the popular 1300 and 1500 saloons. They have wind-down rear windows for extra long loads and the Grand Luxe has a rear platform that lifts out as a picnic table. The roomy four-door saloons have good road holding and manoeuvrability. Door latches concealed under armrests. Maximum of the 1300 is 84 m.p.h. and the 1500 with disc brakes does about 90 m.p.h.

CLOSE-UP
Four-cyl.; o.h.v.; 74 × 75 mm.; 1,290 c.c.; 62 b.h.p.; or 75.4 × 83 mm.; 1,482 c.c.; 81 b.h.p.; 8.5/9.5 to 1 comp.; coil ign.; Solex carb.; 4-speed, 16.22, 9.14, 6.15, 4.45 to 1; cen. lvr.; susp., f. ind. coil, r. coil; 4-door; 4-seat; hyd. brks., disc front; max. 85/93 m.p.h.; cruise 70–80; m.p.g. 28–32; whl. base 8ft. 3½in.; track f. 4ft. 4in., r. 4ft. 3½in.; lgth. 13ft. 11½in.; wdth. 5ft. 2in.; ht. 4ft. 7½in.; g.c. 6in.; turng. cir. 32ft.; kerb wt. 19½–20 cwt.; tank, 12 gals.; 12-volt.

1300—£661 + £139 p.t. = £800
1500—£760 + £160 p.t. = £920

SINGER CHAMOIS

IMPISH junior partner for the Gazelle in the Singer range. A dummy radiator grille in front for those who feel naked without one, even though the engine is at the back. Wood veneers for facia and door capping rails, and a heater blower as standard equipment. Seats are different from those on the Imp, the wheels have trim rings and wider rims, carrying SP 41 tyres.

CLOSE-UP
Four-cyl.; o.h.c.; 68 × 60.4 mm.; 875 c.c.; 39 b.h.p.; 10 to 1 comp.; coil ign.; Solex carb.; 4-speed, 16.59, 8.91, 5.70, 4.14 to 1; cen. lvr.; susp., f. and r. ind. coil; 2-door; 4-seat; hyd. brks.; max. 80 m.p.h.; cruise 75; m.p.g. 40; whl. base, 6ft. 10in.; track f. 4ft. 1in., r. 3ft. 11½in.; lgth., 11ft. 9in.; width, 5ft. 0½in.; ht. 4ft. 6½in.; g.c. 6½in.; turng. cir., 28ft.; kerb wt., 14¼ cwt.; tank, 6 gals.; 12-volt.

Abbreviations—g.c.—ground clearance; susp.—suspension; f.—front; r.—rear; comp.—compression; s.v.—side-valves; o.h.v.—overhead valves; o.h.c.—overhead camshaft; hyd.—hydraulic.

SINGER VOGUE

MORE power is given this popular Rootes model this year, the 1592 c.c. engine yielding 84 brake horse power against the old 62 b.h.p. The engine now has an aluminium cylinder head, and the car a diaphragm spring clutch. Reclining front seats add to all-round luxury, and synchromesh is now on all four forward gears. Add to this front disc brakes and the elimination of all greasing points and you have a very popular car.

CLOSE-UP

Four-cyl.; o.h.v.; 81.5×76.2 mm.; 1,592 c.c.; 84 b.h.p.; 8.3 to 1 comp.; coil ign.; Solex carb.; 4-speed, 13.013, 8.324, 5.413, 3.889 to 1; de Normanville overdrive or BW auto. opt.; cen. lvr.; susp., f. ind. coil, r. half-elliptic; 4-door; 4/5-seat; hyd. brks., disc front; max. 90 m.p.h.; cruise 80; m.p.g. 28-32; whl. base 8ft. 5in.; track f. 4ft. 3½in., r. 4ft. 0½in.; lgth. 13ft. 9½in.; wdth. 5ft. 2½in.; ht. 4ft. 10½in.; g.c. 6½in.; turng. cir. 36ft.; kerb wt. 21½ cwt.; tank, 11 gals.; 12-volt.

£698+£147 p.t. = £845

SKODA OCTAVIA

HOW do they do it at the price? It's one of the mysteries of communist state finance—but you can buy a Skoda for far less than it costs the Czechs at home. All-independent suspension on a chassis made from a single tube. Heater and good tool kit are standard. There's a station wagon and if it's speed you're after, there's the Touring Super Sport with 1221 c.c., twin carburetters and top speed of 85 m.p.h.

CLOSE-UP

Four-cyl.; o.h.v.; 68×75 mm.; 1,089 c.c.; 43 b.h.p.; 7.5 to 1 comp.; coil ign.; Jikov carb.; 4-speed, 20.4, 11.8, 7.6, 4.78 to 1; col. lvr.; susp., f. ind. coil, r. ind. transv. leaf; 2-door; 4-seat; hyd. brks.; max. 77 m.p.h.; cruise 65; m.p.g. 35-40; whl. base 7ft. 10½in.; track, f. 3ft. 11⅝in., r. 4ft. 1in.; lgth. 13ft. 4in.; wdth. 5ft. 3in.; ht. 4ft. 8½in.; g.c. 6½in.; turng. cir. 32ft. 9in.; kerb wt. 17¾ cwt.; tank, 6½ gals.; 12-volt.

£413+£88 p.t. = £501

SKODA 1000 MB

CZECHOSLOVAKIA is making a big bid for export sales with this entirely new rear-engined small car. The light alloy four-cylinder, water-cooled engine is canted over and mounted in unit with the four-speed all-synchromesh gearbox. Body-chassis unit is in steel; front suspension is by wishbones and coil springs, rear by swing axles and coil springs. Reclining front backrests combine with rear seats to form camping beds.

CLOSE-UP

Four-cyl.; o.h.v.; 68×68 mm.; 988 c.c.; 45 b.h.p.; 8.3 to 1 comp.; coil ign.; Jikov carb.; 4-speed, 16.87, 9.41, 6.26, 4.26 to 1; cen. lvr.; susp., f. and r. ind. coil; 4-door; 4-seat; hyd. brks.; max. 74 m.p.h.; cruise 65; m.p.g. 38-40; whl. base 7ft. 10½in.; track f. 4ft. 2⅜in., r. 4ft. 1½in.; lgth. 13ft. 8½in.; width 5ft. 3⅜in.; ht. 4ft. 6½in.; g.c. 7⅜in.; kerb wt. 14¾ cwt.; 12-volt.

SUNBEAM ALPINE

SNATCH bottom gear noiselessly for a quick getaway out of those steep Alpine hairpins with the new all-synchromesh gearbox offered on all Alpines for 1965. Removal of the tail fins has given a sleeker lower line. The two-seater with folding top and winding side windows is still popular with open air enthusiasts, but the fixed head GT coupe has added a new dimension to Sunbeam motoring.

CLOSE-UP

Four-cyl.; o.h.v.; 81.5×76.2 c.c.; 1,592 c.c.; 85.5 b.h.p.; 9.1 to 1 comp.; coil ign.; Solex 2-choke carb.; 4-speed, 13.013, 8.324, 5.413, 3.89 to 1; cen. lvr.; de Normanville overdrive opt.; susp., f. ind. coil, r. half-elliptic; 2-door; 2-seat; hyd. brks., disc front; max. 100 m.p.h.; cruise 80; m.p.g. 25; whl. base 7ft. 2in.; track f. 4ft. 3in., r. 4ft. 0½in.; lgth. 12ft. 11½in.; wdth. 5ft. 0½in.; ht. 4ft. 3½in.; g.c. 5in.; turng. cir. 34ft.; kerb wt. 19¼ cwt.; tank, 9 gals.; 12-volt.

£705+£148 p.t. = £853

SUNBEAM RAPIER

BROUGHT up the hard way as a magnificent rally car, this popular Rootes model now has synchromesh on all four forward gears and inside reclining front seats. The car has sporting looks and a performance to match. It was restyled with lower lines and smaller wheels, and Rapier enthusiasts were quick to appreciate the change. It is a car essentially for the sporting motorist but fulfils ordinary motoring functions just as well.

CLOSE-UP

Four-cyl.; o.h.v.; 81.5 × 76.2 mm.; 1,592 c.c.; 84 b.h.p.; 9.1 to 1 comp.; coil ign.; Solex carb.; 4-speed, 13.013, 8.324, 5.413, 3.89 to 1; cen. lvr.; de Normanville overdrive opt.; susp., f. ind. coil, r. half-elliptic; 2-door; 4-seat; hyd. servo brks., disc front.; max. 95 m.p.h.; cruise 80; m.p.g. 25-30; whl. base 8ft.; track f. 4ft. 1½in., r. 4ft. 0½in.; lgth. 13ft. 6½in.; wdth. 5ft. 1in.; ht. 4ft. 10½in.; g.c. 5¾in.; turng. cir. 36ft.; kerb wt. 21 cwt.; tank, 10 gals.; 12-volt.

£725 + £153 p.t. = £878

TRIUMPH 2000

A SUCCESS from the start Triumph's smooth running six-cylinder saloon sails into its second year with only minor improvements. Front seats are wider and more luxurious; windscreen washer is electric instead of pneumatic. Black padding and satin-finished metal replace colour and chromium glitter on the facia, to heighten the air of quality. Michelotti styling, road-hugging all-independent suspension are strong features.

CLOSE-UP

Six-cyl.; o.h.v.; 74.7 × 76 mm.; 1,998 c.c.; 90 b.h.p.; 8.5 to 1 comp.; coil ign.; 2 Stromberg carbs.; 4-speed, 13.45, 8.61, 5.68, 4.1 to 1; cen. lvr., de Normanville overdrive or BW auto. opt.; susp., f. and r. ind. coil; 4-door; 5-seat; hyd. servo brks., disc front; max. 95 m.p.h.; cruise 80; m.p.g. 24-28; whl. base 8ft. 10in.; track f. 4ft. 4in., r. 4ft. 2½in.; lgth. 14ft. 7in.; width 5ft. 5in.; ht. 4ft. 8in.; g.c. 5½in.; turng. cir. 33ft.; kerb wt. 22½ cwt.; tank, 14 gals.; 12-volt.

£905 + £190 p.t. = £1,095

TRIUMPH HERALD 12/50

DEVELOPED from the ever popular Herald, the 12/50 has all the benefits of independent suspension, no greasing points, taxi-like turning circle, telescopic steering column and interchangeable body panels in case of damage, plus more power and a folding top. Its 1147 c.c. engine develops 51 h.p. against 43 on the normal Herald. And an added attraction are Girling disc brakes on the front wheels.

CLOSE-UP

Four-cyl.; o.h.v.; 69.3 × 76 mm.; 1,147 c.c.; 51 b.h.p.; 8.5 to 1 comp.; coil ign.; Solex carb.; 4-speed, 15.40, 8.87, 5.73, 4.11 to 1; cen. lvr.; susp., f. ind. coil, r. ind. transv. leaf; 2-door; 4-seat; hyd. brks., disc front; max. 77 m.p.h.; cruise 70; m.p.g. 30-32; whl. base. 7½in.; track f. 4ft., r. 4ft.; lgth. 12ft. 9in., width 5ft.; ht. 4ft. 4in.; g.c. 6¾in.; turng. cir. 26ft. 3in.; kerb wt. 16½ cwt.; tank, 6½ gals.; 12-volt.

£525 + £111 p.t. = £636

TRIUMPH T.R.4

NONE of the Standard Triumph models has more than detail changes for 1965, but prices remain stable in a motor show where the price trend is upwards once more. Continued export demand for the TR4 is a strong factor in our export trade, especially to North America. The basic body style is a two-seater convertible with glass side windows. A detachable hard top is an optional extra.

CLOSE-UP

Four-cyl.; o.h.v.; 86 × 92 mm.; 2,138 c.c.; 105 b.h.p.; 9 to 1 comp.; coil ign.; 2 S.U. carbs.; 4-speed, 11.61, 7.44, 4.9, 3.7 to 1; cen. lvr.; susp., f. ind. coil, r. half-elliptic; 2-door; 2/3-seat; hyd. brks., disc front; max. 110 m.p.h.; cruise 95; m.p.g. 25; whl. base 7ft. 4in.; track f. 4ft. 1in., r. 4ft.; lgth. 13ft.; wdth. 4ft. 9½in.; ht. 4ft. 2in.; g.c. 6in.; turng. cir. 33ft.; kerb wt. 20 cwt., 11¾ gals.; 12-volt.

£750 + £158 p.t. = £908

Abbreviations—g.c.—ground clearance; susp.—suspension; f.—front; r.—rear; comp.—compression; s.v.—side-valves; o.h.v.—overhead valves; o.h.c.—overhead camshaft; hyd.—hydraulic.

TRIUMPH SPITFIRE 4

LIKE its namesake, the famous fighter aircraft of World War II, the Spitfire packs a punch. Its 1147 c.c. engine is now offered in three stages of tune to make the top speed anything from 92 to 107 m.p.h. The comfortable body has winding glass windows, lockable boot. A hardtop version is also available. Laycock de Normanville overdrive, operating on 3rd and 4th speeds, is an optional extra.

CLOSE-UP

Four-cyl.; o.h.v.; 69.3×76 mm.; 1,147 c.c.; 63 b.h.p.; 9 to 1 comp.; coil ign.; 2 S.U. carbs.; 4-speed, 15.40, 8.87, 5.73, 4.11 to 1; cen. lvr.; susp., f. ind. coil, r. ind. transv. leaf; 2-door; 2-seat; hyd. brks.; max. 93 m.p.h.; cruise 80; m.p.g. 35-40; whl. base 6ft. 11in.; track f. 4ft. 1in., r. 4ft.; lgth. 12ft. 1in.; wdth. 4ft. 9in.; ht. 3ft. 11½in.; g.c. 5in.; turng. cir. 24ft.; kerb wt. 14 cwt.; tank, 9 gals.; 12-volt.

£530+£112 p.t. = £642

TRIUMPH VITESSE

RE-STYLED instruments and map pocket are among the modifications made to this smooth, small six-cylinder model that comes from the powerful Leyland-Standard-Triumph stable. The car has many distinctions, including all-independent suspension and a 25-foot turning circle. It is the car for the driver with a medium-sized pocket who wants to get places in a hurry. The saloon can be fitted with overdrive.

CLOSE-UP

Six-cyl.; o.h.v.; 66.75×76 mm.; 1,596 c.c.; 70 b.h.p.; 8.75 to 1 comp.; coil ign.; 2 Solex carbs.; 4-speed, 12.06, 7.31, 5.16, 4.11 to 1; cen. lvr., de Normanville overdrive opt.; susp., f. ind. coil, r. ind. transv. leaf; 2-door; 4-seat; hyd. brks., disc front; max. 88 m.p.h.; cruise 75-80; m.p.g. 28-35; whl. base 7ft. 7½in.; track f. 4ft. 1in., r. 4ft.; lgth. 12ft. 9in.; wdth. 5ft.; ht. 4ft. 4½in.; g.c. 6½in.; turng. cir. 25ft.; kerb wt. 18¼ cwt.; tank, 8½ gals.; 12-volt.

£616+£130 p.t. = £746

VALIANT

COMPACT car from the Chrysler group which has caught on in overseas markets, the Valiant has the silky smoothness and soft ride of the transatlantic product in a size which makes it pleasant to drive on British roads. It can be had with a six-cylinder or V8 engine in a range of powers according to carburetters and compression ratios and gearboxes can be three- or four-speed or automatic.

CLOSE-UP

Six-cyl.; o.h.v.; 86.3×79.4 mm.; 2,789 c.c.; 100 b.h.p.; 8.5 to 1 comp.; coil ign.; Holley carb.; 3-speed, 10.4, 6.87, 3.23 to 1; col. lvr. 4 speed opt.; susp., f. ind. torsion bar, r. half-elliptic; 2- or 4-door; 5-seat; hyd. servo brks.; max. 94 m.p.h.; cruise 85; m.p.g. 18-23; whl. base 8ft. 10in.; track f. 4ft. 7½in., r. 4ft. 7½in.; lgth. 15ft. 8in.; wdth. 5ft. 10½in.; ht. 4ft. 5in.; g.c. 6in.; turng. cir. 37ft.; kerb wt. 24 cwt.; tank, 15 gals.; 12-volt.

£1,405+£294 p.t. = £1,699

VANDEN PLAS PRINCESS 4-LITRE

HERE is a big limousine for people with big ideas. Luxury for eight people is laid on with all the lavish extravagance of the biggest B.M.C. model. It has all the sumptuousness of a long-established coachbuilding company plus the experience of a large scale car producer who supplies the 3,993 c.c. engine. No big changes are made this year, and automatic transmission is optional.

CLOSE-UP

Six-cyl.; o.h.v.; 87.3×111 mm.; 3,993 c.c.; 6.8 to 1 comp.; coil ign.; Stromberg carb.; 4-speed, 15.1, 10.3, 6.4, 4.4 to 1; col. lvr., RR Hydra-matic auto. opt.; susp., f. ind. coil, r. half-elliptic; 4-door; 8-seat; hyd. brks.; max. 100 m.p.h.; cruise 80; m.p.g. 16-19; whl. base 11ft. 0⅜in.; track f. 4ft. 10½in., r. 5ft. 2½in.; lgth. 17ft. 11in.; wdth. 6ft. 2½in.; ht. 5ft. 10in.; g.c. 6½in.; turng. cir. 45ft. 6in.; kerb wt. 41¾ cwt.; tank, 16 gals.; 12-volt.

£2,350+£491 p.t. = £2,841

Abbreviations—g.c.—ground clearance; susp.—suspension; f.—front; r.—rear; comp.—compression; s.v.—side-valves; o.h.v.—overhead valves; o.h.c.—overhead camshaft; hyd.—hydraulic.

VANDEN PLAS PRINCESS R

ROLLS-ROYCE engineering for under £2,000. A special 3.9-litre light-alloy six-cylinder engine by Rolls-Royce in a car developed from the 3-litre Princess, with improved suspension, smaller wheels, trimmed tail fins, more rear headroom and horizontal tail lamps. Transmission is Type 8 Borg Warner, new to the British market. Brakes are disc front, drum rear, with vacuum servo and new inertia valve to prevent rear wheels locking.

CLOSE-UP
Six-cyl.; o.h. inlet, s. exhaust; 95.2×91.4 mm.; 3,909 c.c.; 175 b.h.p.; 7.8 to 1 comp.; coil ign.; 2 S.U. carbs.; 3-speed auto., 7.65, 4.62, 3.15 to 1; col. lvr.; susp., f. ind. coil, r. half-elliptic; 4-door; 5-seat; hyd. servo brks., disc front; max. 106 m.p.h.; cruise 90; m.p.g. 14-17; whl. base 9ft. 2in.; track f. 4ft. 5½in., r. 4ft. 5½in.; lgth. 15ft. 8in.; width 5ft. 8½in.; ht. 5ft.; g.c. 6¾in.; turng. cir. 42ft. 5in.; kerb wt. 31¼ cwt.; tank, 16 gals.; 12-volt.

£1,650 + £345 p.t. = £1,995

VANDEN PLAS 1100

TREND-SETTING town-carriage based on the front-drive BMC 1100. It has a Princess radiator grille, large bumpers and wrap-round front indicator lamps. Powered by twin-carburetter 1098 c.c. transverse engine as used in the MG 1100. Front seats are adjustable for rake and reach, with individual folding armrests. Picnic tables fold into their backs. Leather is used for seats; walnut door cappings and facia add touches of luxury.

CLOSE-UP
Four-cyl.; o.h.v. 64.57×83.72 mm.; 1,098 c.c.; 55 b.h.p.; 8.9 to 1 comp.; coil ign.; 2 S.U. carbs.; 14.99, 8.98, 5.83, 4.133 to 1; cen. lvr.; susp., f. and r. ind. rubber-hydraulic; 4-door; 4-seat; hyd. brks., disc front; max. 85 m.p.h.; cruise 75; m.p.g. 35-37; whl. base 7ft. 9½in.; track f. 4ft. 3½in., r. 4ft. 2⅞in.; lgth. 12ft. 2¾in.; width 5ft. 0⅜in.; ht. 4ft. 4½in.; g.c. 6in.; turng. cir. 34ft.; kerb wt. 17¾ cwt.; tank, 8½ gals.; 12-volt.

£740 + £156 p.t. = £896

VAUXHALL VIVA

100,000 Vivas were produced in the first 10 months. Now detail improvements herald a second successful year. Quicker steering goes from lock to lock in 3.14 turns instead of 3.8. Fuel filtration is more efficient. Front seats have better curved backrests and rear backrest is modified. Insulation of body and engine is improved. Parcel shelf, instrument panel, carpets are improved and there is a fitted mat in the luggage boot.

CLOSE-UP
Four-cyl.; o.h.v.; 74.3×60.9 mm.; 1,057 c.c.; 44.2 b.h.p.; 8.5 to 1 comp.; coil ign.; Zenith carb.; 4-speed, 15.53, 9.12, 5.79, 4.125 to 1; cen. lvr.; susp., f. ind. transv. leaf, r. half-elliptic; 2-door; 4-seat; hyd. brks., disc opt.; max. 80 m.p.h.; cruise 70; m.p.g. 40-45; whl. base 7ft. 7½in.; track f. 3ft. 11⅜in., r. 4ft. 0¼in.; lgth. 12ft. 11½in.; wdth. 4ft. 11¾in.; ht. 4ft. 5¼in.; g.c. 5in.; turng. cir. 27ft. 4in.; kerb wt. 14 cwt.; tank, 7 gals.; 12-volt.

£436 + £92 p.t. = £528

VAUXHALL VELOX/CRESTA

TWO important changes come out in these 1965 models. The 2.6 engine is increased in size to 3.3 litres, giving extra power of getaway and a higher speed, and the front grille has been radically changed. Engine power goes up from 113 b.h.p. to 128 b.h.p., with a choice of three or four all-synchromesh gearbox. Four-speed version has central floor mounted control. Individual front seats, fully reclining on Cresta.

CLOSE-UP
Six-cyl.; o.h.v.; 82.55×82.55 mm.; 3,293 c.c.; 128 b.h.p.; 8.5 to 1 comp.; coil ign.; Zenith carb.; 3-speed, 8.97, 5.14, 3.45 to 1; col. lvr., overdrive, 4-speed or Hydra-matic opt.; susp., f. ind. coil, r. half-elliptic; 4-door; 6-seat; hyd. servo brks., disc front; max. 101 m.p.h.; cruise 90; m.p.g. 19-24; whl. base 8ft. 11¼in.; track f. 4ft. 6¼in., r. 4ft. 8¼in.; lgth. 15ft. 1¼in.; width 5ft. 10¾in.; ht. 4ft. 8¼in.; g.c. 6¼in.; turng. cir. 36ft. 6in.; kerb wt. 23¾ cwt.; tank, 10½ gals.; 12-volt.

Velox—£710 + £149 p.t. = £859
Cresta—£795 + £167 p.t. = £962

Abbreviations—g.c.—ground clearance; susp.—suspension; f.—front; r.—rear; comp.—compression; s.v.—side-valves; o.h.v.—overhead valves; o.h.c.—overhead camshaft; hyd.—hydraulic.

VAUXHALL VICTOR

COMPLETELY new bodywork brings the popular Victor and performance-plus VX 4/90 right up to date, but main mechanical elements are the ones that have been developed and refined over several years in the previous models. More space for passengers, more comfort and quieter running are attractions which combine with new accessories and proved mechanical elements to give the Vauxhall sales curve another upwards impetus.

CLOSE-UP

Four-cyl.; o.h.v.; 81.63 × 76.2 mm.; 1,594 c.c.; 69 b.h.p.; 8.5 to 1 comp.; coil ign.; Zenith carb.; 3-speed, 13.2, 6.74, 4.125 to 1, 4-speed opt.; col. lvr.; susp., f. ind. coil, r. half-elliptic; 4-door; 5-seat; hyd. brks., disc opt.; max. 80 m.p.h.; cruise 70; m.p.g. 28-34; whl. base 8ft. 4in.; track f. 4ft. 2¾in., r. 4ft. 4⅜in.; lgth. 14ft. 5¼in.; width 5ft. 4in.; ht. 4ft. 8in.; g.c. 7in.; turng. cir. 33ft. 6in.; kerb wt. 19¾ cwt.; tank, 10 gals.; 12-volt.

VAUXHALL BEDFORD BEAGLE

MARTIN WALTER, the coachbuilder produces this four-seater station wagon called the Bedford Beagle, using the mechanical parts of the Vauxhall Viva. There are two side doors and two at the rear. Spare wheel is in a cradle below the rear floor. The big side windows have sliding centre panes. There are chromium bumpers and wing mirrors, bright metal windscreen frame insert and a parcel shelf under the instrument panel.

CLOSE-UP

Four-cyl.; o.h.v.; 74.3 × 60.9 mm.; 1,057 c.c.; 41 b.h.p.; 7.3 to 1 comp.; coil ign.; Zenith carb.; 4-speed; 15.53, 9.12, 5.79, 4.125 to 1; cen. lvr.; susp., f. ind. transv. leaf, r. half-elliptic; 4-door; 4-seat; hyd. brks.; max. 80 m.p.h.; cruise, 70; m.p.g. 40; whl. base, 7ft. 7½in.; track f. 3ft. 11⅜in.; r. 4ft. 0¼in.; lgth., 12ft. 6¼in.; width, 5ft. 8in.; ht. 4ft. 9½in.; g.c. 5in.; turng. cir., 29ft.; kerb wt., 13 cwt.; tank, 7 gals.; 12-volt.

£513 + £108 p.t. = £621

VOLKSWAGEN 1200 DE LUXE

UNCRUSHABLE "beetle", still the top-selling import in the U.S.A. The 26-year-old basic design is retained but since its introduction there have been 3,000 improvements. The latest include larger windows all round, sun visors pivoting sideways, slimmer front seat backrests to increase legroom, heater controlled by levers instead of a rotary knob. The air-cooled engine is designed to cruise flat-out without tiring. The gearbox is a joy.

CLOSE-UP

Four-cyl.; o.h.v.; air-cooled; 77 × 64 mm.; 1,192 c.c.; 40 b.h.p.; 7 to 1 comp.; coil ign.; Solex carb.; 4-speed, 16.63, 9.01, 5.77, 3.89 to 1; cen. lvr.; susp., f. and r. ind. torsion bars; 2-door; 4-seat; hyd. brks.; max. 72 m.p.h.; cruise 72; m.p.g. 38; whl. base 7ft. 10½in.; track f. 4ft. 3in., r. 4ft. 2¾in.; lgth. 13ft. 4¾in.; width 5ft. 0½in.; ht. 4ft. 11in.; g.c. 6in.; turng. cir. 36ft.; kerb wt. 14½ cwt.; tank, 8¾ gals.; 6-volt.

£517 + £109 p.t. = £626

VOLKSWAGEN 1500

SPARKLE is added to solid VW virtues in the S model which has twin carburetters and a compression of 8.5 : 1, giving 54 h.p. against 45 for the single-carb model. It is identified by bright strips along the sides and plated fairings round the indicators. Adjustable backrests, steering lock, parking lamps, headlamp flasher are included. Top speed is 84 m.p.h. The finish is famous. Both saloons and station wagons are available.

CLOSE-UP

Four-cyl.; o.h.v. air cooled; 83 × 69 mm.; 1,493 c.c.; 45 b.h.p.; 7.8 to 1 comp.; coil ign.; Solex carb. (1500S 2 carbs., 54 b.h.p.); 4-speed, 15.67, 8.50, 5.44, 3.67 to 1; cen. lvr.; susp., f. and r. ind. torsion bar; 2-door; 4-seat; hyd. brks.; max. 81-84 m.p.h.; cruise 81; m.p.g. 30; whl. base 7ft. 10½in.; track f. 4ft. 3½in., r. 4ft. 5in.; lgth. 13ft. 10½in.; wdth. 5ft. 3¼in.; ht. 4ft. 10in.; g.c. 6in.; turng. cir. 36ft.; kerb wt. 17¼ cwt.; tank, 8¾ gals.; 6-volt.

£815 + £171 p.t. = £986

Abbreviations—g.c.—ground clearance; susp.—suspension; f.—front; r.—rear; comp.—compression; s.v.—side-valves; o.h.v.—overhead valves; o.h.c.—overhead camshaft; hyd.—hydraulic.

VOLKSWAGEN KARMANN-GHIA

GET Ghia of Turin to design it, persuade Karmann the famous coachbuilders of Osnabruck to build it, add the Volkswagen 1500S mechanical parts with the twin-carburetter engine and you have the recipe for an eye-catcher that won't mind hard work. Take your choice from coupe or convertible, with seats for two and a folding seat at the rear for luggage or children.

CLOSE-UP
Four-cyl.; o.h.v.; air-cooled; 83×69 mm.; 1,493 c.c.; 54 b.h.p.; 8.5 to 1 comp.; coil ign.; 2 Solex carbs.; 4-speed, 15.67, 8.50, 5.44, 3.67 to 1; cen. lvr.; susp., f. and r. ind. torsion bar; 2-door; 2/4-seat; hyd. brks.; max. 90 m.p.h.; cruise 90; m.p.g. 34; whl. base 7ft. 10½in.; track f. 4ft. 3½in., r. 4ft. 5in.; lgth. 14ft. 0⅜in.; wdth. 5ft. 3¾in.; ht. 4ft. 5⅜in.; g.c. 5½in.; turng. cir. 36ft. 4in.; kerb wt. 18½ cwt.; tank, 8¾ gals.; 6-volt.

£1,055+£221 p.t.=£1,276

VOLVO 122S

SLIPPED disc sufferers should try Volvo's new seats, designed under medical guidance. Seat height and backrest angle are variable and there's adjustable support for the small of the back. Other features of a fast, conscientiously built car for 1965; new radiator grille, new interior styling, heater ducts for rear passengers, stainless steel hub caps, galvanised underbody panels. Station wagons (with two or four doors) now have servo brakes.

CLOSE-UP
Four-cyl.; o.h.v. 84.14×80 mm.; 1,780 c.c.; 90 b.h.p.; 8.5 to 1 comp.; coil ign.; 2 S.U. carbs.; 4-speed, 12.8, 8.16, 5.58, 4.1 to 1; cen. lvr.; overdrive opt.; susp., f. ind. coil, r. coil; 4-door; 5-seat; hyd. brks., disc front; max. 100 m.p.h.; cruise 85; m.p.g. 28-35; whl. base 8ft. 6¼in.; track f. and r. 4ft. 3½in.; lgth. 14ft. 7½in.; width 5ft. 3¾in.; ht. 4ft. 11½in.; g.c. 7⅞in.; turng. cir. 32ft.; kerb wt. 22 cwt.; tank, 10 gals.; 12-volt.

£909+£191 p.t.=£1,100

VOLVO P.1800

PRODUCTION of this well-equipped sports coupe has been transferred from Jensen in Birmingham to Sweden. Its robust engine is derived from that of the 122S saloon but with higher compression. Overdrive is standard in England giving a top speed of nearly 110 m.p.h. Seats are in leather, facia and sun visors are padded. The brakes (discs in front) have vacuum servo assistance.

CLOSE-UP
Four-cyl.; o.h.v.; 84.14×80 mm.; 1,780 c.c.; 100 b.h.p.; 9.5 to 1 comp.; coil ign.; 2 S.U. carbs.; 4-speed, 14.27, 9.07, 6.2, 4.5 to 1; cen. lvr. overdrive; susp., f. ind. coil, r. coil; 2-door; 2/4-seat; servo brks., disc front; max. 110 m.p.h.; cruise 95; m.p.g. 28-30; whl. base 8ft. 0½in.; track f. and r. 4ft. 3½in.; lgth. 14ft. 5½in.; wdth. 5ft. 7in.; ht. 4ft. 2½in.; g.c. 6in.; turng. cir. 31ft.; kerb wt. 24 cwt.; tank, 10 gals.; 12-volt.

£1,366+£286 p.t.=£1,652

WARTBURG

EAST German export at a bargain price. Full-sized family saloon with three-cylinder two-stroke engine of 991 c.c. and front wheel drive. It does nearly 80 m.p.h. and 32-35 m.p.g. Included in the price are fully reclining seats, vanity mirror, coathangers, glove compartment, map pockets, headlamp flasher, screen washer, cigarette lighter, lockable petrol filler, illuminated engine compartment, three ashtrays, pile carpets. Flat floor and 18½ cu. ft. boot.

CLOSE-UP
Three-cyl.; two-stroke; 73.5×78 mm.; 991 c.c.; 50 b.h.p.; 7.3 to 1 comp.; coil ign.; BVF carb.; 4-speed, 15.89, 10.35, 6.55, 4.62 to 1; col. lvr.; susp., f. ind. transv. leaf, r. transv. leaf; 4-door; 4/5-seat; hyd. brks.; max. 77 m.p.h.; cruise 70; m.p.g. 30-32; whl. base 8ft. 0½in.; track f. 3ft. 10½in., r. 4ft. 1⅜in.; lgth. 14ft. 1½in.; wdth. 5ft. 1⅞in.; ht. 4ft. 9in.; g.c. 7½in.; turng. cir. 39ft. 9in.; kerb wt. 18½ cwt.; tank, 9⅝ gals.; 6-volt.

£446+£94 p.t.=£540

Abbreviations—g.c.—ground clearance; susp.—suspension; f.—front; r.—rear; comp.—compression; s.v.—side-valves; o.h.v.—overhead valves; o.h.c.—overhead camshaft; hyd.—hydraulic.

WOLSELEY HORNET

A NIPPY little car which is really an enlarged Mini with bigger boot and luxury trim inside. Its 998 c.c. engine gives this slightly higher-class car sound acceleration and a good cruising speed. The makers have retained the famous Wolseley radiator grille scaled down to size. Here is the ideal run-about or second car for the not-so-poor. Already very popular, now has Hydrolastic suspension.

CLOSE-UP

Four-cyl.; o.h.v.; 64.58×76.2 mm.; 998 c.c.; 38 b.h.p.; 8.3 to 1 comp.; coil ign.; S.U. carb.; 4-speed, 13.657, 8.176, 5.317, 3.765 to 1; cen. lvr.; susp., f. and r. ind. rubber-hyd.; 2-door; 4-seat; hyd brks.; max. 74 m.p.h.; cruise 65; m.p.g. 42-45; whl. base 6ft. 8⅛in.; track f. 3ft. 11¾in., r. 3ft. 9⅞in.; lgth. 10ft 8¾in.; wdth. 4ft. 7½in.; ht. 4ft. 5in.; g.c. 6⅜in.; turng. cir. 31ft.; kerb wt. 11¾ cwt., tank, 5½ gals.; 12-volt.

£478+£101 p.t.=£579

WOLSELEY 16/60

SHARP keen lines from the Italian Pininfarina designer plus the know-how of the great British Motor Corporation produce a well-shaped, adequately powered car of typical Wolseley distinction. It is a four- to five-seater with the famous BMC 1.6 litre engine. Synchromesh the upper three of its four forward gears, and Borg Warner automatic suspension is optional.

CLOSE-UP

Four-cyl.; o.h.v.; 76.2×88.9 mm.; 1,622 c.c.; 55 b.h.p.; 8.3 to 1 comp.; coil ign.; S.U. carb.; 4-speed, 15.64, 9.52, 5.91, 4.3 to 1; cen. lvr. BW auto. opt.; susp., f. ind. coil, r. half-elliptic; 4-door; 4-seat; hyd. brks.; max. 80 m.p.h.; cruise 70; m.p.g. 26-33; whl. base 8ft. 4½in.; track f. 4ft. 2⅝in., r. 4ft. 3⅜in.; lgth. 14ft. 6½in.; wdth. 5ft. 3½in.; ht. 4ft. 10⅞in.; g.c. 5⅞in.; turng. cir. 37ft.; kerb wt. 22½ cwt.; tank, 10 gals.; 12-volt.

£693+£145 p.t.=£838

WOLSELEY 6/110 MARK II

TRADITIONAL Wolseley comfort and style are enhanced by new trim, smaller wheels, improved suspension, better brakes and a new gearbox with four speeds instead of three. Six greasing points have been eliminated and there is a new triple-silencer exhaust system. There are adjustable backrests for front seats, leather upholstery and polished wood instrument panel. Hydrosteer power-assisted steering and Normalair air conditioning are options.

CLOSE-UP

Six-cyl.; o.h.v.; 83.34×88.9 mm.; 2,912 c.c.; 120 b.h.p.; 8.23 to 1 comp.; coil ign.; 2 S.U. carbs.; 4-speed, 10.31 8.1, 5.11, 3.92 to 1; cen. lvr., BW. overdrive or auto opt.; susp., f. ind. coil, r. half-elliptic; 4-door; 5-seat; hyd. servo brks., disc front; max. 102 m.p.h.; cruise 85; m.p.g. 18-22; whl. base 9ft. 2in.; track f. 4ft. 5¾in., r. 4ft. 5¼in.; lgth. 15ft. 7½in.; width 5ft. 8½in.; ht. 5ft. 0½in.; g.c. 6¼in.; turng. cir. 41ft.; kerb wt. 31 cwt.; tank, 16 gals.; 12-volt.

£975+£215 p.t.=£1,190

WOLSELEY 1500

THIS ever-popular car has been in production seven years and still it is in favour with the family motorist. Wolseley owners particularly appreciate the well-balanced shape and 1.5 litre engine that seems to go on forever. There is synchromesh on the second, third and top gears, and the car brakes particularly well with Girling hydraulics. It has a wonderful heart and an easy-on-the-eye appearance to match it.

CLOSE-UP

Four-cyl.; o.h.v.; 73×88.9 mm.; 1,489 c.c.; 53 b.h.p.; 8.3 to 1 comp.; coil ign; S.U. carb.; 4-speed, 13.56, 8.25, 5.12, 3.73 to 1; cen. lvr.; susp., f. ind. torsion bar, r. half-elliptic; 4-door; 4/5-seat; hyd. brks.; max. 78 m.p.h.; cruise 70; m.p.g. 30-35; whl. base 7ft. 2in.; track f. 4ft. 2⅞in., r. 4ft. 2¼in.; lgth. 12ft. 9¼in.; wdth. 5ft. 1in.; ht. 4ft. 11in.; g.c. 6½in.; turng. cir. 34ft.; kerb wt. 17¾ cwt.; tank, 7 gals.; 12-volt.

£550+£116 p.t.=£666

Abbreviations—g.c.—ground clearance; susp.—suspension; f.—front; r.—rear; comp.—compression; s.v.—side-valves; o.h.v.—overhead valves; o.h.c.—overhead camshaft; hyd.—hydraulic.

246

NEW 4.2 litre, 6-cyl. twin overhead camshaft, advanced design of race proved Jaguar XK engine. 3 carburettors. Dual exhausts. Increased acceleration and extra flexibility in lower and middle speed range.

NEW Borg Warner Model 8 Automatic Transmission for the Mark Ten incorporates dual drive range giving option of first or second speed starts to suit road conditions and driver requirements.

NEW 4-speed all synchromesh manually operated gearbox for both 'E' Type and Mark Ten models with hydraulically operated diaphragm clutch giving lighter pedal pressure. Overdrive available on Mark Ten.

NEW Improved effortless braking. Marles 'Varamatic' Bendix Power Steering, exclusive to Jaguar. A new concept of accuracy of response, and precision at top speeds, cruising, cornering or parking. 2¾ turns lock to lock.

JAGUAR ANNOUNCE
TWO NEW 4·2 LITRE MODELS

to join the current range of Mark Ten, 'E' Type, 'S' model and Mark 2 Jaguars

To meet a world wide demand for Jaguar cars which, whilst retaining all the refinements synonymous with the marque, offer even greater performance, Jaguar proudly announce the new 4.2 litre Mark Ten and 'E' Type models. Many new features are incorporated, all of which are designed to bring increased comfort and safety to "a special kind of motoring which no other car in the world can offer."

The 4·2 Mark Ten Saloon

This new, more powerful model retains all the luxury of spacious seating for five, fine leather upholstery, folding arm rests, reclining front seats, folding tables, deep pile carpets, all round independent suspension, self-adjusting disc brakes on all wheels and incorporates many NEW features including NEW 4.2 litre XK Engine, NEW Automatic or Manual gearbox, NEW 'Varamatic' Power Steering (available on no other production car in the world), NEW Hydraulic Brake Servo, NEW variable fresh air heating with independent control for each side of the car. Pre-engaged starter for cold weather efficiency. Alternator to provide higher charge at lower engine RPM. New "increased circulation" cooling system.

FROM £2156.0.5 (INC. P.T.)

The 3.8 Litre Mark Ten continues unchanged. From £2023.2.1 (inc. P.T.)

The 'S' model

The Mark 2

The 4·2 'E' Type G·T Model

Preserving the basic design and aerodynamic styling for which the 'E' Type is world famous—with its independent front and rear suspension and 4 wheel disc brakes—this new model offers many major advancements including NEW 4.2 litre XK engine. NEW Manual gearbox. NEW pressurised cooling system and cross flow radiator. NEW hydraulic braking system with lower pedal effort. NEW "shaped" seating with adjustable squabs. Pre-engaged starter for cold weather efficiency. Alternator to provide higher charge at lower engine RPM. Improved lighting, giving greater penetration and spread.

OPEN SPORTS £1896.4.7 · FIXED HEAD COUPE £1992.17.11 (INC. P.T.)

The 3.8 Litre 'E' type models continue unchanged. Open sports £1829.15.5 · Fixed head coupe £1914.7.1 (inc. P.T.)

The 3.4 & 3.8 Litre 'S' Models
With impeccable body styling and spacious interior the 'S' model incorporates fully independent suspension—self adjusting disc brakes on all wheels, reclining front seats. 19 cu. ft. luggage boot, twin petrol tanks. Automatic or manual transmission.
3.4 LITRE FROM £1670.5.5 • 3.8 LITRE FROM £1759.13.9 (INC. P.T.)

The 2.4, 3.4 & 3.8 Litre Mark 2 Models
As the 'Motor' says "A car of brilliant versatility." Docile in town traffic with the most exhilarating open road performance. Supreme safety and road holding. Disc brakes on all wheels. Available with automatic or manual transmission.
2.4 LITRE FROM £1348.17.1 • 3.4 LITRE FROM £1463.12.11 • 3.8 LITRE FROM £1557.17.11
(INC. P.T.)

JAGUAR *on Stand 116 Earls Court*

LONDON SHOWROOMS 88 PICCADILLY W.1

247

The magnificent HUMBER IMPERIAL

Supreme luxury and elegance with silent 3 litre power. Completely equipped with fully-automatic transmission, power steering, electrically adjustable shock absorbers, fully-reclining Reutter-type front bucket seats, West of England cloth seat trim, radio, rear heater and backlight de-mister, spot and fog lights. A new conception of executive luxury.

ROOTES MAKE IT

The 'top-value' HILLMAN MINX DE LUXE SALOON

The most remarkable car in its class. Now even greater value for money with new all-synchromesh gearbox, new 7½" diameter clutch; new, lighter steering, dished steering wheel; new, redesigned front seats, dimmable warning lights. This, and an 80 m.p.h. performance, and front disc brakes, makes the stylish Hillman Minx de Luxe today's most outstanding value.

FOR EVERYONE TO

The exciting SUNBEAM ALPINE

With its 100 m.p.h. performance the Alpine gives you all the thrill of competition motoring — with luxury, too. Instant, responsive power, swift acceleration, all-synchromesh gearbox and the assurance of servo-assisted brakes (discs at the front), and there's the extra comfort of adjustable seating, with pedals and steering wheel adjustable, too. And there are no greasing points to worry about. Sports Tourer or Gran Turismo Hardtop. Fully-automatic transmission available as an extra.

A REALLY SUPERB

The elegant SINGER VOGUE ESTATE CAR

New power, new elegance, new comfort. The perfect choice for the motorist who wants luxury and performance with sturdy, load-carrying capacity. Fully-reclining front seats, all-synchromesh gearbox, diaphragm clutch are other new features. Also the new-style, more powerful Vogue Saloon. And Singer Gazelle Saloon.

Products of
ROOTES MOTORS LIMITED

London Showrooms & Export Division: Rootes Ltd · Devonshire House · London W.1.

248

The luxurious, sporting HUMBER SCEPTRE

This fine Humber, with its brisk twin-carburettor
1.6 litre engine has sports performance – plus a host of
superb built-in features. All-synchromesh gearbox,
fingerlight steering, self-cancelling overdrive on top and
3rd gears, servo-assisted braking with discs at front,
adjustable steering wheel, heating and ventilation.
And, of course, there's the famous Humber luxury comfort
with fully reclining front seats.

POSSIBLE

The revolutionary HILLMAN IMP

Today's most advanced full-size light car. The Imp has
everything you want . . . economy, roominess and lively
performance. Seats 4 in comfort, with estate car convenience.
80 m.p.h. 40–45 m.p.g. All-synchromesh gears.
All-independent suspension. Remarkable road-holding.
No greasing is needed and servicing once only every
5000 miles.

OWN

The 'top performance' SUNBEAM RAPIER

The car that has won fame and success all over the world.
The car that combines luxury and an outstanding rally-
winning performance. 95 m.p.h. with spacious beautifully
appointed comfort. New features include all-synchromesh
gearbox, improved suspension for superior roadholding.
Built-in equipment includes front disc brakes, servo-assisted
all round, easily regulated heating and ventilation.
Overdrive available as an extra.

MOTOR CAR

The incomparable SINGER CHAMOIS

The first small car with limousine luxury and a wealth of
refinements at no extra cost. Finely upholstered comfort for four
with estate car space when you need it. All-synchromesh
gearbox for easy change. Smooth 80 m.p.h. performance with
acceleration from 0 to 50 m.p.h. in 15 seconds. Economical
40–45 m.p.g. All-independent suspension. No greasing points,
with routine servicing at 5000 mile intervals.

FROM THE REVOLUTIONARY HILLMAN IMP
TO THE LUXURIOUS HUMBER IMPERIAL

See them at the MOTOR SHOW

superior car-care products from the makers of SENSATIONAL turtle wax

–THE ONCE-A-YEAR LIQUID CAR WAX!

Superb Turtle Wax products *care* for your car . . . keep it in showroom condition. That's because Turtle Wax make the finest range of specialised products for the motorist in Britain today!

TURTLE WAX is Britain's fastest selling liquid car wax. Glossy hard shell finish lasts up to one full year! Easy to apply, it cleans, protects and polishes in one quick operation.

ZIP WAX CAR WASH boosts your shine—adds Turtle Wax as it washes! Floats away grease and grime . . . safely and surely. Sachets 10d. 12-wash cans 7/6 or big 20-wash cans 11 -.

BUMPER WAX sprays on in seconds. Contains Turtle Wax for a glossy hard-shell finish that protects chrome for months—aerosol 12/6.

CHROME CLEANER cleans safely, easily, quickly. Removes spotting—even rusty patches. Contains Turtle Wax for a lustrous wax protection—5/6.

DE-ICER Instantly clears windscreen and headlights of ice, snow, sleet . . . iced-up locks and doors too. Giant aerosol to last all winter—7/6.

UPHOLSTERY CLEANER — silicone foam in pushbutton can, cleans leather, plastic, vinyl and fabric quickly . . . easily. Actually repels dirt! Big canister 12/6.

COLOR-BAK restores paint colour to 'new car' appearance instantly, easily. Removes stains, revitalizes dull fading patches. 20 oz. can 11/-.

TURTLE WAX SUPERIOR CAR-CARE PRODUCTS

Whatever makes it go ... Ferodo makes it STOP!

once again nearly every car at the Motor Show is fitted with **FERODO** *anti-fade brake linings*

Ferodo Limited, Chapel-en-le-Frith, Derbyshire, England.   *A Turner & Newall company*

Whichever car you choose it's **AUTOMATICALLY SAFER** with **Britax** 'TERYLENE' belts

STAND 385

BRITAX Automatic Safety Belts
THE WORLD'S MOST ADVANCED DESIGN

★ *Automatic freedom to move*
★ *Automatic protection in emergency*
★ *Automatic retraction when not in use*
★ *Automatic adjustment to any wearer*

Prices from **£5.15.6**

BRITAX Static Safety Belts

Prices from **£4.4.0**

Be sure to call at Stand No. 385 and see a demonstration of the unique advantages of Britax Belts.

ALSO ON OUR STAND
BRITAX power-operated WINDO-LIFT

gives push-button control of both front windows. Another Britax safety feature.

For further details ask your garage or accessory dealer, or write to: **BRITAX (London) LTD., Chertsey Road, Byfleet, Surrey.**

JOIN THE JET SET

It's not exactly a club, because no subscriptions are asked for, and anyone who wants to can join. Some people in the Jet Set have Rolls-Royces, others have hairy sports cars, but most, of course, have ordinary, everyday cars. In short, people in the Jet Set are just like other people. Except for one thing : they pay a few pennies less per gallon for their petrol. Do those few pennies matter? Well, they add up to a few shillings on every tankful. And how many times a year do you fill your tank? Lots of times.

Jet 100 A supergrade petrol, specially recommended for high performance cars.

Jet 97 The premium petrol bought by the majority of the Jet Set. A petrol for the cars that fill the showrooms.

Jet 94 Petrol for the smaller, lower compression engine.

Jet Thrift A well-named commercial grade.

This is the badge. You don't wear it, you simply look out for it.

JET

DENNIS MAY writes another of his attractive guides for gadget-addicts

And to start with

LIGHT

as for instance
on the right ☞

on a

DARK

SUBJECT

Ready to beat the winter's fogs with Lucas's Pathfinder & Projector sealed-beam lights.

OFF AND ON

Alexanders make clip-on stone guards to protect your lamps—seen fitted, below, and ready to clip on (below left).

Variety—"A great source of pleasure, Sir"—vowed Johnson two centuries ago, and its old magic works again as Showland's gadget addicts hither-and-yon from clips to clocks, from joints to jacks, from fans to felts, from locks to lamps . . . .

Lamps? Well, we could start here as logically, or illogically as anywhere else. Joseph Lucas's chandlery display includes a line that is claimed to be the first all-British sealed-beam headlamp. See it on Stand 213.

Sealed-beam units, whatever their application, are expensive, so it makes sense to protect them properly. Foreseeing this need, Alexander Engineering nip into the breach with meshwork stoneguards of the type that had an earlier vogue on sports cars in the 20's and 30's. Well chromed and an aesthetic asset rather than a liability, these miniature grilles are a good defence against flying stones and hedge-hopping birds.

Now back to illumination, as such, and the Halroy automatic parking lamp, product of Wells Electronics Ltd., 42 Botolph Lane, London, E3. Without even the drop of a hat, a cadmium-sulphide photoelectric cell switches the Halroy on at dusk, off at daybreak. This transistorised gizmo consumes a mere milliamp during daylight hours. Just the thing for the ever-growing legion of urban motorists who don't own a garage or even a car sized bit of the earth's crust.

Statistics show that car theft is a form of crime that does pay, but the accessory vendors are out to make it pay less well, less often.

For instance (1) :— The Krooklok, by Johnson and Starley Ltd, Northampton. "In essence an extensible metal bar with a hook at each end". The nether hook grapples the clutch or brake pedal, the upper one the rim of the steering wheel. You just set the bar for length, snap-to a tumbler lock, and walk away leaving a wheel that can't be turned, a brake that can't be applied or a clutch that can't be freed. Looks good value at 47/6.

For instance (2) :— The Carstop, by Bradville Ltd., Bradex House, Boston Parade, London, W.7. Four-way headache for male-factors—kills both the ignition and electric fuel pump current, puts an earth on coil and distributor, sets the horn blaring if an attempt is made to start the car. Can't be forgotten because you have to switch it off to start the engine, on to stop it. A lot of ingenious hardware for 59/6.

For instance (3) :— Key-Leather's new immobilizer, crux of which is a secretly sited switch which, a mite less ambitiously, just cuts the ignition and starts the horn tootling if any monkey business starts. Cheapest of the lot at 25/-. Stand 266.

For instance (4) :— New Era gear-lever lock by Ecurie Rossignol Ltd., 1a Caroline St.,

continued on Page 63

continuing on the gadget prowl with DENNIS MAY

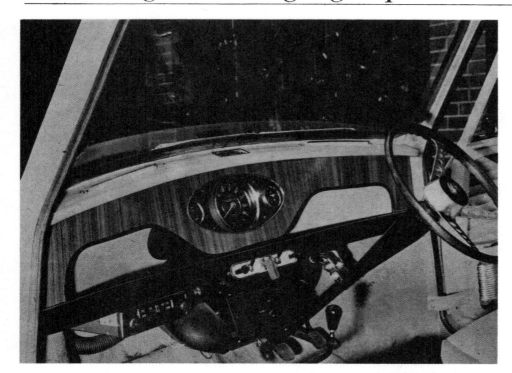

LOOKING CLOCKS IN THE FACE . . .

A new easy-to-fit dashboard panel for BMC Minis comes in walnut finish Warerite from T. G. Supplies (Autofactors) Ltd. Below, Smith's range of supplementary dials range from an ammeter at £1 7s 6d to an impulse tachometer at £9 15s (and if you do not know what an impulse tachometer is, there are plenty who do).

continued from Page 61

Birmingham, 3. Bottom end of a hardened steel arm, claimed to be hacksaw-proof, is made fast to the car floor, top end strangleholds the shift lever in whatever position you care to leave it. Price, 50/-. Fits many B.M.C. models, some Fords.

Purveyance of bits and pieces specially for Minis is becoming an industry in its own grounds. Here are a few on account:—

A. Sets of Wickertrim adhesive panels, to give your Mini Traveller or Countryman that perambulating-basket look which sophisticates rate so highly these days. Each kit comprises six sheets, shaped to fit specific areas of the body. Makers are Dalmas Ltd., 215 Charles St., Leicester, and most factors stock it.

B. Simplified version of a racing jack, enabling either side of a Mini (i.e., port or starboard wheels) to be hoisted clear of the ground in considerably less time than it takes to read this paragraph, instead of tedious minutes. Makers are Multi Motors Ltd., 74 Whitton Rd., Hounslow, Mddx. Price £3/16/0.

C. Rubber switch extenders for headlamp and wiper controls, useful for short-armed Minimen and Minimaidens who otherwise can't reach these switches without a bit of a stretch. Extender's soft material removes risk of impalement in a shunt. Half-a-crown a pair from Nera Motor Factors Ltd., 332 Kennington Rd., S.E.11.

D. Two separate and competitive facia panels for Minis, one by Rokee Ltd., 115 Worship Lane, E.C.2., at £6/18/6 a time, the other by T. G. Supplies (Autofactors) Ltd., 98 Leagrave Rd., Luton, Beds.—£1/19/6 or £2/5/0, according to the type of Mini. Former is polished walnut veneer on a plywood base, and can be installed by any competent do-it-yourselfer with a minimum of tools, latter press-fits and is formed in decorative laminate, ⅛in. thick.

E. Fitted carpets for Mini front compartments, marketed by Cornercroft, the wheel-trim people (Stand 217) and made for them by Dunlop. These are three-strata jobs—bonded underfelt, then a thick rubber layer, finally close-packed Nylon-Courtelle pile. Available in five colours. Pre-pierced for pedals. Prices from £5/12/0.

Next-up for scrutiny—two topping-up aids, their functions unrelated. The first is a Smith Motor Accessory Division product (Stand 206) —Bluecol Top-Up Mixture for winter radiator safeguarding: one-third Bluecol, two-thirds water. With a graduated bottle of this slurp handy (4/- for 30 fluid oz.) you can stop worrying whether your periodic cooling system replenishments are dangerously diluting the contents.

Topper-up no. 2 is a battery maintenance adjunct, by John Sydney Ltd., 1 Streatham Place, S.W.2. Instead of keeping your domestic supply of distilled water on a shelf in your garage, where friends will help themselves to it when you're not looking, it follows you around on your travels in an unbreakable plastic reservoir anchored somewhere under the bonnet. The bottle incorporates a screenwash-type pump and has a delivery tube of whatever length it needs to reach the battery. Price 15/11.

Reclining seats, based on elaborate mechanisms, used to be strictly for the well-heeled, but their increasing adoption by volume production car manufacturers is putting the accessory makers on their mettle. One accessory maker anyway—Restall Brothers Ltd., Floodgate St., Birmingham, 5. This firm, experienced as suppliers of tip-back seats to

continued on Page 64

TUNING-IN *to more gadgets*

continued from Page 63

the motor industry, are now offering their Recliner as a conversion for in-service cars of current or recent vintage. Either Restall or your local garage will do the make-over for you. It costs £12/10/0 per seat.

Talking of seats, two reel-type safety harness retractors—Borg-Warner's Roll-a-Belt and Irving Air Chute's Stowaway—are darkening the Earls Court door for the first time. Borg-Warner's stand is 331, Irving's 364. These roughly similar devices promote tidiness, prevent belts from getting dirty and transmitting the dirt to the wearer's clothes, constitute a silent reminder to *wear* the belts, cut out the clatter of unrestrained buckles swinging against adjacent hardwear.

Can you see where you're going? You can? Always? In that case, Trico's new SR-12 Anti-Smear (Stand 265) isn't for you. But it will be for anybody who is plagued by windscreen film (fall-out from smog or diesel fumes, for instance). The chemical fluid comes in a plastic squeeze-bottle, price 6/9 in the first instance, 4/3 for reloads. Anti-Smear is effective on wiper blades as well as the screen itself.

Something else in a related vein is the Kwik-Wype screen cleaner (why not Quick-Wipe, for mercy's sake?), by Invicta Plastics Ltd., Oadby, Leicester. This clever little tool has a combined handle and reservoir for a water-cum-detergent mix, the grip forming a "T" with a head having a sponge on one face and a squeegee blade along one edge. Squeeze the handle and the goo emerges through the sponge. In repose, the Kwik-Wype (suffering lexicographers!) nests in a plastic bag.

From screen purging to clothes hygiene is a short hop, so let's make it—with encouragement from Holt Productions Limited on the one hand, Minicleans Ltd. on the other (1 East Dulwich Rd., S.E.22). The Holt line, Spot and Stain Remover by name, is claimed to kill any grease your suit may pick up during roadside wheelchanges, etc., and "lifts the stain to the surface, where it dries to a white powder". This can be lightly brushed away, leaving no ring.

Miniclean is selective, the individual and disposable tubes forming the one-and-eleven-penny pack having their own specific "quarries" —grease, tar, wine, tea, what-hast-thou. Most chemists carry Miniclean.

Well, that takes care of the clothes you *wear* en route, but how about protecting the suit you dangle from a hanger in the rear compartment? Conway Car Accessories Ltd. (Stand 239), specialists in seat covers, steering wheel gloves and headrests, tackle this one with their Car Wardrobe. Just the job for fastidious chaps who object to reaching their week-end or holiday rendezvous with their lady-killing gear looking like a dishcloth. Made in plastic, simulating hide. Price 29/6.

If winter comes, can spring be far behind? Yes, probably, but let's not be defeatist about it. When the season of motoring picnics and kindred frolics comes round again, we may be glad we made a mental note of the Simplus Gadabout collapsible armchair. Uniquely, it "folds in two dimensions with one movement . . . rolls into so compact a shape that it can be carried like an umbrella". Even without the model girl who adorns it in our photograph, it makes a handsome and inviting piece of al fresco furniture in the rigged-for-action stance. Framing is light alloy tubing, seat fabric water-resistant Tygan. £5/19/6 including P.T., from Simplus Products Ltd., Wilson Rd., Huyton, Liverpool.

As a companion piece for the Gadabout, the new Pritchard picnic table commends itself.

All-metal construction, stove enamelled top measuring 27 by 15½in., legs made from light alloy and slightly splayed for stability. Folded, the table assumes a shape like a rather large book; weight 6½lb. Makers: W. H. Pritchard Ltd., Caledonian Works, Wednesfield, Staffs.

Desmo (Stand 223) never enter Earls Court without something new to show, and they aren't starting now. A sample eye-catcher from the Desmo list is the aluminium Universal Roof Rack—light, pleasantly styled, easy to fit and adaptable to practically every car on the road. Price 99/6. Another good line from the same source is the 551 Door Buffer/Reflector, killing two birds with one stone as it safeguards door edges and gives visual warning of what's up when you open your car door at night.

"Worth Looking At", runs the Smiths' slogan, leaving it to the reader to look either at the instruments advertised or at the girl who somehow always infiltrates the picture. But even standing in their own grounds, girl-less, the latest Smiths' supplementary instruments, modernistically styled and designed to incorporate internal illumination, are worth looking at. See them all—oil and water thermometers, oil pressure gauges, clocks, ammeters, impulse tachometers and the rest—on Stand 206.

Worth Looking At. If Smiths hadn't thought of it first, that would be a spot-on blanket slogan for the whole shooting-match of accessory exhibits at Earls Court, 1964. Happy looking.

TAKE IT EASY

Push-button or manually tuned—Radio-mobile all-transistor radios take some of the strain off driving . . . and for picnics or a roadside break, the Gadabout folding seat—light and compact—is useful.

AND STOP!

The new Brodex "Carstop", left, is an ingenious automatic "vehicle immobilizer" for under £3. It cuts out ignition and fuel pump, prevents "under the bonnet" starting, and sounds the horn if a thief in spite of that still tries it on.

Published by Beaverbrook Newspapers Ltd., Fleet Street, London, E.C.4 and printed by L.T.A. Robinson Ltd., London, S.W.9

REFLECTIONS ON A CAR HEATER COMPONENT

Just look at that gleaming finish! Obviously the paint job can't affect the performance of a car heater, but the attention SMITHS pay to such detail, can! SMITHS have adopted the revolutionary new electrolytic painting process for their heater components. It eliminates paint 'tears'; prevents the clogging of apertures and threads; ensures that all surfaces are evenly and permanently coated, thus giving increased durability. Whether it's researched thermal efficiency or painstaking paint jobs, SMITHS take care to see that you get the very best in car heating and demisting equipment.

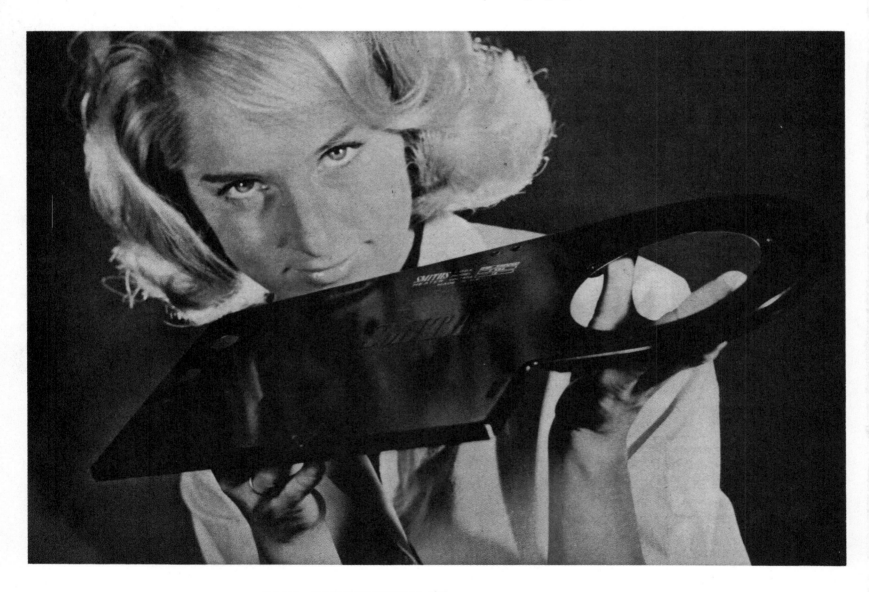

SMITHS

SMITHS MOTOR ACCESSORY DIVISION

LONDON N.W.2.   GLADSTONE 3333

Daily Express Motor Show Review 21 Oct. 1964